AN

for a Canal from

ECTICUT RIVER,

proposed Route to the

OSON.

tion of the Commissioners

win, Engineer.

826.

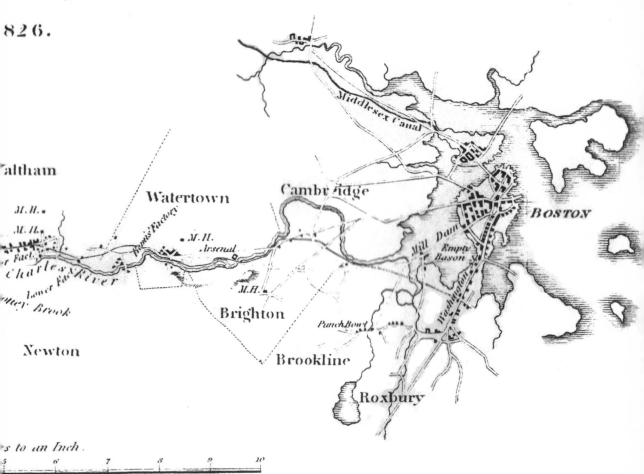

Waltham

Watertown

Cambridge

Middlesex Canal

BOSTON

Charles River

M.H.

M.H.

Bemis Factory

M.H.

Arsenal

Lower Fact.

Brook

M.H.

Brighton

Punch Bowl

Mill Dam

Empty Bason

Washington

Newton

Brookline

Roxbury

s to an Inch.

5   6   7   8   9   10

Enjoy

Cliff Schinger

BUILDERS *of the* HOOSAC TUNNEL

BUILDERS *of the* HOOSAC TUNNEL

BALDWIN · CROCKER · HAUPT · DOANE · SHANLY

CLIFF SCHEXNAYDER, PE

Peter E. Randall Publisher
Portsmouth, New Hampshire
2015

© 2015 Clifford J. Schexnayder
First edition 2015
Printed in USA

ISBN13: 978-1-942155-07-2 hardcover
ISBN13: 978-1-942155-08-9 ebook

Library of Congress Control Number: 2015937906

Published by Peter E. Randall Publisher
5 Greenleaf Woods Drive Suite#102, Portsmouth, New Hampshire 03801
www.perpublisher.com

Distributed by University Press of New England, Dartmouth College
1 Court Street, Lebanon, New Hampshire 03766
www.upne.com

Frontcover: Photo looking out of the east portal. Thomas Doane's survey lining tower is seen to the right but the enlargement of Herman Haupt's bore has not commenced so the photograph was probably taken shortly after December 1863. From an old stereoscopic card. Card says Hoosac Tunnel & Vicinity, American Views, reverse side says: Photographed and Published by Geo. W. Moore, Athol, Ma.

Book design: Grace Peirce

To my love, Judy

We do nothing alone—someone encourages us and stands with us through life. Judy has always been there supporting all of my endeavors. Even when words are not spoken, I am confident of her support. Love is a wonderful thing.

This book was a Labor of Love supported by Judy's Love.

Contents

Preface

Like Thomas Merton I can truthfully say "I know these hills!" Merton, author of *The Seven Storey Mountain*, makes the statement while riding a train through the Delaware Valley in 1941. In my case, the knowledge came slowly over the years 1990 to 2014. With my friend Jerry Kelly, and many times unaccompanied, I ventured into the quietness of the Hoosac Mountain and the Deerfield River Valley. Jerry and I climbed the rock faces and enjoyed the beauty of the woods in spring, summer, and fall. Later, after Jerry had shown me the way, I struggled through the snows of winter to experience the cold the tunnel builders felt. I have seen the icicles at the east entrance hanging almost to the tracks and at the west entrance the evening sun illuminating the tunnel bore for a thousand feet. Walking in the woods during late fall and watching the low water of the river reveal the remains of Doane's crib dam, I was once joined by a black bear.

The Smithsonian Institution's Dibner Library of the History of Science and Technology is located in the bowels of the National Museum of American History. Most visitors to the museum pass the doors of the Dibner Library without a clue about the wonderful information secreted on the other side. I was one of the fortunate who, having received a Dibner Library Resident Scholar award, spent many an hour on the other side of those doors. It was an experience rather like that of C. S. Lewis's Lucy, who climbed into the wardrobe and discovered a magical land. I met no White Witch, but the experience produced this book—the result of a wonderful adventurous journey.

History as taught in the classroom is often boring—especially in high school. All too often, it is just a recitation of dates, names, and places. In reality, history is people and their struggles. People—hardworking men and women—built this land of ours. This story of the Hoosac Tunnel is all about people—dreamers and doers, a Grand American epic—and it embraces this country from the Atlantic coast of Massachusetts to the prairies of Iowa.

The completion of the five-mile Hoosac Tunnel was one of the great engineering achievements of nineteenth-century America. Up until 1916, the Hoosac, which is 7,645 meters (25,081 feet) in length, was still the longest tunnel in North America. By accident, the challenge of tunneling the Hoosac Mountain taught men how to use nitro-glycerin without blowing themselves up in the process. To bore through mile after mile of hard rock, machinists and tinkerers produced a reliable percussion rock drill. And the ingenuity of two men on the west side of the Hoosac Mountain led to perfection of the electric blasting cap. Those three achievements moved the business of tunneling into the twentieth century.

The Hoosac Tunnel work was a confrontation between man and mountain. This huge challenge brought together many of America's greatest engineers and enhanced their legacies as civil engineering greats.

Acknowledgments

Mary Ann Lambert, my wonderful "cuz" (cousin) who once had a house in Clarksburg, Massachusetts, and one day while I was visiting said, "Let's go see the Hoosac Tunnel—you *do* know about the Hoosac Tunnel?" She later gave me a copy of Carl Byron's book, *A Pinprick of Light*, and as a result these pages came into being.

Peg Monahan-Pashall, the editor who holds Hawthorne and the Transcendentalists as her literary heroes and who plays the fife with Middlesex County Volunteers is a special person. Everyone should be blessed with an editor like Peg. Her encouragement, penetrating questions, and guidance have made this book a much better read. She especially liked the line in chapter 1 about the fifers coming over the mountain.

Jerry Kelley, Hoosac Tunnel amateur archaeologist from Boston and a hiking partner who led me up into the Berkshire forest where the leaves now hide the crumbling survey towers that guided the miners through the Hoosac Mountain.

Kirsten van der Veen, at the Dibner Library of the History of Science and Technology, Smithsonian Institution Libraries, whose help in navigating the Smithsonian system was vital to finally transforming an idea into reality.

S. Diane Shaw, Special Collections Cataloger, Acting Head of the Dibner Library of the History of Science and Technology, Smithsonian Institution, was the other person who introduced this engineer to library research.

Katharine C. Westwood, the lively spirit who once shepherded the Special Collections in the North Adams Public Library, where a trove of material awaits the patient reader. Kacy, as she is known, could always find another interesting item, but, more important, she always gave the searcher encouragement.

Susan M. Roetzer, Director of the Fitchburg Historical Society, who introduced me to so many wonderful and knowledgeable volunteers in Fitchburg.

Stanley L. Brown, amateur historian in the village of Florida, Massachusetts, on top of the Hoosac Mountain, who provided old pictures of the works on the east side of the Mountain and tales of his father finding picks and chains in the rock pile below the Hoosac Tunnel's west shaft.

James (Jim) A. Ward, Guerry Professor of History (retired) at the University of Tennessee at Chattanooga and author of *That Man Haupt*, who read the Haupt chapters and, together with his wife, entertained me in their Chattanooga home.

Paul W. Marino, the history man of North Adams, who in a driving rainstorm tromped through the village's graveyards pointing out the headstones of men who died building the Tunnel.

Anna Fahey-Flynn, Reference Librarian at the Boston Public Library, who unfailingly found old newspapers in the library's collections and sent electronic copies of requested articles.

Father Robert of the Most Holy Trinity Monastery in Petersham, Massachusetts, who read chapters and provided a quiet place for reflection.

Kathy Brandes, a sharp-eyed editor hiding somewhere on the coast of Maine, cleaned up my typing and grammatical errors and made this book a much better read.

Thank you, my good friends and supporters—it has been a wonderful journey.

Introduction

WHILE PATCHES OF SNOW began to appear on the Hoosac Mountain in October 1867 signaling the approach of the Christmas season, a devastating accident caused a small crowd to stand silently watching a brave Thomas Mallory being lowered into a gaping black hole, a hole straight down into the bowels of the Hoosac Mountain. Before long, a cold chill unrelated to the temperature gripped the crowd: Mallory was hauled up lifeless. Although he was revived, the sight of this one lifeless man was a shock—one filled with sorrow as deep as the 580-foot shaft. On everyone's mind was the question: "How many lives will the Mountain claim before the Tunnel is punched through?" It was even on the minds of those who championed this daring work.

The engineers finally pierced the Mountain horizontally on Thanksgiving Day in 1873, but the price of success was high. Achieving daylight through the Hoosac Mountain consumed the lives of more than a hundred Irish, Cornish, and French miners. An 1873 newspaper article reported 136 men were killed during the construction of the Hoosac Tunnel, but most histories of the 1880s and later give the number as 195. No explanation has been found for this difference, but recent efforts using news articles and vital records put the total number of deaths much lower. (One of the problems in attempting a count of the deaths is how to classify men who, while employees at the Tunnel, died by falling in the river after drinking too much or froze to death while trying to get home in an inebriated state.)

Through the early part of the nineteenth century, tunneling was accomplished by the strength of strong arms swinging sledgehammers against steel drills held by a "shaker," who rotated the steel after each ringing blow, and black powder was the only blasting agent. As a result the work of boring the Hoosac Mountain dragged on slowly from the early 1850s until the middle of the Civil War. Then, in late 1863, the engineers decided to speed the effort by excavating a shaft from the top of the Hoosac Mountain down to the Tunnel level, some 1,028 feet. From the bottom of this shaft—sited almost equidistant from the two openings of the Tunnel on the eastern and western sides of the Mountain—the miners would begin hammering on the rock with their steel drills, hoping to meet their brothers working from the exterior headings. Because of its location, this hole was dubbed the central shaft.

By mid-January 1864, the miners working in the shaft had excavated twenty-four feet and reached the rock of the Mountain.[1] A year and a half later, in July 1865, the shaft reached the 200-foot mark.[2] On 1 August 1867, realizing the continuing difficulty of excavating the shaft the commissioners put the task into the hands of the contracting firm of Dull, Gowan and Company of Harrisburg, Pennsylvania.

Directly above the fifteen-by-twenty-seven-foot ellipse-shaped central shaft was a large wooden building several stories tall. This building housed the hoisting machinery used to lower the miners into the shaft and to remove the blasted rock. As the shaft progressed deeper and deeper into the Mountain, wooden platforms or landings were erected in the shaft at irregular intervals. Each platform had openings for the buckets carrying miners or broken rock. Besides the hoisting machinery, the building over the shaft held shops and space for storing tools and the pumps used for removing water from the shaft. The new contractors inherited the contents of the shaft building as well as equipment for lighting the shaft with naphtha gas (gasoline). The naphtha gas was kept in an iron tank about 100 feet from the large building over the shaft.[3]

Around noon on Saturday, 19 October 1867, the miners fired a blast at the bottom of the shaft. After the smoke cleared, thirteen miners descended 581 feet[4] into the dark hole. At one o'clock, just as the first bucket of shattered rock was hauled up, someone attempted to start the naphtha lighting system. When he did so, the gas ignited and immediately engulfed the shaft building in flames. The hoist operator tried to lower a bucket to the miners below. But before he could complete the operation, the flames drove him from the controls of the hoisting machinery.

Steel drills and other tools were stored on the first platform below the hoist. As the fire consumed the building over the shaft, burning timbers fell into the shaft. Soon the first platform was consumed and the trapped miners were skewered by steel drills. The burning timbers also rained down on the doomed miners, leaving no hope for their survival.

Men from the village of North Adams on the west side of the Hoosac Mountain rushed up the 1,000 feet of steep mountain road to help but their exertion was for naught. The building could not be saved and the burning platforms in the shaft prevented any rescue attempt. After the fire burned itself out a large timber was cantilevered out over the black void of the shaft and a brave workman volunteered to descend into the abyss. At four o'clock on Sunday morning, a hushed crowd watched Thomas Mallory disappear into the gloom of the pit.

After forty minutes, an unconscious Mallory was hauled to the surface. The North Adams paper reported Mallory was revived, "only after the most vigorous efforts."[5] He made two more attempts to find survivors but both times foul air extinguished his lamps and left no question as to the fate of the miners. If they had survived the rain of steel and burning timbers, the lack of air surely had settled their fate. The pit provided a deep grave for almost a full year before new pumps could be installed, the shaft pumped out, and the bodies recovered. The list of dead from the accident included twelve Irishmen and one Frenchman.

Hoosac central shaft: the descent of Thomas Mallory (courtesy of North Adams Public Library)

The effort to tunnel the Hoosac Mountain was plagued by many terrible accidents but this was the most dramatic and deadly. As the silence of winter covered the Mountain, many voices rose against the Tunnel, but the Governor remained defiant: "We shall ride through this rocky wall."[6] So the men returned to the dark bores on each side of the mighty Hoosac Mountain and the work continued. Work at the central shaft did not resume, however, until June 1869, after new hoisting machinery and pumps were installed. With the new equipment, the miners finally reached the Tunnel elevation after sixteen more months of hard mining.[7]

Besides those men who pounded the steel drills by the light of a tallow candle, the nineteenth-century quest to tunnel five miles through the rock of the Hoosac Mountain and build a railroad across the northern part of Massachusetts touched the lives of such American notables as Transcendentalists Ralph Waldo Emerson and Henry David Thoreau; paper-manufacturing magnate Alvah Crocker; China trader John Murray Forbes; railroad financiers John E. and Nathaniel Thayer of Boston; America's first native civil engineer, Loammi Baldwin Jr.; three generations of Baldwin-trained engineers, including John W. Brooks, Samuel Morse Felton, Thomas Doane, and Charles S. Storrow; and many Massachusetts governors, but particularly Civil War-era Governor John A. Andrew. The challenge of digging the longest tunnel in the United States also drew engineers from beyond the borders of Massachusetts. Three of the most renowned were Herman Haupt, former chief engineer for the Pennsylvania Railroad; H. B. Latrobe, former chief engineer for the B&O Railroad; and Walter Shanly, an engineer and railroad constructor from Canada. They all labored mightily against Massachusetts political forces and the rival Western Railroad to complete the work. Together these men—and the women who stood by them during repeated trials and disasters—succeeded not only in building a railroad tunnel but also in moving the art and science of tunneling into the modern age.

1

A Path Over the Mountain

When the Indian trail gets widened, graded, and
bridged to a good road, there is a benefactor, there is a
missionary, a pacificator, a wealth-bringer, a maker
of markets, a vent for industry.
— Ralph Waldo Emerson, "Civilization," in
In Society and Solitude (Boston: Houghton Mifflin,
1904), 2.

LONG BEFORE THE DUTCH sailed up the Hudson River in 1609 and Pilgrims came to settle on the Massachusetts coast in 1620, a narrow footpath across the Hoosac Mountain in western Massachusetts linked trade routes on the east and west sides of the Mountain. To the west, the footpath joined a corridor of rivers and trails that crossed central New York from the Hudson Valley to Lake Erie. The Indians called it "The Long Trail," although in reality it was a series of rivers and lakes joined by short portage trails. When engineers later came to build the Erie Canal, they followed the Indians' Long Trail as they dug their "Big Ditch."

The footpath over the Hoosac Mountain connected rivers on each side of the Appalachian Mountains. It was the crucial link completing a continuous trade route westward from the Atlantic Ocean to the Great Lakes. On the east side of the Hoosac Mountain, the footpath descended rapidly to the Deerfield River, where snowmelt waters from the Hoosac and mountains farther north powered the river's flow eastward and into the Connecticut River. The final leg of the route for those wanting to trade with the coastal tribes of Long Island Sound was the south-flowing Connecticut River.

The Indians to the west of the Appalachian Mountains traded Great Lakes copper for wampum made from seashells by the Indians of Long Island Sound. Climbing the 1,000-foot, almost-vertical western face[1] of the Hoosac Mountain was hard, but the footpath over the Mountain was a short seven miles,

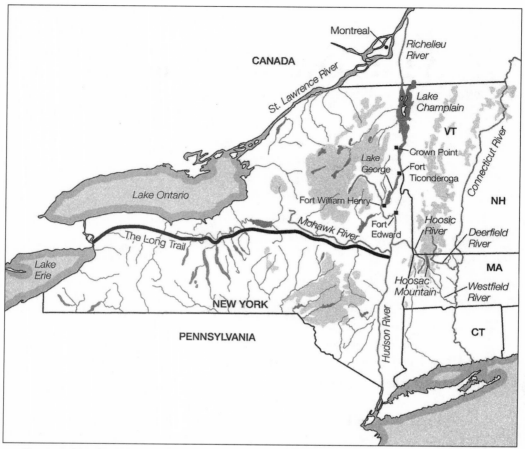

The Long Trail across central New York

and it connected the waters of the Hoosic and Deerfield rivers. The Hoosic River flowed northwestward from the Mountain for sixty miles before joining the Hudson River twelve miles above its confluence with the Mohawk River. The Deerfield River flowed thirty-five miles southeastward before joining the Connecticut River.

To the south and north of the Hoosac Mountain, the obstacle of the Appalachian Mountains was far greater, expanding to forty miles in width. Here only one mountain, the Hoosac, stood between the two rivers, but it was a vertical mass rising to the clouds, a barrier of stone separating the two river valleys. It was a wall to be scaled by those interested in wealth from trade. The Indian footpath was the most direct east–west trade route; in the nineteenth century, men dreaming of a direct trade route via a railroad connecting Boston and Albany would follow the same path worn hard by the repeated passing of Indian moccasins.

In the Algonquian language, *Hoosac* meant the "stone place" or "stony country."[2] The Indians applied the name to both the west-flowing river and the Mountain, but later geographers used slightly different spellings for the two features. The distinct spelling resulted from Europeans trying to put the Indian pronunciation into their continental languages. On the land patent granted to Maria van Rensselaer and others in 1688, the mountain is noted as *Hoosick*, whereas early eighteenth-century maps note the river as *Hoosuck*.[3] Similarly, *Rensselaer* is the more common spelling of Maria's name, but the patent and the family Bible have it as *Renssalaer*. Modern maps identify the river as the Hoosic and the Mountain as the Hoosac.

Maria's father-in-law, Kiliaen van Rensselaer, a major investor in the Dutch West India Company, was awarded a large land grant in the area of present-day Albany. While Kiliaen never visited America, his youngest son, Jeremias, settled there in 1654 and married Maria van Cortlandt of New Amsterdam (New York City) in 1662. Jeremias and Maria occupied the land-lord's house—two rooms with an attic—on the estate. When Jeremias died in 1674, Maria assumed responsibility for raising their six children and managing the Rensselaerswyck property, a 700,000-acre swath of forest on both sides of the Hudson River.[4]

Individual Indian tribes controlled movement on the rivers and trails in their territory, but articles of trade moved the length of the Long Trail and over the Hoosac Mountain to and from the Atlantic coast. Each tribe traded with its immediate neighbors and thus goods passed along the route. The Shinnecock, Pequot, and Narragansett tribes, residing along the coastal plains adjacent to Long Island Sound at the mouth of the Connecticut River, created exquisite and highly prized belts of wampum from the purple shells of the quahog and the white shells of whelk clams. The Mahicans of the Hudson Valley and their western neighbors, the tribes of the Iroquois League, prized wampum greatly. The value of the wampum belts thus increased with distance from the coast. The coastal Indians of Long Island Sound traded their finely crafted wampum to the Pocumtuck tribe of the upper Connecticut Valley and in exchange received copper from as far west as Lake Michigan. The copper from the Indians of the Great Lakes had moved eastward via one Iroquois tribe to its eastern neighbor and then to the Mahicans. Knowing the coastal tribes lacked copper and valued it highly, the Mahicans hauled the copper over the Hoosac Mountain, seeking

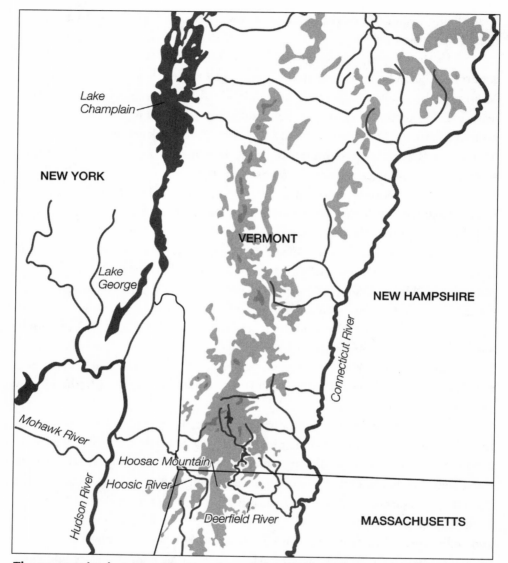

The mountains between the Hoosic and Deerfield Rivers

wampum belts from the Pocumtucks. The Mahicans, who controlled the Hudson Valley, were the middlemen in the east–west flow of copper and wampum.[5]

The easiest way to travel long distances with trade goods was by canoe, so the trade route followed the rivers. When the Mahicans wanted to trade with the tribes of the Connecticut Valley, they loaded their dugout canoes and floated down the Mohawk River to its junction with the Hudson River. Once there, they stroked their paddles hard and pointed their canoes upstream against the current until they found the Hoosic River flowing toward them with the morning sun. Turning east into the rising sun, they paddled up the Hoosic River under a canopy of lofty white pines. It was still an Earth resembling the fifth day of creation.

When Timothy Dwight, the president of Yale College, traveled the Hoosic River Valley in the early 1800s, he described it as "uncommonly romantic and delightful." The river, he said, is "one of the handsomest streams in the world, over a fine bed of pebbles and gravel."[6] In the lower part of the valley to the west of the Hoosac Mountain and closer to the Hudson, there were "luxuriant meadows and pastures green to the water's edge." Farther up the valley in Vermont, the forest became a succession of maple, beech, and evergreens. Dwight had made his way up the Hoosic from New York in mid-October, when he noted that the deciduous foliage was already changed by the frost into successive shades of straw color, orange, and crimson to reddish brown. In another month, the water seeping from the sides of the Mountain would form massive sheets of ice and these would sparkle like stars in the sun's winter rays.

Sixty miles from the Hudson, at the western edge of the Hoosac Mountain, the river split into two branches. Each branch was no more than a shallow stream, but they were very different in character. The southern branch, the Ashuilticook (Ashuwillticook), was a smooth-flowing and winding brook, while the northern stream, the Mayunsook, was a rushing torrent.[7]

Reaching this split in the river, the Mahican trading parties would pull their dugout canoes ashore. These dugouts were too heavy to carry over the Mountain, so the Indians concealed them in the vines and mountain laurel of the forest until needed for the journey home. Frequently, the traders camped on the Hoosic's banks. It was a place to rest before climbing the steep western face of the Mountain. On the west side of the river, away from the Mountain, was a ledge of hard rocks where the Indians found quartzite, from which they fashioned arrowheads. In later years, English settlers found piles of "small glass-like chips about as big as a four pence [slightly larger than a half inch],"[8] marking the industry of the Indians along the river.

It was pleasant along the Hoosic. Here the Great Spirit provided a spring to feed a basin some twenty feet in diameter with warm water and in early summer strawberries and partridge berries grew wild. Dwight remarked how "the meadow strawberry of this country is the best fruit of the kind which I have seen."[9] Game was plentiful here and it was easy to catch fish, so the Indians relaxed before climbing the Mountain.

As the morning sunshine poured its gold onto the east side of the Mountain, the Indians, with trading goods on their backs and pouches of new arrowheads, moved off in single file up the trail. Countless generations of their predecessors had passed over the Mountain on this route, and by the 1600s, the trail had become a beaten track, a sunken path, through the maple, oak, hemlock, beech, and pine. It passed a mound the Indians believed held the bones of their giant ancestors[10] and crossed sacred ground, a place belonging to the spirits where even the bravest of warriors sometimes faltered in fear. This was because a southeast wind would rumble through the hills and produce an echo like bellows pipes, but when the wind stopped the forest became quiet, very quiet. The Indians believed the echo sounds were the voice of the Great Spirit announcing his presence and anger because they were traversing his domain. A Mahican—who would face the fiercest Mohawk warrior with his deadly war club or fight a powerful bear without fear—approached this place with apprehension. It was a realm best left to the rule of the wolf and the eagle. The Mountain was a barrier to cross, not a place to linger. Besides believing the summit of the Mountain was inhabited by evil spirits, the Indians knew there was little game to hunt on its heights. As a result, they were always eager to make the descent to the shelter of the valley on the other side.[11]

The Hoosic Valley quickly receded into the distance as the braves forced themselves up the trail. Reaching the western crest of the Mountain, the view to the north and south was a panorama of peaks. These wooded undulations, which stretched as far as the eye could see, were the Berkshire Hills, part of the Appalachian Mountains. The distance across the top of the Hoosac Mountain was only a mile and a half. It was so narrow the braves could see both the Hoosic River to the west and the Deerfield River to the east without changing the position of their eyes.

After crossing the slight valley perch atop the Mountain, there was a lower eastern ridge to negotiate before the path descended 1,400 feet into the narrow valley of the Deerfield River. The Deerfield Valley at this location was very narrow. Here, close to the Hoosac Mountain, the Indians proceeded into a gorge. The true valley was further to the east, but the Indians knew the swift-flowing Deerfield River would lead them through the mountains to the wide valley of the Connecticut River, where the Pocumtucks had wampum to trade. The Indians considered the Hoosic and Deerfield rivers, pointing to the pathway over the Mountain, gifts from the Great Spirit.

At times, the footpath over the Mountain was used by war parties, but usually the climb was made by those carrying trade goods. This route existed long before the Dutch fur traders arrived in the Hudson Valley. It was in use long before the French, seeking beaver pelts to finance their explorations of Canada, struggled to survive the killing cold of Acadia. By the time the first Europeans arrived, the moccasins of the Indians had pressed the trail into a well-defined passageway through a forest of trees with trunks measuring as much as four feet in diameter and reaching more than 100 feet toward the clouds.

When the Europeans did arrive in 1609, the lands of the Hudson River Valley were still home to the Mahicans. The Mohawks were their neighbors to the west. The Mohawks and the four other tribes on the land south of Lake Ontario in present-day New York State were allied in the Iroquois League. Their tribal names from east of the Hudson Valley to Lake Erie were the Mohawks, Oneidas, Onondacas, Cayugas, and Senecas. They called themselves the Ho-De-No-Sau-Nee, or the "people of the longhouse,"[12] because, instead of living in tents like many tribes, they built long wood-framed houses covered with tree bark rather than skins. The Mahicans and the tribes of the Iroquois League lived in fixed palisaded villages referred to as castles. The women of these tribes were farmers who cultivated corn, beans, and squash. While they were tied to the castles and the crops, the braves roamed the countryside to hunt and fish.

In the 1620s, the hunting grounds and castles of the Mahicans extended some eighty-five miles up the Mohawk River or west from the Hudson River.[13] As late as 1680, when Kiliaen van Rensselaer, Maria's father-in-law, purchased land from the Mahicans, the westward edge of the tract was defined as a two-day journey westward from the Hudson. Later, increased unity among the tribes of the Iroquois League allowed the Mohawks to push the Mahicans eastward to the banks of the Hudson River, but another cause of the Mahican eastward migration was the tribe's willingness to sell large tracts of its western lands to the Dutch.

Until 1609, when two French men and their captain, Samuel de Champlain, paddled with sixty of their Indian friends down the lake that would bear the captain's name, and Henry Hudson sailed up the river that would bear his name, the Indians who used the Long Trail and the trail across the Hoosac Mountain knew nothing of "grape juice" or crabapple brandy, or the "lightning weapons of the sky."[14] Yet early encounters with the men from Europe would determine the state of relations for the next two centuries.

The first contact between the Mohawks and the French initiated a bitter and lasting feud. In one firing of their European weapons, the French explorers unknowingly created permanent hate. The animosity of the Iroquois League would stalk the French until their final defeat by the British and their Mohawk allies during the French and Indian War in 1760. Those defeats would force the French in 1763 to surrender all of North America east of the Mississippi (except for the city of New Orleans) to the British.

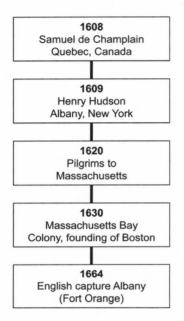

1608
Samuel de Champlain
Quebec, Canada

1609
Henry Hudson
Albany, New York

1620
Pilgrims to
Massachusetts

1630
Massachusetts Bay
Colony, founding of Boston

1664
English capture Albany
(Fort Orange)

Early Explorers

Entering Canada by way of the St. Lawrence River, the French explorer Samuel de Champlain, with twenty-eight adventurers, spent the winter of 1608–9 in a fortified trading post they built at Quebec. The fur trade was the financial engine supporting Champlain's adventures of discovery, and he looked to the Algonquin, Huron, and Montagnais Indians, who lived north of Lake Ontario and along the St. Lawrence River, to serve him as guides and supply him with valuable pelts. The reception these hardy French explorers received was a winter of numbing cold with little snow; snow would have helped to insulate their cabins. The Frenchmen quite literally experienced the chill of the tomb, and only eight[15] of Champlain's band remained alive to glimpse the coming of spring. The survivors welcomed the increasing warmth of the sun as the valley of the St. Lawrence slowly transformed itself into a sea of green. This small band had stayed alive by clinging to the hope that the Indians would provide them with mountains of beaver pelts.

The experience of Henry Hudson in September 1609 was quite different, but Hudson came with a different intention. He had not come to stay—he was seeking a water passage to China and the Spice Islands (Indonesia). When he sailed his clumsy, 85-foot, 80-ton *Half Moon* (*Halve Maen*) up the Hudson River, it was a Mahican chief who offered him beaver pelts. But those pelts stimulated the Amsterdam merchants and turned the eyes of other European adventurers toward North America. The early Dutch and French explorers used many different spellings in recording the name of this tribe—Mahicanor and Mahikander are the most common versions in the seventeenth-century Dutch documents—but Mohican, Mahikan, Mahiecan, Maykan, Muhheakunn, Moheakun, and Mohegan are also found in reference to these Native Americans who resided in the upper Hudson Valley.[16]

The Dutch and French came to trade iron axes, knives, hatchets, woolen blankets, and later muskets for beaver pelts. Early European traders tended to stay in their enclaves, with the Indians bringing the beaver pelts to the fortified posts. Quickly, the tribes realized the importance of trade-route control. Wealth came to those who controlled the trade routes, and the scale of the resulting wealth increased with the degree and range of control. With this realization, the trail over the Hoosac Mountain became a route of strife, a place where blood was spilled for the next 260 years as the Indians, French, and English—all jealous competitors—fought to maintain their trade monopolies.

The Mohawks of the Iroquois League and the Mahicans were the first of the tribes to receive firearms from the Europeans, and those weapons gave them a major advantage over their foes.[17] But before they received "lightning weapons" from the Dutch, the Mohawks were astonished by these new armaments.

Mortal Enemies

After a vessel arrived from France with critically needed supplies for Champlain and his frozen adventurers in June of 1609, his Algonquin, Huron, and Montagnais friends demanded Champlain help them against their enemies to the south, the Mohawks. Because Champlain was dependent on these Indians to guide him into the Canadian wilderness and to supply him with pelts, he acceded to their entreaties. By canoe, some three to four hundred Algonquin, Huron, and Montagnais led Champlain southward on the narrow and shallow Richelieu River to the open waters of a lake he later described as of great extent, 80 or 100 leagues long.[18] As he traveled deep into the country of the Mohawks, many of his Indian allies departed. Champlain affixed his own name to the lake during this voyage in July 1609. The river and the lake were an invasion route the Indians had used many times, and it would be followed by French, British, and American armies until the close of the American Revolution.

While traveling at night, Champlain and two other brave Frenchmen, plus only sixty Algonquin, Huron, and Montagnais warriors,[19] met a Mohawk flotilla at the southern end of Lake Champlain. As the Mohawks moved toward the shore and erected a barricade, war cries echoed across the water. Champlain's allies fastened their canoes together in the darkness and remained on the lake answering the cries of the Mohawk, but they delayed their own landing until daybreak. When day broke, the Algonquin, Huron, and Montagnais canoes approached the shore. As the Mohawks, with painted faces and wooden armor, came out of their barricade and moved forward—flourishing stone war clubs, stone hatchets, and stone-tipped lances—the Frenchmen stayed hidden behind their allies. In tight ranks, the Mohawks approached Champlain's allies like a forest phalanx. The two forces shouted and employed ritual movements to build courage and frighten, but then the Algonquins opened their ranks, letting the fiercest warriors of North America gaze upon a demon wearing breastplates, cuisses of steel (plate armor to protect the front of the thighs), and a high-crowned helmet of forged metal with a large plume of white feathers. The plume of feathers marked him as a captain in the service of the first Bourbon king of France, Henri IV. Champlain described the encounter and the result of firing his short-barreled *arquebus à rouet*:

> *I looked at them and they looked at me. When I saw them getting ready to shoot their arrows at us, I leveled my arquebuse, which I had loaded with four balls, and aimed straight at one of the three chiefs. The shot brought down two, and wounded another.*[20]

After this first flash of exploding black powder, Champlain's two French comrades, kneeling behind the trees, fired their arquebuses into the flank of the Mohawk formation, felling the third chief. Seeing their leaders mortally wounded by "flashes of lightning," the Mohawks' tight fighting formation disintegrated. They abandoned the field and fled into the depths of the forest.

In June of 1610, there was another historic fight between the Mohawks and the French with their Algonquin, Huron, and Montagnais allies at the junction of the Richelieu and St. Lawrence rivers. Again the fire from the captain's wheel-lock arquebus was devastating. Nonetheless, the Mohawks made him feel the sting of their arrows. The head of one lodged in his neck, but his Indian allies took close to ninety Mohawk scalps and another fifteen prisoners. Champlain's only reason for participating in these struggles between the warring tribes was his dependence on the goodwill of the Algonquin, Huron, and Montagnais. At the time he fired his weapons against the Mohawks, they were not his enemies. His motives were trade and the wealth generated by the pelts his allies supplied.

The iron balls Champlain blasted into the Mohawk chiefs sealed in blood his brotherhood with the tribes along the St. Lawrence River, but those same iron balls embedded in the Mohawks a lasting hatred of the French. Seeing the effect of Champlain's weapons, the Mohawks limited their forays into the St. Lawrence Valley for the next thirty-three years,[21] but soon they went looking for friends to supply lightning weapons.

Fortified Posts

After Henry Hudson, sailing for the Dutch West India Company, had shown the way, the Dutch established Fort Nassau on Castle Island in the upper Hudson River in 1614 or 1615. Soon, however, these early adventurers learned about the river's spring floods, which reclaimed the ground of the island. So in 1624 a new outpost, Fort Orange, was erected on the west bank of the Hudson River five miles south of its confluence with the Mohawk River. Both forts were named after the leading noble family of the Netherlands, the House of Orange-Nassau.

Cohoes Falls on the Mohawk River, just above that river's junction with the Hudson, made it necessary for the Indians to portage their loaded canoes to reach the Hudson River safely. Consequently, Fort Orange was sited along the portage trail so the traders could intercept the Indians as they portaged around the falls with their pelts. The Dutch West India Company needed settlers at this fort who could supply the garrison with food, so in 1652 the town of Beaverwyck[22] (Beverswyck) was established on the west bank of the Hudson River just north of Fort Orange. The Dutch word *wyck* means quarter, ward, or district, so the name meant "place of the beaver," since collecting beaver pelts was the principal business of both the fort and the town. While the town was developed under the assumption that the settlers would be productive farmers, most of those who ventured up the Hudson to Beaverwyck quickly turned from farming to the fur trade, a much more rewarding occupation. The town's two main streets are today part of Broadway and State streets in Albany.

While the English colonists in New England had strict laws forbidding provisioning the Indians with muskets, the Dutch traders at Fort Orange were not so principled. Early on, they provided the Mohawks with muskets in exchange for pelts. George Bancroft, Harvard graduate and American historian, stated in his 1843 edition of the *History of the United States*: "The Mohawks . . . having, through commerce with the Dutch, learned the use of fire-arms, seemed resolved on asserting their power in every direction."[23] The fierce Mohawks, with their European weapons, strove never to permit the northern tribes to trade with the Dutch or English unless they themselves served as the intermediaries. Their desire to control the fur trade was a significant driver behind the ensuing Indian warfare.

With their weapons, the Mohawks soon inflicted a severe defeat on the Mahicans and established control of the forest to the west of Fort Orange. In the spring of 1664, the Dutch Governor, Pieter Stuyvesant, convinced the Mohawks and Mahicans to "bury the hatchet," which was the way the Indians spoke of a peace treaty. However, later in the year the British sailed up the Hudson and took possession of Fort Orange.

Now the area was an English dominion and the place was renamed Fort Albany after the Duke of York's second title. Realizing the importance of Indian allies, the English immediately brought the Mohawks and the Mahicans together and concluded a treaty of peace and alliance with both tribes. To the Mohawks was granted the special concession "that they may have free trade, as formerly."[24] Although the Mohawks considered themselves an independent nation, they well understood that their commercial interests at this point lay with the English. This attitude would manifest itself time and time again during the many wars France and England waged along the boundary between New France (as Canada was then called) and the English colonies of Massachusetts and New York. New France was occupied mainly by adventurers who exploited the wealth derived from trading with the Indians while the English colonies were settled by men and women struggling to build lasting communities in the New World.

The English fully recognized the importance of their alliances with the Iroquois League and especially with the Mohawks. Colonel Thomas Dongan, governor of New York, wrote King James II stating the value of maintaining an alliance with the Five Nations and the Mohawks: "The Five Nations are a bulwark between us and the French and all other Indians." Such an alliance was required in the interest of trade, and Dongan understood the importance of trade. Even though France was master of the Great Lakes, England drew the trade of the West to itself down the Long Trail, which was controlled by the Mohawks and their Iroquois League brothers. While the French might bring canoes laden with pelts from Lake Superior, English traders, escorted by their Indian allies, would venture as far west as Mackinaw, Michigan.[25]

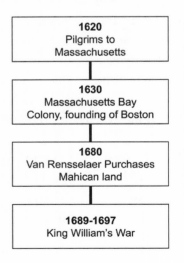

1620
Pilgrims to Massachusetts

1630
Massachusetts Bay Colony, founding of Boston

1680
Van Rensselaer Purchases Mahican land

1689-1697
King William's War

Escalating Hostilities

The English displacement of the Dutch in the Hudson Valley disturbed the French along the St. Lawrence River. Nevertheless, open warfare between the English and French did not occur until King James II (1633–1701) was driven from the English throne by William, Prince of Orange, in 1688. When King William III (1650–1702) and his queen, Mary II, led England into the League of Augsburg in 1689, to resist France's invasion of the

Rhenish Palatinate by King Louis XIV, the European conflict quickly asserted itself on the English–French frontier in America. In Europe it was known as the War of the Grand Alliance—England, Spain, and the Holy Roman Empire—against France. To the colonists in New York and Massachusetts, it was King William's War. Even though Indians had made forays both eastward and westward across the Hoosac Mountain for generations before the English and French came to dispute that corner of the New World, four major periods of strife in Europe between France and England would now bring treachery and warfare on a new scale to the route. Occasionally, however, during the opening years of the eighteenth century, before the border strife made it too dangerous, a lone Mahican and his squaw would tramp the trail eastward over the mountain to a trading post on the Connecticut River, where they found better exchanges than those offered in Albany. Wampum was still the medium of exchange, but the squaw with beaver pelts packed high on her back went over the mountain seeking a metal knife or woolen blankets, and the brave, leading the way, hoped to secure a musket.[26]

During the summer of 1688, the English had mediated a peace between the French and the Iroquois. As part of the agreement the French promised to restore to the tribes several Iroquois chiefs they held captive.[27] The French, however, failed to release the captive chiefs. This breach of faith drove the Iroquois to resolve revenge against the French. In late August 1689, before the European powers formally declared war, the Mohawks and their Iroquois brothers resumed the struggle against New France. Some fifteen hundred Iroquois[28] attacked the French settlement at Lachine, next to Montreal, setting fire to every house and slaying every inhabitant they encountered. The Iroquois then moved against the town of Montreal and its fort—with devastating effects. They remained in command of the fort until mid-October, when, with winter approaching, the braves departed for their longhouses in central New York. The Montreal disaster threw the French into complete disarray and the governor of New France, Marquis de Denonville, ordered a complete pullback of French garrisons farther to the west. His order included evacuating and razing the French fort on Lake Ontario.

As a consequence, Denonville was recalled and Count de Frontenac was appointed governor. Frontenac, a man of bold action, had, during a previous term as governor of New France (1672–1682), sent La Salle to explore the course of the Mississippi River. It was La Salle who gave the name Louisiana (in honor of King Louis XIV) to the land watered by the Mississippi. Frontenac had previously served France in Holland, Italy, and Germany; owing to his valor and skill, he now held the rank of marshal.

Frontenac astutely planned his response to the Montreal massacre. Instead of trying to find the Iroquois in the wilderness, he marched against the English settlements. The Algonquin and Abenaki tribes, allies of the French, with their faces painted and their quivers filled with arrows, took up the hatchet against the English. War whoops soon broke the solitude of the forest trails as the Indians moved southward, raiding English homesteads and settlements. Armed and advised by the French, the Indians pressed the French monarch's territorial claims in blood.

Together with their Indian allies, the French made three successful thrusts southward in 1690. Schenectady, New York, was attacked during the night of 8 February 1690 by a frostbitten party of French and Indians who had waded through deep snow for twenty-two days to reach the western outpost of the empire. Salmon Falls on the New Hampshire–Maine border was burned and pillaged in March. Next the raiding force turned eastward toward Casco Bay, Maine, where they sacked and burned the village of Falmouth and wooden Fort Loyal, carrying northward into captivity those they did not slay. Bleaching bones lay strewn on the soil for two years before a white man again visited the site and buried them.[29] These forays all bore the mark of Frontenac's skillful planning.

After the brutal attacks of 1690, the English resolved to launch a two-pronged offense designed to trap the French in a pincer. A land force would strike at Montreal via the historical route up lakes George and Champlain. At the same time, a fleet would sail north along the Atlantic seaboard and then down the St. Lawrence River to attack Quebec. Together with their Mohawk allies, the English colonists pushed north in 1692, reaching Lake George. There they began fashioning canoes, but a lack of supplies forced the colonists to abandon any attempt to penetrate farther north.[30]

While the land army sat at Lake George, a fleet of thirty-four English ships sailed from Boston and reached Quebec on 16 October. The ships were too late. In early September, Frontenac had received news of how the force of English colonists and Mohawks on Lake George had turned back. As a result Frontenac had concentrated his garrisons at Quebec. When the admiral of the English fleet demanded the city surrender, Frontenac dismissed him with scoffs. Realizing they were outmanned, the men from New England reboarded their ships and sailed for home. Their two-pronged attack on Canada was an utter failure.

Frontenac, who was never idle, changed tactics and struck the Mohawk castles in February 1693. His winter attacks were so successful at surprising the Indians in their redoubts that fear forced them to disperse into the safety of the forest. But English soldiers and militia from Albany, together with the Mahicans, rallied to the relief of their Mohawk allies. The bitter strife of this first conflict, which consumed so many English frontier settlements and Mohawk castles, continued until 1697.

While the border strife of King William's War was a bloody affair, the path over the Hoosac Mountain remained peaceful, as there were still no settlements in northwestern Massachusetts for the French to attack. Robert Morden's 1675 and 1685[31] maps of New England show the coastal area filled with huddled villages, but beyond and to the west the map is an empty void, except for Northampton, Springfield, and Enfield on the Connecticut River.

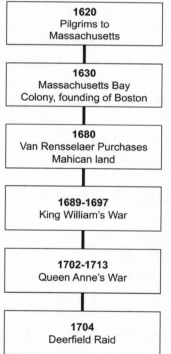

| 1620 |
| Pilgrims to |
| Massachusetts |

| 1630 |
| Massachusetts Bay |
| Colony, founding of Boston |

| 1680 |
| Van Rensselaer Purchases |
| Mahican land |

| 1689-1697 |
| King William's War |

| 1702-1713 |
| Queen Anne's War |

| 1704 |
| Deerfield Raid |

The Treaty of Ryswick, which ended the conflict, brought only a short suspension of hostilities. Five years later, France and England went to war over the succession to the Spanish throne. In Europe it was known as the War of the Spanish Succession, but the colonists gave it the name of the reigning English monarch, Queen Anne. Queen Anne's War would prove to be a long and murderous quarrel, particularly for the colonists living on the frontier. The settlements on the western side of the Hoosac Mountain and in the Hudson Valley were saved from most of the terror during this clash because the Mohawks and their Iroquois brothers had buried the hatchet with the Algonquins. The Iroquois refused to break their treaty with the Algonquins, and even though the Algonquins were allied with the French, they likewise would not make war on the Iroquois.

This peace between the Algonquins and Mohawks did not, however, protect the frontier settlements of Massachusetts and New Hampshire on the eastern side of the Hoosac Mountain. Only forest wilderness stretched northward to Canada from Deerfield Village, situated on the Deerfield River's east bank just southwest of the river's confluence with the Connecticut River. The village was located on the old trade route, and occasionally friendly Indians came over the Hoosac Mountain to trade. But on an intensely cold morning in February 1704, with the snow four feet deep, Deerfield Village fell to a raiding force of French and Indians.[32] The settlement was protected by a palisade, but the snow had drifted high against the wooden wall, rendering it no obstacle to the snowshoed invaders. Fifty-four of the inhabitants were killed,[33] and after the town was burned to the ground, another 100 were marched through heavy snows into captivity in Canada.[34] The Deerfield slaughter was one of the bloodiest of many similar raids during Queen Anne's War.

In December of that same year, two heavyhearted Massachusetts men, John Sheldon and John Wells, followed the old Indian trail over the Hoosac Mountain as they made their way from Deerfield to Canada searching for the captives and their own family members. John Sheldon's wife and daughter Mercy, age three, had been killed in the raid, but his other children had been marched to Canada.[35] On his first trek, Sheldon was successful in purchasing the freedom of his daughter-in-law, Hannah, who was twenty-three at the time of her capture. He crossed the Hoosac Mountain a second time on the same mission in January of 1706 and in April of the following year, he made a third trek across the Mountain. After those three trips, Sheldon finally reclaimed his three children—Mary (sixteen at time of capture), son Ebenezer (twelve), and son Remembrance (eleven)—from Indian villages near Montreal.[36] This brave man was actually able to rescue a total of 113 English captives from different parts of the colonies, but some of those taken in the Deerfield raid were never released. John Wells was not so fortunate; he was killed in 1709 while trying to save another colonist from a band of marauding Indians.[37]

Four years after the Deerfield raid, far to the east of the Hoosac Mountain, the settlement of Haverhill, Massachusetts—a cluster of thirty log cabins beside the Merrimack River—met a similar fate in late August.[38] While Haverhill was only forty miles north of Boston, the settlement marked the edge of the frontier. It had once before experienced the common tragedy of many frontier settlements when, toward the end of the previous war, it was burned and pillaged by the Indians.

There were few English successes during Queen Anne's War. Another coordinated attack on Canada with the same objectives as the failed "pincer" expeditions of 1692 was proposed. Again the plan was to attack Montreal via the Lake Champlain route and Quebec by sea. An English squadron of more than ninety vessels left Boston on 30 July 1711, bound for Quebec. The squadron, which included seven veteran regiments from England, began the ascent of the St. Lawrence River in mid-August. On the evening of 22 August, as the ships moved upriver, they were wrapped in a thick fog. Because of an easterly breeze, the fleet's pilots advised all ships to lie with their heads to the southward.[39] The orders were followed, but before the pilots and captains realized what was happening, the ships were carried toward and onto the north shore. Morning light of the following day revealed eight ships shattered on the rocks and more than 800 men lost. Sir Hovenden Walker, the admiral of the fleet, deemed it impossible to proceed. When news of the naval disaster reached Boston, the troops who had begun marching northward from Albany to attack Montreal were immediately recalled.

The only success experienced by the English colonists was the 1710 capture of Port Royal in French Acadia. The hazards and sorrows of Queen Anne's War finally came to an end in 1713 with the Treaty of Utrecht. This time, peace settled over western Massachusetts and the Hoosac Mountain trail for thirty years, and with the peace, settlers swarmed into the Connecticut and Deerfield River Valleys.

A Long-Suffering Saxon

Captain Moses Rice of Worcester, Massachusetts, purchased from Gershom Keyes 2,000 acres of Deerfield Valley land in 1741. This plantation lay about halfway between the village of Deerfield and the Hoosac Mountain.[40] Based on the deed of transfer recorded in Springfield, Rice was the earliest settler in the area. He was originally from Sudbury, but in 1722, when he was twenty-eight, Rice moved to Worcester, then a small settlement some forty miles west of Boston. This was two years after he had married Sarah King. As a member of the Worcester militia in 1724, he was posted in Rutland, a settlement ten miles northwest of his home. He had earned his title of captain when he became the leader of a cavalry company while living in Worcester.

Captain Rice and his wife moved to their property on the Deerfield River in 1743 and began clearing land for a homestead.[41] When Moses and Sarah made the journey westward from Worcester into the wilderness, to what was then known as "Boston plantation No. 1,"[42] they had seven children, aged thirteen to twenty-three, but it is not recorded if the entire family removed at this time.

The site of their homestead, twenty-two miles west of Deerfield Village, would in 1765 be encompassed by the town of Charlemont. A hundred years further on, Rice's ancestors would still be farming the land, but they would also be exerting themselves to replace the old Indian trail over the Hoosac Mountain with a railroad tunnel through the Mountain.

In May of 1739, Ephraim Williams Sr. and Thomas Wells ventured through the forest west of the Hoosac Mountain and surveyed three townships "on and near the Hoosuck River" by the needle of a surveying instrument.[43] At the time, the Hoosic Valley was still covered by virgin white pine. The Indian trail pointed the way over the Mountain, but there was not a road or bridge anywhere in the valley, and there were no settlers. Settlers from the east did travel the Indian trail, but they found the Hoosic Valley close to the Mountain too narrow for their liking. They said the land "would not raise beans"—which meant it would not raise beans or anything else—so all of those early pioneers continued westward.[44]

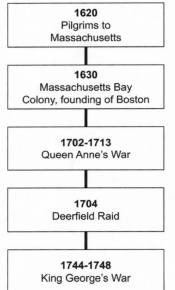

1620
Pilgrims to
Massachusetts

1630
Massachusetts Bay
Colony, founding of Boston

1702-1713
Queen Anne's War

1704
Deerfield Raid

1744-1748
King George's War

Still France and England continued to contest the wilderness on both sides of the Mountain. Beginning with a conflict between England and Spain in Europe, war between the two ambitious nations who stalked one another in North America broke out in 1739 for the third time. The hostilities escalated when France joined Spain against England, and by 1744 the European strife brought the English frontier settlements into conflict with the French in Canada. What was termed the War of the Austrian Succession in Europe had begun when Prussia invaded the Austrian province of Silesia.[45] In North America, the war was known as King George's War (George II, 1683–1760).

During the interlude of peace before King George's War, the authorities in New England worked to erect a chain of stockades and blockhouses from the coast of Maine to the territorial border with the colony of New York.[46] In western Massachusetts, these frontier blockhouses were sited to control the well-trodden Indian trails leading from the southern end of Lake Champlain to the English settlements in northern Massachusetts. From the Connecticut River westward, the forts were located north of the Deerfield River and spaced about five miles apart.

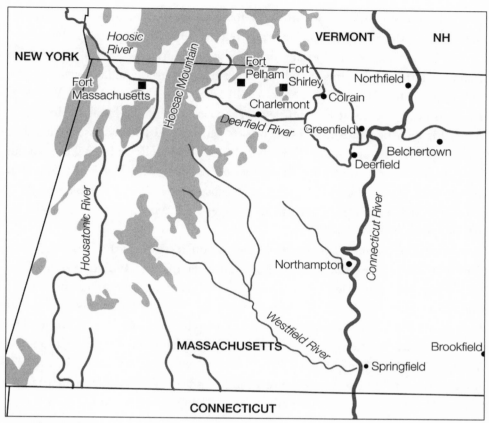

The line of forts

Fort Massachusetts

By the fall of 1744, militiamen were billeted at Fort Shirley; the next spring, Captain Moses Rice, the valley's first settler, supplied the timbers for Fort Pelham.[47] Both of these forts were located about five miles north of Rice's homestead on the Deerfield River, with Pelham being the westernmost stockade on the east side of the Hoosac Mountain. To guard the route of the Hoosic River and the Indian trail over the Hoosac Mountain, Lieutenant John Catlin and soldiers from the two forts on the east side of the Mountain tramped westward over the Mountain in the early summer of 1745 and built Fort Massachusetts.[48] Like the forts on the east side of the mountain, this was a sixty-foot-square blockhouse of hewn and doweled logs. It was approximately two miles west of where the Indian trail began to ascend the mountain.[49] The white pine walls of the fort were twelve feet high, with the logs being hewn to six-by-fourteen inches and stacked edgewise in nine courses. The builders used dowels of red oak to hold the pine logs together.

Command of the border forts in western Massachusetts rested with Captain Ephraim Williams Jr., whose father had surveyed and laid out the three townships in the Hoosic Valley six years earlier. The thirty-year-old Williams made his headquarters at Fort Shirley, on the east side of the Hoosac Mountain. When his men had to travel between forts Shirley and Massachusetts, it was a hard trek of twenty-five miles. From Fort Shirley, they followed a makeshift road down to Moses Rice's and then a trail along the Deerfield River to the Indian trail up and over the Hoosac Mountain. Because of the difficulty in hauling flour across the Mountain from Deerfield Village, Fort Massachusetts received its supplies from Albany, New York.[50]

In 1746, while Captain Williams was off recruiting, the Reverend John Norton traveled over the Hoosac Mountain via the old Indian trail to Fort Massachusetts. The minister was well trained, having graduated from Yale College in 1737.[51] When this chain of frontier forts was established, Reverend Norton entered the service of the colony as chaplain for the isolated outposts. His narrative of events after his trek across the Hoosac Mountain begins: "Thursday, August 14, 1746, I left Fort Shirley in company with Dr. Williams [the medical officer assigned to the forts and no relation to Captain Williams] and about fourteen of the soldiers; we went to Pelham Fort, and from thence to Captain Rice's, where we lodged that night."

Crossing the Mountain the following day, Reverend Norton and the doctor found the fort low on supplies and most of the men in ill health. The next day, Norton sent his escorts back to Deerfield with a letter appealing for supplies. Two days later, before help could arrive from Deerfield, the French and their Indian allies, a force of more than 900, surrounded Fort Massachusetts. The defenders numbered only thirty, counting three women and five children.[52] In their weakened condition, and with so few against so many, the defense of this outpost lasted a single day. On 20 August, Fort Massachusetts was surrendered to the French, who, after first raising and then lowering the French flag, put the torch to its hewn log walls. As flames consumed the fort, Reverend Norton and the other prisoners found themselves plodding toward Canada. Benjamin Simonds, a young soldier of nineteen or twenty, was so sick and feeble he could not walk. Usually the Indians killed anyone who could not keep up during these marches into captivity, but on this occasion, Simonds and the other weakened captives were fortunate—the French commander had promised his Indian allies a reward for bringing the prisoners alive and well to Canada. The Indian guarding Simonds carried the sick man on his back for several days.

At first the weather was good as the prisoners tramped the trail northward to where the French had left their boats on Lake Champlain. But after three days it began to rain, and the rain continued for several weeks. A bedraggled band of prisoners arrived at Quebec in mid-September. Of the original thirty defenders of Fort Massachusetts, one soldier had been killed defending the fort and one sick soldier died on the trail, but, during the second night out, Mrs. Smead gave birth to a baby girl, so twenty-nine prisoners were delivered to the French authorities. Fourteen of those twenty-nine would live to be exchanged the following year for Frenchmen being held in New England. Young Benjamin Simonds, one of the exchanged captives, would thirty years in the future perform yeoman service as a militia commander during the Revolutionary War.

The French had succeeded in planting their fleur-de-lis in Massachusetts, but the attack immediately changed the attitude of the Iroquois, who until then had remained neutral in the conflict because their hatchet was still buried with the tribes to the north. After the capture of Fort Massachusetts, the Mohawks accepted the hatchet against the enemies of the English.

Captain Williams had the blockhouse rebuilt and regarrisoned during the summer of 1747, and he moved his headquarters into the new Fort Massachusetts. The French and their Indian allies assaulted the new fort in August of 1748, but under Williams's personal direction, the defense was successful and the attackers were driven off with the loss of only one man. This second attack came from the south and east, so it is possible the French had come over the Hoosac Mountain on the old Indian trail. While the Treaty of Aix-la-Chapelle (or Treaty of Aachen) was concluded in Europe only a month after this second attack, the hostile feelings on the frontier did not die. The Mohawks and the Mahicans were disappointed when the English quit fighting.

In a conference at Albany, the Indians informed Governor George Clinton of New York that "the axe of the French is sticking in the heads of our people." The Mohawks told him, "We will keep the hatchet in our hands," and the Mahicans in a similar vein said, "We will keep our hands on the cocks of our guns."[53] The forests and the trails would remain dangerous for another three years, especially the trail across the Hoosac Mountain. Even so, many of the men who came over the Mountain to garrisoned Fort Massachusetts now cleared plots of land west of the fort and settled in the lower Hoosic Valley away from the Mountain.

Towns in the Valleys

In 1749, the General Court of Massachusetts appointed a committee to lay out house lots in the west township surveyed by Ephraim Williams Sr. ten years earlier and to lay out another township, East Hoosac, six miles square. The community established on the Hoosic River in the original township, beyond the site of the old fort, was first known as West Hoosac, but in 1765 it incorporated as Williamstown. Sixty lots were sold by the colony in 1750. Benjamin Simonds, the captured soldier back from Canada, purchased lot number 22 and became a farmer in Williamstown. Twelve other Fort Massachusetts soldiers purchased lots, and their commander, Ephraim Jr., took title to two lots. The house Simonds built, on the fifteen-rod-wide main street, became a welcoming tavern on the north bank of the Hoosic River at the site where the Indians used to camp.[54] These settlers soon planted fields along the river, and the flowers of the flax they cultivated turned the valley a beautiful blue. They used the flax to make cloth and to feed their cattle.

In the case of the East Hoosac Township, however, the committee, "not believing in the doctrine of [following] instruction,"[55] failed to make the township six miles square as directed. Abutting the west slope of the Hoosac Mountain, it was laid out seven miles in length, north to south, and five miles in width, east to west. Ephraim Williams, for his services and a promise to "build and keep in repair for twenty years a grist mill and [a] saw mill," received from the General Court of Massachusetts a grant of 200 acres of land in the East Hoosac Township.[56] He sent Jedidiah Hurd, a builder of mills from Woodbury, Connecticut, to erect the required mills on the Hoosic River at a spot later forming the center of a town at the western base of the Hoosac Mountain. Hurd threw a dam across the river to capture the power of its water and proceeded to erect a gristmill on the west bank. On the east side of the Hoosic, he built the required sawmill. A trestle bridge below the mills connected Ephraim Williams's new mills. The bridge had "no railing except a huge log on each side,"[57] but Hurd, respecting the power of the river's spring freshets, took care to set his bridge on strong abutments.

In late 1746, when the French and Indians had poured down from Lake Champlain and captured Fort Massachusetts, Moses Rice had fled his homestead for the safety of Deerfield Village. After the fight at Fort Massachusetts, the Indians came over the Hoosac Mountain trail and burned Rice's homestead. But when peace returned, Moses and Sarah ventured west again to rebuild their homestead on the trail beside the Deerfield River.[58] Aaron Rice, second son of Moses and Sarah, was authorized by the "proprietors" of the town to build a corn mill and a sawmill in 1753. The authorization required him to grind for a sixteenth (he could retain as payment a sixteenth of the ground meal) and no more, and saw boards at the same rate as in Deerfield Village.

To the east of Rice's homestead, at the cataract of the Deerfield River, the village of Shelburne Falls sprang to life as more settlers moved into the lower valley. In the other direction, between Rice and the Hoosac Mountain, settlers established farms in the narrow valley along the trail. There Rice's descendants would persevere. Son Aaron married Freedom French of Deerfield in 1754, and they brought eleven more Rices into the valley during their fifty-four years of marriage.

A century later, but before the railroad penetrated the valley, Henry David Thoreau hiked up the Deerfield River from the town of Greenfield on the Connecticut River and commented about a Rice descendant who lived close to the eastern base of the Hoosac Mountain.[59]

> *He kept many cattle and dogs to watch them, and I saw where he had made maple sugar on the sides of the mountains. I remarked, that it was a wild and rugged country he inhabited, and worth coming many miles to see. "Not so very rough neither," said he. He was earthy enough, but yet there was good soil in him, and even a long-suffering Saxon probity at bottom.*[60]

Soon after Thoreau's visit, Erastus Rice, together with others of such "Saxon probity," would set his mind and money to driving a railroad tunnel through the Hoosac Mountain.

The French and Indian War

The peace of Aix-la-Chapelle did not last, and yet another conflict engulfed the colonies, the French and Indian War. The previous treaty had made no provision for removal of the French forts at the southern end of Lake Champlain. Those French ramparts stood as permanent threats over the northern border settlements of the English in New York and Massachusetts. In 1752, the governor of New France moved to implement the instructions he had received to take possession of the Ohio Valley and remove the British presence from those lands. At the confluence of the Allegheny and the Monongahela rivers, where Pittsburgh now stands, he established Fort Duquesne in 1754. This was land claimed by the Virginia colony of the English. Their colonial grant read, "from sea to sea," so Virginia claimed the lands west of the Appalachian Mountains. Learning of

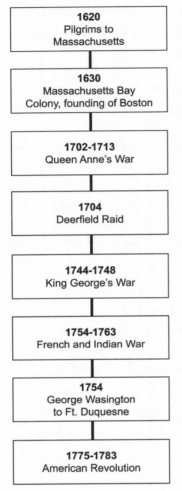

the French incursion, Virginia's colonial governor sent out Lieutenant Colonel George Washington to support Virginia's claim to the Ohio Valley by force of arms. The twenty-two-year-old Washington won a minor engagement but was then defeated when a larger party of French arrived from Fort Duquesne. Those two clashes were the first engagements of the yet-undeclared French and Indian War. Though the European counterpart, the Seven Years' War, would not begin until 1756, the echo of Washington's guns drifted to Canada. English and French soldiers, together with their Indian allies, assembled to purge the forest of their enemies.

In June of 1755, a band of Indians swooped down the trails from Canada and attacked Moses Rice in the field of his homestead on the east side of the Hoosac Mountain. The Indians killed the captain and took several of his family members to Canada as prisoners.[61] During the following month, the Indians fell upon settlers in the Hoosic Valley north of Fort Massachusetts, burning homes and destroying cattle. Next, they burned and pillaged Bakerstown, New Hampshire, on the east side of the Hoosac Mountain beyond the Connecticut River.

The problems of supplying Fort Massachusetts during the previous war had been predictable, so in June 1753 Massachusetts granted funds for marking out a road eastward from the western part of the province. Consequently, sometime after mid-1753, a road was cut over the Hoosac Mountain. The Indian trail—marked only by a rut beneath the forest cover—was now passable for ox-drawn wagons. A map of the Bernardston Grant made from a 1765 survey shows a "Hoosuck road,"[62] which must have been this first road. On the Deerfield side, the ascent of the Mountain was very steep, and for years afterward travelers could look over the cliffs and see the bones of oxen that had slipped while struggling to pull heavily loaded wagons over the Mountain.

Once again the French were using the Richelieu River and Lake Champlain as their primary route for attacking the settlements in New York and western

Massachusetts. To protect this avenue of approach, the French had established a fort at Crown Point, on the southern end of Lake Champlain, in the 1730s. Colonel William Johnson, superintendent of Indian Affairs for the British and a man the Mohawks respected, decided to destroy this menace. With the intent of marching on the French fort at Crown Point, he assembled a militia army in Albany. From the Connecticut Valley in Massachusetts, the militia companies of Belchertown and Northampton came trudging over the Hoosac Mountain on the new but very crude Hoosuck wagon road. Captain Nathaniel Dwight of Belchertown recorded in his journal how his company and one led by Captain William Lyman of Northampton came together in Deerfield on 25 September 1755 while marching to join Colonel Johnson at Lake George. With "the piercing note of the fife" stirring the blood, 126 men marched west over the Hoosac Mountain.[63]

Ephraim Williams, past commander of Fort Massachusetts, accepted a provincial commission as a colonel in Johnson's army. After arriving in Albany to rendezvous with Johnson, he took time to complete a new will and testament. His association with western Massachusetts and the Hoosic Valley ran deep, dating from his father's township surveys of 1739. There were also his years as commander of the northern forts, including Fort Massachusetts. Colonel Williams had strong ties to the valley, so in the will he drew up while in Albany, he granted funds from his estate for the establishment and maintenance of a free school in the west township—Williamstown.

From Albany, Colonel Williams marched up the Hudson with Johnson's army until they reached the falls where the river turns sharply to the west. At this point, some fourteen overland miles separated the Hudson River from the south end of Lake George. Johnson left part of his army at the falls to establish Fort Edward, while he and Colonel Williams pressed onward, cutting a crude road to Lake George. Reaching Lake George, Colonel Johnson began to construct Fort William Henry. On Sunday night, 7 September 1755, Johnson learned that the French had paddled down Lake Champlain and marched overland to place themselves between his two forts. The next morning, Johnson sent Colonel Williams southward, with a force of 1,000 militiamen and Mohawks, to find the French. Riding at the head of this force, Colonel Williams was killed by the first volley from a French ambush. With the loss of their commander, the militiamen and the Mohawks quickly retreated back to Fort William Henry. The man who had made so many trips over the Hoosac Mountain on the old Indian trail was dead. His frontier forts in Massachusetts would rot away once peace returned to the colony, but from the bequest of the will he executed in Albany,

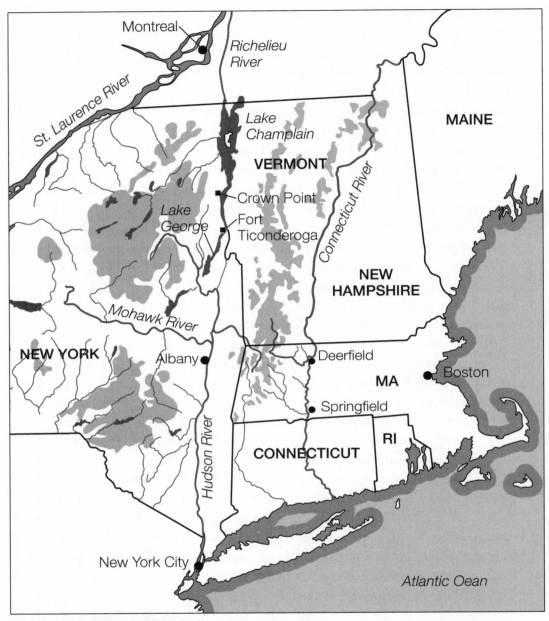

Forts of the French and Indian War

a free school was established in the west township. With time, this free school grew into an eminent center of learning named in his honor, Williams College. Colonel Ephraim Williams may never have envisioned the need for a college in the west township (Williamstown), but today the small seed he planted has grown into one of the nation's leading liberal arts colleges.

What had begun so disastrously ended, later in the day, with the defeat of the French invaders when Johnson rallied his troops. In November, when the Massachusetts troops camped at Fort William Henry were dismissed for the winter, Captain Dwight's men from Belchertown marched homeward over the Hoosac Mountain to the Connecticut Valley. The following year, the French campaign against Fort William Henry resulted in the massacre of the garrison, an event made famous in James Fenimore Cooper's classic *The Last of the Mohicans*. His characterizations of the Indians are filled with inaccuracies, but the descriptions of the routes of travel and the countryside are authentic.

Genesis of a Tunnel

The struggles for the forts on Lake George in 1755 and 1756, and finally the British attack two years later on the French in Fort Ticonderoga, which controlled the entrance into Lake Champlain from Lake George, were more than battles in the struggle between two European powers. These battles served as the training ground for many of the militiamen who would later serve bravely during the American Revolution.

The Treaty of Paris in 1763, which ended the French and Indian War, awarded England all of New France north of the St. Lawrence River. But again the peace would be short-lived; within a decade, the colonists would be throwing tea into Boston Harbor and fighting to free themselves from King George III (1738–1820). Nevertheless, while the peace lasted, the road over the Hoosac Mountain brought a flood of settlers, and those men who journeyed over the Mountain took note of how Ephraim Williams had harnessed the power of the river.

Soon they built water-powered sawmills on the Hoosic River close to the Mountain. The land might not have been suitable for growing beans, but there were tall pines to harvest. Jedidiah Hurd returned in 1762 and replaced his early mills on the Hoosic River with more substantial structures, one gristmill and one sawmill. When folks came to purchase sawed lumber, they did not want the first pieces cut from the log with the tree bark still on it. (These outside boards were known as slabs.) The slab piles beside the sawmills began to grow, and the settlement closest to the Mountain was labeled "Slab City,"[64] although its real name was East Hoosac. To the west and south, where the valley was wider, the new settlers planted fields, built their homes and churches, and established villages.

Beside the road over the Hoosac Mountain, Oliver Parker began keeping a tavern in his log house. His was the first tavern travelers reached as they descended the west side of the Mountain.

Because the first road was very precarious—as was evident from the whitened oxen bones at the base of the cliffs—Samuel Rice, Moses Rice's oldest son, petitioned the General Court of Massachusetts in June of 1762 to be allowed to construct a better road, one not so dangerous.

> *The road over the Hoosuck mountains being at present very dangerous, several creatures having lost their lives thereof, your petitioner hath found a better place for a road, and as there is about 200 acres of Province Land near the Deerfield River, prays for a grant of same, he obliging himself to build a road up said mountain as good as the land will allow of.* [65]

Samuel took on the formidable challenge of building a road through land covered with boulders and along a route crossed by several rapidly running mountain streams. It was a task recorded as requiring muscular strength and much whiskey. By building a series of switchbacks, Rice succeeded in bringing his road up the eastern face of the Mountain. The switchbacks meant he had to construct a longer road, but the design allowed him to provide a gentler ascent. The new road merged with the original Indian trail and a subsequent road just below the point where the Deerfield River makes its sharp turn to the north. Some ninety years in the future, at this location above Erastus Rice's farm, hardy souls dreaming of a tunnel to connect the Hoosic and Deerfield River valleys would begin to scratch the exterior rock of the Mountain with hammers and black powder.

Travel over the mountain became more frequent after Samuel Rice built the second road. In 1771, Joshua Locke petitioned for a grant of land on "Hoosuck Mountain" and permission to build a house of "entertainment." [66] But Locke's tavern was not established very long before another war again brought troops over the Mountain. Seventeen days after "the shot heard round the world" [67] was fired on Lexington Green in 1775, young Benedict Arnold and a single attendant rode into Deerfield Village from Boston. He held a new commission from the Massachusetts Committee of Safety, making him a colonel and appointing him commander of the expedition against the British at Fort Ticonderoga on Lake Champlain. The old fort had been in British hands since the Treaty of Paris in 1763. In Deerfield, Colonel Arnold completed arrangements for fifteen oxen to be delivered to Fort Ticonderoga. His business done, he remounted his horse and continued west over the Hoosac Mountain on Samuel Rice's road.

When Arnold arrived at Lake Champlain, he found that the Green Mountain Boys of Vermont and the militiamen from Pittsfield, Massachusetts, would not respect his commission; they asserted that Colonel Ethan Allen was their chief.[68] Allen, however, allowed Colonel Arnold to be co-commander. So only four days after Arnold's stop in Deerfield Village, the Green Mountain Boys and the Pittsfield militia forced the British fort to surrender. The following day, they took the fort at Crown Point. A fearless Mr. Dickinson of Deerfield came over the Hoosac Mountain driving Colonel Arnold's fifteen oxen and was paid 171 pounds, 13 shillings, and 4 pence when he delivered them to the colonel at Fort Ticonderoga. For their efforts, the colonists not only gained the forts but also the cannons on their parapets.

After the battles at Lexington and Concord, the Massachusetts militia companies forced the British back into the city of Boston. Seeing the militiamen taking up positions to surround the city, General Thomas Gage, the British commander, ordered an attack on the militia's hurriedly constructed fortifications at Bunker Hill. The attack succeeded in securing the fortifications, but Gage and his redcoats could not break the patriots' line. General George Washington arrived in July from Virginia, took command of the ragtag militias, and tightened the noose around the British troops in the city, but he could not drive out the redcoats because the guns of their fleet in the harbor provided, when needed, a protective wall of hot iron.

Then in December 1775, Colonel Henry Knox came from the siege at Boston and proceeded to Fort Ticonderoga. His mission: to drag back to Boston the fifty-nine pieces of artillery captured by Allen and Arnold. The Hoosac Mountain road was too difficult and steep for moving cannon, so Knox took a route much farther south through the mountains. His exploit sealed the British retreat from Boston in March of 1776.

In Charlemont, three of Moses Rice's sons—Aaron, Sylvanus, and Artemas—were appointed to the town's committee of correspondence and safety.[69] At the outbreak of the fighting, a company of minute men was formed in the town, and the service of these men was necessary. Sylvanus, the captain of a company, found himself deployed so frequently he found it necessary to mortgage his farm to raise the funds needed to equip himself.[70]

For almost two years, there was only limited warfare on the upper Hudson and in the Hoosic Valley, but in July 1777 messengers brought troubling news.

Fort Ticonderoga had fallen to the British and the redcoats were on the march southward under General John Burgoyne. Burgoyne's advance caused a flood of men to cross the Hoosac Mountain. First they came from Rowe and Charlemont, just to the east of the mighty Mountain. This group included Samuel Rice, builder of the road over the Mountain.[71] These were followed by other militia hurrying over the Mountain from Deerfield and Greenfield on the Connecticut River. They even came from the towns and villages in eastern Massachusetts. Most marched, but a few rode over the Mountain on horseback.

The first militia units slowed General Burgoyne's southward march by felling trees across the old road of Colonel Johnson's 1755 campaign. By 30 July, when Burgoyne reached the Hudson, he was desperate for provisions, but the area was deserted. The farmers had fled south, driving their cattle before them and burning their fields. Looking to feed his army and secure draft horses, he sent Lieutenant Colonel Friedrich Baum toward Bennington, Vermont, a village on the New York border that was only eighteen miles north of the crumbling remains of the second Fort Massachusetts. The news of Baum's approach brought more men over the Mountain, and Oliver Parker's tavern at the western base of the Hoosac Mountain became the militia's dining hall. Later, Parker claimed that those soldiers in their patched homespun had eaten five oxen in one week's time. Even when many could not pay—or paid in old continental dollars that made a man poorer the more he possessed of them—Parker fed the soldiers who scrambled over the Mountain.

As the militia marched over the Mountain, a veteran leader of the French and Indian War, Bunker Hill, and duty with Washington at Trenton and Princeton, New Jersey, in the winter of 1776–77, journeyed from New Hampshire to lead them. General John Stark, who had retired from the army after crossing the Delaware River with Washington and the victories in New Jersey, now returned to the field to lead the gathering militia.

Stark, like Williamstown tavern keep Benjamin Simonds, had as a young man been a prisoner of the Indians. He had even lived with them for a time. Now the two ex-captives were the general and colonel in command of the militia forces. The two experienced Indian-fighters, with years of experience tramping the hills, positioned their forces to meet the British forces under General Burgoyne, veteran of the Seven Years' War in Europe.

Colonel Simonds hurried his troops from Williamstown to join General Stark. On 14 August, Stark's militia regiments met Colonel Baum's German Hessians five miles from Bennington. Colonel Baum, who had sent for reinforcements, withdrew a short distance to a hill and began digging entrench-ments. The next day, it began to rain and the troops could not load their muskets with the loose black powder without getting it wet. Consequently, instead of fighting, the two armies sat idle and stared at one another through the rain. On the second day, 16 August, the sun came out and General Stark sent two units of his army to attack the British from the rear. As he led them into the fight, he supposedly told his troops: "We must conquer [the British] or tonight Mollie Stark will be a widow." The Hessians were overpowered and Colonel Baum was mortally wounded. General Stark's militiamen took nearly 700 prisoners that day, of whom 400 were German.[72] Many were marched over the Hoosac Mountain road to Boston, but some Hessians abandoned Germany for America and settled in the Hoosic Valley.

After their defeat, many of the Canadians and Indians who were in General Burgoyne's British Army deserted. Still, the Continental Congress was anxious to prevent General Burgoyne from uniting with General Clinton's army, now moving up the Hudson Valley from New York City. Driven by fear, the Congress ordered militia companies from Middlesex and Essex Counties in eastern Massachusetts over the Hoosac Mountain to tighten the noose around General Burgoyne's army at Saratoga, New York. The final contest at Saratoga came in October. General Burgoyne was soundly defeated and surrendered his army. More fighting would occur before Washington's victory at Yorktown ended the Revolutionary War, but after Saratoga, peace descended on the Hoosic Valley.

Peace brought more commerce and settlers over the Mountain. Williams College opened in Williamstown and graduated its first class in 1795. Clad in his regimental coat and continental hat, Colonel Simonds took up the custom of sitting by his front door in his later years and chatting with travelers passing through Williamstown. He had witnessed and experienced many of the events that had changed the old Indian trail into a road connecting the growing cities of Boston and Albany.

The town of East Hoosac developed with two village centers—one in the south and Slab City in the north. The people of the villages decided to name their growing community Adams, in honor of Samuel Adams, the "illustrious leader in the Revolution, signer of the declaration of independence, and later Governor of Massachusetts."[73] With the name change, the two villages came to be referred to as North Adams (at the end of the road over the Mountain) and Adams (farther to the south). There were so many travelers that on 8 March 1797 the Commonwealth chartered the second Massachusetts Turnpike—a toll road "from the west line of Charlemont, in the county of Hampshire, to the west foot of Hoosuck Mountain in Adams, in the county of Berkshire."[74] Construction of the first Massachusetts, a completely different road, was begun the year before. It was located east of Springfield and ran from North Wilbraham though Palmer (a future railroad junction) to Warren.

The route of the second turnpike was westward up the valley of the Deerfield River from Charlemont on the southern bank of the river. When it reached the base of the Mountain, it first made a turn to the south and then resumed its westward direction as it twisted itself up the rock face.

In 1811, a group of North Adams men got together and built a mill to manufacture cotton cloth. A second mill was built in 1813, but the economic effects of the War of 1812 forced the owners to abandon their mills, and they lay idle until about 1820. Transportation was still a problem, but soon more mills would appear across northern Massachusetts. The Turnpike Corporation had been authorized in 1804 to build a bridge over the Deerfield River at the eastern end of its turnpike in Charlemont, but construction of that bridge seems not to have occurred until 1817. The stage road over the Mountain connected North Adams to the towns to the east for another hundred years. In 1833, the Turnpike Corporation was dissolved and the Hoosac Mountain road was opened to free passage.

Mr. Phelps of Greenfield established the first stage line across the Mountain about the year 1814. Phelps's uncovered two-horse wagon, with its body suspended on leather springs, made the trip between Greenfield on the Connecticut River and Albany on the Hudson River once a week. The line proved a success, and later there were more elegant stagecoaches drawn by six or eight spirited horses. A North Adams pastor and writer described the stage ride over the Mountain as a wonderful experience: "The road creeps cautiously up the mountain side—much of the way through the forest, but often revealing the rugged grandeur of the hills."[75] The journey from Boston to Albany could be made in as little as forty-eight hours, but men were dreaming of faster travel and ways to avoid the climb over the Hoosac Mountain.

Before the dream could be realized, the Erie Canal would be carved through the wilderness of the Long Trail, and James A. Garfield, a future president, would walk the towpath of the canal, driving the horses used to pull the canal boats. The Erie Canal would deliver so much trade from the West to New York City that the men of Boston and other eastern cities quickly began to seek ways of improving their own access to the West. The glory of the Long Trail had not died, but the new fight for its commerce would rely on iron rails. The great Erie Canal, like the Indian path, would be superseded by the railroad, but the change was in the future.

In Massachusetts, the descendants of the Puritans who had sent their sailing fleets on trading cruises around the world dreamed of their own canal to the west, but a wall of granite—the Hoosac Mountain—blocked the way. Men and women who had struggled so long and hard to survive on the frontier would not give up easily, though, and a mere Mountain could not block their ambitions.

2

A Dynasty of Engineers

The observant traveller of the Lowell railroad . . .
may see a broad ditch filled with a sluggish stream of
water. He is told perhaps that this was once a portion
of the Old Middlesex Canal.

—Arthur T. Hopkins, "The Old Middlesex
Canal," *New England Magazine* 17, no. 5 (January
1898): 519.

"LAST NIGHT I STOPPED, at dark, on the west side of the meadows, at the mouth of Wickipakick stream, where the level is nine feet above the meadow, at a distance of 5.470 miles from Carter's mills."[1] Writing to General Henry A. S. Dearborn, Loammi Baldwin Jr. penned those lines on 28 August 1825. Dearborn was one of three commissioners appointed the previous February by the General Court of Massachusetts to study the question of building a canal from Boston Harbor to the Hudson River in New York State. The use of the name *General Court*, for the legislative body of the Commonwealth, is a relic from the earliest days of the Massachusetts Bay Colony. To aid the commissioners, the Commonwealth put the task of tramping the wilderness and surveying a feasible route into the hands of its most experienced engineer, Loammi Baldwin.

After the American Revolution, as the new nation expanded across the Appalachians, Massachusetts and other coastal states began to recognize the need for better access to the country's hinterland. While Boston with its port had always been a transportation hub, New York's new Erie Canal dramatically changed the paths of commerce from the west. The middle section of the Erie Canal—ninety-six miles from Utica to Rome—opened in October 1819; by 1822, there were 180 miles of usable canal. Finally, in October 1825, canal boats traveled the full length of the canal, carrying bulk goods from the Northwest Territories—the future states of Ohio, Indiana, Illinois, Michigan, and Wisconsin, plus part of

Minnesota to Albany. The commerce of the Northwest first floated the length of the canal and then continued southward as the Hudson River carried it rapidly to New York City. The success of the Erie Canal instantly caught the attention of all the cities along the Atlantic seaboard. Envious and worried Boston merchants recognized the threat to their city's position of leadership and immediately sought to counter New York's success. They asked—could Massachusetts build a canal to the Hudson River and regain its competitive advantage?

Prior to the America Revolution, Boston—thanks to its fine harbor—stood as a booming commercial center, priding itself on being the first town in North America to reorient its economy from agriculture to maritime commerce.[2] By 1720, Boston was the third-largest port in England's Atlantic empire. In

Loammi Baldwin Jr., the Father of American Civil Engineering (1780–1838)

those early days of the eighteenth century, only the mother country's ports of London and Bristol were larger. Then in 1775, with the start of the American Revolution, British fleets closed Boston's trade avenues, making the great city a ghost town. First the patriot population faded away into the countryside, then the Tories departed for England, and finally many of those who remained died during the 1775–76 smallpox epidemic. The city was quickly reduced to about one-fifth of its pre-1775 population. With the coming of peace, however, fierce ambition and the determination to rebuild drove the merchants of Boston to quickly dispatch a new fleet of sailing ships.

Few roads existed in Massachusetts and the other former colonies and the tracks titled roads were poor, very poor. Consequently, after the revolution, Boston again looked outward for trading relationships. Its maritime traders began sending ships to China, the Pacific Northwest, and Latin America. Resourceful ship owners and trading houses even managed to create a lucrative business of shipping ice from Boston ponds to Charleston, New Orleans, Cuba, and as far as Calcutta.[3]

But trading patterns were changing and New York City was growing much faster than Boston, thanks to its commerce in foodstuffs coming from the Ohio Valley via the Erie Canal. The merchants of Boston watched this change with uneasiness. During the Commonwealth's 1825 session of the General Court, it was resolved to survey routes for a canal across Massachusetts to the Hudson River. Intended to tap into New York's trade, the target of the proposed canal was the Hudson River at its confluence with the Erie Canal. Three commissioners, the Honorable Nathan Willis, the Honorable Elihu Hoyt, and General Henry Dearborn, were appointed to examine possible routes. To assist these commissioners, Governor Levi Lincoln Jr. appointed Loammi Baldwin Jr. as their engineer. At the time, the forty-five-year-old Baldwin was probably the most-experienced and best-trained American civil engineer.

Because there were so few Americans trained in constructing civil engineering works, New York had first looked to England for a chief engineer when the Erie Canal was proposed. Even the federal government had to bring an engineer from France in 1816 to plan coastal defenses. New York soon realized that no English engineer would even consider an assignment in America because of the bitterness and strained relationships caused by the War of 1812. New York then turned to Benjamin Wright, a judge and one of its own. Wright had extensive land-surveying experience but only limited familiarity with the technical aspects of design and construction.

In the early days of the Republic, "judges and lawyers were as a rule surveyors, for they found a knowledge of surveying very useful in determining questions of deeds, leases, etc., and naturally it was from this class of men that the engineers sprang."[4] Wright and those who assisted him had to rely to a large extent on ingenuity to solve many of the technical difficulties of building a canal across central New York. He did, however, have the advantage of experience gained by working with the English engineer William Weston on the Western Inland Lock Navigation Company surveys of the Mohawk River in the mid-1790s. He had also worked with Weston from 1797 to 1799 during the construction of a canal to replace an old Indian portage on the Long Trail between Wood Creek and the Mohawk River, near Little Falls, New York. In fact, all of his work with Weston paralleled the Long Trail of the Indians.

Wright and those who toiled with him in building the Erie Canal learned their engineering by doing, and 363 miles of canal served as their diplomas. Thus, the project has often been referred to as "the first American school of engineering."[5, 6] Although West Point was organized in 1802, Colonel Sylvanus Thayer did not introduce the formal civil engineering curriculum until 1817, the year construction of the Erie Canal began. This was the first comprehensive engineering curriculum offered in the United States. The West Point curriculum model was not imitated by other universities until 1834, when the University of the City of New York and Norwich University in Vermont began their programs.

Loammi Baldwin Jr. was not a product of West Point and had no formal engineering education, for at the time such instruction could only be obtained in Europe. He had, however, received a classical education at Harvard College, and engineering was in his blood—and that blood could be traced back to the very beginnings of the Massachusetts colony.

War of Independence Commander

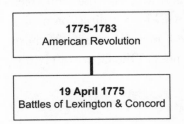

The exact date when Henry Baldwin (?–1697/1698), Loammi's great-great-grandfather, arrived in Massachusetts is not recorded, but it was most likely sometime in the mid-1600s. (His date of birth was not recorded, and there is confusion as to the year of his death.) Henry Baldwin was one of the first settlers in the new town of Woburn, subscribing to the Town Orders in December 1641[7] and serving as a sergeant in the Woburn militia from 1672 to 1685. This would have been during the time of King Philip's War, which began in 1675.[8] The association of the Baldwin family with building began with the son of this first Henry, Henry Baldwin Jr. (1664–1739), Loammi Jr.'s great-grandfather. Henry Jr. erected a sawmill in Woburn. It was probably of the up-and-down type, with a large wooden undershot waterwheel, as was common prior to 1840. Later the mill passed to Henry's son James Baldwin (1710–91). The Baldwins were not yet engineers, but they had become builders. Samuel Sewall, the sometime pastor of the church in Burlington, described James Baldwin in his 1860 *History of Woburn*[9] as "a carpenter, of good repute," and claimed he was the master workman in the 1732 construction of the precinct [Burlington] meetinghouse, which was still standing 130 years later.

Besides owning a sawmill and being a carpenter, James Baldwin was a shopkeeper who bartered in such things as apples, cider, hops for molasses, brandy, and coffee. As had the two previous generations of his family, he worked hard and prospered in Massachusetts. His wife Ruth bore him four sons, of whom three, Cyrus (b. 1740), Loammi (b. 1744[10]), and Ruel (b. 1747), were still alive in the spring of 1775. James's sons had in turn given him three grandsons and one granddaughter before the fateful morning of 19 April 1775, when British troops fired upon American minute men, signaling the beginning of the Revolutionary War. His son Loammi married Mary Fowle, daughter of James Fowle, in 1772, and their first son, Cyrus, was born in June 1773. Mary was again expecting in April 1775, when Loammi marched away, leading three companies of Woburn militia to the fights at Lexington and Concord. After the death of Mary in 1789, Loammi married Margaret Fowle, daughter of Josiah Fowle.

In contrast to the tension in the country, nature provided an early and mild spring in 1775, but on the evening of 18 April, after several days of rain, it turned cold. It was spring, time for turning over the soil, so the men would have been in the fields plowing had it not been for the call to arms. The fruit trees were already in bloom and early grain waved in the fields as militia companies assembled. Years later, Ralph Waldo Emerson would honor the courage of those farmers and shopkeepers turned militiamen with his poem "The Concord Hymn" and its famous lines:

> *Here once the embattled farmers stood,*
> *And fired the shot heard round the world.*

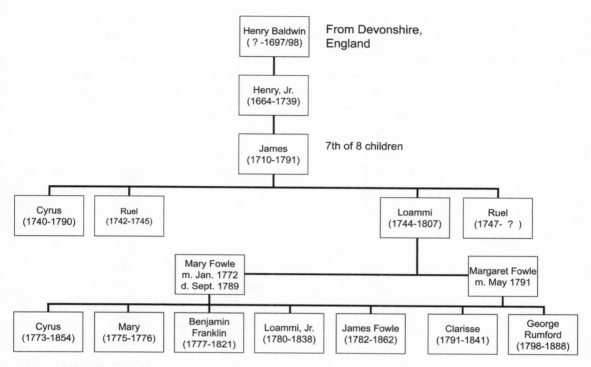

The Baldwin Genealogy

James Baldwin spent only one day of his eighty-one years in the militia, but it was a glorious day. He joined the Woburn men who responded to the drummer's beat in the cold early morning hours of 19 April, when the first shot for liberty was fired on the Lexington Green. Woburn sent some 180 men to answer the alarm, and James—the shopkeeper and sometime carpenter—was doubtlessly wondering whether they could stand and resist the troops under the command of King George III's officers? James's grandfather, the first Henry, had served in the Woburn militia, and now he, with his son Loammi in command, was marching with a latter generation of Woburn men, but this time it was *against* the king's army and not *with* the king's army against marauding Indians.

The messenger had arrived from Medford before first light. He carried Paul Revere's news: "[T]he British are coming out; and if there is any soldier in the house he must turn out."[11] As the church bells rang and a drummer beat the alarm, Major Loammi Baldwin, the future father of an engineering dynasty, quickly assembled the Woburn companies.[12] Major Baldwin later wrote, "The Town turned out extra-ordinary, and proceeded toward Lexington." He was not without experience, having begun his military service in 1768, when he "enlisted himself with His Excellency's Troop of Horse Guards"[13] under the command of Colonel David Phips. Major Baldwin would soon demonstrate his competency as a leader and his ability to persevere in the face of adversity.

Although the Woburn troops, like all the others converging on Concord, were shopkeepers and farmers, the Massachusetts town defense militia structure dated back a century to King Philip's War. The companies included men who had repeatedly experienced hard fights against raiding Indians. They did not move in military array like the British regulars—three abreast and twelve deep in columns—but they assembled with thirty rounds of powder and ball apiece, and they marched rapidly to protect their families. They wore no uniforms, moving across the fields in their homespun linen and weather-beaten hats. Most answered the call carrying long-barreled muskets and wondering whether they would see their wives and children again. Two Woburn men would be shot down and three others wounded by the British. The work that day was about building a new nation. The building of canals and railroads would come later.

When the Woburn militia arrived at the Lexington Green, the English were gone. They had cleared the green and marched off toward Concord with a steady step to the fife and drum. All was silent around the green—the eerie silence that follows a storm of destruction. Baldwin and the Woburn men had arrived too late; they gazed upon a town green stained with blood.[14] Eighteen shopkeepers and farmers had fallen under the volley of the British line; eight of those were dead. Even though they were staggered by the slaughter, the Woburn men did not falter. Baldwin turned his companies down the Concord road to pursue the British. As they neared Concord, there was smoke from burning contraband and confusion, but again the Woburn men were too late. The fight at the Old North Bridge was over and the British were preparing to withdraw.

Baldwin reversed the line of march and led his militia back down the Lexington road to await the British column on its return to Boston. He and many other militia commanders who had hurried their companies to Concord were now repositioning their men to stop the British withdrawal. At Meriam's Corner, about a mile from Concord Village and still five miles from Lexington, the British entered a gauntlet of militia companies fighting Indian style.[15] From behind stone walls and trees, the militia sniped at the redcoat line. The flank guards, which the British had sent out into the woods on the left and right of the road to protect the column, were by these attacks pushed in toward the main column. The Americans quickly took advantage of the situation and moved into the heavy underbrush within fifty yards of the road.

Skillfully, and with a good eye for ground, the thirty-one-year-old Baldwin positioned his Woburn companies in the woods, where the road ascended a hill after crossing Elm Brook. It was a spot where the woods came down to meet the road on one side. At this point, just before the crest of the hill, the road made a turn to the left, forcing the British column to march into the tight angle of the turn. But only a short distance farther, the road turned to the right. In his diary, Baldwin described the fight: "We . . . scatter[ed] and made use of trees and walls for to defend us, and attack them."[16] Between those two crucial turns, Baldwin's Woburn militia waited as the first British regiment came up the hill, driven by the harassing fire from other militia companies. The red line came on at a trot, and the forward companies of the column took the full shock of the Woburn milita muskets when Baldwin ordered his men to fire. At that turn in the road, which later writers would call the "Bloody Angle," shopkeepers and farmers exacted revenge for the Lexington savagery. Eight redcoats died on the spot and another twenty were wounded by the lead of the Woburn men. All of the junior officers in the redcoats' first company were hit almost immediately. British Lieutenant William Sutherland recorded later: "Upon our ascending the height to the road, [the Woburn Militia] gave us a very heavy fire. . . ." Riding in a confiscated buggy, Sutherland, with an ugly wound across his chest, returned to Boston at the rear of the harassed column.

Baldwin was everywhere, waving his saber and encouraging his men.[17] In his diary, he later described the action, saying, "The enemy marched very fast and left many dead and wounded, and a few tired."[18] He had disrupted the British march to such an extent that other militia units were able to greet the column with another ambush before the redcoats finally reached Lexington and the protection of the relief column sent from Boston by General Thomas Gage.

Lord Hugh Percy, commander of the British relief column, deployed his men and cannons, two six-pounders, at Lexington to provide cover for the infantry and grenadiers fleeing from Concord. The Americans instantly took up positions on both flanks of the British position and began sniping at every opportunity. In his diary, Baldwin wrote, "I proceeded on till coming between the meeting-house and Buckman's Tavern with a prisoner before me, when the cannon began to play, the balls flew near me, I judge not more than 2 yards off." When he took shelter with a large group of militia behind Reverend Jonas Clark's meetinghouse on the green, Percy directed his cannons at the meetinghouse.

A cannonball missed Baldwin, but splintered boards showered him as it sailed through the building,[19] so he retreated to a meadow where wisdom led him to lie on the ground out of cannon range.

Returning home to Woburn following his experiences at Lexington and Concord, Loammi Baldwin enlisted in the Continental Army's 38th Regiment of Foot (infantry). The regiment's companies were positioned in the lines of Washington's army surrounding Boston, so he was not far from home. He became the regiment's commanding officer in August 1775. When the Army was reorganized at the close of 1775, the 38th was redesignated the 26th, and on the first of January in 1776, Baldwin was commissioned a colonel in the Continental Army by order of "John Hancock, President of the Congress of the United States."[20] He wrote to his wife from Chelsea on 6 March 1776: "I have had much to do, constantly keeping a party on Noddle's Island for spies to discover all the movements of the enemy."[21] Noddle's Island was a large island located between Hog Island and Chelsea, northeast of Boston. The island was connected to the mainland in the 1940s, and it is now part of East Boston. During the War of 1812, Loammi Baldwin Jr. would direct the building of a fort on Noddle's Island to protect the city. The construction of that fort would be Loammi Jr.'s first major engineering work.

In April of 1776, after pushing the British out of Boston, Baldwin and his troops followed Washington and the Continental Army to New York City and later participated in the faltering retreat into Pennsylvania at the end of the year. These were worrisome and hard times for Baldwin and his family. In June, a letter from his wife brought the sad news that their youngest child, Mary, had died; by the first of August, Baldwin himself was seriously ill. He took a short leave to recover at home, but because of the British offensive in the fall, he hurried back to rejoin his regiment at Fort Constitution, New Jersey. The army's retreat across New Jersey took its toll on Baldwin. In a letter home, he reported: "I have been fatigued all day in the skirmish and exercised at the same time with dysentery which has now followed me for seven weeks." But he still seemed to have a sense of humor, relating, "I have been obliged sometimes to lodge . . . on the bare floor or soft side of a board."[22]

The fight at the Bloody Angle was Baldwin's moment of glory during the revolution, but he was a participant in Washington's daring enterprise of crossing the Delaware River and capturing the Hessian troops at Trenton on 26 December 1776.[23] Sometime in early 1777, he was honorably discharged from the Continental Army for health reasons. He had demonstrated the courage to challenge the professional army of Great Britain, and soon he and his sons would surmount great engineering challenges that other men had warned against, saying the Baldwins were "engaged in a ruinous and impractical project, involving immense expense, and which [they will] never accomplish." Such comments greeted Baldwin when he began construction of the Middlesex Canal.[24] His detractors failed to appreciate how hard he and his sons were willing to work as they sought to develop their engineering knowledge.

Education of an American Engineer

As a lad, Loammi Baldwin attended Master John Fowle's grammar school in Woburn, where he "was taught reading, writing, arithmetic, and the grammar of his own language, through the medium of the Latin."[25] He later trained as a cabinetmaker while he continued to help in the store kept by his father next to their house. Even into his late teens, he would occasionally attend Master Fowle's school to study John Potter's *A System of Practical Mathematics* (1757). Loammi liked to apply book learning to practical purposes, so sometime after 1767 he started a pump-making business while still laboring at his studies. He signed himself Loammi Baldwin *joiner* or Loammi Baldwin *cabinetmaker*, as he considered himself a professional man.

Baldwin had an inquiring mind, and even though he was never a regular student at Harvard, he obtained special permission in 1771, when he was twenty-seven years old, to attend Professor John Winthrop's Experimental Philosophy lectures. His notebooks, with headings such as "Experiments of the Air Pump, Lectures upon Dioptics, Optics, Lences [lenses], Refractions, Hydrostatics, and Hydrolics [hydraulics] & Pneumatics,"[26] illustrate the technical nature of those lectures. Harvard College, located in Cambridge, was "by shady roads and green fields, and easy hills and pleasant ponds,"[27] some eight miles south of Woburn, so on lecture days Baldwin and his friend Benjamin Thompson would discuss the lecture topics while making the trek to class. Thompson, who remained a loyal Tory, would later in life become a noted physicist. For his service to Charles Theodore, the elector of Bavaria, he received the title of Count of the Holy Roman Empire. He then assumed the title of Count Rumford, choosing the name because Rumford (now Concord) was the New Hampshire town where he had begun his career as a humble schoolmaster. Focused by Winthrop's lectures, Baldwin's inquisitiveness led him to fashion rough instruments to repeat the experiments discussed in the classroom; on his own, he continued to work at developing a grasp of mathematics and hydraulics.

Exactly how or from whom Baldwin learned surveying is not clear, but John Winthrop did teach the elements of geometry and surveying until 1779. Even before the revolution, however, Baldwin was engaged in making surveys for land transactions, and in 1773 he was elected for a term of one year as surveyor of highways and roads for the town of Woburn. On several occasions during the revolution, he was employed as an engineer. On 3 June 1775, he wrote to the Massachusetts Congress to request the loan of "some mathematical instruments" (survey instruments) belonging to Harvard College so he could make a survey "of the ground between us and our enemies."[28] Later he reported, "My brother came down in order to help me survey Lechmere Point." Even after he resigned and was released by the army, he continued to render service as an engineer. Massachusetts engaged him in 1779 to "see to the repair of the fortifications in Boston Harbor for immediate defense." As late as 1785, the forty-one-year-old Baldwin attended Dr. Henry Moyer's lectures on the "Structure of the Earth, Hydraulics, Pneumatics, and Mechanics."

Following the revolution, there was little money for engineering works, so few engineers were needed in the new federation. Since there were no engineering schools in the new nation, when a project was proposed, an engineer was enticed to come to America from Britain or Europe. Construction of the Santee Canal in South Carolina, which started in 1786, was accomplished under the direction of John Christian Senf, a Swedish engineer who had served in the Continental Army after being captured with his British employers at Saratoga. He returned to Europe in 1784–85, inspecting hydraulic works in Holland before accepting the canal engineering challenge in South Carolina.[29]

So in 1793, when a group of Medford men, led by James Sullivan, attorney general of Massachusetts, were successful in petitioning the General Court to grant them incorporation for building a canal from the Merrimack River to Boston,[30] their first difficulty was in securing someone with engineering knowledge to direct the work. Loammi Baldwin, the borer of logs for crafting pumps and sometime builder of cabinets, would soon direct his avocation for physical sciences toward a practical application. As a result, he would become the most influential civil engineer in New England.

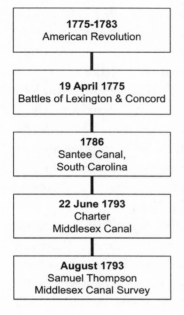

1775-1783
American Revolution

19 April 1775
Battles of Lexington & Concord

1786
Santee Canal,
South Carolina

22 June 1793
Charter
Middlesex Canal

August 1793
Samuel Thompson
Middlesex Canal Survey

The Proprietors

The gentlemen who came together for the canal enterprise were referred to as the "Proprietors" because the bill titled the corporation "The Proprietors of the Middlesex Canal." During the course of the work, they and those who later joined them were the sole sources of the project's construction funds. Each time more money was needed to keep the project going, they would pay stock subscription fees. These were men of commerce who knew the value of efficient transportation, and they fully believed the canal would stimulate their businesses. Their hope was to tap into the timberlands of New Hampshire and furnish an outlet for agricultural products north of Boston. They were convinced the canal would prove a profitable investment.

Blanchard's Tavern in Medford was the site of the Proprietors' first meeting. There they entrusted the management of the corporation to a board of thirteen subscription holders.[31] But the board did not meet to organize until 11 October, when James Sullivan was chosen as president and Loammi Baldwin was voted first vice president.[32] Even before the company was fully organized, a survey was undertaken to site the canal. Samuel Thompson, a magistrate of Woburn and a self-taught surveyor, made this primary examination of the ground in August of 1793.[33] He was assisted by Loammi Baldwin, Judge James Winthrop (the son of Professor John Winthrop), and Benjamin Franklin Baldwin, Loammi's fifteen-year-old son. Benjamin served as the errand boy for the group. The fieldwork took nine days. While it was done very carefully, the directors of the enterprise immediately recognized the work lacked accuracy regarding the elevations assigned to points along the route. Furthermore, they realized that neither Thompson nor anyone else in New England owned an instrument for the accurate determination of elevations. Though it is not known for sure, Thompson's only instrument was most likely a compass with sights. Since a compass is used to measure direction rather than elevation, Thompson and those assisting him could only estimate differences in elevation between ridgelines and valleys.

None of the company's other directors had experience with such matters, so it is plausible Loammi Baldwin was the one who voiced concern about the accuracy of the survey. But it is also possible the directors, who often traveled the route to Boston to conduct their respective businesses, had gained a feel for the rise and fall of the land and so held opinions opposing what Thompson reported. It is known that after the survey was completed, Baldwin went to Boston and met with General Henry Knox, then the secretary of war, and Knox's surveyor, John Hills, to discuss the survey and the problem of accurately determining elevations. In the late 1780s, Knox had suggested a waterway from Boston to the Connecticut River, and in March 1792, he was granted a bill of incorporation for the privilege of opening a canal from the Connecticut River to Boston.[34] In 1791 and again in 1792, Knox employed Hills to conduct preliminary canal surveys across Massachusetts from Boston to the Connecticut River.

John Hills served as a draftsman in the British Army during the revolution and had later acquitted himself with credit as an engineer.[35] Following the war, he remained in the colonies and established himself as a surveyor and draftsman in Philadelphia. During the period when the new country operated under the Articles of Confederation, Knox, as secretary of war, resided in Philadelphia, and it is probable he met Hills there. Some of the Massachusetts maps Hills made for Knox were later used in 1825 by the Boston to Hudson Canal commissioners who employed Baldwin's son Loammi Jr.

Following the meeting with Knox and his surveyor, Baldwin spent three days in Boston with a Mr. Cross, constructing a device to use in ascertaining elevations. There is no surviving description of this device, but the company's vouchers for the period 15 to 21 October 1793 identify the purchase of an iron screw, some loops, and four pieces of cherry wood. It is possible Baldwin, a consummate tinkerer, constructed a plummet level. Such devices for checking elevations dated to the beginning of the Christian era, and French authors provided detailed descriptions of several types as early as 1553. By holding the instrument so the plumb fell vertically, a person could make an elevation sighting along the horizontal bar of such a device. With his new instrument, Baldwin, James Winthrop, and Samuel Jaques, a yeoman farmer (the term applied to small landowners who farmed their own land), spent the following week again trying to ascertain the rise and fall of the land through which the canal would have to pass. This second effort convinced the directors that the services of a professional engineer were indispensable.

Therefore, in November 1793, James Sullivan wrote to Knox in Philadelphia asking for his assistance in securing "a man, who is skilled in the business of canaling."[38] Knox informed Sullivan that a Philadelphia group led by Robert

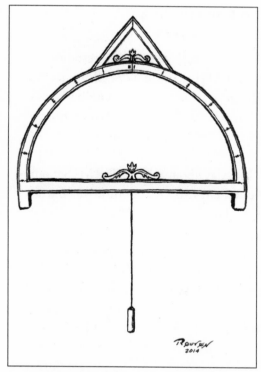

Suspended plummet (plumb bob) level of the sixteenth century (original drawing in *De Re Metallica*, 1556)[36]

A plummet (plumb bob) level and stand of the seventeenth century (original drawing in *La Science des Eaux*, 1653)[37]

Morris had succeeded in securing the services of William Weston, an engineer from England, to help them with canal projects in Pennsylvania. At the time he was hired by Morris, Weston was engaged in building canals in Ireland, and it seems he had previously worked under other engineers directing canal work in central England.[39] Mr. Weston and his bride had arrived in Philadelphia in early January 1793.

Work on the Schuylkill and Susquehanna Canal was already in progress when Weston reached Pennsylvania, so he promptly met with his employers and then left the city to inspect the work. In about two years, the company's financial conditions deteriorated and work was suspended. The plan, however, would not expire with the work stoppage. The idea smoldered until resurrected in 1811 as the Union Canal, with Loammi Baldwin Jr. as the chief engineer.

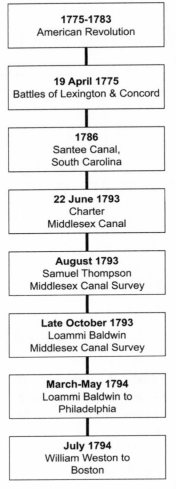

1775-1783   American Revolution
19 April 1775   Battles of Lexington & Concord
1786   Santee Canal,   South Carolina
22 June 1793   Charter   Middlesex Canal
August 1793   Samuel Thompson   Middlesex Canal Survey
Late October 1793   Loammi Baldwin   Middlesex Canal Survey
March-May 1794   Loammi Baldwin to   Philadelphia
July 1794   William Weston to   Boston

A Journey to Philadelphia

With the hope that William Weston would return to Philadelphia, Knox had delayed his response to James Sullivan until February of 1794. But once he informed Sullivan a knowledgeable engineer was working in Pennsylvania, Loammi Baldwin was immediately dispatched to secure his services. In his almanac diary, Baldwin recorded his trip on 10 March 1794: "Monday about 3 O'clock P.M. Set out for the Southern States to ye appointment and at the request of the Directors of the Middlesex Canal to View the Canals. Engage an artist in our service & make such further enquiry as shall think proper."

When Baldwin arrived in Philadelphia on 18 March, he found that Weston was extremely busy in planning not one but two canals—the Schuylkill and Susquehanna and the Schuylkill and Delaware. In addition, Robert Morris had asked him to give attention to the Philadelphia and Lancaster Turnpike, which had been surveyed previously by David Rittenhouse. Like the Schuylkill and Susquehanna Canal, this turnpike project was well underway when Weston arrived. Rittenhouse, who was sixty-four years old at this time, was a self-educated maker of mathematical instruments. Both Baldwin and Rittenhouse had been elected to the American Academy of Arts and Sciences in 1782. This connection might have provided them with a further conduit for discussing matters of science.

Morris and the Philadelphians were reluctant to release their engineer, and Weston was dubious of interrupting his lucrative employment, which garnered him £1,680 per year. This was an enormous salary, equivalent to about $8,000 in 1793 American currency. By comparison, the new republic's vice president, John Adams, received a salary of $5,000.[40] John Rennie, the noted British engineer who worked on the Aberdeen, Great Western, and Kennet Canals in England, had advised the Morris group that £800 to £1,000 per year was a reasonable salary.[41]

Loammi Baldwin, however, seems to have possessed both a keen technical mind and an appreciation for personal relationships. He immediately perceived that Mrs. Weston was the key to securing the engineering services the proprietors desired, so he wrote to Sullivan:

> *Mrs. Weston has more than once expressed a passionate desire of visiting Boston. . . . I dare say that in my important business you will think this a very trifling circumstance to report to you—however after all that our friends have done I declare that almost my only hope of securing Mr. Weston's assistance in season rests on this circumstance.*

To satisfy Robert Morris's concerns about losing the services of his engineer, Baldwin volunteered to assist with the preparation of plans for a bridge across the Delaware River at Trenton. The multitalented Baldwin was a director in the joint-stock company that built Boston's Charles River Bridge in 1785–86, and there is evidence he carried out the survey to determine the river's depth at the bridge site and performed other surveys to determine the required bridge length for the crossing. Later he served as a consultant[42] to the builders, Major Samuel Sewall, the architect, and Mr. Cox,[43] master workman. The work gave Baldwin more knowledge and experience than almost any other bridge builder in America.[44] It was an age of very short bridges, and the Charles River Bridge in Boston was the only permanent bridge in existence to span a river of any size.[45] Major Sewall seems to have been the person primarily responsible for the design of this 1,503-foot-long[46] structure supported on seventy-five oak piers.[47] He was brought to Boston from York, Maine, because of a reputation established when he built a bridge spanning the York River in 1761. Sewall's Bridge is credited as being the first drawbridge engineered and built in America. The other unique feature of Sewall's Bridge was its system of driven piles to support the spans. Baldwin's firsthand knowledge of this engineering feat impressed Morris.

While in the South, Baldwin took time to inspect the locks and canal work on the Potomac River above Georgetown—a pet project of George Washington. In 1785, when the "Patomack Company" was incorporated, Washington served as company president. Because Washington had a keen interest in canals and, even more importantly, because of his desire to open the Potomac to navigation, he conducted several interviews with Weston in 1794. In response to Washington's urgings, Weston would examine the work on the Potomac at Great Falls in March 1795 and submit a report. In his letters, Washington, who was extremely good at judging men, spoke highly of Weston's competence as an engineer. His letters frequently contain complimentary references regarding Weston's skill and judgment.[48]

After obtaining a promise from Weston to visit Massachusetts, Baldwin returned to Woburn in May. His inspections of the Potomac work and his conversations with Weston had added greatly to his knowledge and understanding of canal engineering and lock building, but of equal importance was the fact that he carried back to Woburn a Wye (Y) level. This instrument, borrowed from Weston, was the first such surveying instrument brought to America.

A Wye level is a telescope with crosshairs, but the telescope is mounted so it can be positioned perfectly level before a sighting is made. The telescope rests on a pair of vertical Y posts, hence its name. The Y posts are mounted on a horizontal bar containing a bubble level. Once the instrument is leveled, a surveyor can sight on a graduated vertical rod to accurately determine the elevation of any point relative to another point. With this instrument, measurements of elevation could be made repeatedly and continuously along a route. In Baldwin's case, the elevations he needed to determine were along a canal route.

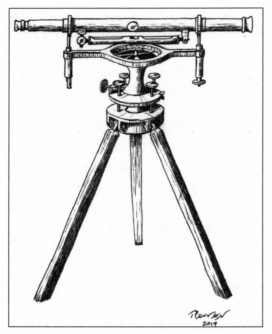

A Wye spirit level[49]

Loammi Baldwin immediately realized the value of Weston's Wye level, particularly after his own experiences in trying to determine elevations along the route of the Middlesex Canal the previous year. James Sullivan, who was quite familiar with and fully appreciated the surveying problem, probably did not have to be convinced of the value to be derived from spending $163.35 to obtain two such instruments and rods from London. In June, the captain of a ship sailing for London carried Sullivan's orders to obtain two Wye levels and two rods from "Mr. Troughton Mathematical Instrument Maker, Fleet Street, London."[50]

Actually, the firm on Fleet Street during this period was a partnership of two brothers, John and Edward Troughton, who were both excellent instrument makers. Their achievements were considerable, as evidenced by the fact that when the British Society of Civil Engineers established a class of honorary members in 1793, John Troughton, the senior brother, was one of two instrument makers invited to join the society. Later, Edward was likewise honored.[51]

A Visit to Boston

As promised, William Weston and his wife, Charlotte,[52] arrived in Boston on 13 July 1794. Baldwin left the entertainment of Charlotte to Boston society while he spirited Weston to the field. Together they spent nine days surveying possible canal routes. This survey work served as a practical course in civil engineering for Baldwin's three sons. Cyrus, twenty-one at the time, was the rod man for the survey. Benjamin Franklin, who was sixteen, served as a chainman with the four-rod or sixty-six-foot chain used to measure distance. Fourteen-year-old Loammi Jr. was responsible for the horses and the two-wheeled carriage with the party's baggage. It can truly be said that Loammi Jr., the man who would later be titled the Father of American Civil Engineering,[53] gained his professional knowledge in the field working at all possible tasks. At this time, Loammi Jr. was well along with his studies at Westford Academy, and he would enter Harvard in another two years. So even though his assignment was to manage the baggage, he was undoubtedly very stimulated by the work, as the future direction of his career bears out.

The results of this Weston-Baldwin survey confirmed what had been suspected: There were significant errors in the original Thompson work. Across the five-mile stretch separating the Concord and Merrimack rivers, the difference between what Thompson reported and the true lay of the land was 41.5 feet. On 2 August 1794, the English engineer submitted his report. It concluded that the proposed canal was feasible: "The ground through which this canal has been surveyed is extremely favorable for cutting."[54] Weston and Baldwin laid out two possible routes for consideration by James Sullivan and the proprietors. But Weston's more significant long-term contribution came from his conversations with Baldwin and Baldwin's sons about engineering work. He instructed Baldwin and his sons about critical engineering questions. Weston explained in detail the issues one needed to consider when forming engineering judgments regarding canal design and construction.

After William Weston departed, all of the engineering for the Middlesex Canal rested on Baldwin's shoulders. On the first of October, the board of directors made him superintendent of the Middlesex Canal at a salary of $1,000 per year. Weston never returned to the project, but Baldwin maintained communication with him, seeking engineering advice and guidance. It was an eighteenth-century correspondence course in canal engineering.[55] Their letters discussed the proper dimensions for the canal, the dimensions of the locks, the important issue of constructing watertight masonry lock walls, and the design of a mechanical means for operating the lock gates. Then as now, the question of which route to select, a question Weston had avoided, came down to nonengineering issues. The proprietors settled upon the more westerly route because "the inhabitants who are thickly settled on the west generally approve the plan."[56]

The Beginning of a Dynasty

As Loammi Baldwin, isolated in Massachusetts from other trained engineers, struggled to apply Professor John Winthrop's Experimental Philosophy lectures to the practical problems of building a canal, he must have had many thought-provoking discussions with his sons. His four oldest sons all worked with their father on the canal. They toiled as laborers and assisted with surveys, and they functioned as overseers and inspectors once they gained experience. The evidence of their professional lives shows that all of his boys shared their father's interest in engineering and were inspired by their close association with the construction of the Middlesex Canal. Cyrus (1773–1854), the oldest, would be employed for many years as manager of the canal's Merrimack terminal. The second son, Benjamin Franklin (1777–1821), was primarily a yeoman farmer. He died suddenly while traveling home from a cattle show in the Boston area but prior to his death, he was often called to work on projects with his brother Loammi Jr. In addition, a number of maps in the Massachusetts archives bear Benjamin's signature as draftsman, so it is apparent he was very active as a surveyor.

Loammi Baldwin Jr. (1780–1838), the third son and the surveyor of the Boston–Hudson canal route, entered Harvard in 1796. During his four years at Harvard, he passed his father's canal work repeatedly as he traveled between Woburn and Cambridge. The impact of being introduced to the Wye level by

Weston must have still been on the senior Baldwin's mind when he sent Loammi Jr. off to college. Count Rumford, his friend from Professor Winthrop's lectures at Harvard, was residing in London during this period, and Baldwin wrote to him seeking assistance in finding a position to nurture the talents of his son Loammi Jr.[57]

Woburn, November 4, 1799

My dear Count, —

I have already told you that I have a son at Harvard College, whose genius inclines him strongly to cultivate the arts. I have thought whether it would not be best to endeavor to provide him a place for a year or two with some gentleman in the mathematical line of business in Europe, who is actually in the occupation of making and vending mathematical and optical instruments in an eminent degree.

He is very lively, ready, and enterprising, and has even sustained a good character. I have raised expectations of his usefulness, if I can but hit his prevailing genius.

Yours sincerely
LOAMMI BALDWIN

He was hoping Loammi Jr. could learn both the art of making optical instruments and the mathematics behind such work. After Count Rumford replied, explaining the high cost and required duration of such a placement, the idea was dropped. Consequently, when Loammi Jr. completed his education at Harvard in 1800, he settled in Groton, twenty-five miles to the northwest of Woburn, to read law under Timothy Bigelow.

The fourth son, James Fowle (1782–1862), was living at home during the first six years of the canal's construction, and he too must have found watching the work stirring. About the time Loammi Jr. graduated from Harvard, James was sent off to Boston to become a merchant. He would, however, soon follow his brother Loammi into engineering and easily make the transition from canal to railroad engineering—something Loammi Jr. never truly managed.

Loammi Baldwin's fifth and youngest son, George Rumford (1798–1888), was a month away from his sixth birthday when the Middlesex Canal was completed, so his exposure to the work was minor—even though the canal literally cut through his backyard playground. But he had a talent for mathematics, and he would follow his brothers into the profession of engineering. As early as his fourteenth year, George was making drawings of Loammi Jr.'s work on Fort Strong in Boston Harbor. At times, he executed projects as an independent engineer and at other times he worked with Loammi Jr.. The Union Canal in Pennsylvania and the Pensacola, Florida Marine Railway for the U.S. Navy were two endeavors in which George assisted Loammi.

Bringing the work on the Middlesex Canal to a successful conclusion was the result of the elder Baldwin's perseverance, careful supervision of details, and continuing study of engineering. The moment of celebration came in the early morning hours of 31 December 1803, when water flowed continuously through the entire twenty-seven-mile length of the canal. To achieve this feat, Baldwin would become the earliest concrete researcher in the United States. He would also lead the way in the development of construction methods and techniques adaptable to the resources available in the new republic. He realized the value of engineering texts, and together with his sons he collected a large professional library. During construction of the Middlesex Canal, those texts helped Baldwin immensely in navigating many construction problems. Upon his death the library passed to his sons.

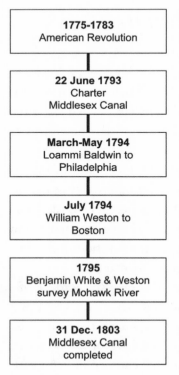

| 1775-1783 |
| American Revolution |

| 22 June 1793 |
| Charter |
| Middlesex Canal |

| March-May 1794 |
| Loammi Baldwin to |
| Philadelphia |

| July 1794 |
| William Weston to |
| Boston |

| 1795 |
| Benjamin White & Weston |
| survey Mohawk River |

| 31 Dec. 1803 |
| Middlesex Canal |
| completed |

Building the Middlesex Canal

Some of the men who labored under Baldwin to build the canal were diligent, hardy workers. Others, however, were—as an Irish man working on another canal noted in a letter—nothing but "old soldiers, and the very refuse of the army."[58] For either type of man, the stout Irish man or the refuse of the army, building a canal and constructing locks were completely new types of labor. The field supervisors were competent builders, particularly in the case of working with wood, but most were barely literate. Consequently, Baldwin had to explain in excruciating detail how to perform many of the necessary tasks. He also had to respect the practices of the era. Men who worked outside every day in the cold and wet of early spring and late fall, and through the summer under the blaze of the sun, expected their grog, a mixture of water and rum, twice a day. Nevertheless, it was a time when a laborer fortunately was versatile—working one day as a blacksmith and the next as a teamster, and possibly later in the week as a mason.

The digging of canal sections was fairly simple, especially if rock was not involved; it was basically the same as digging a ditch. Local landowners or yeoman farmers often accomplished such work, and arrangements for yeomen to complete the excavation of canal sections worked very well in most cases. These men were experienced in digging ditches and removing stumps. The problem for Baldwin was that often the men undertook canal building for secondary income, and work on the canal came after their work on the farm. As a result, delays in completing even short sections of excavation were common. Besides using working yeoman farmers, Baldwin let portions of the canal excavation work to contracting firms. Many of these sections were completed satisfactorily, but there were cases when the contracting firms experienced problems—usually because of unexpected soil conditions. Twenty-seven and a quarter miles of thirty-foot-wide ditch is a mighty task when all you have to work with are spades, pickaxes, and wheelbarrows.

Engineer-in-training Baldwin faced three major technical problems during the course of building the canal. The first problem was in developing a construction method for creating a watertight canal. The second problem had to do with masonry lock construction. In building the stone locks, it was necessary to find a source of cementitious material and then to determine the correct proportions for creating a cement mortar that would provide a waterproof bond between the stone blocks. The third problem was in locating a foundry capable of casting the iron parts for operating the valves and gates needed to control the water flow into and out of the lock chambers.

Farmers could dig trenches and pile up the earthen embankments, but creating a watertight canal was something new—they had no experience to guide them. Leakage in the elevated sections of the canal became a continuous problem for Baldwin, and all of the proprietors felt the need to pummel him with solutions. Many of their ideas bordered on the bizarre. James Sullivan suggested that the banks should be made of a "slimy and glutinous substance." What do those words mean? Engineers in England and Europe had built many canals, and they had developed a practical "puddle gutter" procedure to ensure that elevated canal sections did not leak.

The term *puddle gutter* referred to three-foot-wide walls of "best of earth, clear of stones and rubbish,"[59] built into the embankments on both sides of a canal's trough. Baldwin had knowledge of both puddle-gutter walls and the puddling process, which consisted of chopping and mixing clay with water to obtain a semiplastic paste. Whether he learned this from William Weston or from reading engineering books, it is not clear, but he did know that to build the impermeable walls, the plastic-clay material was supposed to be placed and compacted in thin layers or lifts. Furthermore, puddle material was supposed to be spread as a lining in the canal trough. But creating puddle-gutter walls and applying processed clay as a canal lining was hard work, representing a significant additional cost for completing the project.

The canal seems to have had an initial cost estimate of around $500,000, though at first many believed the canal could be constructed for much less. It was soon realized that the needed labor was expensive (it could not be procured for less than $10 a month with board[60]) and the expense of properly constructing puddle gutters put added strain to the budget. Because of the added cost, the proprietors and their engineer sought other solutions for the leakage problem. First they tried ramming and pounding or compaction of the banks. Then they used loaded ox carts to travel up the finished banks. Baldwin even experimented with admitting water into and then draining canal sections "to season and consolidate the banks."[61] These practices were helpful in controlling the leakage, but they were not completely successful. This "weeping" problem would plague the proprietors until the railroads finally put the canal out of its tearful misery.

The first locks built on the Middlesex Canal were located at the junction of the canal and the Merrimack River. At the time, Baldwin's lock-building knowledge was practically nonexistent. He had corresponded with Weston about the matter, and he had seen the Potomac work. This was the extent of his familiarity with building a lock. Therefore, the proprietors decided that a committee should supervise the building of this first set of stone locks.

The first problem they addressed was the creation of hydraulic cement. In the 1790s and early 1800s, when the locks for the Middlesex Canal were built, a consistent theory for cement had not evolved. English engineers of high repute, including John Smeaton (1724–94), who is sometimes referred to as the Father of Civil Engineering, and others all held different opinions, but builders as far back as Roman times knew that a material manufactured by commingling volcanic pozzuolana and lime would harden under water. Marcus Vitruvius Pollio, an architect and engineer under Julius Caesar, had documented such a mixture.[62]

Among English engineers at the time, the usual practice was to create a cementitious material by mixing trass—a volcanic tuff found in the Westphalia region of Germany—with lime. Smeaton, when building the Eddystone in 1756, had discovered a reference to "Terra Puzzolana" by the French engineer Bernard Forest de Bélidor in his *Architecture Hydraulique*. One can draw an interesting historical link between Smeaton's work and that of engineer Baldwin in Massachusetts. Smeaton's Eddystone Lighthouse was built for the English town of Plymouth from which Pilgrims sailed, and now Baldwin was building for the descendants of the resulting Plymouth Colony in America.

Based on what Smeaton gleaned from Bélidor's work, he decided to perform his own experiments to compare the performance of the trass and the terra pozzuolana secured from Italy. In 1791, years after completing his research, Smeaton published a description of his findings in a volume[63] on the construction of the Eddystone Lighthouse (which he spelled "Edystone"). He provided the proportions of his mix and reported that "Terra Puzzolana" was stronger and better than trass.

The directors of the Middlesex Canal had knowledge about the use of terra pozzuolana in England and tried "to obtain particular information as to compounding,"[64] or, more specifically, the proportions of terra pozzuolana and lime that should be used in the mixture. Smeaton's book held the answer to their questions, and the committee made efforts to obtain a copy, but it was 1798[65] before their agents were able to deliver the book to Boston. Twenty years later, Loammi Jr. would recommend the volume to the Virginia Board of Public Works, stating, "Smeaton's reports are very valuable, and afford more information upon hydraulic labors than any other English book."[66] But the book was not available to his father, and before anything definite was learned about the terra pozzuolana mixture, Aaron Dexter, a member of the proprietors' lock committee and a professor of chemistry and materia medica at Harvard, learned that trass could be procured from the island of St. Eustatius in the Dutch West Indies. Receiving this news, Sullivan immediately dispatched a sloop to secure a load of trass for the project.

Complete blending of the trass and lime was a critical factor in producing strong hydraulic cement capable of enduring the constant wetting-and-drying conditions experienced in a lock. The blending process used in England added the lime to the trass stones before the trass was pulverized. To crush the trass stones, the dry trass–lime mix was subjected to heavy and prolonged beating with a timber. Intermittently the beating was interrupted and the pounded material was mix chopped and turned with a shovel to further blend the lime and the trass.

When the St. Eustatius trass arrived, Baldwin, just as Smeaton had done years earlier, conducted his own trass experiments. As a result of those experiments he formulated a set of proportions for achieving good hydraulic cement. Additionally, he developed a superior method for processing the trass. He chose to first grind the dry trass stones into a fine powder before mixing it with the lime and the water. In Holland, windmills were employed to pulverize trass under grinding stones; since the proprietors had established their own sawmills to provide lumber for building bridges over the canal and other needs, it is possible Baldwin adapted one of these mills for grinding his trass.

Processing the trass with Baldwin's grinding method made it possible to achieve good blending of the trass and the lime with much less effort. Next Baldwin experimented with the proportions of the trass–lime mix. Finally, he concluded that a mixture of two parts trass, one part lime, and three parts sand yielded the best mortar. He further reported, nine months after the opening of the Merrimack locks: "I have found the trass mortar which had been under water since it was first laid almost as hard as stone itself."[67]

Baldwin's employment of hydraulic cement during the building of the Middlesex Canal was probably the first use of such material in the United States, and his research served as the touchstone for the next twenty years. His pioneering work concerning cementaous materials was decades ahead of any other engineer in the United States. When New York set out to build the Erie Canal, it sent engineer Canvass White to England in 1817 to study the canals of the mother country and to learn how English engineers created hydraulic cement from limestone rock. When he returned, he explored upstate New York and located a suitable material. Not until White introduced these materials for creating hydraulic cement was the base of knowledge pushed beyond Baldwin's original research.

Manufacturing in the Colonies

During the colonial period, acts of the British Parliament systematically restricted all forms of manufacturing,[68] so very few iron-furnace operations had been established in the colonies prior to the American Revolution. On the Pawtuxet River in Rhode Island, a venture known as the Hope Furnace managed to open in 1765, producing kettles, nails, and iron hoops. During the Revolutionary War, it produced some seventy-six cannons for the colonials.

During construction of the first Middlesex lock, William Weston, who was still in the United States, supervised the casting of the iron gear mechanisms for the valves necessary to control the flow of water into and out of the lock chamber. He also had the racks, pinions, and other parts cast "from molds of his own forming."[69] The racks consisted of long iron rails that had cogs or teeth on one side. Cogwheels—wheels having teeth along their outer perim-eter—fitted into the teeth of the racks; when these were turned, they caused the valves to open. All of this work was done at a foundry in New York, but later, by the time mechanisms were needed for the other locks, Weston had returned to England. Inquiries in New York by agents for the proprietors were not successful in finding Weston's molds or in locating a foundry willing to undertake the work at a reasonable price. The issue lingered until Baldwin learned of a reputable foundry in Rhode Island operated by the Wilkinson brothers—David, Abraham, and Israel. Israel had been one of the partners in the original Hope Furnace enterprise.

The proprietors sent a representative to Pawtucket to inspect the brothers' foundry, and later, at a meeting in Boston, Baldwin himself had a conversation with a member of the family. An arrangement was reached and wooden patterns were sent to Pawtucket. When the iron pieces were received, however, the rack-and-pinion teeth did not mesh properly. They were so defective that Baldwin had to travel to the foundry and make adjustments to the patterns.

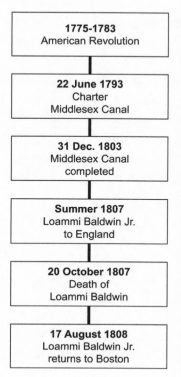

1775-1783
American Revolution

22 June 1793
Charter
Middlesex Canal

31 Dec. 1803
Middlesex Canal
completed

Summer 1807
Loammi Baldwin Jr.
to England

20 October 1807
Death of
Loammi Baldwin

17 August 1808
Loammi Baldwin Jr.
returns to Boston

Success

When water finally passed the length of his Middlesex Canal, the elder Loammi Baldwin's fame as an engineer was assured. Solving the many, many problems that had presented themselves over the ten years he labored to build the Middlesex made Baldwin one of the most knowledgeable civil engi-neers in the country. During the period when the canal was under construction, Loammi Jr. completed his studies at Harvard College and spent four years reading law in Groton. In the year following the opening of the canal, Loammi Jr. would establish a law office in Boston. His father, after retiring as superintendent of the Middlesex Canal, began trav-eling across New England, surveying and serving as a consultant for a host of projects. Baldwin's second son, Benjamin Franklin, assisted him with work in Massachusetts and New Hampshire. Diversi-fying his practice, he directed the building of the India Wharf in Boston, designed by America's first professional architect, Charles Bulfinch of Boston, and traveled to the District of Maine frequently to lay out the town of Baldwin. In 1803, as the Middlesex was nearing completion, he and Benjamin Franklin and Loammi Jr. made surveys for two canals to open the town site to water communication.

Baldwin turned sixty years old the January after the Middlesex Canal was completed, and although he was initially active with many projects, poor health soon began to interrupt his travels. Often one or more of his sons had to perform the fieldwork. After returning from New Hampshire in the late summer of 1807, he became continually weaker until he died on 20 October. By then, Loammi Jr. had closed his law office in Boston and gone off to England in order to make a close examination of British engineering works.

Evaluated strictly in terms of accomplished physical work, the Middlesex Canal achievement proved Baldwin's ". . . abilities were rare and noteworthy and his accomplishment was outstanding."[70] However, Baldwin's greatest achievement from an engineering standpoint was the way he influenced the direction of civil engineering. Loammi Baldwin, Revolutionary War soldier and self-taught engineer, moved civil engineering from practices guided by simple "rules of thumb" to a profession guided by scientific principles. Over the years, his library on engineering topics had continued to grow, and his sons Loammi Jr., James, and George would eventually expand it to almost 4,000 volumes. Returning from England in August 1808, following his father's death, Loammi Jr. brought home some fifty volumes. In 1899, his niece donated the collection to the Woburn Public Library,[71] and in 1914 it was transferred to the Massachusetts Institute of Technology.[72] All of Loammi's sons would work in the profession, but his namesake, Loammi Jr., would take the lead in continuing to advance engineering practice and in mentoring another generation of civil engineers who would look to building railroads instead of canals.

3

Canals vs. Steel Rails

Ascertain the practicability of making a Canal from Boston Harbour to Connecticut River and of extending the same to some point on the Hudson River in the State of New York.

—*Report of the Commissioners of the State of Massachusetts, on the Routes of Canals from Boston Harbour to Connecticut and Hudson Rivers* (Boston: True and Green, State Printers, 1826), 5.

L OAMMI BALDWIN JR. READ law with Timothy Bigelow, in preparation for entering the legal profession[1] but during his four years in Groton, he spent a goodly amount of time considering engineering matters. In 1804, after the Middlesex Canal was completed and while he was reading law, Baldwin wrote an account of his father's canal project for the *Boston Weekly Magazine*. This report was rated by a contemporary as "an excellent piece of technical analysis."[2] Later in 1804, he published a series of articles in Boston's *Columbian Centennial* newspaper entitled "Observations on Dry Docks," which included the suggestion of harnessing the tidal surges in Boston Harbor for powering machinery in mills. His idea of using the ocean's tide would eventually be taken up by others and would provide Baldwin with engineering employment.

During the second year of his law practice, now in Cambridge, Baldwin accepted an engineering commission from the Boston Commissioners of Sewers. Whether his father encouraged the change in career paths is not documented, but once the decision was made, the senior Baldwin lent his full support. Writing again to his old friend Count Rumford, who had moved to France, the senior Baldwin sought his assistance in introducing his son to engineers on the continent.

European conflicts, however, prevented aspiring engineers from gaining access to the continent. Lord Nelson's fleet had won the Battle of Trafalgar in October 1805, and Britain followed up on this naval advantage by blockading

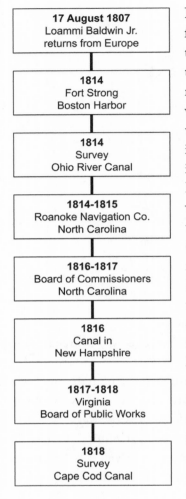

17 August 1807
Loammi Baldwin Jr.
returns from Europe

1814
Fort Strong
Boston Harbor

1814
Survey
Ohio River Canal

1814-1815
Roanoke Navigation Co.
North Carolina

1816-1817
Board of Commissioners
North Carolina

1816
Canal in
New Hampshire

1817-1818
Virginia
Board of Public Works

1818
Survey
Cape Cod Canal

French ports in May 1806. Even lacking a naval force, Napoleon was a threat to England, but he turned his Grand Army eastward in 1806, winning the battles of Jena and Auerstädt. After those victories, the British became more persistent in seeking ways to thwart Napoleon's power, and in 1807 they seized Denmark's fleet to keep it from falling into his hands. So when Loammi Baldwin arrived in England, it was almost impossible to cross the English Channel to visit the French engineering works and institutions. He had particularly wanted to visit L'École Nationale des Ponts et Chaussées (Bridges and Highways) and L'École Polytechnique, the world's leading engineering schools. The Royal Corps des Ponts et Chaussées dated from the thirteenth century, and even though L'École des Ponts et Chaussées was established in 1720,[3] it was not formally organized until 1747.[4] Napoleon, recognizing the state's need for engineers, had authorized the founding of L'École Polytechnique in 1794. Even at this early point in his own career, the younger Baldwin (presumably inspired by his father) was contemplating how to train future engineers. These French schools would later serve as the models for engineering education in the United States.

Loammi Baldwin Jr., like his father, had to learn engineering through self-study because there were still no formal engineering schools in America. The books in his father's library provided him with a solid theoretical foundation for his future profession, and throughout his career he diligently made astute examinations of engineering works whenever the opportunity arose. He clearly stated the purpose for his 1807 trip was to inspect the principal canals, docks, and manufactures in England and France. He considered his visit as an extension of his professional studies.

In the spring of 1823, he would again travel to England to visit canals and converse with the leading engineers. On this later occasion, he crossed the Channel and inspected many of the great works built by French engineers.

An Engineer for Boston

Returning from his first trip abroad in August 1807, Loammi Jr. opened an engineering office in Charlestown, across the Charles River from Boston. These were hard times in New England, as Thomas Jefferson's embargo, in response to the Napoleonic Wars, seriously affected the prosperity of Massachusetts's nautical commerce and Baldwin's chances of employment as an engineer. Because of the embargo's effect on commerce, there was agitation in the New England states for secession from the Union. When actual hostilities with Britain commenced, they would provide Baldwin with his first major engineering engagement. In the spring of 1814, British warships began sailing into the harbors of America's maritime cities, destroying property and vessels. A force of British seamen and marines, in small vessels, even traversed the Connecticut River in April and destroyed twenty-two vessels. The consternation in Boston and along the Massachusetts coast was very great—when the people learned the British had burned Washington in August 1814, the Yankees "had no mind to endure the [same] fate." The citizens of Massachusetts, therefore, "took prompt measures to protect themselves."[5]

> *Governor Strong, whose opposition to the war was intense, listened to this appeal, and at once instituted measures for the defense of the whole line of the coast of Massachusetts and of the District of Maine, its dependent. The high ground on Noddle's Island [now East Boston], known as Camp Hill, was chosen for the site of a new and heavy fort, and it was resolved to place its erection under the supervision of Loammi Baldwin, a graduate of Harvard College, as engineer.*[6]

Loammi's feelings about these events were recorded by his brother James: "He was glad to get into the profession he liked and give up law for good." The Fort Strong project was very similar to the work accomplished by his father thirty-nine years earlier for General George Washington. The inhabitants of Boston and the surrounding towns turned out and toiled like common laborers with their pickaxes, spades, shovels, and barrows. The *Boston Gazette* of 8 October reported: "Fort Strong progresses rapidly. On Saturday the citizens of Concord and Lincoln, to the number of two hundred, performed labor on it; the punctuality of the patriotic husbandmen deserved the highest praise of their fellow-citizens of the metropolis." Fort Strong, named for the governor, was ready for occupancy by 26 October.

After completing Fort Strong, Baldwin found his services in constant demand. Engineer William Weston, who had helped the senior Baldwin survey the Middlesex Canal, had returned to England, and the only other experienced engineer in the country was Benjamin Henry Latrobe (1764–1820). Latrobe was born in Yorkshire, England, but his mother was from a Pennsylvania family. Latrobe learned his engineering in a manner similar to that of Baldwin, first receiving a classical education at a Moravian seminary in Saxony and later completing his education at the University of Leipzig, also in Saxony. After service in the Prussian Army, Latrobe returned to England in 1786. Latrobe, like Baldwin, working for his father, then proceeded to learn the profession by employment in engineering offices. He spent several years in the London office of John Smeaton—the same Smeaton whose book on cement the proprietors of the Middlesex Canal had been unable to procure. Later, between 1791 and 1794, he worked on the Basingstoke Canal in southern England.[7] There is no evidence Baldwin and Latrobe ever met, yet there exists a web of connections throughout their professional lives. After the burning of Washington in 1814, Latrobe was appointed to direct the rebuilding of the Capitol. When he gave up that work in 1817, his successor was Charles Bulfinch, with whom the senior Baldwin had worked in Boston on the India Wharf project.

Canal Surveys

Baldwin's first work beyond his native Massachusetts came in November of 1814, when the state of Kentucky summoned him to perform a survey for a canal around the falls in the Ohio River at Louisville. This was another convergence between the Baldwin and Latrobe careers, for Aaron Burr had invited Latrobe in 1805 to perform a similar survey.

In 1807, President Thomas Jefferson's secretary of the treasury, Albert Gallatin, was directed by a Senate resolution to prepare a report regarding roads and canals. In preparing the report, Gallatin queried the senior Latrobe for his opinions "respecting artificial navigations and canals."[8] In responding to the request, Latrobe offered Gallatin a postscript observation: "It has however occurred to me, that a few remarks upon rail roads might not be unacceptable to you."[9] The report was probably the first printed work to advocate the construction of railroads in the United States, and as such it leads to another intertwining of careers.

Some fifty years in the future, Latrobe's son, also named Benjamin Henry (1807–78), would serve as a consultant to the great trans-Massachusetts work that resulted from Loammi's 1825 canal survey and report to General Dearborn—but the project would no longer be a canal. The senior Latrobe's postscript speculations about railroads, which had appeared in Albert Gallatin's internal-improvements report of 1808, would be borne out, and Baldwin's canal route would be used for a railroad. The challenge of building a tunnel through the Hoosac Mountain would be accepted by a number of the engineers who trained in Baldwin's Charlestown office, and the junior Latrobe would work as a consultant to the Commonwealth on the tunnel project.

After his survey in Kentucky in 1814, Baldwin was drawn farther south when the Roanoke Navigation Company of North Carolina engaged him and his brother Benjamin to survey routes and estimate the cost for canal and riverbed navigation works. Working far afield from cities or even large towns in 1814 and 1815, the brothers made use of rooms in taverns built of rough-hewn timbers. Space in these taverns served as their offices for drawing plans and preparing reports. Meals in such establishments, while sometimes decent, could be an adventure in eating, as the journal of another traveler articulates:

> *Having called for something to eat [the woman served] a dish of pork and cabbage. The sauce was a deep purple, which I thought was boiled in her dye kettle. What cabbage I swallowed served me for a cud the whole day after.*[10]

Benjamin remained in North Carolina directing the fieldwork for the Roanoke firm while his brother repeatedly made the journey across the Appalachians to direct the work in Kentucky.

While the federal government had failed to act on Gallatin's proposals for a national program of financial assistance for improving routes of internal communication, the North Carolina General Assembly in 1815 passed a plan for joint state–private development companies. The direction of these activities was placed under the control of a board of commissioners, which was empowered to employ an engineer and assistant engineer. The following year, the board invited Loammi and Benjamin Baldwin to continue their work in North Carolina by taking up these positions. Both men accepted the offer, though Loammi at the time was engaged with a project in New England, so only Benjamin returned immediately to North Carolina. Subsequently, Virginia in February 1816 created a Fund for Internal Improvement and a Board of Public Works to supervise and aid private companies in constructing roads and canals. After seeking advice from Latrobe as to the knowledge and qualities a competent state engineer should possess, the Virginia board began its search for a capable engineer. Daniel Webster wrote to

Board Chairman Charles Mercer recommending Loammi Baldwin. "As to his reputation as a gentleman and man of character, the most conspicuous gentleman in New England would introduce Baldwin to your knowledge and confidence."[11] When the position of state engineer was offered to Baldwin, he accepted, but he also explained the necessity of completing his existing commitments. "I am now employed by the General Court of Massachusetts to survey for a canal in New Hampshire. I shall finish that immediately and then go to North Carolina to survey for . . . improvements in inland navigation under the act of the government of North Carolina."[12]

Finishing the surveys in New England must have been extremely grueling in 1816. The April 1815 eruption of Mount Tambora in Indonesia, the largest volcanic eruption in recorded history, caused vast amounts of ash and dust to fill the atmosphere around the globe. Different estimates placed the quantity at between eleven[13] and twenty-four[14] cubic miles of rock, ash, and dust ejected into the atmosphere. The dense ash shield from the eruption drifted into the Northern Hemisphere in 1816 and blocked sunlight to such an extent that very cold weather occurred even during the summer months. In New England, it was a summer of frosts. In Vermont, just to the west of where Baldwin was surveying, a foot of snow fell on 8 June, and the drifts were three or four feet deep. Vermont also had snow in August and September.[15]

Although Loammi Jr. did not begin working for the Virginia Board of Public Works until February of 1817, his new position with the state was confirmed on 20 November 1816.[16] When his brother Benjamin completed the survey and report in North Carolina with respect to navigation on the Cape Fear River in early 1817, the board encouraged him to remain, but he politely refused the reappointment offer. As many engineers during this period would soon discover, working for public boards subjected you to the abuse of political factions. Apparently Benjamin was both homesick for New England and tired of working under political scrutiny. His health may also have been a factor for although he was only forty, he would be dead within four years.

Baldwin's first tasks in Virginia were to survey the Rappahannock and Rapidan rivers for the purpose of opening each to navigation. Following those surveys, the board asked him to explore the possibility of creating a waterway/turnpike road over the mountains to the west. The plan was to use the James and Kanawha rivers on each side of the Appalachian Mountains as waterway routes for the greatest part of the distance. The route would follow the James River through its gap in the Blue Ridge Mountains as far as possible. From the headwaters of the James, a mountain road would provide passage to the Kanawha River. The Kanawha was navigable from its confluence with the Ohio River at Point Pleasant to its great falls just below the community of Gauley Bridge where the New River and Scrabble Creek joined to form the Kanawha River. The proponents of the plan believed reaching the Kanawha below the falls would open a through route to the Ohio River. Baldwin's survey, therefore, included laying out 100 miles of road across the mountains to the great falls of the Kanawha.

Writing to his brother Benjamin, Loammi told a familiar story of the travails experienced by all men engaged in backcountry work: "The roads here are terrible." This was the very reason why every state was considering canals. One of his last projects in Virginia was a canal survey down the Potomac River to Alexandria. This followed the route of the original Potomac project and some of the work his father had examined in 1793. It would be another decade before this project would be undertaken as part of the Chesapeake and Ohio Canal, but by then Baltimore merchants had given up on a canal and made the decision to push a railroad along the river and over the mountains to the Ohio River. That railroad work would provide a challenge for Latrobe's son Benjamin Henry.

Completing his surveys in Virginia, Baldwin returned to Massachusetts in the fall of 1818. At the invitation of the Commonwealth, he executed a survey and report for a canal to be built across the neck of Cape Cod.

The Mill Dam

For the greater part of four years, Loammi Baldwin Jr. had been employed by government boards, making surveys and estimating the costs of canal projects from Massachusetts to North Carolina and as far west as Louisville in Kentucky. Finally, in late 1819, he was offered the opportunity to build a major project. The Boston and Roxbury Mill Dam Corporation named Baldwin their superintendent to direct the building of two dams, on top of which toll roads were to be located. Today, in the Back Bay area of Boston, Beacon Street follows the top crest of Baldwin's 1½-mile-long Mill Dam. Massachusetts Avenue approximately follows the crest of the second (or cross) dam. These dams were designed

17 August 1807 Loammi Baldwin Jr. returns from Europe

1814 Fort Strong Boston Harbor

1817-1818 Virginia Board of Public Works

1818-1821 Mill Dam Boston

1821-1822 Union Canal Pennsylvania

1823-1824 Inspection tour in Europe

to create a basin for trapping the high tide waters of the Atlantic. The retained water was then slowly released to drive machinery in a series of mills. With a project closer to home, Baldwin's brother Benjamin again participated as a partner.

It is not clear whether or not Uriah Cotting, the leading proponent of the project, read Baldwin's 1804 mill scheme, but this project was very similar in concept and mirrored the ideas Baldwin had proposed some fifteen years earlier. Cotting, a wealthy Boston real estate promoter, put all of his energy into the mill dam project, even serving as its initial engineer. Through his efforts, a charter for the project was obtained in 1814. Still work did not commence until 1818, but then Cotting died in May of 1819 and the company was now in need of a qualified engineer. Like his father on the Middlesex Canal project, Loammi Baldwin was responsible for both engineering and construction of the mill dam. In fact, he handled everything. He hired the necessary labor, secured needed materials, and drafted all contracts.

Baldwin used two parallel exterior stone walls, backed by small stones, to contain the earthen fill of the dams.[17] The massive exterior stone blocks were laid on a three-course timber (white pine) crib. The first course of the crib was placed directly on the bottom mud of the low land adjacent to the Charles River. This course of four twelve-inch-by-twelve-inch timbers ran lengthwise to the wall. The next course of timbers was laid crosswise to the wall. These were nine-inch-by-nine-inch timbers, spaced about nine inches apart. Finally, another course of five twelve-inch-by-twelve-inch timbers was laid lengthwise. The timbers were joined together with oak treenails (pegs) 1¾ inches square. While the exterior side of the stone walls was vertical, the

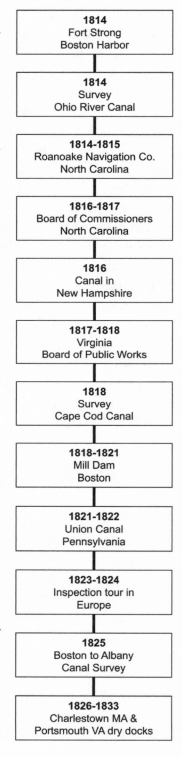

1814
Fort Strong
Boston Harbor

1814
Survey
Ohio River Canal

1814-1815
Roanoake Navigation Co.
North Carolina

1816-1817
Board of Commissioners
North Carolina

1816
Canal in
New Hampshire

1817-1818
Virginia
Board of Public Works

1818
Survey
Cape Cod Canal

1818-1821
Mill Dam
Boston

1821-1822
Union Canal
Pennsylvania

1823-1824
Inspection tour in
Europe

1825
Boston to Albany
Canal Survey

1826-1833
Charlestown MA &
Portsmouth VA dry docks

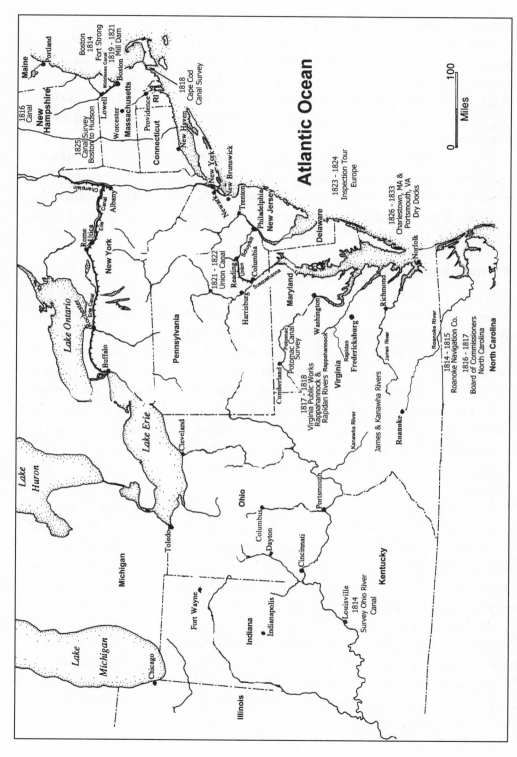

Loammi Baldwin's projects, 1814 to 1833

inner wall created a triangle-shaped structure with a thickness of six feet at the bottom on the timbers and only three feet at the top.[18] The stone blocks came from Roxbury and Weymouth.[19] Other than the work on the Erie Canal, also underway at this time, the two dams, having a total width of fifty feet from outer face of stone to outer face of stone, constituted one of the largest internal improvement projects actually undertaken in the less-than-thirty-year-old American Republic.

Finding labor for the hard work of constructing the dams was a problem, so Irish laborers were "for the first time expressly imported into the country"[20] by a private corporation. The work was completed in June 1821. Two months later, Loammi Jr. journeyed south to assume the position of chief engineer for the Union Canal Company in Pennsylvania.

Pennsylvania Politics

The Union Canal was a resumption of the canal schemes the English engineer William Weston had surveyed almost thirty years earlier, when Loammi's father had traveled to Philadelphia seeking his advice. After the Englishman's arrival in 1793, some three miles of the canal were hollowed out and five locks were built before financial difficulties caused the work to cease. The Union Canal Company was incorporated in 1811 to revitalize those earlier attempts, but the lack of funds stalled the work a second time. In March 1821, however, the Commonwealth of Pennsylvania enacted an Improvement Act, which included a subscription by the Commonwealth to help finance the Union Canal Company. This transfusion of capital allowed the work to resume, and Baldwin received his appointment on 13 September 1821.

Arriving in Pennsylvania in October, Loammi carefully went over the route of the canal. "I want to be sure of my ground before starting so I will have no uncertainty or disappointment later on in the construction."[21] Samuel Mifflin, president of the company, accompanied Loammi during the initial phase of this reconnaissance, and Baldwin recorded that Mifflin "rendered great assistance in examining the ground."[22] It was the type of work Baldwin loved—it was his forte, and he believed everything connected with his employment was satisfactory. As he would often require, Baldwin was given complete control of the work, subject only to the approval of President Mifflin. Writing home enthusiastically, he reported: "[A]t the canal meeting in Philadelphia had the best dinner in a long time, good wine, cigars, songs, and good humor." He was doing what was in his blood, building a canal.

In the field, he overcame the difficulties of cuts through limestone rock and engineering questions concerning adequacy of a water supply, but in 1822 he began to feel pressure from the board of directors and President Mifflin about the cost of the work. Around the same time, the company was experiencing "hostility to the canal in the Pennsylvania legislature."[23] Added to these pressures was the fact that Baldwin's subsequent investigations had revealed a scarcity of water supplies along the canal route the directors had selected. So he advised President Mifflin and the directors about how the contemplated route could be changed. Probably remembering his father's leakage problems on the Middlesex, he also proposed route changes because of ground conditions at locations where he anticipated leakage.

It was not an opportune time to present such proposals. The president and the board did not want to incur additional expenses, even if they were required for prudent engineering reasons. Hoping the changes were not really necessary, they engaged two other engineers to check Baldwin's survey of the route. This was a severe blow to his pride—he took it as criticism of his competence as an engineer. Writing to a friend, he stated, "The news went through me like a bullet. I cannot tell you the insult this is to my reputation."[24] Never one to accept such external control over his work, he wrote to his brother James that he was considering tendering his resignation. He also broached the subject with President Mifflin, but the directors were reluctant to lose their engineer.

By this point in his career, Loammi Baldwin had acquired considerable and varied experience across the country. In addition, he had continued his systematic pursuit of self-education, but now he was learning firsthand a lesson regarding the tension between a governing body trying to stretch limited funds and an engineer who believes there is a professional duty to deliver durable works. This was still a time when many owners believed they knew as much or more about engineering and building than did their engineers.

In the fall of 1822, the board did allow Loammi to employ his younger brother George on the project. George had previously assisted Loammi by drawing sketches of the Boston harbor fortifications and now Loammi recorded, "I fear he will beat me drawing plans." George Baldwin's presence cheered Loammi but did not solve the problem of convincing the board to approve the changes. Engineering arguments did not hold water when compared with politics and financial pressure. An argument between Baldwin and the board about the proper dimensions for the canal locks finally led to the engineer's dismissal. Repeatedly Baldwin was questioned about the proper width of the locks and he repeatedly responded that they should be "twelve and a half feet wide, seventy-five feet long" for a canal twenty-five feet wide at its bottom. This followed the historical proportions stipulated for canals and locks. It matched the lock width to the width of the towboats, and in this case to the dimensions of the feeder canals from which the Union Canal would draw boats. Since the towboats had to pass one another in the canal, the width of a canal established the maximum boat width: approximately half the width of the canal. So, logically, the locks had to be constructed to match the width of the boats. Moreover, Baldwin tried to explain that the canal could not reach its traffic potential if it could not handle the boats operating on its feeder canals. Constructing locks on the Union Canal smaller than those of the adjacent canals would create a situation where a boat's cargo would have to be offloaded onto smaller boats before it could proceed on the Union. Baldwin could not abide such a dim-witted decision.

But common sense was overruled by cost considerations, and President Mifflin directed the locks be only eight and a half feet wide. Writing home in early December of 1822, Baldwin commented, "I terminate my connection [with the Union Canal] on January 7, 1823, for me a day of rejoicing."[25] Holding himself to a higher professional standard, he could not in good conscience build an inferior canal.

Loammi may have written home about rejoicing, but it was not a cheerful time. Just as he had departed for Pennsylvania in September 1821, his wife, Ann Williams Baldwin, had died. The death weighed on Baldwin as he sought to convince Mifflin of the proper course to take in building the canal. Then the final blow to his spirits came in January 1823, just before he started the icy winter journey home. He received news his young son, Samuel Williams Baldwin had died. After receiving this news, he wrote, "[S]o soon after the death of my wife, is hard to take; and doubly so on top of this Union Canal business."[26]

The Scapegoat

Refusing any new engineering assignments, Loammi sailed for Liverpool, England, in April 1823. After he departed, in an effort to justify their actions, the Board of Directors of the Union Canal published selective correspondence relative to the controversy. In September 1823, Charles Vignolles, an English engineer returning to England from the United States, carried Baldwin a copy of the vilifying publication. President Mifflin and the directors continued their attacks the following year. In November of 1824, the "Annual Report of the President and Managers of the Union Canal Company" was published in Philadelphia's *National Gazette*.[27] It touted the success and progress of the work and again justified the decision on the width of the locks.

The citizens of Pennsylvania and Massachusetts were interested in the exchange simply as a public fight. More thoughtful men, however, scrutinized these arguments very carefully. The attacks by Mifflin forced Baldwin to protect his reputation as an engineer by responding to the canal directors. Moreover, he was motivated by his duty as a professional engineer to educate the public about the consequences of the directors' lock decision. He felt obliged to explain how a decision void of fundamental engineering knowledge would lead to a great waste of public funds. In his response and in later writings, Baldwin repeatedly argued that a professional engineer had to be in charge of directing such work. Major projects could not be successfully accomplished by rules of thumb. The challenging work the federal government later entrusted to Loammi Baldwin proved the value of the pains he had taken to make the lock size argument as more thoughtful men than the Union Canal Board of Directors understood his reasoning.

Baldwin's response appeared in the 13 April 1825 edition of Nathan Hale's *Boston Daily Advertiser*. As an additional measure, Baldwin had the response printed in a pamphlet that he distributed to interested parties.[28] The exchange continued in June when Samuel Mifflin responded to Baldwin in the *Daily Advertiser*. Baldwin made a final summary of his arguments and response to Mifflin's allegations in December 1825. His concluding defense was published in the *Daily Advertiser*. During the summer of 1825, he was engaged surveying canal routes between Boston and the Hudson River, and this work forced the delay in his response to Mifflin. Those surveys eventually would lead to the driving of a tunnel through the Hoosac Mountain.

Hale's *Boston Daily Advertiser*, the city's first daily newspaper, would shortly become the mouthpiece for a group of Massachusetts men seeking to wean the Commonwealth from enthusiasm for canals and to proclaim the superiority of railroads over canals.[29] Closely following the progress of railroads in Great Britain, Hale collected extensive printed literature on railways and locomotives. Using this material, he turned his persuasive pen to promoting railroad schemes for Massachusetts. With the chartering of the Boston and Worcester Railroad in 1831, he assumed the presidency, a position he would hold until 1850. Hale would also play an important role in the February 1833 chartering of the Western Railroad. Because of his visionary writings, he is referred to as the Father of the American Railroad.

The Union Canal Company in April of 1823 hired Canvass White as its chief engineer. White was the engineer who had advanced the study of hydraulic cement some twenty years after the senior Baldwin's work. White began his engineering career on the Erie Canal in 1816 under Benjamin Wright, an engineer more attuned to the demands of political boards. Because of health problems early in White's life, he had quit the family farm and moved to Whitestown, New York, where he had worked as a clerk in a country store. At the age of twenty-three, he studied chemistry, mineralogy, mathematics, astronomy, and surveying at Fairfield Academy in New York,[30] but those studies were interrupted by army service during the War of 1812. Fairfield Academy, which opened in 1803, was noted for its instruction in surveying, mechanics, and practical mathematics. The academy developed a reputation during the early 1800s for offering the best engineering classes outside of West Point.[31]

In 1817, New York Governor DeWitt Clinton sent White to England to examine canals, particularly the methods used for their construction. White proved his dedication to the task by walking nearly 2,000 miles of English canals. On the Erie Canal work, he was the engineer/surveyor responsible for locating the best possible route between the Seneca and Genesee rivers. In New York, he had accredited himself as one of the best construction engineers in the country, but in Pennsylvania he acceded to Samuel Mifflin's wishes and designed locks of a narrow width.

The verdict concerning the argument between Loammi Baldwin and the Union Canal directors came in 1828 when the Union was opened to barge traffic. It did not take an engineer to understand the problem—the miniature canal locks prevented the passage of the larger boats using the Pennsylvania Main Line and Schuylkill Canals. As Baldwin had argued, barge traffic could not pass continuously down the system. This restriction was painfully felt by those who had put faith in the canal project. They all came to realize that Baldwin was correct about not just the lock-size question but also many other issues, such as alignment to avoid leakage and to ensure the availability of water at the canal's summit level. The smaller lock width forced the Union Canal Company, beginning in 1841, to tear out the original locks and enlarge them at great expense. The small locks also led to the construction of a railroad on that section of Pennsylvania's Main Line system of canals to Pittsburgh.[32]

For Baldwin, this outcome was more than just an argument about the proper width of canal locks. It represented a tragic example of how an important project, which would have greatly benefited the people of Pennsylvania, could be wrecked when administrators lacking technical qualifications sought to control the work of engineers. Nonetheless, engineers in Massachusetts later would face even greater pressures from political forces opposed to their work.

Engineering Education

Loammi Baldwin Jr. was, however, pleased with the procedure used during the Union Canal work to tutor those seeking to become engineers. A system was established during the work whereby, for a small fee, student engineers gained the privilege of working under the direction of a practicing engineer. While he considered this a good approach and he would adopt it in his own office, he did have concerns because many of the canal engineers who were training men under this system were themselves woefully ignorant.

Baldwin may have gone to Europe to escape the sorrows of losing so many loved ones and the tension of the Union Canal dispute, but the trip served to further advance his engineering knowledge. Before departing he wrote, "I consider my visit to Europe as an extension of my professional studies,"[33] and he took every opportunity to visit all types of hydraulic works including the docks at Antwerp.[34] Exactly a year later he was home in Massachusetts and almost immediately his inspections proved providential for in September of 1824 Secretary of the Navy Samuel L. Southard requested Loammi prepare a plan for constructing a dry dock at Charlestown. Secretary Southard described Baldwin as an individual who "has had an opportunity of inspecting some of the most important docks of Europe." He had, therefore, turned to Baldwin for an opinion on the feasibility and an estimate of the probable cost of constructing a dry dock. Baldwin submitted a detailed design report in November 1824. The submitted design envisioned the use of turning rather than floating gates and pumps powered by steam engines for emptying the dock of water. While in London he had examined dry docks along the Thames River and commented in letters to his brother James how they might be built at little expense. It is not clear if the idea of turning gates was something he had seen during his travels or an original idea based on careful study of the docks in England and on the Continent. Before a definite location was chosen and drawings prepared, he estimated the cost at $280,000.

A Plan to Tunnel the Hoosac

In June of 1825, three months after the Pennsylvania Canal commissioners announced the practicality of their own canal to the West,[35] Baldwin began the task of exploring possible canal routes to intercept the trade of New York's Erie Canal. His younger brother George, at a handsome salary of $3 per day plus expenses, assisted him in this work. "I left George Baldwin, the Assistant Engineer, to make the surveys, and take the levels of various ponds in the vicinity,

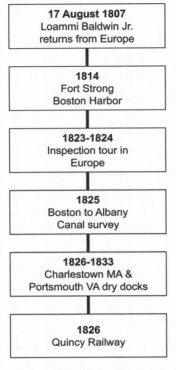

17 August 1807
Loammi Baldwin Jr.
returns from Europe

1814
Fort Strong
Boston Harbor

1823-1824
Inspection tour in
Europe

1825
Boston to Albany
Canal survey

1826-1833
Charlestown MA &
Portsmouth VA dry docks

1826
Quincy Railway

which were considered important as reservoirs or feeders."[36] His survey crew consisted of assistant engineer George, two chainmen, one axman, and a packman to carry the instruments. Baldwin and his brother probably worked with only a compass and a level. In the early 1800s, each of these two instruments typically weighed about ten pounds. But together with the boxes for each instrument and a Jacob's staff to support the compass, their packman was laden with at least forty pounds of equipment.[37]

In heavy timberland, the axman had to clear the brush to provide a clear line of sight between the location of the level and a rod or board having linear units like those on a yardstick. One of the chainmen carried this board. When the rod was held vertically and sighted on through the telescope of the level, the vertical distance to the ground was known. Working from previously known calculations, the surveyor knew the elevation of the level and could, wherever a sighting was taken on the rod, calculate the ground elevations along the line of the survey. The chainmen used a metal chain to measure the distance between points. These chains, made up of 100 metal links, were sixty-six feet long and typically weighed four to six pounds, although some were heavier. To get a good measurement of distance, the chain had to be pulled taut to eliminate any sag. This would have required about thirty pounds of pull.

Since canals required a continuous supply of water to operate, water was always the critical factor in route selection. But locks were costly, so Baldwin's task was to locate a route with a dependable water supply and also a route requiring the least number of locks. The commissioners' report stated: "It being important to avoid more than one summit level, between the Connecticut and Boston Harbour, to prevent the loss of water, which would necessarily be the case, between summits."[38] A southern route Baldwin investigated followed "a portion of one of the routes, surveyed from Connecticut River to Boston[39] by John Hills in 1791."[40] This is the same John Hills with whom the senior Baldwin had conversed about how to conduct a survey for the Middlesex Canal. But Baldwin did not recommend this southern route through Worcester, Brookfield, Palmer, and on to the Connecticut River at Springfield.

Baldwin and the Massachusetts commissioners recommended a canal route of approximately 100 miles. Running northwest from Boston, the route crossed the Nashua River and continued to Fitchburg before turning almost due west. In 1748, during King George's War, when John Fitch's blockhouse homestead had been overwhelmed by the Indians, he was dragged captive to Canada. But, like the men and women of Deerfield, Fitch returned and rebuilt his home on the frontier. In 1764 the community he founded had some forty families and was incorporated as a town, Fitchburg.[41]

The westward course from Fitchburg followed the valley of Miller's River for the last stretch to the Connecticut River.[42] In later years, a railroad would follow the general course Baldwin recommended—first running northwest from Boston up the Charles River to Waltham, then via Concord and Groton, then to Fitchburg, and subsequently due west along Miller's River to Greenfield on the Connecticut River. Baldwin estimated the construction cost for this first part of the route to connect Boston with the Connecticut River at three million dollars.

"The best route from the Connecticut River to the Hudson, was up the valley of the Deerfield River, and down that of the Hoosack [Hoosic]"[43] from North Adams. This was determined by reconnaissance, as there was no need for a survey of the two rivers. There was only one difficulty: Between the two rivers stood the lofty Hoosac Mountain. The commissioners' report recommended a tunnel four miles long to pierce the geological obstruction. Baldwin estimated the cost of creating a tunnel 20 feet wide and 13½ feet high at $920,832.[44] To arrive at this estimate, he calculated the amount of material the builders would have to remove to create the four-mile-long passage and then applied the greatest tunneling cost he could find in his engineering literature. The cost he used was based on the Lehigh Coal Company's tunnel work in blue granite. Professor Edward Hitchcock of Amherst College, the first state geologist for Massachusetts, led the commissioners and Baldwin to believe that the Hoosac Mountain was composed primarily of mica slate and granite. Hitchcock did issue a caution, however, concerning the rock on the North Adams side. He believed "lime-stone or marble" could be expected on the Mountain's western base. To support the estimate, the report stated the "excavation of a tunnel will not be more difficult than the cut through the 'Mountain Ridge,' on the Erie Canal, where the rock, consisting of a mixture of flint and lime-stone" was encountered.

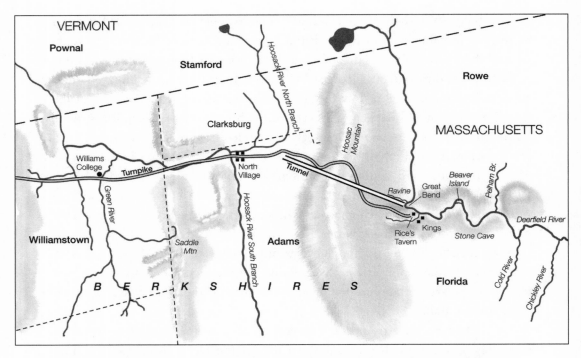

Baldwin's *Boston Harbour to Connecticut and Hudson Rivers* Survey with the Hoosac Mountain Tunnel

The commissioners included in their report to the legislature an unfavorable letter from General Epaphras Hoyt (1765–1850) of Deerfield, a brother of Commissioner Elihu Hoyt. The letter expressed a widespread view of the proposal: "A tunnel four or five miles, through the mountain, composed of primitive rocks, would be a Herculean task—probably too great for the contemplated objective."[45] General Hoyt was a surveyor, and he was high sheriff of Franklin County from 1814 to 1831. At the request of the commissioners, he had made a survey of the Deerfield River Valley and the Hoosac Mountain in September 1825 to ascertain the mountain's height above the Deerfield River. The commissioners, however, were anxious to sell the project, so they stated in the report: "To modern engineers there is nothing novel; no work to be performed which they are not in the constant habit of successfully executing."[46] They also graciously thanked Loammi Baldwin for his engineering efforts: "Indefatigable, energetic, and persevering, he has achieved all that could have been accomplished. During the period he has been employed, in a manner highly satisfactory to the Commissioners, and honorable to himself."[47]

Governor Levi Lincoln's full support for the project and the salesmanship of the commissioners was not sufficient to convince the legislature to appropriate the necessary millions for constructing a canal to the Hudson River. Lincoln even warned the legislature of the steady deterioration of Boston's situation in comparison to that of New York City, as the commerce floating down the Erie Canal and the Hudson River made New York City the new commercial capital of the United States. There would be no canal and no tunnel engineering for Loammi Baldwin; piercing the Hoosac Mountain was in the future for a different mode of transportation. Nonetheless, because of his mentorship of young engineers, Baldwin's engineering ideas did have considerable impact on the construction of the Hoosac Tunnel, and several of his protégés would play major roles in leading the challenging project.

The Quincy Railway

While Loammi Baldwin and his brother were surveying canal routes across Massachusetts, Loammi also took time to serve as a consultant to the Bunker Hill Monument Association for determining the form of the future monument. The association had been incorporated in 1823 with the aim of purchasing the battlegrounds and constructing a suitable memorial. Baldwin used a model to show the association that the monument should be "in the shape of an obelisk, thirty feet square, and two hundred and twenty feet high."[48] When the Marquis de Lafayette[49] arrived in Boston to lay the monument's cornerstone on June 17, 1825, Baldwin was serving as a member of the association's board of directors.[50] General Lafayette's appreciation for the welcome he received manifested itself later in his support of Baldwin's apprentice engineer Charles Storrow's application for the admission to L'École des Ponts et Chaussées in Paris.

More important, though, for immediate future events, was the method used to transport the required granite blocks to the Bunker Hill Monument site. To move the heavy blocks, engineer Gridley Bryant constructed the Quincy Railway. The four-mile-long railroad, often referred to as the Granite Railway because of its purpose, was the first railroad in America. Bryant related:

> *I finally obtained a charter, although there was great opposition in the House. The questions were asked: "What do we know about railroads? Who ever heard of such a thing? Is it right to take people's land for a project that no one knows anything about? We have corporations enough already."*[51]

Gridley Bryant was an ingenious builder. Earlier, while employed to build the United States Bank building in Boston, he applied his inventiveness to the creation of a portable derrick whose design was later used on many projects requiring heavy lifting. After completion of the Bunker Hill Monument, Bryant would apply his talents to building lighthouses along the coast of Maine.[52]

Yet the debates to which Bryant refers reflected a second reason why Baldwin's plan for a canal to the Hudson was tabled. Gentlemen were beginning to consider what was happening in England. In February of 1804, Richard Trevithick demonstrated his steam locomotive at an ironworks in Wales. In 1825, the Stockton and Darlington Railway opened, using a steam locomotive built by George Stephenson. The twenty-mile-long Stockton and Darlington was the first railroad to run on a regular schedule.

In mid-February of 1826, about the time the commissioners' report was published, Nathan Hale, using his *Daily Advertiser* newspaper as a platform to educate the public, entered the debate by stressing the advantages of the railroad. Hale was the editor who, not too many months previously, had published Baldwin's responses to Samuel Mifflin and the managers of the Union Canal Company. He had joined a small group of men dedicated to promoting a railroad network across Massachusetts.[53] The group included Dr. Abner Phelps, who, along with Theodore Sedgwick of Stockbridge, was the leading railroad advocate in the legislature. When a number of legislature members traveled to Quincy for the funeral of President John Adams in July, Phelps convinced several, including Daniel Webster, to visit Bryant's unfinished railroad during the return trip.[54]

The days of cross-country canal building were rapidly passing away, and within ten years the Boston and Lowell Railroad would replace Baldwin's beloved Middlesex Canal. Although Loammi Baldwin Jr. would always believe in canals, he and his brothers would soon turn their talents to railroad engineering. In fact, his brother George worked with Gridley Bryant on the Quincy Railway project,[55] and there is correspondence between Bryant and James Baldwin about the project.[56]

Massachusetts Railroads

Loammi Baldwin was back in Pennsylvania in 1826, surveying a canal for the Harrisburg Canal, Fire Insurance, and Water Company. However, because of opposition to the Harrisburg company, he was forced to suspend operations, and his work was over by summer. In 1824, Baldwin had prepared a plan for a dry dock in Charlestown, but Congress had not taken action. Nonetheless, there was

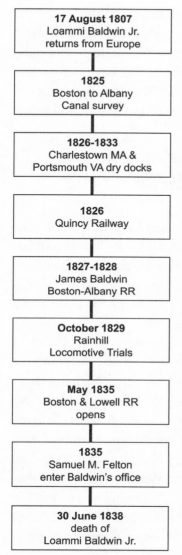

17 August 1807
Loammi Baldwin Jr.
returns from Europe

1825
Boston to Albany
Canal survey

1826-1833
Charlestown MA &
Portsmouth VA dry docks

1826
Quincy Railway

1827-1828
James Baldwin
Boston-Albany RR

October 1829
Rainhill
Locomotive Trials

May 1835
Boston & Lowell RR
opens

1835
Samuel M. Felton
enter Baldwin's office

30 June 1838
death of
Loammi Baldwin Jr.

still interest, and since January he had been communicating his ideas about dry-dock construction to the secretary of the navy. It was the type of work he had studied in Europe, and hydraulic structures were his first love. As a result of his many inquiries and interest in such matters, he was probably one of only two engineers in America who could handle the task—the other being Benjamin Latrobe Sr. As soon as the appointment was offered, Baldwin accepted it. He was to superintend construction of the naval dry docks; in June 1826, he wrote Secretary Samuel Southard that he would begin on 1 August. He and his brother George, who was fresh from the Quincy Railway work, immediately began surveying prospective sites in Massachusetts, New Hampshire, New York, and Virginia.

Their reports and cost estimates went to Congress in January of 1827, and by March the decision was made to build one dry dock at Charlestown, Massachusetts, and another at Portsmouth, Virginia, across the Elizabeth River from the port of Norfolk. President John Quincy Adams of Braintree, Massachusetts, wanted Baldwin appointed as civil engineer for the government. While he was grateful for the president's confidence, before accepting he insisted he have "general authority over the entire project . . ." and permission to employ his brothers. The secretary accepted his terms and Loammi Baldwin, four years younger than his father when the senior Baldwin had started the Middlesex Canal, began organizing his engineering corps. He anticipated employing brothers James and George as resident engineers and dividing his time between the two sites. Almost immediately, this plan was upended when the Massachusetts legislature in June 1827 authorized the appointment of two commissioners and an engineer to make surveys for a railroad from Boston to the Hudson. James stayed on the Charlestown dock work only four months before he submitted his resignation and undertook the railroad survey.

In two short years, Massachusetts had come to realize railroads were the transportation mode of the future, but there was still a wide variety of ideas about exactly what constituted a railroad. The task of studying the matter—and, more specifically, defining what constituted a railroad—fell to the Commonwealth-delegated Board of Internal Improvements. The Quincy Railway used horses to pull the carriages, and this idea of motive power was fixed in the minds of many. The board's final report stated:

> *The most simple and obvious method of construction, is to pursue the route which presents the least inclination, and which requires no power but that of horses, traveling on the road.*[57]

The report prepared by the board's directors recognized the many advantages railroads offered over canals. In the case of a northern state like Massachusetts, railroads could operate even in the winter, when canals would be closed because of ice. As evidence to support this conclusion, their report drew attention to the way the Quincy Railway had cleared snow from its tracks "by placing two planks meeting at an angle in front of a heavy carriage."[58]

James Baldwin submitted his railroad survey report to the Board of Internal Improvements in December 1828. The directors' report concerning the railroad was for the most part prepared by *Daily Advertiser* editor Nathan Hale.[59] The document went to the General Court in January 1829. James Baldwin had investigated three possible routes across the Commonwealth: A southern route through the towns of Worcester, Springfield, and Pittsfield, and then into New York State and on to Albany; a middle route through Princeton, Savoy, and on to Albany (Princeton being about ten miles north of Worcester and the Savoy crossing of the Berkshires being south of the Hoosac Mountain); and a northern route using Loammi Baldwin's canal survey from three years earlier.[60] In their report, the directors stated "that the southern route affords the greatest facilities for construction of the road."[61]

This southern railroad was built in two steps. First the Boston and Worcester Railroad was organized in 1831, and then the Western Railroad was chartered in 1833 to create a continuous line to Albany. The completion of the southern railroad would create a sectional battle between the northern cities of the Commonwealth lacking a through railroad and the southern cities experiencing the benefits of easy travel by railroad. This bitter struggle, however, was still years in the future. In 1826, Loammi Baldwin was in need of the best talent available to assist him with construction of two dry docks.

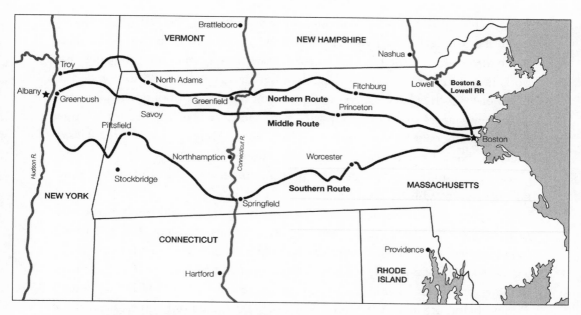

James Baldwin's 1828 survey of three railroad routes across Massachusetts

Dry-Dock Construction

At the time the dry-dock work began, George Baldwin was ill and James Baldwin was off surveying railroads, so Loammi Baldwin wrote to his friend Charles Bulfinch, seeking the names of "good men in the engineering field." Bulfinch at this point had moved from Boston to Washington to complete the unfinished wings and central portion of the Capitol. Finally Baldwin settled on Alexander Parris as his resident assistant for the Charlestown work. Parris had entered Bulfinch's Boston office in 1815 following service in the War of 1812 as a captain of artificers (engineers) in Plattsburgh, New York. To oversee the work at Portsmouth, Baldwin hired Henry Singleton, an established architect from the Portsmouth–Norfolk area. Just as Baldwin had worked on the Bunker Hill Monument, Singleton had in 1824, built a magnificent memorial arch for Lafayette's visit.

Work was underway at both locations by the summer of 1827. The Middlesex Canal had been the crowning achievement for Loammi Baldwin Sr. and the greatest civil engineering accomplishment in the new country until that time. These two granite dry docks would be the greatest engineering works of Loammi Baldwin Jr.

Immediately after his appointment as engineer, Baldwin proceeded to locate the two docks and to develop the plans. In June, construction commenced at Charlestown, followed by a November start in Virginia. The following year, workers began driving piles to create a foundation for the 86-foot-wide and 253-foot-long chambers. Once the foundation for the Norfolk dry dock was in place, newspapers in Virginia reported that the river was jammed with barges carrying lumber cut by local lumbermen and boats bringing granite from Massachusetts. New England stonecutters were imported to shape the giant stone blocks. The granite for the Charlestown dock came from Gridley Bryant's Quincy quarries via the Quincy Railway.

Just as his father had faced the issue of hydraulic cement, Loammi had to investigate the properties of available cementitious materials. It was critically important to the success of the work to find a hydraulic cement capable of providing a good waterproof bond. By the late 1820s, two such materials could be purchased in New York. Peter Mensen and Company of New York[62] was marketing White's Patent Hydraulic Cement, a natural cement manufactured from limestone deposits near Chittenango, New York. These were deposits Canvass White had discovered during construction of the Erie Canal. Cement manufacturers published instructions for mixing the cement with sand to create a good mortar: "To every bushel of the powdered cement add one bushel of sand, mix them together and pass them through a sieve, then add a sufficient quantity of water to make it (by well mixing and working) about the consistency of a soft putty."[63]

The second commercially offered cementitious material was the Rosendale brand. The Rosendale products were natural cements from a limestone deposit near the town of Rosendale in Ulster County, New York.[64] This source was first used during construction of the Delaware and Hudson Canal from 1825 to 1829. The brand name was applied generically to all cements manufactured in the Ulster County region, but Baldwin later identified the product as Remsen's. This was the brand name used by the Howes Cave Lime & Cement Company for their Rosendale cement.[65]

Like his father before him, Baldwin made trial batches and specimens using each of the cements and with different proportions of cement and sand: "I made some pieces of masonry last fall [1826] of each kind mixed in various proportions." He allowed the samples to harden for several months. From his letters it is not clear whether the specimens sat exposed to air or whether he placed them in water, as White had done when first demonstrating the material. Nevertheless, when he broke the different specimens in the spring, he reported, "Remsen's was the best."

Still Loammi was not satisfied, and he continued to test available products. In England the Reverend James Parker had patented in 1796 a natural impure limestone material as Roman Cement. He later sold his patent to James and Charles Wyatt and subsequently moved to the United States. Although nothing more is known about the reverend, there are nevertheless records of Roman Cement being used for construction at the University of Virginia in 1821:[66]

Richmond 1st. June 1821

Received of Andrew Smith five Casks of Roman Cement in good Order,
NO. 55 SMITH'S WHARF, BALTIMORE.

Directions for using the Roman Cement, in making Tanks, Cisterns, Drains, Ponds, Docks, the Fronts of Wharves, Vaults, Sewers, and every kind of Brick and Stone Work, in which Strength is required, or where Wet or Damp are to be excluded.

From an unidentified source, Baldwin obtained samples of Roman Cement and had Alexander Parris conduct experiments, as he had done earlier with the other cements. He later reported to the U.S. Navy: "Roman cement is more expensive than others, but for water cement jobs it should be used in preference to the hydraulic lime of New York manufacture." So it appears Baldwin followed his established practice of always seeking to build quality, even if the cement had to be ordered from England at a greater cost.

Loammi Baldwin had long argued the need for instituting structured programs to train civil engineers, and he had praised the apprenticeship programs introduced on canal works. Answering his own summons, he established similar student-apprenticeship programs at both dry-dock locations. He had a deep appreciation for the value of scientific theory applied to engineering practice, so, under his personal direction, his student engineers received a comprehensive foundation in scientific principles. The two dry-dock projects produced a unique group of highly qualified engineers who would later prove to be leaders in the profession. John Brooks and Charles Storrow, Baldwin's young protégés during this period, would later make significant contributions to the building of the Hoosac Tunnel.

Charles S. Storrow spent from July to December of 1829 reading engineering works in the junior Baldwin's Charlestown office before entering L'École des Ponts et Chaussées in 1830.[67] His admittance was arranged by the Marquis de Lafayette, who graciously supplied him with letters of introduction. Because of Lafayette's letters and influence, Storrow was granted the privilege of attending as a special student.[68] Storrow would later be instrumental in the founding of Harvard's Lawrence Scientific School in 1847.[69]

Loammi Baldwin Jr. was a man endowed with the ability to keep multiple projects going at the same time. In the late 1820s, during the most critical phases of the two dry-dock projects, he designed a stone bridge to provide another route over the Charles River in Boston. Moreover, at the same time the U.S. Navy appointed him consulting engineer to its planning board and had him investigating projects in Pensacola, Florida; Governor's Island, New York; Philadelphia; and Washington. He did, however, call upon his brother George in 1828 to assist him with the Pensacola assignment, as it involved a railroad and he wanted to draw on George's experience with the Quincy Railway. On the Fourth of July in 1828, a ceremony was held in Baltimore to mark the inception of the Baltimore & Ohio Railroad. The B&O, as it was called, would be a transportation system leader—one that Massachusetts would soon follow. In fact, the chief engineers for two of Massachusetts's railroads would come from the B&O work.

Engineer Loammi Baldwin Jr., like his father on the Middlesex Canal, had to deal with numerous practical problems during his dry-dock work, including the design of treadmill-powered pile drivers and derricks to lift the heavy stone blocks. In addition to the challenge of the technical problems, he experienced the "pleasure" of working for the government: "The Gentlemen at Washington don't pay their debts."[70] Later, some of the engineers who were involved in attempting to build the Hoosac Tunnel would be destroyed financially by such spiteful governmental actions.

But Baldwin persevered, finding solutions to the technical problems and responding to political sniping. By May of 1832, the Virginia papers announced: "Plans are ready for the steam dredging machine" to excavate the entrance into the Portsmouth dry dock. When the USS *Delaware* entered the flooded Dry Dock No. 1 at Portsmouth on 17 June 1833, she was the first ship ever to be dry-docked in the United States. The *Delaware*, launched in 1820, was a major ship-of-the-line.[71]

The old fighting ship *Constitution* was docked a week later in the Charlestown dry dock. The *Boston Daily Advertiser and Patriot* described the event:[72]

> *The hull of "Old Ironsides," the frigate* Constitution, *was taken into the*
> *Dry Dock at the Charlestown Navy Yard yesterday morning, under the*

superintendence of Commodores [Isaac] Hull and [Jesse] Elliot, and the whole operation was conducted in fine style. The Yard was handsomely decorated with flags and pendants. The morning was exceedingly unpleasant, the wind being North-East, attended by rain; yet upwards of fifteen hundred persons, including some ladies, were present at 5 o'clock, and great numbers visited the Yard through out the day.

The Charlestown dry dock was transferred to the Navy Department on 9 September 1833. Baldwin told Commodore Elliot, "I give up a subject, which for five or six years has filled me with excitement and has produced alternately hopes, fears, and expectations of various characters, but never a doubt of its ultimate success."[73] The Portsmouth dry dock was transferred on 27 December 1833, but the work was not completed until March 1834.

Recognition

Loammi Baldwin Jr. built well, as evidenced by the fact that Dry Dock No. 1 is still in use at the Norfolk Naval Shipyard and is a National Historic Landmark. The Charlestown Dry Dock was also designated a National Historic Landmark by the National Park Service. Additionally, in 1977 the American Society of Civil Engineers designated the Charlestown and Portsmouth Dry Docks as National Historic Civil Engineering Landmarks. Ten years earlier, the American Society of Civil Engineers had designated Loammi Baldwin Sr.'s Middlesex Canal as a National Historic Civil Engineering Landmark. The two Loammi Baldwins are the only father and son engineers who both have individual projects so designated.[74] The Hoosac Mountain Tunnel that Loammi Baldwin Jr. envisioned in 1825 would also be designated a National Historic Civil Engineering Landmark.

In April 1834, President Andrew Jackson authorized retaining Loammi Jr. as the navy's civil engineer.[75] It was a job he had not sought and was not eager to hold, but he agreed to stay conditionally. It was a temporary arrangement until a replacement could be found to fill the position permanently. His reluctance to accept a permanent appointment seems to have been driven by three very specific motives: (1) his distaste for having to work in a political environment, "They never seemed to consider me anything but a swindler"; (2) the meager salary offered; and (3) the real reason—there was no longer a project to construct. His decision to accept was driven by the hope that a dry dock would soon be authorized for New York. The challenge of building notable projects was his source of energy.

But the navy relieved Baldwin of his duties as civil engineer a month later, and he immediately accepted an assignment from the city of Boston to develop a plan for supplying the city with pure water. Writing to his bother James on 6 June, Baldwin explained, "I am now engaged in surveys and examinations for the government of Boston to ascertain the practicability of bringing a supply of water into the city."[76] He made calculations of the city's consumption of water and estimated its population growth in order to project future water needs. Predictably, he recommended constructing an aqueduct that would deliver water to a reservoir in Roxbury. From a reservoir at such a location, gravity would supply the necessary pressure for delivering water into the city. His proposed system demonstrated a thought process guided by his canal-building experiences. In making calculations to size the distribution system within the city, Baldwin relied on an 1835 publication entitled *A Treatise on Water-Works for Conveying and Distributing Supplies of Water.*[77] This document was being prepared at the time by Charles Storrow, Baldwin's former apprentice engineer and was based on Storrow's studies at the L'École des Ponts et Chaussées. But it was a familiar story: Baldwin's plan would sit for twelve years before the city found the money and courage to address its water problem.

The Middlesex Canal as Hearse

In 1835, another gentleman who would later be involved with the Hoosac Tunnel entered Baldwin's Charlestown office. Samuel Morse Felton, a native of Massachusetts, had managed to put himself through Harvard by teaching on the side. After his graduation in 1834, Felton accepted a position as supervisor of a school for boys in Charlestown. This very talented man related how he became involved in engineering: "About the year 1835, Mr. Baldwin asked me to undertake the instruction of some of the young men then in his office, in physics, mathematics, surveying, and kindred subjects." Felton accepted the invitation. By the end of the year, when he found himself drawn to engineering, he gave up his school position and became a senior Baldwin apprentice.

In the spring of 1836, when the U.S. Navy approached Baldwin about conducting preliminary surveys for a dry dock in New York, he went to the city to meet with the navy secretary and discuss possible dry-dock sites. By June, he submitted a survey report indicating the dock could be built either on Governor's Island or on the East River in Brooklyn. President Andrew Jackson then asked him to comment on the relative advantages of each site. He prepared a second report in which he stated that he preferred the Brooklyn site because the

Brooklyn Navy Yard was already established there. Baldwin completed the plans, but this project, like the one for the Boston water-supply system, languished for years, even though it was authorized. Loammi Baldwin Jr. had built his last dry dock, as work at the Brooklyn yard was delayed until 1841, three years after his death.

During this same period, Baldwin undertook a canal survey for the Morris Canal and Banking Company of New Jersey. The Morris Canal linked the Delaware River with New York Harbor at Jersey City and provided access to Pennsylvania's anthracite coal mines through a connection with the Lehigh Canal. The canal was originally owned by the Lehigh Navigation Company, but it became the Lehigh Coal and Navigation Company after a merger in 1821. Between 1827 and 1829, Canvass White had enlarged and improved the original Lehigh Canal. Initially the system was only a series of small artificial pools that permitted arks loaded with coal to float downstream to Philadelphia. The terminal facilities at Jersey City had not yet been designed, even as the canal was nearing completion. Loammi was, therefore, retained to prepare plans and specifications for the harbor terminus. While Loammi Baldwin was still employed at this late date as a canal engineer transportation modes were changing rapidly.

On 5 June 1830, the Boston and Lowell Railroad was chartered, and James Baldwin's survey of the route was presented to the General Court of Massachusetts a year later. The line of the survey he submitted for the railroad closely followed the alternate Middlesex Canal route his father and William Weston had surveyed in 1793. In the employ of the Boston and Lowell, James's brother George traveled to England in late 1831 and remained there inspecting English railroads for more than a year. While in England, he placed orders for the Boston and Lowell's rails and its first locomotive. This was only two years after George Stephenson's locomotive—dubbed "Rocket"—had won the Rainhill Trials by hauling thirteen tons at an average speed of twelve miles per hour. Sponsored by the Liverpool and Manchester Railway, the Rainhill Trials of terrifying iron monsters—breathing fire and spouting hot cinders—proved the great value of the steam locomotive for powering railroad cars. George Baldwin sent home descriptions of railroad work, together with sketches and copies of plans. He was also able to discuss with George and Robert Stephenson and other English railroad engineers the manufacture of parts and railroad construction techniques.

Canal boats floating on Loammi Baldwin Sr.'s Middlesex Canal carried the granite blocks used as cross ties for the new Boston and Lowell Railroad—in fact, the canal carried most of the materials for the work—but the demise of the canal was assured in 1835, when the railroad opened for service. It could even be said that the canal carried its own hearse: The railroad's Stephenson-built locomotive, ordered from England, was moved to the railroad's Lowell shops via a canal boat making its way up the Middlesex Canal.

James Baldwin wrote to his brother Loammi on 27 May 1835, describing his emotion at the experience of putting a railroad into service: "Monday Mr. Jackson and I went to Lowell & on that day got our Largest Locomotive onto the Track—Tuesday got the Steam up & went moderately down the Rail Road 6½ Miles & back—this was its first movement & she went kindly & well." On Wednesday, James Baldwin and George Washington Whistler—who would later build the Western Railroad of Massachusetts from Worcester to Albany—took the locomotive with tender and passenger car to Boston, where they gathered twenty-four of the directors and stockholders for the run back to Lowell. They made the return trip of twenty-seven miles in one hour and twenty-three minutes. James continued in his letter: "[T]he country people were out on the bridges & banks & the Track laborers swung the hats with huzzas. I am quite weary & fatigued with anxiety & care but one nights rest will restore me especially as we have proved our road & are satisfied."[78] Finally in late summer of 1835, Loammi Baldwin Jr. followed his brothers into railroad work, doing preliminary surveys for the Concord and Nashua Railroad.

Over the following years, there were canals to survey in Georgia and mills to be designed in Massachusetts, New Hampshire, and Maine. The Navy again enlisted his services in 1836 to lay out new Navy Yards in Jersey City and Perth Amboy, New Jersey, and on Great Barn Island (in the East River between Manhattan and Queens, New York, and today known as Ward's Island). By this time, Samuel Felton had assumed charge of Baldwin's Charlestown office and in April of 1837, more responsibility fell to Felton when Baldwin suffered a stroke and could no longer participate in the strenuous fieldwork. Loammi Baldwin Jr., the Father of American Civil Engineering and visionary of the Hoosac Tunnel, died of a second stroke on 30 June 1838.[79]

The man Baldwin had brought into the office to teach physics and mathematics to apprentices took over Baldwin's engineering practice. Five years later, Felton became superintendent and engineer for Alvah Crocker's Fitchburg Railroad. By 1850, Crocker was pushing a railroad westward to Greenfield, and by sheer willpower and perseverance, he would drive a railroad across the northern part of Massachusetts along Loammi Baldwin Jr.'s 1825 canal route. It would be a long and hard struggle, because the folks who had built the Boston and Worcester and the Western Railroads across southern Massachusetts following James Baldwin's survey would battle Crocker every mile of the way.

4

Railroad Crusader

*Instead of the scream of a fish-hawk scaring
the fishes, is heard the whistle of the steam-engine,
arousing a country to its progress!*
— Henry David Thoreau, *A Week on the
Concord and Merrimack Rivers* (Princeton, NJ:
Princeton University Press, 2004), 87.

A S HE DID EVERY week, Alvah Crocker was driving a wagonload of newly manufactured paper to Boston. An ambitious young man, Crocker was the proud owner of a small paper mill on the Nashua River, in Fitchburg village, which now had a population of about 1,800. But to sell the product of his mill, he had to maneuver forty-seven miles of bad roads to Boston each week. The oxen team[1] moved slowly through the cold and Crocker's hands were red, though that was not from the chill.

A Vatman

In the early 1800s, paper was made one sheet at a time by a vatman who lifted a mold of wet fiber pulp from a vat of warm water and pulp. Bending and skillful dexterity were required for the task, and with that task came big red hands—the result of continually dipping one's hands into the warm water and pulp. Red hands were the mark of the trade, and Crocker was his own vatman. In the beginning, he personally made every sheet of paper that came from his mill.

To make his paper, Crocker (and his father before him) used a rag-pulp process dating back some 2,000 years. The pulp was made from old cotton and linen rags that traveling peddlers collected for him from farmers' wives. A hired lass cut the rags into small squares by drawing the cloth across knives Crocker had fixed to a post in the mill. The squares were then reduced to pulp in an oval-shaped wooden vat by a revolving water-powered beater.

Reuven
2014

Alvah Crocker (1801–74)[2]

Crocker built the mill himself, but the log dam to confine the Nashua River[3] cost him $1,500. The revolving beater, driven by water from his dam, was the only mechanized part of the mill. From the beater, the fiber pulp went into a vat of warm water where Crocker used a rectangular wooden frame with a fine woven-brass screen to make one sheet of paper at a time. It was a tedious and time-consuming process, but he was a skilled vatman.

He was only twenty-six when he built the mill, but he had been laboring at papermaking for seventeen years. His father, Deacon Samuel Crocker, had been a vatman before him,[4] and Alvah had followed his father into the trade. To purchase the mill site, Alvah borrowed $3,000, but he owed $12,000 before the mill was operating. To conserve funds, Crocker served during the day as his own vatman and spent one night a week as teamster for the journeys to Boston.[5]

In the early days of paper manufacturing, new mills were often opened by experienced vatmen. As a mill owner, a skilled man with ambition could gain greater financial rewards, and Crocker was a man of aspirations. But his dreams were now resting on borrowed money, so he was working day and night to pay off his debts. Hard work was not new to Crocker, who, as a young boy, worked at someone else's mill for twelve hours a day and took home twenty-five cents.

Now his day stretched into the darkness of night. To reach Boston in winter, he faced a biting wind and a snow-choked road. In spring, deep mud greeted him and rendered the road almost impassable. Even those in the stage business substituted open wagons for coaches in the spring because of the deep mud.[6] In summer, he drove his wagon over a dry road but endured clouds of dust that choked him like smoke from a fire. Even in Boston, the ride was not pleasant, as the wagon lumbering over cobblestone streets made an unbearable din.[7]

Winning the battle with the roads allowed Crocker to sell his paper directly and avoid the greed of the city's commission agents. In the beginning, he had used those men to sell his paper as well as to procure the chemicals he needed. Soon, however, he became convinced they were cheating him; when they told him his balance was $4,000 in their favor, he quickly ended the relationship.[8]

Those night trips to Boston imbued in Crocker a personal appreciation of how badly Massachusetts needed adequate transportation. On a very personal level, he learned the importance of transportation to the success of his business. He had many a lonesome hour to think about the situation. As a result, he would spend forty years on a personal crusade to build a railroad across northern Massachusetts.

The Crocker Family

Crocker's great-grandfather and grandfather had been seafaring men, master mariners. Captain John Crocker, his great-grandfather, was born in England but emigrated to Boston in the early 1700s. Soon after his arrival, he moved up the Massachusetts coast to Newburyport, at the mouth of the Merrimack River. Captain Crocker and his third son, Benjamin Crocker, shared ownership of the brig *Ranger*[10] in the mid-1700s.

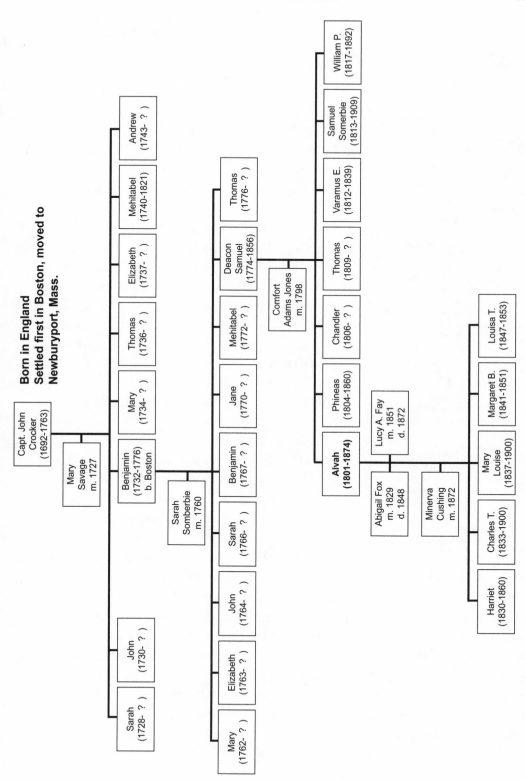

**Born in England
Settled first in Boston, moved to
Newburyport, Mass.**

Genealogy of Alvah Crocker[9]

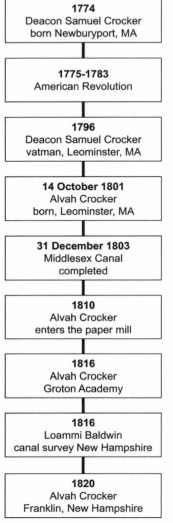

1774
Deacon Samuel Crocker
born Newburyport, MA

1775-1783
American Revolution

1796
Deacon Samuel Crocker
vatman, Leominster, MA

14 October 1801
Alvah Crocker
born, Leominster, MA

31 December 1803
Middlesex Canal
completed

1810
Alvah Crocker
enters the paper mill

1816
Alvah Crocker
Groton Academy

1816
Loammi Baldwin
canal survey New Hampshire

1820
Alvah Crocker
Franklin, New Hampshire

The eighth child born to Benjamin and Sarah Crocker was a son, whom they christened Samuel; years later, he would become Deacon Samuel Crocker. Samuel grew up in Newburyport but probably never knew his father, as Benjamin died in 1776—two years after Samuel's birth. His death occurred immediately after losing all his property in a fire.

The years of the American Revolutionary War (1775–1783) were trying times for American sailors and shipowners. Salem merchant Elias Hasket Derby had his schooner *Jamaica Packet* intercepted by the British navy and carried into besieged Boston, where it was burned when the British troops evacuated the city.[11] Before March of 1776, he lost three other vessels to the British. But Derby would thrive, and his namesake descendant would join Crocker's railroad crusade.

The loss of her husband left Sarah Crocker and her nine children to rely "upon the cold charity of the world without a dollar."[12] In that era, church and family supported those in need, so when Samuel reached the age of eleven, a Richard Clark took him in to learn the process of making paper by hand.[13] Clark owned a paper mill on the Neponset River in Dorchester, south of Boston. It seems Clark engaged the lad because an earlier Crocker had been party to the founding of the Episcopal Church in his town. Over the next eleven years, Samuel became a skilled vatman.

In 1796, Samuel was offered the generous wage of $5 per week, exclusive of board, to become a vatman at a new mill in Leominster, Massachusetts, a small village about forty miles northwest of Boston. The usual vatman pay at the time was $4.50, but William Nichols and Jonas Kendall,[14] who had come together to start the first paper mill in Leominster, were in need of an experienced man for their one-vat, one-engine mill.[15] One other factor might have influenced Nichols to make the generous offer: At a time when vatmen were notorious for drinking grog while they worked, Samuel Crocker was "a rigid uncompromising puritan."[16]

Drawn by the offer, twenty-two-year-old Samuel Crocker moved to Leominster in 1796. Two years later, Samuel married Comfort Adams Jones of Medway, Massachusetts. In a house close to the paper mill, Alvah Crocker, the first of Samuel and Comfort's seven sons,[17] was born on 14 October 1801.[18] His parents were so poor friends would remark years later that Alvah was "brought up by the rugged hand of poverty."[19] When he was only six, his mother began sending him out in the summer months to "drop corn" and "rake hay" for farmers. Soon he was employed permanently, with his father, in the Nichols and Kendall paper mill. Recalling the experience, he stated, "I was put into a paper factory at the tender age of eight years."[20]

As a child laborer in a paper mill, Alvah worked as a layboy, separating the damp sheets of paper from the felts on which they had been placed for squeezing in the screw press.[21] He was allowed remission from his labors for six to eight weeks each year to attend school, but, because of the family's circumstances, there were few books available to him.

The poverty of his household did not, however, defeat the lad in his drive to obtain an education. He had tremendous ambition and found ways to supplement his limited schooling. His employer, Mr. Nichols, allowed him to borrow books from his personal library, and J. G. Kendall, a lawyer and son of Jonas Kendall,[22] gave him carte blanche use of his library in return for sweeping the office.[23] After working for eight years in the Leominster paper mill and wringing what education he could from meager opportunities, Crocker managed to accumulate enough funds to pack himself off to Groton Academy (now known as Lawrence Academy).

Groton Academy, incorporated in 1793,[24] provided higher education for those considering college attendance. Alvah Crocker, a self-reliant sixteen-year-old youth with $60 in his pocket,[25] traveled the twelve miles to Groton for his only period of extended schooling. This would have been approximately fourteen years after Loammi Baldwin had resided in Groton while reading law. When his funds were exhausted, Crocker returned to the Leominster paper mill. By this time, he was skilled at making a perfect sheet of paper of uniform thickness.[26] In 1820, offered the opportunity to improve his earnings, he moved to a mill in Franklin, New Hampshire, some eighty miles up the Merrimack River from where his grandfather had resided.

After two years in New Hampshire, he returned to Massachusetts as a vatman in General Leonard Burbank's Fitchburg paper mill. Burbank had built his first Fitchburg paper mill in 1801, but the small mill had been destroyed by fire, and now Burbank was attempting to restart the business.[27] Fitchburg, was located on the North Nashua River, five miles beyond Leominster. It could boast of one mail stage a week to Boston.[28] Alvah's father, Deacon Samuel Crocker, soon joined Alvah in Burbank's mill.

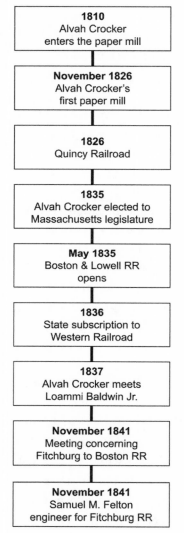

1810
Alvah Crocker
enters the paper mill

November 1826
Alvah Crocker's
first paper mill

1826
Quincy Railroad

1835
Alvah Crocker elected to
Massachusetts legislature

May 1835
Boston & Lowell RR
opens

1836
State subscription to
Western Railroad

1837
Alvah Crocker meets
Loammi Baldwin Jr.

November 1841
Meeting concerning
Fitchburg to Boston RR

November 1841
Samuel M. Felton
engineer for Fitchburg RR

The New Mill Owner

Alvah Crocker had come to Fitchburg with ambition. After three years in the Burbank mill, the young man left Burbank and acquired a mill site of his own. In 1826, he embarked on this enterprise with $800 he had saved and funds he borrowed from a friend of his mother.[29]

His first mill, like most mills of the period, was an unpretentious affair, and, because of limited funds, it was not built in the best location. The only land he could afford was in a birch swamp; to further conserve his funds, he cleared the land himself. But he did hire a builder to construct the dam. It was a typical mill,[30] a wood-frame structure adjacent to the river with a waterwheel to power the beating-machine roll. His beating machine was probably built by a local millwright using a section of tree trunk as the roll. The roll would have been positioned in a waist-high oval wooden tub so the rags were dragged against metal knives as it rotated. This was the final step in reducing the rags to pulp. Dipping his hand mold into the pulped fibers, Crocker would have worked his magic and created a perfect sheet of paper. He invested in a screw press for squeezing the water out of the paper sheets, and there was a loft where the damp paper was hung for drying over wooden poles fixed horizontally. Firewood for warming the workrooms and heating water in large iron kettles would have come from the surrounding area, probably supplied by farmers, but he might have been forced to cut his own wood. His son later recorded that at the time the local farmers feared that "an 'increased' manufacturing population might vitiate the morals of the town."[31] After overcoming all obstacles, in November 1826 Crocker began making paper in his new mill.

Alvah Crocker's timing for entering the paper business could not have been much worse. Less than a year later, the first Fourdrinier papermaking machine was put into operation in New York.[32] A second Fourdrinier arrived in America from France in December 1827, and it was producing paper by the following year.[33] George Spafford, a millwright who had successfully assembled this second machine in North Windham, Connecticut, foresaw the revolution these machines would bring. A confident mechanic, Spafford set to building Fourdrinier machines together with mechanics James Phelps and Charles Smith.[34] Their first machine began making paper in May of 1829 and sold for $2,462.[35] Therefore, at a time when Crocker was already in debt, he was forced to borrow another $10,000 to purchase a mechanical papermaking machine and to rebuild his mill structure to accommodate all of the supporting equipment. A complete papermaking system—Fourdrinier-type machine with dryer and cutting machine plus sundries—cost more than $4,300 in 1830, but Crocker understood that this mechanical contraption eliminated the need for a vatman.

If Crocker had not learned perseverance from his childhood, the financial hardships he shouldered at this time surely would have defeated him. To make matters worse, nature conspired against him in the spring of 1829: The Nashua River flooded the birch swamp and destroyed his mill.[36] He immediately went to work rebuilding, and his younger brother Samuel Somerby Crocker, age sixteen, joined him in his labors for the next two years. So, with the help of family, he overcame another obstacle. In fact, Crocker felt so confident of the future that he traveled to Jaffrey, New Hampshire, and married Abigail Fox in August 1829.[37] Bringing his bride home to Fitchburg, he built her a house on the hill above the new mill.[38] But money was still a precious commodity, so he began serving at the Calvinistic Congregational Church as master of the singing school. Abigail presented him with a daughter in December of the following year, and the master's pay of $13 a year helped him support his growing family.

As a mill owner, his standing in the community improved, and Alvah Crocker was elected "hog reeve" in 1830.[39] These were still the days when stock grazed on the town common, and the town's hog reeve assumed custody of animals that strayed into the cultivated fields of neighbors. In addition, the hog reeve was responsible for appraising damages and ordering restitution, so it was a position requiring someone of good character. The following year, 1831, he was made a tithingman, or peace officer. The term comes from early English law enforcement, when towns were broken into small groups—ten families equaled a tithing—and the elected leader held the title.

Alvah Crocker's next call to civic duty came in 1834, when he was still hauling his paper to Boston at night.[40] The town charged him with securing the property for a road it wanted to build westward along the Nashua River. Again he found opposition from the farmers. This time they were opposed to selling rights-of-way at reasonable prices. So, taking matters into his own hands and assuming more debt, he bought the whole valley west of town. Unknowingly, the town had done him a great favor. After purchasing the valley, he presented the town with the necessary land for the road. Not only did his generosity benefit the town, but, more important, the remaining land provided him with good sites for future paper mills. The birch swamp had served its purpose, and now it was time to move to higher ground, away from the threat of the spring freshets.

Though Crocker still had a considerable burden of debt, his business was growing—as was his family. Charles T. Crocker was born in March 1833. Two years later, Crocker took the next step in expanding his business with the purchase of the old Burbank mill where he and his father had been employed. He immediately installed new and improved drying cylinders in both of his mills.[41] Procuring the necessary quantity of rags was becoming a problem, so he began to experiment with palm-leaf fibers for making paper pulp. The fibers were unsuitable for making writing paper, but they served well for manufacturing wallpaper, which was then coming into vogue. So he expanded his product line. In the fall of 1835, he was elected to the House of the Massachusetts General Court and transportation was on his mind. His nighttime wagon rides to Boston had made transportation a cause he would proclaim for the rest of his life.

A Railroad Dreamer

In 1830, Massachusetts chartered the Boston and Lowell Railroad, and in 1831 charters were granted to the Boston and Providence and Boston and Worcester railroads. By 1835, all three of these pioneer railroads were operational. The forty-four-mile Boston and Worcester represented the first step in achieving Boston's long-sought connection with the Hudson Valley. Workmen had turned the first shovelful of dirt for the Boston and Worcester in August 1832, and trains were running from Boston to Newton by April 1834. Before the first train ran those eight miles, Boston men still desiring to draw freight from the Erie Canal secured a charter on 13 March 1833 for the Western Railroad Corporation to build from "the terminus of the Boston and Worcester Railroad to the line of the State of

New York."[42] When completed, this line was celebrated as the realization of all that Henry Knox and Loammi Baldwin had advocated so many years earlier. The only problem was that the Western Railroad followed the southern route surveyed by James Baldwin, not his brother Loammi Baldwin's northern route.

The Western Railroad would later prove to be the nemesis of Alvah Crocker's efforts to build a railroad across the northern tier of Massachusetts, but in the 1836 legislative session he voted affirmatively for a state subscription of $1 million in Western Railroad stock. This state aid was needed to support completion of the railroad. If it had not been ". . . for his zealous advocacy, it is more than probable that the subscription would not have been made. . . ."[43] Twenty-six years later, when he was fighting for support of his Troy and Greenfield Railroad, Crocker reminded the senate that "some twenty-five Northern Massachusetts men" had supported the Western in 1836.[44]

As early as 1829, there was agitation for a railroad in northern Massachusetts. In July of that year, someone writing under the pseudonym "Franklin" inserted a letter in the *Columbian Centinel* of Boston advocating a railroad from Boston to Brattleboro, Vermont. The proposed railroad was to pass through Leominster and Fitchburg.[45] Consequently, that fall the architect Solomon Willard was employed by Andrew J. Allen, a Boston merchant, to reconnoiter a route to Fitchburg. In December, he presented outlines of several different routes, including extensions as far north as Brattleboro, Vermont.[46] This was only four years after George Stephenson had proved the practicality of steam locomotives at the Rainhill Trials in England and fully a year before the American steam locomotive "Tom Thumb" ran on the tracks of the Baltimore & Ohio Railroad. But Massachusetts had seen a demonstration of a railroad's hauling abilities when the horse-drawn Granite Railway opened in 1826, transporting the stone for the Bunker Hill Monument. Willard had been the superintendent of the monument project,[47] and he had supported Gridley Bryant, builder of the railway, when he faced strong opposition in the legislature.[48]

The next call for a railroad to Fitchburg came in 1837, the year Crocker's second daughter was born and a year after he completed his term in the legislature. The men of Fitchburg first considered a line eastward to connect at Lowell with the Boston and Lowell Railroad. Then attention focused on a line to the south. A meeting was held and a committee was chosen to investigate the southward route and a connection with the Boston and Worcester Railroad at Framingham, some forty miles away. Crocker personally paid for surveys of these two routes.

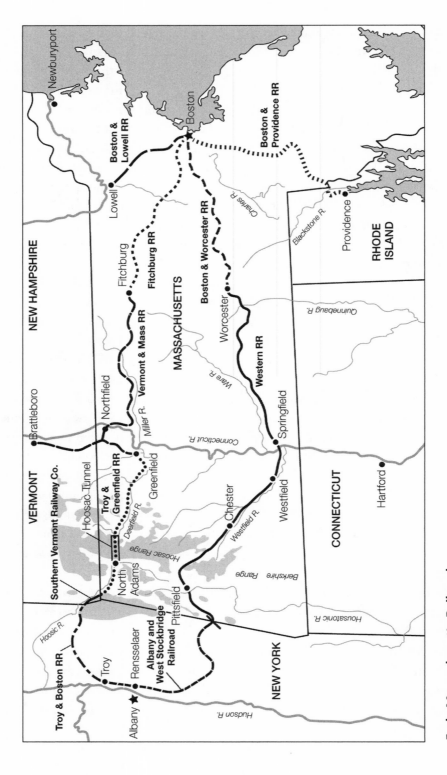

Early Massachusetts Railroads

A favorable report was forthcoming concerning the route to Framingham, so another committee was chosen to present a petition to the legislature for a charter, but the matter died from neglect. The neglect may have been the result of the trying financial conditions the country experienced that year. Martin Van Buren had become president in March 1837, but the financial troubles of the time stemmed from the attacks of his predecessor, Andrew Jackson, on the Second Bank of the United States and its president, Nicholas Biddle. Land speculation was also one of the causes of the 1837 financial panic. The loss of stability in the banking community caused Crocker and many other businessmen to suffer severe losses. In Boston, fifty or sixty merchants and traders failed in the first month of 1837.[49]

To save cash, Crocker closed the old Burbank mill, but still he "found the inside bottom of his pocket" empty.[50] Only the timely repayment of an old loan made to a friend saved him from his protested notes. The friend traveled from Alabama and paid him in "Nick Biddle's bills" (Bank of the United States bills)—this was rather astonishing, for there was little currency in circulation at the time.[51]

Even in these difficult times, Crocker continued his mission to "find a way to bring Fitchburg nearer to Boston." Ralph Waldo Emerson relates how Crocker desired to meet Loammi Baldwin, "the best engineer in the state." As Emerson tells the story, Crocker was finally successful in meeting the busy man because Baldwin's wife and Crocker's mother had been dearest friends. When Crocker approached Mrs. Baldwin, she invited him to visit on a Sunday afternoon, supposedly saying, "I will see that Mr. Baldwin shall answer all your questions."[52]

After the financial storm of 1837 subsided, the next five years proved good for business, so men once again turned their attention to connecting Fitchburg with Boston. On 11 November 1841, a notice appeared in the *Fitchburg Sentinel* calling citizens to a meeting at the town hall the following evening "to adopt such measures as they might think proper" concerning a railroad from this place to the city of Boston.[53] The editor of the *Sentinel*, W. S. Wilder, later related that the origin of the meeting was a conversation in his reading room. The gentlemen present had all espoused the town's need for a railroad to Boston, but Crocker had expressed no faith in the project because of the past failures in promoting a line. But one of the participants in the conversation drafted the meeting notice and Wilder published it in the *Sentinel*. Although his third daughter had been born only three days earlier, Crocker attended the meeting.

He immediately took a leadership role, being voted a member to the Committee of Correspondence and Enquiry,[54] which was instructed to develop definite plans for a railroad. Fortunately, that fall Crocker was reelected to the lower house of the Massachusetts General Court.[55]

Railroads were still new and there were strong prejudices against those "teakettles on wheels" whose smoke was a terrible nuisance and whose noise prevented hens from laying. Crocker's old nemeses—the farmers—were against all railroads just as they had been against mills and roads. At a meeting for the Old Colony Railroad, a speaker protested, stating, "[T]he opening of such communication with Boston would affect the price of oats and destroy the business of the stage proprietor."[56] Tavern-keepers joined the teamsters to put every possible obstacle in the way of railroad construction.[57] But again Crocker persevered, and a second meeting was held in Fitchburg before the end of December. He reported that "the people of Concord have been aroused to the importance of aiding in the project."[58] So, with support from Concord, a railroad convention was organized. Delegates from the towns above and below Fitchburg were summoned to the Massasoit House in Waltham on 11 January 1842.[59]

About a hundred delegates from towns along the proposed line gathered at the convention. Crocker addressed them, "calling attention to the feasibility and advantages of an independent route" to Boston instead of simply a connection to one of the other railroads.[60] Abraham T. Lowe of Boston, a director of the Boston and Worcester Railroad,[61] also addressed the convention, giving encouragement. It seemed the time had finally arrived for Crocker's dream of better communication with Boston.

In 1841, civil engineer Samuel M. Felton, the successor to Loammi Baldwin's Charlestown engineering practice, had surveyed and constructed the Fresh Pond Railroad to Charlestown.[62] The line connected the Fresh and Spy Ponds, just northwest of Harvard, with the Charlestown wharf. It was a short-line railroad built solely for hauling ice to Boston.[63] At Crocker's meeting with Baldwin in 1837, it is possible the great engineer had recommended Felton to him. Whatever the circumstances surrounding Felton's presence, when a Committee of Survey was organized, he was chosen as the engineer for the Fitchburg Railroad.[64] He made the preliminary survey of the route for obtaining a charter from the legislature.[65]

Alvah Crocker, ever the optimist, was assigned to a committee charged with meeting with the directors of the Fresh Pond Railroad, which Felton had just completed. The Fitchburg Railroad wanted to use the completed Fresh Pond track. Crocker's committee was also charged with submitting the railroad's petition for a charter to the legislature, where there was opposition from the leading men of the Western Railroad. Senator James K. Mills, Boston merchant and the largest Western Railroad stockholder,[66] spoke against the charter, saying, ". . . a six-horse stagecoach and a few baggage wagons will carry all the freight from Fitchburg to Boston."[67] Though Mills and other Western men voted against the charter, Crocker's energy garnered success. The bill to charter the Fitchburg Railroad Company passed the legislature on 2 March 1842.[68]

The Fitchburg Railroad

Chartering the Fitchburg Railroad proved a costly personal victory for Alvah Crocker. While "the local papers along the route teemed with editorials in favor of the project,"[69] there were strong feelings among farmers, teamsters, and tavern-keepers against his railroad.[70] People were fearful the railroad would be ruinous to their livelihoods, and, being the leading advocate of the railroad, Crocker was the prime target of the opposition. When fires of mysterious origin consumed his paper mill and one belonging to his brother, Samuel S. Crocker, the assumption was that someone in opposition was the culprit. When asked whether everything had burned, Crocker remarked, "Yes everything, except the mortgage."[71]

Even before the charter was approved, the railroad began holding meetings in towns along the line—Cambridge, Watertown, Waltham, Concord, Groton, and Lancaster—to solicit stock subscriptions.[72] In Fitchburg, however, there were still strong feelings against the railroad because no decision had been made about where the railroad would terminate. There existed a strong sectional division between "Old City" and "Up Town" as to a depot location.[73] Despite the dissent in Fitchburg, at a meeting in Concord on 13 July, the company was organized and Alvah Crocker was elected to

2 March 1842
Fitchburg RR
Charter

13 July 1842
Crocker & Elias H. Derby
elected directors Fitchburg RR

Spring 1843
Chief Engineer Felton
advertises first contract

15 May 1843
Work begins on the first
27 miles of Fitchburg RR

August/September 1843
Crocker and Derby
tour RRs in Europe

21 August 1843
Crocker purchases
iron rails in England

15 March 1844
Vermont & Massachusetts
Railroad chartered

5 March 1845
First train arrives
in Fitchburg

14 May 1845
Crocker resigns
presidency Fitchburg RR

December 1850
Vermont & Massachusetts RR
reaches Greenfield, MA

the first board of directors.[74] He would later serve as board president during the construction period. At the Concord meeting, Crocker enlisted as an ally Elias H. Derby, an eminent railroad counsel from Boston. Derby was also chosen as a Fitchburg director at the Concord meeting. The two soon became troubadours chanting the benefits of low fares and low freight rates for the new road.[75]

The son of the great Salem merchant of the same name, Derby was an 1824 graduate of Harvard College. He read law in Daniel Webster's office and was an early proponent of railroads in Massachusetts. When elected a director of the Fitchburg Railroad, he was still serving and actively involved as a Western Railroad director.[76] The intense battles between the Western and the northern Massachusetts railroads were still in the future, but Crocker was marshaling his forces. Derby believed in the idea of siphoning off Erie Canal freight, and he was squabbling with his fellow Western Railroad directors over the issue of low freight rates from New York to Boston.[77] After losing that battle in 1843, he did not stand for reelection as a Western Railroad director in 1844. Some twelve years in the future, William H. Swift, after his time as president of the Western Railroad, would publicly label Derby's low-rate ideas a "preposterous principle laid down by certain men ignorant of the subject."[78] Swift was a Massachusetts native and a West Point–educated engineer.

Alvah Crocker and the new railroad had chosen wisely. Derby worked hard to sell the Fitchburg's stock in Boston, and even before all of the stock was sold, men were sent out along the route to buy land for the railroad. In Concord, they encountered the Transcendentalists Ralph Waldo Emerson, Henry David Thoreau, and Nathaniel Hawthorne. Emerson moaned about the progress but sold a slice of his Walden Pond property for a railroad right-of-way. He then invested the proceeds in Fitchburg Railroad stock.[79] The state charter required $600,000 of stock be subscribed before the company could commence operations. Even with Crocker's and Derby's efforts to sell the stock, it was the spring of 1843 before sufficient cash was collected and Chief Engineer Samuel Felton could leave his grading work on the Bunker Hill Monument[80] to advertise the first Fitchburg Railroad contract.[81]

Men of moderate wealth—the manufacturers, mechanics, and even the disinclined farmers along the route—bought shares, "much of it in small amounts of from one to ten hundred dollars."[82] At $100 a share, Emerson subscribed to twelve shares, Crocker took fifty-one, and engineer Felton bought fifty-four. The firm of John E. Thayer & Brother, leading figures in Boston finance, took 657 shares.[83] Massachusetts men of substantial wealth were beginning to invest in railroads, and soon such men would link themselves with competent engineers capable of protecting their investments.

As early as 1839, John E. Thayer, Nathaniel Thayer, and John M. Forbes—either with others or individually—began to invest in New York railroads that paralleled the Long Trail of the Indians.[84] These men, who had made their fortunes as China traders, were experienced in directing such far-flung enterprises as railroads. Although never personally engaged in the China trade, Elias H. Derby was also an investor in many railroads with this group of men.

In 1846, these men discovered that the Philadelphia, Wilmington, and Baltimore Railroad (the PW&B) was deeply in debt. Sensing an opportunity, they purchased four-fifths of the PW&B's stock.[85] John Thayer's firm led the PW&B purchase. To protect and foster their investment, Forbes was instrumental in getting William H. Swift out of the army—his resignation was accepted on 31 July 1849—and he became president of the PW&B soon afterward.[86] His older brother, General Joseph Gardner Swift, was the first gentleman to graduate from West Point. William Swift entered the U.S. Military Academy in 1813 at the age of thirteen. Because he was ordered in December 1818 to accompany Major Stephen Long's expedition to the Rocky Mountains, he was absent from the academy for his final exam, yet the army placed him at the end of the class roll and commissioned him in July 1819.[87]

On loan from the U.S. Army, Swift had served from 1836 to 1840 as resident engineer with the Western Railroad. In 1847, he designed and then built—over two seasons—a skeleton iron tower lighthouse on the Outer Minot Ledge off Boston Bay. On 16 April 1851, the structure was destroyed, with the loss of its two keepers. It was probably Swift's only failure, but the poor quality of iron and additions made to the structure by the keepers were contributing causes for the loss. The state of knowledge of the processes needed to produce good-quality metal materials was still in its infancy. Later, the issue of metal quality would also challenge Crocker's efforts to tunnel the Hoosac. In 1850, Swift returned to Massachusetts as president of the Western Railroad. With that move, Thayer would steal Crocker's chief engineer, Samuel Felton, and send him south to replace Swift as president of the PW&B.[88]

Forbes, from his time in China, was well connected with the British banking house of Baring Brothers and Company, and through this trusted relationship he could draw significant financial support for his railroad projects in the United States. He would later lead investor groups that built a connected series of east–west railroads reaching to the Missouri River and after the Civil War, his railroads would reach as far west as Denver. His trusted chief engineer, John W. Brooks, for those undertakings came out of Baldwin's Charlestown office, where he had been trained by Samuel Felton. A tight band of Boston finance men and engineers was beginning to coalesce in the 1840s. Though Elias Derby had access to the finance men, they were not willing to subscribe to any additional Fitchburg stock in 1843, so Crocker was still searching for additional stock subscriptions.

Crocker and Derby found their solution when an experienced railroad contractor came looking for work. S. F. Belknap from Windsor, Vermont, spent 1842 in Maine constructing the Portland, Saco & Portsmouth Railroad (PS&P).[89] With the PS&P work completed, he traveled south in 1843 looking to build another railroad. Thirty years later, Derby, when reminiscing about the financial woes that had so bedeviled the Fitchburg Railroad in its first year, stated that Belknap came forward and bought the last 1,500 shares, $150,000 worth, of railroad stock necessary to reach the state-mandated $600,000.[90]

The firm of Belknap, Gilmore and Co. was then put under contract to build the first twenty-seven miles of the Fitchburg between Fresh Pond and Groton.[91] Derby, appearing before a legislative committee in 1873, referred to Belknap as "that prince of contractors." His evaluation must have been unanimous, for Belknap eventually built the entire line. His contracts required him to supply all material except the rails.[92] But material—other than rails—was not the biggest problem. At a time when the cuts through the hills and embankments across the valleys for a railroad were made by men wielding picks and shovels,[93] labor was the critical need.

Belknap brought good railroad men to the job, including a sixteen-year-old tracklayer named James Harvey Strobridge from Albany, Vermont.[94] Strobridge later went to California and became superintendent of construction for the Central Pacific Railroad. It was he who pushed the Central Pacific over the Sierras to meet the Union Pacific Railroad in 1869 at Promontory Summit, in the Utah Territory. Crocker spent days haunting the Boston wharves for Irish immigrants escaping hard times at home. Meeting the Cunard steam packets, he found men glad to bend their backs to the pick and shovel sixteen hours a day for sixty cents.[95] By August 1843, Belknap, with Crocker's help, had 700 men working to build the railroad.

As the gangs of Irish laborers smoothed the route for the railroad, Felton was busy designing bridges, writing contracts, and formulating specifications. His specifications required the contractor to prepare a roadbed "composed of free sand and or gravel for a depth of two feet" and be accountable "for leaving gates or fences of land owners open." The bridge specifications required "oak piles not less than 14 inches average diameter, driven to a firm bearing." Felton also put a clause in the contract that "contractors will not be allowed to consign their contracts without the consent of the Engineer or Agent."[96] Loammi Baldwin had prepared Felton well as a civil engineer and manager of projects. This issue of contract assignment would later cause innumerable problems when the Hoosac Tunnel work was contracted to builders. While Felton was busy pushing the work, Crocker and Derby turned to the problem of obtaining iron rails.

In early August of 1843, Crocker and Derby sailed from Boston on the Cunard packet to purchase rails and investigate the construction of railroads in Europe. Out in the Atlantic on 5 August, Crocker recorded in his diary "a most delightful day for the first time in my life saw a whale spouting."[97] They maintained a hectic pace as they tried to see everything and talk to every railroad engineer and manager in England and France. In London, they had planned to call on Isambard Kingdom Brunel, son of the French civil engineer Sir Marc Brunel, but, to their dismay, he was out of the city. Before going on to build twenty-five railways, Isambard had worked with his father and served as the resident engineer for the 1,300-foot-long Thames River Tunnel in London. (The Thames River Tunnel was the first successful tunnel under a navigable river. While designed for horse-drawn carriages, it was originally used only for pedestrian traffic. Between 1865 and 1869, it was converted for use by trains and later became part of the London Underground system.)

From the editor of *Railway Magazine* Derby and Crocker obtained letters of introduction to the managers of the principal British railways. By 21 August 1843, they had received proposals for 4,000 tons of rails and were pleased to be offered the iron at $23.75 per ton. A new American tariff, however, would add another $25 per ton[98] to the cost. (There had been no tariff on railroad iron imported into the United States between 1832 and March 1843.)

Two days later, they crossed the English Channel to France. Traveling to Paris via the Paris and Rouen Railway, Derby noted a major difference between Puritan New England and France: "Each of our companions has a bottle of claret beside him and a long and slender roll of bread."[99] In Paris they visited the Louvre and admired Notre Dame before beginning their study of the country's railroads. Their hectic pace then continued, with stops in Baden-Baden, Heidelberg, and Frankfurt in early September. Before returning to England, they inspected a railway yard in Antwerp. In his diary, Crocker made sketches of bridges and railroad stations. He also paid close attention to the materials used in constructing the stations and rolling equipment. Whenever the opportunity arose, he and Derby questioned managers and engineers about costs and operational logistics.

Returning to London, they made arrangements for the shipment of the iron rails to Boston. After this, Crocker and Derby spent several days traveling the country on different English railways. They took the Manchester and Leeds Railway to Leeds and passed through numerous tunnels, including the two-mile-long Summit Tunnel. Derby kept his own detailed notes on the number and cost of tunnels. Finally, back in Liverpool on 18 September, they called at Baring Brothers and Company, the merchant bankers who acted as agent for many American railroad enterprises, including the Western Railroad. Crocker and Derby completed their business and bade farewell to England on the fast packet *Acadia*.[100] The troubadours arrived back in Boston on 2 October at four in the morning.

The Western Railroad

Over the years, the Commonwealth of Massachusetts had provided financial aid to several railroads, including the Eastern, the Boston and Maine, the Norwich and Worcester, and the Western.[101] But the Fitchburg Railroad was financed entirely with private capital and received no financial aid from the Common-wealth. When the Western Railroad was chartered, its authorized stock capital-ization was limited to $2 million.[102] But in January of 1836, after the company was organized and the stock subscribed, the directors realized that driving a railroad through the mountains of western Massachusetts would require much, much more money. President Jackson's war on Nicholas Biddle's bank had caused financial problems for Crocker, but it also gave the Western an opportunity to appeal for state aid. When Bostonians petitioned the legislature for a state bank to fill the vacuum left by the loss of the Bank of the United States, the direc-tors of the Western Railroad joined the petitioners and added a proviso to the bank charter bill requiring the new state bank to purchase $1 million of Western stock.[103] The Jacksonian Democrats in the legislature, fearful of a "monster" money institution, divorced the railroad provisos from the bank bill, but to gain their victory over the bank, they had to give the railroad what it wanted.[104] By a separate act, the legislature increased the Western Railroad's capitalization to $3 million and directed "the Treasurer of the state to subscribe $1 million to the stock of the road."[105] The 1836 bill of commonwealth generosity to the Western additionally specified that three of the Western's nine directors be appointed by the Massachusetts General Court.[106]

Once state backing was assured, the Western was able to collect from private investors the first two assessments on its stock, so construction commenced in January 1837.[107] The stockholders paid two additional assessments during 1837 and the work proceeded smoothly. The first twenty-seven miles were graded and ready for rail by January 1838. But as the work progressed and the engineers completed surveys west of the Connecticut River, the cost estimate for building the line was revised upward to $4 million. Adding to this harsh reality, the financial panic worsened during the year and the railroad found it could not squeeze any additional stock assessments from its private investors. With no private capital available, the Western Railroad's directors again turned to the Massachusetts legislature, pleading that suspension of the work would totally waste the already expended private capital. Again the legislature was responsive, creating $2,100,000 in sterling bonds on 21 February 1838 and assigning them to the Western Railroad.[108] Baring Brothers and Company sold the bonds on consignment and used the proceeds to pay for rails the Western purchased in England.[109] There was one particularly interesting provision in the loan act, and when Massachusetts made a similar bond award to support tunneling the Hoosac Mountain, it would cause much debate. The Act of 1838 specifically required that any premium received on the sale of the bonds go into a sinking fund to retire the thirty-year bonds at maturity,[110] and Massachusetts bonds, because they were issued in sterling, sold at higher prices, thus bringing the requirement into effect.[111]

By October 1839, the fifty-four miles of Western Railroad track between Worcester and Springfield were opened to traffic, but before the trains steamed to the Connecticut Valley, the Western again appealed to the legislature for funds. The problems of correctly estimating the cost of the work sprang from two sources. First, like Loammi Baldwin's canal-building experiences in Pennsylvania, management for the projects used low cost estimates to obtain legislative approvals. Then, as more engineering work was performed in the field, the true enormity of the task became obvious. In Pennsylvania, management had refused to listen to engineer Baldwin; in Massachusetts, as the engineers sought routes to Albany through the hills west of Springfield and gained a better understanding of the difficulties, the cost estimates rose. Since management of the Western Railroad resided with men determined to build the best possible railroad, they were forced to return repeatedly to the legislature for financial help.

During the debate for a second loan, the Western men met opposition from Northfield's Samuel C. Allen Jr.,[112] who suggested that the Commonwealth purchase control of the railroad. In 1839, the legislature had found the idea of the Commonwealth owning a railroad to be repugnant, so on 23 March 1839 it had authorized another issue of Commonwealth bonds, amounting to $1,200,000. These bonds were not so easily disposed of, because the railway bubble had been pricked in England. In fact, it was October 1839 before Baring would even agree to handle the bonds.[113]

The Western found itself short of funds again in early 1841. Driving the railroad through the mountains beyond Springfield had required twenty-one costly bridges,[114] of which several, it should be noted, were still in use in 2015. Although the road was graded for a single line of track, the railroad's board of directors ordered the engineers to build all bridges except the one over the Connecticut River for a double-track railroad. President Thomas B. Wales and the directors were convinced that flimsy bridge construction was false economy.[115] Earlier, when the directors had made the decision to employ the West Point–educated engineers Gibbs McNeil, William H. Swift, and George W. Whistler, there had been much debate about economical construction practices.[116] The West Pointers had solid railroad experience, but a director spoke against the military men, saying such engineers were charmed more with the beauty of a bridge "than the plain and homely attributes of utility and economy."[117] The issue of utility and economy versus solid construction would later lead to much debate concerning the character of those constructing the Troy and Greenfield Railroad and tunneling the Hoosac Mountain.

For now, the Western men could point out that the railroad built by their West Point engineers was solid and durable. But solid construction translated into the need for another million dollars. When the Western Railroad men of Pittsfield and Springfield arrived in Boston to plead their case and tout the benefits that would accrue to the Commonwealth, this third appeal was not well received. There were even charges of mismanagement. Nevertheless, after a bitter debate, the Western representatives were partly successful. The legislature granted the railroad another $700,000 in Commonwealth bonds on 12 March 1841.[118] When the first train huffed and puffed over the mountains from Boston to Albany, the Commonwealth of Massachusetts held $1 million of Western Railroad stock and had provided the railroad $4 million of its credit in sterling bonds. The City of Albany, New York, had also contributed $1 million in bonds. Private stockholders held only $2 million of Western railroad stock.[119]

The result of having obtained such a large portion of its financing by the use of bonded debt was that the Western now had to establish very high freight and passenger rates to pay off the bonds. If the Western failed to make the necessary interest payments and contributions to the sinking fund for redemption of the bonds at their maturity, the Commonwealth of Massachusetts was liable for making up the default, as the money had been raised with Commonwealth bonds rather than with railroad company bonds. Even Elias Derby's strenuous campaigns for low rates could not change this reality. The Western's high freight and passenger rates generated a great many complaints, and these would serve to support Crocker's efforts to build a competing railroad across northern Massachusetts.

The Vermont and Massachusetts Railroad

Alvah Crocker watched these money maneuvers by the men of the Western Railroad and plotted his strategy for a direct-line railroad connecting the towns of northern Massachusetts with Boston and Albany. As early as 1831, engineer James Hayward reported the results of a survey for a railroad from Boston to Ontario,[120] and during the early planning for the Fitchburg Railroad, the idea was to eventually extend the line into southern New Hampshire and Vermont.[121] Crocker and the directors of the Fitchburg saw the bounty of the Erie Canal and originally planned to capture a share by way of Lake Champlain, with an extension to Lake Ontario or a point above the lake on the St. Lawrence River. From Fitchburg, the line could have proceeded northwest and cut across the corner of New Hampshire. But in 1840, the Granite State declared war on the railroads. Specifically, the New Hampshire legislature passed an act prohibiting the use of eminent domain by railroads to obtain land at reasonable prices. The act had a chilling effect on the promotion of railroads in that state[122] and turned Crocker's sights toward potential alliances in Vermont. Immediately after arriving home from Europe, he proceeded to Montpelier, to lobby the Vermont legislature's Committee on Roads. It was a hard trip, as he recorded in his diary: "I have this week met four audiences and traveled more than 100 miles."[123] During the trip to Vermont, Crocker's wallet was stolen, he endured stage delays, and he even had to walk the last twenty miles home. But he achieved his purpose.

On 17 October, he met with Charles Paine, Vermont's ex-governor, to discuss railroad matters.[124] Paine served two terms as governor and had stepped down from his second term only four days before their conversation. Crocker was thinking about Brattleboro, Vermont, on the Connecticut River as the terminal point for the railroad he wanted to build through the towns to the west of Fitchburg, and Paine wanted a north–south railroad through his state, especially through Northfield, where he owned a mill for processing wool. Crocker's persistence, and doubtlessly some horse trading with Paine, paid off. On 31 October, two weeks after his visit, the Vermont legislature approved Act no. 56, which granted a charter to the Brattleboro and Fitchburg Railroad Company of Vermont. This act gave Crocker the legal grounds for continuing his railroad westward into Vermont towns on the Connecticut River. Specifically, the charter conveyed the right to build from Brattleboro, Vermont, to the Massachusetts boundary line to meet any railroad from Fitchburg.

In early 1844, as part of his deal with Paine, engineer Samuel Felton was in Vermont surveying a route for the Vermont Central Railroad.[125] By enduring the travails of the trip and making some shrewd agreements, Crocker was closer to realizing his dream of tapping the bounty of the West with a northern Massachusetts railroad.

Back home in Massachusetts, Crocker appeared in Boston at the winter 1844 session of the Massachusetts General Court, seeking a charter for the Vermont and Massachusetts Railroad Company with the right to build a railroad to the state line of either Vermont or New Hampshire.[126] Crocker kept secret the fact that the Fitchburg Railroad already had an agreement with Paine, granting the Vermont Central an exclusive line to Boston. By their private agreement, Crocker's Fitchburg Railroad would not join the Rutland and Burlington Railroad, which was to run north–south in Vermont, and Paine's Vermont Central would not join the Northern Railroad, which cut across New Hampshire toward Lowell, Massachusetts. On 15 March 1844, as the Western Railroad awakened to the competition, the legislature gave Crocker his charter. The Vermont and Massachusetts companies authorized by these two charters were united as the Vermont and Massachusetts Railroad Company in November 1844. At the organizational meeting, Alvah Crocker was elected a director; in March 1845, he became president of the new railroad. At the time, he was still president of the Fitchburg Railroad.

Even before the Vermont and Massachusetts Railroad Company charter was granted, Crocker was off to Washington, DC, in February 1844 to lobby for a remission of the tariff on railway iron. This duty had doubled the cost of the iron rails for the Fitchburg Railroad.[127] The "Railroad Iron Bill" of 1832, by means of a drawback (refund), had effectively eliminated the 25 percent ad valorem tariff on railway iron imported by states or incorporated companies. By 1842, Pennsylvania iron interests were pushing hard for a protective tariff, and their success in gaining a tariff act had imposed a $25 per ton tariff on iron, effective the third day of March in 1843.[128] The passage of the 1842 bill was quickly followed by a flood of requests from railroad companies, including one from Crocker and the Fitchburg Railroad, praying for relief from the new import duties. The new tariff had gone into effect just before he and Derby negotiated to buy the iron rails from England for the Fitchburg Railroad.

Crocker was also in Washington to try to secure a postal contract for the Fitchburg Railroad.[129] He presented the railroad's tariff plea to the chairman of the Committee of Finance in the Senate and buttonholed senators in the corridors of the Capitol. He even went so far as to publish pamphlets about how the duty on iron rails discouraged the building of railroads.[130] His persistence got him an interview with Senator James Buchanan from Pennsylvania on 4 March. It was Buchanan who, by offering an amendment to the revenue bill of 1841, had led the drive to reinstate a tariff on iron.[131] Crocker was not pleased with the outcome of the interview, as Buchanan stated that he would "persist in opposing the remission of duty."[132] General Winfield Scott gave Crocker a letter propounding the military value of good railroads,[133] but the powers in Washington persisted in opposing the remission of the duty.

Toward the end of April 1844, Crocker went to Philadelphia to visit the Baldwin Norris Locomotive Works, where he discussed purchasing a Baldwin engine for the Fitchburg Railroad. His efforts in Washington had met constant delays, so in early June he toured the Baltimore & Ohio Railroad. Again Crocker closely examined everything about the line and its construction. He noted that the B&O used broken stone to fill in between the cross ties to a depth of a foot, at a cost of $1,300 per mile. Also, for the first hundred miles they had used snakehead rails (the name applied to the practice of spiking down a strap of iron on top of wooden rails to avoid the cost of iron rails). Upon his return to Washington in June, the news was not what he wanted to hear: "Found my R.R. bill had gone by the board." Three days later, departing the city, he wrote, "took leave of this degraded hollow-hearted place Washington. A place which of all other places I loathe and abhor."[134] Twenty-eight years later, however, he would be sitting there as a representative from Massachusetts, considering tariff bills then before the House of Representatives.

While Crocker was in Washington, the controversy about where to locate the Fitchburg depot commenced in earnest. Residents in the lower part of town championed their undeveloped section, while businesses in the upper town believed the railroad should terminate there. Adding to the controversy was the fact that Crocker owned most of the open land in the lower town. Even

Snakehead rails, wood rail with iron strap

though he was not a member of the directors' committee that made the decision to purchase his land in the lower town, he was subject to much abuse. Chief Engineer Felton reported to the directors that there was not enough open acreage to accommodate the railroad in the upper town, but the weekly *Fitchburg Sentinel* and many citizens accused Crocker of unduly influencing the decision. Local holders of Fitchburg Railroad stock dumped their holdings and depreciated the stock price below par. Before the controversy was over, there were few Fitchburg Railroad stockholders left in the town. Later, however, many would regret their rash decision to dump the stock. The railroad proved a success, and stockholders received dividends ranging from four to ten percent during its first ten years of operation.[135]

On March 3, 1845, the *Fitchburg Sentinel* announced:

FITCHBURG RAILROAD OPENED THROUGH TO FITCHBURG

On and after Wednesday, March 5th, and until further notice, passenger trains will run over the Fitchburg railroad as follows:

Up trains, leave Charlestown at 7 A.M., 1½ and 5 P.M.

Down trains, leave Fitchburg at 6½ and 10 A.M. and 4½ P.M.

A freight train will run both ways over the road daily.

S. M. Felton, Engineer

Henry David Thoreau, while living in his cabin on Walden Pond, wrote about awaiting the coming of the train each morning: "I hear the iron horse make the hills echo with his snort like thunder, shaking the earth with his feet, and breathing fire and smoke from his nostrils."[136] Thoreau was short of stature but firmly built, with strong hands and skillful in the use of tools;[137] when he built his cabin overlooking the pond in 1845, he used boards from James Collins's shanty. He paid the Irishman Collins, who had labored with the track gang building the Fitchburg Railroad, $4.25 for the shanty. Thoreau paid the money on an April evening before Collins and his wife moved on following the railroad work.[138]

The newly married Nathaniel Hawthorne had moved with his bride to Concord in June of 1842. The next year, he penned his short story "The Celestial Railroad" as the track gangs did their work beyond the Old North Bridge. While Crocker and Derby celebrated, the two Transcendentalists drank it in and composed very different lines of verse about the iron horse. Two years of hard work by Crocker, Derby, and Felton had given Fitchburg a direct-line railroad to Boston. Thoreau, it should be noted, actually contributed more than verse to Crocker's railroad efforts. Edmund Quincy Sewall, who as a lad had attended Henry and John Thoreau's Concord Academy, would apply his schoolboy geometry lessons as he ran surveys for Crocker's next railroad project.[139]

The shrill of the whistle from the locomotive "Charlestown" announced the arrival of the first train into Fitchburg on 5 March 1845—a day crowned with a gray sky and cooled by sleet and rain.[140] It matched the mood of many in the Fitchburg crowd, still angry about the depot decision. But in the other towns along the line, the weather did not dampen the celebration—people turned out with flags and banners in Leominster. The *Fitchburg Sentinel* described the event in only three terse and tense sentences, while other papers, such as the *Bunker Hill Aurora*[141] of Charlestown, congratulated Crocker and recorded that the Fitchburg Band provided "fine music."

The moisture and the chilly reception failed to daunt the indefatigable Crocker. Even as he descended from the train, his vision of a great main-line railroad across the northern tier of Massachusetts to the West was crystallizing. He now believed that Loammi Baldwin's 1825 canal survey pointed the way—maybe the two men had even discussed it during their 1837 meeting. The previous January, Crocker had written to Felton that he planned to "tap the very sources of Clinton's canal."[142]

Alvah Crocker's original dream had become a reality—iron rails now carried trains from Fitchburg to Boston on a regular schedule. He had overcome the skeptics and the challenges, but the success was only the first segment of a railroad to connect all of northern Massachusetts directly with Boston. On 14 May 1845, he met with the board of the Fitchburg Railroad and resigned from his position as president. The Fitchburg was built and was hauling people and freight; now there was another railroad to build. To keep the Fitchburg Railroad operating smoothly, Samuel Felton moved from engineering to management and became superintendent of the Fitchburg Railroad, while Crocker turned his attention to building the Vermont and Massachusetts Railroad.

Construction of the Vermont and Massachusetts commenced in September 1845, and the line opened in stages. From Fitchburg to the Connecticut River Valley, the line traversed the corrugated landscape of the northern Massachusetts highlands. Those conditions made construction much more difficult and costly. Capitalists looked at the rugged country of northern Massachusetts, with only small settlements and little industry, and quickly decided the railroad's prospects of achieving early financial returns were limited. Still Crocker labored onward, selling stock one share at a time. After listening to him for hours, farmers would buy one share just to get him out of their homes.[143] In 1847, the British railroad boom collapsed, making his efforts to raise funds even more difficult—the collapse affected interest rates and the availability of money. The inability to raise capital by the sale of stock forced Crocker in 1849 to finance the railroad by selling long-term railroad company bonds. The struggle for capital to build the Vermont and Massachusetts was a preview of the financial and political brawl to come with the next railroad Crocker chartered.

The rails of the Vermont and Massachusetts reached Baldwinville, about twenty miles west of Fitchburg, in September 1847; before the state legislature met in 1848, Crocker had pushed the line to Athol, another ten miles.[144] The first train reached Brattleboro, Vermont, on 20 February 1849,[145] after construction of a bridge across the Connecticut River and the laying of rails northward on the west bank of the river. Originally the line southward to Greenfield, Massachusetts, was considered a spur line, but when it was completed in December 1850, Greenfield immediately became the terminal for the combined Fitchburg and Vermont and Massachusetts Railroads.[146] The Fitchburg and the Vermont and Massachusetts were now only thirty-five miles north of Springfield, the Western Railroad's home. Alvah Crocker, busy promoting the final link in his chain of railroads to the Hudson resigned from the presidency before the rails of the Vermont and Massachusetts reached Greenfield. Thomas Whittemore, a Boston clergyman and financier,[147] was named president of the Vermont and Massachusetts in late 1849.[148]

The Tunnel Scheme

A happy New Year to you, my beloved husband!
May it preserve to you all your blessings, confirm
all your virtues, realize all your hopes! May it ripen
your peaches, multiply your strawberries, extend your
grapes, & build your RAILROAD!

—Susan Sedgwick to Theodore Sedgwick,
January 6, 1828, Sedgwick Papers,
Massachusetts Historical Society

PAPER MAGNATE ALVAH CROCKER had spent countless hours convincing individual farmers to buy Vermont and Massachusetts Railroad stock. He invested so much time in those face-to-face visits because they gave him the opportunity to educate and build support for the coming struggle to complete his vision of a continuous railroad between Boston and Albany. It was a vision bitterly opposed by the Western Railroad.

A Visionary Scheme

In late March of 1847, the *Amherst Express* announced "that a survey of a route to Troy from Greenfield, Mass. via Deerfield River will soon be made."[1] So, as the surveyors toiled in the Deerfield River Valley, Crocker spoke at town meetings across northwestern Massachusetts, promoting the benefits of a through-line railroad to Boston. He was a one-man traveling show, delivering hundreds of lectures. A local paper would carry an announcement:

> *RAIL ROAD MEETING:*
> *A meeting of all those interested in the extension of the Fitchburg, and Vermont and Massachusetts Railroad through the vallies of the Deerfield and Hoosic Rivers to Troy, thereby connecting Boston and many other towns in Massachusetts, by way of Troy, with the Great West.*[2]

15 March 1844
Vermont & Massachusetts
Railroad chartered

10 May 1848
Troy and Greenfield Railroad
chartered

13 November 1848
Southern Vermont Railway
chartered in Vermont

29 March 1849
First patented
American percussion drill

22 November 1849
Troy and Boston Railroad
chartered in New York

October 1850
Gilmore and Carpenter sign
short tunnel contract

December 1850
Vermont & Massachusetts RR
reaches Greenfield, MA

8 January 1851
T&G RR start of construction
ceremony, North Adams

February 1851
Samuel Felton to Philadelphia,
Wilmington, & Baltimore RR

13 May 1851
$2,000,000 state aid bill
defeated

The following week, Crocker would appear, cultivating support for what the Western Railroad men would tag "the tunnel scheme"—a railroad through the Hoosac Mountain. *The Weekly Transcript* (North Adams) reported, after Crocker's visit there in November 1847, that delegates had filled the Baptist Church to overflowing and the engineer had said that "a nearly level track could be obtained by tunneling Hoosic Mountain a distance inside of four miles. . . ."[3]

In early 1848, Crocker carried a petition to the Massachusetts General Court for a railroad to extend westward from Greenfield, Massachusetts, "to meet or connect with any railroad that may be constructed from any point at or near the city of Troy, on the Hudson River, in the state of New York."[4] The petition immediately drew the hostility of the Western Railroad men, who considered such a road an encroachment on their route to Albany, New York.[5] Addison Gilmore, president of the Western Railroad, called the idea of tunneling the Hoosac ". . . a novel, a visionary scheme."[6] In the legislature, Crocker and his Troy and Greenfield Railroad associates were quick to stress the inadequacy of the Western's service and the lack of the Commonwealth's support for transportation improvements across the northern part of the Commonwealth. He wrote: "[T]he northern part of this Commonwealth will reap the same advantages it has so freely contributed by its votes, to give the Southern portion thereof by the Western Road."

As a representative in the lower house of the General Court, Crocker had voted for Commonwealth support to the Western Railroad. A majority of the General Court, believing in the doctrine of free competition, granted a charter to the Troy and Greenfield Railroad or T&G. Governor George N. Briggs signed the act chartering the T&G on 10 May 1848.[7] The first meeting to organize the company was held on 1 June 1848 at the Mansion House in Greenfield, but directors were not chosen until 5 April 1849.[8] The first directors were Jenks Kimball, John Vincent, Samuel Potter, Cephas Root, William Keith, Daniel Wells, Erastus Rice, Ebenezer Maynard, and Wendell T. Davis. They chose Judge George Grennell Jr. of Greenfield as president at a meeting on 11 April.[9] Judge Grennell, a Dartmouth graduate who was well connected politically, had served in the Senate of the General Court from 1825 to 1827 before being elected to the U.S. Congress in 1829 for five terms. The Troy and Greenfield Railroad charter marked the beginning of a bitter, mudslinging, twenty-five-year war with the Western Railroad, as the Springfield men of southern Massachusetts strove to protect their railroad monopoly.

On the western side of the Hoosac Mountain, the railroad Crocker envisioned would follow the Hoosic River from North Adams across the southwest corner of Vermont and on toward the Hudson River Valley to reach Troy, New York. Therefore, once he had the Massachusetts charter for the Troy and Greenfield Railroad, he returned to Vermont seeking the necessary charter for a railroad across the southwest corner of the Green Mountain State. This line was named the Southern Vermont Railway Company, and a charter was granted by the Vermont State Legislature on 13 November 1848.[10]

With authority to build a railroad to the New York state boundary, Crocker now visited Troy and proclaimed his railroad vision. The men of Troy were eager to compete with Albany, so Crocker's efforts were well received. On 22 November 1849, railroad enthusiasts in Troy successfully organized the Troy and Boston Railroad. This railroad, with tracks reaching from the city of Troy to the Vermont border, was only thirty-five miles long, but it provided the connecting link for Crocker's line to the Hudson River. At a ceremony with military companies, the mayor of Troy turned the first shovel, and construction of the Troy and Boston commenced in June of 1850,[11] but it progressed by fits and starts in a piecemeal fashion. The work reached Eagle Bridge, twenty-three miles from Troy, in February 1852, but then progress slowed as the railroad's backers watched developments in Massachusetts. Crocker and the Troy and Greenfield Railroad struggled to sell stock subscriptions and find contractors willing to accept the challenge of tunneling the Hoosac Mountain. The Troy and Boston was pushed another four miles to Hoosick Falls Junction by mid-1854, but the final eight miles, to the Vermont line, were not completed until March of 1859.

By charter, the Troy and Greenfield was capitalized at $3.5 million—the tunnel was estimated to cost $2 million, and $1.5 million was needed for the land

and railroad—but the backers could find few stock purchasers. Judge Grennell later recalled: ". . . the labors, travel, efforts and expenses incident to getting subscriptions for stock [was] a slow and weary process."[12] Northern Massachusetts was desperate for railroad facilities, and Crocker, together with the townspeople along the road, expected the state to come to their aid just as it had done twenty years earlier for the Western Railroad.

Western Railroad Opposition

Edward Hitchcock, the Massachusetts state geologist and president of Amherst College, reported that the Hoosac Mountain ". . . was composed mainly of mica and talcose slate [containing talc]."[13] On the west side, at the foot of the mountain, he noted that some limestone should be found, but he attached no particular significance to its occurrence.[14]

Limestone, a sedimentary rock, is formed from the remains of shells deposited on a seabed. As such, it is chemically a calcium carbonate material that will react under the influence of diluted hydrochloric acid. Rainwater, which contains a weak carbonic acid, will therefore deteriorate limestone as it passes through cracks and fissures in the rock. The resulting weathered material is very unstable, and a debris flow can result when the rock is excavated.

Hitchcock deduced that the rock was dipping steeply and striking at nearly right angles to the tunnel alignment. Testifying before the General Court of Massachusetts on 31 January 1854, Hitchcock went so far as to say that ". . . I do not believe that it would require any more masonry for its support than would be necessary for a good sound stick of timber with an auger-hole bored through it." Hitchcock had the "impression" that because the tunnel was so low in the mountain, it would be "below where the groundwater percolated." Consequently, he expected it to be dry after the miners drove the Hoosac bore beyond the portals. Having visited the Hoosac Mountain many times, Hitchcock felt confident in making these statements about the nature of the rock and the structure of the mountain.

Being a consummate realist about the task of driving a five-mile tunnel through the Hoosac Mountain using only muscle power, Crocker sent Samuel Felton and A. F. Edwards, the Troy and Greenfield's chief engineer, to Europe in 1850 seeking information about the invention of a powered drill. [15] Crocker had seen a report claiming that ". . . 22 feet of solid rock [could] be got through per day." *Scientific American* commented about the report, stating that "the English occasionally announce new discoveries. . ."—a comment based more on wishful thinking than fact. The editors of *Scientific American* were correct when they questioned the power drill report but such news was enticing. In July of 1853, the *American Railway Times* reported on a demonstration at a Quincy quarry where a steam drill had sunk four-inch-diameter holes at the rate of ten inches in eleven minutes. This drill was even advertised for sale in the *Railway Times*,[16] but there must have been problems, as it was never tried in the Hoosac bore.

It was the great hope of Crocker and the tunnel men that someone would perfect a mechanical rock drill, and over the ensuing years they and their contractors would examine the claims of many inventors. Jonathan J. Couch of Philadelphia patented the first American percussion drill on 29 March 1849.[17] The Couch drill was a large and unwieldy affair. It used a hollow piston to aim a steel drill that was launched like a lance. Couch's contraption was not a success. Two years later, on 11 March 1851, Couch's former assistant, Joseph W. Fowle, received his own patent for a percussion drill.[18] The two men had gone their separate ways even before Couch received his patent. Fowle's ideas eventually would provide the genesis for a workable drill, but in the 1850s Fowle did not have the financial resources to support his inventive ideas.

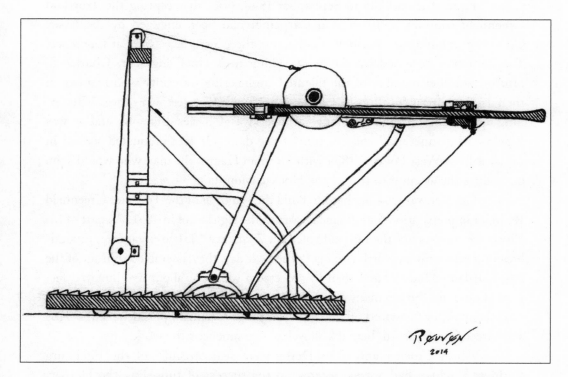

J. J. Couch's patented percussion drill (U.S. Patent no. 6237, 27 March 1849)

In February of 1851, Samuel Felton left Crocker and the Fitchburg Railroad. The Boston financiers had recognized his talent and sent him to Philadelphia to manage the Philadelphia, Wilmington, and Baltimore Railroad for them. (A decade in the future, during the Civil War, Baldwin's former engineering student would again be involved with Crocker's efforts to drive a railroad through the Hoosac Mountain.) Chief Engineer A. F. Edwards continued with the work, and, relying on Hitchcock's statements, pronounced tunneling of the Hoosac Mountain feasible. He developed a plan for a twenty-one-foot-by-twenty-foot horseshoe-shaped tunnel, estimating the cost at $1,968,557. Assuming manpower only—since no reliable powered drill had yet been located—he calculated the tunnel could be completed in 1,556 working days.[19] The location survey for the Troy and Greenfield Railroad was filed in 1850. Gilmore and Carpenter signed a contract in October of 1850 to construct the short tunnel at North Adams and the road from there westward to the Massachusetts–Vermont state line.[20, 21] Gilmore, in partnership with S. F. Belknap, had built the Fitchburg Railroad. John A. Carpenter had also worked on the Fitchburg and began working with Gilmore in 1845.

From August 1845 to September 1848, prior to accepting the Troy and Greenfield contract, Gilmore and Carpenter had been engaged by the Essex Company in building a masonry dam across the Merrimack River at Lawrence. The dam was designed by the Essex Company's chief engineer, Charles S. Storrow, another member of the talented engineering fraternity who had begun their engineering education in Loammi Baldwin's Charlestown office.[22] Beginning in 1846, Storrow's assistant engineer was Charles Bigelow, and it was Bigelow who supervised construction of the dam. He had graduated second in his class from West Point in 1835 with Herman Haupt, the man who would soon be leading the attempt to tunnel the Hoosac Mountain.[23]

Crocker was working hard to build the standing of the Troy and Greenfield Railroad in preparation for a financial plea to the legislature in 1851. As part of his effort, the directors of the railroad voted on 7 January 1851 to organize a groundbreaking ceremony in North Adams.[24] The next day, they assembled in front of the North Adams House,[25] and then in procession went out about five hundred feet west of town for the ceremony. The town band and Reverend Crawford[26] accompanied them. After Crawford offered a prayer, Judge Grennell, president of the Troy and Greenfield Railroad, hefted a shovel and commenced the work.[27]

Alvah Crocker and Elias Derby were still directors of the Fitchburg Railroad,[28] which had a great interest in the success of tunneling the Hoosac, but the two men did not hold official positions with the Troy and Greenfield. Success would be tied to local political support, so they allowed local men to assume the railroad's management positions. At the annual meeting in Charlemont on 4 February 1851, the majority of those chosen as directors resided in towns along the route. There were two from Greenfield, one from Charlemont, one from Buckland, one from Florida (Erastus Rice), three from North Adams, one from Williamstown, and three representing Boston and Cambridge. Six days later, the directors chose a new president, Henry Chapman of Greenfield.[29] Judge Grennell had not been thrown out, and he definitely had not abandoned the road, but his talents were needed elsewhere. Later in the year, he served as counsel to the petitioners for a loan from the Commonwealth to the Troy and Greenfield.[30]

Based on the tunneling plan and estimate prepared by Edwards, the railroad petitioned the legislature in 1851 for $2 million of state aid.[31] The Troy and Greenfield men argued the need for their railroad, stating: "[T]he West is the undoubted granary of the Union, and must supply New England with most of her breadstuffs."[32] To counter claims the Mountain could not be bored, and to prove the feasibility of the work, they presented cost data on railway tunnels in England, including the famous 1.8-mile-long Box Tunnel—the longest railroad tunnel then in existence—and the tunnels constructed by the Baltimore & Ohio Railroad. (It seems apparent that as early as 1843, when Crocker and Derby had visited England and attempted to meet with Isambard Kingdom Brunel, builder of the Box Tunnel, they were gathering data to support their future plans.) The estimate prepared by Edwards was explained to the legislators and a cross section of horseshoe-shaped tunnel was submitted. Finally, they offered Samuel Felton as a witness, but the committee did not deem his appearance necessary.[33]

The Western Railroad men contended that the Commonwealth, being an owner in their railroad, would not find it in its interest to help a rival project.[34] The matter went to the Joint Standing Committee on Railroads and Canals, which heard the petition. The committee did not accept the Western's argument and unanimously reported in favor of granting state credit to the Troy and Greenfield.[35] Both sides then continued to argue and publish their claims in the newspapers. The Western men started a rumor that the Greenfield men had agreed to support Charles Sumner in his bid for the U.S. Senate[36] and had thereby sold their souls to gain votes. The *Worcester Palladium* carried a story originally from the *Pittsfield Sun* claiming that five times the $2 million "would have to be rolled up before a locomotive could come bellowing out of the bowels of that mountain."[37] On the other side, a story appeared in the *American Railway Times,* describing a tunnel-boring machine. It was a contraption resulting from Yankee mechanical genius, and such machines would soon be tried against the rock of the Hoosac Mountain.[38] In the Senate, the third reading of the bill granting the loan of state credit passed twenty-one to eleven in April, and northern Massachusetts believed victory was theirs.[39] The Western Railroad turned up the congressional pressure and issued a memorial (written statement of facts or a petition presented to a legislative body) urging the Commonwealth not to support a competing line and pointing out the fact that little private money deemed it wise to invest in the railroad.[40] On 13 May 1851, the House voted and the bill went down to defeat 237 to 129. The *Weekly Transcript* of North Adams asked, "We should like to know how much it has cost the Western Railroad for its opposition to it, and to what account the amount is to be charged?"[41]

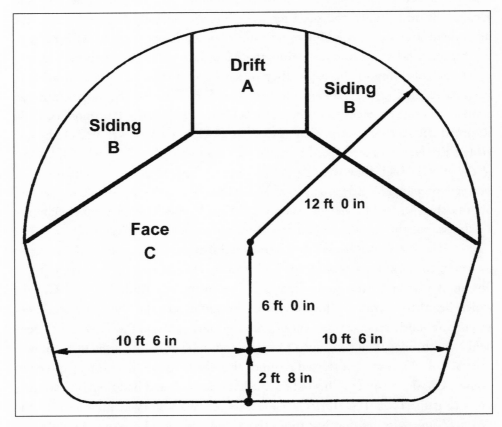

Tunnel cross section recommended by A. F. Edwards, chief engineer, 1851

A Tunnel-Boring Machine

Crocker and the men of the Troy and Greenfield Railroad were not so easily defeated. It was announced in July that the railroad would "commence the work of tunneling on the east side of the mountain, so as to demonstrate to the next legislature . . . the feasibility of the project."[42] True to their word, on 25 September 1851 contractors commenced operations "near the confluence of Truesdell Brook [later changed to Cascade Brook] and the Deerfield River, about a half mile above Erastus Rice's."[43] It was further reported in the *American Railway Times* that "the proprietors of a rock cutting machine, who . . . examined the rock of the mountain have made proposals to the Directors for building a machine to bore the tunnel with, and putting it in operation, and all at their own expense."[44] The report was true, and by February 1852, eighty men were working on the east side of the mountain—not digging a tunnel but preparing an approach for a monster boring machine.[45] The gentlemen who had made the offer held legal title to Charles Wilson's patented machine for excavating tunnels. On 29 October 1851, Joseph C. Batchelder of Cambridge, R. Butler of Quincy, and Richards, Munn & Co. of Boston signed a contract with the Troy and Greenfield Railroad—represented by President Henry Chapman and directors Cephas Root and E. G. Lamson—to provide a 75-horsepower stonecutting machine. The contract specified a machine to bore a tunnel twenty-four feet in diameter through the Hoosac Mountain,[46] and they would be paid $100,000 if the machine progressed into the mountain at a rate of six feet per day. If the borer could progress at eight feet per day, they would receive $150,000 for the machine.

Joseph Richards and Luther Munn, together with Lysander Richards and John S. Lyons, had been in the granite-quarrying business since 1829.[47] Their quarry was located in Quincy, and they probably had a business relationship with Wilson. In 1828, Joseph Richards had patented a bush hammer for cutting and dressing stone,[48] and Wilson had applied the same principle to his boring machine. Additionally, one of Wilson's machines for dressing stone was set up in the Quincy quarry of Richards and Munn in 1853.[49]

Wilson,[50] a mechanic from Springfield, obtained a letter patent for a stonecutting and stone-dressing machine in 1847.[51] Several of these machines were manufactured and used by the Empire Stone-Dressing Company of New York City. The president of Empire, Charles T. Shelton, requested a committee from the American Institute of the City of New York visit his works at the foot of 29th Street and examine Wilson's machines in operation.[52] The institute honored Shelton's request and pronounced Wilson's invention "the best Stone-dressing machine." As a result, in 1852 Wilson was awarded a gold medal by the American Institute for his stone-dressing machine.[53] Quarry men and entrepreneurs in both Massachusetts[54] and New York[55] believed they could replicate Wilson's ingenious stonecutting machine on a larger scale to bore through the Hoosac Mountain. Maybe because of Shelton's salesmanship, newspaper scribblers expressed great confidence in the Wilson machine and its ability to solve the problem of piercing the mountain. In February 1852, *American Railway Times* reprinted a story from the *Franklin Democrat* of Greenfield that announced how a "working model satisfies everybody who sees it." And: "The machine itself cannot fail to fulfill all that is expected of it."[56] Even before work started at the Mountain to prepare a face for the machine, the mechanics at John Souther's Globe Works[57] in South Boston set to work building the monster stonecutter.[58] Visitors and newspaper editors searched for words to describe the tunnel borer. Words like "gigantic" and "ponderous mass of iron" were typical.[59]

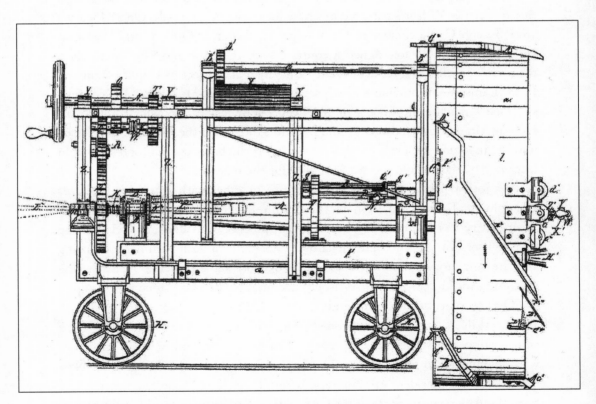

Charles Wilson's machine for excavating tunnels (U.S. Patent nos. 14,483 and 17,650)

The *American Railway Times* announced in early May of 1852 the plan to deliver most of the parts for the "big borer" to Greenfield by railway, "and thence by teams to the mountain."[60] The main shaft, however, was so heavy many towns in the Deerfield River Valley would not permit it to pass over their bridges. Therefore, it was shipped via the Western Railroad to North Adams and hauled over the mountain. The *Railway Times* reported the machine had a 75-horse-power steam engine, as stated in the contract, but the editor of the *Springfield Republican* wrote that it had a 100-horsepower engine.[61] Mr. Batchelder, one of the owners, testified at the legislative hearing on 23 March 1853 that "the whole cost of the machine was $25,000."[62] The *Railway Times* added the comment that, "in case of a failure, half the loss falls on the contractors for supplying it and half on the inventor."[63]

Before the first of July, all of the component parts were scattered at the eastern base of the Hoosac Mountain, where an army of mechanics began to assemble the monster.[64] The tunnel contractor had prepared a face of solid rock just to the side of the actual tunnel alignment. The carriage of the machine was set in front of this rock wall, and the men, using a derrick, hoisted the iron spokes and shafts into place as they slowly bolted the mass together. The large wheel on which the rock cutters were mounted was twenty-four feet in diameter;[65] this matched the twenty-four-foot tunnel diameter proposed by the engineer Edwards. The cutters or grinders were mounted on the edge of the large wheel. The center "shaft as big as a barrel"[66] was twenty feet long. Powered by the steam engine, the shaft caused the large wheel with the cutters to revolve and grind a foot-wide circular trench in the rock. The shaft also drove a five-inch-diameter center drill. The plan was to drive the machine three feet into the mountain[67] and then withdraw it a safe distance for blasting the rock within the circular trench by loading the center bore with powder. Once the rubble was cleaned away after the blast, the borer would attack the mountain again, and the drill-and-blast procedure would be repeated. While it was being assembled, the owners charged visitors a twenty-five-cent admission fee to view the monster.[68]

The borer's first attack on the rock of the Hoosac Mountain was on 6 August 1852.[69] At the bottom of the rock face, it penetrated three or four feet, but because the face was not perfectly vertical, the cutters did not touch the rock at the top of the circle. The test lasted about forty minutes before the cutters along the outer edge of the large-diameter wheel failed. Unfazed, the builders returned to Boston to fabricate "heavier and firmer" cutters.[70] They wanted to order steel from England for the cutters, but the shipment would have meant

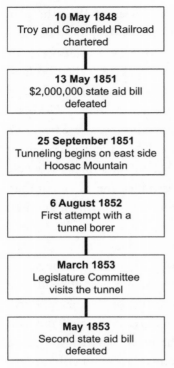

10 May 1848
Troy and Greenfield Railroad
chartered

13 May 1851
$2,000,000 state aid bill
defeated

25 September 1851
Tunneling begins on east side
Hoosac Mountain

6 August 1852
First attempt with a
tunnel borer

March 1853
Legislature Committee
visits the tunnel

May 1853
Second state aid bill
defeated

months of delay, so a supply was secured from the Jersey Steel Works.[71] On 7 September, there was a demonstration of the borer for the directors of the Troy and Greenfield Railroad[72] and on 13 October, there was a demo for a group of men from Troy, New York.[73] After the October demonstration, it was reported that new and larger cutters were being prepared at the machine shop in Boston. London's *Civil Engineer and Architect's Journal* reported that Wilson "confidently expects to be able to overcome all the difficulties."[74]

Another Legislative Battle

While the excitement was all about the tunnel borer, Crocker was rubbing shoulders with the opponents of the Troy and Greenfield Railroad. On 24 August 1852, a general railroad convention was convened in Springfield to discuss experience in construction, rates of fare, and the exchange of reports. In attendance were Thomas Hopkinson of the Boston and Worcester Railroad (in fact, he was appointed chairman of the convention) and William H. Swift of the Western Railroad.[75] Alvah Crocker served on the construction committee charged with investigating whether it was "expedient to cover railroad bridges."[76] The issue was between preserving the timber bridges from decay or exposing them to fire hazard from engine cinders. This was a convention primarily of railroad presidents, so the construction committee reported that the covering-of-bridges issue was more properly left "to experienced bridge builders or engineers." The convention did provide Crocker with a chance to meet with allies and adversaries in a congenial atmosphere. With or without the tunnel borer, the Troy and Greenfield Railroad still needed state aid to bore the Hoosac, so this was a chance to build support and scout the opposition.

The backers of the Troy and Greenfield were again before the legislature in February of 1853 with another petition for assistance. Six days before the first hearing, an article appeared in the *American Railway Times* discussing the tunnel borer in detail. The article stated that although there were still changes necessary because of vibration problems—which necessitated the replacement of bolts after only two hours of operation—the machinery moved in perfect harmony. The concluding paragraphs of the article described how during the trials the borer had cut into the rock a total distance of twenty-five linear feet. The unnamed author then stated that the directors of the railroad were satisfied with the machine and were sure of success. Their confidence allowed them to suspend operations until "a more auspicious season" when the machine could be put in motion after a few hours' notice.[77] In the legislature, other men were not so sure about the directors' confidence, and the Western Railroad definitely did not want to see the state grant $2 million in aid to a potential competitor.

The verbal battle between the two railroads commenced on 9 February at the first session of the legislative hearing. Crocker's friend Elias Derby and attorney J. M. Keith, representing the Troy and Greenfield, had only begun to explain the petition when Ansel Phelps, counsel for the Western Railroad, interrupted, saying, "It has an ancient, and a fish-like smell."[78] Derby then made some comments about the membership of the special committee, noting that George Bliss, former president of the Western Railroad, was the Speaker of the House. When Phelps asked whether Derby was insinuating that the Western had packed the committee, Derby replied, "I mean to suggest that it is very obvious we have not packed the committee." The Committee did agree to visit the Hoosac Mountain and witness the operation of the tunnel borer.

Charles Wilson's tunnel borer against the Hoosac Mountain

Accompanied by some twenty other members of the legislature and invited guests, the Committee left Boston via Crocker's Fitchburg Railroad on

15 March.[79, 80] Arriving in Greenfield a little after noon, the party of fifty or sixty persons[81] was welcomed by the citizens, "who feel a lively interest in the projected tunnel."[82] After being hosted in Greenfield, the party continued on to Shelburne Falls, the next town on the proposed route of the railroad. The following day, they proceeded up the valley of the Deerfield River to Rice's Hotel, located about three-fourths of a mile from the tunnel. At Rice's, the group was joined by one delegation from North Adams and a second from Troy, New York.

From there, the crowd set off to examine the borer. It was one of those crystalline winter days when the air is so clear, but it was very cold, only two degrees above zero. The borer was sitting against the Hoosac Mountain, the large wheel crisp with frost. The mechanics raised steam, and in fifteen minutes the cutters of the wheel cut another four inches of groove into the rock. Acknowledging the temperature, the legislative report stated: "[T]he operators did not dare test the machine to the extent of its capacity."[83] After the demonstration, the different groups ascended the Mountain in sleighs and traveled to North Adams. The railroad paid Batchelder and his associates $200 for operating their borer for those fifteen minutes.[84]

The next day, the committee journeyed along the route of the railroad from North Adams to Williamstown. Those seven miles, graded by Gilmore and Carpenter, were ready for rails. Continuing along the proposed route, the legislators proceeded down the valley of the Hoosic River to Pownal, Vermont, before crossing into New York. Beyond Hoosick Falls, they boarded cars of the Troy and Boston Railroad and traveled on to Troy. Taking the Hudson River Railroad, the committee went to New York City to examine the Wilson stonecutting machines in use at Shelton's Empire Stone-Dressing Company. The previous June, Shelton had placed advertisements in the *New York Times*, offering to form a company "for tunneling mountains for Railroad purposes," using machines built under Wilson's stonecutting patent.[85] In 1852, he had also come into possession of the Albert Eames patent for an improved Wilson stone-dressing machine.[86] When the legislative committee arrived, the smaller machines at his works were set in motion, making horizontal and vertical cuts in blocks of Connecticut red sandstone and Hudson Valley graywacke (another type of sandstone).

After the junket, the committee returned to Boston, where hearings resumed on 23 March. A. F. Edwards, chief engineer of the Troy and Greenfield, was called to testify about the rock in the Hoosac Mountain and his cost estimate. This included discussion about the cost of tunnels in England, including the Box Tunnel. James Hayward, who with James Baldwin had made the original survey for a railroad from Boston to the Hudson River,[87] appeared for the Troy and Greenfield to testify about the cost of long tunnels. He had traveled to Europe to study railroad construction and had inspected many tunnels, including the most costly, the Box Tunnel—which Edwards had already mentioned—and the Bletchingley Tunnel. Hayward closed his testimony by stating, "I think two millions of dollars will be ample to tunnel the Hoosac,— it leaves a large margin."[88] During cross-examination by Ansel Phelps, he admitted he had not personally constructed any long tunnels. When asked about water, Hayward replied, "I think there would be no trouble with water in the Hoosac Tunnel."[89]

Before closing, Elias Derby brought Edwards back to testify about his surveys. In particular, Derby wanted the hearing record to contain a detailed comparison of the length, curves, and grades on the Western Railroad versus those of the Troy and Greenfield Railroad. Finally, Derby presented data from the Western Railroad's annual reports to show that the railroad was failing to deliver trade from the West to Boston and that the Western Railroad had repeatedly received state aid.

The battle of words continued as Phelps responded to Derby's arguments. Phelps and the Western Railroad attacked the proposal of the state granting aid to the Troy and Greenfield on four points: (1) the tunnel was not feasible, (2) the Western already provided adequate communication with Albany, (3) no railroad could compete with the Hudson River, and (4) the tunnel would cost the Commonwealth too much money. These points of discussion would change over the years, but even in 1853 it was clear that the first and last points contradicted one another, as the last admitted only the want of money prevented the tunnel from becoming a reality while the first claimed it was not possible to complete the tunnel. To make his point about time and money, Phelps called upon William Swift, then president of the Western Railroad. Swift was asked why the Western had not tunneled Mount Washington when he was the field engineer building the line. He replied that the issues were time and expense. Swift also noted that his Mount Washington decision had taken into account the fact that the tunnels on the Baltimore & Ohio Railroad had each cost more than the original estimates. Swift did make one prophetic statement when he observed that during the digging of England's Box Tunnel, it was necessary to pump out four million gallons of water daily, and water was always a costly problem when excavating a tunnel. "The practical difficulty in tunneling is met with in the water."[90] Phelps reiterated this fact in his closing speech. "It is pretty evident that there will be . . . more millions of gallons of water, than probably any engineer ever dreamed of."[91] He added snidely "that travelers from this section [meaning Massachusetts] going west to any part of New York along the line of the New York Central roads require it [the Tunnel] for their accommodation."[92] He may have had knowledge about Boston investors beginning to think in terms of a railroad to Chicago, or it could have simply meant that men should not be leaving Massachusetts for the West. Finally, after eight weeks, the hearing came to an end on 6 April.

The fate of the bill hung in the balance for almost two months, until the Senate debate and vote at the end of May in 1853. During the debate, the supporters, calling on Loammi Baldwin's reputation, reminded their colleagues about his $920,000 cost estimate. Senator Clark of Roxbury, chairman of the Tunnel Committee, argued against the petitioners, stating that he "looked upon the whole project as visionary and ill-advised."[93] After Clark's remarks, the vote resulted in a twenty-two-to-eighteen defeat for Alvah Crocker and the Troy and Greenfield Railroad. Senate President (Judge) Charles H. Warren was one of those who voted against the bill. Via telegraph, the news of the vote reached North Adams at half past four in the afternoon. The town soon displayed its displeasure with the vote by rigging an effigy of Judge Warren. Before the townspeople hung it from a hotel on Main Street, it was soaked in turpentine and stuffed with powder. At dark, when it was set afire and the ashes fell to the street, the town's "Saxe Horn Band played a mournful dirge."[94]

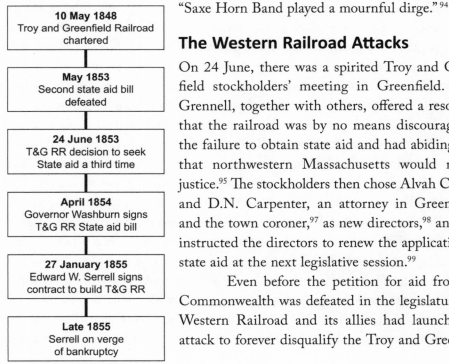

10 May 1848
Troy and Greenfield Railroad chartered

May 1853
Second state aid bill defeated

24 June 1853
T&G RR decision to seek State aid a third time

April 1854
Governor Washburn signs T&G RR State aid bill

27 January 1855
Edward W. Serrell signs contract to build T&G RR

Late 1855
Serrell on verge of bankruptcy

The Western Railroad Attacks

On 24 June, there was a spirited Troy and Greenfield stockholders' meeting in Greenfield. Judge Grennell, together with others, offered a resolution that the railroad was by no means discouraged by the failure to obtain state aid and had abiding faith that northwestern Massachusetts would receive justice.[95] The stockholders then chose Alvah Crocker and D.N. Carpenter, an attorney in Greenfield[96] and the town coroner,[97] as new directors,[98] and they instructed the directors to renew the application for state aid at the next legislative session.[99]

Even before the petition for aid from the Commonwealth was defeated in the legislature, the Western Railroad and its allies had launched an attack to forever disqualify the Troy and Greenfield

Railroad from receiving aid from the Commonwealth. In May 1853, Massachusetts organized a convention to amend the Constitution of the Commonwealth; two weeks later, the newspapers reported on a motion "to restrict the legislature from loaning the Commonwealth credit and contracting debts, except for paying its expenses or for public safety, unless sanctioned by a vote of the people."[100] On a motion by Alpheus R. Brown of Dracut, a town served by the Boston and Lowell Railroad, a special committee of thirteen was appointed to report on the expediency of amending the constitution as proposed.[101] After Mr. Brown's motion was ordered, Charles Mason of Fitchburg countered by offering a motion "that the Committee on the Frame of Government, consider the expediency of providing that it shall be incompetent for the legislature to refer to the people, for their approval or ratification, any legislative act other than such as have reference to amending or altering the Constitution."[102]

Brown was appointed to the special committee he had suggested, but there were also members with a direct interest in the Hoosac Tunnel—Milo Wilson of Shelburne and Ephraim Tower of Florida. The Committee on the Frame of Government recommended that Brown's special committee be in charge of the question, and it was so ordered. When called to present their report on 22 June, Brown stated that his committee had made progress but had reached no conclusion. A week later, another effort was made to bring the matter to a vote, with Western Railroad men offering several resolutions to limit the ability of the legislature to lend money. These were all rejected. On 8 July Mr. Stetson of Braintree gained the committee floor and waved a copy of the *Plymouth Rock* containing an article that stated after watching the maneuvers at the convention: "Whig intrigue and political duplicity stood out in such bold relief. I wish it were otherwise, but yet I am forced to the conclusion, that much of the debate to-day was influenced by the money of the Western Railroad. In the main it is a strike at the Hoosac Tunnel."[103]

On 8 July, there was another attempt by the Western allies to force a vote on a constitutional amendment prohibiting the Commonwealth from lending its credit to any corporation. The Hoosac forces had the Western's amendment ruled not in order. A vote was finally taken on Saturday, 9 July, and the convention rejected the amendment to limit state aid to corporations by 137 to 104. One of those voting against the limitation was Francis W. Bird of Walpole. Not too many years in the future, Bird would become a fierce foe of the Hoosac Tunnel, but in 1853 he did not want to limit the state's ability to aid corporations. Immediately after the vote, Joel Giles of Boston, who had voted with the Hoosac Tunnel men, offered a resolution to accomplish the Western's purpose:

the General Court could not grant aid "without a two-thirds vote in the House of Representatives and the Senate in its favor."[104] His resolution passed 114 in the affirmative to 76 opposed. The Western's game remained alive, as Giles's resolution was ordered to a second reading.

Over the Sabbath, the Hoosac men must have prayed hard, for on Monday Charles Thompson of Charlestown moved a reconsideration of the vote. His motion prevailed and the yeas and nays were again ordered for Giles's motion requiring a two-thirds vote to approve state aid. This time, the Hoosac men had all of their supporters in attendance and defeated the motion 200 to 120. The fight had been fierce, but the convention tactics of the Western Railroad team served to prepare Crocker and the Hoosac Tunnel men for the 1854 legislative session, when another petition for aid to tunnel the Hoosac Mountain would be filed.

Back to the Legislature

The campaign for the Tunnel loan began in earnest during the fall. On 30 September 1853, the first issue of the *Hoosac Gimlet* appeared in Fitchburg. (The name referred to the small hand tool used for boring holes—not the cocktail made with gin or vodka and a touch of lime juice.) The *Gimlet*'s editor was A. X. Auger Handle, obviously a fictional character, and it was a pure propaganda sheet. The masthead slogan was "Devoted to the Great Bore." The editor and printer, Mr. Screw Propeller, urged the people of Fitchburg to "bring their influence to bear upon the Legislature." The advertisements were about Tunnel meetings in Fitchburg, one on the third of October and another on the eleventh. Crocker and Derby were both speakers at the latter meeting.[105] Three resolutions of the convention set forth the arguments to be used in seeking aid from the Commonwealth: "That the Northern half of Massachusetts is entitled to participate in the State aid which has given so great an impulse to other sections of the State. The tunnel will do more for the towns and cities upon the line and for the great seaport of the State than any enterprise yet commenced in old Massachusetts. Massachusetts' citizens are entitled to the shortest, cheapest, and best route to the Western States."[106]

In August, the *Barre Patriot* carried a short article about a new tunnel borer. This machine, "instead of leaving a core to be removed by blasting, as the Hoosac machine does," cuts the entire face.[107] Ebenezer Talbot of Windsor, Connecticut,[108] received U.S. patent no. 9,774 on 7 June 1853 for a machine to bore cylindrical tunnels. Further articles extolling the machine appeared in the *American Railway Times* on 1 December 1853 and 26 January 1854. These explained how a Talbot machine, constructed at the Woodruff & Beach Iron Works in Hartford, Connecticut, was then being tested by the Harlem Railroad. Talbot was in fact a foreman in Woodruff & Beach's factory.[109]

In April of 1853, Charles T. Shelton, the promoter of the Wilson tunnel-boring machine, together with others, formed the Hudson River Stone-Dressing Company.[110] Samuel Woodruff and Henry Beach were stockholders in this company. D.N. Carpenter must have seen the articles and communicated to Shelton his interest in the Talbot machine. Shelton's reply to Carpenter's inquiry was printed in the *Weekly Transcript*: "In the opinion of those acquainted with this machine and the rock of the Hoosac Mountain, it will perforate there at least ten feet per day."[111] But Shelton's hopes for the success of the Hudson River Stone-Dressing Company, and Carpenter's hopes for quickly boring the Hoosac, proved unfounded. The rock of Harlem easily defeated the iron of Talbot's cylindrical tunnel-boring machine.[112]

Crocker and the Troy and Greenfield Railroad supporters presented their petition for aid on the opening day of the 1854 legislative session.[113] On the second day, as before, it went to a joint special committee for consideration. There was opposition from the Western Railroad as expected, but the constitution fight served the tunnel promoters well; they were united and they were prepared. Charges did fly from the two opponents, with each accusing the other of bribing legislators. An investigation followed, and both sides had to provide statements of their lobbying expenses. The Western reported spending $4,546 and the Troy and Greenfield $5,282.[114] Each claimed the majority of their expenditures were for printing petitions and legal counsel. Because the Commonwealth still owned a considerable amount of Western Railroad stock, it was then claimed it had expended public funds to fight a rival.[115]

On 21 February, the special committee gave a favorable report, with loan terms substantially the same as those imposed on the Western Railroad.[116] The aid bill passed the Senate on 9 March 1854. Three weeks later, the House gave its approval but added a minor amendment. The bill therefore had to go back to the Senate, which gave its approval, sixteen to seven, on 21 March. After the vote, the editor of the *Boston Daily Advertiser* wrote: "[T]he tunnel will never be completed. . . . it will be abandoned long before it is finished." The *Advertiser*'s editor and publisher was Nathan Hale, an 1804 graduate of Williams College, but, more significantly in this matter, a man intimately connected to the Western Railroad.

Governor Emory Washburn, who had been chairman of the committee responsible for providing the Western with its first loan, was now presented a legislative act in support of a rival northern road.[117] Northern Massachusetts erupted with elation when the 1817 graduate of Williams College signed the bill granting the Troy and Greenfield Railroad $2 million in Commonwealth bonds. Alvah Crocker's perseverance had triumphed against the naysayers. One writer examining the record a century later attributed the success to Crocker's "subterranean political manipulations."[118]

Aid from the Commonwealth did not come gratis, however. The bill required the railroad to give the Commonwealth of Massachusetts a first mortgage on all its assets as security that the loan would be repaid. With each installment, 10 percent had to be set aside immediately as the nucleus of a sinking fund from which the loan would be repaid. The first installment of the state bonds would only be provided after the railroad had $600,000 of its stock subscribed and 20 percent had been paid to the company. This meant that $120,000 had to be collected from the stockholders—a steep prerequisite, as the company had only been able to collect $56,000 in the first three years of its existence.[119] At the beginning of 1854, there were 1,028 persons owning Troy and Greenfield Railroad stock; of these, 620 owned only one share and another 201 owned only two shares. It was a railroad largely owned by the farmers living along the line.[120]

Edward W. Serrell, Contractor

It had taken three years of battles in the legislature. It would take four years of attacking the rock of the mountain before the first loan installment would be paid to the railroad. The bonds of the Commonwealth would be provided in installments tied to completion of the railroad and boring of the tunnel. To collect the first $100,000 installment, the Troy and Greenfield had to complete seven miles of railroad and 1,000 feet of tunnel.[121] The notices in the papers of late April did not mention the conditions of the legislative act. In the *American Railway Times*,[122] the announcement read:

> *To **Contractors**. Hoosac Tunnel. The Troy and Greenfield Railroad Company having obtained an act for a loan of Massachusetts State Bonds for two million of dollars, invite examination with a view to proposal for the construction of a Tunnel through the Hoosac Mountain.*
>
> *The payments will be monthly, about seventy-five per cent cash and twenty-five per cent in the Stock of the Company, reserving from both ten percent.*
>
> *No Contractor need apply who has not means and experience.*
>
> *Otis Clapp, President*

Clapp, a homeopathic pharmacist, had his establishment on School Street in Boston.[123] Although he owned only two shares of Troy and Greenfield stock,[124] he had been named a director in 1852.

In June 1854, the Executive Committee of the railroad, which consisted of Clapp, Derby, and Carpenter, wrote a long article about the Hoosac Tunnel in the *American Railway Times*.[125] In the piece, they stated that, like the issue for the Western Railroad, the state was providing sterling bonds, which commanded a premium on the London exchange. Therefore, it was expected the bonds would actually produce $2.2 million to $2.4 million. This fact was obviously known by all, but ten years later it would be claimed the railroad had cheated the Commonwealth because of this premium. Trying to comply with the $600,000 stock-subscribed requirement, the railroad men proposed that the tunnel contractor would take "one-fifth of payments in stock." Herman Haupt would later use this technique to satisfy the requirements of the act when he was the contractor, and tunnel critics would accuse him of fraud.

By the fall of 1854, Crocker and the railroad had found a contractor interested in the Commonwealth's $2 million pledge: Edward W. Serrell of New York. Serrell was an enterprising and knowledgeable engineer with extensive construction and engineering experience, having previously built railroads and large bridges. He attended the school of the General Society of Mechanics and Tradesmen[126] of the City of New York before taking up civil engineering under his father, William, and elder brother John J. Serrell.[127] His first railroad experience was with the Central Railroad of New Jersey, which he joined in 1845 as an assistant engineer.[128] From 1846 to 1847, he was an assistant engineer for the Erie Railroad.[129] In 1848, he served under Colonel George W. Hughes, chief of the U.S. Army's Corps of Topographical Engineers in Panama, leading one of the exploratory parties for the Panamanian railway.[130] In 1854, Serrell published an interesting article in the *Journal of the Franklin Institute* about an instrument for rapid surveying. While in Panama, Colonel Hughes had charged Serrell with making an accurate survey of the Chagres River. To speed the survey, sights needed to be taken at great distance. Serrell created a special instrument for this by mounting a thirty-inch German telescope on his transit, using beeswax and black thread; for the crosshairs, he relieved his pet monkey "of the finest hairs" at the root of his tail. With this improvised instrument, he was able to survey eighteen miles of river per day.[131]

After his return from Panama, Serrell prepared the plans and supervised the construction of the Queenston–Lewiston Suspension Bridge across the

Niagara River between Lewiston, New York, and Queenston, Ontario.[132] He completed the bridge, six miles below Niagara Falls, in March of 1851.

Scientific American made note of the fact that the estimated cost of the Lewiston Bridge, which stretched 841 feet across the river, was only $30,000, while the 1,010-foot Wheeling Suspension Bridge in West Virginia had cost $139,000.[133] Reports written after the Lewiston Bridge was completed, however, did place its cost at $56,000.[134] The difference between the construction costs for the two bridges might be an indicator of Serrell's lack of the financial resources necessary for carrying out large projects. He repeatedly bid low for work because he needed income to pay the bills from previous projects. It was a business strategy for failure.

After an examination of the Hoosac Mountain in late 1854, Serrell penned his observations for the *Journal of the Franklin Institute*:[135]

> *Whether the tunnel shall be worked from both ends only, or whether shafts shall be employed, has yet to be determined.*
>
> *Wilson's machinery, which was constructed before the loan was obtained from the State, and was tried at the easterly side of the mountain, is said to be defective in many particulars, but the inventor has modifications of plans with which he confidently expects to be able to overcome all difficulties.*
>
> *Gardner has invented a system of drills.*
>
> *By some of these machines, or by something else not yet contrived, or by the old fashioned method of drilling by hand and blasting, the excavations have to be made.*

On 27 January 1855, Serrell signed a contract with the Troy and Greenfield Railroad to construct the railroad and tunnel for $3.5 million.[136] The *American Railroad Journal* reported Serrell could receive another $200,000 because of the anticipated premium on the Commonwealth bonds. The *Journal* also stated that Serrell expected to use a combination of tunneling devices in order to complete the tunnel in four years.[137] On 21 February in North Adams, a meeting was held at the Baptist Vestry, with Serrell, Crocker, and President Clapp speaking.[138] But in April the North Adams paper reported that Serrell had not begun work because he was waiting for the railroad to raise the $220,000 it had pledged in the contract.[139]

Serrell's Money Problems

Presently Crocker was back seeking help from the legislature. A bill was introduced to allow certain towns in Franklin and Berkshire counties to subscribe to Troy and Greenfield stock. While the bill made its way through the legislature, engineers and laborers finally appeared along the line of the railroad. By the middle of May 1855, Serrell had let subcontracts, and about a hundred men were in the field.[140] Then, in August, the papers announced that another tunneling machine, being constructed at the Novelty Works in New York, was "of an improved construction, designed to open a drift way of eight feet diameter."[141] This was another Wilson tunnel borer.

Things were looking up for Crocker and the Troy and Greenfield. At the stockholders' meeting in August, the company voted to accept the terms of the loan act; this was a formality conducted because some had questioned the legality of the company's previous action to accept the loan. It was also voted to authorize the issue of the Commonwealth bonds to Serrell, "to enable him to raise funds on the same."[142] To gain this concession, Serrell agreed to take a larger share of the railroad's stock—in fact, he agreed to take all of the stock not otherwise subscribed. At the time, it was not much of a concession, as Crocker in June had experienced a second success in the legislature, enabling towns to subscribe to the stock,[143] and towns along the way were already holding meetings to vote on taking stock.[144] North Adams held a town meeting in June to consider taking two hundred shares at $100 a share. The town did stipulate, however, that it would not be liable for an assessment of more than 50 percent until the line was completed from North Adams to the Vermont state line.[145]

The work again commenced and good progress was made on the little tunnel in North Adams, but Serrell's money problems soon became evident. The *Pittsfield Sun*, in its 13 December edition, carried a story about a fight at the eastern base of the mountain "between a party of North Adams people and the Irish labors of the work."[146] To ease his financial burden, Serrell was subcontracting the work and letting the lower-tier contractors finance their own portions, but some of these contractors had their own financial problems. One contract passed from one subcontractor to another until one D.N. Stanton of North Adams, who had not been paid, filed an attachment. With the attachment, D.N. and John C. Stanton, together with William W. Fitch of Hartford, Connecticut, took over the subcontract[147] with E. W. Serrell and Company.

The Stantons proved to be competent builders, and Serrell gave them additional subcontracts, some of which had previously been held by other contractors. This led to a fight on the east side of the Mountain in which several Irish workers had their skulls broken and apparently died, because the newspapers called it murder.[148] The grisly deaths marked the beginning of the dangerous business of tunneling the Hoosac. The Irish had been working for a Mr. Hull, but he had failed to pay them, so the tunneling there was suspended. When the Stantons and their men appeared to take over the work, the Irish resisted, "saying no one should work there until they had been paid what Mr. Hull owed them."[149]

Soon after the fracas, the North Adams newspapers reported "that the probability is that the contract for the whole work road will eventually pass into the hands of the Messrs. Stantons, unless the work progresses immediately, under Serrell."[150] Remembering Serrell's promises from the previous year about having a thousand men on the job, and now with the troubles in North Adams, the T&G became skittish about its contractor. Serrell worked hard to sell Troy and Greenfield stock and raise funds, but financial success always seemed to fly away. Although the towns along the line were meeting to consider the matter of subscribing to stock, and North Adams had voted five-to-one to take $20,000 worth, no funds had yet appeared.

Crocker and Serrell had tried to get the Commonwealth to purchase 2,500 shares of the Troy and Greenfield stock,[151] but the bill died in committee when the legislature adjourned. Attempts to sell stock in Boston[152] were also disappointing. Because the stock had not been sold, Serrell was forced by the contract to take it, but it had no value. Men would not accept stock as payment for their work. Although Serrell was on the verge of bankruptcy, he was reluctant to give up the pot of gold he believed awaited him in the Hoosac Mountain.

With his Troy and Greenfield Railroad contract in hand, Serrell went looking for men with money. Believing William A. Galbraith, an attorney, and William Brown, a businessman—both of Erie, Pennsylvania—could supply him with the necessary capital to keep the job afloat, he brought in the two men as partners. His connection to these men possibly stemmed from his work as assistant engineer to the commissioners of the Erie Railroad in 1846 and 1847. Soon, however, the three partners realized that they were unable to raise the necessary funds from their own resources;[153] by late 1855, Serrell, Galbraith, and Brown were in serious financial trouble. Debts were accumulating and no funds were coming in from Crocker and the Troy and Greenfield Railroad. Crocker's grand railroad plan now rested in the hands of William A. Galbraith, who set out to seek capital in his home state of Pennsylvania.

6

The Pennsylvania Railroad Engineer

Where the object if to increafe the produce of labour,
. . . that mode which will convey the moft goodf for the
leaft money will confequently be the beft.

—Robert Fulton, "On the Formation
of Canals, and the Mode of
extending them into every District"[1]

ERMAN HAUPT, A RAILROAD engineer from Pennsylvania, gave five and a half years of his life trying to punch a tunnel through the Hoosac Mountain for Alvah Crocker's Troy and Greenfield Railroad. It began in December of 1855 and went on until July of 1861, when he ceased boring into the heart of the Mountain. Haupt labored mightily to realize his dream of constructing the longest railroad tunnel in the United States. He was defeated not by the Mountain but by William S. Whitwell, an engineer for the Commonwealth of Massachusetts, who arbitrarily cut off the flow of Commonwealth funds to the work. During those five years, Haupt led an army of Irish and Cornish miners who hammered drill steel into the gneiss, limestone, and slate of the Mountain. By the grit and perseverance of these miners, Haupt caused the rock of the Mountain to yield ever so slowly. At the great bend in the Deerfield River where the Mountain met the water, his steel-driving men penetrated almost 2,400 feet into the Hoosac Mountain. This total distance was not all to full specified Tunnel dimensions but included the penetration of the header. His smoky black hole proved men could tunnel the Mountain, and Haupt's success terrified the men of the Western Railroad. Then the Civil War unleashed its fury across the country and the fury of Massachusetts politicians denied Haupt his ultimate success.

Haupt was a man blessed with an acute scientific intellect and an enormous capacity for hard work, but his decisiveness and bluntness created problems.

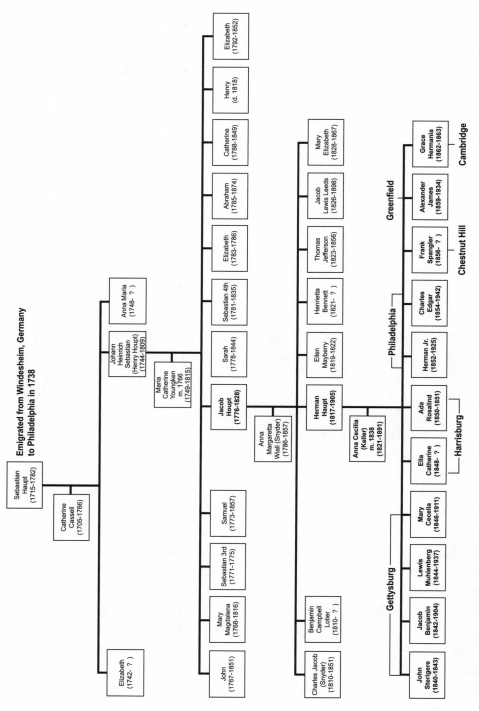

Herman Haupt Genealogy

Being formally trained as a civil engineer at West Point, he considered the Hoosac Tunnel strictly from an engineering perspective—a problem to solve. The magnitude of the work was a challenge, the challenge of a lifetime, and he wanted to be the one credited with defeating the Mountain. After Massachusetts politics and the cronies of the rival Western Railroad finally succeeded in driving him from the bowels of the Mountain, and then in taking the Troy and Greenfield contract from him in April 1862,[2] he stated his commitment to the challenge: "What I chiefly desire . . . [is] proving that this great work, so long ridiculed as visionary and impracticable, is really susceptible of accomplishment. . . ."[3]

Palatine Immigrants

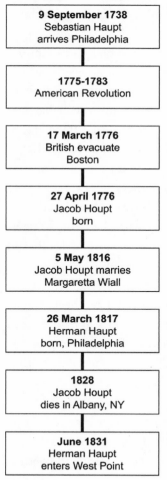

9 September 1738
Sebastian Haupt
arrives Philadelphia

1775-1783
American Revolution

17 March 1776
British evacuate
Boston

27 April 1776
Jacob Houpt
born

5 May 1816
Jacob Houpt marries
Margaretta Wiall

26 March 1817
Herman Haupt
born, Philadelphia

1828
Jacob Houpt
dies in Albany, NY

June 1831
Herman Haupt
enters West Point

Haupt's German ancestors arrived in Pennsylvania some forty years before the Revolutionary War, but they were newcomers compared with the Baldwins of Massachusetts, who arrived a full century before the German migration. The patriarch of the Haupt family in the New World was Sebastian Haupt (1715–82), who, along with 349 other immigrants from the Palatinate (Pfalz) region of Germany, first sighted Philadelphia from Captain Walter Sterling's ship, the *Glasgow*.[5] Two generations later, the line of Sebastian and his first wife, Catherine Cassell, produced the future Hoosac Tunnel engineer, Herman Haupt.

Sterling's *Glasgow* had departed from the port of Amsterdam, made a stop at Cowes, on the Isle of Wight, and then proceeded across the Atlantic with its cargo of immigrants. The Germans arrived in Philadelphia on 9 September 1738. Sebastian Haupt brought with him his Old World barrelmaking skills and listed his occupation as a cooper. To accommodate the English phonetic pronunciation of his name, Sebastian changed the spelling from Haupt to Houpt after arriving in the colonies.[6,7] In about 1760, he bought a mill property of 108 acres in Upper Dublin Township, Pennsylvania. His son Johann Heinrich, or Henry, was born there in 1744.

When he reached maturity, Henry took up the miller's trade and married Maria Catherine Youngken in May of 1766. Her original family name was Junghen, which became Jungen, and then Youngen before finally becoming Youngken.[8] As Sebastian had done, Catherine's French Huguenot family had changed its name to something more phonetically English. In 1770, Henry and Catherine moved to the Valley of Durham Creek in Bucks County, Pennsylvania, about eight miles south of Easton,[9] where he established a profitable business milling flax to produce linseed oil.

Henry and Catherine's fourth son, Jacob, was born on 27 April 1776, a month after the British troops evacuated Boston and sailed past the guns of the senior Loammi Baldwin's engineering works. In May 1778, Henry signed the oath of allegiance to the Commonwealth and later joined Captain George Heinlein's Durham Militia.

All of Henry's sons were raised "in strict obedience to church discipline" and "after the manner of the Germans."[10] Each son, as soon as he was able, left the home of their father. John departed in 1788 but returned four years later to work the mill. Samuel, the third son, moved to New York State, and Sebastian, the fifth son, went to Alabama—never to return. At the age of fifteen, Jacob moved to Philadelphia, where he initially found employment as a clerk.[11] Later, he and his brother-in-law, Abraham Piesch, who was married to Jacob's younger sister, Sarah, entered into a profitable partnership as owners of several clipper ships plying the trade routes to the Orient. Their trading business flourished until 1798, when, during revolutionary France's undeclared war with the United States, the French navy, aided by privateers, captured or destroyed most of Jacob and Abraham's ships.

Undaunted, Jacob used the inheritance from his father's estate and again invested in the shipping business—but his timing could not have been worse. When the War of 1812 erupted between the United States and England, fifteen of his ships were in the Far East. The blockading British fleet standing at the approaches to the Delaware River soon captured all of Jacob's second fleet.[12] Thus ended his interest in maritime commerce, and he turned to mercantile trade in Philadelphia.

After decades as a bachelor, forty-year-old Jacob Houpt married Anna Margaretta Wiall Snyder in May of 1816. Margaretta had been granted a divorce from her previous husband, Andrew Snyder, because of his "excessive ill conduct and gross infidelity."[13] From her first marriage, Margaretta had one son, Charles, and an adopted son, Benjamin Campbell Lotier.[14] So when Herman was born at home on the west side of Fourth Street, between Race and Arch in Philadelphia,[15] on 26 March 1817, he was the third son in the household. Including the two boys from her first marriage, Margaretta would eventually have eight children in her care. Their daughter Ellen died young, and son Benjamin Lotier joined the navy sometime before 1828. He was never heard from again.[16]

Herman (sometimes spelled Hermann), the future Hoosac Tunnel engineer, was often told by his mother that he was "born under the sign of the fish,"[17] meaning he was a Pisces. But as a gullible young boy, he would look at the large gilded fish hanging over the entrance of a tackle store on Philadelphia's Front Street and wonder whether he had entered the world through the doorway of that store. During his childhood in Philadelphia, his father and a Henry D. Steever jointly operated a grocery store on Second Street. The young Herman first attended Mrs. Wilson's school on Vine Street and later Mr. Pardon Davis's at Fromberger's Court. The centers of his life—home, store, and school—were all in a four-square-block area not far from the Philadelphia waterfront.

Life without a Father

Herman Houpt's secure urban life came to a halt when he was nine years old. Because of failing eyesight, his father, Jacob, quit the mercantile business and moved the family to a small farm in Woodville, New Jersey, thirteen miles north of Trenton. There he opened a crossroads country store and the city-bred youngster became acquainted with farm work. Some sixty years later, Herman remarked that it was "a very distasteful employment for a boy brought up in a city,"[18] particularly the task of loading manure. Because there were no schools in the Woodville area, the move temporarily marked the end of Herman's formal education.

In August 1828, Margaretta delivered Herman's sister Mary Elizabeth; a month later, Jacob departed for Albany on a Hudson River steamboat. He undertook this arduous journey to visit his older brother Samuel in Little Falls, New York. It was not to be a social visit but rather a humbling trip to beg for a loan, as the family was sinking under a load of debt. But before the steamboat even reached Albany, Jacob was struck down by an attack of apoplexy, probably a stroke. In Albany, the paralyzed man was carried from the boat to the home of physician Elisha S. Burton, and he died before word of his condition even reached his family.

With five young children to care for, Margaretta sold everything to pay most of their debts. Then, with scarcely a penny to her name, she moved her brood back to Philadelphia.[19] She rented a house on Second Street and supported the family by making and selling laces and trimmings. To ease her burden, she shipped Herman off to live in the country with his cousin, Catherine Evans, a kindly woman who was the daughter of Jacob's younger brother Henry. She and her husband had a farm on the turnpike between Philadelphia and Bethlehem. At the time, they still had four children Herman's age living at home, so Herman spent the winter enjoying the company of his cousins.

When he rejoined his mother and siblings in Philadelphia, there was no money for his schooling, but Margaretta made arrangements with schoolmaster John Brown. In exchange for helping out at the school, he was admitted tuition-free. In 1830, John B. Sterigere, a family connection and friend of President Andrew Jackson, offered Herman an appointment to the U.S. Military Academy at West Point.[20] There was only one problem: Herman was only thirteen and the minimum age for attending West Point had, since Captain William Swift's days, advanced to fourteen. Margaretta, the ever-resourceful mother, produced a falsified birth certificate, but the deception was discovered in Washington and the secretary of war withdrew the appointment. Nevertheless, the secretary renewed the appointment the following year.[21] With the appointment, Herman Houpt changed his name back to his grandfather's "Haupt." Sterigere had pointed out to him that "Houpt" had no meaning, whereas "Haupt" implied chief or principal: Hauptstrasse, for example, indicates the principal street of a town.

Cadet "Le Petit"

With much anxiety, four-foot-nine-inch Herman Haupt made a lonely steamship journey up the Hudson to West Point in June of 1831. When he entered the walls of the stone bastion on the plateau overlooking the Hudson, the instructors assigned Haupt to a company of runts.[22] For two years, he was called "Le Petit," the little fellow. His classmates included the future Civil War general George G. Meade. Meade graduated nineteenth in the class of fifty-six; Haupt, because of his initial lackadaisical attitude, ranked thirty-first.

Once Cadet Le Petit realized he could master the academics, he became overconfident. This led him to engage in late-night card games and other frowned-upon activities, and he accumulated an excessive number of demerits. Confidence sustained him many times in his career, but overconfidence also caused him many problems. The day of reckoning came at the end of the second year, when he appeared before the Board of Visitors and the faculty for the yearly examinations. After he finished the exams, he felt certain his performance in mathematics had been flawless, but he feared he had failed French. A failure in French, together with his demerits, meant dismissal from the academy. The two-week wait for the examination results was a period of despair and soul-searching for the sixteen-year-old Haupt.

Later he spoke of this as the turning point in his life. Cadet Le Petit, who entered West Point at fourteen, had lacked maturity, but he matured during those two weeks after the examinations. Haupt's memoirs contain the statement that "the Bible was almost a sealed book"[23] in Jacob Houpt's home—young Herman had received no religious training at home and had rarely attended church. But while awaiting news of his fate, he read the Bible for the first time. He approached religion and the existence of a Supreme Being much as an engineer would demonstrate a Euclidean proof. Step-by-step, in mathematical fashion Haupt convinced himself that the Creator existed. His religious conversion, and the deep faith it produced, comforted him through many later trials.

Herman Haupt at age 34 (courtesy Manuscripts and Archives, Yale University Library)[24]

Anna Margaretta Haupt (courtesy Manuscripts and Archives, Yale University Library)[25]

Finally, word arrived from Washington: Haupt's mathematics perfor-
mance had saved him; he could continue at West Point as a third-year cadet.
His standing, however, had dropped to the bottom 15 percent of the class.
During that summer, Superintendent Sylvanus Thayer, whom Haupt believed
was unfriendly toward him, was replaced by Major René DeRussy, who granted
Haupt leave to visit his mother in Philadelphia. During those first two years at
West Point, Haupt had grown and developed physically. He now stood a head
taller than Margaretta.

Though Haupt improved his behavior and concentrated on his studies,
rising almost to the middle of the class, his earlier performance seriously affected
his standing. In that era, all West Point cadets received an engineering education,
but when Haupt graduated, his low academic standing kept him out of the army's
elite Corps of Engineers. On 1 July 1835, he was offered instead an assignment in
the Third Infantry and a commission with the rank of brevet second lieutenant,
effective 30 September 1835.[26]

It was a boom time for railroads in the United States, and engineers were
in great demand, especially those from West Point, the nation's preeminent engineering school. The need for civil engineers was so great that under the General
Survey Act of 1824, Congress had authorized the temporary release of engineers from the military to work for either state or private groups building internal
improvements.[27] These engineers made surveys and superintended construction
of railroads and canals. In 1831 alone, active-duty army engineers surveyed the
routes for two railroads and supervised the construction of three others.[28]

Railroad Engineer

During this period, West Point graduated more men than there were officer
vacancies in the U.S. Army, so many graduates did not accept commissions. They
found it more lucrative to find employment in the civilian sector.[29] Haupt's own
resignation from the army was accepted effective 30 September 1835,[30] and he
took a job with the Philadelphia engineer Henry R. Campbell. Campbell was
chief engineer for several railroads in eastern Pennsylvania, including the Philadelphia, Germantown and Norristown Railway. He was also a designer of locomotives. At a starting salary of two dollars a day, Haupt worked as a draftsman,
"making drawings of locomotives on the largest size of drawing paper, showing
every bolt and rivet."[31] All of the parts used in building a locomotive in that
era were shaped by hand, and skilled but uneducated mechanics did the work.
Therefore, Campbell, like Middlesex Canal engineer Loammi Baldwin Sr., had

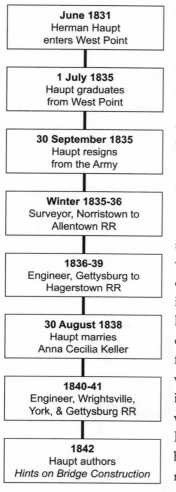

June 1831
Herman Haupt
enters West Point

1 July 1835
Haupt graduates
from West Point

30 September 1835
Haupt resigns
from the Army

Winter 1835-36
Surveyor, Norristown to
Allentown RR

1836-39
Engineer, Gettysburg to
Hagerstown RR

30 August 1838
Haupt marries
Anna Cecilia Keller

1840-41
Engineer, Wrightsville,
York, & Gettysburg RR

1842
Haupt authors
Hints on Bridge Construction

to communicate his ideas in graphic detail. Campbell also gave Haupt "much practical instruction in reference to the construction of bridges."[32] Those lessons later led Haupt to analyze carefully how the structural components of bridges react to loads.

Early locomotives had only two driving wheels, which limited their ability to pull a load because they lacked adhesion between the drivers and the rail. Because of this problem, the management of the Philadelphia and Columbia Railroad in 1834 had to put out a notice: "The locomotive engine . . . will depart daily when the weather is fair, with a train of passengers' cars. On rainy days, horses will be attached."[33] When Haupt joined Campbell's office in 1835, the engineer was designing America's first locomotive with four driving wheels. It had a four-wheel leading truck followed by four drivers and no rear wheels under the cab; therefore, it was referred to as a 4-4-0, indicating the wheel arrangement. Campbell patented the design in 1836, and the first one, the *George Washington*, was completed by James Brooks[34] in May of 1837.[35] Haupt's drafting work was probably part of Campbell's effort to develop this four drive wheel locomotive. The Campbell locomotive became known as the "American type."

During the winter of 1835–36, Campbell acquiesced to the eighteen-year-old draftsman's plea for the opportunity to gain practical experience as an engineer in the field. He assigned Haupt to survey a railroad line along Perkiomen Creek, between Norristown and Allentown, Pennsylvania.

This field assignment was quickly followed by a survey for a line from Downingtown to Norristown. Haupt loved fieldwork so much that even winter cold did not bother him. He allowed: "[I] have broken through the ice in streams and continued to work with pants stiffly frozen rather than cause the party to quit work."[38] He quickly completed his field assignments and drew the profiles for the proposed lines. He also calculated the quantities of earthwork to be excavated in building the lines. When the Commonwealth of Pennsylvania sought engineers for a railroad between Gettysburg and Hagerstown, Maryland, Campbell recommended his young protégé. In June 1836, nineteen-year-old Herman Haupt, just a year out of West Point, journeyed to Gettysburg to take a position as principal assistant engineer under John P. Bailey, chief engineer of the eastern division.

Henry R. Campbell's 4-4-0 locomotive[36, 37]

The two most important elements for a good railroad location are the absence of steep grades and the lack of sharp curves. The payload a steam locomotive could haul was severely reduced by the presence of sharp curves and even a slight increase in grade. Such features also meant train speed was reduced.[39] Haupt had a unique ability to locate routes where grade and curvature were kept to a minimum, and Bailey quickly came to appreciate his competence in laying out a superior line and doing so rapidly. The chief engineer soon "left everything in regard to location and construction in . . . [Haupt's hands]."[40]

Herman Haupt had found his calling; he thrived on being out in front with his compass, discovering a suitable line for the survey party. In wooded terrain, his axmen cut away the trees and bush to give clear sight lines between the survey stations where the transit was set up.[41] At night, Haupt sat up working out the traverse—often at a camp in the woods—by the light of a burning rag in a cup of pork fat.

Marriage

After he completed the location in 1837 and moved into Gettysburg, Haupt lived first at the Eagle Hotel and then at Nancy Miller's boardinghouse. Another boarder, Professor William Reynolds of Pennsylvania College, prodded Haupt about the fact that he had not been baptized. While he attended Sabbath services regularly, Haupt had never established a connection "with any Christian denomination" or particular church.[42] Reynolds's questioning caused Haupt to declare himself a Lutheran, and the next day he called upon Reverend Benjamin Keller, pastor of the local Lutheran church. The very next evening, Keller baptized Haupt. On Good Friday of Easter week, he was confirmed with the church's regular confirmation class. During the ceremony, Haupt stood and knelt on the altar next to the pastor's daughter,[43] Anna Cecilia Keller.[44] Later Haupt reminisced: "I attended to my duties closely, and had but little fondness for society, parties I detested and avoided." The young lady recorded in her diary that her eye had followed the young engineer for quite some time, and soon she captured him. Not long afterward, as he escorted Anna home from a wedding party in York, Pennsylvania, Haupt proposed. He was twenty and Anna only sixteen, so the Reverend Keller asked them to wait one year.

Anna Cecelia Keller, age 16 (courtesy Manuscripts and Archives, Yale University Library)[45]

Haupt purchased land on Seminary Ridge just west of the village and built a brick home, which he called Oakridge. Twenty-six years later, during the Civil War, he moved Union troops and supplies by railroad to this corner of Pennsylvania in support of his former classmate George G. Meade. During the Battle of Gettysburg, Confederate General James Longstreet, West Point class of 1842, positioned his batteries in front of Haupt's former home[46] in order to fire across the valley at the Union's defenses south of the village.

Haupt and Anna Cecilia were married at six in the morning on 30 August 1838. After a short honeymoon, the couple settled into Oakridge. During the early years of his residency in Gettysburg (1837–39), Haupt, while still surveying state railroads, taught civil engineering and architecture without compensation at Pennsylvania College.[47] (The college changed its name to Gettysburg College following the Civil War battle.) Haupt continued doing state railroad work until 1839, when a new administration in Harrisburg let many of the engineers go. During his last year with the state, he patented a relatively simple truss-bridge design.[48]

Oakridge, the façade toward Gettysburg, built by Haupt in 1837 (courtesy Manuscripts and Archives, Yale University Library)[49]

Oakridge on Seminary Ridge in Gettysburg National Military Park (2008 photograph C. J. Schexnayder)

Benjamin Latrobe

From 1840 to 1841, Haupt worked as an assistant engineer for location and then supervising construction for Samuel W. Mifflin on the Wrightsville, York & Gettysburg Railroad. Mifflin was a distinguished location engineer (surveyor of railroad routes) from Wrightsville, Pennsylvania,[50] and Haupt's association with him perfected the young engineer's already considerable skill at locating railroad lines. So while Loammi Baldwin Jr. had tussled with one Pennsylvanian named Samuel Mifflin, whose engineering was suspect, this Samuel Mifflin (no known relationship) was more attuned to good engineering practice. Haupt's association with Samuel Mifflin would help his engineering career considerably. The first step toward recognition came when Mifflin made him responsible for building several railroad bridges for which plans had already been prepared.

Haupt believed the bridge designs were deficient, so he began a detailed review of how to calculate the strength of timber truss bridges. He soon discovered that only one other engineer was attempting to calculate the strength of such bridges.[51] Benjamin H. Latrobe II, a railroad engineer with the Baltimore & Ohio Railroad, calculated the strains imposed on the timber bridges he designed.

Latrobe's route to the engineering profession was similar to the crooked journey of Loammi Baldwin Jr. He had been exposed to his father's engineering work, on the United States Capitol and the Baltimore Cathedral at a young age in the same manner Baldwin had followed his father's building of the Middlesex

Canal. After attending St. Mary's College in Baltimore, Latrobe read law, like Baldwin, and was admitted to the bar in 1825. He even practiced in the profession for a short while. His brother, John Hazlehurst Boneval Latrobe, attended Georgetown College in Washington, DC, before entering West Point in 1818. John stood at the head of his class and was only five months from graduation when he resigned from the academy in December 1821[52]—a decision forced by his father's death in late 1820. "It was clearly my duty to take my father's place and be at the head of the household,"[53] said John. Under the weight of his new responsibilities, he learned the practice of law and in 1828 became chief counsel for the Baltimore & Ohio Railroad.

Benjamin Latrobe quickly sought to "give Blackstone [the legal profession] the go-by and start at the foot of the engineering ladder."[54] He appealed to his brother John for help in obtaining a position with the Baltimore & Ohio. In 1830, he started in the field as a surveyor's rodman, and, like Haupt, he rose rapidly. In 1832, when he was made principal assistant to the chief engineer, Jonathan Knight, he was tasked with designing the railroad's bridge over the Patapsco River at Relay, Maryland. He created a 612-foot-long, sixty-foot-high viaduct using eighty-six-foot granite arches. The Thomas Viaduct—named for Philip E. Thomas, first president of the Baltimore & Ohio Railroad—is still in use and is now one of the oldest railroad bridges in the world. At the time it was built, it was the largest bridge in America and the first railroad bridge built on a curve.

After such an achievement, Latrobe was appointed in 1835 as chief engineer of the Baltimore and Port Deposit Railroad (B&PD). This railroad was incorporated to build a route from Baltimore to the Susquehanna River. The previous year, Latrobe had surveyed the proposed route. The B&PD was one of four railroad companies later amalgamated to create the Philadelphia, Wilmington, and Baltimore Railroad.[55] While with the B&PD, Latrobe built three bridges of considerable length "over rivers of moderate water depth, but almost unfathomable mud."[56] Having completed the B&PD work, Latrobe returned in 1836 to the Baltimore & Ohio Railroad with responsibility for building the line from Point of Rocks, Maryland, to Harpers Ferry. In 1842, when Jonathan Knight resigned, Latrobe was appointed chief engineer. Much later, after Herman Haupt had been forced from the Hoosac Tunnel project, Latrobe would be involved as a consultant to the Commonwealth of Massachusetts.

College Professor

Haupt, his interest piqued about bridge design, set out to develop a theoretical basis for the design of timber bridges. His initial investigations involved building models of bridge structural systems. He also began to take measurements of the loads on the members of existing bridges around Gettysburg as trains passed over them. He reported his findings in an eighteen-page pamphlet titled *Hints on Bridge Construction*, which he printed privately in 1842.[57] Haupt did not acknowledge his authorship, so the cover of the pamphlet simply stated: "By an engineer."

HINTS

ON BRIDGE CONSTRUCTION,

BY AN ENGINEER.

Title on the cover of Herman Haupt's first book

Haupt continued his efforts to understand how loads are transferred between structural members and to create a theoretical model for the determination of timber-bridge capacity. Finally he felt confident enough to prepare an engineering text to describe "the ways by which the strains [on a bridge] can be estimated and the relative sizes of the timbers accurately determined."[58] He completed the manuscript in 1846, four years after the publication of *Hints on Bridge Construction*, but it took him another four years to find a publisher. As he related in his *Reminiscences*,[59] the reason for the publication delay was that no publisher could find an engineer who was capable of reviewing the work. In the meantime, he did describe his ideas in an article in the *Journal of the Franklin Institute*.[60]

D. Appleton and Company of New York finally accepted Haupt's *General Theory of Bridge Construction* in 1851.[61] This time, the book's cover announced Herman Haupt, civil engineer, as the author. Shortly after its publication, it was adopted as a text in the engineering schools of West Point, Rensselaer Institute (now Rensselaer Polytechnic Institute), Yale, and Union College. Haupt's theoretical approach to bridge design gained him national stature as a civil engineer.

While working for the Wrightsville, York & Gettysburg Railroad during the winter of 1840–41, Haupt contracted ague, a disease similar to malaria. Believing it would help him recover from the chills, fever, and sweating seizures, doctors advised him to try a change of climate. Consequently, in 1841 he moved to a farm outside of Centerville, Maryland,[62] on the Eastern Shore, where he again tried his hand at tending animals and plowing. It did not take him long to discover once again that farm work was not to his liking.

When Pennsylvania College offered him a regular teaching position, he packed up and moved back to his Oakridge home. But by the time his family was settled in Oakridge, the depression of 1841–43 affected the college's finances and it withdrew the teaching offer. The resourceful Haupt then opened his own academy for boys, with his younger brother Lewis Haupt teaching French and William B. Harrison teaching Latin, Greek, and German. At his Oakridge Select Academy, Haupt taught mathematics, drawing, and natural science. Anna became the surrogate mother for twenty-five boys who boarded in their home and a dormitory Haupt constructed adjacent to the house. The boys' academy was a success, so in 1845 Haupt and Anna opened a similar institution for girls. It was a pleasant time for the family, and their academies began to draw students away from Pennsylvania College. In response, the college trustees absorbed Haupt's boys' academy and named him head of the mathematics department at the college.[63]

The Pennsylvania Railroad

While Herman and Anna were tucked away at Gettysburg teaching school, the seaboard states north and south of Pennsylvania were busy improving their primitive overland transportation systems. Boston, Philadelphia, and Baltimore were leading commercial cities, but each was fearful that New York's Erie Canal would forever exclude them from access to trade with the West. In response to the Erie Canal, the Commonwealth of Pennsylvania came to believe in the glory of canals. Pennsylvania therefore patched together its Main Line canal system,[64] a series of canals with inclined railroads using stationary engines to pull rail cars up and over the Allegheny Mountains. At the five inclines on each side of the mountains, the railroad cars were fastened to a rope and the stationary steam engines at the top drew the cars up or lowered them down the mountain separating the sections of canal. In the early 1830s, it was the pride of Pennsylvania, but a journey from Philadelphia to Pittsburgh on the Main Line Canal was a torturous trip. It required unloading and reloading at each interface between the railroad incline and the canal boat, and Philadelphia merchants soon found it preferable to ship their goods west via New York's Erie Canal. (The original document of the city charter issued on 18 March 1816 has the "Pittsburgh" spelling

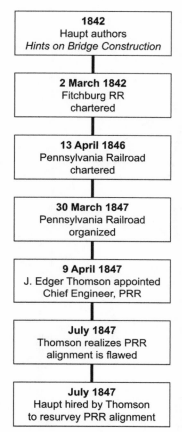

1842
Haupt authors
Hints on Bridge Construction

2 March 1842
Fitchburg RR
chartered

13 April 1846
Pennsylvania Railroad
chartered

30 March 1847
Pennsylvania Railroad
organized

9 April 1847
J. Edger Thomson appointed
Chief Engineer, PRR

July 1847
Thomson realizes PRR
alignment is flawed

July 1847
Haupt hired by Thomson
to resurvey PRR alignment

of the city's name; printed copies of the document used the "Pittsburg" spelling. In 1891, the United States Board of Geographic Names recommended the spelling be "Pittsburg," but this was reversed in July of 1911, and the "Pittsburgh" spelling was restored. The Pittsburgh spelling will be used from here forward.)

Baltimore merchants reacted to the Erie Canal by organizing the Baltimore & Ohio Railroad (B&O)—a feat they accomplished with no state financial support. The B&O's engineering department was set up in May 1828, and construction of Maryland's railroad to Ohio began on 4 July 1828. The B&O courted the Pennsylvania legislature and gained the right to build its road to Pittsburgh, the third largest city west of the Appalachian Mountains, but this success sparked opposition from Philadelphia.

Thomas Cope, a leading Philadelphia merchant, noted in his diary on 18 February 1846: "[L]eft home for Harrisburg [the capital] . . . to oppose the scheme of the B. & O. R. R. Co. in their attempt to rob us, on our soil, of the western trade."[65] Philadelphia merchants recognized that the Main Line Canal system was a failure, and the transportation improvements in New York and Maryland presented an acute threat to their financial interests. Consequently, led by merchants such as Cope, Philadelphia interests succeeded on 13 April 1846 in their efforts to have the legislature grant a charter of incorporation to the Pennsylvania Railroad (PRR). The company was not formally organized, however, until 30 March 1847. At the organizational meeting, thirteen directors, including Cope, were chosen from Philadelphia's elite. The directors were all businessmen: six merchants, four manufacturers, two bankers, and one who was both a merchant and a manufacturer.[66] The following day, the board elected one of its members, Samuel V. Merrick, as the Pennsylvania Railroad's first president.

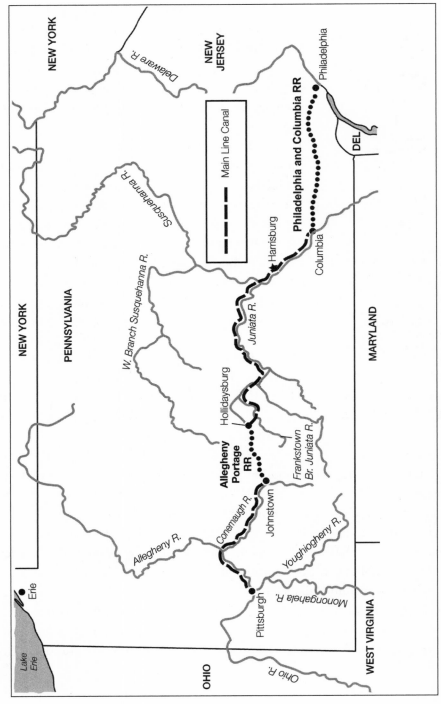

Pennsylvania's Main Line system of railroads, inclined railroads, and canals

Merrick was a successful manufacturer of steam engines, boilers, and fire engines. His firm supplied the engines for the steam frigate USS *Mississippi*, Commodore Matthew C. Perry's squadron flagship when he opened Japan to the West in 1853. From 1839 to 1841, Perry was in Philadelphia, personally supervising the construction of the *Mississippi* at the Philadelphia Navy Yard.

In 1816, at the age of fifteen, Merrick had traveled to Philadelphia from his home in Hallowell, Maine. He first entered his uncle's mercantile firm to learn the wine business, but, four years later, he embarked on a career of manufacturing machinery.[67] He had received a public school education in Hallowell before going to Philadelphia, so now he turned his mind to learning mechanical engineering through self-study—there were no schools offering training in the mechanical arts. His personal experience led him and William H. Keating in 1824 to organize The Franklin Institute of the State of Pennsylvania for the Promotion of the Mechanic Arts (now The Franklin Institute), in Philadelphia.[68] Although Merrick had extensive knowledge of the manufacture of steam engines and boilers—having supplied engines for the USS *Princeton*, USS *San Jacinto*, and USS *Wabash*, in addition to the *Mississippi*—he lacked railroad experience. Not a single member of the Pennsylvania Railroad's board had any railroad engineering, construction, or operating experience.

The challenge of building a 250-mile cross-state railroad to Pittsburgh excited Haupt. He applied to Merrick for an engineering position, but the haughty Merrick quickly let Haupt know that engineers were "as plentiful as blackberries,"[69] even ones who had published articles in his *Journal of the Franklin Institute*. Haupt's services evidently were neither wanted nor needed. Disappointed, the acclaimed bridge engineer scurried back to Gettysburg with little hope of working on the great project.

Chief Engineer John Edgar Thomson

Notwithstanding his rude comments to Haupt, Merrick and the railroad did need engineers. On 6 April 1847, shortly after the Haupt interview, he and the directors had "a long debate on the organization of the Engineering Department."[70] Three days after that debate, which took place at the Hall of the Franklin Institute, the directors voted to hire John Edgar Thomson as chief engineer at $4,000 per annum, and two assistant engineers at $3,000 per annum.[71, 72] Thomas Cope wrote that the men were "all natives of Pa. & highly recommended. We think they will form a strong corps."[73]

Thomson was a seasoned railroad man. He had learned surveying and engineering from his father, also John Thomson, at a time when it was still a craft. When summoned by the Pennsylvania Railroad, he was employed as chief engineer for the Georgia Railroad, a position he had assumed in 1834 at age twenty-six.[74] At the time, the Georgia Railroad was the longest continuous railroad in the country operated by one company.[75] Thomson built the railroad's line from Augusta to Marthasville, where it connected with the Western & Atlantic Railway, owned by the State of Georgia. Marthasville—a metropolis of five shacks—had previously been a survey location southeast of the Chattahoochee River named Terminus. Thomson renamed the place Atlanta.[76]

Thomson had begun his railroad career as a surveyor for the Philadelphia and Columbia Railroad (P&CRR), built by the Commonwealth of Pennsylvania as part of the Main Line, to link Philadelphia with the Susquehanna River canal system. While working on the P&CRR in the late 1820s, Thomson came to the attention of Major John Wilson, who made Thomson his principal assistant engineer in 1829, with responsibility for constructing the first twenty miles running west out of Philadelphia. Thomson later worked for Wilson on the Camden and Amboy Rail Road and Transportation Company (C&A), the first railroad in New Jersey and the third in the United States. Completing his work with the C&A, he surveyed and estimated the cost of a line to Baltimore for the Oxford Railroad Company. Following those assignments, he traveled to England and Scotland to broaden his knowledge of railroad engineering.

This talented man followed a career path similar to the trajectories of Loammi Baldwin Jr. and Canvass White. All three men gained practical knowledge in the field and then expanded their perspective by scrutinizing English and European work. Back in the United States, Thomson was hired by the Georgia Railroad Company of Augusta. He had probably been recommended by Major Wilson, who, prior to coming to Pennsylvania, was an engineer in Charleston and then state civil and military engineer under South Carolina's Board of Public Works from 1818 to 1822.[77]

Although the Pennsylvania Railroad was headquartered in Philadelphia, Thomson operated out of Harrisburg because all of the line's new construction stretched from Harrisburg westward to Pittsburgh. He was going to build a railroad across the Allegheny Mountains, some of the most unwelcoming railroad terrain in the eastern United States. Merrick and the board did have some appreciation for the task before them, so they decided to divide the line into two divisions: the Eastern Division from Harrisburg to Altoona and the Western Division from Altoona to Pittsburgh.

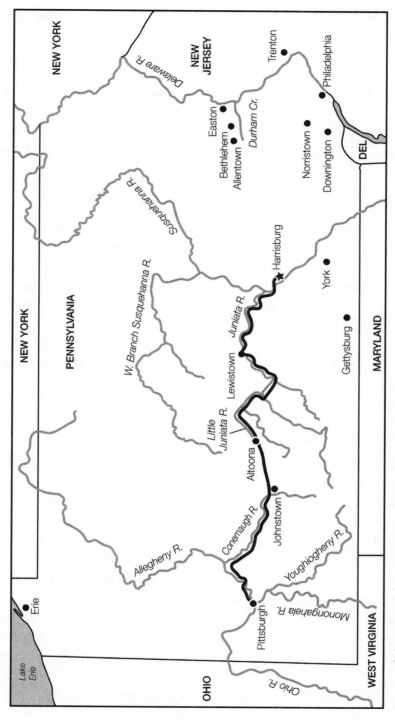

Route of the Pennsylvania Railroad, Harrisburg to Pittsburgh

The Pennsylvania Railroad board hired Edward Miller as associate engineer for the Western Division. After attending the University of Pennsylvania, Miller had learned his engineering on the Lehigh Canal under Canvass White. In 1831, he crossed the Atlantic and spent several months examining railroad practices in England.[78, 79] Returning to Pennsylvania, he served as chief engineer for the Catawissa Railroad (CRR). To construct the CRR, which runs south from Williamsport, following the West Branch of the Susquehanna River, and then east, following the main branch of the river, Miller had to excavate a 1,200-foot-long tunnel through rock. Later in his career, he was chief engineer for the New York and Erie Railroad.[80]

William B. Foster Jr.[81] was the board's choice for the Eastern Division's associate engineer position. Foster had been a canal engineer working in Pennsylvania and Kentucky.[82] President Merrick wanted Miller and Foster to report directly to the board, but Chief Engineer John Thomson demanded they report to him, and the chain-of-command disagreement marked the beginning of a running series of management disputes. Eventually these disputes would split the board.[83] The engineering divisions were further subdivided into thirty-mile segments, each under a principal assistant engineer. Samuel W. Mifflin, for whom Haupt had worked on the Wrightsville, York & Gettysburg Railroad, was one of the principal assistant engineers[84] responsible for a ten-mile segment within the Eastern Division under William Foster.

The Thrill of Challenge

Maryland's B&O Railroad was pushing its line to Pittsburgh at this time under the franchise it had obtained from the Pennsylvania legislature. The B&O franchise, however, contained a stipulation whereby it would be revoked if the Pennsylvania Railroad raised $3 million in stock subscriptions, with $1 million paid, and put fifteen miles of its line under contract at each end by 30 July 1847. The Pennsylvania Railroad was not organized until the last day of March 1847 and Thomson was still in Georgia until late April, so by the time he arrived in Harrisburg, he had only three months to select the first two sections of line and find contractors to perform the work. By early June, when his engineers had identified the alignment, he sought the board's authorization to begin letting contracts. It seems that Merrick expected Thomson to consult with him about all contracting matters, while Thomson sought to retain contracting authority in his own hands. Director Cope recorded in his diary: "I called by invitation on Pres. Merrick at the office of the Penna. R.R. Compy. He read to me the private correspondence

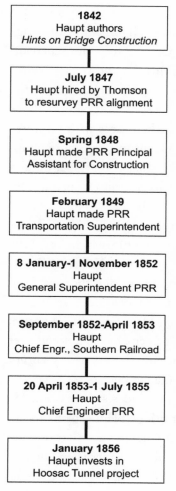

1842
Haupt authors
Hints on Bridge Construction

July 1847
Haupt hired by Thomson
to resurvey PRR alignment

Spring 1848
Haupt made PRR Principal
Assistant for Construction

February 1849
Haupt made PRR
Transportation Superintendent

8 January-1 November 1852
Haupt
General Superintendent PRR

September 1852-April 1853
Haupt
Chief Engr., Southern Railroad

20 April 1853-1 July 1855
Haupt
Chief Engineer PRR

January 1856
Haupt invests in
Hoosac Tunnel project

between himself & Jno. Edgar Thomson, Engineer in Chief, from which it appears that jealousies exist as to their relative prerogatives, powers & rights."[85] But Thomson did, on 8 June, receive authorization from the Road Committee of the board to place fifteen miles under contract at each end.

Thomson, whose methodical approach frustrated many, walked every hill and valley of some sixty miles of proposed alignment in July. From this visual survey, he realized that the proposed railroad location was flawed. Assistant engineer Mifflin was conscious of Thomson's need for a new alignment survey before it would be possible to put contractors to work, so he recommended Herman Haupt as an excellent engineer who could correct the alignment rapidly. Mifflin wrote to Haupt in Gettysburg and instructed him to immediately see Thomson in Harrisburg.

At their meeting, Haupt took Thomson's aloof personality as arrogance, and he came out of his interview with grave doubts about working for the Pennsylvania Railroad's chief engineer. Mifflin, a man of few words, told Haupt, "Don't be a fool, take the position and ask no questions. You can help him and . . . he will not be ungrateful."[86] It would prove the best career advice Haupt ever received.

A year after his West Point classmates, including Second Lieutenant George G. Meade, sailed off with General Winfield Scott to conquer Mexico, supported by Commodore Perry commanding the USS *Mississippi*, powered by Merrick's steam engines, Herman Haupt marched off to survey the Pennsylvania Railroad south of Mexico, Pennsylvania.

Foster assigned Haupt a four-and-a-half-mile section along the Juniata River. Thomson had figured that the survey would take two or three weeks to correct. In four working days, Haupt finished reworking the alignment. Finding it hard to believe that the work had been done well, Foster made a personal inspection. Once he convinced himself of Haupt's ability, he kept him busy on the alignment for the rest of 1847 and into 1848.

Haupt's letters home recorded the difficult conditions during this pressure-driven winter, as he sought to correct the flawed alignment of the original survey. He wrote Anna, whom he addressed as "Cis": "Rain, got drenched," and the next day, "Rain turned to snow." On the third day, he wrote, "cold," the single word probably reflecting both the weather and his mood. When the sunlight was strong, the men succumbed to snow blindness, a most painful affliction. Sometimes they tried to prevent it by blackening their faces with mixtures of charcoal and pork fat. During all these hardships, Haupt was continuing with his bridge studies. He had his survey rodman, a cabinetmaker by trade, build a large model bridge according to his design ideas. This model and Haupt's studies caught Thomson's attention.

As Haupt later related, Thomson made a surprise visit to his office one blustery winter day. While Thomson stood silently warming himself, he spied the bridge model, which Haupt had supported between two chairs. Noticing Thomson's attention, the young engineer began expounding his bridge theories. Two days later, division subassistant engineers appeared in Haupt's office asking for instructions. In typical Thomson fashion, he had given Haupt no official notice, but the youthful alignment surveyor suddenly held a principal assistant engineer position, responsible for a thirty-mile segment of the line. It was a very abrupt promotion, but characteristic of the way Thomson conducted business.

Thomson now had additional duties for Haupt besides survey work. He sent Haupt a penciled note accompanied by a roll of bridge plans—plans for all of the bridges on the line. The short note read, "I would like to have your opinion about these."[87] Haupt, in his usual precise fashion, detailed the merits and defects of each design and returned his notes to Thomson. When the relocation of the line between Harrisburg and Lewistown was completed in the spring of 1848, Thomson took Haupt into his Harrisburg office and created a new position in the organization for him. Young Haupt, only thirty-one, was now the Pennsylvania Railroad's principal assistant for construction.[88]

Haupt was responsible for reviewing all of the alignment surveys and plans for construction of the railroad. One of his most critical responsibilities was construction of the railroad's Susquehanna River Bridge, five miles above Harrisburg. This 3,680-foot-long wooden structure, built for a single line of track, had twenty-three spans, including one that straddled the Pennsylvania Main Line Canal. While Haupt was out of the state in March of 1849, six of the spans were destroyed when a violent wind caused unusually high waves on the river. The bridge was still under construction, so Haupt redesigned the structural system to produce a much more robust bridge.[89] Years later, his opponents would use this bridge failure to demean his abilities as an engineer.

When Haupt assumed his new position, he always presented his construction recommendations to Thomson before passing them on to the field engineers. Soon, however, he won Thomson's complete confidence, and construction matters were left entirely in his hands. In fact, Haupt became a close friend of the man he once thought so arrogant. His friendship with Thomson lasted until the man's death in 1874. Writing in 1861, Haupt stated: "[I]f there is a man living for whom I have labored more than any other, that man is J. Edward Thomson. . . . In this I was influenced not by hope of reward but by considerations of personal regard."[90]

Railroad Management

With forethought, Thomson began fashioning an organization to operate the railroad when the first section of the Pennsylvania opened. He named Haupt superintendent of transportation in February 1849 and charged him with development of the organizational details. Hoping to learn from the successes and mistakes of others, Thomson sent his man to visit the principal railroads in New England.[91] Haupt questioned officials of the New York and Erie, the Boston and Providence, Alvah Crocker's Fitchburg, and the Western Railroad of Massachusetts.[92] He interviewed personnel, studied the organizational structures, collected business forms, and evaluated machinery and operational procedures. Upon his return to Pennsylvania, Haupt worked with Thomson to fashion a highly centralized plan of operation that drew from the information he had gathered as well as Thomson's experiences with the Georgia Railroad.

Thomson's choice of Haupt as superintendent of transportation did not sit well with President Merrick and his allies on the board who wanted their own man in the job. It was also possible that Merrick still smarted because Thomson had hired Haupt after Merrick had rebuffed the young engineer with contempt. Additionally, there was continual bickering between the Merrick faction and board members friendly to Thomson. After visiting the railroad's office in June 1848, Thomas Cope wrote: "[T]he secy. informs me that jealousies & bickering have crept into their counsels. . . ."[93] Merrick declared Haupt "unfit for the position of superintendent." He also stated that Haupt was "too young, and entirely inexperienced."[94] Over Merrick's objections, the board approved Haupt as superintendent of transportation, but it also required Thomson to assume the position of general superintendent. To mollify Merrick, the board had made Thomson responsible for Haupt's performance.

Thomson had repeatedly clashed with Merrick, and this new confrontation led to Merrick's resignation as president on the first of September in 1849. Merrick resigned after he sought to oust Haupt as a means of embarrassing Thomson.[95] Their clash was part personality conflicts, but other issues were involved. Merrick's hostility to Thomson and Haupt masked an internal board fight concerning his salary as president. A split had occurred in the board, and one faction demanded that unless Merrick could act as both president and engineer, he should not be paid the $5,000 salary he demanded. This faction wanted to reduce the president's salary to $2,500.[96] Merrick forever blamed Haupt for his fall from power at the Pennsylvania Railroad, even though the dispute in fact centered on how the railroad was to be managed.

Prior to the advent of the railroads, a company's board managed the day-to-day operations of a business. Railroad companies, by the nature of their technical complexities and the fact that they operated over such large geographical areas, required a different business model. Management had to be involved in the operational aspects of the business at all times. Someone had to have minute-by-minute knowledge of the location of every steaming train, and this was beyond the capabilities of most board members. These men had their own businesses to manage and could not devote the necessary time to running a railroad. In the late 1840s, this was not apparent to many on the railroad's board.

Although no longer president, Merrick remained on the board, and he would cause further troubles as the Pennsylvania Railroad sought a solution to running multiple trains in two directions over a single line of track. The board selected William C. Patterson as the railroad's second president, and the first section of the railroad opened for passenger service in September 1849. On opening day, the railroad scheduled over its single track both an eastbound train leaving Lewistown at 10 a.m. and a westbound one leaving Philadelphia at 7:30 a.m. President Patterson, a close friend of Merrick, chose to use the day to harass the new superintendent of transportation, and the president's actions almost caused the railroad's first wreck.

When the westbound train, with company officials and other notables on board, reached Harrisburg, Patterson ordered an unscheduled halt. He did this on his own authority, without consideration for how two trains would run on a single track—that was Haupt's problem. Haupt, who was aboard the president's train, inquired about the unexpected delay. As soon as he learned what Patterson had ordered, he realized that the unplanned stop would cause a head-on collision. He immediately sent an engine over the line to stop the eastbound train.[97]

The charade between the general superintendent and the superintendent of transportation ended on 8 January 1851, when Thomson resigned his oversight position. Without much discussion, Haupt was named general superintendent and the position of superintendent of transportation was abolished. H. J. Lombaert, who had experience with New England railroads, became Haupt's assistant superintendent.

Still, Haupt's precision and brisk style made him a lightning rod for criticism. The board was repeatedly irritated with him because he destroyed, by careful analysis, their preconceived notions about costs and rates for freight and passengers. When Haupt was called before the board about a rate schedule the board had issued, he detailed cost factors the directors had not even considered. The embarrassed Merrick waved Haupt away, remarking, "That is not a heavy loss for the Pennsylvania Railroad, not enough to make a fuss about."[98]

The disputes about how to organize the management continued for another two years, during which Thomson and Haupt were involved with solving operational problems twenty-four hours a day. The company's president and the merchant princes and bankers of Philadelphia on the board were unable to grasp the intricacies and problems created by running multiple trains on a single track. Finally, in February 1852, the stockholders ousted Merrick and Patterson and elected Thomson to the railroad's board. The next day, the new board elected Thomson president of the Pennsylvania Railroad.

Believing his continued employment might jeopardize Thomson's candidacy for the board, Haupt had, before the election, given the newspapers the impression he would be resigning from the Pennsylvania Railroad. Therefore, he felt honor bound to do so and submitted his resignation after the election. But when Thomson and the new board rejected the resignation, Haupt agreed to stay with the railroad for the time being.[99] In August of 1852, Thomas A. Marshall, president of the Southern Railroad of Mississippi, wrote to Thomson seeking an engineer who could take charge of location surveys for the railroad's route to the Alabama state line.[100] Eager to construct their east–west railroad across Mississippi, the road's directors had hired a local individual as their engineer. He presented the company with a survey so riddled with errors that its flaws were obvious even to the merchant-class directors with no technical training.[101] Thomson passed the letter to Haupt, and by September the Southern Railroad had a new chief engineer,[102] although Haupt's resignation from the Pennsylvania was not effective until 1 November 1852.

Before leaving for Mississippi, Haupt sold his home in Gettysburg and moved Anna and the five children to Philadelphia.[103] Thomson, who from his days with the Georgia Railroad still had professional links to many railroads in the south, advised Haupt to visit lines in South Carolina, Tennessee, Georgia, and Alabama on his way to Mississippi. Haupt did so, stopping often to confer with local railroad officials as he made his way to his new headquarters in Mississippi.[104] In less than four months, Haupt completed the Southern Railroad surveys and was back in Philadelphia. In 1853, he published his *Report of the Final Location of the Southern Railroad from Brandon, Mississippi, to the Alabama Line, in the Direction of Charleston and Savannah*.[105] The report was not just a technical treatise on the location of Mississippi's Southern Railroad; it also presented Thomson's vision of a railroad system that would connect the entire country. Haupt used the report to assert the benefits of railroads joining northern and southern cites and the need for their westward extension into Texas. He even envisioned a linked railroad system stretching to the Pacific coast.

Haupt's mentor Edward Miller, who had taken over from Thomson as chief engineer of the Pennsylvania Railroad, resigned in early February 1853. Miller had been with the Pennsylvania Railroad since the earliest days of the enterprise. The other original associate engineer, William B. Foster Jr., had left the railroad for another stint at canal engineering, but he returned later to serve as a vice president. The timing of Haupt's return to Philadelphia could not have been better; on 20 April 1853, he was named chief engineer of the Pennsylvania Railroad.[106]

Tunneling Experience

The railroad was pushing hard to complete the line between Altoona and Pittsburgh and to double-track the entire Main Line. In the *Sixth Annual Report of the Chief Engineer*, issued in January 1853, Miller reported: "[T]he most formidable work on the route is the Summit Tunnel through the Allegheny Mountain. Its length is 3,570 feet and it has been driven from both ends, and from three working shafts, two of which are 200 feet deep."[107] Thomson had started the tunnel in 1850; his 1851 report had stated: "[T]wo shafts to work it have been commenced, together with a sufficient amount of the eastern approach to open the face of the tunnel for working the drift."[108] In this same general vicinity, it had taken the state two years to hammer and blast the 901-foot-long Staple Bend Tunnel of its Portage Railroad.

In the 1850s, miners advanced tunnels by using black powder, a very weak explosive, loaded into hand-drilled holes. When the powder was fired, they hoped the blast would have the power to shatter the rock of the mountain. The rate at which a tunnel could be advanced was determined by the muscle power drilling the blast holes, which were created by pounding steel drills into the rock with ten-pound hammers. Men like the legendary "John Henry" could swing a ten-pound hammer against the steel drills for hours on end, and it was their strength and endurance that determined the success or failure of the work. In hard rock, a three-man crew might take three hours to hammer a one-inch-diameter hole thirty-six inches deep. Progress on the Staple Bend Tunnel had been about eighteen inches a day, typically involving twelve hours of labor with water pouring through the tunnel ceiling like rain and the constant danger of falling rocks.

The Pennsylvania Railroad's Summit Tunnel was Haupt's introductory course in tunnel engineering and the problems associated with underground work. Thomson predicted that "the [Summit] tunnel will prove the most tedious job."[109] When Haupt assumed responsibility, the tunnel headings had been joined and the bore penetrated completely through the mountain, but there was still much work to be done before trains could pass through. In his 1853 report, Miller had warned about the presence of a four-foot-wide vein of coal in the tunnel and "fire-clay and perishable shales." These features made the tunnel roof very treacherous. His report further warned that "about a half mile of the tunnel will require arching"[110] with bricks. The previous year, Thomson had warned the railroad's board that "progress . . . has not been as great as anticipated, in consequence of the great flow of water encountered."[111] Water and bad rock were common problems in tunnel work. Haupt and others attempting to bore the Hoosac Mountain would soon learn plenty about the difficulties imposed by water and bad rock.

In his first report to the Pennsylvania Railroad stockholders, in January 1854, Chief Engineer Haupt stated the difficulties of advancing the Summit Tunnel:

> From the treacherous character of the material in the Allegheny Mountain tunnel, frequent falls occurred before the roof could be supported, and from this cause the quantity of material that required removal was twice as great as would have been necessary had the rock been of a solid and permanent character. In the middle shaft from 120 to 175 gallons of water per minute were pumped and discharged at the top of the shaft.[112]
>
> Nearly the whole of the tunnel will require arching.[113]

A month after Haupt's report, the entire length of the Pennsylvania Railroad from Harrisburg to Pittsburgh was opened to traffic. Feeling great pressure to have the line in service, Haupt opened the track before the arching was completed, and it remained unfinished for another year. The railroad's 1855 annual report detailed the remaining work on the line: "[A]rching of the tunnel under the summit of the mountain, the roof of which had been previously made safe by supporting it with heavy timbers."[114] The arching was proceeding slowly because passing trains constantly interrupted the work. Haupt and Thomson both believed it was more important to place the line in service and produce revenue than to worry about completing all of the construction details. The tunnel would be arched, but it would take longer to accomplish under their scheme.

In mid-1853, when the railroad needed additional funds to keep construction work going, Haupt proved successful at saving the railroad cash. He managed to persuade the contractors working on the line to accept Pennsylvania securities in place of cash payments. The contractors "agreed very generally to accept the stock and bonds of the company at par in payment for work and materials at cash prices, rather than suspend operations."[115]

Thomson traveled to England in late 1853 in an attempt to sell $1 million of railroad bonds. But the threat of war in the Crimean Peninsula had financial circles in a panic, and he was able to place only $230,000 worth of bonds. Haupt and the railroad's management were forced to limit cash outlays during this period. Haupt's success at using securities for contractor payments tainted his perception of railroad finance for years to come and influenced his approach to financing the Hoosac Tunnel work.

By April 1855, there was very little unfinished construction,[116] so the moderately wealthy Haupt informed the company that he would accept compensation only when actually employed. On 1 July, he resigned as chief engineer and the position was abolished.[117] In November, the common councils of the City of Philadelphia, which held a large block of the railroad's stock, elected Haupt as one of the Pennsylvania Railroad's directors, and he held that position until December of 1856.[118]

Herman Haupt thrived on challenges, and his work for the Pennsylvania Railroad had become routine. Since 1851, he and his railroad friends had been investing in real estate along the route of the Pennsylvania Railroad, so now he turned his attention to organizing coal and timber companies that could be serviced by the new railroad. He and a group of associates, including Thomson, Alexander J. Derbyshire (a director of the company from 1851 to 1855), and

Thomas Scott (who would become president at Thomson's death), were linked in a complex web of financial dealings.[119] While Derbyshire had been a member of Merrick's committee when Haupt was charged with insubordination,[120] he would later prove to be a true friend. Under Thomson's tutelage, Haupt was drawn into a network of men who invested their capital in promising development schemes.

Probably because of his association with such men and his experience with the Summit Tunnel, Samuel M. Lane, a director for the North Western Railroad of Pennsylvania,[121] approached Haupt in December 1855 about the practicality and cost of tunneling the Hoosac Mountain. A friend named William A. Galbraith had offered Lane an interest in the contract to bore the Hoosac, and Lane was intrigued by the thought of easy money. Galbraith had written Lane about the project on 1 December 1855.[122] In his letter, Galbraith stated: "[W]e want men rather than money, and attention and management more than capital. Mr. Serrell and I will raise a considerable part [of the capital] from our own means."[123]

William Galbraith was the son of Judge John Galbraith. As a young lawyer, John Galbraith had lived in Butler, Pennsylvania, where he had established the county's first newspaper.[124] He later moved his practice north to Erie and became the county judge. Samuel Lane was also from Butler. Prior to his railroading days, he had been a storekeeper in Butler,[125] and he had served as a councilman in 1850.[126]

Haupt reviewed the proposal Lane had received from Galbraith and pronounced the project feasible, but he wanted to visit the site before advising Lane about investing his money. Before the month of December was out, Haupt traveled to Massachusetts and then returned to Philadelphia virtually bubbling with enthusiasm about the project. While in North Adams, Massachusetts, Haupt scrutinized the boring of the "Little Hoosac Tunnel," by D. N. Stanton and his partners. This was a 324-foot-long tunnel through a rock ledge that blocked the route of the railroad from the village of North Adams to the Vermont border.[127] Stanton's work was impressive. His men were working three shifts a day, driving the bore with muscle and black powder. The rock they were mining was mica schist—just as Amherst geology professor and state geologist Edward Hitchcock had predicted. He had also said that the interior of the Hoosac Mountain was dry and no water problems would be encountered. For the Little Hoosac Tunnel, at least, his predictions were true.

Based on his experiences with the Pennsylvania Railroad and working with the mercantile men of Philadelphia, Haupt envisioned a similar situation for the Massachusetts project. He expected substantial Commonwealth backing for the project and generous support from the commercial men of Boston. Haupt also believed the work could be completed at a profit to the contractors, considering the state loan of $2 million, the stock subscriptions already sold, and the prospect of additional subscriptions from Boston.

The thirty-eight-year-old Haupt was fascinated by the challenge of such a grand project. Lane was interested in a return on his investment, so, after hearing Haupt's glowing assessment, he immediately invested $20,000 in Edward Serrell's contract. Lane assured Haupt that Serrell was a reputable contractor. So, in January 1856, an excited Haupt invested $20,000 in the Hoosac Tunnel project.[128] Lane was convinced that Serrell had adequate financial backing,[129] something Lane must have been told by Galbraith. This financial information was also passed to Haupt. Without making his own inquiries about Serrell, Haupt accepted Lane's assurances.

The new partnership of Serrell, Haupt, and Company—with Serrell, Galbraith, Brown, Lane, and Haupt each agreeing to invest $20,000 and assume equal obligations—was organized on 7 January 1856. On the very first day of their company's organization, the partners negotiated a contract with the Troy and Greenfield Railroad. The contract specified that the investors would assume the risk of constructing the railroad and tunnel for a lump sum of $3,570,000. The contract also included a stipulation requiring the railroad to have $210,000 in paid-in stock subscriptions by 15 May 1856.[130] The clause was meant to assure the contractors as to the railroad's ability to pay for the work until it progressed to the point where it was possible to collect the first installment of the $2 million in Commonwealth of Massachusetts scrip. To receive those funds, the contractors would have to finance the building of the railroad and the boring of the hole into the Hoosac Mountain from their own pockets and those of the Troy and Greenfield Railroad.

7

Quick-Profit Friends

How often do we see . . . in the paper an
Irishman crushed, suffocated in a cave-in . . .
Blown to bits, —ten, twenty Irishmen buried alive
Perils to which honest Pat is constantly subjected, in the
*   hard toils for his bread.*

—Unidentified New York minister, in
George Potter, *To the Golden Door*
(Boston: Little Brown, 1960), 165

A T THE TIME HERMAN Haupt invested in Edward Serrell's contract to build the Troy and Greenfield Railroad, he envisioned his place in the history of engineering as the one who tunneled the Hoosac Mountain. He thought there was money to be made, but, more important, he saw himself as the consulting engineer to a great work. The possibility of the need to actually manage the work and deal with the various political factions in the Commonwealth of Massachusetts never occurred to him.

Partnerships

Based on Haupt's visit to North Adams and his analysis of the work, both Haupt and Lane were convinced that the $100,000 the five partners were supposedly investing in the company would allow Serrell to complete seven miles of railroad and 1,000 feet of tunnel. To Haupt, seven miles of railroad in a river valley was nothing. After all, he had mastered the difficulties of the Summit Tunnel, in the Alleghenies, so even the thousand feet of tunnel in Massachusetts did not seem insurmountable. Once this piddling amount of work was accomplished, the partners assumed, they would be able to collect their first $100,000 in bond scrip from Massachusetts and the Commonwealth would fund the rest of the work. They would be on their way to guaranteed profits. The reality of the Mountain and dealing with Massachusetts politicians proved to be completely different from what they expected.

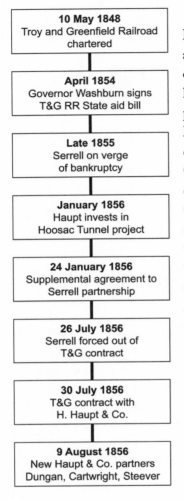

10 May 1848
Troy and Greenfield Railroad
chartered

April 1854
Governor Washburn signs
T&G RR State aid bill

Late 1855
Serrell on verge
of bankruptcy

January 1856
Haupt invests in
Hoosac Tunnel project

24 January 1856
Supplemental agreement to
Serrell partnership

26 July 1856
Serrell forced out of
T&G contract

30 July 1856
T&G contract with
H. Haupt & Co.

9 August 1856
New Haupt & Co. partners
Dungan, Cartwright, Steever

Less than a week after investing his money, Haupt started to realize the difficulties of the work and to begin uncovering the true financial condition of his partners. The first revelation was that Serrell had no money to meet his monetary obligation to the partnership. As the cold January winds beat on the Mountain, Haupt slowly learned the equally chilling details of Serrell's tangled finances. E.W. Serrell and Company was devoid of capital and sinking under a debt load exceeding $100,000.[1] Serrell and William Galbraith were not looking for management help, as stated in the letter to Lane, but instead were on the verge of bankruptcy and desperate for someone to bail them out. Their financial situation, it turned out, had long preceded Galbraith's letter to Lane. As Lane and Haupt learned further details, they quickly demanded a revised partnership agreement to protect them from Serrell's burden of debt. Consequently, two and a half weeks after the partnership was formed, a supplemental agreement was executed with Serrell and Galbraith. The new agreement, dated 24 January 1856, contained language to shield Lane and Haupt from legal liability for Serrell's previous debts. After the January revelations about the company's finances, Haupt, who wanted to be involved only as a consulting engineer, found himself fully engaged in trying to untangle the partnership's financial mess so the company could proceed with the business of driving a tunnel.

Haupt soon learned that, notwithstanding the new agreement between the partners, no one was going to work for the company or supply it with needed materials because it was common knowledge Serrell and Company did not pay its bills. Haupt and Lane were not legally responsible for Serrell's earlier debts, but the new company was not going to be viable until money was found to pay Serrell and Company's past debts. An impression of financial strength was more important to renewal of the work than who was legally responsible for the old bills.

But Serrell's financial condition was not unique, in February, Haupt learned another cold fact: None of his other partners—Lane, Galbraith, and Brown—had the resources to fulfill their $20,000 pledges to the company. Even Lane, who had drawn Haupt into the project, had financial problems. His North Western Railroad in Pennsylvania was not profitable, and its financial difficulties were pressing on Lane more each day. The North Western would struggle along for another two years before the situation became so dire that the railroad could not even pay the interest on its bonded debt. Finally, in July of 1859, it was sold in foreclosure to its bondholders.[2]

Haupt was the solitary member of the group not burdened by outstanding debt. Lane, seeing no opportunity for quick profits and not wanting to be dragged further into the financial quagmire, withdrew before the end of February, when the remaining partners relieved him of all responsibility and liability.[3]

At the same time, the Troy and Greenfield Railroad was not doing any better at fulfilling its own contractual obligations. Alvah Crocker had struggled to build his business and then to build railroads as far as Greenfield, but he had always succeeded through perseverance. The Baltimore & Ohio and the Pennsylvania Railroads both had teetered on the edge of failure because of financial and political adversity, but the leaders of each had persevered and reaped great rewards. Crocker's only business plan was hope and continued perseverance. He had watched other Massachusetts railroads receive Commonwealth aid when their money ran out, and he hoped to tap the same source. So in 1856, when the T&G was unsuccessful at selling its stock or at least in accumulating paid-in subscriptions, he again appealed to the Commonwealth for financial support.

He presented a petition to the General Court entreating the Commonwealth to purchase $150,000 worth of the railroad's stock.[4] Because the T&G had no collateral, the petition offered the Commonwealth the privilege of appointing men to the company's board of directors. This was similar to the arrangement the Commonwealth had made with the Western Railroad when it applied for support. The gentlemen of the General Court were not interested in such a proposition, so the railroad, like its contractors, was strapped for funds. The difficulty of paid-in stock subscriptions would trouble the T&G for another four years and lead to accusations of fraud against Haupt. The Hoosac Tunnel project could not go forward without money. But fate had flashed her kindly eyes on the T&G, since Galbraith had found a man who wanted to build the country's longest tunnel and who had friends willing to risk their money.

To salvage Serrell's company and the Tunnel contract, Haupt turned to his Pennsylvania Railroad associates. Using his personal property as collateral, he arranged a $100,000 loan from George Howell and Christian Spangler, directors of the Pennsylvania Railroad,[5] and Horatio Burroughs, a successful Philadelphia merchant. Nevertheless, as fast as Haupt solved one financial problem, another surfaced from the tangled mess that Galbraith and Serrell had previously created while trying to build the Tunnel on the backs of small subcontractors.

D. N. Stanton and partners, who were successfully driving the "Little Hoosac Tunnel" Haupt had inspected when he visited North Adams in December, withdrew from the work and assigned their contract to another local firm, Ballou and Simmons. Haupt, who was now running the affairs of the partnership, at first refused to recognize the transfer and tried to put the contract's obligation on Serrell and Galbraith as being a subcontract executed before the new company was organized.[6] Nevertheless, the threat of a civil suit forced Haupt to negotiate. He settled the Ballou and Simmons claim by giving them 1,300 shares of his personal stock in the Allegheny Railroad and Coal Company. The stock had a par value of $25 per share, and when Haupt made the transfer, it had a market value of $10 per share. As part of the settlement agreement, Haupt guaranteed he would redeem the stock for $12 per share if they wanted to sell at the end of three years. Ballou and Simmons accepted his stock offer on 30 January 1857, and their contract with E. W. Serrell and Company was canceled.[7]

It was now apparent that success in boring a tunnel through the Hoosac Mountain would depend on Haupt's ability to find more than the $100,000 he had already raised to pay Serrell's old financial obligations. To meet those obligations, Haupt would again have to turn to friends in Philadelphia. He obtained a $60,000 investment in the Hoosac contract from John Edgar Thomson and Thomas A. Scott of the Pennsylvania Railroad; Pat McAvoy; Horatio Burroughs (who had already participated in one loan); and Andrew Eastwick (a pioneer locomotive builder from Philadelphia).[8, 9] As investors, these five men purchased an 11 percent interest in the contract the company held with the T&G Railroad. But as soon as Haupt found more money, Galbraith produced more outstanding obligations. In late May, Galbraith informed Haupt the company would have to pay $30,000 in maturing obligations over the next five months.[10] During the first half year of Haupt's involvement, the work of actually driving the Hoosac Tunnel languished as he sought to correct the financial situation.

At this point, Galbraith, who had contributed no money but who, because he was an attorney, had been handling all of the partnership's business matters, recommended to Haupt that it might be wise to ease Serrell out of the company. It is unclear how much Galbraith knew about all of Serrell's financial problems before the new partnership was formed, but after six months of struggle to correct the financial condition of the partnership, Haupt's tolerance toward Serrell had come to an end. Taking Galbraith's advice, he forced Serrell out of both the partnership and the construction contract. On 26 July 1856, Serrell wrote to the directors of the Troy and Greenfield Railroad: "Gentlemen, by an amicable arrangement made this day between H. Haupt and Wm. A. Galbraith on the one part and myself on the other, my interest in the contract for building the Troy and Greenfield Railroad is relinquished and the gentlemen above named are authorized to surrender the contract and make such new arrangements in their own name as they can agree upon with the Board of Directors. . . ."[11]

To rid himself of Serrell, Haupt was overly generous to a man who had undoubtedly swindled him. Haupt agreed to assume most of the remaining debts from Serrell's old company and to pay Serrell $16,000 for his 5,987 shares of Troy and Greenfield Railroad stock. For Haupt, the only favorable stipulation in the agreement was a restriction on when Serrell would receive payment for his shares. Serrell would be paid only when Haupt was successful in obtaining the first two installments of the Commonwealth loan; half of the amount would be payable after receipt of each Commonwealth installment. By a further generous term, Haupt agreed to allow Serrell $5,000 in Troy and Greenfield Railroad bonds annually for six years and $2,500 in the railroad's stock for as long as the work continued.[12] As was the case with all the partners who were accepting bonds and stock as payment from the railroad, these instruments would have no value until the Hoosac Tunnel was completed and trains were running between Troy, New York, and Greenfield, Massachusetts.

Repeatedly in his career, Haupt was overly generous to men who fraudulently represented themselves to him in business endeavors. At the Pennsylvania Railroad, Haupt had proved very good at picking men for positions of responsibility. He would also demonstrate this business acumen when he worked for other railroads after his Hoosac Tunnel days, but when it came to choosing men to be partners in his own business affairs, charity overrode judgment more often than not. Those years after his father died, when he and his mother had been thrown on the mercy of others, seemed to forever haunt his personal dealings with other men. Many men had shown him kindnesses when he was in need—including the schoolmaster John Brown in Philadelphia and then John Sterigere, who arranged his appointment to West Point—and those experiences seemed to have shaped Haupt's behavior. He all too frequently conducted his personal business affairs in an excessively generous manner. But he also may have convinced himself that this was the price he had to pay to rid himself of Serrell and proceed with becoming the engineer who tunneled the Hoosac Mountain.

With Serrell gone, a new firm, H. Haupt and Company, was formed. By agreement, Haupt and Galbraith apportioned the Hoosac Tunnel contract, after allowing for the 11 percent interest held by the Philadelphia men—two-thirds to Haupt and one-third to Galbraith. William Brown, who had contributed nothing during the preceding six months of financial struggle, was dropped from the new company.[13]

At the end of July, the Troy and Greenfield Railroad, realizing that no one else was willing to assume the risk of such an immense undertaking and appreciating the fact that it was unable to comply with the paid-in subscription requirement of the previous contract, negotiated a new contract with H. Haupt and Company. The total price for building the railroad from Greenfield to the Vermont state line and driving the four and a half miles of single-track tunnel through the Hoosac Mountain was set at $3,880,000.[14] This was based on an estimated tunnel length, as the true distance of a tunnel through the Hoosac Mountain was still unknown. No surveys of the railroad's tunnel alignment had yet been accomplished, as money matters had constantly drawn all from seriously considering the engineering issues. This new contract specified a tunnel with a clear opening so there would be eighteen feet above the rail and fourteen feet of width. The only cash the railroad had to offer was from the sale of stock, so most of the contract value was still in the Massachusetts bonds to be paid in installments by the Commonwealth as work was accomplished.

The 30 July 1856, contract apportioned to H. Haupt and Company:[15]

$2,000,000	*in Commonwealth of Massachusetts bonds*
900,000	*in 6% mortgage bonds of the Troy and Greenfield Railroad Company*
598,000	*in capital stock of the Troy and Greenfield Railroad Company*
382,000	*in cash, payable in such proportions monthly, as estimated by the engineer.*
$3,880,000	

In truth, the railroad's cash on hand to pay the contractor was much less than what was stated in the contract. From its earliest days through to the end of 1856, the Troy and Greenfield had sold only $121,412 worth of company stock.[16]

This new contract with the T&G had one other interesting twist concerning the 5,987 stock subscriptions H. Haupt and Company now held (which had originally been paid to E. W. Serrell and Company). The T&G would credit performance of contract work as payment for calls on the stock subscriptions. This was titled "stock credits" in the contract.[17] This clause relieved Haupt and Company from having to pay cash to the T&G as the work proceeded, but it added a complication concerning the requirement stipulated in a later Commonwealth Loan Act about paid-in stock subscriptions. Because there was still no cash available for payments from the T&G, Haupt was again forced to find new investors to finance the work. He had toiled for almost seven months, but almost none of his efforts had gone into building a railroad or tunneling the Mountain, and now he needed operating capital to finance the building of that first 1,000 feet of the Tunnel. Only by launching into the work would he be able to secure the first payment from the Commonwealth. Haupt was desperately in need of new partners who could contribute cash, not more debt.

Once again he returned to his haunts in Pennsylvania, seeking financial support. This time he found the engineering firm of Dungan, Cartwright, and Company willing to invest $87,000 at the rate of $10,000 per month. There were three partners in the firm: Charles B. Dungan, Henry Cartwright, and Henry D. Steever. Some twenty years earlier, Steever and Haupt's father had jointly operated the grocery store on Second Street in Philadelphia. The Dungan, Cartwright, and Steever company specialized in gas and water works and had built gaslight plants in Albany, New York; Charleston, South Carolina; Hartford, Connecticut; Newark, New Jersey; and Washington, DC.[18] Before an agreement was executed with Haupt on 9 August 1856, Henry Cartwright personally went to Massachusetts and inspected the proposed Tunnel work. Haupt and his new partners believed $87,000 would provide sufficient capital to finance the work until the conditions had been met for receiving the first installment from the Commonwealth.

To aid his new partners in raising their capital contribution, Haupt lent the trio $125,000 in Troy and Greenfield Railroad bonds, which were to be used as collateral against any loan they could arrange. Haupt, who was still hoping to remain in Pennsylvania and be involved in the Tunnel project only as a consulting engineer, refused to take responsibility for the day-to-day management of the work. So Cartwright, who was an accountant,[19] agreed to go to North Adams and oversee the subcontractors Haupt had hired. (Later events would prove Cartwright a true friend as Haupt struggled with the project.) Haupt went back to

Massachusetts in August to survey the alignment of the railroad between Green-field and the Tunnel, but once the survey was completed, he returned to his Chestnut Hill home in Philadelphia.

With Cartwright in North Adams directing the work and money in hand to pay the miners, H. Haupt and Company began to make headway boring into the Hoosac Mountain. For the moment, there was a respite from the troubles of unpaid bills and unfaithful partners. The Mountain was brilliant with color as the leaves changed with the cooler weather, and everyone's spirits were raised when the North Adams *Weekly Transcript* reported that workmen were being hired to tunnel the Mountain.[20] By February of 1857, the *Weekly Transcript* would detail progress on driving the Tunnel: "[A]n advance of more than six hundred feet into the rock has been made on the east side of the mountain."

Massachusetts Politics

During the winter session of the General Court in 1856, while Haupt was being drawn into the project by Serrell's representations and the exciting challenge of constructing the longest tunnel in the country, Alvah Crocker and the Troy and Greenfield Railroad appealed to Massachusetts for further aid. The petitioners make much of the fact that the ". . . contractors have associated with them some of the strongest and ablest men, commanding considerable capital, who have made some of the tunnels in Pennsylvania."[21] The efforts by Crocker and the rail-road were stymied by what the newspapers called "altogether too much lobbying and log rolling in the House."[22] The leaders of the opposition were again the men of the Western Railroad, who wanted to protect their Boston-to-Albany rail monopoly. The newspapers candidly identified the foe: "[T]he Western Rail-road has struggled hard and earnestly against the project."[23] This was something Haupt had not expected. In Pennsylvania, the Commonwealth and particularly the City of Philadelphia had stood firmly behind the Pennsylvania Railroad. In Massachusetts, there was already a cross-state railroad, and it considered itself threatened by this proposed line across the northern part of Massachusetts.

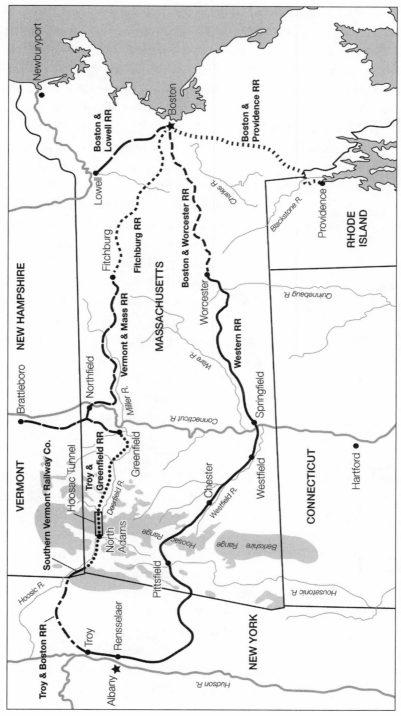

Cross-Massachusetts railroad routes, with the Western Railroad in the south connecting Boston to Albany

Defeats in the General Court were nothing new for Crocker. He was a veteran of many battles on Beacon Hill, beginning with those to obtain the charters for his two other railroads across northern Massachusetts. He would not be turned away easily. Herman Haupt was similarly honed by many a trial. Difficulties served to stimulate both Crocker and Haupt, so each increased his exertions.[24] After a year of struggle, Haupt realized that he faced two critical problems: (1) the need for cash to keep the work going and (2) the time required to bore five miles of tunnel through the Hoosac Mountain. It was apparent that it would take an army of stout Irishmen a lifetime of pounding steel drills to create all of the blast holes necessary to shatter the rock of the Mountain.

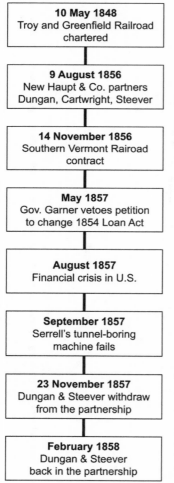

10 May 1848
Troy and Greenfield Railroad chartered

9 August 1856
New Haupt & Co. partners Dungan, Cartwright, Steever

14 November 1856
Southern Vermont Rairoad contract

May 1857
Gov. Garner vetoes petition to change 1854 Loan Act

August 1857
Financial crisis in U.S.

September 1857
Serrell's tunnel-boring machine fails

23 November 1857
Dungan & Steever withdraw from the partnership

February 1858
Dungan & Steever back in the partnership

Strong men hammering on drill steel to create twenty-inch-deep blast holes in the rock were not going to complete this Tunnel. Haupt probably had known this fact from the beginning, but he, like Crocker, always had faith in his ability to solve any problem. Each man thrived on adversity. Crocker, after spending those lonely nights driving his wagon load of paper to Boston, believed in a mainline railroad across the northern part of Massachusetts. Haupt simply believed in his own ability as an engineer.

Ten years in the future, mining techniques would slowly change—primarily because of the struggles of boring the rock of the Hoosac Mountain. But when Haupt attacked the Mountain in the 1850s, an advance of two or maybe two and a half feet per day was considered excellent. The rate of advance was controlled by how fast the necessary blast holes could be drilled. The mining of the Mountain was accomplished by eight-man crews, each led by a foreman and working by the light of tallow candles stuck in rock crevices. To attack the rock, these hardy men had only their muscles and hammers. The men worked an eight-hour shift,[25] while one foreman worked twelve hours directing one and a half shifts.

At the rock face on the east side of the Mountain, four men "drivers" pounded steel star drills with nine- to twelve-pound hammers. (The term star referred to the shape of the steel at the business end of the drill.) Each drill was held by one of the other four men in the crew. The man who held the drill steel steady for the hammers was called the "shaker," because his job was to rotate the steel after each ringing blow. After each hammer strike, a slight turn was necessary to loosen the rock chips and keep the steel from binding in the hole. Contrary to popular fiction, a man did not sling a hammer for eight hours; the driver and shaker would at intervals switch jobs. The drill steel star became dull very quickly, therefore a shaker would withdraw the drill and rapidly position a replacement quickly, so as not to break the rhythm of the driver. A "walker" would gather the dull steels and carry them to a blacksmith outside the Tunnel. During the years Haupt had men attacking the Mountain, two blacksmiths were constantly busy sharpening drill steels during the day shifts, and one blacksmith continued to sharpen steel throughout the night.[26] At the east face in the hard rock of the Mountain, the drillers went through about 225 pounds of the best English steel per month in 1860.[27]

Once all of the blast holes were drilled, the foreman loaded them with black powder and then tamped in the fuses. The fuses were cut at different lengths so the powder in the different holes would ignite a moment or two apart. While the foreman did his dangerous work of loading and tamping the holes, the men retreated behind a wall of stone or heavy timbers. When everything was ready, the foreman had to light the multiple fuses and retreat across the rough floor of the tunnel as fast as his legs would carry him. After the blast, the broken rock was taken from the Tunnel in small carts hitched to mules.

The full face of the Tunnel was excavated in a two-step process. Haupt had Cartwright organize the work with a lead crew of miners first excavating the top six and a half feet of the face, known as the "header." Then a second crew followed, taking out the lower part of the face. This allowed two crews to advance into the mountain at the same time while not interfering with each other's work. They were separated by a sufficient distance so that a blast by one crew did not endanger the other. Once the header crew had advanced well into the Mountain, Haupt had a fan installed outside the Tunnel to push fresh air into a fourteen-inch-diameter painted cloth tube.[28] This cloth tube was tied high up along the side of the Tunnel. As the header work advanced, tube extensions were added so the air from the fan exited the tube close to the rock face at the header and forced the foul air from the blasts out of the Tunnel.

Early in 1857, Crocker, with Haupt at his side, tramped into the Massachusetts General Court with another petition on behalf of the Troy and Greenfield Railroad. Their aim was to restructure the Loan Act of 1854. To both Crocker and Haupt, it was clear that the only way to keep the work going was to have a regular and reliable flow of capital. Their petition did not ask for more money. Its only purpose was to change the requirements of the 1854 act so the Commonwealth would make the loan payments more frequently. Under the original act, the T&G had to complete five miles of railroad and 1,000 feet of tunnel to earn $100,000 in Commonwealth bonds; at the rate the miners were then advancing into the Mountain, two years of work would be needed to obtain the first payment.

Thev petition sought to uncouple the construction of the Tunnel from the required railroad work. It modified the earlier statute so payments of $50,000 would be made separately for each five miles of completed railroad or each 1,000 feet of tunnel. The total loan amount would remain the same, $2 million, but the payments could now be earned separately for building the railroad and digging the Tunnel. The logic of their request flowed from the Tunnel contractor's desperate need for funds to keep the work progressing into the mounntain. Under the terms of the 1854 act, a contractor in need of funds would seek to construct the easiest sections of railroad first in order to qualify for the Commonwealth bonds. The act was in effect forcing such a contractor to build unconnected sections of railroad. If the requirements were changed, it would be possible to build the railroad continuously from Greenfield westward through the towns of Shelburne Falls and Charlemont. Then, once there was a continuous railroad up the Deerfield Valley, the T&G could begin to earn revenue by running trains. This revenue could then be used to defray the cost of tunneling the Mountain.

The battle lines were already drawn, but with each petition to the General Court, the positions became more entrenched and the debate more vicious. Daniel L. Harris, a civil engineer and president of the Connecticut River Railroad, served as the hatchet man for the Western Railroad, which was closely connected to his railroad. Harris was a resident of Springfield, a town dependent for its prosperity on the Western Railroad. The Western Railroad transshipped Connecticut River Railroad freight to Albany and Boston, and in 1852 the Western helped the Connecticut River Railroad with its debt by granting it a loan of $100,000.[29]

There was one additional factor driving Harris's opposition: He was an engineer with a large financial interest in bridge building. The firm of Boody,

Stone, and Harris held the rights to build Howe truss bridges in all of New England.[30] Years later, it would be noted that Harris was "committed to the excellences of the Howe [bridge truss] patent."[31] Haupt's bridge innovations menaced the Howe truss patent and the income Harris derived from building those bridges. William Howe, inventor of this bridge system, was from Springfield. He developed his truss system, which he patented in 1840, while building a bridge for the Western Railroad at Warren, Massachusetts. So Harris had many financial reasons for leading the opposition against the Troy and Greenfield Railroad and the Hoosac Tunnel. It is interesting to note, however, that there was a relationship between Harris's firm and Crocker's Vermont and Massachusetts Railroad. Boody, Stone, and Harris had built the bridges along the line of the Vermont and Massachusetts.

For Crocker and Haupt, the fight resembled Hercules against the "Hydra of Lerna": every time they answered an argument, Harris and the Western raised three more claims. The Western Railroad men, believing Haupt had made little progress boring into the Mountain, sought to encourage the Joint Special Committee hearing the petition to visit North Adams and inspect the work. This was a mistake. The attention and effort that Cartwright and Haupt had brought to the project over the preceding six months was clearly evident to the members of the committee. Their report of the visit was carried in the *Weekly Transcript* on 7 May 1857:

> *In conclusion, the committee says that the representations which have been made by the Troy and Greenfield Railroad Company, in relation to the condition and character of the work, are correct and trustworthy.*[32]

On the east side of the Hoosac Mountain, the committee found 274 feet of full-face Tunnel eighteen feet high and fourteen feet wide completed, and the heading six and a half feet high by ten feet wide extended another 274 feet. There were three gangs of men working the east face of the Tunnel each day, except Sunday, and the rock was so firm that no arching support was required. On the west side of the Mountain, 185 feet of heading had been driven, but heavy timbers were needed to support the crumbling ground.

There are no drawings of the timbering systems used by Haupt, but years later, when the Commonwealth took over the work, a small timber-supported bottom header was driven to drain off the water trapped in the material. This was followed by a top header to install the timbers necessary to support the roof of the Tunnel. Both of these headers were excavated and their timber supports were installed in advance of the main heading and the remainder of the timber support work. The Commonwealth engineers would learn later that a bottom drainage header was critical to excavating the Tunnel on the western side of the Mountain, as no amount of timber cribbing would support the material if it was fully saturated.[33] But this systematic method of advancing into the west face of the Hoosac Mountain was still ten years in the future. In 1857, Haupt remained hopeful that his miners would soon reach solid rock and the timbering would not be needed.

After the General Court received the report of the visiting committee, Harris obtained a week's postponement of the bill's consideration. When the committee reconvened, he insisted the Troy and Greenfield Railroad provide a copy of its contract with the men from Pennsylvania. Daniel Carpenter, president of the Troy and Greenfield, deflected the request by stating it was injurious to the interest of the contractors, and the committee accepted his position.[34]

But the Hydra continued to raise new issues. Harris next went into the General Court and read several anonymous letters published in the Greenfield *Gazette and Courier* denouncing the railroad and its petition before the General Court. He hoped to prove that the citizens of Franklin County, through which the T&G traversed, were unsympathetic to the railroad's argument for relief. Under questioning, however, it came out that Harris was the author of the so-called anonymous letters, and he was driven from Beacon Hill in embarrassment. The bill then passed both houses of the legislature by wide margins and was sent on to Governor Henry J. Gardner.[35]

Governor Gardner had come to power in 1854 with the Know-Nothing Party's sweep of all but two seats in the General Court. Officially, Gardner was a member of the American Party, but this loosely organized group was commonly referred to as the Know-Nothing Party, because the party had arisen from secret societies opposed to the flood of Irish immigrants driven to America by the Irish potato famine in the late 1840s. When a member of the American Party was asked about his participation in the party, he would always say that he "knew nothing."

The following year, Gardner defeated Republican Julius Rockwell, and even the Republicans endorsed the Gardner candidacy in 1856. While campaigning in 1856, Gardner had visited North Adams and the Tunnel work, declaring himself in favor of the Troy and Greenfield efforts to tunnel the Hoosac.

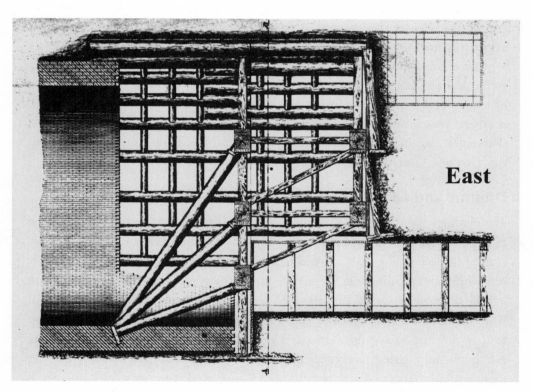

Timber supports that were used to advance the Tunnel into the west face of the Hoosac Mountain when the Commonwealth took over the work (courtesy The State Library of Massachusetts)

Nonetheless, the political winds in 1857 were blowing in another direction, and Gardner "returned the bill to the legislature with his almighty veto."[36] The political storm leading to Lincoln's election as president in 1860 had begun, and the antislavery members of the Know-Nothing Party were moving into the ranks of the Republican Party. This change of political issues weakened Gardner's political base and probably motivated his veto.

In his attempted appeal to strong progressive sentiments in eastern Massachusetts, Gardner added insult to the injury the veto inflicted on the towns of northern Massachusetts by declaring that it would be "simply ridiculous for the state to embark in this preposterous scheme."[37] The House side of the General Court easily overrode the Governor's veto, but the override failed by a single vote in the Senate. The Western Railroad, Daniel Harris, and the Governor had won the 1857 legislative battle.

Having been so close to victory, Haupt was devastated. Nevertheless, the lost battle proved fortuitous, as it gave the Tunnel supporters the necessary impetus to win the war. The towns of northern Massachusetts once again came to realize they had to join together and act in concert. If they failed to do so, they would have no mainline railroad, and their only connection to Boston would be by some poorly run branch line of the Western. In the fall elections of 1857, the northern towns demonstrated their new spirit. Governor Gardner received less than eight percent of the vote in the Franklin and Berkshire County towns along the Troy and Greenfield Railroad.

Dreams and Fantasies

The concern about how many years it would take to bore a tunnel through the Hoosac Mountain was detailed in the July 1857 issue of Zerah Colburn's weekly journal, *American Engineer.* Colburn had just returned from England and knew something about tunneling. He had begun his career as an apprentice draftsman in the railroad shops in Lowell. His article on tunnels discussed the rate at which a tunnel could be advanced by manpower alone. It also called attention to a significant issue engineers faced when tunneling under a high mountain. Although the digging of vertical shafts was the common technique for gaining more working faces and reducing the total time needed to drive long tunnels, it was not possible, or not easily possible, to use this technique with a mountain as high as the Hoosac. The article cited the conditions at the Hoosac as an example of a deep tunnel where shafts would not be practical. The author's calculation—based on an assumption of four miners and four drillers working continuously, twenty-four hours a day, on only the two faces—led to the conclusion that Haupt would need twenty-two years before the east and west headings of the Hoosac Tunnel would meet.[38] This estimate of time matched perfectly with an average advance of two feet per day and crews working six days per week. (Sunday was still considered sacred in Massachusetts.) Haupt was aware of this fact, and it was actually one of the reasons he accepted the challenge of the project. He viewed the Hoosac as the opportunity to develop and perfect a mechanical drilling machine. He believed it would be possible to excavate the Tunnel much more rapidly with such machines, and the Hoosac Tunnel provided him with a giant laboratory for testing his ideas. Moreover, he had already begun work on developing a mechanical drill.

In January of 1857, a tunnel-boring machine[39] Serrell had ordered and Haupt had inherited when he took over the contract arrived in North Adams. This iron contraption built by the Novelty Iron Works, located on the East River in New York City weighed more than forty tons and was powered by two forty-horsepower steam engines. The Novelty Iron Works was one of the country's great shipbuilding establishments. Four years in the future, the firm would fabricate the turret and machinery for the Union Navy's ironclad *Monitor.* This borer was another machine designed by Charles Wilson, whose earlier monster had penetrated all of twelve feet into the Hoosac Mountain before the steel of its gears and cutters disintegrated. After arriving in North Adams, Serrell's machine was carried piece by piece over the mountain to the east face of the Tunnel. This labyrinth of wheels, gears, and rock cutters cost Haupt $22,272.[40]

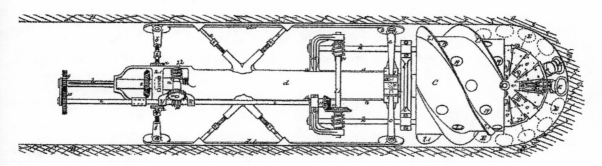

Charles Wilson's second machine for tunneling rock, U.S. Patent no. 14,483. The rotating main shaft carries a front wheel of cutters that rotate at right angles to the axis of the Tunnel.

The new machine was designed to cut an eight-foot-diameter hole in the rock by means of revolving cutter wheels mounted around a truncated cone.[41] After the pieces reached the east side of the Mountain and were assembled in late August of 1857, the workmen moved it up against the Mountain for a trial. On 2 September, the *Hoosac Valley News* reported: "[T]he borer, which was on trial last Wednesday gave a practical demonstration of its utility. . . . The machine is now being made ready for another trial."[42] Two weeks later, the machine had gone into winter quarters—the paper reported the situation as a hibernation![43] The truth was that this machine, like its forerunners, was a failure, and its rusting hulk would sit against the Mountain for years to come. Such mechanical contraptions were simply ahead of their time, by more than ninety years, in terms of engineering knowledge and industry's ability to produce steel strong enough to hold together under the stress of continually grinding and beating on rock. Later enemies of the Tunnel would point to the rusting monster as visible evidence of Haupt's failure. It would be the theme of many ridiculing articles by the Tunnel's opposition. But this was not the kind of machine Haupt envisioned. He had little faith in such monster machines, but he did believe a mechanical rock drill could be perfected.

The previous fall, while Crocker and Haupt were planning their petition to change the terms of the Loan Act, William Galbraith was also busy. On 14 November 1856,[44] he executed a contract for H. Haupt and Company to build six miles of line for the Southern Vermont Railroad (SVRR). These six miles across the southwest corner of Vermont would connect the SVRR with the Troy and Greenfield at the Massachusetts border above Williamstown. To the west, it would connect with the Troy and Boston in New York State. The Troy and Boston had reached the Vermont state line in August of 1852. [45] The linkage of the three railroads would provide a continuous line from Troy, New York, to North Adams.

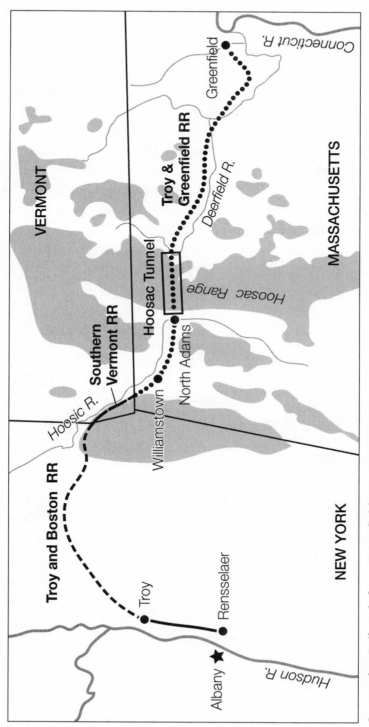

Connecting Railroads from Greenfield, MA to Troy, NY

The arrangement Galbraith made for building the Vermont line was similar to the one Haupt and Company had made in the General Court concerning the Troy and Greenfield. Again Haupt and Company was pledged to work for stock and bonds. There would be no immediate cash—only the $200,000 in company stock and bond paper. Somehow during the early part of 1857, Haupt found time to return to North Adams from Boston and lay out a route for the Southern Vermont Railroad. In addition, he designed all of the bridges while waging the fight on Beacon Hill. The survey was done, the plans were ready, but there were no subcontractors willing to work for the paper and no foundry was willing to supply the rails unless it was paid in cash.[46] The towns of Vermont wanted the railroad, but finding the money to finance the work was just as difficult as finding money for the T&G.

After Governor Gardner's veto, Haupt penned a letter to Cartwright, giving instructions on how to proceed with the work. The letter, probably at Haupt's urging, was later published in the *Weekly Transcript*. In it, he informed the people of his intention to "expend upon the seven miles west of [North] Adams, all the money the people of Adams and Williamstown are willing to contribute, and no more." This was the line from North Adams to the border between Massachusetts and Vermont. But because of "the insertion of the 'executive knife into the heart' of the tunnel project," he was forced to confine his efforts to driving the Tunnel "with all possible expedition."[47] He had to focus his efforts on gaining the first loan installment before funds ran out.

Financial Woes

The late spring and early summer of 1857 proved disastrous for Haupt and his efforts to drive the Tunnel. In May, he realized that his partner Galbraith had not been completely honest with him about Serrell and the debts of the original Serrell–Galbraith partnership. Galbraith was proving to be as much of a drag as Serrell's debts. Even though the attorney had no capital to contribute, he was an endorser and therefore liable for partnership debts equaling some $60,000. Like Lane, he had become involved in the project in hopes of a quick profit. He was not an engineer and had no stomach for a long struggle whose only reward might possibly be a place in history, so he was seeking a way out. Haupt and Galbraith reached an agreement whereby the attorney would receive ten percent of any future profits, if they should accrue from the contract; $20,000 in Troy and Greenfield Railroad Company bonds; $5,000 in Southern Vermont Railroad bonds; and, most important from Galbraith's respective, release from liability for the firm's debts.[48] After the agreement was finalized, Galbraith sent a letter to the Troy and Greenfield, resigning his directorship and asking the railroad company to appoint Haupt in his place.[49]

The effects of Governor Gardner's veto also rippled through events later in the year. The Governor had used the Tunnel bill veto as part of his reelection campaign, and the papers, while reporting on the campaign, carried news of the veto to Philadelphia. The revelation of the Governor's veto and the animosity to the Tunnel in Massachusetts impacted the ability of Dungan, Cartwright, and Company to raise the funds to meet their obligations to Haupt. In fact, even before this news reached Philadelphia, their own business had been teetering on the brink of failure. Haupt had once again become involved with a group of men who were overextended financially. The previous August, when the partnership with Haupt was formed, Dungan, Cartwright, and Company was struggling under half a million dollars of debt. They, like Galbraith and Lane, had hoped that quick Tunnel profits would be their salvation. But Governor Gardner's veto had seriously jeopardized both Haupt's tunnel boring firm and Dungan, Cartwright, and Company. In fact, there were financial difficulties nationwide—caused by events in Europe.

The ratification of the Treaty of Paris in April 1856 ended Britain's participation in the Crimean War. The war had drained European funds out of American railroads, but many European countries depended upon American crops to feed their people during the war, and the need for food powered the American economy. Things changed, almost immediately, when the war ended. Armies of men were released back to their farms. Abruptly, European purchases of American agricultural products ceased—creating a financial crisis in the United States. The crisis erupted in full force on 24 August 1857, when the Ohio Life Insurance and Trust Company's New York City office ceased operations. Across the country, banks and railroads failed. And, in the midst of all these financial failures, Haupt's beloved mother, Margaretta, died on this black day in August.

The week before the crisis, Haupt decided that the necessary length of tunnel had been excavated to qualify for the first installment of the Commonwealth bonds, so he told Cartwright to suspend all work: "This is quite as far as it is expedient for us to proceed until some portion of our expenditures shall have been returned to us."[50] Though it was later found they needed to accomplish more work before the Commonwealth money would be forthcoming, the decision proved providential. In October, one of Haupt's notes was called; before the financial crisis passed, some of his property was seized by the sheriff and sold to pay creditors. During October, while scrambling to pay his bills, Haupt moved to protect his personal property by placing the title to his home and his holding in the Clearfield Coal and Lumber Company in Alexander Derbyshire's name as security for a loan.[51] Together with Horatio Burroughs and others, Haupt and Derbyshire had been and were still business partners in numerous Pennsylvania coal properties. During this crisis, and through many others in the future, Derbyshire proved a true friend to Haupt.

When the financial situation finally caused Dungan, Cartwright, and Company to fail, two of the partners, Dungan and Steever, sought to separate themselves from the Tunnel contract. Previous partners had withdrawn or been pushed out at Haupt's urging, but this time Dungan and Steever were fearful the H. Haupt and Company liabilities would cause them further distress. The official separation came on 23 November 1857. With the exception of Cartwright, who had been in Massachusetts directing the work in the field and who stayed with Haupt, the other members of the firm had contributed little. It had been an exceedingly trying year, but Haupt was still drawn to the challenge of tunneling the Hoosac Mountain, and Governor Gardner's defeat in the fall elections gave him hope for legislative success in 1858.

Ready to try again at loosening the requirements of the 1854 Loan Act, Haupt traveled to Boston in early January 1858. This time, he had not even started his lobbying efforts before the bill died in committee. The legislature was still spooked by the financial panic of the previous year, and no one could be swayed to do anything that looked like loosening the doors to the Commonwealth's treasury. Looking elsewhere for funding help, Haupt retraced his steps to Philadelphia, and again Alexander Derbyshire came to his aid. Derbyshire offered $30,000 at six percent interest. Derbyshire's confidence and friendship was so great that he did not even require Haupt to provide any security for the loan.

Haupt and the faithful Henry Cartwright, whom Haupt always referred to as "Brother H," reviewed the situation and laid their plans for the coming year. The two men believed the $30,000 of cash in hand, together with $40,000 in credit, would carry the work forward until they qualified for the first installment of the Commonwealth loan. Derbyshire's money gave them hope for the future. Things even looked better when Derbyshire and Haupt actually signed the papers for the loan in February. Derbyshire, the constant friend, provided Haupt with $33,000 instead of the promised $30,000. Haupt was once again ready to attack the Mountain.

His old partners Dungan and Steever soon learned that Haupt was back in business and suddenly the partnership had promise. Dungan and Steever believed they could now reap some easy money. Yielding to Cartwright's exhortations on behalf of his old partners, Haupt executed a new partnership agreement in February 1858, bringing Dungan and Steever back into the Troy and Greenfield contract.[52] They were guaranteed 10 percent of any profit and had no liability for the company's debts. Why Haupt ever agreed to this renewed partnership cannot be explained rationally, but, until the day he died, Herman Haupt always seemed to have believed in the better side of all men. Galbraith, Dungan, and Steever were now hangers-on, contributing nothing but continually looking for a payout from H. Haupt and Company. The only thing Haupt gained from the new arrangement was a clause requiring Dungan and Steever to return the $125,000 in Troy and Greenfield bonds he had lent them. These were to be returned before they received any share of the profits. Yet even this was not a real gain, as Haupt was entitled to this even without the new contract.

The welcoming of Dungan and Steever back into the partnership led to a new contract with the Troy and Greenfield Railroad Company. Haupt now made a second bad move, and it would affect his later appeals in the legislature. When he executed the new contract with the railroad, H. Haupt and Company gained everything the T&G owned. Anything accruing to the Troy and Greenfield would go directly to H. Haupt and Company to pay for the tunnel work. H. Haupt would receive all payments on stock subscriptions, credits from the Commonwealth bonds, even any revenue from the operating segment of the railroad. Additionally, H. Haupt and Company would not be liable for any of the T&G's debts.[53] The Troy and Greenfield Railroad would now exist only to serve as a conduit for passing funds to Haupt's firm. As a company, the Troy and Greenfield Railroad was a myth: "Its alpha and omega was Herman Haupt."[54] The man from Pennsylvania had "lost the buffer of the Troy and Greenfield Railroad a Massachusetts company standing between him and the opposition."[55] To many in Massachusetts, Haupt was an outsider who sought to rob the Commonwealth. By the summer of 1858, Haupt was a member of the Troy and Greenfield Railroad's board of directors, the company's general agent, and its chief engineer. He was positioned just as the papers were claiming.

After the swift defeat in the legislature, Haupt turned for support to the towns connected by the railroad. In 1855, Alvah Crocker and friends had pushed a bill through the legislature, allowing towns along the railroad to subscribe to T&G stock. Haupt set out on a crusade to proclaim the benefits of the railroad in every community between Greenfield, Massachusetts, and Pownal, Vermont. As a good promoter, he first provided the newspapers in each local region with details of his future construction plans. On 27 January 1858, the *Hoosac Valley News* of North Adams announced: "A well authenticated rumor, states the Messrs. Haupt & Co., are soon to re-commence operations upon the Tunnel, and the road leading from the west side of the mountain, to the Vermont State Line."[56] Two weeks later, the *Adams Transcript* in its "Local Intelligence" column, stated: "[F]rom the State line at Williamstown, to within a mile of Adams, six miles are graded and ready for rails. All the unfinished expensive work is on the remaining mile near Adams. . . . We understand that it is the wish and intention of the contractors to finish up this mile, if funds can be raised by the company or from other sources for this purpose."[57]

Haupt followed the newspaper assault with town meetings in Buckland, Charlemont, Rowe, Heath, Florida, North Adams, and Williamstown.[58] He spoke plainly and convincingly about the need for the towns to subscribe to Troy and Greenfield stock so the railroad connections could be completed on both sides of the mountain. The meetings were successful in gaining subscriptions and, maybe more important, in building support for the work. The appeal struck a responsive chord as the towns remembered well the mistreatment received from the Governor and the General Court. The citizens of northern Massachusetts regarded those political actions as being directed at both the railroad and their towns. When Haupt made his case in Williamstown in early April, he was supported by Reverend Dr. Mark Hopkins, president of Williams College. The *Hoosac Valley News* reported: "The town voted the maximum subscription that evening and then celebrated by firing canon and ringing of church bells."[59] Though all the money was not paid in immediately, Haupt's efforts were rewarded with the towns of Massachusetts subscribing to $145,600 worth of stock. True to his pledges, the papers soon reported the work had "resumed at several points on the line of the railroad between North Adams and Pownal."[60] The money was important, but Haupt had also built vital support for future battles in the legislature. Regional fervor would translate into political collaboration in support of the railroad and the Tunnel.

To qualify for the desperately needed first loan payment, the law required Haupt to complete seven miles of railroad, including the laying of the iron rails. So Haupt went looking for a foundry to supply the necessary rails on credit. This time, he turned to family friends. Haupt and his wife were longtime friends of General John Ellis Wool of Troy, New York. Abandoning his law practice in

Troy when war broke out with Great Britain in 1812, Wool joined the U.S. Army and rose to the rank of colonel during that war. During the Mexican War, he won acclaim for superintending the organization of the Western volunteer regiments. He later served as second in command to General Zachary Taylor at the Battle of Buena Vista. In 1858, the seventy-four-year-old general was commander of the Department of the Pacific.

The general's nephew, John A. Griswold, was owner of the Rensselaer Iron Works and president of the Troy City Bank. He was very close to General Wool, having as a youth made his home with the general. Thanks to the general's intervention, Haupt was able to secure $35,000 in credit at the Troy bank for purchasing the seven miles of rails he needed. Like the builder of Haupt's tunnel-boring machine, the Novelty Iron Works, Griswold's firm would in four years be part of the syndicate building the ironclad *Monitor.*

On the fifth of June, the *Adams Transcript* announced to its readers, under the banner "Rapid Progress of the Railroad to Troy": "[T]he whole road from North Adams to New York State line is now lined with men." With a wry tone, it added that "the Western Railroad Co." would transport the rails for the line.[61] While this short railroad was being pushed as rapidly as possible, Haupt and Cartwright were also focusing their efforts beyond the first installment of the Commonwealth loan. After the first thousand feet of the Tunnel had been driven, there was the need to complete a second thousand feet of bore to qualify for the next loan installment, so the crews of sturdy Irishmen kept hammering away steadily at the bowels of the Mountain.

On the east side of the Mountain, by Haupt's calculation, progress was twenty feet per week, but the heading on the west side was another matter. Only with luck and great exertion could they advance even five feet a week, and often the Mountain reclaimed this short advance in a surge of flowing mud. As the crews advanced the West Bore, they had to place a mass of timber cribbing to support the crumbling rock. Professor Hitchcock's predictions about sound rock were not proving true. Tunneling is always dangerous work, but it was especially perilous on the west side of the Mountain, and every effort to advance the bore met a creeping soup of crumbling limestone and water. Haupt still insisted on believing the west-side miners would soon reach stable rock and their progress would improve. Meanwhile, even the requirement for another seven miles of railroad was not being neglected—the papers reported Haupt was out between Greenfield and Shelburne Falls surveying routes for the next section.

Success, Distractions, Suspension of Work

A contract was made with H. Haupt and Company, by which they agreed to complete the road and tunnel for $3,880,000; and the work was carried on at the east and west end of the tunnel until 1861, when the contractors abandoned the enterprise.
—Rev. Elias Nason, *A Gazetteer of the State of Massachusetts* (Boston: B. B. Russell, 1874), 211.

10 May 1848
Troy and Greenfield Railroad chartered

1858
Haupt and Stuart Gwynn work to develop a drill

6 October 1858
Haupt receives first bond installment

December 1858
Southern Vermont Railroad completed

26 March 1859
Revised Loan Act signed by Governor Banks

AFTER ALMOST TWO YEARS of struggle, Haupt and Cartwright finally reached the elusive goal as prescribed by the 1854 Loan Act to qualify for $100,000 of Commonwealth of Massachusetts bonds: complete seven miles of railroad and bore 1,000 feet of tunnel. In early August 1858, the *Adams Transcript* reprinted a notice from the *Greenfield Democrat* announcing that Haupt had made application "to the Governor and Council for the first installment of State aid for the Troy and Greenfield Railroad."[1] But nothing with the Hoosac Tunnel was ever easy.

A Plan for Success

The Tunnel was designed with a slight rise in elevation from the portals to the middle. At the middle there would be a short level section to connect the two inclines. These slopes provided drainage and made it easier for the mules dragging the carts to haul the excavated material away from the face of the bore.

As the work progressed, a wooden railway was laid on the Tunnel floor for the carts used to haul the blasted rock to the entrance of the bore. On the east side of the Mountain, the waste was dumped just outside of the Tunnel entrance at the edge of the Deerfield River. Haupt had plans for harnessing the waterpower of the Deerfield River, and he expected to use the waste from the Tunnel for constructing a dam.[2]

Even in the hard rock on the east side of the Mountain, water was raining from the roof of the bore and a stream flowed constantly toward the river in a ditch beside the wooden track. But Haupt and the Tunnel advocates were not worried about water. Haupt was now pondering ways to speed the work, and because he still did not have a mechanical drill, he had begun to consider shafts to open up more faces from which his miners could attack the Mountain. Writing to General Wool in September, he stated: "[T]he shafts would be but 750 feet deep, and the water to be pumped after reaching the grade of the road, and excluding surface drainage, would probably be less than 10 gallons per minute."[3]

As with his consideration of the water, Haupt did not believe ventilation would be a problem as the bore advanced. To provide fresh air for the crews deep in the Mountain, he made calculations and sized ventilation fans to push the volume of air necessary. At the East Bore, which now stretched more than 1,000 feet into the Mountain, a single mule walked in circles to power his ventilation system. The mule's motion was geared to drive a sixteen-inch-diameter fan used to force air into the Tunnel. Haupt hoped to harness the waterpower of the Deerfield River at a later date to drive his fans and power other machinery.

Sterling Bonds

Finally, in August of 1858, the physical requirements of 1,000 feet of tunnel and seven miles of track, as prescribed by the Loan Act, were accomplished. But Haupt immediately faced technical and legal hurdles before he could collect any money. First, he had to respond to questions about the quality of the ties used for the track. Then he faced a more serious matter. The Loan Act's first installment was conditioned on the Troy and Greenfield Railroad's having $600,000 of stock subscriptions, with 20 percent of the stock's par amount (the face value) actually paid to the railroad by the subscribers. Because the stockholders were paying for their stock over time most had not paid the full amount when they agreed to purchase shares. To satisfy the Loan Act the stockholders had to pay in $120,000 on their railroad for stock subscriptions before Haupt could collect the Commonwealth installment. This financial requirement had to be met.

Haupt argued that the town subscriptions, which he had worked so hard to garner, should be counted as paid-in subscriptions, but the attorney general would not accept his reasoning. Finally, he reverted to a clever sleight-of-hand maneuver.[4] The contract he had executed with the railroad in February 1858 specified that H. Haupt and Company should receive any funds paid to the T&G for stock subscriptions. The T&G had become only a pass-through agent to H. Haupt and Company. So one day he borrowed $100,000 from a bank, paid it to the Troy and Greenfield Railroad for the stock he and his partners were holding, and received $100,000 back from the railroad—per the contract requirement for payments to the contractor. The attorney general ruled that the transaction was entirely within the law,[5] but a few years later, Haupt's opponents point to this ploy as evidence that he had swindled the Commonwealth.[6]

Haupt's next set of hurdles developed within the Troy and Greenfield Railroad Company itself. First, D. N. Carpenter, president of the company, refused to hold a board vote on a motion authorizing transfer of the Commonwealth bonds to H. Haupt and Company. Despite the clauses in Haupt's contract, Carpenter wanted the T&G to keep the bonds and use the money to pay its own obligations. Haupt finally overcame his argument by agreeing to pay Carpenter's salary for a year. It was bribery, but in late August the Troy and Greenfield Railroad did present its letter to the Commonwealth, authorizing issuance of the bonds to H. Haupt and Company. When the authorization was presented to the state treasurer's office, the treasurer asked Haupt to delay three weeks so they would not have to clip a coupon off each bond. Sometimes, as with his partners, Haupt could be too accommodating; he agreed to wait.

After the postponement, Haupt arrived at the treasurer's office to receive the bonds, but the treasurer refused his demand. Elias H. Derby, who had championed and labored mightily for the Troy and Greenfield during the early fights in the General Court,[7] had entered an attachment against the company for his fees.[8] Derby had faced the best arguments of the Western Railroad crowd and had won several victories for the Troy and Greenfield Railroad, but even though he remained a champion of the T&G, he still wanted to be paid for his services. Alvah Crocker had enlisted Derby early to the cause of a railroad through the northern tier of Massachusetts, and the two had been like troubadours chanting the praises of the Fitchburg, the Vermont and Massachusetts, and now the Troy and Greenfield Railroad. In 1855, Derby had argued in favor of a Commonwealth loan to the Vermont and Massachusetts Railroad,[9] and in 1853, at the Constitutional Convention, his persuasiveness had helped to defeat the Western and its henchmen when they tried to include a clause prohibiting Commonwealth loans to private enterprises—a prohibition aimed directly at the Troy and Greenfield Railroad.

Instead of meeting Derby face to face and settling the matter, Haupt hired a lawyer to negotiate a $3,036.74 settlement.[10] Finally, after two and a half years of struggle, on 6 October 1858, H. Haupt and Company received £22,500 in sterling bonds from the Commonwealth of Massachusetts, equivalent to $110,475 because of the exchange rate at the time.[11] Haupt was no doubt happy—he may even have been ecstatic—but his lack of consideration in handling Derby's claim probably cost Haupt an important supporter. Keeping the Hoosac project going required persistence and drive, but sometimes Haupt's direct approach caused him to make unnecessary enemies or at the least to drive supporters out of the Troy and Greenfield camp. In future political battles, Derby could have done yeoman service and provided Haupt with good practical advice about Massachusetts politics.

While Haupt was in Boston struggling to collect the loan money, the first locomotive ran over the seven-mile Troy and Greenfield track west of the Hoosac Mountain. To the excitement of the residents along the line, the twenty-four-ton locomotive "Richmond" of the Pittsfield and North Adams Railroad, a branch line of the Western Railroad, ran through the little tunnel and over Haupt's bridge in North Adams as a test. But it was a seven-mile line to nowhere, so, after collecting the money from the Commonwealth, Haupt immediately turned his attention to completing the Southern Vermont Railroad, which would fill in the gap between the T&G and New York's Troy and Boston Railroad. The completion of the SVRR would finally provide a continuous railroad from Troy to North Adams.

To push construction of the Southern Vermont Railroad, Haupt moved to Pownal, Vermont, and took personal charge of the work. Winter had set in, and he had to cope with bitter cold: "Yesterday I came to Adams in one of the worst storms I have experienced for some years, the wind was driven horizontal and it was only at intervals that the eyes could be opened to see the road."[12] Now that he had received the first Commonwealth loan installment, contractors had faith in the railroad and were willing to accept railroad stocks and bonds in payment for their work, so for a time he did not have to go begging for money.

Anna Cecilia came up to Vermont from Philadelphia and created a home for the family in a boardinghouse.[13] Haupt's sons Jacob and Lewis worked with him in supervising the contractors.[14] Jacob was fifteen and Lewis was only thirteen at the time, but Lewis, like the young Loammi Baldwin sixty years earlier, was drawn to his father's work. Lewis would later graduate from West Point, seventh in a class of sixty-three, and be commissioned in the Army Corps of Engineers. He resigned from the army in August 1869 going on to spend twenty years as a professor of mathematics and engineering at the University of Pennsylvania. President McKinley, in 1897, appointed Lewis to a commission created to study the feasibility of a Nicaraguan canal linking the Atlantic and Pacific oceans. When the Panama site was finally chosen, he then served as a member of the Panama Canal Commission.

On 11 December, the *Adams Transcript* announced: "[T]he last rail of the iron track connecting this village with Troy, was laid on Friday, near the state line." The six miles of railroad[15] across the corner of Vermont was finished, and trains would now run between Troy and North Adams. Immediately Haupt refocused on the challenges of the Hoosac Mountain.

The Hoosac Tunnel work had presented Haupt with the opportunity to test his ideas about the development and manufacture of a mechanical drill, but, in the fall of 1858, Haupt wrote to General Wool, explaining he had not been "able to devote any time or attention to the introduction of machinery" into the tunneling operations.[16] The glory associated with the Tunnel challenge and the mechanical-drill idea were the two things that had originally drawn Haupt into the project. As other men draw energy from food, Haupt drew his energy from technical challenges. Now, with his finances in better shape, he sought to develop the mechanical drill he needed to speed the Tunnel work.

In 1848, Jonathan J. Couch of Philadelphia had employed Joseph W. Fowle to build a working model of a rock-drilling machine of his design. Couch and Fowle then carried out experiments with the contraption. The Couch drill was a large, unwieldy machine with its own steam boiler to provide the pressure for driving the lance. Couch's machine looked like a crossbow mounted on the back of an elephant, but it was the first patented American percussion rock-drilling machine.

While the two men were able to demonstrate their drill, and it would drill holes in a block of granite, it was not a commercial success. As with the monster tunnel-boring machines previously tried against the Hoosac Mountain, their machine was not capable of holding together when subjected to the vibrations caused by steel constantly pounding against rock. This drill and those that immediately superseded it were forever breaking down and required more mechanics to keep them operating than men required to drill the Tunnel by sweat and muscle power.

Couch rock-drilling machine, U.S. Patent no. 6237, 27 March 1849[17]

After Couch and Fowle parted ways in 1849, Fowle, a man of imagination and vision, developed his own drill, which received Patent no. 7972 on 11 March 1851. Fowle's first improvement was to abandon Couch's hollow-piston idea and attach the drill steel to the operating piston of the drill. He stated: "[T]he drilling-tool is attached directly to the cross-head of the engine. . . . [It is] an elongation in a direct line of the piston-rod."[18] Following Couch's hollow-piston idea, Haupt, together with the brilliant but erratic mechanic Stuart Gwynn, began in 1858 to develop a drill.

Legislative Success

Haupt was off to Boston in early 1859 for what was becoming the annual battle with the General Court of Massachusetts. He was once again trying to loosen the terms of the 1854 Loan Act. This time, he had two objectives: (1) he did not want to fight the battle of paid-in subscriptions the next time he applied for an installment, so he petitioned that the town subscriptions be considered as "paid-in," and (2) he returned to his 1857 request to make construction of the Tunnel and of the railroad separate requirements so he could collect portions of the loan at shorter intervals. This time his usual antagonists, Daniel Harris and the Western Railroad, made an argument contradictory to their prior pronouncements. In the past, they had argued it was impossible to drive a five-mile tunnel through the Hoosac Mountain, but the lieutenant governor and a legislative committee had visited North Adams during the summer of 1858 and had seen the progress Haupt and Cartwright were making in boring through the Mountain.

In February 1859, while the General Court was considering the Tunnel questions, Haupt's West Point classmate Captain Charles H. Bigelow visited the Tunnel with his father-in-law, ex-governor George N. Briggs. After they exited Haupt's bore, the newspapers reported that they both pronounced themselves firm believers in the "practicability of the work."[19] After graduation, Captain Bigelow had gained a commission in the Corps of Engineers, serving eleven years before resigning. He now held the chief engineer's position for the Essex Company at Lawrence, Massachusetts, under Charles S. Storrow. Briggs had served Massachusetts as Governor for seven terms between 1844 and 1851. These were men of standing in the councils of Massachusetts. When they acknowledged that the Tunnel work was possible and progressing, Harris and the Western Railroad changed their tactics and claimed Haupt was being overpaid and robbing the Commonwealth: "Mr. Haupt is building the tunnel at $75,000 per foot . . . and is going to get through the mountain so quick that he will be immensely rich."[20]

The Governor's 1857 veto had served to strengthen the solidarity of the Berkshire legislators, and the residents of northern Massachusetts towns now viewed the Western Railroad as selfish and lordly. Haupt's speaking tours and town meetings, while primarily designed to encourage stock subscriptions, had given the towns a new sense of purpose. All now comprehended that the true difficulty was to overcome the obstructionist opposition of the Western Railroad—the trouble was political and not a question of boring a hole through the Hoosac Mountain. The consequence of this realization gave Haupt his first real victory at the State House on Beacon Hill. In the Senate, Haupt's bill passed twenty-one to ten; in the House, the vote was 167 to 54. The Western Railroad men tried to amend his request, but "all the amendments, designed to fetter it, had been previously rejected almost 3 to 1."[21] On 26 March 1859, the new Republican Governor, Nathaniel P. Banks, signed the bill, which separated the payments for driving the Tunnel and building the railroad. The bill also specified construction of a single-track tunnel eighteen feet high and fourteen feet wide,[22] which matched what was in Haupt's Troy and Greenfield contract, but now the specifications were confirmed by the General Court.

A huge struggle for political leadership positions had taken place in Massachusetts during the fall 1858 elections, and this time Haupt and the

Tunnel supporters had been on the winning side. Massachusetts Republicans defeated the Know-Nothing Gardner that fall, but there was also an internal struggle in the Republican Party, which was split into two hostile camps: the Bird club (whose members held radical, extremist, and abolitionist views) and the Banks faction (which was more moderate and conservative, with a practical vision).[23] The Bird club took its name from its leader, political gadfly Francis W. Bird of Walpole, and included John A. Andrew, who would eventually succeed Banks as Governor. This group of abolitionist Republicans put forth a candidate in 1857, but most of the radicals stuck with Banks, who had an understanding of engineering work and supported the Tunnel. Early in his life, he had worked in Boston as an apprentice on Loammi Baldwin's Mill Dam.[24] Banks proved to be a stout supporter of Haupt and the Tunnel project.

Governor Banks would later have his own problems with Andrew, but it was Haupt who would suffer most from Bird and Andrew. When Banks won the Republican nomination for a second term in 1859, the radical Andrew drafted the convention's resolutions and limited his praise of Banks to only a comment on his "firmness, economy, and ability."[25] There was no love lost between the two Republicans and their respective groups.

Many of the arguments used against Haupt during the legislative battles revolved around a claim that a Pennsylvania bunch was going to make large profits at the expense of Massachusetts. Bird would later pun, in one of his pamphlets attacking the Tunnel and Haupt, along these lines.[26] To blunt some of those "outsider" allegations, and for personal reasons, Haupt moved Anna and the family to Massachusetts, taking a house in Greenfield. But he did not make a clean break with Pennsylvania, deciding to keep the house he owned outside of Philadelphia.[27]

Even with the £22,500 of Commonwealth bonds, Haupt again began to have cash problems by the summer of 1859. The Troy and Boston Railroad had signed a lease with Haupt in November of 1858 to operate its trains between Troy and North Adams, using the tracks of the Southern Vermont Railroad. As soon as Haupt had completed the construction of the Vermont link, the Troy and Boston began the service. To stimulate business, the Troy and Greenfield ran an excursion train from North Adams to Troy for its stockholders one Saturday in June.[28] But the New York men managing the railroad refused to make any payments on their $20,000-per-year lease until Haupt made improvements to both the tracks of the Southern Vermont and the seven miles of the Troy and Greenfield west of North Adams. Haupt had built expediently so the line could be opened and begin to generate revenue as soon as possible. This approach followed the practice of the Pennsylvania Railroad, which opened the Summit Tunnel in the Alleghenies to traffic and then completed the arching. Once the railroad was in service, it was much easier and cheaper to use the railroad to haul construction materials to where they were needed. Haupt seems to have adhered to this practice in constructing the Southern Vermont. Nevertheless, the Troy and Boston wanted the line upgraded immediately. Haupt would follow this same expedient practice while building the railroad on the east side of the Hoosac Mountain, and his detractors in the General Court would use it against him during future battles. They would never mention or recognize the benefits that had immediately accrued to the communities west of Greenfield. Those benefits to the mill towns were significant. In the case of North Adams, on the west side of the Mountain, the Troy and Boston had carried on its short line 1,500,000 pounds of cotton and 750,000 pounds of wool, first in raw material and then in manufactured articles, by summer's end in 1859.

The cash situation once more became so bad it forced Haupt in July to visit New York in an effort to find investors willing to take Southern Vermont Railroad bonds. His efforts were unsuccessful, so he had to resort to borrowing to meet the July expenses. In August, he was able to get a $5,000 loan in Boston. It was not much, but, by being frugal, he hoped to keep the work going another month or two. The money problem caused him to reduce the crews in the Tunnel, and he remarked, "I am sick, tired, and disgusted with financiering and with the intolerable meanness and selfishness with which it brings me in contact."[29] At the Pennsylvania Railroad, J. Edgar Thomson had handled the money matters, but now Haupt had to assume the management responsibility for the large cash flows necessary to keep the project going. It was a new task for the disciplined engineer.

The Three Stooges

At this time, Haupt was also discouraged by the struggle against the semiliquid rock at the west bore, a material he called "porridge stone." Digging into this slop was incredibly difficult and expensive work. The workmen described the job as like handling a "shovelful of ells [eels]." With the timber arching the men had to put in place to keep the header open, it was costing more than a hundred dollars for every foot he advanced the Tunnel. By the end of October, the west header had been advanced only 277 feet.

Haupt's solution to the porridge-stone problem was avoidance. Every-thing he tried had failed, so until he could devise a solution for mining this

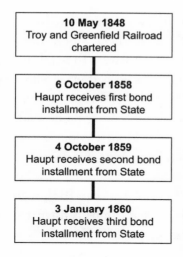

10 May 1848
Troy and Greenfield Railroad chartered

6 October 1858
Haupt receives first bond installment from State

4 October 1859
Haupt receives second bond installment from State

3 January 1860
Haupt receives third bond installment from State

difficult material, he decided to move 3,000 feet east up the Mountain and start a bore from the bottom of a shaft. George Rice[30] sold him a plot of land, which lay in the line of the Tunnel, and Haupt hired a subcontractor to begin digging a vertical shaft down to the elevation of the Tunnel. At this location, away from the face of the Mountain, he was hopeful of finding solid rock. His plan was to have crews mining in both east and west directions once the shaft reached the Tunnel grade. This, he figured, would allow him to decrease the time necessary to complete the Tunnel. The North Adams and Greenfield papers reported his plans in June 1859: "H. Haupt & Co. have a contract with a company of whom Sidney Dillon is a member, to sink a shaft in the west slope of the Hoosac Mountain 250 feet, and excavate 2,200 feet of the Tunnel on the Troy and Greenfield Railroad."[31]

At this new location, Dillon's workers encountered layers of weathered limestone with pockets of clay and sand or pockets of quicksand, and by September the *Adams Transcript* reported that the site was found to be impractical for the excavation of a shaft. Haupt then selected another location farther up the Mountain and purchased it in his own name.[32] Mr. Dull, a subcontractor, began sinking a shaft that would have to be 270 feet deep. Soon the newspapers reported: "This shaft has been sunk until what is presumed to be the solid rock diverging from the mountain has been reached, and the blacksmiths . . . [are] sharpening the drills for regular rock splitting business."[33] "Rows of cabins, not worth the name of dwellings"[34] became part of the landscape. Swarms of women and children crowded around the excavation and filled the site with chatter, but the real air of excitement came from the great sheds of machinery and the miners working day and night.

Over the years, Haupt had constantly juggled several tasks simultaneously, and mid-1859 was no exception. While trying to keep the Irish crews hammering away at the next 1,000 feet of bore and searching for other sources of funds, he was busy surveying the route of the railroad up the Deerfield River Valley from Greenfield to Shelburne Falls. He had started this task once before, but it seems he had not reached a final decision. It was an especially difficult location for a railroad because of the limited land available between the Deerfield River and the steep slopes of the mountains. He labored to find a suitable route in the incredibly picturesque but very narrow eastern end of the Deerfield Valley, which was more like a defile where it emptied into the Connecticut River. To build this stretch of railroad, he faced a challenge as difficult as any he had experienced in Pennsylvania. In fact, Haupt feared it would not be possible to construct this section of railroad for the amount allowed by the Loan Act. So yet again he made the rounds, prodding the towns on the eastern side of the Hoosac Mountain to take out stock subscriptions. He laid the groundwork by making statements to the papers: "Mr. Haupt is now engaged in making a carefully adjusted location along the valley of the Deerfield on the route prescribed [in the Loan Act], with the view to ascertain whether a line can be obtained . . . that can be constructed with the means which can be made available for that purpose."[35] His efforts at persuading the citizens of Greenfield to support the railroad were rewarded. The town subscribed to $30,000 of stock,[36] and Haupt had crews grading the line within a week of the vote. Since he and his family now resided in Greenfield, these were his fellow citizens, and they considered him a friend, not an outsider from Pennsylvania. He promised his neighbors that "the first three miles [would be] graded before cold weather."[37]

On 11 September 1859, by the light of their tallow candles,[38] the men in the Tunnel, with the help of Eliza the mule pulling the dump cart, cleared the 2,000-foot mark, and Haupt applied for his second installment of the Commonwealth loan. After a committee of the Governor's Council certified the claim, he received £11,200 on 4 October. Accusers later would claim Haupt was overpaid because the Commonwealth valued the bonds at $4.44 to the pound, but the 1859 exchange rate was $4.90 to the pound, so he actually collected close to $54,900. These statements or claims were not quite correct, because he was obliged by the Loan Act to immediately put ten percent of each payment into a sinking fund to pay off the Commonwealth bonds. Therefore, he had only $49,410 from this second payment to use in financing the work. But Haupt's success in getting the Commonwealth to make another payment created an unexpected problem.

Dungan, Steever, and Galbraith, his partners, who had invested little money and no sweat in achieving the results, smelled money. During November, an unpleasant meeting of the partners occurred in Troy, New York, with the three stooges spouting a demand for Haupt and Company to pay a dividend. They bullied him by insisting that he had to declare a dividend or they would refuse to allow him either a salary or relief from his personal liabilities.[39] Cartwright seems to have remained neutral, perhaps feeling guilty about his role in persuading Haupt to allow Dungan and Steever back into the partnership. This time, Haupt did not allow the partners to talk him into something foolish, which was fortunate, because in late December he was again strained financially.

One factor contributing to Haupt's financial problems was his employment of Stuart Gwynn to develop a mechanical rock drill. Haupt described Gwynn as "a queer fellow . . . [who] cannot be driven."[40] When Haupt hired him, Gwynn was attempting to fabricate a drill along the lines of Couch's patent for a drilling engine capable of working underwater.[41] From his shop in South Boston, Gwynn now began to work with Haupt to perfect a drill for the Hoosac Tunnel work. Haupt desperately needed a mechanical drill—a machine with the ability to drill three-inch-diameter blast holes faster than his crews of hammer men and shakers could do.

In 1864, Gwynn would obtain two drilling-machine patents of his own, but in 1859 he and Haupt were still struggling to solve a multitude of small but serious mechanical difficulties, each of which had to be overcome in order to produce a machine that could withstand the stresses of drill steel continually beating on rock. The two men did produce a working model, but, as Haupt admitted: "It revolves well whenever we start it in a new place in the rock, but stops turning as soon as it strikes a hard spot."[42] Their drill would penetrate twelve inches of hard granite in twelve minutes,[43] but it was prone to breakdowns. Also, individual drill parts were constantly breaking when the drills were tested, so Haupt knew there was much more work to do in perfecting the design.

As he had promised his neighbors in Greenfield, a three-mile section of railroad was finished on their side of the Mountain in December, so Haupt applied for payment of another loan installment on 29 December. There were no political or legal problems this time, and he received £11,300 in Commonwealth bonds on 3 January 1860.[44] This was equivalent to approximately $55,483 before the sinking-fund payment. Even with the financial trials, it had been a good year. A correspondent from Boston visited the Tunnel in September and published a story in the *Boston Bee*:

> *There we were and the rapid ringing of the hammer, the regular "thud" of the drills, and the trundling of the cars, laden with the fragments of the mountain's bowels, wrested away by the . . . steady industry of the Irishman, . . . convinces us that in spite of wiseacres in State street, and doubters in Springfield, . . . the Hoosac Mountain is being tunneled.*[45]

Haupt's problem was not that Springfield doubted the Mountain could be tunneled—it was the exact opposite. Springfield and the Western Railroad feared his success and the emergence of a rival railroad. It was a deep-rooted hostility born of fear, and that fear grew more intense with Haupt's every success.

With another payment in hand from the Commonwealth, Haupt could not forestall his greedy partners, Dungan, Steever, and Galbraith. In early January of 1860, the trio appeared unannounced at Haupt's home in Greenfield. Haupt's argument against their demands centered on the uncertain condition of the company's financial position and his claim of having no extra money.[46] Bookkeeping was not Haupt's forte, and when he produced the company books, his single-entry system of accounting failed to convince the partners there was a cash-flow problem. This time, Haupt caved to their demands. The three stooges each pocketed $10,000 in cash and $10,000 in company notes. To Cartwright, the faithful superintendent of the work, he promised $20,000, but how the payment was to be split between cash and notes was left undefined. In all probability, Cartwright was not with his former partners when they descended on Haupt, because Haupt made the $20,000 pledge in a letter to Cartwright about two months after the January meeting.

During his years at the Pennsylvania Railroad, Haupt developed and instituted a financial accounting system for the corporation. The system he established allowed the company to accurately determine cost and to manage the business. By 1851, he was carefully analyzing the operating figures and making rate recommendations to John Thomson. In 1852, when he was general superintendent, he replied in detail to "a large number of stockholders of the company requesting information in reference to the management of the road." In his responses, he said, "I confine my attention to a watchful supervision of the expenditures . . . [achieving a lower] cost of running the trains per mile than on any other important railroad."[47] Yet, his own bookkeeping during the Hoosac Tunnel years was atrocious. He never seemed to know exactly how much he owed or when his notes were due.

Following his January largesse, Haupt discovered that the company was more than $4,000 short of the cash needed to meet its April expenses. He confided to Cartwright: "I now see what I feared at the time, the making of the January dividend was a great and probably a fatal error."[48] Haupt's accommodation of the partners can be attributed to two factors: (1) his bookkeeping was terrible and never up-to-date, and (2) he did not like confrontation. The Western Railroad was a known enemy he was prepared to fight, but Dungan, Steever, and Galbraith were associates to whom he had feelings of loyalty.

At the Pennsylvania Railroad, Haupt had demonstrated his skill at identifying men of ability. Before he left for the railroad survey in Mississippi, he called Thomson's attention to Thomas A. Scott, who was then the agent at Hollidaysburg Junction. Based on Haupt's recommendation, Scott was appointed assistant superintendent in charge of the Western Division. Scott would later become president of the Pennsylvania Railroad after Thomson died. But the man who could identify management talent in Pennsylvania could not seem to pick competent and supportive partners for his own Hoosac Tunnel endeavor. He treated other men with respect and seemed to lack the ability to harbor distrust of partners.

Possibly his actions were tempered by the religious tenets formed during the time when he feared expulsion from West Point at the end of his second year. As late as 1904, he wrote to his son Charles Edgar about the foundation of his beliefs. His letter stated that Christians "imagine and persuade themselves that religion consists in joining some church and listening to sermons, . . . and forget that humility and self denying services for humanity are the distinguishing characteristics of the true Christian."[49] He was successful as a professional engineer by his education, research, and continued study, and he was challenged and excited by large, complex projects. The science of organization and management of these kinds of projects was in its infancy at the time, and while he excelled as an engineer working within an organization, he lacked the attributes to merge his technical talents with the combined roles of capitalist and manager.[50]

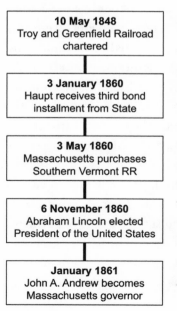

10 May 1848
Troy and Greenfield Railroad chartered

3 January 1860
Haupt receives third bond installment from State

3 May 1860
Massachusetts purchases Southern Vermont RR

6 November 1860
Abraham Lincoln elected President of the United States

January 1861
John A. Andrew becomes Massachusetts governor

Feejee the Mermaid

As sure as the arrival of cold weather across the Berkshires in January, Haupt was off in early 1860 for his yearly pilgrimage to the General Court. He was once again appealing the payment restrictions of the Loan Act. This time, he needed relief concerning the paid-in subscription requirement or he would not be able to collect a fourth installment. Even with the change to the 1854 Loan Act the previous year, which allowed the Troy and Greenfield to count the town subscriptions as paid-in, it was clear that the subscription requirement could not be met when he applied for a fourth payment under the Loan Act. Additionally, Haupt was seeking an amendment to allow smaller payments on a regular schedule. His periodic financial difficulties caused incessant anxiety and distracted him from the technical problems of tunneling the Mountain and building the railroad.

With so many newspapers reporting his success against the Mountain, the Western Railroad and Daniel Harris, for the fourth consecutive year, attacked Haupt's petitions. As they had done the year before, the issue was character and the quality of his work. The *Hoosac Valley News*, an organ supporting the effort to tunnel the Mountain, recognized these attacks on Haupt's character and stated: "[T]he *Springfield Republican* and Mr. Harris, who as the mouthpiece and ear trumpet for the Western Railroad . . . are again trying to poison the public mind regarding the honesty of Mr. Haupt."[51] As a result of the accusations, the legislature appointed a committee to investigate whether the Commonwealth had paid for an inferior railroad. The chair of this committee was Moses Kimball, a veteran member of the legislature from Boston.

Kimball happened to be a close friend of Daniel Harris, and he would, beginning in 1864, serve as a Commonwealth director on the board of the Western Railroad. But he had another interesting claim to fame. It was from Moses Kimball that the showman P. T. Barnum had leased Feejee the Mermaid. Moses and his brother David owned the Boston Museum and had acquired the mermaid from a sailor in Boston. Both Kimball and Barnum knew it was the upper body of an ape stitched onto the body of fish, but it drew great crowds and made money for the two men.

The committee's report was assembled in a manner rather like the configuration of Feejee, and its slant was predictable: The prime complaints were that the work "has not always been done in the amount and quality required" and "the stock subscriptions have not been obtained."[52] An additional concern of the committee was the Southern Vermont Railroad. Kimball and the committee believed the Commonwealth of Massachusetts should have control of the Southern Vermont. The report of innuendos Kimball shepherded through the committee did not have the intended effect, or at least the effect desired by the Western Railroad.

The friends of the Tunnel used the report to draft legislation to correct the deficiencies, but their bill also corrected the parts of the Loan Act that Haupt found troublesome. This bill passed the legislature and set a schedule of payments for the work: $30 for each foot of tunnel heading excavated and $20 for each foot of bottom excavation. It also set aside $650,000 for building the railroad from Greenfield to the Tunnel. The track construction was to be paid proportionally,[53] based on the value of work completed as compared to the total estimated cost of the line.[54] Not knowing Haupt's actual expenses—which even he did not know—the proportioning was based on the Commonwealth's estimate of values. The approved bill did include a requirement to ensure the quality and measurement of work completed. Going forward, all work would be certified by an engineer appointed by the Governor and commissioned by the Commonwealth. The bill dropped the requirement for stock subscriptions and accepted only the finished work as security. It also enumerated the construction specifications with much more exactness as a means of ensuring the quality of the Commonwealth's security. Under the Loan Act, certain costs for building the railroad and excavating the Tunnel could not be claimed. These included land damages and costs related to the sinking of shafts. "These things were outside of the items that were to be paid for, or aided by the commonwealth's money."

The manner in which the legislature chose to address the Southern Vermont Railroad issue became a windfall to Herman Haupt. The bill ordered the Troy and Greenfield Railroad to purchase the Southern Vermont and pledged the Commonwealth to supply the necessary $200,000. Because H. Haupt and Company held all of the Southern Vermont Railroad stock, Herman Haupt was richer by $200,000 on 3 May 1860 after trading the stock for the Commonwealth's money.

It did not take long for Haupt's partners to come calling with hands extended for another dividend. Steever congratulated Haupt for his success before the legislature, saying, "I never faltered in my belief that the Hoosac Tunnel enterprise would in the end be O.K. provided your life should be spared."[55] Next Dungan inquired, "How much [might I] consider at my disposal of the proceeds of these bonds?"[56] What followed was another rowdy meeting of the partners in Troy on 6 May. Haupt once again pleaded against a dividend, but this time he used a clause in their 12 February 1858 contract and some interesting logic. By the contract, profits from the Southern Vermont were to be split among the partners in the same proportion as profits from the Troy and Greenfield. Haupt argued that there were no profits on the T&G work, so there should be no dividend. When this argument failed, he quoted another clause from their partnership contract. This clause called for the profits from the Southern Vermont to be used "for carrying on the work on the Troy and Greenfield Railroad as long as this may be required for that purpose."[57] His erstwhile friends would not be deterred by such arguments.

While they admitted that there had been no profits from the T&G work, the precedent had already been set when Haupt had allowed the dividend payment from the previous issue of Commonwealth bonds. So now a dividend could be paid from the Southern Vermont funds. Finally, in frustration, Haupt paid his four partners $50,961.90.[58] He had once more agreed to questionable largesse at a time when the company owed the Commonwealth loan sinking fund $32,000. To pay this debt, Haupt desperately tried again to raise cash. Furthermore, Dungan had never returned Haupt's Troy and Greenfield bonds, as required by their contract and as he had promised when the first dividend was paid. Haupt's bookkeeping had yet again been an issue of heated discussion. This time, the matter was settled when Steever and Cartwright took the ledgers. Haupt would not see the company books again until 1875, after other men had punched a hole through the Mountain.[59]

Understandably, Haupt was distressed after the meeting, but he had only himself to blame for these confrontations. Notwithstanding his amazing largesse when he had allowed two of these men back into the company after they had jumped ship during previous financial troubles, his critical mistake was sloppy and careless bookkeeping. The partners were able to manipulate the arguments because the books were close to useless for proving profit or loss and the flow of company money could not be traced. Haupt apparently never made the effort required to keep the books up to date. When the partners questioned him about expenditures, there was nothing to support his claims of how he had used the funds. So they believed that Haupt had taken funds to pay personal debts while failing to distribute proportionate amounts to all members of the firm. The rub was that no matter how he argued his honesty, the accusation was true. Because he had procured the funds and fought the battles, Haupt felt he was entitled to take a salary from time to time and to draw what was "sufficient to keep the Sheriff off [his] back in Massachusetts."[60] The partners, of course, saw the matter differently.

Galbraith, the Harvard Law School graduate, had made an investment of not quite $15,000 in the original E. W. Serrell and Company. Later it was Galbraith who suggested that Serrell be eased out of the partnership. When drawing Lane into the first partnership, Galbraith had not honestly portrayed the financial condition of the company, and later he quite possibly used Haupt to clean up debts he and Serrell had accumulated so that he would not be held liable. In the bargains he struck removing his early partners, Galbraith was retained in the company. Over time, Haupt found Galbraith a drag, but it is not clear whether he ever distrusted the man. For Galbraith, the railroad and Tunnel business was simply an investment for personal gain. After the second dividend, he had probably recovered all of his investment and may even have made a few dollars. Years later, when Haupt was still petitioning the Massachusetts legislature for his money, Galbraith had moved on and was engaged in real estate investments in Chicago.

The situation with Dungan and Steever was quite different. They had initially supplied capital to Haupt when he was in desperate need. Later, their own debts forced them to quit contributing to the partnership, and their fear of Haupt's debt caused them to withdraw completely. Their claim on H. Haupt and Company for a dividend was based on the contention that their contributions had saved the firm from bankruptcy. They believed that if they had not contributed the funds when they did, there would have been no H. Haupt and Company in 1860. Haupt made a counterclaim, asserting that it was the failure of their firm that destroyed his credit in 1857. There was some truth in both arguments, and Haupt paid the desired dividend, but it was clear Galbraith, Dungan, and Steever saw the project only as a financial deal, whereas Haupt was pouring his life into tunneling the Hoosac Mountain. His dedication sprang primarily from his desire to be in the vanguard of the engineering profession—he was completely self-assured and thought he could solve any engineering problem. But, as evidenced by his career after the Tunnel experience, he never learned to judge financial risk. With predictable results, he continually invested his capital in ventures that promised fantastic returns.

Haupt's careless bookkeeping reflected a larger and more serious problem: He was constantly pulled in various directions and tried to handle everything personally. Over the previous four years, his partners—except for Cartwright—had never joined in the management of the work. It was Haupt alone who sought to perfect a mechanical rock drill, dealt with the labor strikes, had to continually negotiate contracts, and performed the engineering—not to mention the time he devoted to seeking relief before the General Court of Massachusetts. At least Cartwright, the accountant, did move to North Adams and was faithful in handling the day-to-day matters necessary for keeping the crews pecking at the Mountain. Maybe things would have turned out differently if he had made use of Cartwright's accounting skills.

In early June, Haupt escorted Colonel Ezra Lincoln, the newly appointed Commonwealth engineer, through the work.[61] Next came an inspection visit by Governor Banks,[62] creating considerable excitement among the workmen and in the towns on both sides of the Mountain. Banks and his party even ventured into

Haupt's dark hole, and observers of the Governor's party spoke of how "a sense of awe, if not alarm came over all as they progressed into the cavernous depths, whose darkness was only relieved by the lanterns of the guides and the tallow candles which surrounded the workmen at the farther end."[63] Banks was treated to the simultaneous firing of several holes loaded with black powder, and the *Hoosac Valley News* reported: "[Y]ou can imagine huge cannon in the distance, dealing death and woe in battle, to produce such effects." When the Governor emerged into daylight, his face clearly showed his relief at leaving the smoke and noise of the hammers. The newspaper scribbler was an unknowing prophet. In only a few short years, Banks would be facing the cannons of Southern armies belching fire from black powder; he might well have looked back to consider whether the Hoosac might have been a safer place. In fact, Stonewall Jackson would twice defeat armies under the command of Banks. Like Haupt, the men of the southern Confederacy loved him, but for a different reason—he would lose such great quantities of supplies that they dubbed him "Commissary Banks."[64]

Colonel Lincoln, charged with approving Haupt's requests for draws against the loan, was a civil engineer and surveyor with considerable experience. Prior to his appointment as Commonwealth engineer, he had prepared designs for the Boston Public Garden and for numerous streets in the city. In 1849, he had been a member of the Commission on Harbor and Back Bay Lands. The two engineers, Haupt and Lincoln, developed an amiable working relationship. Their mutual friendship would last throughout Lincoln's tenure as engineer for the Commonwealth. Under the new Tunnel Act, progress was compensated on a regular basis. Because Haupt was dealing with a Commonwealth engineer who was not biased by the Western Railroad, it was the only period when he did not have to constantly beg for funds in order to maintain progress.

Even with the financing under control, there was still a multitude of daily struggles to keep the miners advancing into the Mountain from the eastern and western sides of the mighty Hoosac. Tunneling was backbreaking work, and almost four miles of Mountain still had to be pierced. The work was dangerous and workmen were repeatedly crushed or maimed by falling rocks. At the troublesome bore on the western side of the mountain, a rock falling from the roof of the Tunnel crushed the leg of William Johnson, a native of England and veteran of the Crimean War who had signed on as a laborer only four days earlier. His leg and body were so mangled that he died of internal injuries a few hours after the accident.[65] Even outside of the Tunnel, it was dangerous work. As a possible solution to the bad ground problem on the western side, Haupt decided to extend an open cut into the Mountain as far as possible. A Thomas Burns was working in the cut when the bank collapsed on him. Buried against his crowbar, he was bruised badly.[66]

On the east side of the mountain, "Eliza," the mate to the mule walking in circles to push air to the face of the bore, steadily pulled cartloads of broken rock out of the Tunnel.[67] The bore had now passed the 1,500-foot mark. Eliza proved a more dependable worker than some of the men—in and out of the dark hole, she never faltered—but she did not have to work where the men loaded and fired the blasts of black powder. Eliza was always safely away from the face of the excavation when a blast was fired—or misfired.

Men were blown to pieces when loaded drill holes detonated before everyone could reach cover, or when a foreman went to check a hole that had not fired.[68] In only a short time, the North Adams papers would be carrying similar stories from battlefields far to the south, but the human damage from explosions is the same—"blowing off the upper portion of his head, terribly mutilating the rest of his body, and he survived . . . only twenty-four hours."[69]

Still Haupt was optimistic. He placed an order for rails from the Rensselaer Iron Works and, while speaking in Greenfield, promised his audience the Troy and Greenfield Railroad would be open to Shelburne Falls by summer 1861.[70] Haupt contracted the work of grading the alignment of the railroad to Shelburne Falls to B. N. Farren.[71] Farren had come to the tunnel work with Haupt in 1857 from Pennsylvania, and had served Haupt well as the overseer of the bore on the east side of the Mountain. Now Farren struck out on his own. He would be one of the few who stuck to the tunnel work until the very end. The overseer's job at the east bore now went to John Cartwright, the brother of H. Cartwright Haupt's faithful supporter.[72]

The War of Southern Rebellion

Freed temporarily from the need to beg constantly for funds, Haupt began to devote more attention to development of his mechanical rock drill. After he and Gwynn tested another drill in May 1860, he acknowledged in a letter to Cartwright that the test had not been a stunning success.[73] At the end of June, Gwynn had an improved model ready, and he wrote to Haupt's wife, Anna: "I do not hesitate to say, the Hoosac can be tunneled by machinery, and we have the machine to do it."[74] But in October, disaster struck when the foundry where the drill was being manufactured burned.[75] Haupt's investment of some $2,500 in the prototype drill and a summer's worth of work went up in smoke with the building.[76] But the plans were saved, and Gwynn would later have another drill manufactured, but the fire was an omen of future events for both Haupt and the country.

These were tense times both at the Tunnel and throughout the nation. One day, a discharged hand, Dan Keefe, took his grievances literally into his own hands. Standing at the eastern portal, he brandished a club and prevented the workmen from entering. He was finally removed, but then he returned and had a six-round prizefight with Harry Hawking, a shaft hand, for $2 a pot (the amount of money wagered on the fight.) Harry sent Dan to the grass four times before "the rioter took his departure."[77] A few months later, Haupt faced a similar political fight.

In the fall of 1860, as the nation raced toward civil war, the Republican Party selected Abraham Lincoln as its candidate for president. In Massachusetts, John A. Andrew, an abolitionist, was the party's candidate for Governor. On Election Day, the sixth of November, Lincoln carried Massachusetts with sixty-three percent of the vote. Andrew's margin was just as impressive—he was elected Governor with the greatest popular majority Massachusetts had ever seen.

South Carolina passed its ordinance of secession on 20 December, and Mississippi, Louisiana, Florida, Alabama, Georgia, and Texas followed suit within six weeks. Andrew would lead the Commonwealth of Massachusetts through America's bitter Civil War, and he would prove to be a stout supporter of Lincoln and the Union but not of Herman Haupt, President Lincoln's railroad engineer.

Though Lincoln would not take office until 4 March 1861, Andrew, immediately after taking his oath of office on 2 January, placed the Commonwealth's troops on alert to aid the Union. On 12 April Confederate forces opened fire on Fort Sumter and Andrew sent Massachusetts troops to the South almost instantly when Lincoln called for 75,000 volunteers. The Governor mustered the troops and sent them on their way, but it took the untiring efforts of Samuel Morse Felton to deliver them to Washington. To defend the republic in its darkest days, Felton, Loammi Baldwin's former apprentice engineer and the first engineer for Alvah Crocker's Fitchburg Railroad, rushed the Massachusetts troops southward over his Philadelphia, Wilmington, and Baltimore Railroad.

Only by his personal inventiveness in avoiding the vicious pro-South crowds in Baltimore did he achieve the movement of the Massachusetts troops to Washington. As a border state, Maryland had many Southern sympathizers, and crowds in Baltimore destroyed the railroad tracks through the city. The mobs also attacked the stopped train carrying the Massachusetts Sixth Regiment as it was being rushed to defend Washington on 19 April. In Philadelphia, Felton received this news by telegraph. Next came news that the railroad bridges south of the Susquehanna River had been burned. Anticipating such disruption, Felton had before the first trains departed for Washington conceived a plan to move the troops via an alternate route. He ordered the ferry *Maryland* to take on coal and stand by at Perryville on the Susquehanna River to carry the troops. After his railroad delivered the troops to Perryville, the *Maryland* and other boats hauled them to Annapolis, within easy reach of Washington. The next day, Felton again used this railroad/ferryboat route to move General Benjamin F. Butler's Massachusetts Eighth Regiment.[78]

Because of Andrew's and Felton's initiatives, the blue-coated troops quickly moved into the field between the Washington, D.C. and the Confederate forces forming in Virginia. Until the bridges could be rebuilt and the Baltimore crowds controlled, Felton's route moved a host of Northern regiments to strengthen the line protecting President Lincoln and the Capitol.

Previously, Felton had played a key role in spiriting Lincoln into Washington from Pennsylvania after Allan Pinkerton (of Pinkerton's National Detective Agency) reported plots to kill the president-elect even before the inauguration. As president of the Philadelphia, Wilmington, and Baltimore Railroad, Felton was able to direct Lincoln's movement south to the capital. Later, Felton would serve as a commissioner overseeing the construction of the Hoosac Tunnel, even while continuing to direct his railroad during the stress of the wartime urgency.

Looking over the change in administration he would face in January 1861, Haupt was fearful not because of the approaching sectional hostilities but because the new Governor was a friend of Francis W. Bird, his nemesis in past legislative battles. He therefore took the initiative late in 1860 and achieved a temporary success, but it was gained at the price of precipitating the termination of his Tunnel dream.

Haupt's need for enterprise began in December, when, because of illness, Ezra Lincoln was unable to inspect the Tunnel and certify payment of the November issue of bonds. When appointed Commonwealth engineer in May, Lincoln had expressed "a disinclination to accept the appointment" because he suffered from attacks of sickness in the winter months, and those "might compel me to resign."[79] He had engaged Charles L. Stevenson of Charlestown "as an assistant to make estimates in detail of the whole cost of the road to the easterly end of the Tunnel, and the various monthly estimates."[80] Stevenson was well trained, having been another of those who had learned their engineering in Loammi Baldwin's Charlestown office under Felton. While Stevenson prepared the estimates for the payments to Haupt, the Loan Act required the Commonwealth engineer to go over the work before signing the certificate.

Because of his illness, Lincoln informed Governor Banks that he felt obliged to resign. Haupt, after so many years of struggle, was not to be denied his payment because an engineer suffered from an attack of inflammatory rheumatism. He was moreover concerned because he did not know Andrew's views toward the Tunnel loan, but he definitely knew that Andrew had political friends who were fiercely opposed. Haupt's plan was to have Lincoln resign and then to have Stevenson appointed Commonwealth engineer. There were only three weeks remaining in Banks's term as Governor, so Haupt drafted a letter of resignation for Lincoln and not so subtly included words to recommend Stevenson for appointment as a replacement.

Early on the morning of 12 December, Haupt carried the letter to Banks—so early he caught the Governor eating his breakfast. Banks accepted Lincoln's resignation and, on the same morning, recommended Stevenson to the Governor's Council for confirmation. Haupt even attended the council meeting. When the recommendation was confirmed, Haupt went to the secretary of state's office to have the commission drawn. Before nightfall, a messenger delivered the commission to Banks for signature and Haupt proceeded to have Stevenson sign the estimate for the Commonwealth funds. That evening, Haupt appeared before Banks with the estimate. Only at this point did Banks have second thoughts about the matter—he was concerned that both Stevenson's commission and the estimate bore the same date. To satisfy Banks's concerns, Haupt hurried, a second time, to Lincoln to obtain a certificate of explanation. (In fact, all he did was get Lincoln to sign a blank piece of paper; Haupt wrote the explanation himself.) In one day, Haupt had managed to get both his November estimate and the appointment of an acceptable Commonwealth engineer.[81] The next day, he collected for H. Haupt and Company a credit of £26,500 ($130,115) against the Commonwealth loan.[82] In the process, however, he had managed to bruise the ego of the incoming Governor.

In January 1861, when Andrew stepped into the Governor's office, Haupt came to appreciate the consequences of his brash maneuvers. As a politician, Andrew was acutely aware of the polarization between northern and southern Massachusetts caused by the Hoosac Tunnel issue. While he had no strong personal position on the Hoosac Tunnel, he wanted to keep his political options open. But Haupt's affront to his position as Governor gave Francis Bird and the Western Railroad the opening they needed.

Primarily because of the perceived slight from Haupt, Andrew refused to sign the order for the December Commonwealth loan payment—in the press of business when leaving office, Banks had forgotten to sign the order. In addition, Commonwealth engineer Stevenson received a note from the Governor requesting he resign. When Haupt asked for a meeting, Andrew refused. He bluntly wrote to Haupt, "[I]t is clear on the face of it that the appointment of C. L. Stevenson, made as it was and when it was, ought to have been resigned to me."[83] The Governor's wrath was forestalled temporarily when the Governor's Council decided that the engineer's appointment was only to complete Lincoln's term, and Stevenson should continue in office until June. The council also affirmed continuation of the loan payments.[84]

To add to Haupt's troubles, in late December his partners were again badgering him to declare a dividend, and Dungan was insinuating he was dishonest. The partners knew H. Haupt and Company had received more than $200,000 in Commonwealth loan payments since the last dividend at the beginning of 1860. It also seems that Dungan, Cartwright, and Company was again in desperate need of cash.[85] Haupt was too exhausted to resist their demand, and a $60,000 dividend was declared in January. Half of the amount was paid in cash, with the partners accepting notes for the second half.[86] Even with the dividend, Steever the ex-partner of Haupt's father, claimed Haupt owed the company $18,000. The wrangling continued, with Steever even taking the dispute to Alexander Derbyshire. Later, when Haupt requested a $4,000 loan from Derbyshire, who had been a faithful financial supporter, he was refused. Finally, in April 1861, Haupt resigned as treasurer and general manager of the company. Cartwright then assumed those roles. The fights with the Governor and with his partners had totally distracted Haupt from the engineering aspects of building the railroad from Greenfield to the eastern end of the Tunnel.

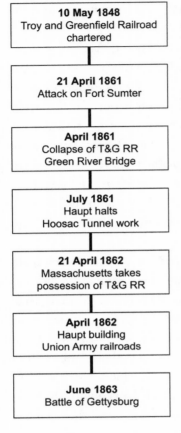

10 May 1848
Troy and Greenfield Railroad
chartered

21 April 1861
Attack on Fort Sumter

April 1861
Collapse of T&G RR
Green River Bridge

July 1861
Haupt halts
Hoosac Tunnel work

21 April 1862
Massachusetts takes
possession of T&G RR

April 1862
Haupt building
Union Army railroads

June 1863
Battle of Gettysburg

Reunion at Gettysburg

During the winter of 1860–61, the thirty miles of railroad between Greenfield and the eastern end of the Tunnel were put under subcontract. The work proceeded while Haupt was tied up in Boston first with Governor Banks and then with Governor Andrew. In addition, the dispute with his partners over dividends and his bookkeeping continued through April. In mid-February, Haupt admitted to Cartwright: "I have not seen the work or been on the road for nearly three months."[87] If he had not been so distracted, things might have been different, but in April one span of the bridge over the Green River at Greenfield collapsed, killing one workman and injuring two others.[88] Haupt had designed the bridge, which was still under construction at the time of the accident. In fact, the collapse occurred during a test when "several cars heavily loaded with iron were passing over it."[89] Before the General Court of Massachusetts, engineer Charles Stevenson would later testify that the failure was caused by "a defect in one of the iron castings,"[90] and not to any problem with the design. Stevenson stated: "[T]he designs for the bridge were submitted to Colonel Lincoln, who gave them more examination at that time. . . ." Stevenson's own review "found that, theoretically, it presented a greater amount of resistance to the weight liable to be brought upon it than is usual with the Howe and Pratt bridges, which styles are in very general use on all railroads."[91]

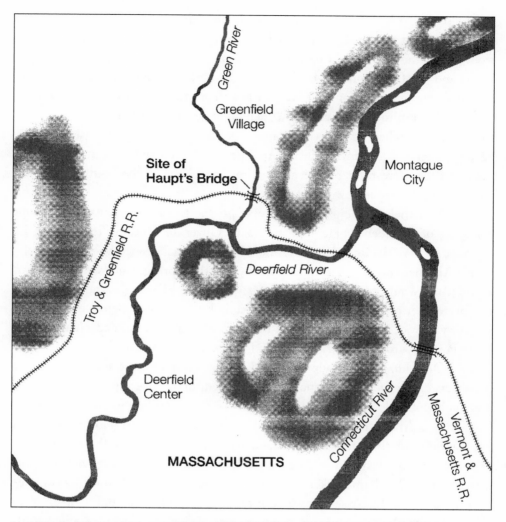

Location of Haupt's Troy and Greenfield Railroad bridge at Greenfield

On top of Haupt's troubles with Governor Andrew, the bridge accident provided Haupt's enemies and the enemies of the Tunnel yet another opportunity to undermine him. Daniel Harris, through his friend Moses Kimball, resumed the campaign against the Tunnel project. Harris wrote Kimball calling for the "removal of this rickety structure [the Green River Bridge]"[92] and Haupt. Based on Harris's harangues, Kimball was soon advising Governor Andrew that the Troy and Greenfield Railroad was a sham and the work for which the Commonwealth was paying was flawed—all of the work, not just this collapsed bridge.

Haupt seems to have been oblivious to the changing political winds. Work on the Tunnel and the grading and track laying continued, with regular payments from the Commonwealth. Engineer Stevenson was approving the monthly esti- mates and the Commonwealth bonds were being handed over to H. Haupt and Company without question. But Haupt was still pushing an extremely challenging project with a minimum of capital. When all of the dividends and expenses were totaled and matched against the Commonwealth payments, there was a measly $2,262.42 left in the bank at the end of April 1861.[93] Possibly Haupt was further distracted, as were most people at the time, by events in the South. The long, bloody Civil War was now underway.

Nonetheless, the steady progress and the timely payments gave Haupt a feeling of confidence. He even wrote to Governor Andrew to say that he expected to have the line from Greenfield to the Tunnel opened by the end of the year.[94] Another encouraging development came that spring, when Stuart Gwynn reported he would soon have another drill ready to be tested. And, because of Haupt's earlier position with the Pennsylvania Railroad, President Lincoln's new secretary of war, Simon Cameron, a Pennsylvania man, appointed Haupt to the West Point Board of Visitors for the end of the academic year.

On 5 June 1861, Haupt departed Massachusetts for the academy. During his absence, the Stevenson appointment expired, and Governor Andrew imme- diately appointed William S. Whitwell as the Commonwealth engineer.[95] Whitwell, a Massachusetts native, had worked as an engineer on railroads in Pennsylvania in the early 1830s. Then, when construction of the Boston and Worcester Railroad began in August 1832, he was employed, together with his brother-in-law William Parker, as an engineer with the B&W until its comple- tion. Parker would later serve as superintendent of the Boston and Worcester, so Whitwell was closely connected to adversaries of the Troy and Greenfield Rail- road. Whitwell's family seems to have had a close friendship with the Merricks in Philadelphia, as his sister Lucy C. Whitwell Parker recorded in her diary a trip she and her mother made to visit Mrs. Merrick, the wife of Samuel V. Merrick, the former Pennsylvania Railroad president. Whether or not any of these past associations came into play in subsequent events is not clear, but the first thing Whitwell did as the Commonwealth engineer was to send an assistant engineer, a Mr. Henche,[96] with orders to check Stevenson's June estimate.

After Henche returned with an estimate that exceeded Stevenson's, Whitwell decided to visit the project himself. Haupt, in a letter to Cartwright, claimed that Whitwell "took a dose of Harris at Springfield on the way"[97] to the

Tunnel. But when Whitwell made his own estimate, it came out even higher than the one his assistant had calculated. His solution? Ignore the calculations and cut Haupt's June earnings by approximately $40,000.

Haupt realized the seriousness of the situation, but he wanted to get whatever he could out of the Commonwealth for the finished work even though Whitwell was still questioning the previous estimate. He told Cartwright they had to be prepared to suspend all operations and discharge the workforce if the next estimate was lowered. Haupt was weary of the constant haggling, the threat to his personal finances, and the abuse he received from the Springfield and Boston press as well as from his own partners. He still yearned to be the engineer who built the longest tunnel in the country. And he believed that the Commonwealth, after investing so heavily in the undertaking, would have to continue the work. He welcomed a respite, but to pursue his objective of completing the work, he planned to pressure the administration by inserting "a proper paragraph in the papers to give a right direction to public sentiment."[98]

Haupt's supporters, the Tunnel promoters, even claimed Whitwell was in the pay of anti-Tunnel forces, but it is more likely he was simply embracing the Governor's attitude toward Haupt. Whitwell handled the June estimate for the work in a similar manner, so on 12 July 1861, nine days before the Battle of Bull Run outside of Washington, H. Haupt and Company ceased all work on the Tunnel. Haupt remained in Massachusetts, trying to overcome the political challenges and defending his performance. Francis Bird became a crusader not so much for the Western Railroad but more as someone who believed the Tunnel was a waste of Commonwealth money. In January of 1862, Haupt went before a legislative committee investigating the Troy and Greenfield Railroad Company. Shortly after that appearance, Bird penned a pamphlet, *The Road to Ruin or the Decline and Fall of the Hoosac Tunnel*, in response to Haupt's remarks. Haupt had submitted a detailed written statement about the Tunnel and Commonwealth Engineer Whitwell. After that first pamphlet, Bird unleashed his acid pen a second time and produced *Facts vs. Illusions: Being a Reply to H. Haupt's latest Misrepresentations relating to the Troy and Greenfield Railroad*.

Haupt responded by publishing his own pamphlets: *The Rise and Progress of the Hoosac Tunnel* and *Haupt's Memorial*. The *Memorial* was specifically aimed at influencing members of the legislature while he and Alvah Crocker worked to salvage the project. Governor Andrew was now committed to his position and could not change without an admission that his engineer had made mistakes. At that point, events on Southern battlefields intervened, and the man who had been accused of building a shabby bridge over the river at Greenfield was summoned to erect countless bridges quickly under hostile conditions.

In March 1862, Union General George B. McClellan began his drive up the peninsula between the York and James Rivers in Virginia to capture Richmond. At the same time, General Irvin McDowell and his Army of the Rappahannock were ordered to move southward to threaten Richmond. In response, the Confederates destroyed the northern Virginia railroads that were crucial for the movement of McDowell's supplies. So on Tuesday, 22 April 1862, Secretary of War Edwin M. Stanton wired Haupt in Boston, summoning him immediately to Washington.[99] By Thursday, Haupt was in Washington conferring with Stanton; by Saturday, he was Colonel Herman Haupt, aide-de-camp on General McDowell's staff.

Eight days after receiving the wire from Washington, Haupt was in the field directing three companies of soldiers—none of whom had had any experience in track laying or bridge building—in a struggle to put the Richmond, Fredericksburg, and Potomac Railroad back in service. By the following Sunday afternoon, General McDowell rode across Haupt's new bridge spanning Accokeek Creek.

Haupt performed nothing short of a miracle—or a series of miracles. In less than a month, he had trains running to Fredericksburg. To accomplish the feat, he had directed his workforce of soldiers in bridging the formidable Potomac Creek. On 23 May, President Lincoln made a trip over the line to visit General McDowell, after which the president remarked, "That man Haupt has built a bridge across Potomac Creek 400 feet long and nearly 100 feet high, over which trains are running every hour and, upon my word, gentlemen, there is nothing to it but beanpoles and cornstalks." In Massachusetts, they were accusing him of shoddy work, but in Washington the president was proclaiming him a genius.

In June, when General John Pope assumed command of the Union Army, he assigned control of the railroads to his Quartermaster Department and Haupt went back to Massachusetts to write his pamphlets and fight battles in the General Court. But in early August, after the Union defeat at the Battle of Cedar Mountain, the War Department telegraphed Haupt again: "Come back immediately; cannot get along without you; not a wheel moving on any of the roads." Pope had completely bungled the railroad supply system. Haupt's distinguished service this time brought him the offer of a commission as a brigadier general.

As the Confederate and Union Armies converged on Gettysburg in June of 1863, General-in-Chief Henry W. Halleck sent Haupt to restore the railroad system Confederate General Jubal A. Early was busy destroying. General Early, West Point class of 1837, had been an underclassman with Haupt. Now there would be an unfriendly reunion of classmates at Gettysburg. While Confederate General James Longstreet's artillery fired from the front lawn of Haupt's former home in Gettysburg, Haupt's rail service was supplying another classmate, Union General George G. Meade, with tons of supplies and transporting the wounded back to hospitals in York, Harrisburg, Philadelphia, and Baltimore.

Shortly after the Battle of Gettysburg, Governor Andrew decided it was time to rid himself of Haupt's continual appeals to the General Court of Massachusetts for redress. Through his influence with the administration, the Governor urged Secretary of War Stanton to try to force Haupt to relinquish his voluntary position and accept the general's commission in the Union Army. Cameron was removed by Lincoln from the Secretary of War position on 14 January 1862 and sent to Russia as a minister. Stanton had assumed the Secretary of War duties on 15 January 1862. Both the Governor and the secretary misjudged their man. Haupt decided that his honor was under attack in Massachusetts, so he refused the commission and retired from army service. His personal battlefield was in Massachusetts, so he returned there to continue his fight with the Governor. It would be a long-drawn-out affair, and he would never return to the Hoosac Tunnel work. At the time, however, he quipped to friends that he was the only man "ever guilty of the crime of refusing to become a general."

Haupt's fate regarding the Tunnel was sealed. The day before he received Stanton's first telegraph and journeyed to Washington, the Massachusetts legislature, on 21 April 1862, approved the appointment of three commissioners to report on the most economical method for completing the Tunnel. While the commissioners' section of the bill did not eliminate the possibility of Haupt's return, a second part authorized the Governor "to take possession of the railroad under the mortgages."[100] But Alvah Crocker and the Hoosac Tunnel supporters managed to insert a small paragraph into the bill granting H. Haupt and Company the right of redemption—the legal right of a mortgagor to reclaim property by paying an amount equal to the fair market value of the assets securing the lien, in this case securing the Massachusetts bonds—for ten years.

9

A Line of Baldwin-Trained Engineers

When publishers no longer steal,
And pay for what they stole before,—
When the first locomotive's wheel
Rolls through the Hoosac tunnel's bore;—
TILL then let Cumming a blaze away,
And Miller's saints blow up the globe;
But when you see that blessed day,
THEN order your ascension robe!

—Oliver Wendell Holmes, "Latter-Day
Warnings," in *The Complete Poetical Works of Oliver
Wendell Holmes*, 1908 ed., 154.[1]

RANCIS "FRANK" BIRD AND the leaders of the Western Railroad had misread their man. Governor John Andrew might not have appreciated those who dared to trample on his prerogatives, but he was too much the consummate politician to turn his back on the citizens and towns across the northern tier of Massachusetts. Or, perhaps more important, he heeded the money men of Boston. One of them, John Murray Forbes, a leading Boston businessman who always "worked in the background, usually without status or position,"[2] was Andrew's strong right arm during the Civil War era. Forbes, who had made his fortune as a China trader while still a young man, was now dealing in railroad stocks. He was used to thinking in terms of trade routes across vast distances, around the globe to Canton and Hong Kong.[3] The idea of a through railroad from Boston to Albany was something Forbes clearly understood. In fact, he was already thinking of rails well beyond Albany.

Whether it was for personal reasons or to satisfy the Western Railroad is not clear, but Andrew had forced Haupt's removal from the Hoosac Tunnel

230

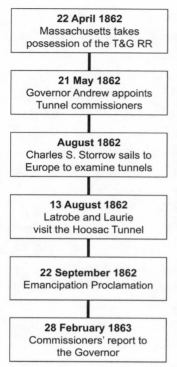

22 April 1862
Massachusetts takes possession of the T&G RR

21 May 1862
Governor Andrew appoints Tunnel commissioners

August 1862
Charles S. Storrow sails to Europe to examine tunnels

13 August 1862
Latrobe and Laurie visit the Hoosac Tunnel

22 September 1862
Emancipation Proclamation

28 February 1863
Commissioners' report to the Governor

project. His payback came in the 1861 election, when the citizens in the northern towns along the railroad refused to vote for him. Those were the same voters who swept him into the Governor's mansion by a four-to-one margin in the 1860 election. So while the Union ironclad *Monitor* loaded its cannons with black powder and fought the Confederate ironclad *Merrimac* (CSS *Virginia*) off Loammi Baldwin's dry dock in Norfolk, Virginia, another battle raged in the Massachusetts legislature. This battle would soon put Baldwin-trained engineers in charge of the Tunnel work.

When Herman Haupt appeared in Boston to expound his claims against the Commonwealth, the engagement with his detractors was as fiery as the shots of the *Monitor* and the *Merrimac*. The opposition sought every opportunity to vilify both Haupt and the Troy and Greenfield Railroad, but the Massachusetts legislators were unable to reach a decision. Finally, on 21 April, a compromise bill took the contract from Haupt and suspended the work, pending the findings of three commissioners appointed by the Governor [4] to investigate the project and recommend a course of action. The bill gave Governor Andrew the perfect solution for satisfying all parties to the argument while appearing to be completely neutral. Andrew gained political cover from any future Tunnel decision; Alvah Crocker gained time to organize his Tunnel supporters; and Frank Bird, together with the Western Railroad gang, hoped the ravages of nature would wreck everything Haupt had accomplished and literally close the Hoosac bore with crumbling rock and water and thereby shut down the Tunnel dream. They expected rain and snowmelt to wash away whole sections of the railroad embankment Haupt had hastily built between Greenfield and the Tunnel. It was similarly their expectation that the Tunnel would fill with water, especially the work on the west side of the Mountain and the water would speed the rotting of the timber cribbing used to support Haupt's bore into the porridge stone of the Hoosac Mountain's western slope. Bird and friends therefore anticipated the mass of the mountain soon collapsing the weak porridge stone and sealing the Hoosac bore forever.

Frank Bird, standing firm with the opposition, considered Governor Andrew an ally and quickly wrote, confirming his belief: "The universal impression entertained by his most intimate friends, was that he was opposed to the tunnel."[5] Bird's opinion gave the foes of the Tunnel confidence, but the struggle had taken many turns over the years, so Bird pressed his immediate advantage. What nature did not attack, Bird's pen sought to bury under sarcastic words in the pamphlets he gleefully scribbled. In retrospect, he acknowledged the truth of the matter four years later: "Although the act [which launched the commissioners' investigation] nominally seemed to contemplate the prosecution of the work on the road and Tunnel by the State, . . . it made such prosecution subject, in both cases, to the approval of the Governor and Council."[6] To contend with the physical fact of Haupt's success, as evidenced by a hole burrowed half a mile into the eastern flank of the Mountain, Bird sought to spread confusion. The gaping hole proved the Tunnel was feasible. Consequently, Bird who had been a divinity student at Brown University,[7] called upon his preaching talents and transformed himself into a showman. Standing in front of a legislator he had buttonholed, he would audibly rub two stones together in his hand while challenging the man with the question, "Sir, would you build a railroad into a closet?"

The rickety track from Greenfield to Shelburne Falls, and the graded roadbed scraped out of the hillsides from Shelburne Falls westward toward the black hole in the flank of the Hoosac Mountain, quickly began to deteriorate as the clouds hugging the Mountain dispensed rain and snow. The spring rains quickly flooded Haupt's 310-foot-deep west shaft and, for lack of maintenance, his pumping machinery died a rusty death. Each succeeding day, the weight of the Mountain twisted and bent the mass of wooden timbers supporting the 600 feet of Tunnel into the mass of the porridge stone on the Hoosac's west flank. It seemed the miners had been correct in calling the stuff a mass of "ells," and now the "ells" were trying mightily to escape Haupt's timber cage. The sorry condition of the railroad and its continual deterioration were easy targets for Bird's arguments. Even so, the first 100-foot hole into the porridge stone was now supported by a tube of bricks. This tube, built by B. N. Farren, whom Haupt had brought from Pennsylvania, remained as proof that the "ells" of the Mountain could be defeated.

The Commissioners

After the Tunnel legislation passed, the two sides directed their attention toward influencing the appointment of the commissioners. As the letters poured into the Governor's office faster than the snow and rain falling on the Mountain, the deft politician Andrew coolly handled the situation. Practicing great care, he proceeded with the selection of commissioners. In a letter from Philadelphia, Bird advised the Governor to create a commission with no engineer.[8] It was the kind of thinking Loammi Baldwin had encountered in Pennsylvania when trying to build the Union Canal and having to explain why the locks should be a certain width. Decisions by men who did not understand engineering principles had cost Pennsylvania dearly.

Others wrote letters with recommendations for specific individuals and stated their bias, ". . . although a Tunnel Man Judge R. has not at all been mixed up with the lobbying."[9] Some were more subtle, pleading the case based on political party affiliation, but their nominations were suspect from the perspective of the Tunnel supporters. At the end of May, Andrew sent invitations to three extremely qualified and respected railroad men. Each gave the outward appearance of being without bias toward either the Tunnel or the Western Railroad. Each had years of railroad experience and none had had any involvement in the previous Tunnel fights. Two had mastered the engineering profession by working in Loammi Baldwin's Charlestown office. At the time of their appointments, all three were heavily engaged in running their respective railroads, yet each willingly accepted the Governor's request to serve.

At forty-two years of age, John Woods Brooks was the youngest commissioner and a man "unknown outside of a very narrow circle in Boston."[10] His early mentor in Baldwin's office, and now a fellow commissioner, was Samuel M. Felton, age fifty-two. The oldest commissioner was Alexander Holmes, age fifty-nine. Possibly because Brooks was close at hand, with an office in Boston, he served as the commission chair. But the position also may have been conferred on him because of his close working relationship with John Murray Forbes. At the time of his appointment, Brooks was involved with multiple railroads across the Midwest, all of which were controlled by Forbes and his Boston associates. Brooks was president of the Michigan Central Railroad; a director for the Chicago, Burlington, and Quincy Railroad in Illinois; and a director for the Hannibal and St. Joseph Railroad in Missouri. All of these roads were controlled by what came to be termed "the Forbes group," and Brooks served as their operations man in the field. He was a Massachusetts native, but because most of his work was in the Midwest, he made Detroit his home from 1846 until 1857.

The other two commissioners were also railroad presidents. Alexander Holmes was president of the Old Colony Railroad in Massachusetts and Rhode Island and Samuel M. Felton was president of the Philadelphia, Wilmington, and

Baltimore Railroad. Felton had a strong connection to Crocker and the Fitchburg Railroad, having been the road's first chief engineer and its superintendent for five years before moving to Philadelphia in 1851—a move precipitated by another group of Boston financial men.

The War of Rebellion, as the Civil War was referred to in Massachusetts, now overshadowed the Tunnel issue. Governor Andrew was admired as a strong supporter of the Union cause, but he came to realize that his dismissal of Haupt had turned the Tunnel advocates against him, and they were bent on turning him out of office. The citizens of the northern part of the Commonwealth considered Andrew a traitor as evil as any man in the Southern armies fighting against the Union. So as the Tunnel commissioners quietly went to work on the engineering issues in the fall of 1862, the Governor set to work repairing the political fallout from his decision to force the Troy and Greenfield Railroad into foreclosure and thereby bring the Tunnel work to a halt. With the November elections drawing near, he visited the Tunnel, spoke in North Adams, and assured the residents that their Tunnel was of great commercial importance to Massachusetts. He promised to give a fair hearing to the matter of completing the project, and, as a clincher, he stated his belief that the balance of the $2 million loan would be sufficient to complete the work.[11]

Alvah Crocker, in a speech before the Massachusetts Senate in the spring of 1862, had attacked the Governor and the Western Railroad for joining forces to "bitterly oppose the Troy and Greenfield road." He defended Haupt and Cartwright as having been "much maligned" by these same forces.[12] In September, however, after the commissioners were appointed, Crocker's attitude changed, and he publicly stated: "Governor Andrew was not to blame for the discontinuance of the work."[13]

To the public and even to the enemies of the Tunnel, one important fact seems to have gone unnoticed. Commissioners Brooks and Felton held their railroad positions at the pleasure of the mercantile aristocracy of Boston, an aristocracy with major investments in a network of railroads not just in Massachusetts but across the country. These same men of finance also held stock in Holmes's Old Colony Railroad.[14] This aristocracy, including John M. Forbes, was composed of the men whom Dr. Oliver Wendell Holmes Sr. would later label "Boston Brahmins."[15]

Pagan Capitalists

During the period when Samuel Felton was running Loammi Baldwin's Charlestown office, John Brooks interned under Felton and Baldwin. Brooks later gained his first railroad construction experience working on the Boston and Maine Railroad.[16] He must have proved himself a capable engineer, because he was soon appointed chief engineer of the Boston and Maine. This was only three years after he had entered Baldwin's office, and he had yet to celebrate his twenty-first birthday. He was, therefore, a chief engineer three years before Felton held a similar position with the Fitchburg Railroad. In 1843, Brooks moved to upstate New York to become superintendent of the Auburn and Rochester Railroad (A&R), at an annual salary of $3,000.[17] It is not clear whether this move was made simply to accept the lucrative engineering offer or whether Brooks was sent explicitly to protect the interest of Boston financiers who had become interested in New York railroads. At the time, the Boston firm of J. E. Thayer and Brother—the same men who would later send Felton to protect their investment in the Philadelphia, Wilmington, and Baltimore Railroad—held a large block of Auburn and Rochester stock.[18] Additionally, David A. Neal of Salem, who was head of the Eastern Railroad in Massachusetts, probably held an interest in the Auburn and Rochester. In 1846, he converted the Auburn and Rochester Railroad bonds he was then holding into stock.[19] William Sturgis, another Boston financier, was a director of the Attica and Buffalo Railroad in 1843. Through his firm, Bryant & Sturgis, John M. Forbes was drawn into New York railroad investments for the first time in 1843.

Prior to his move to New York, John Brooks married Charlotte L. Dean and removed himself from engineering for a spell. From 1840 until he moved to the Auburn and Rochester Railroad, he was involved primarily in a lumbering business, so something had enticed him to resume engineering work and make the 400-mile move. Had the money men of Boston sent him as a scout? He made the move less than a year after Erastus Corning first proposed joining the separate railroads running across New York State into a single through line. Or did his wife's family, who still had connections in New York, propose something to beckon him westward? Charlotte's father had served as a Universalist itinerant preacher in central New York before moving to Boston in 1813.

The timing of Brooks's move to New York seemed to be aligned with the efforts Erastus Corning had made to create a railroad link across New York from Albany on the Hudson River to Buffalo on Lake Erie. Corning, an Albany merchant, financier, and owner of an extensive ironworks, saw

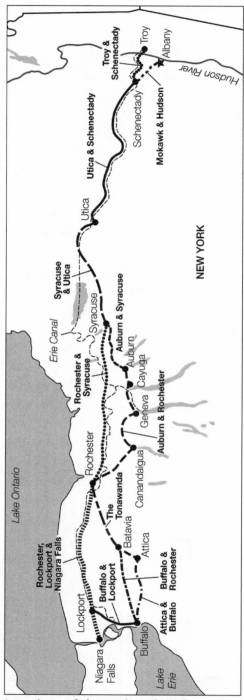

Locations of the early railroads across New York

railroads as an expanding market for his iron. Men like him, who were already trading with the communities of the "old northwest," recognized the great commercial value of railroads. He purchased his first railroad stock in 1831—joint ownership of 130 Mohawk and Hudson Railroad shares.[20] Seizing opportunities, he became a major investor in other New York railroads and then served as president of the Utica and Schenectady Railroad.

There was another connection or question about Brooks's motives for joining the Auburn and Rochester. Robert Higham, an assistant engineer with Corning's Utica and Schenectady Railroad during its construction, moved next as engineer to the Auburn and Rochester. After completing the road's construction, he was retained as superintendent. Then Brooks arrived to replace Corning's former engineer and superintendent. Just as he had done with the management at the Boston and Maine, Brooks and Corning soon built a close relationship of respect and trust.

Ahead of his time, Corning understood the potential of one continuous railroad across New York, but he needed additional capital to bring his vision to fruition.[21] Exactly how the connection was initially made is not clear, but, in the early 1840s, Boston capital began to support Corning's railroad ventures. John Forbes, together with John E. and Nathaniel Thayer and their firm J. E. Thayer and Brother, were soon tightly bound to Corning as investment partners in New York railroads. These men represented some of Boston's leading financiers. John E. Thayer had been instrumental in establishing the Boston Stock Exchange in 1834. The firm J. E. Thayer and Brother was organized in 1839, when his younger brother, Nathaniel, joined the business.

When the Thayers began investing in New York railroads, they were already involved with the Philadelphia, Wilmington, and Baltimore Railroad. In fact, their firm served as the transfer agent for that railroad, which was completely controlled by Boston men. Perhaps the Corning-Thayer relationship originated through social connections, as Nathaniel's wife, Cornelia, was the daughter of Stephen van Rensselaer, whose estate was in Troy, New York,[22] where Corning's first mercantile business was located.

In 1844 and 1845, the Thayers helped Corning market Utica and Schenectady Railroad securities in Boston. During this same period, Bostonians, led by the Thayers, were investing heavily in the Auburn and Rochester, Auburn and Syracuse, Attica and Buffalo, and Syracuse and Utica Railroads. These short lines would in only a few more years be combined and become Corning's New York Central Railroad.[23] Then, suddenly, all of these men set their sights farther west.

Seeking to improve cross-state transportation, Michigan yearned to replicate the railroad systems of the Eastern Seaboard states, so its leaders reached into the state's coffers in the 1830s and began building three east–west railroads across the wilds of the state. But the financial panic of 1837 intervened and doomed Michigan's plans. Halting all work on two of the three roads,[24] Michigan concentrated on constructing its central railroad, which was projected to run from Detroit to St. Joseph on Lake Michigan. To complete their route westward, the Michigan planners envisioned a steamboat connection between St. Joseph and Chicago. At the time, Chicago was a not-so-booming town of fewer than 25,000 souls. By January 1846, the central road—or Michigan Central Railroad, as it came to be called—had been pushed 143 miles westward from Detroit to Kalamazoo. Corning and the Thayers were both holders of the internal-improvement bonds the State of Michigan had issued to finance its railroad dream. In addition, Corning had another connection with the Michigan Central. Early railroads did not have solid iron rails—they used wooden rails, on top of which iron straps or bands were nailed. The iron straps[25] for the Michigan Central—a half-inch thick by two and a quarter inches wide—had come from Corning's Albany ironworks, and Michigan still owed him for that iron.

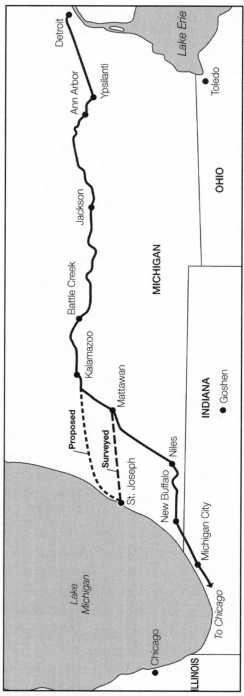

Proposed, surveyed, and built routes of the Michigan Central Railroad

The Michigan Central was a success in terms of business, but it had been constructed poorly, so it was literally falling apart under the trains. The strap rails were too flimsy for the heavy loads the road carried, and they had to be replaced frequently—or, often, after an accident. The top of the spike holding the strap iron on the wooden rail would wear off and the end of the iron would stick up in the air. When the next train came over the line, the broken rail would ride over the wheel of a car and pierce the floor where passengers were sitting. The rail would bite a passenger like a snake, so, during early railroad days, these offensive pieces of iron were known as "snakeheads." On the Portsmouth and Roanoke Railroad, a snakehead derailed a locomotive and tore into the first coach, fatally injuring two passengers. The *Frisco-Man*, a news sheet of the St. Louis–San Francisco Railway Company, reprinted a 20 May 1844 item describing a snakehead accident: "The cars on the railroad a short distance east of Rome, New York, came in contact with a snakehead on Saturday morning, which threw several of the passenger cars and the mail car off the track, the crash was tremendous and the cars were torn to splinters."[26]

So while the state slowly pushed its strap-rail line toward St. Joseph, the tail of the road was crumbling into nests of snakeheads. When Forbes rode over the line in 1847, he wrote, "We found the road in the most deplorable condition, the iron broken up often into pieces not a foot long, and sometimes we could not see any iron for some feet, only wood."[27] The dim prospect of the railroad ever being completed caused some in Detroit to agitate for the sale of the road to private interests. In 1844, an unsuccessful attempt was made to authorize the sale of the three state-owned railroads.

In the latter part of 1845, John Brooks went to Michigan to examine the Michigan Central. He carried letters of introduction from the Thayers in Boston and Corning in Albany,[28] so it might be presumed he was sent to protect their investment in the road. After his inspection of the Michigan Central, Brooks traveled to Boston and provided a detailed appraisal of the road.[29] He saw an opportunity in Michigan, and his encouraging report stressed the financial possibilities of the Michigan Central. Based on Brooks's assessment, the Thayers and Corning probably viewed purchase of the Michigan Central as an investment opportunity and as a way to protect the money they had already sunk into the State of Michigan bonds. In mid-January 1846, the Thayers wrote to Henry B. Gibson, president of the Auburn and Rochester, giving instructions for Brooks to return to Michigan and attempt to purchase the Michigan Central. They also sent Brooks a draft of the charter he was to wrangle from the Michigan legislature.[30] With the help of James F. Joy, a Detroit lawyer who would work with Brooks on many future railroad deals, the desired legislation passed in March 1846.[31]

During his struggles with the legislature, Brooks kept Corning and the Thayers informed about his progress, and it seemed there was a new crisis every day. An attempt was even made to amend the bill to keep the pagan capitalists of the East from attempting to run trains "on the Sabbath" and to require the directors to attend church at least twice every Sunday.[32]

Forbes and Brooks

Even though Brooks was close to Corning, evidence of his true allegiance is gleaned from the list of names he slipped into the Michigan railroad bill as incorporators. It contained only names of Boston men, including John E. Thayer and John Murray Forbes. Corning immediately protested, so one Bostonian was dropped to make way for the man from Albany. The purchase price was $2 million, but the State of Michigan would accept its outstanding improvement bonds as payment. This provision allowed the State to retire some of its debt and effectively gave the purchasers a 30 percent discount by using the depreciated bonds.[33]

The purchasers had to guarantee that the tracks would be completed as far as the shore of Lake Michigan in three years and to replace the old strap rails with iron rails weighing sixty pounds to the yard. At first, there was difficulty selling the stock of the new Michigan Central, but once John Forbes agreed to accept the presidency, the subscription was easily completed.

On 23 September 1846, the new owners took possession of their property. John Brooks was named superintendent by his Boston sponsors and given the task of rebuilding the shabby property and completing the last fifty-six miles to Lake Michigan. From the start, Forbes displayed strong confidence in Brooks, and he was not disappointed. Their first year of working together cemented their union of trust and reliance.

Several months later, the State of Michigan sold its other partially built railroad, the Michigan Southern, to a group of New York investors. Interestingly, George Bliss of Springfield, Massachusetts, late of the Western Railroad, was appointed head of the new Michigan Southern.[34] Bliss, originally a lawyer, had been instrumental in wringing financial support from the Commonwealth of Massachusetts for the Western Railroad in 1835.[35] Initially he served as a director and agent of the Western Railroad, but from 1842 until February 1846, he was president.[36] By 1851, Forbes and Brooks realized they were in a race to Chicago with this southern rival led by a Western Railroad man. Brooks managed to get his first train into Chicago on 21 May 1852, one day ahead of the challenger.[37] A year later, Forbes's evaluation of Brooks clearly showed his respect for his superintendent: "The more I see of the difficulty of getting good managers for other roads and other large things, the more am I satisfied with Brooks."

Soon Forbes and Brooks were applying the lessons learned in building and driving the Michigan Central into Chicago to other railroads reaching farther west. Even before they reached Chicago, the Forbes group had purchased an interest in the Aurora Branch Railroad. This railroad had been chartered by the Illinois General Assembly in February 1849 and opened in September 1850. On 22 June 1852 it was renamed the Chicago and Aurora Railroad.

It was only twelve miles long, but it had trackage rights into Chicago. In February 1852, Brooks was named a director of this minuscule road. At almost the same time, however, an unrelated opportunity in Michigan temporally diverted the attention of Forbes, Corning, and Brooks. It proved a severe test, but it also proved their ability to complete large projects in remote areas.

The copper boom on Lake Superior spurred the State of Michigan in 1853 to offer 750,000 acres of land in exchange for construction of a ship canal and locks on the St. Mary's River (in French, Ste. Marie), which connects Lakes Superior and Huron. The river is only sixty-three miles long, but it drops twenty-one feet in a single stretch of only three-quarters of a mile. This short section of the river is known as Sault Ste. Marie (*Sault* in Old French means "leap" or "waterfall"), and the river at this location literally leaped over the rocks. Construction of the desired canal and locks at Sault Ste. Marie would allow ore-carrying ships to pass between the two lakes. Forbes, Corning, Brooks, and Joy, their lawyer, together with Erastus Fairbanks of Vermont and others, organized the Saint Mary's Falls Ship Canal Company in New York. With Brooks as their engineer, they accepted Michigan's challenge to build the canal and locks in a short two years—short because severe winter weather at this Canadian border location limits the work season.

The general agent whom Forbes and Corning sent to Sault Ste. Marie had no engineering experience, so the ultimate responsibility for the project's success fell on Brooks. The agent handled the hiring and paying of the laborers needed to perform the work, and the purchasing of materials and supplies, but Brooks had to provide the engineering skill. In a paper read before the American Society of Civil Engineers, an engineer who supervised construction of a second set of locks at Sault Ste. Marie twenty years later described the challenge Brooks inherited: "The locality was almost as uncivilized; the resources of the surrounding country were almost as undeveloped, as when white men first set eyes upon it two centuries before."

Brooks, using knowledge from Loammi Baldwin's experience in building the dry docks for the U.S. Navy, planned and pushed the work at Sault Ste. Marie. But even before the Sault Ste. Marie locks were finished, Forbes and Brooks began to work on building a railroad westward from Chicago. The Chicago, Burlington, and Quincy Railroad was organized in 1855.[38] The corporation was in fact only a name change authorized by the Illinois General Assembly for the Chicago and Aurora Railroad, but Forbes would use it to absorb and unite several railroads that were already under the umbrella of his financial group, which now controlled a through railroad from Detroit to the Mississippi River at the Iowa border. Forbes, an extremely shrewd and well-informed financier, was fully committed to the concept of an east–west railroad system[39]—the same type of operation Alvah Crocker was striving to build on a smaller scale between Boston and Albany.

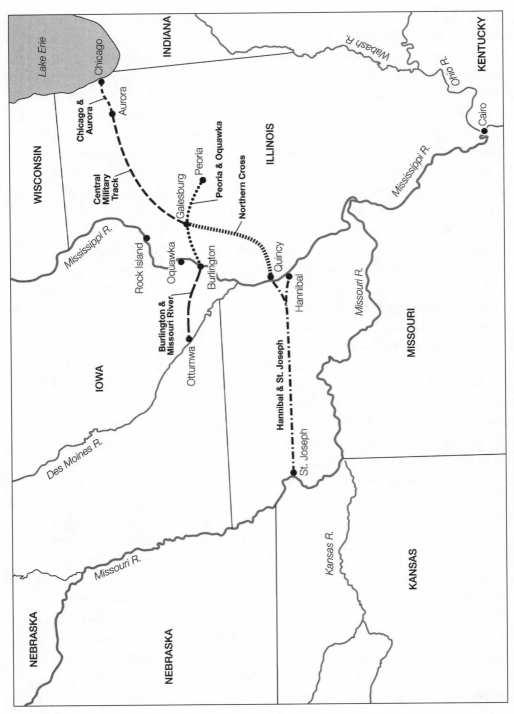

The Forbes railroad system west of Chicago prior to the Civil War

From the Mississippi River, Brooks next pushed the rails of Forbes's Hannibal and St. Joseph Railroad westward across Missouri. The iron bands reached St. Joseph on the Missouri River in February of 1859.[40] At the same time, the Burlington and Missouri River Railroad in Iowa, which was being shepherded by engineer Thomas Doane, reached Ottumwa on the Des Moines River.[41] Twenty months later, in 1862, when Brooks was appointed a commissioner to investigate the Hoosac Tunnel, he was serving as president of Forbes's Michigan Central Railroad but living just south of Boston in Milton.[42] "Brooks was a man Forbes admired extravagantly,"[43] and in 1857 he had persuaded Brooks to settle on his estate in Milton. Though his office was in Boston, Brooks was an active executive who made frequent trips west to the numerous railroad properties owned by the Forbes group.[44]

Charles S. Storrow

The formal document appointing the commissioners for the Hoosac Tunnel was issued by the secretary of the Commonwealth on 22 May 1862. It directed the commissioners to report on "the most economical, practical, and advantageous method of completing said road and tunnel."[45] The next day, Governor Andrew sent a personal letter to Samuel Felton, whose Philadelphia, Wilmington, and Baltimore Railroad was then serving as the primary route for delivering troops from northeastern states to Washington and the critical theater of war in Virginia. The Governor expressed his appreciation for the fact that Felton was occupied with the cause of the country (the Civil War) because of his position as president of a vital railroad, but he still hoped to have his judgment and experience to guide him concerning the Tunnel.[46]

In late February of 1861, Felton had secretly and safely delivered President-elect Abraham Lincoln to Washington by delaying the regular night train on the pretense that a package of important documents needed to be sent to Washington.[47] The individuals conspiring to assassinate the president-elect during those days were keeping a lookout for the special presidential train. By secretly placing Lincoln on the regular train, Felton left the conspirators waiting for a train that never appeared. The heavy burden of delivering troops during the war would finally compel Felton to retire after a stroke led to his paralysis in the fall of 1864. In May 1862, when Governor Andrew originally sought his services for the Hoosac Tunnel, Felton was preoccupied with directing the movement of federal troops via his railroad in order to stop General Stonewall Jackson in the Shenandoah Valley. Additionally, his Philadelphia, Wilmington, and Baltimore

Railroad was then moving supplies to Washington in support of General George McClellan's Peninsula Campaign against Richmond.

Alvah Crocker, whom Governor Andrew had appointed to manage the care of wounded Massachusetts soldiers,[48] was also feeling the pressure of the war, but he found time to write Felton, the builder of his Fitchburg Railroad, on 25 May 1862, asking him not to decline the appointment.[49] Besides being urged to accept the commission, Felton was besieged by young engineers who were looking for positions with the commission's prominent engineers.[50] Several consulting engineers would be hired to assist the commissioners, and they, too, would be engineers of stature.

On 9 June, John Brooks wrote to Felton seeking a date for a meeting in Massachusetts. In the letter, Brooks noted that he was "sorry for the job but glad of the company."[51] Things then began to move quickly. Brooks and Alexander Holmes approached the Governor about hiring Charles S. Storrow,[52] another engineer who had been mentored and inspired in Loammi Baldwin's Charlestown office. The two men wanted to send Storrow abroad to gather recent information on the most economical methods for driving tunnels.[53] The Governor approved the request and Storrow departed his home on 28 July to obtain reliable data on European experiences.[54]

Brooks and Felton could not have found anyone better prepared for the mission to Europe. Storrow was a brilliant man who, on the advice of Loammi Baldwin, had turned to engineering upon graduating from Harvard in 1829. He graduated first in a Harvard class that included such notable minds as Oliver Wendell Holmes Sr. and Benjamin Pierce. After graduation, Pierce taught mathematics at Harvard for forty years, served as director of the U.S. Coast Survey from 1867 to 1874, and was a founding member of the National Academy of Sciences.[55] Storrow's senior mathematics thesis, titled "Of the Celestial Motions,"[56] examined changes in the gravitation of the moon's orbit. The science of such motions had taken a great leap forward from Aristotle's ideas, which had placed the Earth at the center of the universe, when Sir Isaac Newton (1642–1727) advanced his concepts of motion and force in his small tract the *Principia* (1687). So Storrow applied the laws of Newtonian physics to create his thesis.

In 1832, when Storrow returned from his studies at L'École des Ponts et Chaussées in France, something Loammi had encouraged him to do, he became an assistant engineer under James Baldwin, who was then building the Boston and Lowell Railroad.[57] He was the only engineer then engaged who had actually seen a working railroad or steam locomotive. While Storrow was studying in

Europe, Loammi sent letter after letter encouraging his young protégé to make inspection trips to as many projects as possible. The only hindrance to following the advice was financial, because Storrow was almost out of funds by late 1830. In fact, he was seriously thinking of returning home early. His plans changed when his family's earlier hospitality to William Lawrence in Paris was rewarded. Though Amos Lawrence had never met Storrow, he was so appreciative of the hospitality shown his son William that, when he learned of the young student's need for funds, he sent him a loan of $500,[58] which facilitated a tour of engineering works in England during July and August of 1831. While traveling across England, Storrow rode on George Stephenson's Liverpool and Manchester Railroad and recorded in his journal, "The sensations are such as I never felt before, whirling along with such wonderful rapidity."[59] He calculated the train's top speed at more than thirty-two miles per hour and took time to sketch cross sections of the roadbed used to support the iron rails. He was just the man to help Loammi's brother build the Boston and Lowell Railroad.

Upon completion of the Boston and Lowell in 1836, Storrow was named general manager of the road. Ten years later, he resigned the position to become chief engineer and agent for the Essex Company, formed to develop the waterpower of the Merrimack River.

As chief engineer, Storrow was charged with building a mill town on the Merrimack River at Bodwell's Falls, twelve miles downstream from Lowell, where the thirty-two-foot drop at Pawtucket Falls[60] had been developed in the 1820s. On the company's 4,000 acres of land,[61] he would design and build the streets, bridges, railroad, and commercial buildings for the new town of Lawrence, plus a large overflow dam to divert the water of the Merrimack to the textile mills. The dam was his foremost engineering challenge. Because the mills were to be located along canals on the sides of the river, any flood current would have to pass over the crest of the dam. At this location on the river, the dam would need to be more than thirty feet high and at least 900 feet long. No overflow dam of that size then existed in either the United States or Europe on a river comparable to the Merrimack.[62]

Once Storrow joined the Essex Company and accepted responsibility for building the mill complex, he moved his family to Lawrence. His design for a 943-foot-long dam was completed in mid-1845 and a contract was let in July. Needing a qualified assistant, Storrow convinced Captain Charles Bigelow, Haupt's West Point classmate, to resign his commission and supervise construction. Storrow, Bigelow, and the contractors labored for just over three years to complete the massive stone dam at Lawrence. But even before the dam reached its full height, mills were erected. So by midsummer 1848, with the water rising behind the unfinished stonework, the mill turbines began to turn, driving the spindles. When the major building work at Lawrence slowed in 1860, Storrow moved back to Boston. He remained with the Essex Company until 1889, when he finally retired at the age of eighty.

Benjamin Henry Latrobe (courtesy of the Smithsonian Institution Libraries, Washington, DC)

Benjamin Henry Latrobe, II

While Storrow was preparing for his mission to Europe in 1862, the commissioners and Crocker continued to receive letters from those with vested interests in the Tunnel. Haupt wrote to Felton, requesting that he make arrangements with Stuart Gwynn to test a gang of four steam drills. These were the drills Haupt and Gwynn had spent years trying to perfect. Haupt also recommended his subcontractor B. N. Farren to Felton, saying he was "intelligent and energetic."[63]

Farren wrote to Crocker, pleading his own case and stating that he stood ready to resume work at the Tunnel with only twenty-four hours' notice.

Many in northern Massachusetts had expectations that the commissioners would speedily resume the work. Those with such high hopes should have read the *Hoosac Valley News* of North Adams, which correctly affirmed the commissioners' intentions—that they were "unwilling to proceed till they have further knowledge of the subject of making big tunnels."[64] The commissioners' decision to send Storrow to Europe was a signal; the Tunnel work would not be resumed immediately. In early August, the *American Railway Times* published an unsigned letter that complained about the "unwarrantable extravagance to send an agent to Europe on a salary of $3,000, to find out what he could ascertain as well in the Boston Public Library." The letter writer was, however, favorably inclined to support a two-month investigation of American tunnel work by B. H. Latrobe.[65] This Latrobe was the son of the B. H. Latrobe who in 1808 had offered secretary of the treasury, Albert Gallatin, a few remarks on railroads. The younger Latrobe went on to serve as chief engineer for both the Baltimore and Ohio (B&O), and the Northwestern and Virginia Railroads. Besides being an accomplished bridge builder, he was, as Haupt had learned, unquestionably the most experienced tunnel builder in the United States.

With the approval of the Governor and the Governor's Council, Storrow proceeded to Europe,[66] and the commissioners engaged Latrobe and James Laurie as consultants. As location and construction engineer for the B&O, Latrobe had directed the construction of the B&O from Harpers Ferry to Cumberland, Maryland. This stretch of railroad, completed in November 1842, was his baptism in the trials of tunnel work. Building westward from Harpers Ferry to Cumberland, the B&O and Latrobe drove three tunnels, the longest being 1,200 feet in length.[67] Later, as chief engineer of the B&O, he built the road on to Wheeling, Virginia (later West Virginia). Between Cumberland and Wheeling, he built twelve tunnels. The Kingwood Tunnel on this part of the road was 4,132 feet long[68]—at the time, the longest railroad tunnel in the world.[69] To speed the work, he excavated three shafts, which enabled his crews to bore the tunnel from eight faces. The depth of the shafts varied, but they averaged 170 feet.[70] He also excavated a long, deep cut at each end to reach solid rock. His experiences with the Kingwood Tunnel would influence his Hoosac Tunnel recommendations. The natural rock at the Kingwood Tunnel caved badly in places, and Latrobe employed cast-iron arches to protect the workmen.[71] These arches were later covered with brick-and-stone arching. Between 1838 and 1866, Latrobe directed the boring of forty-four tunnels[72] and stood as America's master tunnel builder. The technique for digging these tunnels and the shafts was the same as for the Hoosac: strong men with big hammers.

Using hammers, steel drills, and black powder, crews of miners attacked the rock of the mountains separating Latrobe's B&O Railroad from Wheeling.[73] Blasting was an imprecise science, and the strength of black powder was often inconsistent. The powder would sometimes yield spectacular but deadly results. Once the holes were drilled into the rock, the powder was poured in and some poor devil lit the fuse—a strip of brown wrapping paper soaked in saltpeter. If there was too much saltpeter, the fuse burned rapidly—to the blaster's peril. The only improvement from the earliest days was the introduction of a safety fuse by William Bickford in 1831. This machine-made paper cord with a core of powder burned at a predictable rate, so the man lighting it had an idea of how much time he had before the rock fragments showered him.[74]

Even before the newspaper published the letter urging the commissioners to seek the opinion of Latrobe, Felton had made contact with the distinguished engineer. In fact, Felton, whose railroad terminated in Baltimore, was probably already well acquainted with Latrobe before he made the contact. Besides the Hoosac Tunnel commitment, Latrobe would work closely with Felton in 1863 as a consulting engineer. Felton engaged him in connection with the design and construction of a bridge the Philadelphia, Wilmington, and Baltimore Railroad was building across the Susquehanna at Havre de Grace, Maryland.

Latrobe was also acquainted with railroads in Massachusetts and had previously met Charles Storrow. Following the same advice Loammi Baldwin had given to Storrow, Latrobe made a working tour of American railroads in November and December of 1837. At the time, Storrow was the general agent of the Boston and Lowell, and he had escorted Latrobe over the road. Felton wanted to arrange a joint visit with Latrobe to the Hoosac Tunnel in late July 1862, but Latrobe had other business in Pittsburgh. When his business was concluded, however, he wrote Felton to say he was available to visit the Tunnel after the first of August.

Latrobe was tasked with examining the Tunnel and Laurie was to survey the entire route of the railroad from Greenfield to North Adams. Over the years, Laurie had become a leading consulting engineer for bridges, and there was the issue of Haupt's failed bridge over the Green River above Deerfield. In 1836, Laurie had been chief engineer in charge of construction for the Norwich and Worcester Railroad. During that project, he built in 1837 what many believe was

Engineering experience timeline (1836–1856) for Commissioners Samuel Felton and John Brooks and their consultants.

Alvah Crocker
- 1837: Visits Loammi Baldwin
- 1842–1843: Fitchburg RR chartered; Crocker & Derby to Europe

Samuel M. Felton
- 1836–1837: Joins Loammi Baldwin
- 1838–1839: Assumes Baldwin's practice
- 1841: Engr. Fresh Pond RR
- 1842–1843: Engr. Fitchburg Rail Road
- 1843–1847: Superintendent Fitchburg Rail Road
- 1850: Europe to study drills
- 1851–1856: President Philadelphia, Wilmington, Baltimore Rail Road

John W. Brooks
- 1836–1837: Tutored Baldwin's Office
- 1838–1839: Engr. — 1840–1841: Chief Engr. Boston & Maine RR
- 1840–1842: Lumbering
- 1842–1843: Tutored Felton's office
- 1843–1845: Engr. Auburn & Rochester RR
- 1845–1850: Michigan Central Rail Road; Superintendent
- 1853–1854: Pres. Burlington & Missouri Rv. RR
- 1854–1855: V. President St. Mary's Ship Canal
- 1856: Pres.

Thomas Doane
- 1845–1847: Engr. Vermont Central RR
- 1848–1849: Engr. Cheshire Rail Road
- 1851–1852: Charlestown Office

Charles S. Storrow
- 1839–1842: Manager, Boston & Lowell Rail Road
- 1845–1848: Develop water power Merrimack Rv.
- 1849–1852: Engr. and agent Essex Company

Benj. Henry Latrobe
- 1837–1839: Engr. Baltimore & Ohio Rail Road
- 1837–1840: Visits Storrow at Boston & Lowell
- 1839–1842: B&O to Harpers Ferry – 3 tunnels
- 1844–1850: Chief Engr. Baltimore & Ohio Rail Road
- 1847–1852: B&O Cumberland to Wheeling – 12 tunnels (4,132 ft Kingwood)
- 1850–1853: Chief Engr. North-Western & Virginia RR
- 1851–1853: 23 tunnels (longest 2,700 ft)

James Laurie
- 1836–1839: Chief Engr. Norwich & Worcester RR
- 1837: Taft Tunnel 300 ft first RR tunnel in US
- 1840–1843: Troy & Schenectady RR
- 1844–1847: Survey Providence & Plainfield
- 1848–1849: Boston office
- 1850–1852: Engr. New Jersey Central RR
- 1852–1854: New York office
- 1854–1856: Chief Engr. Nova Scotia RR

Engineering experience of Commissioners Samuel Felton and John Brooks and their consultants

the first railroad tunnel in America, the Taft Tunnel at Bundy Hill, Connecticut.[75] In addition, he had considerable experience in locating railroads in the Northeast and in Nova Scotia.

Latrobe and Laurie jointly visited the Hoosac on 13 August 1862 and began their respective tasks. At the same time, Brooks began the tedious business of preparing an audit and examining outstanding claims against the Troy and Greenfield Railroad for work performed on the road and at the Tunnel.[76] Latrobe would open his report by stating: "Upon my first view of this great undertaking, I said to myself, here is, indeed, a tunnel through the body of a mountain. All tunnels heretofore executed have been through spurs or crests of mountains."[77] His comment reflected not only the task of tunneling the Mountain but also the magnitude of the responsibility placed on the commissioners. By mid-December, Governor Andrew was prodding these eminent engineers for answers.

Commissioners' Report

With the results of the 1861 election on his mind, Governor Andrew wrote the commissioners and asked the question everyone was thinking: Should the work be taken to completion? If their answer was going to be positive, he wanted to announce it in his address at the opening of the General Court session on 9 January. Thinking in terms of his gubernatorial legacy and the public's perception of him as a warmonger because of his stout support of Lincoln and the Union cause, he pressured Brooks repeatedly about the commissioners' decision. Writing to the commissioners, he wanted to know whether their conclusion was going to be positive concerning resumption of the work. He told Brooks that if they recommended the Commonwealth proceed, "I want to get hold of it and show during . . . my administration some honorable progress . . . so as not to go out of office like King David who was forbidden to begin the Temple of God because he was only a 'man of war.'"[78] Three days later, he again wrote to Brooks. Possibly the two men had spoken in the meantime, because this letter gives the impression that Andrew believed the commissioners were going to support a renewed effort to drive the Tunnel through the Hoosac Mountain. "I am very anxious to be in possession of the main results . . . [so as] to make proper allusions . . . in the address on the 9th. It will be of great importance to seize that occasion to give [the] correct impressions, before log rolling, discontent, jealousies, and posturing efforts are stirred up in the legislature."[79]

Andrew fully realized the Tunnel battle in the legislature would be bloody, as bloody as those being fought by the Blue and Gray armies in northern

Virginia. In the Hoosac Tunnel battle, no quarter would be given and there would be no one to comfort the wounded, whereas in Washington the ambulances would deposit the wounded at one of the many hospitals.

Louisa May Alcott, who had studied in Henry David and John Thoreau's Concord school, rode Crocker's Fitchburg Railroad to Boston at this time on the first leg of her trip to Washington as an angel of mercy to "go nurse the soldiers."[80] She wrote, "[T]here they were! 'our brave boys,' . . . so riddled with shot and shell, so torn and shattered."[81] The commissioners' report would consign many a man to a similar fate by the same medium—explosions of black powder in the bowels of the Hoosac Mountain.

As the month of December wore on, Brooks was extremely busy assembling data for the report and reviewing the analyses submitted by engineers Latrobe, Laurie, and Storrow. The reason behind Forbes's faith in Brooks was evidenced by the man's meticulous attention to every detail. He carefully reviewed the reports by the three consulting engineers and, on finding calculation errors or misstatements, immediately requested corrections.[82] By the 1860s, Brooks was practiced in executing large projects, and his years of experience in examining engineering reports had given him a well-developed sense of the physical meaning behind the numbers in a document. When the numbers in a report did not seem to jibe with reality, he would immediately check the report in greater detail and make his own calculations to understand why the data did not agree with his view of reality. It was an ability honed by experience as a chief engineer. When Brooks asked Latrobe to check some calculations, the reply immediately came back confirming Brooks's intuition. Latrobe admitted that he was "mortified at the mistake,"[83] as he too possessed years of experience and understood this ability.

Forbes and Brooks worked well together because they both adhered to the same principles. One principle concerned serving the public, and both men believed this could only be done well if the railroad was profitable.[84] Early on in his association with Brooks, Forbes had commented about the engineer's energy and zeal, and at the same time he had taken note of two other characteristics: Brooks's thoroughness and his tendency to do too much himself instead of delegating.[85] Now, just as Forbes had noted, those two character traits caused Brooks to be tardy in delivering the commissioners' report to Governor Andrew.

Consequently, as the nation entered the third year of bloody war, and as the Emancipation Proclamation[86] issued by President Abraham Lincoln came into effect on the first of January in 1863, all Andrew could do was lay the groundwork for the positive report he was expecting. The day after the Central

Pacific Railroad Company held its groundbreaking in Sacramento, California, to begin the transcontinental railroad, Andrew remarked to the Massachusetts legislature that the Hoosac Tunnel commissioners he had appointed were able, impartial, and skillful. Without the report in hand, this was all he could say, but he did conclude his address by calling for unanimous support if the report was "favorable to the active pursuit of the enterprise."[87] The Governor then turned his attention to organizing the 54th Massachusetts Regiment, which Secretary of War Edwin M. Stanton had finally authorized after the Emancipation Proclamation took effect. It was the first black regiment recruited in the North, and Andrew gave it his careful attention.

In late February, Brooks finally delivered the commissioners' report to the Governor. It stated exactly what Andrew had hoped for—and what he needed for his political career. In transmitting the report to the Senate of the General Court, Andrew wrote, "[T]he report of the Commissioners establishes the feasibility of the grand enterprise of tunneling the Hoosac Mountain." He went further and affirmed his assent to the opinions of the commissioners. In the report, Brooks and his fellow commissioners estimated that a railroad from Greenfield to North Adams, with a tunnel through the Hoosac Mountain, would cost the Commonwealth $5,719,330. This figure included what the Commonwealth had already expended under the previous legislation and had paid to Herman Haupt. Because the expected cost to the Commonwealth was now projected well beyond the $2 million of the 1854 Loan Act, Andrew urged legislation to provide additional funding and "render the prosecution of the enterprise practicable by the commissioners."[88]

Brooks was the primary author of the main body of the report, which contained the figures to support his estimate of the cost, but the appendices written by Latrobe and Laurie were of more interest to newspaper editors. Latrobe asserted that the question of tunneling the Mountain had moved from the abstract to proven practicality by the work Haupt had accomplished. This statement was reprinted in the *American Railway Times*.[89] Latrobe also applauded Haupt's alignment of the Tunnel, stating that it "seems to have been established with great care."[90] But he followed this statement with a proposal to raise the grade of the Tunnel portal on the west side of the Mountain. Haupt and the workmen had struggled mightily to penetrate the semiliquid porridge stone at the western base of the Mountain, but years of effort had resulted in a bore of slightly less than 600 feet. Latrobe's solution based on his Kingwood Tunnel experience, was to let that part of Haupt's work sink into the porridge stone.

Latrobe's B&O tunneling experience spurred him to recommend that the engineers increase the slope of the roadbed between the North Adams station and the western portal of the Tunnel. This change would raise the portal elevation twenty-five feet.[91] He was hopeful this change would literally lift the work out of the worst material. Nevertheless, he recommended one further adjustment. He believed the Tunnel portal should be moved back into the mountain 500 feet and an open cut should be made through the porridge stone. This would minimize the length of Tunnel the miners would have to bore through "ells." Even with these changes, Latrobe believed masonry would still be necessary to support the roof of the Tunnel for a good part of the 3,000-foot distance between the new portal location and Haupt's shaft on the west side of the Mountain.

The *American Railway Times* also saw fit to quote Latrobe's recommendation to sink two shafts "in the valley between the mountain summits."[92] As an engineer with more tunnel experience than any other American, he considered two shafts essential to ensuring the correct alignment of the Tunnel through the Mountain and to providing the necessary ventilation for such a long tunnel. The commissioners would take his caution to heart, and later their engineers would devote considerable thought, attention, and effort to keep the crews digging in the right direction.

When Latrobe attempted an estimate of the cost and time to complete the Tunnel, he made two very succinct comments. While he believed water would not be a problem—based on his examination of Haupt's bore on the east side of the Mountain—he went on to say that "the quantity of water to be encountered in the more central parts of the tunnel" was the most unpredictable element of progress and expense.[93] Then, as a closing note, Latrobe stated that his cost estimate was based on "the common mode of working by hand drills." He had no confidence that future tunneling machines could solve the problem of boring the Hoosac. After examining the junked tunneling machine rusting on the Mountain, he wrote, "I could only look upon it . . . as a misapplication of mechanical genius."[94]

Storrow's "Report on European Tunnels" was attached to the commissioners' report as an appendix. It contained complimentary references to what Haupt had accomplished and his concept for directing the work. His report noted that an experienced tunnel contractor in England was favorably impressed by Haupt's decision to have rising grades from both portals, thereby facilitating the removal of materials and the drainage of water.[95] This same gentleman, like Latrobe, unhesitatingly stated the need for a shaft in the center of the Hoosac

Tunnel for ventilation purposes, but he warned of the likely difficulties if water was encountered either while digging the shaft or when tunneling away from the shaft.

The English tunnel contractor supplied Storrow with a detailed description of a terrible accident that had occurred in 1857 at the Hauenstein Tunnel in Switzerland while the miners were attempting to mine a shaft down to the floor of the tunnel. The wood used to line the shaft had caught fire and collapsed, along with a mass of earth, onto the unfortunate workmen below.[96] As the tragedy unfolded, other miners rushed to rescue their trapped comrades. The reports differed, but approximately thirty-one trapped workers and eleven of those attempting their rescue died either from lack of oxygen or by being buried under the collapsing mass (some reports claim a total of sixty-four miners died). It was a prophecy of the grim destiny awaiting those who provoked the Great Spirit of the Hoosac Mountain.

Storrow's extended analysis of the seven-mile-long Mont Cenis Tunnel under the Alps between France and Italy clinched the argument for completing the Hoosac Tunnel. He emphatically stated his conviction about a Tunnel through the Hoosac Mountain: "As regards the feasibility of completing such a work, I entertain no doubt whatever."[97] Storrow had spent days with Germain Sommeiller, the Italian engineer directing the Mont Cenis bore, and their discussions convinced him of the Hoosac project's feasibility. Many of the things Storrow observed and described in his detailed report would soon find their way into practice as the commissioners directed a renewed attack on the Hoosac Mountain.

Sommeiller, like Haupt, had devoted a great deal of attention to developing a usable drilling machine, preferably a portable one. This led him to concentrate on developing a machine powered by compressed air—a pneumatic drill. Haupt had attempted to do the same thing, though he had come to the conclusion the drill should be powered by steam. Storrow described the Sommeiller drills as "weighing 300 or 400 lbs. apiece, and . . . about 8 ft in length." But even those drills were too heavy and bulky for one man to handle, so Sommeiller mounted a gang of nine drills on a carriage that ran on a railway track in the center of the tunnel. When Storrow questioned Sommeiller about using large machines for excavating the full section of the tunnel, like those tried at the Hoosac, the engineer unhesitatingly expressed his lack of faith in such monsters.[98]

Storrow made numerous visits into the interior of the Mont Cenis Tunnel and closely observed the mining operations for hours each time. He later wrote,

"I wished to see with my own eyes whether the machines in use were but an untried experiment . . . or whether they were actually and uniformly at work."[99] His final analysis of the drilling machines was favorable in terms of the time required to bore the mountain, but he did not believe they would reduce the cost. At the same time, he was extremely impressed with Sommeiller's use of compressed air. He regarded it as a "great instrument in the hands of the engineers. It provided pure air for breathing, the wind to drive away the noxious vapors after a blast, and the power to run the drills."[100] His report detailed Sommeiller's use of waterpower to drive his air compressors. In his concluding paragraphs, Storrow made recommendations for powering air compressors. The commissioners should either erect steam engines or build a dam across the Deerfield River at the eastern portal of the Hoosac Mountain in order to create waterpower to drive the compressors. The compressed air could be used to ventilate the work and possibly to put mechanical drills into operation.

Another important note in Storrow's report related to the survey work necessary to guarantee the headings from each side of the Mountain would converge. He described how the engineers at Mont Cenis had built stone survey observatories—structures that ensured the stability of the survey instruments while taking sightings of the line. From a structure placed on the summit of the mountain and two others placed opposite the tunnel portals, the line of the tunnel was established and projected into the bore. The engineers working for the commissioners would soon emulate this technique in western Massachusetts.

The Laurie Appendix

The final appendix to the commissioners' report was the work of James Laurie, who spelled out two interesting facts about the location of the Hoosac Tunnel. First, on the eastern side of the Mountain, the portal had originally been located in a ravine, and torrents of water rushed down this ravine to the Deerfield River whenever a storm battered the Mountain. The difficulty of trying to control the water gushing down the ravine convinced Serrell to move the line of the railroad 150 feet south. Haupt's miners used Serrell's more southerly alignment as they penetrated the Mountain, and Laurie fully approved of this.

Serrell who had held the first contract to tunnel the Hoosac, was now an army engineer. When the Civil War began, he organized and served as commander of the 1st New York Volunteer Engineers, but in mid-1863 he became chief engineer for X Corps (10th Corps of the Union Army). The connections between the many Hoosac engineers and politicians were uncanny. Four

months after Governor Andrew received the Tunnel report, his 54th Massachusetts Regiment would lead the attack on Fort Wagner in Charleston Harbor, and
Serrell would be the engineer officer providing support. Serrell the builder had
traded the black powder and splintered rock of tunneling for the black powder
and shell fragments of war.

The second alignment issue was on the western side of the Mountain.
There the portal grade was lowered some thirty feet, with the expectation of
reaching solid rock sooner. In light of what Haupt actually encountered, Laurie
and Latrobe both thought this elevation decision should be reconsidered.

On several points, Laurie's report was the one most critical of Haupt's
performance. But it must be remembered that James Laurie may not have been
completely unbiased in his evaluations, since he had a close relationship with
Daniel L. Harris, the mouthpiece for the Western Railroad in attacking Haupt
and the Hoosac Tunnel enterprise. In fact, Harris had started his railroading
career in 1837 as a rodman under Laurie, surveying the line of the Norwich and
Worcester Railroad. He had also worked with Laurie as an assistant engineer on
the Troy and Schenectady Railroad in New York.[101]

Regarding the location of the route between Greenfield and the Tunnel,
Laurie believed the original location by A. F. Edwards presented no objectionable
features and compared favorably with the alignment of the Western Railroad.
He then praised Edwards's work: "His location had been made to obtain the best
possible line which the ground admits of, and in some respects exhibits much
boldness of design."[102] After this introduction, he noted that this alignment by
Edwards was abandoned and "a new one adopted, evidently with the intention
of obtaining the cheapest possible road." Here he was referring to the alignment
Haupt had surveyed and used in building the road westward from Greenfield to
the Hoosac Mountain. But Laurie's harshest comments were reserved for Haupt's
Green River Bridge.

Here again there is a conflict, as Laurie's friend Harris held the rights to
Howe truss-bridge construction in New England, and Haupt had fashioned his
own design instead of using a Howe truss. Laurie, his Scottish blood showing,
bluntly declared the superstructure unsafe and insufficient, and the stone and
workmanship of the piers very inferior. "I know of no bridge of the height of
this where the masonry is so poor, and I have some doubts of its sufficiency to
resist the jar and strain it will be subjected to by the passage of heavy trains."
He added: "No wooden structure can be made creditable on the present location
and piers."[103]

Laurie followed his evaluation of the bridge with a few comments addressing Haupt's defense of the design. Haupt had compared the design of the Green River Bridge to the Susquehanna Bridge on the Pennsylvania Railroad, but Laurie reminded those unfamiliar with that bridge about its failure. It "was destroyed by an ordinary gale of wind before it was entirely completed, for want of proper and sufficient bracing." After the failure, Haupt had redesigned the structural system and had included in his book on bridge construction an explanation about the arched ribs of the Susquehanna Bridge being its main support. Laurie quoted from Haupt's book and made much of the fact that this arched-rib support method was not the issue with the Green River Bridge. Its deficiency was in the sizing of the chords, and Laurie was very pointed in his criticism.[104] A truss bridge has vertical, diagonal, and horizontal members tied together to create continuous series of panels; the horizontal members of the panels are referred to as chords. The vertical posts serve to brace and keep the chords spaced apart. The upper and lower chords carry the load of the bridge to the piers.

Then turning his attention to boring the Mountain, Laurie stated that he saw no reason why drills such as those used at Mont Cenis could not be adopted at the Hoosac, and he fully supported Storrow's idea of a dam across the Deerfield River to power air compressors. He reiterated the arguments of both Latrobe[105] and Storrow[106] concerning the size of the Tunnel—that it should be large enough to accommodate a double-track railway.[107] His words about size served to remind and direct the attention of the Governor and the legislature to the original Troy and Greenfield Railroad proposal: a twenty-four-by-twenty-and-a-half-foot tunnel to accommodate two tracks. But the Loan Act of 1854 had changed the requirement by stating "that it might be built for one or more."[108] Then, based on that act, the contract between the Troy and Greenfield Railroad and H. Haupt and Company permitted him to build for a single track. That size change was confirmed in 1859, when the legislature authorized a tunnel fourteen feet wide by eighteen feet high, thus reducing the tunnel width by ten feet.

The other major change Laurie advocated was a reiteration of Latrobe's counsel to raise the grade of the west portal and the open cut into the Mountain as far as possible before attempting to tunnel through the porridge stone. By his estimate, an open cut was probably cheaper than attempting to tunnel, even if it was necessary to build heavy masonry walls to support the high banks of the proposed cut.

In the end, the three consulting engineers employed by the commissioners were all in agreement—a tunnel could be driven through the Hoosac Mountain. Each had looked at the situation based on personal experiences, yet each made very similar recommendations: change the elevation of the west portal, construct a double-track tunnel, attempt to develop a mechanical drill powered by compressed air, and—for ventilation purposes and to speed the work—excavate a vertical shaft close to the midpoint of the Tunnel. Brooks endorsed these recommendations and concluded by asserting: "The only course which seems to us as free from embarrassment, and likely to lead to a successful result, is for the State to undertake the work on its own account, controlling its own agents, and holding them responsible for the integrity of their management."[109] The commissioners' report had sufficient criticism of Haupt's work to justify Governor Andrew's decision to withhold payments, yet it pronounced the work feasible, thus giving him political cover to reconnect with the citizens in the northern tier of the Commonwealth. The *Hoosac Valley News* immediately proclaimed: "[T]he Commissioners and Governor have not disappointed us in their report."[110]

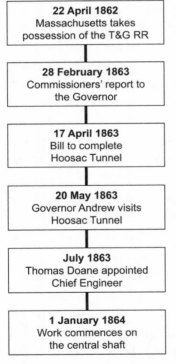

22 April 1862
Massachusetts takes possession of the T&G RR

28 February 1863
Commissioners' report to the Governor

17 April 1863
Bill to complete Hoosac Tunnel

20 May 1863
Governor Andrew visits Hoosac Tunnel

July 1863
Thomas Doane appointed Chief Engineer

1 January 1864
Work commences on the central shaft

The Smith Mortgage

In April 1863, Governor Andrew, together with the friends of the Tunnel, prevailed over the lingering opposition and passed a bill to immediately resume the work, using the remaining portion of the original $2 million Commonwealth aid appropriation.[111] The bill allowed the work to commence under the general supervision of the commissioners already appointed. So John Brooks, president of the Michigan Central and director of several other western railroads in John Forbes's empire, now had the added task of tunneling the Hoosac Mountain.[112] Though legal issues remained to be resolved, the papers announced the work would be resumed immediately. The most critical issue, however, was the validity of the Commonwealth's claimed Troy and Greenfield Railroad ownership. The 1854 Loan Act to aid the Troy and Greenfield Railroad had authorized the issue of $2 million in Commonwealth bonds, but in turn it required the railroad to execute a mortgage assigning its property to the Commonwealth if the money in the sinking fund should be insufficient. By foreclosing on this mortgage, Governor Andrew wrested control of the Tunnel work from Haupt.[113] But there persisted a cloud as to the validity of the Commonwealth's title. In July of 1855, when the Troy and Greenfield Railroad had entered into a contract with Serrell, it had issued construction bonds valued at $900,000. These bonds were passed to Serrell and later to Haupt as payment for their work in building the railroad and tunneling the Mountain. Because the railroad did not have cash to pay Serrell or Haupt, the idea was for the contractor to use the bonds as security to raise money to pay the workforce or to purchase railroad iron. Such financial arrangements were used by many railroads to raise capital for construction. The bonds could be used as collateral behind bank loans of cash.[114] The problem now, in terms of who had ownership of the T&G's property, was that these bonds were backed by a mortgage assigning the railroad's property to the holders if they were not redeemed at face value. Trustees for the bonds were J. V. C. Smith, Paul Adams, and John G. Davis of Boston. Taking the name of the first trustee, this argument about ownership came to be known as the "Smith mortgage."[115] Therefore, both the Commonwealth and the holders of these Troy and Greenfield bonds held a mortgage on all Troy and Greenfield Railroad property.

Brooks, in the commissioners' report, had pointed to the existence of the Smith mortgage. In his opinion, the first mortgage did not conform with the Commonwealth statutes concerning railroad mortgages. He also believed the Smith mortgage was defective, because the railroad had acted without obtaining a variance from the legislature. In late July, he again raised the issue of the Smith mortgage in a letter to Governor Andrew and specifically requested an opinion from the Governor's Council concerning whether the Commonwealth had clear title to all the property of the Troy and Greenfield Railroad.[116] Andrew was aware of this problem, so in early June he had appointed a committee to inquire into the Smith mortgage. He also directed the committee to obtain an opinion "in writing" from the attorney general.[117]

The issue of the Smith mortgage would linger for another two and a half years. Finally, in September 1865, the Supreme Court of Massachusetts would declare the Smith mortgage invalid and the mortgage held by the Commonwealth as the original. The Commonwealth's mortgage had been executed at the time of the first Loan Act in 1854. "To clinch the matter, the Court held that these bonds were technically invalid in any case, since their maturity was at thirty years, whereas the statutes limited the life of railroad bonds in general to twenty years."[118] Nonetheless, the squabble about the validity of the bonds was not over. When the Tunnel was finally completed Haupt and other bond holders would press their mortgage claim against the State. The *American Railroad Journal* had predicted a dispute from the beginning, while warning those involved about the ownership of the bonds. The *Journal* proclaimed: "[S]omewhere near half the amount went into the hands of Mr. Haupt, the late contractor and engineer of the road; and it is safe to say that the State will not escape their payment."[119]

Engineers from Crocker's Fitchburg Railroad

Cloudy mortgage or not, the commissioners now had authority to proceed with the work, and Governor Andrew wanted to see progress. Therefore, to show his commitment, the Governor and his council passed over the route and visited North Adams on 20 May 1863.[120] Three days later, the commissioners gave notice, in accordance with the provisions of the legislation, they were ready to proceed. Nevertheless, it was 26 June before the Governor and the council gave their approval to begin work. None of the commissioners had the time to devote to directing the great project on a daily basis, so a search was underway for a capable chief engineer. It was yet another month before John Brooks could write to Samuel Felton to say that Thomas Doane had accepted the position of chief engineer.[121]

Doane, Felton, and Brooks were closely associated, each having learned engineering in Loammi Baldwin's Charlestown office. After his tutorage in Charlestown, Brooks had pursued his own career. But Felton and Doane had remained and in turn succeeded to the office and Baldwin's original practice. Doane, who had learned engineering under Felton, had joined the office about four years after Loammi's death, so he probably never met Baldwin. When Felton departed for Philadelphia, Doane inherited the practice and office. In 1863, the office was still located at 21 City Square[122] in the Bunker Hill Bank building between Chelsea and Main in Charlestown.[123] When Thomas's brother, John Jr., joined him in the practice of civil engineering, the firm name became T. & J. Doane, Jr.[124] Together they would continue to practice civil engineering and surveying from this Charlestown office until Thomas Doane's death in 1897.

Thomas Doane spent three years with Felton in Baldwin's old office. The last two years coincided with construction of the Fitchburg Railroad, so it is probable Doane and Crocker had known one another since the earliest days of that line. Engineer Doane was an efficient man who practiced the profession with the same attention to detail exercised by the office's first engineer.[125] He could trace his ancestry to Deacon John Doane, a Puritan who arrived in Plymouth around 1630, and, from his training under Felton, Thomas Doane was well schooled in the Baldwin philosophy of high-quality building. This Baldwin trait—exhibited when Loammi senior sought to build stone locks for the Middlesex Canal and when Loammi junior struggled with the canal owners in Pennsylvania—would now be exhibited by Brooks and Doane as they assumed control of the Hoosac Tunnel work.

During his early career, Doane was continually associated with railroad projects within the web of Alvah Crocker's business dealings. The railroad deal between Crocker and Charles Paine to link their railroads in Vermont caused Felton in early 1844 to survey Paine's Vermont Central Railroad. In July of 1844, Felton was appointed chief engineer of the Vermont Central.[126] The next year, Doane followed his mentor, taking charge of the Windsor White River Division of the Vermont Central.[127] S. F. Belknap, Elias Derby's "prince of a contractor," also moved north and contracted to build sections of the Vermont Central.[128] Later, William E. Babbitt,[129] another Felton protégé from Baldwin's office, became chief engineer of the Vermont Central.

A web of relationships existed between Crocker, the Tunnel promoter, and the commissioners—first to Felton and then to the fraternity of engineers who had passed through Baldwin's old Charlestown office. Completing the connection to Alexander Holmes, the third Tunnel commissioner, Felton's student Samuel R. Johnson had earlier labored for the Old Colony Railroad. Moreover, Crocker's old troubadour friend Elias H. Derby had preceded Holmes as president of the Old Colony Railroad. There were also Forbes and Brooks connections to Holmes. In 1848, Derby represented Forbes as petitioner before the Rail-Road Committee of the Massachusetts legislature on behalf of the Old Colony Railroad when the line was trying to gain a route into Boston.[130] And Brooks, a few years before becoming a commissioner, was involved in a second mortgage bond of the Dorchester and Milton Branch Railroad Company to the Old Colony Railroad.[131]

Thomas Doane, after completing his work with the Vermont Central, moved to Walpole, New Hampshire, in 1847 as a resident engineer for the Cheshire Railroad.[132] The Cheshire first laid its rails northwestward from Crocker's Vermont and Massachusetts Railroad at South Ashburnham, Massachusetts, to Winchendon, a town on the New Hampshire border. This section of railroad opened in October of 1847.[133] Crossing the border, the route continued on the same northwesterly line to Troy, New Hampshire,[134] a section that also opened in 1847. When Doane arrived, he pushed the rails farther northwest to Bellows Falls, on the Vermont side of the Connecticut River. He completed this work in late 1849, when the Cheshire Railroad provided the tie between Crocker's Vermont and Massachusetts Railroad and Charles Paine's Vermont Central Railroad. The Crocker–Paine agreement of 1843 was fulfilled, so Doane moved back to Charlestown in December 1849 and took over Samuel Felton's engineering practice.

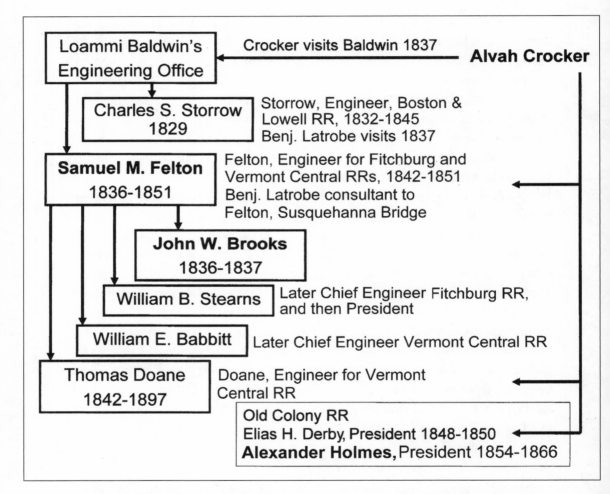

Engineers mentored in the Charlestown office started by Loammi Baldwin and their relationships to Alvah Crocker, plus Crocker's connection to Alexander Holmes

While in Vermont and New Hampshire, Doane found time for more than just engineering work. The *New Hampshire Sentinel* of Keene, along the route of the Cheshire Railroad to Bellows Falls, announced on 5 November 1850 the marriage of Mr. Thomas Doane and Miss Sophia D. Clark of Brattleboro, Vermont.[135] Over the next decade, Doane and his wife would reside in Charlestown and, until called by Felton to the Hoosac Tunnel, he would perform engineering work for all of the railroads running into and out of Boston.[136]

While Herman Haupt was fully occupied rushing thirty trains a day to Gettysburg in support of his West Point classmate George Meade,[137] engineers Brooks and Doane were planning their attack on the Hoosac Mountain. On 4 July 1863, the defeated General Robert E. Lee began the withdrawal of his Confederate Army from Gettysburg. Later reports claimed the train of wagons carrying his wounded stretched for more than fourteen miles. Unfortunately, there would soon be similar agony and a trail of wounded and dead miners in Massachusetts at the Hoosac Mountain.

A New Alignment

In August, the *Hoosac Valley News* of North Adams reported that the Tunnel work would be resumed immediately and the necessary men were being recruited.[138] Brooks and Doane were making preparations and planning to attack the mountain in typical Baldwin-esque manner. Based on Storrow's understanding with Germain Sommeiller, four pneumatic drills were ordered from Europe.[139] The possibility of securing mechanical drills for the miners was exciting news along the route of the Troy and Greenfield. Local papers announced that an agent had been sent to Europe to secure "a model of the excavating apparatus now in use in the great Alpine tunnel under Mount Cenis."[140] The other news was not so exciting, and it did not appear in the papers, but the people soon noticed there was no work on the route of the railroad between Greenfield and the east portal of the Tunnel. The unsettled issue of the Smith mortgage caused the Governor and Brooks to defer repairing Haupt's abandoned railroad.[141]

This lack of work on the railroad caused the papers in September to wonder whether Governor Andrew was "playing honest." "There is a large and growing crowd who suspect the Governor don't mean to do anything, but to keep up a show for his own interests, in this matter."[142] Soon, however, Doane arrived in North Adams[143] and began working on a new Tunnel survey.

Haupt—or maybe it was Serrell before him—had fixed the direction of the Tunnel based on two lines or azimuths, one from the east and one from the west side of the Mountain. These two azimuths intersected at a slight angle near the center of the Mountain. Serrell, a practiced engineer, knew from his experience in Panama how to survey a railroad route through rough terrain. Haupt, also a practiced engineer, had surveyed a route for the Pennsylvania Railroad through the Allegheny Mountains. The reality of building a railroad exactly to a survey line was a challenge each man understood. Both men had appreciated the difficulty of keeping the miners—who were digging from both sides of the Mountain—on the same line. So, by using an intersecting line, they eliminated the possibility that the miners working from opposite sides would pass like two giant worms in the mass of the Hoosac. Even if the excavations were slightly off the survey line, the two bores would cross, and a small arc could be used at the meeting point to make a transition for the rails.

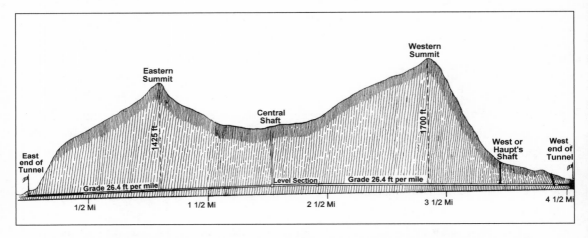

Profile of the Hoosac Mountain, viewed from the north, at the Tunnel line with slight upward angle from each end and level transition in the middle

When the commissioners assumed responsibility for the work, the existing west portal position and west shaft were fixed on one line, and the Tunnel driven from the east portal was along the other line. Doane and Brooks, following the recommendations of the consultants, Latrobe and Laurie, decided to abandon Haupt's work at the old west portal and to establish a straight-line Tunnel through the Mountain. But this new line had to intercept the west shaft, as they did not want to dig another 300-foot-deep hole, and it needed to encompass as much of the existing Tunnel on the east side of the Mountain as possible. There was some flexibility because Haupt's bore on the east side was twelve to fourteen feet wide, and the new plan was for a larger Tunnel that would accommodate a double-track railroad.[144] To establish this new line, Doane set crews to work from the east portal, clearing a twenty-foot-wide swath up and over the Mountain. As the trees and brush were cleared on the steep slope above the portal, a survey crew followed with an ordinary railroad transit, establishing a line.

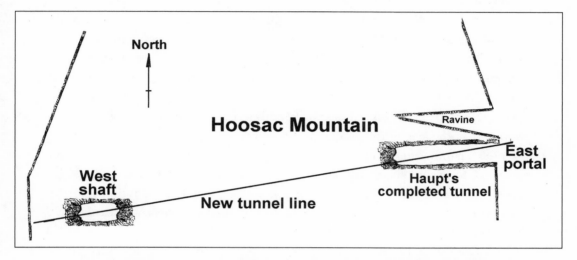

Doane's new Tunnel line connecting Haupt's east-end bore and west shaft

The side of the Mountain was so steep that the horizontal distance between survey points could not be measured directly, so Doane used trigonometry to calculate the horizontal distance of the Tunnel. The survey crew establishing the line set stakes at irregular distances, but the horizontal length between stakes probably never exceeded sixty-six feet. This is because a sixty-six-foot Gunter's chain, the same type Loammi Baldwin Sr. had used for the Middlesex Canal survey, was still the standard device for measuring distance. The sixty-six-foot length may sound awkward, but it was the standard because ten square chains equaled an acre, and land surveying was, until the arrival of the railroads, the main employment of surveyors. In 1867, a 100-foot steel tape for surveying would be patented. The 100-foot tape would soon be referred to as a "surveyor's chain."

Between the stakes, Doane's crew set in the ground to mark their survey points, they used the Gunter's chain to measure the distance parallel to the surface of the Mountain. The surveyors took particular care in making these measurements. They would later correct the measured distance for the tension on the tape and the air temperature when the measurement was made. These individual measured distances between stakes were the hypotenuses for the mathematical right triangles Doane used to calculate the horizontal distance of the Tunnel through the Mountain.

To determine the elevation of the points along the line, two other survey parties with leveling instruments followed the transit party.[145] Each of these parties worked independently so their results could be compared and checked. By the level measurements, Doane knew the changes in elevation between the survey points. These changes represented the length of the vertical leg of each right triangle. Knowing the length of the hypotenuse and the length of the vertical leg, he applied the Pythagorean theorem to calculate the horizontal distance between each stake. It was tedious work, both in the field and in the office, yet to people on both sides of the Mountain there was no sign of progress. There were no miners hammering steel, but Doane was establishing the engineering control necessary to ensure successful completion of the work. Later Doane would be accused of wastefulness, because there was no measurable penetration into the Mountain, but without his commitment to this survey, there could easily have been two dead-end bores into the bowels of the Hoosac Mountain.

Even with Doane's careful efforts, the line lacked the necessary precision to guarantee success. In his December report to Governor Andrew, Brooks explained how the new line entered the Tunnel at the east end near the northerly side of the portal and passed diagonally through Haupt's work before leaving it at the heading near the southerly side. Then, as the line neared the western face of the Mountain, it passed through the west shaft. He continued his comments about the line by acknowledging that it was not "established with the required accuracy but is sufficiently near for immediate practical purposes. It will be necessary in another season to procure proper instruments and establish permanent signal stations upon the prominent points of the mountain for reference points and use during the whole construction of the work."[146] (The signal-station idea was borrowed from Storrow's observation of the Mont Cenis Tunnel survey control.) The three Baldwin engineers were now obviously in close communication.

Focusing on the need for proper instruments, Doane ordered two large transits with astronomical eyepieces from John H. Temple of Boston.[147] John Troughton, who made the instruments for Loammi Baldwin's Middlesex Canal work, had been received into the British Society of Civil Engineers as an honorary member because of the quality of the survey instruments he crafted.

Doane ordered the transits necessary to survey the Hoosac Tunnel from a man of similar stature. Temple was elected to the American Academy of Arts and Sciences in 1845 because of the quality of his instruments.[148] So now, seventy years after the senior Loammi Baldwin had set out for Philadelphia to procure a leveling instrument for his Middlesex Canal project, Thomas Doane required a high-quality instrument to build the Tunnel that Baldwin's son, Loammi Jr., had proposed back in 1825.

Preparations

While Doane was running a survey line over the Hoosac Mountain in the fall of 1863, Herman Haupt was relieved from duty with the Union Army. When called to Washington by Secretary of War Edwin M. Stanton in April 1862, Haupt had refused to accept a commission because he wanted the freedom to return to Massachusetts and fight his personal battle with the Commonwealth. So each time a commission was offered, even at the rank of brigadier general, he declined. Consistently he said that "the country could command his services whenever they needed, but he could not part with control of his time when his presence in the field was not necessary."[149] Some claimed Governor Andrew was behind Secretary Stanton's demands for Haupt to accept the commission, which had already been confirmed by the Senate. Andrew was a good friend of Stanton's, and it was whispered that he used his connections with the administration to try to keep Haupt out of Massachusetts. Finally, in the fall of 1863, Stanton set a deadline for Haupt to make a decision; when the date passed, Colonel Daniel C. McCallum, former superintendent of the Erie Railroad, was appointed brigadier general in Haupt's place.

The survey activity on the Mountain did not satisfy many in northern Massachusetts. One paper reported that the "work has commenced on both faces," while another ridiculed the effort, saying there were "two men and a boy at each end, with a State Engineer to hold a candle."[150] Doane and Brooks were getting ready for the long haul—the very long haul of digging a five-mile tunnel—so most of the 1863 work was preparatory. In addition, Doane began building a better class of shanties, with small cellars and shingled roofs, for the workmen and their families. Brooks wrote Governor Andrew that "the good behavior, self respect, and industry of men are more or less affected by the character and decency of their houses."[151] He continued by commenting on the need for company stores, "to bring the supplies for the men and their families near to the work without introducing intoxicating drink and other evil influences."[152] He and Doane were building whole villages, complete with a company store at each end of the Tunnel as well as at the location of the proposed central shaft.

On the Deerfield River at the east end, the commissioners purchased twenty-nine acres near the Tunnel for the necessary buildings and other conveniences incidental to the work. Based on Storrow's report about the drills at Mont Cenis, Brooks seemed confident that an operational air drill could be procured from Europe or developed in New England. As a result of those hopes, Doane was preparing to build a wooden crib dam on the river, about a mile above the east portal. Using heavy timbers cut from the forest along the Deerfield River, he would have the men stack them in a chain of multiple "log cabins"—called cribs—across the river from bank to bank. To hold these cribs in place, and to resist the pressure of the water, each crib would be filled with rock.

The plan was to use the water behind this seventeen-foot-high structure to power air compressors. The engineering experiences of both Storrow and Brooks were evident in the dam project. Doane designed an overflow structure similar to Storrow's masonry dam on the Merrimack, and the details of the control gates for diverting the water into the channel leading to the compressors reflected Brooks's work with Baldwin on the dry dock in Boston and his later experience with the Sault Ste. Marie locks. Toward the end of October, some fifty men were employed preparing the dam site, and before the first of the year, Brooks reported that Doane had "about 1,200 logs cut for its construction."[153]

But the critics were correct when they claimed very little mining had been done during the first six months the Tunnel was under the commissioners' control. Many believed all the activity of building villages and surveying was a ruse to extend the suspension of real work. At the end of the year, Brooks wrote to Governor Andrew detailing the accomplishments and plans for the next year. He explained his thoughts regarding drainage and his concern about water in the Tunnel. Because "the stratification of the rock is presented to the work nearly at right angles it is thought that the drainage" could be achieved at less expense if put through a culvert in the center of the bore.[154] He also changed the sequence of the mining. The heading that had previously been driven at the top of the section would now be driven at the bottom. He had three reasons for this change: (1) the drainage would be more efficient; (2) it would be possible to have an unbroken line of tracks for the removal of material; and (3) enlargement could be begun at many different points. In the whole length of the eastern Tunnel, the old track and ballast were removed. The change in alignment and the need to correct the bottom grade necessitated this track work. After correcting the bottom grade,

Doane's miners at the eastern end did enlarge approximately two hundred feet of the Tunnel to the new dimensions.

The workforce in the field numbered about three hundred men, collected mainly from Canada and from immigrant ships arriving in New York.[155] Once the site was located for excavating the central shaft, ten and a half acres of land were purchased. Doane excavated a test pit there and hit rock at twenty-five feet. At the west shaft, the old timber cribbing was bulging inward, so it was replaced. The old timber floor for the pumping and hoisting equipment had rotted away, so it was replaced with stone and brick. Once the water was pumped out, Doane began driving the Tunnel headings in both directions. At the west end, twenty-two acres of land were purchased. The commissioners and Doane spent time considering the materials encountered at the west portal. Reflecting on the obvious challenge, Brooks wrote that it "is a heavy piece of work. The cut at the portal is estimated to be about eighty feet deep it may be more or less depending on where suitable rock to commence the tunnel may be found."[156]

The plan for executing this deep excavation was to divide the cut into four levels or benches. Doane began work on the upper bench and relied on horsecarts for hauling away the material. A double-track railway and cars were used to haul away the material excavated from the second bench. The third and fourth benches would not be started until the upper two had advanced far enough to provide workspace.

Brooks purchased twenty-four carts and turntables for this heavy excavation.[157] These preparations were completely in character with the way Brooks went about his work when no one was monitoring his expenditures. In the mid-1850s, when Forbes had stepped down as president of the Michigan Central Railroad, Brooks had assumed the presidency. Able to operate independently and away from Forbes's watchful eyes, he spent large sums of money between June of 1855 and June of 1857 to thoroughly repair and reequip the Michigan Central. With pride, he stated his accomplishments in the annual reports of those years: "The property of the Company has never been in better condition than now."[158] But he also reported expenditures of more than $1.5 million to achieve this. Consequently, in late 1857, when the depression hit, Forbes had to step in and rescue the railroad from ruin by raising $2 million in fresh capital.[159]

With Governor Andrew pushing to see some progress at the Tunnel, Doane began excavating the central shaft on New Year's Day in 1864. He chose to puncture the Mountain with an ellipse-shaped shaft. The long axis was twenty-seven feet and lay parallel to the centerline of the Tunnel, but it was one foot north of the centerline. The width of his ellipse was fifteen feet.[160] His choice of an ellipse was probably driven by a desire to have the greatest possible distance between the two points that would be used later to establish the line of the Tunnel at the bottom of the shaft. A point could be dropped by a plumb bob from where the centerline crossed each edge of the ellipse at the top of the shaft. But for now, more than a thousand feet of rock would have to be excavated before that survey problem would have to be faced. When rock was reached the hard work began. Doane's records testify to the hardness of the rock and the effort required to advance the shaft even one foot. On average, excavating one foot required fifty man-days of labor, 286 dulled drills, and thirty-seven pounds of black powder.[161] Between April and November 1865, the men driving the shaft used more than two tons of black powder. Much work lay ahead before trains would be able to pass through the Hoosac Tunnel.

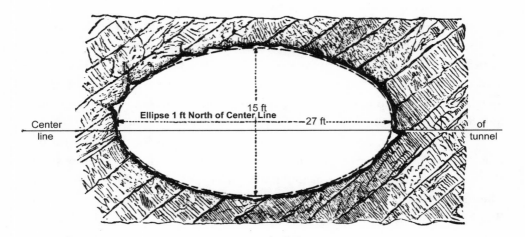

Hoosac Tunnel, cross section of the central shaft

10

American Inventive Genius

Half Froth, half Venom, [he] spits himself abroad,
In Puns, or Politicks, or Tales, or Lyes,
Or Spite, or Smut, or Rymes, or Blasphemies.

—Alexander Pope, *Epistle to Dr. Arbuthnot,*
2 August 1734

ITH WESTERN MASSACHUSETTS BURIED deep under winter snows of early 1864, Doane's miners ventured into the silence of the early morning dark to continue the state's attack on the Hoosac Mountain. Even Francis Bird, the vilifier of Herman Haupt,[1] believed the chief engineer's preparatory activities during 1863 would lead to great progress in 1864. His reflections on the possibility of successfully driving the Hoosac Tunnel would spur Bird, Boston's "Don Quixote, to renew [his] attack on the old Boar."[2] With renewed activity deep in the bowels of the Mountain, the Hoosac Valley newspapers now added a second sad saga to their litany of Civil War tragedies. Week after week, papers on both sides of the Mountain reported war casualties affecting valley families: "Capt. Lawrence Hopkins of Williamstown wounded and has suffered the amputation of his limb; Peter Galligher, North Adams, wounded in the foot; James H. Sheldon, North Adams, wounded in the leg; C. M. Babbitt, of the 37th regiment, of South Adams, lost an arm."[3]

The second litany described the casualties at the Tunnel. During the cold early months of winter, with the temperature dropping below ten degrees, Tunnel workers were often found lying in the snow with shirts and jackets frozen to them.[4] If the cold did not kill a man, there was always the unpredictability of the black powder used to blast the rock. "Last week . . . an Englishman, who was working on the East entrance of the Hoosac Tunnel, was instantly killed by a blast."[5]

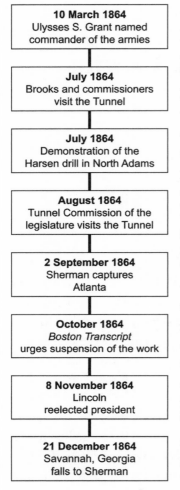

10 March 1864
Ulysses S. Grant named
commander of the armies

July 1864
Brooks and commissioners
visit the Tunnel

July 1864
Demonstration of the
Harsen drill in North Adams

August 1864
Tunnel Commission of the
legislature visits the Tunnel

2 September 1864
Sherman captures
Atlanta

October 1864
Boston Transcript
urges suspension of the work

8 November 1864
Lincoln
reelected president

21 December 1864
Savannah, Georgia
falls to Sherman

Porridge Stone

Even with the new vigor of the commissioners' attack, mining the porridge stone at the west header bedeviled Doane just as it had Haupt before him. Doane's failure to discover a way to drive through the sticky porridge stone slop was the perfect opening for Frank Bird, who renewed his personal attacks on the Tunnel and its supporters. Bird, a paper-mill owner, was then a legislator and member of the Governor's Council. He had been vicious in his attacks on Haupt. Now this pamphleteer, with a great-grandmother who traced her roots to the same family as Nathaniel Hawthorne,[6] the author and Transcendentalist friend of Emerson and Thoreau, would turn his pen on the commissioners and their engineer. He was not bashful about attacking individuals, but he primarily stuck to a theme of describing how the Hoosac Tunnel was wasting Commonwealth monies. While he was not directly aligned with the men of the Western Railroad, he made common cause with them against the Tunnel. Though some did not believe Bird was a vindictive man, his motives might have been tainted by the fact that in 1847 the Norfolk County Railroad had bypassed East Walpole, where his home and paper mills were located. The loss of railroad access was a blow to his enterprises.

He was a "tall, thin, wiry-looking man."[7] In 1848, he organized and chaired the "Bird Club," which until 1871 was a political center in Massachusetts. Beginning in 1860, members of the club assembled regularly on Saturday afternoons for dinner at Young's Hotel in the financial district of Boston. Dinner was just the excuse—the purpose was to discuss political affairs and expound abolitionist and other liberal views. Although he was generally opposed to Governor Nathaniel Banks, Bird had served on the Governor's Council during the Banks administration. Bird being a liberal with progressive ideas, never invited Banks to attend a "Bird Club" dinner. Tunnel supporters would claim Bird provided free dinners at the club as a means of lobbying against the Tunnel.[8] Together with

Governor John Andrew, Bird was one of the strongest supporters in forming the black 54th Massachusetts Regiment in March of 1863. Commissioner John Brooks would soon learn that Francis Bird's written arguments were equaled by few men and were always punishing. Even with the protective shield offered by John Murray Forbes, Commissioner Brooks would be vilified publicly by Bird.

Engineers John Brooks and Thomas Doane had overcome many challenges, but the porridge stone of the Hoosac Mountain's west flank was a mystifying problem. So, adhering to the recommendation of Benjamin Latrobe, their first solution was to raise the grade of the tunnel. This change caused the abandonment of Haupt's bore on the west side of the mountain. Latrobe's other recommendation was also followed, and the workmen therefore proceeded with an open cut some three hundred feet into the flank of the Mountain before they started the new bore.[9] While the open cut was moved forward, the newspapers reported that test holes were being sunk on the west slope of the Mountain to try to locate solid rock.[10]

The advance of the bore was very slow, so while the two engineers struggled to find a workable solution, Bird scribbled away with his acid pen, mocking their every attempt. For the moment, the thrust of his argument was about how the porridge stone continued to defeat the state engineers. With graphic accuracy, Bird described the problem: "In its normal condition it is tough and hard, like rock, but when exposed to the combined influences of air and water, it runs away like quicksand; or, if pent up, it becomes 'porridge.'"[11] For emphasis, he quoted a workman as saying, "Be jabbers, ye might as well try to shovel a cart load of live ells [eels]!" This description and other discouraging words were laid before the public in a long article published in the *Boston Daily Advertiser*. Later, the *Scientific American* reprinted Bird's article, thereby imposing a scientific imprimatur on his dark assessment of the enterprise.

In July of 1864, Brooks and the other commissioners visited the work to review the progress and encourage their engineer.[12] While they were in North Adams, a William Harsen[13] of Greenpoint (a section of Brooklyn), New York, demonstrated his portable pneumatic rock drill (U.S. Patent no. 31,430: 12 February 1861) on a large piece of Hoosac Mountain rock. The rock had been hauled into the yard of the James Hunter Machine Company especially for the trial. After the drill punctured a two-and-a-half-inch-diameter hole six inches into the rock, the local paper enthusiastically reported: "[T]his invention will probably be the drill which will penetrate the bowels of the Hoosac Mountain."[14] Maybe the commissioners were impressed, but, as with so many pronouncements that had been made about drills by Haupt and others, it was wishful thinking.

After the open cut into the west flank of the Hoosac Mountain was completed, Doane started a new bore into the Mountain. He succeeded in driving more than 100 feet by building a stout framework of heavy timbers and planks to hold the Tunnel walls and ceiling in place, but the flow of water steadily increased as the miners advanced. Water poured down from the ceiling, rushed in from the sides, and boiled up from the bottom of his bore. The deluge from the bowels of the Mountain soon caused Doane to halt the work and continue with the open cut past the point where a large spring bled water continuously from the very heart of the Mountain. Even as this revised plan proceeded, Doane began to form a plan and make preparations to arch the troublesome west section of the Tunnel with brick. By mid-August of 1864, an excellent bed of clay was located especially for making bricks.[15]

A week later, the Tunnel Committee of the legislature visited the Tunnel to inspect the work of Doane and the commissioners. The group included Moses Kimball, owner of Feejee the Mermaid. Like Bird, Kimball had been an adversary of Haupt. While Bird did not accompany the politicians, he seemed to have called on the Greek god Poseidon to serve his cause. The *Hoosac Valley News* reported that the gentlemen "got a through wetting by heavy rain,"[16] and what Bird had not yet accomplished with his pen was almost achieved by the rains. The waters of the Deerfield River rose so high it was feared the coffer dam protecting the east header would be carried away and the Tunnel would be flooded. Fortunately, the dam held and the work continued.

When the Governor's Council (also known as the Executive Council) visited the tunnel for two days in late October, Bird again declined the opportunity to view the engineers' accomplishments, and this time his influence over the weather miscarried and the Great Spirit of the Mountain provided sunshine. Commissioner Brooks personally escorted the party as it examined both the east and the west headings and the central shaft.[17] Nonetheless, Bird's associates at the *Boston Transcript* used the occasion once more to editorialize against the Tunnel project. The editor suggested the work should be suspended due to the war effort.[18] The papers of western Massachusetts, including the North Adams paper, responded, calling the Boston writer a "disinterested and philanthropic editor . . . , certainly."

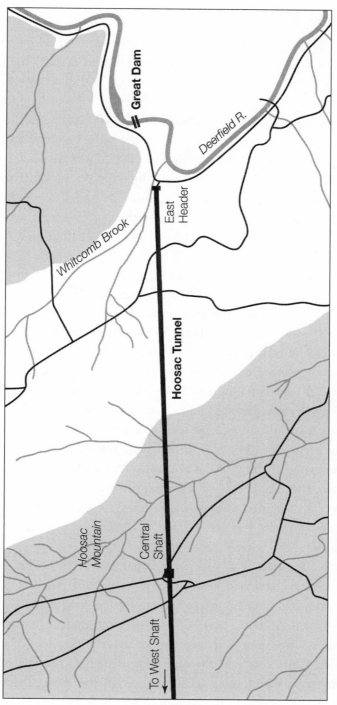

Location of Doane's Great Dam on the Deerfield River

1864—Tunnel Progress

By the fall of 1864, Doane had almost nine hundred men pecking at the Hoosac Mountain with their picks, shovels, hammers, and steel drills.[19] The sight of these men spread between the east and west headings, and at what was then called the Great Dam on the Deerfield River, made every Tunnel supporter extremely happy. The Great Dam was upstream, above the east heading of the Tunnel. The original east heading driven by Haupt was now being enlarged and reshaped to the line and grade Doane had carefully surveyed. Under his plan, both the west and the east headings proceeded into the Mountain on a slight rising grade. To connect the two rising grades, Doane planned to have a short section of level grade in the middle of the Mountain below the central shaft. By using a rising grade from the two portals, water would always drain naturally from the Tunnel.

The height and width of the Tunnel had been increased to enable it to accommodate two tracks. All of the old Haupt heading penetrating into the east side of the mountain was being utilized, but the change in grade and size meant that the crews had to lower the excavation closest to the Tunnel entrance and widen the full length of the old bore. By August, the widening work reached about a quarter of a mile into the Mountain, and carts were steadily running in and out, hauling blasted rock. Doane organized the drilling crews into gangs of four men each. To save the men from having to learn new drilling patterns constantly, a gang always worked holes in the same heading positions at the face of the Tunnel. Two shifts were now used to advance the work. Before beginning their drilling a gang would come in and blast the holes made by the previous shift. The lowering of the grade was completed by December 1864, when the crews reached the old bench of Haupt's discontinued effort.[20] Because the commissioners had decided to press the heading forward using a bottom instead of a top-bench approach, the first months of 1865 were spent taking out Haupt's bench and starting the bottom heading.

The flooded west shaft was pumped out and a new hoisting machine was put in place. Doane was well aware that it would take years to mine through the Hoosac Mountain, so he was prepared for the long haul. Everything was upgraded. He even erected a new building over the shaft. Down the shaft, 4×4 timber guideways were set to receive two safety cage elevators. His plan was to run the loaded dump cars into the cages, hoist them to the top, and then send them out on tracks to dumping locations beyond the shaft. This would eliminate lowering hoist buckets to the bottom of the shaft, loading blast rock into the buckets, and then having to offload the rock into other cars at the top of the shaft.

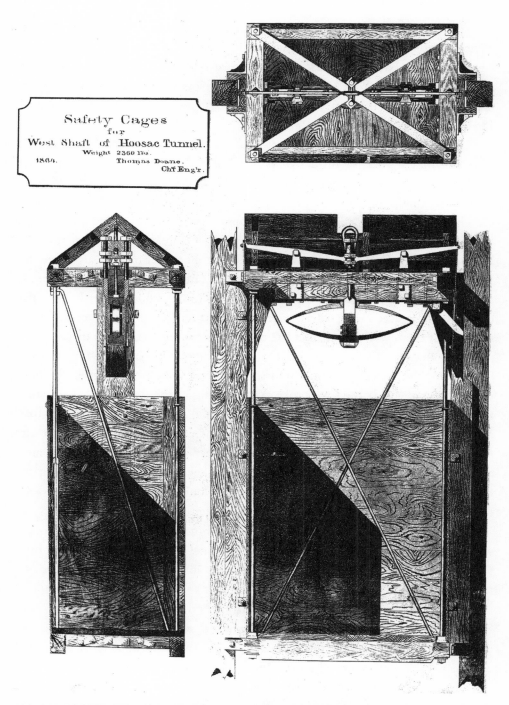

Thomas Doane's 1864 drawing of west-shaft elevator safety cages (courtesy The State Library of Massachusetts)[21]

Elisha Otis, in Yonkers, New York, had developed an elevator safety device to stop an elevator cage if the hoisting rope failed. In 1854, Otis demonstrated his safety device in the Crystal Palace at the Exhibition of the Industry of All Nations in New York. After the exposition closed, he and his sons began to manufacture and sell this safety device, but they did not patent the device until 1861.

Before moving to Yonkers, Otis had worked in Green River, Vermont, and in Albany, New York, so his activities were all within close proximity of North Adams and the Hoosac Tunnel. There is no direct evidence to connect Doane or Brooks personally with Otis, but the possibility exists because, while in Albany, Otis had tinkered with an idea for a safety brake for trains. Another possibility is that someone told the engineers about seeing the Otis elevator brake at the New York exhibition. Still a third possibility is that Charles Storrow suggested the safety brake based on the knowledge he gained examining tunnels in Europe. In 1845, Pierre-Joseph Fontaine, an engineer for a mining company in France, had developed a similar spring safety system for cages in his employer's mines. Soon fourteen of them were installed at the company's pits in northern France.

Whatever the case, when Doane designed the elevators for the west shaft, they had a steel-pointed chisel safety device to stop the cage if the hoist rope should break. If the rope broke, a leaf spring at the top of the cage (which was held tight while there was tension on the rope), would release, and the chisel arms on each side would be forced outward. The extended chisels then cut into the timber guide members and stopped the cage.[22] There were very few elevators at this time, but in another twenty years, as they became more common, the trade magazine the *Manufacturer and Builder* would often report elevator accidents, including ones at Boston City Hall and the Parker House Hotel.

Doane's activities to improve the machinery did not slow the Tunnel work, as he kept the crews busy driving the Tunnel eastward and westward from the bottom of the west shaft while the new equipment was being installed. By the end of 1864, he reported that ninety-six feet of Tunnel had been driven east and west from the bottom of the shaft.[23] Tunnel progress encouraged the Tunnel supporters, but the digging of the central shaft is what drew the most attention; the North Adams paper reported that on one Thursday in August some 112 curious persons had ventured up the Mountain to see the work.

Once Frank Bird and the Western Railroad realized that Governor Andrew would bow to political pressure and let the Hoosac Tunnel proceed, the Tunnel antagonists sought to emphasize the increased cost of the work as a means of enlisting others on their side of the argument. Therefore, they were supportive of the act allowing the work to proceed under the commissioners with the stipulations of increased tunnel dimensions to accommodate a double track and the requirement to sink a central shaft. Both requirements would add to the cost of completing the tunnel. Doane and the commissioners were now proceeding to build what was prescribed, not what they considered prudent, and soon Bird would shout, "The expense is not prudent!"

Doane put S. A. Keene, a man with "great experience in shafting and mining,"[24] in charge of the central shaft work. By August, the pit reached forty feet into the rock, and, at the urging of the North Adams paper, even more visitors were coming up the Mountain to watch the drillers and see the huge derrick.

The publisher of the *Hoosac Valley News and Transcript* was most impressed by the huge derrick Keene had erected to hoist the blasted rock from the shaft. The derrick's mast was sixty-five feet high, with seven guylines to steady it. A fifty-four-foot boom reached out over the shaft from the mast of the derrick. This first derrick could lift ten tons, but its sole source of power was a single horse, the steed would be replaced later by a steam-powered derrick. A 100-horsepower steam engine with three large boilers was already on-site, and workmen were wrestling with the pieces to complete its assembly. On the ground next to the shaft, iron rails were laid within reach of the derrick boom. Rail trucks, assisted by a horse, hauled the cars loaded with broken rock down a declivity to where it was dumped. To support the earthen sides of the upper shaft excavation and to keep rainwater out of the hole, there were plans to wall the upper portion "with solid masonry laid in water cement."[25] This wall, with its interior face set back ten feet from the shaft proper, would have a base width of ten feet and was to extend ten feet above the natural ground surface. The *Hoosac Valley News and Transcript* concluded its August "Hoosac Tunnel" story with the comment that this was "the most gigantic commercial enterprise ever entered upon in these States since the Pilgrims trod old Plymouth Rock."[26] When the cold winds of January 1865 began to greet the visitors, the shaft was down a further ten feet into the rock of the Mountain.

The Great Dam across the Deerfield River

Preparing for the day when a functional pneumatic drill would be perfected, Doane pressed construction of the[27] rock-filled timber-crib dam across the Deerfield River. The dam would supply the necessary waterpower to drive the air compressors he planned to build. He chose a site for this dam about three-quarters of a mile upriver from the Tunnel's east portal.[28]

The dam was a joint effort of engineers who had trained in Loammi Baldwin's office, plus one newcomer. In the "Report of Chief Engineer" for 1864, Doane identified Hiram F. Mills as the engineer at the dam.[29] A native of Bangor, Maine, Mills was an 1856 civil engineering graduate of Rensselaer Polytechnic Institute in Troy, New York. Since 1835, Rensselaer had offered a one-year course in civil engineering. But in 1846, Benjamin Franklin Greene assumed leadership of the school, and by 1849 he had instituted a three-year engineering program based on the French École des Ponts et Chaussés model, so Mills and Charles Storrow had a kinship in hydraulic engineering. The Great Dam of the Deer-field River was designed and built based on knowledge gained in constructing Loammi Baldwin's dry docks for the Navy in Boston and Norfolk, John Brooks's experiences with the locks at Sault Ste. Marie, and Storrow's Great Stone Dam at Lawrence. Mills completed the design details under his Baldwin-trained mentors. Storrow must have regarded him very highly, because Mills took his place when he vacated the Essex Company's chief engineer position in 1869. Mills would likewise continue the hydraulic studies begun by James Baldwin, George Whistler, and Storrow on the Lowell power canals. In all likelihood, the calculations for energy requirements for the envisioned Hoosac turbine-driven air compressors were based on the data from measurements by these engineers. Their files of hydraulic data dated back to 1841.

The Deerfield dam, with a crest length of 250 feet,[31] proved to be a large expense at a time when an operational pneumatic drill was still a dream. But Doane was probably following orders from Brooks, who, together with Crocker, was confident machinists in Fitchburg would produce a reliable drill. This gave Francis Bird yet another opportunity to criticize. He was extremely caustic about the dam, calling it ". . . one of the most extraordinary features of the enterprise" and adding a snide comment about the drills: ". . . to drive the drills in case any can be found which will work."[32]

On the west side of the river, along the base of the Mountain, Doane had men excavating a channel from the reservoir behind the dam to where the compressor building would be erected, immediately north of the Tunnel portal. The dam and the channel would create a water drop of thirty feet, to power the turbine-wheel-driven compressors.

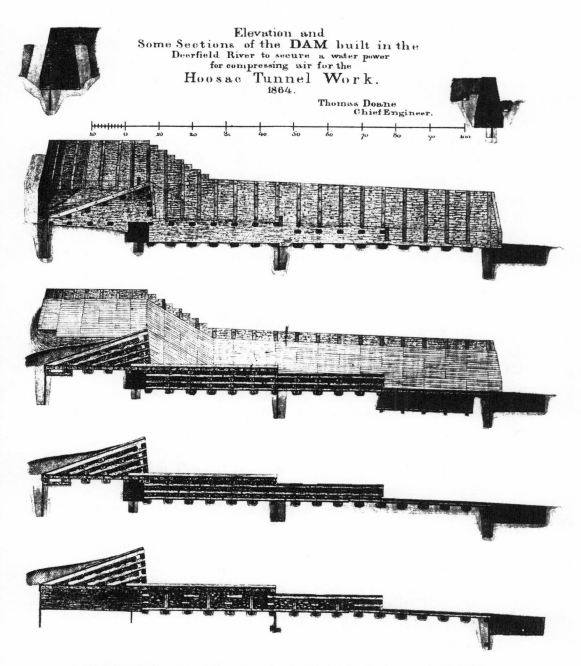

Rock-filled timber-crib Great Dam across the Deerfield River (courtesy The State Library of Massachusetts)[30]

The timber cribs of the dam were tied to the rock of the riverbed with one-and-a-half-inch-diameter steel rods. These extended ten feet into the rock below the bed of the river. The cribs were held together with steel rods of similar diameter. Once a timber crib was completed, it was filled with stone from the canal excavation. This timber-and-rock structure was designed to be overtopped without damage during a flood. Consequently, it had three aprons dropping in terraces to receive the water coming over the dam and to dissipate the energy of such violent flows. To prevent undermining of the dam, during times of flood, a concrete wall extended six feet below the bottom of the river at the lower end of the last apron. The timber crib wall spanned the full width of the river. (Doane in his Chief Engineer's report of 19 September 1864 put the dam height at twenty feet while the commissioner's report has it as seventeen feet. [33])

The *Commissioners' Report* issued at the end of 1864 stated that $450,000 had been drawn from the state treasurer for work during the year, and $252,017.79 was for the Deerfield dam, the compressor building, and the purchase of machinery. The amount actually expended in excavating the Tunnel was a miserly $162,565.45.[34]

Porridge Stone and Rotgut Whiskey

The difficulty of excavating the west-side approach through porridge stone was evident in the excavation cost numbers in the *Commissioners' Report*. In working the open cut and attempting to start a new portal on the west side of the Hoosac Mountain, Doane spent $83,684.31, whereas the enlargement work on the east side of the Mountain had cost only $46,709.51. During 1864, no work was attempted on the railroad between Greenfield and the east portal of the Tunnel, supposedly because the Smith-mortgage question had not been settled by the courts.[35] But in March of 1865, the Massachusetts Supreme Judicial Court ruled the second mortgage of the Troy and Greenfield Railroad to Smith and others was invalid and constituted no lien upon the railroad.[36]

Doane's most vexing challenge, after the porridge stone, was the sale of rotgut and rum in North Adams. Even though he had built boardinghouses for the workmen, these hardworking fellows needed more than a roof to ease their minds about the dangers of the work. Regularly the North Adams paper reported stories such as: "Two tunnel men, under the influence got into a huge fight on State Street, and made music for a few moments."[37] While the fights might have provided minor amusement to townsfolk, the rum often led to tragedy. "Patrick Durgan, a workman of the tunnel of industrious habits, but who occasionally had a spree, in an intoxicated state. . ." fell into the Hoosic River one evening and sank to the bottom before anyone could reach him.[38] To no avail, Doane complained about the rum sales in the village. He repeatedly voiced a warning about how they were disruptive to the orderly conduct of the work.[39] In his "Report of Chief Engineer" for 1864, he wrote, "At the East End and Dam we have been successful in keeping liquors away . . . consequently everybody has been orderly and quiet. But at the Central Shaft, West Shaft, and West End liquor sold within the limits of Adams . . . has occasioned much trouble and has interfered with the orderly conduct of the work."[40]

In late 1864, Herman Haupt returned to Boston and tried to persuade the Massachusetts legislators to pay his claim for liabilities still owed to H. Haupt and Company, but, more important, to release him from liabilities Massachusetts claimed he owed the Commonwealth. He was also fighting a suit the Commonwealth had brought against him for alleged over issue of Commonwealth scrip. At the time, Governor Andrew and the Commonwealth chose to disregard most of his claims, but Haupt did have one claim Massachusetts could not ignore. He personally held title to the land where the west shaft was located and he again pressed his claim for payment with interest. In May 1865, the legislators finally passed an act directing the commissioners, "with the aid and advice of the attorney-general . . . to inquire into the existing title to the shaft at the west end of the Hoosac Tunnel and the land upon which said shaft is located."[41]

In November 1864, Abraham Lincoln had been reelected president and, far to the south, the War of Rebellion continued, with General William Tecumseh Sherman marching through Georgia and capturing Savannah four days before Christmas. For the people west of the Hoosac Mountain, there were a few personal items of good news from the war. For instance, Alexander Harrington of South Adams was paroled and returned home from the infamous Southern prison at Andersonville, Georgia, where at this time 33,000 Union prisoners were being held in squalor.[42]

In North Adams, the year came to a close with William Harsen again demonstrating a rock drill in the yard of the James Hunter Machine Company. This drill had a ratchet arrangement to automatically turn the drill after fourteen strokes, just as a shaker did after every strike of the hammer when men were doing the work by muscle power. This new drill punctured a three-inch hole through a two-foot rock in less than twelve minutes.[43] Fourteen years in the future, Long Island's *Newtown Register* would expound about Harsen's rock-drilling machine, which by then was ". . . exclusively employed on all large public works."[44] In 1864, however, the machine was still not capable of hammering continuously on Hoosac rock.

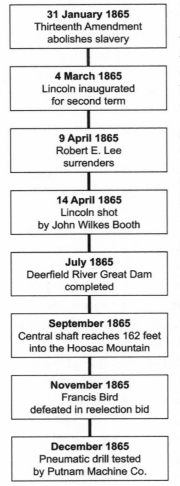

31 January 1865
Thirteenth Amendment
abolishes slavery

4 March 1865
Lincoln inaugurated
for second term

9 April 1865
Robert E. Lee
surrenders

14 April 1865
Lincoln shot
by John Wilkes Booth

July 1865
Deerfield River Great Dam
completed

September 1865
Central shaft reaches 162 feet
into the Hoosac Mountain

November 1865
Francis Bird
defeated in reelection bid

December 1865
Pneumatic drill tested
by Putnam Machine Co.

1865—Relentless Bird Attacks

As the New Year dawned, General Robert E. Lee's Army of Northern Virginia found itself pushed south of Richmond and trying to hold off General Ulysses S. Grant from behind earthworks at Petersburg, Virginia. The boys in blue and the boys in gray then became engaged in tunneling—just like the Hoosac miners—as they tried to burrow under the opposing army's fortifications. In Boston, Frank Bird continued his personal war against the Hoosac Tunnel and its engineers, Thomas Doane and John Brooks. In every council Bird entered, he expressed his consternation about the idea of driving a tunnel through the Hoosac Mountain at Commonwealth expense, and then he repeated his arguments again and again. He was like Don Quixote tilting at the windmills of Spain, and some even began to refer to him as Don Q.[45] So while the *Pittsfield Eagle* rejoiced and reported progress "of 16 feet a day into the solid rock of the mountain,"[46] Bird issued another anti-Tunnel pamphlet: *The Hoosac Tunnel: Its Condition and Prospects.*[47] His skill with the pen allowed him to pinpoint every problem Doane was working so diligently to solve. But he also wrote with the malice of a fiend, and his closing remarks lambasted the commissioners as being "ignorant of the actual state of things."[48] With the Tunnel work in such good hands and obviously progressing, Don Q was joined in opposition by his own Sancho Panza—Daniel Harris, the hostile voice of the Western Railroad. (Sancho Panza was Don Quixote's loyal sidekick in the novel *Don Quixote.*) The *Boston Transcript* suggested that because of the greatly increased price of labor and materials caused by the war, and the Commonwealth's vast expenses, work on the Tunnel should be suspended for the present![49] Even Herman Haupt, feeling he had been wronged by John Brooks and the commissioners, joined the chorus against the

Tunnel: "It is for . . . the legislature, to determine whether you will permit operations to be carried on at the expense of the State treasury, which exhibit, and have exhibited from first to last, such an entire absence of calculation and intelligent investigation."[50] Haupt was a very good engineer, and presumably would have acknowledged the progress on the Tunnel, but his pride and his feeling of having been wronged by the Commonwealth may have spurred those remarks.

The attacks by Bird grew more intense as a result of a public humiliation he suffered at the hands of a Tunnel man. In January of 1865, when Bird was elected to the Governor's Council, he declined to take the required oath to support the Constitution of the United States.[51] As with many Massachusetts abolitionists, this was Bird's way of showing his anger at the U.S. House of Representatives for not passing the Thirteenth Amendment (abolition of slavery). The U.S. Senate had passed such an act in early 1864, but the House did not follow the senior branch's lead. No matter how principled his stand, the War of Rebellion was daily claiming the lifeblood of many a Massachusetts man, so his refusal quickly drew an outcry in the Massachusetts Senate. Soon the press followed with harsh words against such a stand:

> *The brave boys in blue were laying down their lives on that very day in*
> *its defense and support, but a man elected to be an advisor and councilor*
> *of Governor Andrew declined to take an oath to support it.*[52]

Senator Paul A. Chadbourne, a professor at Williams College, patriotically offered resolutions declaring Bird's council seat vacant. To Governor Andrew's embarrassment, Bird's refusal went on for several days. Finally Tappan Wentworth, chair of the Massachusetts Senate, notified Bird that a vacancy would be declared if he did not comply with the Constitution of the United States and take the oath. Wentworth, a Tunnel supporter, would later write of the incident: "The love of office of course predominated over principle. . . ."[53] As Bird continued to harass the project and slander the engineers, these remarks and other similar incidents would be published and used against Don Q by Tunnel supporters.

The Joint Special Committee of the General Court, appointed in 1864 to report on the Troy and Greenfield Railroad and the Hoosac Tunnel, finally delivered its opinion: The railroad was in the undisputed possession of the Commonwealth. The committee, somewhat chagrined, then noted that no progress had been made on the construction of the railroad between Greenfield and the eastern end of the Tunnel.[54]

The failure of the Tunnel commissioners to begin work on constructing the railroad from Greenfield to the Tunnel was a well-known fact, so the next part of the legislators' report was most interesting. It pointed out that the legislation of 1862 had directed the commissioners to "cause the said railroad to be completed" without unnecessary delay. But the report further noted that the legislation also provided "that the road shall not be constructed without the approval of the Governor and Council." The Joint Special Committee, in reviewing the evidence, concluded that because of opposition to the enterprise in the Governor's Council, a compromise had been worked out to allow the Tunnel work to advance—but, by a gentleman's agreement, no work was permitted on the railroad. While the report did not name Bird, it did point directly to the Governor's Council, and Bird was the council member most adamantly in opposition.

Perseverance

After the bottom of the Tunnel's east heading was brought to the grade established by Doane, the bore had a slight rising grade of eighteen feet per mile[55] as it advanced westward from the east header. A drain was then excavated in the middle of the Tunnel floor, allowing water to flow naturally out of the Tunnel and into the Deerfield River. A track was put down over the drain for the small railcars used to haul the excavated rock to daylight beside the river. At the river, the broken rock was dumped down a steep, seventy-foot bank.

By February, the miners reached the end of Haupt's top heading[56] and started the fifteen-foot-wide-by-six-foot-high bottom heading westward into the Mountain. Haupt had advanced his work by taking out the top of the Tunnel first, a top heading. This change to the sequence of mining—excavate the bottom first—was initiated by Doane and the commissioners because it allowed the immediate extension of the dump-car track and helped the removal of excavated material.[57] Later in the year, the contractors working at the east heading imported fourteen mules for hauling the dump cars loaded with broken rock.[58] The bottom heading was, moreover, premised on the prospect of a workable drill. With mechanical drills, the miners would easily be able to drill in any direction—even up.

Two months later, the carnage of the cruel war, far to the south, slowly came to an end—beginning with the 9 April surrender of General Robert E. Lee and his Army of Northern Virginia to the Union forces under General Ulysses S. Grant at Appomattox Court House. But tragedy followed only five days later, when John Wilkes Booth entered Ford's Theatre in Washington, DC, and shot

President Lincoln. Lincoln died the next day, 15 April. Across the South, some were still ready to fight. But in June, General Kirby Smith in the Trans-Mississippi Department, whose divisions had put the Union Army under General Nathaniel P. Banks into a hasty retreat down Louisiana's Red River in 1864, surrendered the last organized Confederate forces. The Red River campaign was a bitter pill for the former Massachusetts Governor who had supported Haupt and the Tunnel work.

While there were celebrations in the North and struggles to survive in the devastated South, the human carnage at the Tunnel continued. The foreman on the night shift at the west shaft lost part of his cheek and nose when the black powder exploded unexpectedly and drove his tamping iron through his face. [59]

To control the water running down the Hoosac Mountain into the ravine of Whitcomb Brook, just to the north of the entrance to the east bore, a small dam was constructed about 150 feet above the Tunnel portal. This location was below the point where a second smaller brook added its waters to the Whitcomb stream. The point where the two brooks joined was known as the Cascade. (Maps from the time when the Tunnel was being excavated use the Whitcomb Brook name. Modern maps record the stream beside the Tunnel as Cascade Brook, and a stream below the Tunnel entrance is named Whitcomb Brook. The earlier maps name the modern Whitcomb Brook as Newman Brook.) During rainstorms, the combined flow down the lower end of Whitcomb Brook would send torrents of water toward the Tunnel entrance. In fact, this was the reason Serrell had modified the Tunnel alignment back in the 1850s. From the pond behind this small dam, Doane now laid a three-inch pipe down the ravine and into the Tunnel to provide water for washing out drill holes. [60] By using water with force enough to clean out the debris from the holes, no additional dust was created in the Tunnel. [61]

Work inside the Tunnel at the east end was now organized in eight-hour shifts, with blasts of black powder made every two hours. The only stoppage occurred on the Lord's Day. Doane directed there be no work from midnight Saturday to midnight Sunday. But drilling of blast holes was still accomplished by the strength of a man's arm—one man holding the drill and the other with the hammer striking the blows. To keep the "John Henrys" supplied with sharp drill steel, there were now three forges in a blacksmith shop at the entrance to the bore. [62]

Through a twelve-inch pipe laid in the drain trench, Doane, like Haupt before him, forced pure air onto the face of the work. Nonetheless, a visitor in the fall reported: "At the extreme end where the miners are at work . . . the heat of the numerous lights and the smoke from the blasts [make] the air very close and uncomfortable."[63] The air pipe was extended as the work progressed, so low-pressure air was always pumped to the most forward point of the advance.[64] Later, an eight-inch pipe for sixty pounds per square inch air[65] for the drills would also be located in the drainage trench.[66]

Doane began to erect buildings on the hillside above the east portal and just north of Whitcomb Brook. These were for the workforce and for staff offices. One large building served as a boardinghouse for mechanics and foremen. The lower floor of another large two-story building was used as a company store; the upper floor held a school for sixty to seventy children. During the week, the wives of the workmen took their young children to the upper-floor school, and on Sundays they scolded husbands for not attending the morning Catholic Mass, or, if they were Baptist, the afternoon service.[67] No liquor was sold in the company store. Doane took a keen interest in his workforce—he was concerned about the welfare of his workmen as well as their families. This was a practice well beyond what was common for the times. The wives of the workmen now had small houses with cellars and shingled roofs built by the Commonwealth, instead of the shanties found on most construction sites or like the one purchased by Thoreau from the Irish man building the Fitchburg Railroad.

The Great Dam of the Deerfield was completed in July, and the canal from the reservoir on the river to the compressor building was ready by September. The walls of the compressor building, constructed of rock excavated from the tunnel, had not yet been completed, but by year's end, it stood at the edge of the Deerfield River above the bend at the Tunnel entrance. The air compressors required a solid foundation, so large limestone blocks were hauled over the mountain from Adams.[68] A turbine wheel of 100 horsepower was already on-site, having arrived in late January, and a small air compressor was purchased for drilling-machine experiments.[69]

At the site of the central shaft atop the Hoosac Mountain, the Commonwealth completed the purchase of a 250-acre farm. Such a large area was needed not just for the shaft but also to supply wood to fuel the boiler and timber for the shaft buildings Doane planned to erect. Having to lift all of the shattered rock out of the shaft meant that progress was slow, but the shaft extended 162 feet into the mountain by September 1865.[70] Doane and the miners managed to reach this depth without any report of serious accidents.

The work at the west shaft continued to progress eastward. A new 100-horsepower engine with three heavy boilers was installed to power the pumps, lifting equipment, and a future air compressor necessary for the anticipated pneumatic drills.[71] Since the commissioners were optimistic that a workable drill would soon be available, the James Hunter Machine Company of North Adams was engaged to build an air compressor.[72]

The mining eastward into the Mountain from the west shaft now extended 260 feet. When the mining to the westward reached a point about 300 feet from the shaft, soft ground was encountered, causing the westward work to be suspended.[73]

The problem of the porridge stone at the west heading was still delaying the work. All attempts at advancement into the Mountain were slow, very slow, and costly, very costly.[74] In late September of 1865, water rushed in on the workers, and all attempts to tunnel through the "live ells" had to be terminated.[75] The "ells" of the Mountain had defeated each and every one of Doane's strategies for boring the west flank of the Hoosac. For the year, he could report only 331 feet of header advance, and even this section might soon collapse, as the large-diameter timbers used to support the bore showed signs of severe distress.[76] In an attempt to locate good rock, he had wells dug farther up the Mountain, but these only established the existence of more rotten material awaiting his miners. One paper reported, "It is yet a matter of experiment, except that a necessity exists for masonry the whole distance from the entrance to the western shaft."[77]

In October, Alvah Crocker—"the faithful war horse of the Tunnel enterprise"[78]—visited North Adams. It was the political season, and Crocker, always watchful of men with political ambition, was accompanying General Benjamin Franklin Butler, who was seeking a seat in the U.S. Congress. His father, John Butler, had fought with General Andrew Jackson at the Battle of New Orleans in the War of 1812, and the son had joined the Massachusetts Militia as a third lieutenant in 1839. By 1855, Benjamin Franklin Butler had risen to the rank of brigadier general in the militia. He served one term as a state senator in 1859 and was very active in national Democratic politics, so he was made a general in the Union Army because of a desire to gain Democratic Party support for the war. However, after Butler's failed performance in attacking Fort Fisher in December 1864 (first battle of Fort Fisher), General Grant persuaded President Lincoln to remove him from command of the Department of North Carolina and Virginia. The order simply said, "[R]epair to Lowell, Mass., and report by letter to the Adjutant General of the Army."[79] He would not succeed in his quest for a House seat until 1867. Crocker made a short speech and alluded to the first Tunnel meeting in the Baptist Church vestry seventeen years earlier.[80] Governor Andrew visited the Tunnel project a week later.[81]

Even Francis Bird was observed, in October 1865, "sneaking over the Hoosac Tunnel works with his pockets filled with the very hardest specimens of rock he could find."[82] But when the votes were counted in November, Francis Bird went down to defeat in his Walpole district.[83] Many were happy about the outcome, but the defeat only served to give the Tunnel antagonist even more time to compose vicious attacks on Brooks, Doane, and the Tunnel.

Attacks by Boston Newspapers

Immediately after the November elections, the Boston-based *American Railway Times* launched a series of attacks to persuade the newly elected legislature to revisit the Tunnel issue. The principal argument used by the *Times* against the Tunnel was the continuing drain on Massachusetts revenues. The paper claimed the money could be better spent and that the entire matter was "prejudicial to the political morality of the State."[84] At the end of November, the *Railway Times* once more attacked the Tunnel in an article signed "Civil Engineer."[85] In the same edition, the editor called attention to the attack article and issued a call for the Commonwealth to "appoint a competent Engineering Commission, composed of men of largest experience and commanding talent." It was a very prejudicial statement against the existing commissioners, who represented the foremost collection of railroad engineering talent in the country—men who before the Civil War had built railroads halfway across the country and who throughout the war had kept their roads operating effectively during a time of extreme need. The final line in the editor's plea was the most interesting, as it borrowed the reference previously used against Francis Bird: "It is certainly not wise to continue the expenditures for the present Quixotic tilt against the 'hidden difficulties' of the proposed tunnel."[86] A week later, the editor yet again questioned the idea of continuing the Tunnel, citing eleven-year-old documents written by Haupt when he was chief engineer of the Pennsylvania Railroad.[87] The *Railway Times* and Bird had referred to Haupt as a shyster a few years earlier when he was trying to tunnel the Hoosac—now he had become an authority to be quoted.

The tactics of the Tunnel opponents would wear on Doane and the commissioners and begin to bear fruit. When a party from the Senate visited the Tunnel in early fall of 1865, the *Adams News & Transcript* reprinted an account from the *Boston Courier*. The *Courier*'s scribbler noted that Herman Haupt had penetrated 2,394 feet into the east side of the Mountain, but now the Doane heading had reached only 2,700 feet[88]—not much progress for more than two years of work. The *Courier* did explain the need to create a uniform grade and the change from a top to a bottom header, but it failed to mention the larger Tunnel diameter imposed by the General Court. Moreover, the article once more informed readers about the way the men were penetrating the Hoosac: "[T]he work continues to be done by hand, one man holding the drill, while others strike with a sledge. . . ."[89] After years of promising statements, there was still no workable mechanical drill.

Brooks and Doane, however, had not given up on finding a workable pneumatic drill, and the first official notice of their efforts was a single line in the *Commissioners' Report* for 1865. It stated that some drills under development at the Putnam Machine Company shop in Fitchburg were tested on 16 December 1865 in that city.[90]

Although Samuel Felton's "stroke of paralysis" in the autumn of 1864 had caused him to resign from his position as a Hoosac Tunnel commissioner early in 1865, he had recovered sufficiently by September 1865 to accept the presidency of the Pennsylvania Steel Company, but he would never again be directly connected with the Tunnel.[91]

The Pennsylvania Steel Company was specifically organized for the manufacture of steel railroad rails. Felton was later one of the organizers of the Northern Pacific Railroad, and he would serve as a director of the road in the early 1870s. The interconnection of engineers from the Hoosac drama would continue for years into the future. In 1881, several years after Felton stepped down from his position with the Northern Pacific, Herman Haupt was named general manager of the Northern Pacific Railroad.

As a result of Felton's resignation, Alexander H. Bullock of Worcester, who had succeeded Andrew as Governor of Massachusetts in January 1866, appointed John W. Brooks, Alexander Holmes, and James M. Shute of Somerville, Massachusetts, as Hoosac Tunnel commissioners. The appointment of Shute, who was not an engineer, was the first crack in the control of the project by engineers. Shute's strength lay in local politics. In January, Herman Haupt again returned to Boston to voice his claims against the Commonwealth. One of Haupt's first efforts was a long conversation with Commissioner Shute, seeking to convert the new commissioner to his view of the Tunnel situation and to explain how he had been wronged. It would be a trying legislative session for both Haupt and the Tunnel supporters.

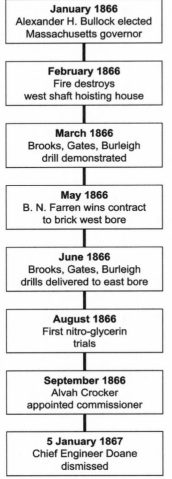

January 1866
Alexander H. Bullock elected
Massachusetts governor

February 1866
Fire destroys
west shaft hoisting house

March 1866
Brooks, Gates, Burleigh
drill demonstrated

May 1866
B. N. Farren wins contract
to brick west bore

June 1866
Brooks, Gates, Burleigh
drills delivered to east bore

August 1866
First nitro-glycerin
trials

September 1866
Alvah Crocker
appointed commissioner

5 January 1867
Chief Engineer Doane
dismissed

1866—A Year of Turmoil

As the legislative battles opened in Boston, catastrophe struck at the Hoosac Mountain. Almost three months of work were lost when a February fire consumed the hoisting house at the west shaft. The rebuilding effort did provide Doane the opportunity to install improved hoisting machinery, but it meant more money spent with no progress on the Tunnel. Then, when the miners again tried to extend the bore westward from the shaft, water began to pour in so rapidly that Doane deemed it unsafe to proceed,[92] and work in the westward direction was wholly suspended. To facilitate removal of the water, Doane commenced excavating an eight-foot-by-fifteen-foot shaft at a location about 264 feet west of the west shaft. Because of its location farther down the slope of the Mountain, the water lift would be reduced almost eighty feet, making the pumping much easier.[93] Once the west-shaft hoisting house was rebuilt, the eastward heading from the west shaft progressed satisfactorily until the end of November, when the miners encountered a water-filled seam of fractured rock. When they broke through the rock covering the seam, a virtual river poured into the Tunnel. The water came in so rapidly the men were standing in two and a half feet of water two days later, as the pump could not keep up with the flood.

The outside air temperatures were beginning to dip to freezing, but the Tunnel's massive rock walls kept the interior temperatures fairly constant, in the mid-fifties. It was miserable working in the water, but at least it was not freezing. After the pump speed was increased and the plunger was enlarged to handle the flow, the miners were again able to begin work on 12 December. But the next day, when even greater quantities of water began to pour into the Tunnel at the heading, work was suspended. By New Year's Day in 1867, the water stood almost ten feet above the grade at the foot of the shaft.[94] When the work was suspended because of this flooding, the eastward heading had reached a point 414 feet from the shaft.

A Brick Tube

After years of trying to tunnel or open-cut into the west side of the Hoosac Mountain in hopes of finding solid rock, Doane finally decided to build a brick tube through the sloppy porridge stone. A contract was arranged with B. N. Farren in May 1866. He would first build 174 feet of tube in the existing open excavation. Then he would proceed to both tunnel and build the brick tube another 200 feet into the Mountain. The Commonwealth would furnish the necessary cement and the bricks, but Farren would be charged $9 per thousand for the bricks. The interior shape of the tube was a series of twenty-six-foot arcs. The bottom was determined by an arc drawn from the centerline of the tube at its uppermost interior point. The width was twenty-six feet, and a radius of thirteen feet described the top of the tube.[95]

Farren was from Doylestown, in Pennsylvania's Bucks County. It is not clear when Haupt brought him to the tunnel work but it seems to have been very soon after Haupt first became involved. Farren was definitely from Haupt's environs in Pennsylvania.[96] He set his crews to work on 7 June, and by December the brickwork had entered the Mountain. But even before he began working, the point selected for the start of the brick tube was moved about twenty-five feet farther west, so he actually built 199 feet of tube in the open cut. When the tube was started at the western end of the cut, it was laid with five courses of brick and the arch had six, but the soft ground soon caused this to be changed to eight bricks thick all the way around. The top support timbers from the upper gallery of the mining operation were left in place to support the soft ground while the arch was being built under them. To help remove water from the Mountain and stabilize the ground, side drains were excavated ahead of the tunneling. As the tube brickwork proceeded into the Mountain, these drains were later filled with stone, but some openings were left in the brickwork to serve as drains into a culvert below the roadbed for the rails.

On the east side of the Mountain, what previously had been called the compressor building was now known as the machine shop, because the upper floor housed lathes, a planer, a bolt-cutting machine, and a saw table. Three turbine wheels were installed under the building, and a fourth pit stood ready to receive another turbine. Above the turbines on the basement floor, two air compressors were ready to supply air to the hoped-for pneumatic drills. Air would also be pumped to the blacksmith shop at the entrance to the Tunnel. The first compressor was installed in January of 1866. It had four cylinders, each thirteen inches in diameter and with twenty inches of stroke (the distance the piston moves in the cylinder). A second compressor was in place by October. It was slightly larger than the first, having four twenty-five-inch cylinders with twenty-four inches of stroke.[98] To clear the Tunnel of smoke, this second compressor was operated for about two hours after each blast.

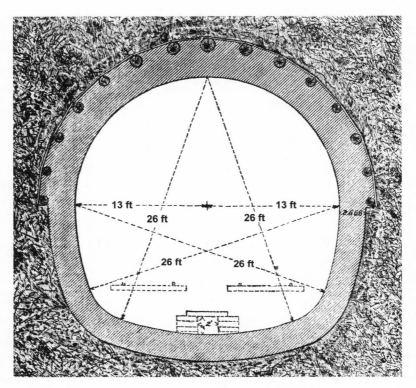

B. N. Farren's brick tube through the porridge stone[97]

The Continuing Quest for a Pneumatic Drill

The Putnam brothers, John and Salmon, were machinists who built and repaired textile and paper machines. They were originally from Peterboro (the name was later changed to Peterborough), New Hampshire, where their father, John, had a farm and practiced the scythe-maker's trade. Their grandfather, also John, was a fifth-generation Putnam who had served in a Minuteman company during the Revolution. He, too, was a scythe-maker. They could trace the family back to a John Putnam who sailed from England in 1634 and landed in Salem, Massachusetts, where he became a prosperous farmer.[99]

John, the older of the brothers, learned scythe-making from their father. Their mother, Mary, blessed the family with thirteen children. Of these, eight daughters and three sons lived to maturity. Needing to help support the family, John, when he reached the age of fourteen, was apprenticed to a machinist in Mason Village (now Greenville), New Hampshire, some ten miles southeast of his family's home. His five-year apprenticeship was only a little better than what Alvah Crocker had experienced in his youth. John worked fourteen hours a day, for which he received one dollar per day and was allowed four weeks of school each year. Before he completed the apprenticeship, his father died. Completing his training, John rented part of the shop in Mason Village and began manufacturing cotton cloth-making machinery. In 1835, his brother Salmon joined him as an apprentice. The brothers attempted to start a business in Trenton, New Jersey, but their partners abandoned them. After that failed adventure, they found employment in East Wilton, New Hampshire, at Deacon Smith's cotton factory, but fate was still against the young men—the mill burned down shortly after they arrived. Another opportunity arose almost immediately at Samuel Wood's cotton factory in the small village of Ashburnham, Massachusetts—seventeen miles due south of their family farm. After a few months as employees, the brothers rented space from Samuel Wood and began business as J. & S. Putnam.[100] Business proved slow in Ashburnham, so in 1838 they moved seven miles away to the 2,000-strong metropolis of Fitchburg and leased a twenty-foot-by-thirty-foot room from Alvah Crocker in the former General Leonard Burbank paper mill,[101] the mill on the Nashua River that the very forward-looking Crocker had purchased in 1835. It was the same mill in which both Alvah and his father had once plied their papermaking skills.

For seven years, the Putnams grew their business from simply repairing machines to manufacturing new ones. As a result, Crocker erected a new brick building in 1845, and the brothers moved their shop into its bottom floor. This brick structure, again with access to waterpower, gave them ten times as much space for their growing business. But calamity struck once again. On the night of 7 December 1849, the building burned.[102] Like Crocker, they were hardworking men, and in two weeks they were back in business, using machines salvaged from the fire and quickly repaired. The next year was especially trying, as they had no insurance to help them recover from the fire losses. But somehow they managed to pay off their debts, and Crocker erected another building on the same spot to serve as their shop. At about this time, their mother, Mary, joined her sons in Fitchburg for the final years of her life.

Charles R. Burleigh, a steam-engine builder who had previously worked in East Boston, joined the Putnams in 1850. About a year earlier, Charles H. Brown had joined the brothers—in fact, Brown purchased a one-third interest in their company. John and Salmon and their two new mechanics reorganized the business in August of 1854 as a partnership, naming it the Putnam Machine Company.[103] In 1855, Charles Burleigh and Charles Brown patented a steam engine, and the patent was assigned to the Putnam Machine Company. Four years later, the partnership was reorganized as a stock company, with Burleigh as a stockholder and director.[104] During the Civil War, the primary business of the company changed to the manufacture of heavy guns.[105] In April of 1865, as Robert E. Lee was surrendering, the Putnam Machine Company delivered to the government a pair of eleven-inch cannons, each of which weighed more than twenty-one tons.[106]

The Putnams and their company had over the years developed a close relationship with Alvah Crocker. This relationship stretched back thirty years before the Hoosac commissioners contacted them to fabricate a pneumatic drill based on drawings and plans the commissioners provided.[107] Some sources allude that Crocker—who was more attuned to the changing political situation and the impact of the attacks by Bird and the Western Railroad—recognized that Thomas Doane's slow, deliberate approach could spell the doom of his cherished enterprise. The necessity to show rapid progress in tunneling the Hoosac Mountain was made very clear to Crocker during the 1866 fight in the General Court for continued funding. If costs could not be controlled and progress improved, all would be lost and citizen Bird together with the Western Railroad would triumph. Hand drilling was just too slow and too expensive, so it is almost certain Crocker was involved with encouraging Burleigh and the Putnams to devise a workable pneumatic drill to speed the work.[108]

Before joining the Putnam Machine Company, Charles Burleigh had an earlier career even more diverse than that of the Putnam brothers. Born into a large family in Waterville, Maine,[109] he was a mere boy when he began working at the blacksmith shop of William Brown. On turning eighteen, he left Waterville and signed on as a sailor for a three-year whaling voyage. After his experiences at sea, he moved to Boston, where he was employed by Otis Tufts. Why he moved away from Boston is unclear, but the tale was told that, while in Shanghai on his whaling voyage, the young Burleigh happened to see a machine marked "Manufactured by Putnam Machine Company, Fitchburg, Mass."[110] The story has some substance, but it is more likely that his friend Charles Brown was the one who induced Burleigh to join him at the Putnams' shop. Brown had worked with Otis Tufts, and he preceded Burleigh to Fitchburg.[111] In Fitchburg, people pointed out Burleigh as the man with the long beard, or the heavy black beard, and they spoke of him as a man who did not trifle.[112]

Sometime in 1864, the commissioners had secured the plans for three different drilling machines.[113] One of these sets of plans was probably for the Sommeiller pneumatic rock drill Storrow had observed at the Mont Cenis Tunnel. In his report on European tunnels, Storrow stated that Germain Sommeiller gave him a "drawing on a scale of one fifth the full size, which shows the latest pattern."[114] Because both Jonathan J. Couch and Joseph A. Fowle had patented their drills, it would have been possible to obtain from the U.S. Patent Office information and drawings showing their ideas in detail. Years earlier, Haupt had looked at the Couch and Fowle drills. As a result of those examinations, he and his mechanic, Stuart Gwynn, had followed Couch's ideas as they sought to develop a workable drill. Haupt later went so far as to claim that the hollow piston with a lance-type drill was separately invented by Gwynn.[115]

The efforts of Haupt and Gwynn had ended abruptly when the Commonwealth took over the Hoosac Tunnel work. But Gwynn did receive two drill patents of his own in 1864. The last one, no. 44,862, was still of the Couch hollow-piston design, but Gwynn added a ratchet to rotate the drill steel. In 1865, Haupt obtained two successive patents, again following the ideas of the Couch drill. His later patent added a gripper to regulate the feed of the drill steel. The drills that William Harsen demonstrated for Doane in North Adams were of a design similar to the Couch hollow-piston idea, but they had a ratchet to rotate the piston and drill steel together.[116]

Believing he could perfect a Couch-type drill, Burleigh initially followed the path of the Haupt and Harsen efforts. This work produced the W. Brooks, S. F. Gates, and C. Burleigh drill, which they patented on 6 March 1866. Stephen Gates was a machinist who in the 1850s had been superintendent of the Locomotive Building Department of the Lowell Machine Shop.[117] He held a patent for a slide valve. While Brooks, Gates, and Burleigh held Patent no. 52,960, the right to use the drills in the construction of the Hoosac Tunnel was assigned to the Commonwealth of Massachusetts.[118]

A delegation from the legislature traveled to Fitchburg via special train in late March 1866[119] to witness a demonstration of the drill.[120] Haupt even joined the men for the trip and carefully observed the operation of the drill. After the demonstration, he praised the commissioners' drill, but he then asserted the drill was different in no essential feature from his own, apart from an improvement in the feed. Maybe in hopes of influencing his audience, he even let it be known he hoped to sue for patent infringement because the essential features were covered by his two 1865 patents.[121] After delivering those comments in Fitchburg, Haupt returned to Boston and composed a twelve-page explanation of how the drill he had seen followed his patents. On the last page, however, he told the commissioners it was not his "practice to cherish resentment."[122] The following year, he would publish a small booklet titled *Tunneling by Machinery* to reassert his claim as the inventor of the drills.[123]

Shortly after the delegation's visit, an enthusiastic report of the demonstration appeared in the *Worcester Palladium* and was immediately reprinted in the *Adams Transcript*,[124] whose editor described how the drill penetrated twenty-three inches into a block of granite in less than twelve minutes. Moreover, the idea of using compressed air to power the drill had impressed the visitors, and the news report concluded with the statement: ". . . thus the tunnel will have a constant supply of fresh air by the same power that drives the drill." Believing they had finally found a suitable drill, the Tunnel commissioners ordered forty.[125]

Fights in the Legislature

Haupt stayed in Boston buttonholing senators and representatives as he sought a favorable bill to address his many claims for unpaid compensation. It was the eleventh year of his personal involvement in the Hoosac Tunnel saga, and his battle with the Commonwealth would continue for many years in the future. This time, however, his old adversary, Francis Bird, was working with him and even lobbying legislators on his behalf. In fact, Haupt had buried the hatchet with both Bird and Daniel Harris of the Western Railroad. Together this team of newfound friends was successful in the House, but Crocker prevailed in killing their bill in the Senate. Crocker and the Tunnel men were fearful such a bill would have an impact on their own appropriation request, which was necessary to keep the Tunnel work going. Writing to Henry Cartwright in early May, as the 1866 session was rapidly drawing to a close, Haupt explained how Crocker and other Tunnel men had killed his relief bill. He also revealed that he and Bird had been in daily communication during the previous week.[126] The last line of his letter expressed a wish for the Tunnel appropriation to fail and thus punish Crocker for his treachery.

The battle to continue the Tunnel was intense. Four days after writing to Cartwright, Haupt penned a letter to his wife, telling her that John Brooks had presented a communication against Haupt's claims to the Tunnel Committee. The committee chair, who was supportive of the Tunnel project, got an order to have it published. But the printer allowed Haupt to see this report, and he immediately set to work scribbling a rebuttal. Three days later, when the Senate reconvened, Haupt and his friends were successful in having his reply combined with the statement by Brooks. Haupt gloated in the small victory, saying it was a ". . . most bitter pill for Mr. Brooks and his friends."[127] Two days later, Brooks collapsed in a state of paralysis just as he completed his testimony against Haupt's claims in the Senate. As had occurred with Samuel Felton in 1864, the strain of keeping the Michigan Central running during the war and dealing with all of the politics surrounding the Tunnel had taken their toll on Brooks. He would eventually recover, but for days he lay in a room at the Tremont House Hotel below Beacon Hill and could not be moved.

The Tunnel men got their appropriation of $900,000 to continue the work, and Haupt succeeded in having a commission appointed to review his claims and the counterclaims of the Commonwealth, but no money was immediately forthcoming from the Commonwealth to the man from Pennsylvania. By August, Brooks was improving but could not resume his commissioner duties. Therefore, about the first of September 1866,[128] Governor Alexander Hamilton Bullock appointed Alvah Crocker to succeed Brooks as the lead commissioner. The legislation providing additional funds for the Tunnel contained a clause directing the Governor to appoint a consulting engineer, so on 1 August, Benjamin Latrobe was again engaged to advise about the Tunnel project. Felton and Brooks, the two Baldwin-trained and experienced railroad engineers, were now gone from the Tunnel Commission—in fact, the new commission lacked anyone with engineering experience. Engineer Thomas Doane, who had trained under Felton in Baldwin's office, was now reporting directly to Alvah Crocker, the paper manufacturer. Crocker was now a rich man, but he still harbored that long-held dream of a railroad across northern Massachusetts. It was not just a matter of a railroad or a tunnel—it had become a personal challenge.

Around the middle of June, when the first batch of drills from the Putnam shops were delivered to the east heading of the Tunnel, Doane immediately put them to work.[129] Stephen Gates arrived to superintend their use. According to the commissioners, these drills were reported to weigh 240 pounds each,[130] but the *American Railway Times*[131] had the weight of the drills at 210 pounds. In either case, these were not tools a single man could handle easily, so they were mounted on a carriage of Doane's design. The carriage could hold several drills in place at one time and it allowed the drills to be aimed in any desired direction. The carriage frame had steel wheels and rode on the tracks used for the dump cart.[132]

Unfortunately, the new drills were not a success. The constant jarring from banging on the rock of the Mountain quickly rendered them inoperable.[133] The longest run for an individual drill before one of its eighty parts shattered was five days. By applying a large force of mechanics, however, a fair number were kept in service for a few months. The crews using the drills penetrated fifty-four and a half feet in the month of September, which was seven feet greater than the 1866 monthly average. But the number of working drills diminished with repeated use. Even Charles Burleigh admitted that "these drills were kept in operation at the Tunnel for several months, with very unsatisfactory results, and at great expense."[134] After he visited the Tunnel in August to inspect the work and performance of the drills, his conclusion dampened everyone's spirits: "I became perfectly convinced that the Brooks, Gates, and Burleigh Drill could never be made to do the work, it being wrong in principle."[135] Now, with both Felton and Brooks gone, and after so many years of stress defending the Tunnel, seventy-one-year-old Commissioner Alexander Holmes submitted his resignation in August. Years later, he testified before a legislative committee that "Crocker was the governing man at the tunnel."[136] He then went on to say that Crocker believed the organization of the Tunnel work was faulty and they needed to reduce the number of "scientific men."

Charles Hudson of Lexington would subsequently be appointed commissioner to fill the seat vacated by Holmes.[137] He was a most interesting choice. Besides being a politician who had served as a state representative, a state senator, and as a U.S. Representative from 1839 to 1849, Hudson had been president of the Lexington and West Cambridge Branch Railroad. But his last connection with railroading was as a state director overseeing the Boston and Albany Railroad which had come into existence by the amalgamation of the Boston and Worcester with the Hoosac Tunnel's nemesis, the Western Railroad. But Crocker obviously knew this man well, because Hudson had been "one of the first and most active to organize the Vermont and Massachusetts Railroad."[138]

Nitro Trials

With Crocker in charge and the question of the Smith mortgage settled by the courts, work on the railroad from Greenfield to the east portal of the Tunnel became a priority. Bids were solicited from contractors, and the *Adams Transcript* announced in early October that a contract with B. N. Farren[139] awaited action by the Governor and the Governor's Council. Farren, whom Doane had previously engaged to excavate and brick the west-header tube, was now going to build the entire railroad on the east side of the Mountain. He was to complete the road to Shelburne Falls by November 1867 and to the Tunnel by mid-July 1868. The contract was quickly approved, and work commenced in Greenfield on the second-to-last Monday in October. At the same time, the commissioners leased this unbuilt line to the Vermont and Massachusetts Railroad. Crocker would soon have a railroad stretching from Boston through Fitchburg and on to the Hoosac Tunnel. The lease, which was valid only until the Tunnel was completed, called for yearly payments of $30,000.[140]

Except for one pier, the masonry of Haupt's Green River Bridge was to be taken down so the bridge could be rebuilt on a straight line instead of a curve. The *Commissioners' Report* for 1866 noted that "all of the bridges on the line are to be 'Howe's Truss,' and equal in strength and durability to any in New England."[141] Had Crocker made peace with Daniel Harris, the Western Railroad mouthpiece, by publicly stating that the rebuilt road to the Tunnel would only have Howe truss bridges? Such a decision ensured patent payments to Harris. Crocker was certainly putting his personal stamp on the work that had been his dream for more than twenty years, but he was not an engineer.

To shatter the mica and quartz rock of the Hoosac Mountain with black powder required holes drilled very close together, lots of drill holes. This had been the decisive factor driving the search for a mechanical drill. But the problem, it seemed, could be approached in another manner. Doane realized early on that it would be possible to improve the rate of penetrating the Hoosac Mountain if they could use a stronger blasting agent to shatter the rock. During his many years as chief engineer, he had been seeking a stronger explosive and a way to fire several charges at the same time. In his report for 1866, he stated: "It has been my continual desire since entering upon this work . . ." to fire charges simultaneously and to find a more powerful explosive compound.[142] During the summer when the Burleigh drill was being tested, Doane conducted his first explosive experiments.

Colonel Taliaferro Preston Shaffner, representing the United States Blasting Oil Company, spent three days[143] at the west shaft's eastward bore in August, demonstrating his explosive compound against the rock of the enlargement.[144] What his company possessed and Shaffner came to demonstrate was Alfred Nobel's nitro-glycerin.[145] The company held the American patents for this new explosive compound. In addition, Colonel Shaffner personally held a patent for an electrical blasting machine.[146]

Working on the six-foot-high and fifteen-foot-wide enlargement, Shaffner's nitro-glycerin allowed the crews to advance fourteen and a half feet in three days. Obviously, this new explosive was much stronger than black powder. Doane thought it was eight times more powerful. The colonel's "magneto-electrical" system fired the shots, but the electrical firing was unsuccessful, as only five charges could be fired at one time, and this was inadequate. Two other electrical blasting machines the commissioners had ordered from Europe arrived shortly after the nitro-glycerin tests, and Doane was able to fire as many as thirty-one charges simultaneously with these machines, which were called frictional ebonite battery machines. He explained in his report that a blast of several holes at the same time allowed each charge to help the others tear the rock away. Other benefits from using electrical firing were reduced risk of accidents and the elimination of the smoke from a burning fuse.

Simultaneous firing with the frictional ebonite battery machines from Europe was also tried in the central shaft. Even without the more powerful explosive, progress was increased almost twenty-five percent with simultaneously firing. When Colonel Shaffner returned to North Adams on 8 October with more nitro-glycerin, the experiments were again impressive. The *Adams Transcript* reported that the miners took three days to clear away the rock that a single blast had ejected.[147] This time, all of the shots were at the east heading from the west shaft, and all were fired with electricity.

Then, in late November, experiments with another explosive compound—called Dr. Ehrhardt's Powder—were tried on the east side of the Mountain. When the powder was fired, however, it drove the miners from the Tunnel because of the very disagreeable gas the blast created. Tests were then tried at the central shaft for a week, ending with disastrous results when the stuff fired prematurely, killing one miner and injuring three or four others.[148]

After Burleigh visited the Tunnel, he returned to the Putnams' shops in Fitchburg and set to work to perfect a drill capable of holding together while constantly beating on hard rock. He followed Joseph Fowle's approach and attached the drill steel directly to the piston rod. To rotate the drill steel, he followed William Harsen's idea whereby the piston and drill rotated together. He filed an improvement notice for the earlier patent on 27 November 1866, and sixteen of the improved Burleigh drills were sent to the Tunnel before the end of the year. These performed much better, averaging five days of hard work in the Tunnel before needing repairs—and, more importantly, the needed repairs were minor.

Doane was very close to solving the critical problems associated with speeding the Tunnel work. The new Burleigh drill looked very promising, his Deerfield River Dam stood ready to capture the waterpower of the river to drive the air compressors and provide the air for the drills, simultaneous electrical firing of shots was already speeding the work, and a source of nitro-glycerin would surely make a major contribution to the rate of progress. From the engineer's point of view, 1867 held promise. But tunneling remained a very dangerous job, and the day after Doane filed his annual chief engineer's report with the commissioners, there was a fatal accident at the central shaft. A spark from the lamp on the visor of one of the workmen fell into the powder being prepared for a blast and caused a premature explosion. One man was killed, a second was very seriously injured, and two others were badly hurt.[149] Doane had been well aware of this danger to the men handling explosives. Carrying a live flame on their heads was not a good situation. In his report, he had a single line mentioning experiments with the use of naphtha gas to provide lighting for the workmen.

Believing the work was now well in hand, and feeling the need to reduce expenses, in early January 1867[150] Commissioner Crocker abolished the chief engineer position and reduced the engineer corps to a single resident engineer. On 5 January, Thomas Doane's association with the Hoosac Tunnel reached an abrupt end. All of the engineers who had trained in Loammi Baldwin's Charlestown office had now departed from the project that Loammi had proposed forty years earlier.

11

Nay an Engineer

Why is it that the Commissioners of it are all non-professional?
I mean non-professional in an engineering sense.
One is a paper maker, another an ex-clergyman,
and another a manufacturer of newspaper type.

—J. A. Haven, "The Hoosac Tunnel
Commissioners," *American Railway Times* 19, no. 18
(4 May 1867).

I N 1847, ALVAH CROCKER's Fitchburg Railroad erected in Boston a magnificent granite-walled station with battlement towers at each corner of the facade.[1] When the station was torn down in 1927 one tower—the Jenny Lind tower—was dismantled and transported to Cape Cod where it was re-erected. Jenny Lind (Johanna Maria Lind), the "Swedish Nightingale," was a renowned opera singer who the impresario P. T. Barnum brought to the United States in 1850 for a series of concerts. She was to give a concert in the hall of Crocker's station but all who wanted to attend could not crowd into the building. The story of the incident claims that to prevent a riot the lady climbed onto this seventy foot tall tower and gave her performance. This is probably the reason the tower was preserved but it should also be remembered Barnum liked to create such stories.

From this station on Causeway Street, trains carried travelers from the "Hub City" as far as Greenfield, on the Connecticut River in western Massachusetts. Beginning in 1865, those who wanted to venture on to North Adams made the journey up the Deerfield Valley and the eight miles over the Hoosac Mountain in elegant stagecoaches pulled by six horses. These stagecoaches, belonging to Barnes and Company deposited passengers in North Adams on the steps of a hotel as grand as the Fitchburg's station in Boston.

Washington Gladden, the Congregational minister in North Adams, described this hotel as "quite a phenomenon in a village. . . ."[2] Located on Main

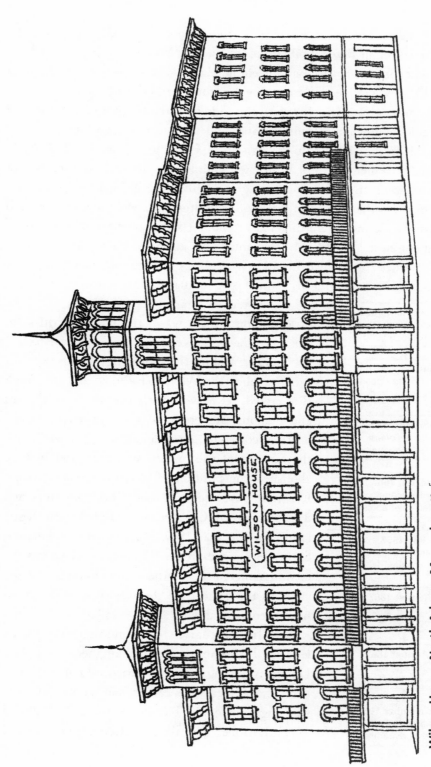

Wilson House, North Adams, Massachusetts[5]

Street, the Wilson House was so large its ground floor housed the post office, the telegraph office, eight stores, a billiard room, and the Masonic Hall. In early 1867, Alvah Crocker arrived at this magnificent hotel and took up residence.[3] All of the Baldwin-schooled engineers were now gone from the Hoosac Mountain Tunnel work, and non-engineer Crocker, with the consent of the Governor, held the dual offices of chief engineer and commissioner under the title of superintendent.[4]

In his January address to the legislature, Governor Alexander H. Bullock, a lawyer and a former mayor of Worcester, said not a word about the removal of Thomas Doane or any of the other engineers from the Tunnel work. He did, however, mention the section in the 1866 legislation whereby the Governor and the Governor's Council were directed to appoint a competent and experienced consulting engineer. Accordingly, Benjamin H. Latrobe of Baltimore was again employed by the Commonwealth and charged to examine the work and report directly to the Governor and his council on a regular basis.

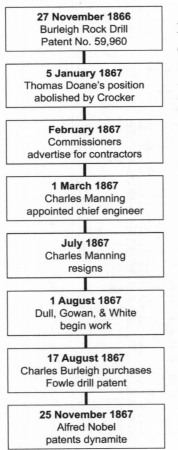

27 November 1866
Burleigh Rock Drill
Patent No. 59,960

5 January 1867
Thomas Doane's position
abolished by Crocker

February 1867
Commissioners
advertise for contractors

1 March 1867
Charles Manning
appointed chief engineer

July 1867
Charles Manning
resigns

1 August 1867
Dull, Gowan, & White
begin work

17 August 1867
Charles Burleigh purchases
Fowle drill patent

25 November 1867
Alfred Nobel
patents dynamite

After so many years of effort and so little progress, there was a trainload of critics "to denounce the work as a stupid and expensive folly."[6] So Crocker, feeling the mounting pressure against the Tunnel by the Western Railroad and the Frank Bird crowd, set to work with a fury to cut expenses and demonstrate progress. He reduced the engineering corps to a single chap, dispensed with the services of the master mechanic, and in June abolished the position of superintendent of labor. Everyone involved with the work now reported directly to Alvah Crocker. In the report to the legislature for the year 1867, the eloquent explanation for these changes read: "[I]n all cases where the commissioners believed the salary paid was of more value to the State than the service rendered, men have been discharged."[7]

In February, the commissioners hired Charles P. Manning as chief engineer to replace Doane. Manning was an experienced railroad engineer who, fifteen years earlier, had served as a division engineer for the Baltimore and Ohio Railroad under Latrobe. It is likely Latrobe recommended him for the position at the Tunnel. Manning's Sixth Division on the B&O line to Wheeling had included the Board Tree Tunnel—one of the first major railroad tunnels in the United States—so Manning's tunneling experience stretched back to the early 1850s.[8] At the Board Tree, he and Latrobe had resorted to iron arching to hold troublesome faulted rock in place.

When the new chief engineer reported to the Hoosac Mountain work on 1 March, Crocker would not allow him to perform any duties. Commissioner Charles Hudson wrote that Manning was "treated with cold neglect and was not allowed to have any voice in the business of the tunnel. . . ."[9] After four frustrating months, Manning resigned. Crocker had nothing personal against the engineer, but he sought complete control, and any engineer with an independent mind was not welcome in North Adams or at the Hoosac Mountain. Nonetheless, Crocker provided Manning with a glowing letter of recommendation, including testimony that Manning was a man of "great professional skill."

Later in the year, Crocker would employ W. P. Granger, a thirty-three-year-old North Adams man, as assistant engineer. During Doane's tenure, Granger had been employed as the resident engineer at the west shaft and had received a salary of $1,350 per year, while Doane was receiving $4,000.[10] He had not learned his engineering under the exacting tutelage found in Loammi Baldwin's Charlestown office, and he lacked the experience and stature necessary to challenge Crocker's decisions. This junior engineer was now the only fellow possessing a semblance of professional skill on the country's most difficult engineering project. By early January 1868, Granger would begin signing reports over the title "Resident Engineer."

While Latrobe would later praise many aspects of Crocker's management, he would, in his gentlemanly style, make it clear that their thoughts concerning numerous engineering issues diverged.[11] Crocker always addressed Tunnel questions in terms of dollars spent today, while Latrobe sought to consider risk and to take a long-term view. By his training and experience as an engineer, Latrobe knew how to analyze both the technical and the financial aspects of engineering tasks. At the B&O, he had learned to look at work and cost as a single entity driven by employee considerations, consumption of energy, and performance of machines.

Even with all of his energy and dedication to the Tunnel, Crocker was in a very difficult position. He realized the performance of John Brooks as the lead commissioner had been less than satisfactory because many Tunnel opponents could say progress was not proportional to the funds expended. Consequently, in the chaos of the massive enterprise, Crocker struggled to demonstrate progress while playing Scrooge with the funds. Everything had to be done as inexpensively as possible. Necessary purchases of equipment and machines would not be approved if it was possible to repair old machines or purchase something cheap to serve the immediate need. His penny-pinching approach was radically applied to the water problem at the west shaft.

The increased flow of water into the east and west headings from the west shaft had forced the suspension of all mining in December 1866. Before his dismissal, Doane had recommended the commissioners spend $50,000 for "two bull engines" and pumps to remedy this flooding situation. The term *bull engine* refers to the crank mechanism of the machine—the piston reciprocates inside the cylinder while the cylinder simultaneously rotates about a fixed point. Such an arrangement is excellent for pumps. Its name originated from an action against a Mr. Bull by James Watt to protect his single-acting pumping engine.[12] Bull had used the rotating-cylinder mechanism when manufacturing pumps for Cornish mines.

While Commissioner James Shute considered the purchase of the two engines a large expense, he approved the suggested purchase and passed the matter over to Crocker, who was the only other commissioner at the time. Crocker concurred about the cost, took no action, and began looking for a way to solve the problem on the cheap. So, as the months rolled by, mining at the west shaft remain stalled because of the flooding.

More Accidents

Tunneling is always hazardous work, and with the added pressure to speed the work, the Hoosac became as deadly as the Gettysburg and Shiloh battlefields of a few years earlier. Miners in Europe driving the heading from the French side of the eight-and-a-half-mile Mont Cenis Tunnel experienced only thirty-six deaths during fourteen years of work.[13] But the Hoosac Tunnel had always been a place where human bodies were crushed under rocks, blasted into unrecognizable pieces by explosives, or pounded senseless by large timbers. With the lack of engineering leadership, the Hoosac would claim almost as many lives in one year as the French lost in all their years of tunneling Mont Cenis.

Reports of death underground always brought a crowd of wives from the shantytowns around the diggings. When "a limp body in earth-stained overalls and a torn black shirt was carried out into the sun a sobbing woman hid the eyes of her small children in her skirt."[14] Over the years, the scene was repeated regularly. Still the human moles continued to burrow the Mountain, often humming the Irish driller's song:

> *Drill, ye Tarriers, drill*
> *For it's work all day,*
> *for the sugar in your tay,*
> *Down beside the railway*
> *And drill, ye Tarriers, drill*
> *And blast and fire.*[15]

The first deadly accident of the year occurred on 18 March, when a premature discharge killed a miner named Key. Two other miners were seriously hurt by the force of the explosion.[16] This mishap was a trifling event, however, compared to what Fred Trombly (spelled Twombley in some accounts) experienced. He was working at the bottom of the central shaft when an iron drill fell from above and pierced him through. It struck him in the abdomen, came out of his body just below the knee, passed through the two-inch plank on which he was standing, and continued deep into the earth and rock under the plank. To release the poor man, his coworkers had to drive the drill back through the plank before it could be withdrawn from his body. When his punctured body was finally freed, they hoisted him the 325 feet to daylight and carried him home. Though the man was beyond help a doctor was summoned as a matter of course. The accident occurred on a Friday, but Trombly lingered until Saturday before death finally released him from his agony.[17]

The workmen were not the only ones who suffered. In May, measles broke out among the families on the east side of the Mountain. In the crowded conditions of the work camps, this extremely contagious children's disease struck more than fifty youngsters.[18]

The third death of a miner occurred later in May, when a fuse hung fire (the charge failed to fire[19]). Then just as the workmen returned to clear the blasted rock at the Tunnel face it exploded. When firing black powder, the miners would count the explosions to tell whether all the holes had fired, but the count was wrong on this occasion, and Michael Devine was killed by flying rock.[20]

Pneumatic Drill Success

The Tunnel commissioners, since taking charge of the work in 1862, had looked at seventy or eighty patented drill machines and reached the conclusion none were capable of useful work.[21] Two years after engineer Charles Storrow visited the Mont Cenis Tunnel in 1862, the commissioners sent their chief assistant engineer, a Mr. Brown, to Mont Cenis to procure a sample drill. But, at the time, Germain Sommeiller, the engineer directing the Mont Cenis work, told him they were dissatisfied with the drills and were seeking to manufacture an improved model.[22] In the Massachusetts Senate Report no. 59 on the Hoosac Tunnel,[23] detailing Tunnel expenditures through the year 1866, it was claimed that "about $13,000 was spent" on experiments to construct the Brooks, Gates, and Burleigh drill. This figure did not include the cost of manufacturing the drills tested by Doane at the Tunnel. The total cost over four years of the Common-wealth's effort to develop a workable drill was about $100,000, and the Brooks, Gates, and Burleigh drill was a total failure. Those opposed to the Tunnel would point to the fact that a Brooks, Gates, and Burleigh drill capable of standing up only a single day to the abuse of pounding rock two hundred times a minute cost $400, whereas a reliable Colt revolver only cost $10 and lasted a lifetime.[24] As a consequence of the attacks against the Tunnel in the legislature, Crocker and the commissioners decided to expend no further funds on drill development. At the same time, though, they let it be known that if individuals experimented at their own expense and succeeded in manufacturing a drill capable of effective and continuous work, there would be a substantial payment.[25] Hence Crocker encour-aged Burleigh to continue his efforts to perfect a useful rock drill.

So at his own expense, Burleigh continued trying to develop a reliable mechanical drill. He next pursued Joseph Fowle's ideas and created a machine with the drill steel attached directly to the engine piston.[26] This was a completely new machine weighing 372 pounds,[27] but it was based on Fowle's concept of direct action (U.S. Patent no. 7972 of 1851).[28] The critical feature, designed to keep the drills from destroying themselves, was the way Burleigh caused air to be vented to the back of the cylinder with each blow. When the piston and attached drill steel recoiled after striking the rock, this exhaust air acted as a cushion. Several drills of this new design were delivered to the Tunnel for testing on the first of November in 1866, and the diligent inventor of the Burleigh Rock Drill obtained U.S. Patent no. 59,960 on 27 November 1866.[29]

At this time, Crocker was so tightfisted about Tunnel expenses he did not even repay Burleigh the $35 cost of shipping the first drill to the Tunnel.[30] In late 1866 and into 1867, as Burleigh delivered his drills to the Tunnel, his only compensation was for the cost of materials and labor to produce each machine. After the Tunnel was completed, he would end up petitioning the legislature for compensation—a petition that would also include the cost of protecting his invention.

Joseph Fowle later told the story that a sharp solicitor in Boston was keeping a keen eye on the Tunnel commissioners' search for a rock drill and Burleigh's labors at the Putnam Machine Company in Fitchburg. Fowle further claimed that the solicitor offered, at his own risk and expense, to take up the case for a patent extension just when the first term of Fowle's 1851 drill patent was to terminate.

Burleigh Rock Drill at the east portal (courtesy of the Smithsonian Institution Libraries, Washington, DC)

The Patent Act of 1836 provided a fourteen-year term and, in certain circumstances, an extension of "seven years from and after the expiration of the first term."[31] The solicitor was successful, and Joseph W. Fowle received Reissue Patent no. 2275 on 5 June 1866.[32] This enterprising solicitor was J. B. Crosby of Crosby, Halsted, & Gould, Solicitors of American and Foreign Patents,[33] located at 34 School Street in Boston. The man was very qualified for his work, being both a mechanical engineer and a solicitor of patents.[34] He even signed as a witness for Fowle on the extension application in August 1865. Fowle's story of the patent solicitor's scrutiny is convenient, but Stephen Gates, in testimony before a legislative committee, claimed it was Fowle who was continually watching the efforts of the commissioners to develop a mechanical drill.[35]

The patent solicitors were very sharp at their business, so less than a month after the reissue patent was signed, the Tunnel commissioners and Putnam Machine Company received letters claiming that the Brooks, Gates, and Burleigh drill was "a direct infringement upon"[36] the Fowle patent. This first threat was ignored as only a few trial drills were produced based on the Brooks, Gates, and Burleigh design, but after the drills Burleigh later designed proved their worth in late 1866 and on into 1867, Charles Burleigh, to protect his interest, purchased the remaining four years and five months[37] of the Fowle patent for $10,000. This transaction was consummated on 17 August 1867. It included a provision absolving the Putnam Machine Company from any liability for the Brooks, Gates, and Burleigh drills it had previously built and delivered to the Tunnel.

In 1872, Fowle and his solicitor would appeal to the U.S. Senate and House of Representatives to grant a further seven-year extension on his patent. In the appeal, he acknowledged he had only received $5,000 from the patent sale to Burleigh. The solicitor had done very well, and, seeing the success of the Burleigh drill, he obviously looked for further gain. The bill was sponsored in the Senate by Orris S. Ferry of Connecticut, who at the time was chairman of the Senate Committee on Patents. The bill passed in the Senate,[38] but this time many other inventors were aroused by the special treatment requested and addressed some heated letters to members of the House about the matter. Professor De Volson Wood of the University of Michigan, who held two rock-drill patents, presented Congress with a letter detailing the inconsequential nature of what Fowle and his solicitors claimed.[39] The solicitor and Fowle were not successful in their second attempt at robbery. As forceful as the letters against the petition had been, the defeat was most assuredly engineered by Alvah Crocker, friend of Charles Burleigh and the Putnams—and, at the time, a member of the U.S. House of Representatives from the Ninth District of Massachusetts.[40]

At the same time when Fowle and his solicitors were battling with Burleigh for money, Thomas Doane, while still at the Tunnel in 1866, was planning for the future—a future with mechanical drilling machines. In his last report as chief engineer, he noted: "The two machines drill at about the same rate, but the second one [the new Burleigh Rock Drill] is likely to prove much more durable than the first."[41] From his training, Doane sought to anticipate challenges, so he had been studying the problem of how a man could control and direct the action of a drill weighing more than two hundred pounds. Drill holes are not random punctures in the rock face—they are placed in a pattern so the explosive, even black powder with its great racket and smoke, would efficiently tear the rock from the Mountain. Understanding this, Doane wrote, "When a heading is driven by hand, it is possible and usual to locate each hole in such a place, and drive it in such a direction, as will enable it to get the most rock dislodged. The fact that machine labor cannot do this as well, has been one great argument against its use."[42]

In the spring of 1866, when the members of the legislature visited the Putnam shops in Fitchburg to witness a demonstration of the Brooks, Gates, and Burleigh drill, the 210-pound monster was mounted on an iron column about five inches in diameter.[43] Even at this early date, Doane was ready to describe his solution to the problem of holding the heavy machine drills in position. When used in the Tunnel, the drills were to be mounted upon his iron frame supported on small railroad wheels. This would allow the frame or carriage to be run forward against the face of the rock for the drilling operation and then easily moved back out of danger when the workmen were ready to discharge a blast.

Mounted on the Doane carriages, the heavy drills could be aimed and held in any direction. This matched the versatility of the universal-motion drill machine Burleigh had created. Pointed in any required direction, a drill would still operate, and, just like the shakers or tarriers who held the drill steel during hand drilling, the Burleigh drill partially rotated the drill steel with each stroke of the piston.[45] The Doane carriage held a drill in place where desired, and it was not even necessary to make a small hand-drilled hole as a starter for aligning the heavy drill. The new Burleigh drills, together with the Doane carriages, were going to change the whole approach to boring holes in the rock of the Hoosac Mountain.

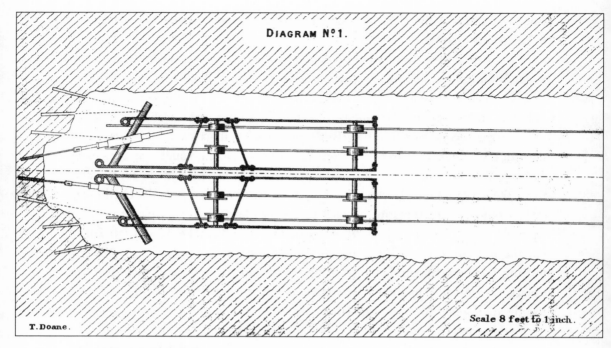

DIAGRAM N°1.

Scale 8 feet to 1 inch.

T. Doane.

Doane drill-carriage drawing, 1867 [44]

In his report to the governor and the Governor's Council, Latrobe explained how the success of the drilling machines supported the decision to change to a bottom heading. With hand drilling, the top heading is best, because it serves as a platform for the advance group of miners and thus avoids the need for scaffolding. It also permits the later enlargement to be accomplished by downward vertical drilling—a very great advantage in hand drilling.[46] With a machine drill mounted on a carriage, downward vertical drilling no longer offered an advantage. Also, when using machine drills mounted on a carriage it would be necessary to keep the top heading too far ahead of the enlargement because of the need to have a sufficient safe distance for retiring the carriage while blasting.

Crocker's faith in Charles Burleigh changed the whole approach to tunneling the Hoosac Mountain. The Burleigh drill was a dramatic success. It was just what John Brooks and Herman Haupt had worked so unsuccessfully to create. For the seven months before the drills were introduced in the Tunnel, progress on the six-foot-by-fifteen-foot heading averaged fifty-five feet per month. Once the Burleigh drills were introduced, the heading progress for the next seven months averaged 116 feet, and the heading area was increased to eight and a half by twenty-four feet.[47] Crocker could now brag that the rate of progress had doubled and the area excavated had increased two and a quarter times. The introduction of the Burleigh Rock Drill into the Hoosac Tunnel marked the beginning of modern tunneling. Mechanically powered rock drilling was no longer a dream or an inventor's tinkering—it was finally a practical reality.[48]

Contracting the Work

Doane had finally succeeded against the porridge stone at the west header by extending an open cut into the Mountain and using stout stone retaining walls to hold back the tremendous force the Mountain exerted against his trench. Then, after clawing his way farther into the Hoosac's western flank with the open cut— which was easier than trying to support a Tunnel bore—he had contracted with B. N. Farren to construct a brick tube within the most easterly section of open cut. Once this section of tube was completed Doane covered it with dirt to avoid the need for more retaining walls.

Latrobe was impressed with what Farren had accomplished in the battle against the porridge stone. In fact, Farren's outstanding performance spurred Latrobe to recommend to the Commonwealth the advantage of contracting out the Tunnel work. He began encouraging Commissioners Crocker, Shute, and Hudson to move away from the day-labor system. Latrobe pressed his thoughts by stating that the work ". . . may be so divided as to let out to individuals, or firms of contractors, at stipulated prices, with advantage in many ways."[49] The *American Railroad Journal* wrote: "He [Latrobe] favors the contract system, as the most economical to the State."[50] But such controversial ideas would lead to a tremendous political fight in 1868.

In early February of 1867, the *Adams Transcript* carried a notice that the state commissioners had ". . . advertised for proposals for continuing the work at both the eastern and western approaches, and sinking the central shaft."[51] Similar notices in circulars and as advertisements in newspapers invited contractors to submit proposals for taking up the work on various parts of the project.[52] The notices directed the contractors to send their proposals to Commissioner James Shute in Boston and specified 10 March as the date for the opening of proposals. Subsequently, the date of the opening was extended to the first of April. Before that date, some of the contractors who visited the Mountain to inspect the work tendered their proposals directly to Commissioner Crocker in North Adams. Later, Shute accused Crocker of opening the proposals he received before the set date, and he alluded to other maneuverings by the on-site commissioner. Never-theless, when all of the proposals were opened, the commissioners judged the offer by Messrs. Dull and Gowan to be the best. Dull and Gowan were the principals in a contracting partnership in Harrisburg, Pennsylvania. It was not clear how this decision was made, as no documentation of the prices the commis-sioners received was ever published. However, Dull and Gowan had completed a very difficult tunnel for the City of Chicago in November of 1866, and there was widespread publicity about that accomplishment.

The two-mile-long tunnel to draw water from Lake Michigan for the population of Chicago presented unique challenges because it was driven under Lake Michigan but Dull and Gowan completed it in less than three years. This success gave them credibility as contractors capable of undertaking the difficult job of tunneling the Hoosac. The Chicago tunnel was not as large in diameter as the Hoosac Tunnel, being only a little over five feet in diameter, and the majority of it was in the clays under the lake. Moreover, there was no rock involved, so black-powder blasting was not required. Following the technique used at the Hoosac, these men laid a temporary railroad in their tunnel and used small cars pulled by mules to carry the debris out to the mouth of work. Another similar feature was the lining of their tunnel with bricks, as Farren was then doing at the bore into the troublesome west side of the Hoosac Mountain.

In June, two months after the opening of proposals, the newspapers began asserting that there was a contract between the Commonwealth and Messrs. Dull and Gowan to excavate 6,400 feet of Tunnel on the east side of the Mountain and to complete the sinking of the central shaft.[53] Subsequently, Shute accused Crocker of further intrigues, which, from Shute's perspective, supposedly caused additional delays in the execution of the contract. In the following year, Shute issued a pamphlet providing a detailed list of improprieties by Crocker. One specific complaint accused Crocker of having opened a proposal from Mr. C. L. White. This proposal allegedly was the lowest received, but it had been withdrawn. After the proposal by Dull and Gowan was judged the best, Crocker then delayed the award of a contract for four months until he had persuaded Dull and Gowan to accept White as a partner. The exact identity of White, this third partner for the Hoosac work, is not clear. The North Adams newspaper reported that the delay was caused by the contractors' having to provide the Common-wealth with a construction bond on the million dollars' worth of work they were undertaking. Commissioner Charles Hudson, confirmed Shute's charge about White, stating that Crocker's opposition to the contract ". . . manifested itself in a more tangible form, by forcing into the firm a third party, who was a stranger to the old firm."[54]

Finally, everyone except Commissioner Shute seemed to be satisfied, and the contractors went to work on the first of August. Under the contract, Dull and Gowan plus White had two years to complete the agreed-upon work. The *Adams Transcript* praised Crocker and the commissioners for devoting their entire time to the project.[55]

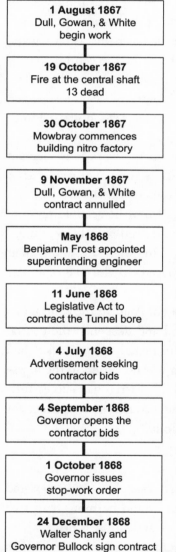

1 August 1867
Dull, Gowan, & White
begin work

19 October 1867
Fire at the central shaft
13 dead

30 October 1867
Mowbray commences
building nitro factory

9 November 1867
Dull, Gowan, & White
contract annulled

May 1868
Benjamin Frost appointed
superintending engineer

11 June 1868
Legislative Act to
contract the Tunnel bore

4 July 1868
Advertisement seeking
contractor bids

4 September 1868
Governor opens the
contractor bids

1 October 1868
Governor issues
stop-work order

24 December 1868
Walter Shanly and
Governor Bullock sign contract

Shute may not have been an engineer, but he had closely tracked the cost of the Tunnel work. Based on the information he had accumulated, he was able to express his concern based on actual work data: "My only apprehension—the prices paid [by the contract] being hardly a third of the cost to the State during the previous year—was that the contractors might be unable even to sustain themselves."[56] The North Adams paper reported the contract was with Messrs. Dull, Gowan, and White,[57] but an *American Railway Times*[58] article about the matter made no mention of White.

In order to be able to begin work immediately, the contractors leased all of the State's machinery and buildings at the east header and at the central shaft. The agreement with the Commonwealth required them to return everything to the Commonwealth in the same condition as when it was leased, except for inevitable wear and tear.[59] Latrobe, in his "Report of Consulting Engineer" for 1867, noted that the machinery at the central shaft was well designed and substantially constructed, but he added that the machines were proving "inadequate to the increasing service required . . . as the depth of the shaft increased."[60] The contractors, who were of the same opinion, immediately made arrangements for additions and improvements.

Providing light for the work in the bowels of the Mountain was always a problem. News reporters who ventured into the hole wrote about the "blackness" of the interior.[61] The engineers did have kerosene lamps for their work, but since the earliest days, light for the miners had been provided by candles stuck on their hats or on the rocks where they worked. Sometimes a miner would take some wood into the bore and make a small fire on a rock for warming coffee.[62] In that case, the light was only a minor secondary benefit. Probably because the central shaft was a limited vertical space, kerosene was more common for lighting.

At the central shaft, the contractors inherited from the Commonwealth an interesting contraption called a gasometer, a device for the manufacture of gas from liquid gasoline. In 1865, the commissioners had the mechanism constructed with the intent of using the gas to improve the lighting in the central shaft.[63] They installed suitable piping reaching into all the work areas and used the system from November 1865 until the first of April in 1867. However, they then decided the system presented too great a danger,[64] and the gasometer stood unused until the work passed to the contractors.[65]

Whether commissioners or contractors directed the work, one element stayed the same at the Hoosac Mountain—death. Less than two weeks after Dull, Gowan, and White assumed management of the central-shaft work, two miners, Marshall O. Tower and William Dunn, fell from the scaffolding onto the rock floor below. Tower died immediately and Dunn lived only a few hours.[66] Each such event brought a "crowd of worried wives" to the work site, and if their men were not involved, the women "melted away relieved that for one more day tragedy had passed them by."[67]

It was not an auspicious beginning. By the end of August, the contractors had driven 123 feet of Tunnel header at the east end and deepened the central shaft by thirteen and a half feet. The results failed to match what Crocker had achieved a month earlier. Their progress in September was no better, so the newspaper scribblers wrote about the west bore, where B. N. Farren had successfully completed his first brick-arch tube contract and had taken a new contract for another five hundred feet farther into the porridge stone.[68]

Into the Depths of Hell

The north village of Adams, on the Hoosic River, had, as early as 1840, boasted twenty-two cotton looms in its mills; by 1870, there would be more than two hundred. It was a village of crowded boardinghouses and mills, a place where millworkers labored thirteen hours a day under dangerous conditions. As early as 1838, Nathaniel Hawthorne had visited the area and recorded in his notebook:

A steam-engine in a factory to be supposed to possess a malignant spirit.
It catches one man's arm, and pulls it off; seizes another by the coat-tails,
and almost grapples him bodily; catches a girl by the hair, and scalps her;
and finally draws in a man and crushes him to death.[69]

Whether he saw these events or simply recorded what he heard is not clear. In this case, he wrote it like a story. The dangers the mills presented were different in nature, yet just as real, as those faced by the American, Irish, and French Canadians who came to mine the Hoosac Mountain.

At the east end, the central shaft, the west shaft, and the west end, children now poured in and out of squalid shacks where women, speaking foreign tongues, were busy cooking and caring for their babies. The miners, roughly dressed men, black with grime, returned to these makeshift communities when their shifts were over.[70] These were men who could say, like Jonah, "Down I went to the roots of the mountain; the bars of the nether world were closing behind me forever."[71]

On 24 October 1867, a local headline screamed: "Terrible Accident at the Central Shaft."[72] On Saturday afternoon, 19 October, the contractors fired a black-powder blast at the bottom of the central shaft. When the smoke cleared, thirteen miners descended in one of the buckets used to draw up the broken rock and convey miners to and from the bottom of the shaft. By this time, the shaft had reached 580 feet below the surface of the Mountain. It would have been a long climb down but to go down and to return the men usually rode the buckets. As the digging had proceeded deeper and deeper into the Mountain, the workers had erected wooden platforms in the shaft. These were spaced from twelve to twenty-three feet apart vertically. The platforms were connected by stairs or ladders and had openings for the passage of the buckets. But the lower platforms, including the last, which was still seventy feet from the bottom, did not have connecting ladders because they would have been destroyed by flying rock each time the miners fired a blast.

At this time, mounted on the heavy stone wall Doane had built around the central-shaft excavation, there was a large wooden building containing shops, tools, machinery for pumping water from the shaft, and offices. This building completely covered the mouth of the shaft. Just outside of the wall was the derrick with its operator's room, and while the tank containing the gasoline for the gasometer was about one hundred feet beyond the derrick engine, the gasometer itself was in a small room close to the derrick engine and directly under the operator's station. Moreover, the pipes between the gasoline tank and the gasometer went directly under the derrick engine.[73]

Several weeks before the fateful day, the commissioners had ordered eight barrels of gasoline for the contractors. When the order was delivered, the gasoline sat in the North Adams depot. Then, on Friday, it was carried up the Mountain to the central shaft and placed in the tank, ready to supply the gasometer.[74] At almost the same instant when the engineman for the derrick had raised the first bucketload of broken rock sent up by the thirteen miners, R. R. Peet and George Goodwin opened the door to the gasometer room.[75] Peet had worked as a clerk[76] at the central shaft for three years during the tenure of the commissioners, and the contractors had retained him when they assumed control of the work. By accounts at the time, Peet was thoroughly experienced with the operation of the gasometer. A short time before the two men went into the gasometer room, Goodwin had discovered that the retort on the machine was too full. (A retort is a vessel in which a substance is heated for the purpose of collecting the resulting gaseous products.) So the two men were preparing to draw off some of the gasoline. When Peet, with lantern in hand,[77] opened the door, the gasoline ignited in a wall of flame. Both men escaped in a rush, with Peet being burned on the head and face. The derrick engineman, in his station above the gasometer, had already dumped the load of broken rock,[78] and he was about to lower three miners to the bottom of the shaft in the bucket. These three scrambled away, and the engineman attempted to lower the empty bucket to the miners below.

But it was already too late to effect a rescue. The flames immediately drove the badly singed engineman from his post above the gasometer. Even if he could have started the bucket downward, the fire had instantly consumed almost everything. The wooden derrick poles gave way and the bucket lunged down the shaft. At the same time, the air pumps stopped working, so pure air was no longer being pumped to the men below.[79] "In less than half an hour the entire structure fell"[80] into the shaft, with the burning timbers and flames landing on the first wooden platform below the surface. On this platform were stored drills, hammers, and chisels for the miners. Once the flames consumed the wooden beams of the platform, some three hundred sharp iron drills, weighing half a ton, plunged down the abyss and onto the miners below.[81] The usual stoicism at the recurring accidents this time gave way to hysteria.

The collapse of the building completely closed the mouth of the shaft on:

James Burnett[82] (Bennet[83])
James Cavanaugh (Cavenough[84]), leaving a wife and two children
Thomas Collins[85] and his brother, Peter[86] (Patrick[87]) Collins
Patrick Connolly, leaving a wife and seven[88] (or six[89]) children
Thomas Cook, leaving a wife and two children[90]
John Curron[91] (Curran[92, 93])
James Fitzgerald[94]
Edwin (Edward[95]) Haskins[96] (John Harkness[97])
James McCormick[98] (McCormice[99])
Joseph Messier[100]
Thomas Mulcare[101] (Mulone[102])
Michael Whalen[103]

News of the disaster quickly reached North Adams, and the village firemen rushed up the Hoosac Mountain with their engine. Despite all their efforts, it was well into the evening before the fire was extinguished and the charred timbers were removed from the opening. Finally, at four the next morning, Thomas Mallory, a workman with experience as a sailor, was lowered into the black hole on a rope. The story in the North Adams paper the following week made it clear there was a large audience of spectators, including the wives and children of the miners to watch this daring man descend into the pit. After forty minutes, he was drawn up—unconscious. He was revived, but the words he immediately stammered were devastating. He had found the bottom of the shaft filled with water on which floated burned timbers, but there was no trace of the miners. He made a further attempt on Monday afternoon. When he reached the wreckage of the last platform this time, some seventy feet from the bottom, the air was so bad his lamp went out, and he had to be drawn up. Mallory made two more attempts after Monday, but the outcome was always the same. Each of his trips into the flooded pit produced the same announcement: "All I can find is charred timbers and foul air." It was more than a year before the thirteen bodies were recovered.

The villagers and those who had stood vigil on Saturday night and Sunday morning were heartbroken for the destitute families. In the churches of North Adams, collections for the victims' families raised more than $2,000[104] and the contractors provided the families with a little money. Even the commissioners came forward, furnishing the families a few dollars, accommodations, fuel, and provisions.[105]

Crocker devoted only a paragraph to the accident in his *Commissioners' Report* at the end of 1867. In an appendix to the report, titled "Accident—Casualties," there was an account describing the gasometer and a summary of lost property: the shaft building, together with a large amount of material and machinery, including five hundred cords of wood and 35,000 feet of lumber. Only Shute pointed a finger: "This work was in charge of the person who had been forced into the firm of Dull and Gowan."[106] Because the contractors had leased the machinery, the loss fell upon them and not on the Commonwealth. At such a distressing time, this was the only consolation the papers could report.

With no pumps or other machinery available for draining the shaft, no work could be accomplished, so all of the workmen at the central shaft were discharged immediately. The Governor and his council annulled the contract with Messrs. Dull, Gowan, and White on 9 November, and no one later mentioned who really paid for the lost machinery.

Less than a month after the accident, and a day before the Governor's decision to annul the contract, a correspondent for the *New York Times* visited the site. The reporter noted that there were patches of snow on the Mountain, and the water in the shaft reached a depth of more than one hundred feet.[107] Cold winter winds were blowing hard, and the disastrous death of the thirteen miners cast a very dark shadow over the Mountain. As never before, the whole affair of tunneling the Hoosac was being seriously questioned. The final blow for Alvah Crocker came on 30 October, when ex-Governor John Andrew died at his residence in Boston at the age of forty-nine. The passing of the man who had driven Herman Haupt from the Hoosac Mountain and had put the work in the hands of the commissioners seemed an omen marking the end of the whole affair. At this point, Andrew's commissioners had spent more money and accomplished less than Haupt.

Seizing an opportunity, the Western Railroad used the tragedy to launch an attack against the idea of a bore through the Hoosac Mountain. Their spokesman this time was former Lieutenant Governor Joel Hayden, who, at a late-November meeting in Northampton, expressed a belief that the Commonwealth would not complete the Tunnel.[108]

Tri-Nitro-Glycerin

New Yorkers were startled one fine Sunday morning in November of 1865 by an explosion on Greenwich Street in front of the Wyoming Hotel. The explosion was so great that it broke the glass in every window on both sides of the block. Pedestrians were thrown down and the pavement was broken up. A milkman who was riding past the Wyoming was taken away from the street stunned, mutilated, and bleeding.[109] The explosion occurred when a hotel porter tossed a small box of chemical oils out into the street gutter. An account in the *New York Times* stated that the box "had hardly struck the curbstone when the explosion occurred."

George Mordy Mowbray, a chemist from England who immigrated to the United States in 1854, reported the New York incident and several others in his 1872 book *Tri-Nitro-Glycerin as applied in the Hoosac Tunnel, Submarine Blasting, Etc., Etc., Etc.* All were incidents caused by boxes containing chemical oils. Yet Crocker was searching almost frantically for these chemical oils— nitro-glycerin—that the railroads absolutely refused to carry because it was "hair-trigger stuff." "It was said to be so sensitive the scraping of a fiddle was enough to set it off." [110]

Crocker had visited New York in February 1867, endeavoring to procure the stuff, but he was not successful. As always, the former papermaker was persistent, and in July he made contact with Mowbray, who was living in Titusville, Pennsylvania, a booming region where oil was producing wealth for those who drilled productive wells.

Back in 1866, when Chief Engineer Doane had been conducting experiments with nitro-glycerin, he had taken note of announcements Mowbray twice placed in *Scientific American* magazine.[111] So perhaps Doane passed the announcements to Crocker and thus spearheaded the search for Mowbray. Once Crocker made contact, he invited Mowbray to visit North Adams. During the visit, the superintending commissioner drafted a contract whereby the chemist would construct the laboratory necessary for the production of tri-nitro-glycerin at his own expense, but it would be on a convenient site furnished by the Commonwealth. By a clause of this contract, the site was to have a supply of water and sufficient space for the necessary buildings. Mowbray knew the fear everyone had about transporting nitro-glycerin, so he recognized there would be no competition for his explosive from any sources beyond North Adams. Because of his experience in the oilfields of Pennsylvania, he was confident of his ability to produce a superior explosive.

Mowbray was already a chemist of considerable experience when he crossed the Atlantic to the United States at the age of forty. Now he was presented with an opportunity to enter the explosives business in an ownership position, instead of working for someone else, and the Commonwealth would provide the real estate for his laboratory. This was, however, at the same time that Crocker was pressuring Dull and Gowan to accept Mr. White as a third partner, so, perhaps because of uneasiness about the central-shaft contract, the other commissioners did not see fit to ratify Crocker's agreement with Mowbray. When Dull, Gowan, and White began work in August 1867, Crocker turned the nitro matter over to them. Following the accident at the central shaft, when Crocker once more took control of the work, he again asked Mowbray to visit North Adams.[112]

After Mowbray came to the United States with his wife, Annie Fade, they settled in the New York City area. Five years later, his wife's sister, Eliza Fade Siddons, came to the United States from Egypt with her less-than-one-year-old son, Henry Siddons, and they moved in with the Mowbrays. Their move was precipitated by the death of Eliza's husband shortly after Henry was born. Immediately after Eliza's arrival, she burned to death in an explosion at a friend's home in Brooklyn. George and Annie Mowbray took in her young son, and it appears they adopted the lad, because he became known as Henry Siddons Mowbray. Later, during the Mowbrays' years in North Adams, the boy's teacher at Drury Academy, the town high school, encouraged the lad's interest in art, and he became an artist of some repute.

During his early period in New York, Mowbray was employed by Schieffelin Brothers, a drug and chemical house in the city. When the oil boom began in Pennsylvania, his employers sent him to investigate opportunities. Colonel Edwin Drake, who is popularly credited with having drilled the first oil well in the Titusville area, sat down to discuss business with Mowbray, the agent for Schieffelin. After the two men had puffed their way through a box of Cuban cigars, two hundred barrels of oil at thirty-five cents a gallon were on their way to the Schieffelin Brothers chemical house in New York. Soon thereafter, George Mowbray, Annie, and Henry took up residence in Titusville. The oil boom must have excited Mowbray, for shortly after this, he appeared to have been working as an independent chemist and was no longer affiliated with Schieffelin Brothers. He joined John A. Mather and two other gentlemen in drilling a well on the Morey farm, but their well was not successful.[113]

Mowbray next contributed his scientific skill to the refining of petroleum into kerosene for lamp fuel, and he established the William H. Abbott Refinery near the corner of Spring and Brown Streets in Titusville.[114] Soon he received a patent for an oil-well ejection pump (U.S. Patent no. 45,464, dated 13 December 1864). On 21 January 1865, Colonel E. A. L. Roberts increased the flow in an oil well by firing eight pounds of black powder in the Roberts Petroleum Torpedo at a depth of 465 feet. Colonel Roberts was a dental technician by profession but he had learned about explosives during service with a New Jersey regiment during the Civil War. Leaving the Army, he constructed an oil-well torpedo of his own design. Others had been blasting oil wells for more than five years, but Roberts was astute enough to patent his design (U.S. Patent no. 59,936). Roberts was more of an entrepreneur than a freelance operator. He charged $100 to $200 per torpedo, plus a royalty of one-fifteenth of the increased oil flow, and he viciously protected his patent.

Soon after this, Colonel Roberts began to realize that nitro-glycerin was a much more powerful blasting agent than the black powder he was then using. As a result, he and Mowbray turned their attention to manufacturing nitro-glycerin. This is probably the point at which Mowbray began to concentrate on the techniques to produce this temperamental high explosive. High explosives detonate at supersonic speeds—a shock wave—while low explosives like black powder decompose by a flame front. Mowbray studied the work of Ascanio Sobrero, the Italian chemist who in 1847 first made nitro-glycerin, and he researched the work of other European chemists. Mowbray, the British chemist, and Roberts, the oilfield pioneer, established a factory near Titusville, but they suspended the operation when they found that the article—then termed "soup"[115]—could be purchased much more cheaply in the East.[116]

Roberts did not actually try nitro-glycerin in his torpedo until 1867. When Roberts decided to purchase nitro-glycerin instead of continuing to work at making the explosive in late 1866, Mowbray resolved to look for other opportunities beyond the oilfields of Pennsylvania. In December 1866, he placed the nitro-glycerin advertisements, which Doane had seen, in *Scientific American*. Mowbray had gained the necessary knowledge about the chemical process, had built one factory for producing the explosive, and had developed a theory about the connection between purity of the product and safety. At this time, he still believed it was safer to transport the "soup" at temperatures above seventy-five degrees, as he thought the danger of an unexpected explosion increased with lower temperatures.

Great minds met: Crocker knew what he wanted and Mowbray was ready to leave the oilfields. They quickly revived their previous agreement, and, by 30 October 1867, the chemist was in North Adams beginning his operations. On a ten-acre site[117] down the Hoosac Mountain from the west shaft, Mowbray erected a two-story laboratory/factory.[118] Some five hundred feet farther away, and at the extreme edge of the property owned by the Commonwealth, a magazine was constructed for storing the nitro-glycerin.

George Mowbray's "Nitroglycerine Works," below the west shaft (courtesy of the North Adams Public Library)

On the second day of 1868, Mowbray moved into his laboratory and began testing the manufacturing apparatus. The plan was to use the explosive first in the east header of the west shaft, so Mowbray worked out a scheme to place an electric blasting machine in the timekeeper's office above ground, instead of in the damp Tunnel. He ran the firing wires from the machine down the shaft. At the bottom of the shaft, these wires were connected to the wires leading to the explosive in the drill holes. Once everything was ready and the miners had withdrawn some three hundred feet from the face, the charges would be fired.

The Intractable Alvah Crocker

In 1867, the route of the Troy and Greenfield Railroad from the west bore of the Hoosac Tunnel to North Adams was still very much under discussion. In the autumn of 1866, Benjamin Latrobe had suggested improvements to the route previously surveyed. Chief Engineer Charles Manning, during his short tenure, had surveyed a line between the Tunnel and the village in early 1867, but his line was not materially different from the one surveyed earlier by Doane.[119] Crocker was still not satisfied and he did not want to spend any unnecessary money at the time, so he deferred the purchase of the necessary land. The selection of this route was an issue Crocker well understood from years earlier, during his battles to locate the Fitchburg depot. This time the question did not involve the location of a station in the village so it was slightly different than the fight in Fitchburg. The two endpoints of the line were defined by the west portal of the Hoosac Tunnel and the existing location of the Troy and Boston Railroad station in the village, so the focus was on how to connect those two endpoints. It was almost a repeat of the question Loammi Baldwin Sr. had faced in locating the Middlesex Canal: What was the value of the land the railroad would have to purchase? Latrobe admitted Crocker's point: "The question of land damages and cost of real estate in the approach to and passage through the village, which is referred to in [my report of last year], has however, so grown in importance, (as I then predicted,) and so formidable are the claims of property owners . . . I gave special attention to a suggestion . . . for a change in this part of the route."[120] No decision was reached, and no definite action would be taken by the superintending commissioner.

In many respects, the year could be rated a gloomy failure. Despite criticism and ridicule, Crocker went grimly forward as the Tunnel opponents gathered their strength for the coming battle in the General Court. The tragic central-shaft accident and the departure of Dull, Gowan, and White caused many to stop and reflect on whether this undertaking was worth the sacrifice. Had there been too many muffled explosions underground—yielding a burst of flame together with a shower of rock, bits of cloth, and fragments of charred flesh? Some who previously were believers and supporters began to question whether it was possible to tunnel the five miles though the Hoosac Mountain.

Although Crocker had made missteps in trying to cut costs, he had a good sense of what was really important and critical to achieving success. As 1867 ended, he had these decisive elements solidly in his grasp:

- Burleigh was now producing a reliable drill. The drill had proven itself and the shop in Fitchburg would soon be turning out many more with further improvements. More compressed-air machinery was necessary to drive additional drills, but the compressors could be purchased.

- Mowbray was ready to produce a more powerful explosive that had proved its worth in 1866 during Doane's trials at the heading from the west shaft.

- Crocker could point to one real success. On New Year's Day of 1868, the faithful and resourceful B. N. Farren opened the Troy and Greenfield Railroad between Greenfield and Shelburne Falls.[121]

Crocker won the initial battle for controlling the fate of the Tunnel. By early February, the two commissioners who had accused him of abusing his office were gone: Governor Bullock removed Charles Hudson on the last day of January and James M. Shute resigned. In their place, the governor appointed two strong Tunnel supporters—Senator Samuel W. Bowerman of Pittsfield and Honorable Tappan Wentworth of Lowell.[122] Wentworth was the gentleman who, in 1864, had threatened to declare Francis Bird's Senate seat vacant if he did not take the required oath to support the Constitution of the United States. Bowerman was a native of North Adams, having been born there in 1820. After graduating from Williams College and being admitted to the bar, he first set up a practice in South Adams. In 1857, he moved to Pittsfield. Two years later, Bowerman was elected to the Senate of the Massachusetts General Court for a single term, but Pittsfield returned him to Beacon Hill in 1866 as a member of the House. In 1867 and 1868, he was returned to the Senate.[123]

In late February, the wooden building over the west shaft again caught fire, but this time the village firefighters did not have so far to travel. The blaze was extinguished before any serious damage resulted.[124] A week later, the Tunnel commissioners announced their decision to rebuild the buildings at the central shaft and to purchase new machinery. The buildings were erected in the spring, and the Putnam Machine Company of Fitchburg delivered new machinery during the summer. Finally, on 15 September, operations were underway to remove the water from the shaft. This was done using a large bucket attached to a new derrick. Most certainly, the decision was made to haul out the water instead of pumping it because of the amount of floating wreckage—all of the charred timbers and other debris would have clogged the pumps. It was slow going, because there were so many floating boards and because of the need to remove the protruding remnants of platform timbers. Six bodies were found and recovered on 14 October, almost exactly a year from the date of the accident. The other seven were removed over the next eight days.[125] Crocker later reported that the waterlogged remains of all the miners except for one were recognizable, and all were properly interred in the cemetery at North Adams.[126]

Another Latrobe Engineer

Crocker still could not suffer engineers, and by April 1868, W. P. Granger, who had signed himself as resident engineer, was considering departure from the project. Besides Crocker's independent manner, the possibility that the General Court might end the project caused Granger anxiety about his job. A young engineer named Arthur Beardsley, referred to as an assistant engineer, departed after less than a year of employment. Beardsley was university-trained, having completed a degree in civil engineering from Rensselaer Polytechnic Institute in 1867. From the Hoosac project, he would go on to organize civil engineering programs first at the University of Minnesota and later at Swarthmore College in Pennsylvania. Engineer Granger would finally depart in August, after accepting a position with the White Mountain Extension Railroad in New Hampshire.

In early February, when the new commissioners were announced, a letter in the *American Railway Times* noted the changes and expressed "wonder that the new appointees have had no engineering education or practical experience in works of public improvement."[127] Pressure was again mounting against the Tunnel, and someone must have encouraged Crocker to have an engineer around. In May, Crocker finally relented, and Benjamin D. Frost was appointed superintending engineer.

A most interesting fact about the new engineer was that he had served as the resident engineer in 1852 at the Board Tree Tunnel of the Baltimore and Ohio Railroad under Charles Manning. When their last child was born, Frost and his wife named the lad Charles Latrobe Frost. But Frost was a Massachusetts man, originally from Wayland, a small town between Boston and Worcester. Before entering engineering practice, he had in 1845 obtained an A.B. degree from Rutgers College in New Jersey, and then he spent an additional year studying at Harvard as a resident graduate before returning to Rutgers and completing an A.M. in 1848.[128]

Benjamin D. Frost superintending engineer

Crocker's hoped-for speedier penetration of the Hoosac Mountain, through the use of nitro-glycerin, did not occur. Mowbray experienced production problems when he tried to use acids ordered from American firms. He found them to be far below the required purity. Although the sulfuric acid he purchased seemed to be satisfactory, he needed a higher-quality nitric acid. He was able to produce a small quantity of good-quality nitro-glycerin early in 1868, using acids imported from Europe.[129] These acids were of the required purity for the exacting chemical process he was performing.

The difficulty of locating nitric acid manufactured to the necessary purity forced Mowbray to produce his own, so he constructed an "acid house." It was a well-ventilated building 150 feet long, containing eleven two-foot-diameter stills. But he also needed retorts (glass or earthenware vessels with long necks used for condensing the acid vapors), and these had to be specially produced, as they were of a unique pattern.

Therefore, there was only limited use of Mowbray's tri-nitro-glycerin, as he called his product, during the first part of 1868. What he did produce prior to the first of August was used for excavation enlargement. Finally, in August, the production of nitro reached a level where it met the needs of the eastward-mining operation from the west shaft. While the nitro-glycerin use in August proved a short-lived test, the results were encouraging.

Superintending Engineer Frost reported the following when using simultaneous blasting by electric battery:

1. Fewer holes had to be drilled in proportion to the area of face carried forward.
2. Deeper holes were possible: The best nitro-glycerin performance occurred when the average depth of the bore hole was forty-two inches, versus thirty inches for black powder.
3. Nitro-glycerin rarely failed to take out the rock to the full depth of the hole.[130]

Frost further remarked on the necessity of retraining the men to successfully employ the new pneumatic drills, explosive material, and fuses.[131]

Decision in Boston

While the arguments in Boston were about to become heated, very heated, concerning tunneling the Hoosac, the thermometer at the Mountain stood at twenty-four degrees below zero and the local paper reported "a large body of snow and glorious sleighing."[132]

In Boston, the cold January weather of 1868 chilled the lawmakers scurrying into town for the annual legislative session of the General Court. All were preparing for a battle royal, maybe the final battle. Many speculated that the thirteen bodies at the bottom of the central shaft had put the Tunnel to rest. Herman Haupt arrived to present his claim for $300,000 owed his company for Hoosac Tunnel work performed some seven years earlier.[133] Maturin M. Ballou of North Adams and D. S. Simmons of Greenfield, sensing an opportunity for a quick dollar, filed a claim against Haupt for unpaid services during construction of the Troy and Greenfield Railroad. If Haupt was going to get any money by his persistent efforts, they wanted part of the treasure—just like Haupt's old do-nothing partners. Ballou and Simmons were the pair who had worked on the "Little Hoosac Tunnel" in North Adams as subcontractors to Edward Serrell. Haupt had given them 1,300 shares of Allegheny Railroad and Coal Company stock in 1857, and they had agreed that their contract was canceled. It was really a debt Haupt had inherited from Serrell when he first became involved with the work. Now the pair claimed the stock was worthless and therefore they had never been paid.[134] Few in Massachusetts were favorable to Haupt's claims, but the Tunnel Committee exercised integrity and ruled against the claim of these thieves.[135]

Then, as the cold winter weather began to break and the legislative session wore on into April, the Tunnel Committee visited the works.[136] The committee visit was followed a week later by the arrival of one hundred members of the General Court, who also wanted to enjoy an excursion to the beautiful Berkshires. After almost five months of speeches, name-calling, arm-twisting, and what the North Adams paper called "unexpected perils from false friends,"[137] the climax of the legislative season came on 11 June[138] with the passage of a Tunnel bill. This piece of legislation incorporated what Latrobe had been expounding for years. The act required the use of the contract system: "After the first day of October next, no part of this appropriation shall be used in payment of work done excavating the tunnel, unless the same be done under contracts approved by the governor and council."[139] The act of the General Court appropriated $5 million[140] for the completion of the Tunnel by the contract method. This was money exclusively for tunneling the Mountain; the final railroad work would be handled only when it was clear the Tunnel would be completed. The legislation also contained a clause limiting what Crocker was allowed to do during the interval leading to the Commonwealth's execution of a construction contract.

While the Act of the General Court required the use of the contract system to accomplish the work, it did allow Crocker and the commissioners to spend $250,000 of the appropriation before 1 October 1868.[141, 142] After a construction contract was negotiated, the Board of Commissioners would be abolished and supervision of the project would be turned over to a superintending engineer appointed by the Governor. All these conditions were spelled out in the legislation. If Crocker wanted to see his cherished Tunnel completed, he would soon have to relinquish control.

This largesse by the General Court made Francis Bird livid, and he immediately issued one of his vindictive pamphlets—*The Last Agony of the Great Bore*.[143] He found fault with every word of the legislation, and he clearly feared the Governor would ignore the word *engineer* and reappoint Crocker as superintendent. He deemed the requirement to withhold 20 percent of each amount due the contractor until completion of the work a "perfectly illusory pretense of security."[144] He even assailed the stipulation that the Governor and his council, and not the Tunnel commissioners, execute the contract. His assault on this point led him to attack the attorney general, who would have to rule if the intent of the legislation was not followed. "The attorney-general was born and brought up and practiced law for years in Greenfield—in a community where tunnel-on-the-brain has long been a chronic disease."[145] His bitter attack filled ninety-six pages with such words and phrases as "treacherous arts," "rogue," "resolved to ruin," "log-rolling," "tobacco-chewing," and "first-rate horse jockey"—all squeezed together in small type. Bird would soon be answered by a pamphlet—written under the pen name of Theseus—reminding everyone of his refusal to support the Constitution of the United States.[146] But while Frank Bird remonstrated in his usual shrill manner, the solicitation of contractors began. The 4 July 1868 issue of the *American Railway Times* carried a block advertisement.[147]

Before the end of July, parties interested in the contract were visiting the project and seeking information for preparing their bids.[148] The pleasant weather of summer also brought legislators who wanted to leave the heat of the city and enjoy a visit to the mountains. On Thursday, 6 August, 100 members of the General Court made an inspection tour of the Tunnel work.[149] In anticipation of a contractor taking over the work, most of the workmen at the east end had been discharged in July.[150] But the specifications had not been completely set forth, so instead of accepting bids on 12 August as hoped, the receipt of proposals was postponed until the first of September.[151]

The role Benjamin Latrobe played in bringing the General Court and the Governor to this monumental juncture is found in his diary for 1868.[152] While Alvah Crocker may not have put much stock in engineers, Governor Bullock obviously had come to trust the advice of Latrobe. Bullock served three one-year terms as Governor and was noted for restoring the financial health of Massachusetts after the Civil War, including paying many of the Commonwealth's wartime obligations. He would now bring financial responsibility to the troubled Hoosac Tunnel project.

On Saturday, 22 February, Latrobe made the trip from New York City to Boston via a railroad sleeping car. Arriving in Boston, he paid two dollars a day for his room at the Tremont House, on the southwest corner of Tremont and Beacon Streets. This fashionable hotel, the first with indoor plumbing, was a regular haunt of the gentlemen who made up the Massachusetts General Court. On the Monday morning after his arrival, Latrobe met with Governor Bullock. There was another meeting on Tuesday morning, this time including all three of the Tunnel commissioners Bullock had appointed. While he seldom mentioned the specific issues discussed, Latrobe did on this occasion record that the Governor made a speech to "us to let bygones be bygones." Wednesday morning, Latrobe met Crocker and Wentworth at the State House, and the diary's only note says, *No conclusion.* On Thursday, Latrobe took the train to Shelburne Falls. After disembarking, he boarded a sledge, which carried him the rest of the way up the Deerfield Valley to the Tunnel. The very next day, he was back in Shelburne Falls in time to catch the 8:15 a.m. train to Fitchburg, where he visited the Putnam Machine Company shops and had dinner with the mayor. On Saturday, after stopping at the Tremont House in Boston, he went to Stonington, Connecticut, and caught the ferry across Long Island Sound to New York City.

To Tunnel Contractors

The Commissioners of the Troy and Greenfield Railway and Hoosac Tunnel, acting for the State of Massachusetts, invite proposals until 12th day of August next, for completing said Tunnel, either in separate contracts for three different sections of the work, or in one contract for the whole.

Ample sureties will be required from parties who may be contracted with, and the Governor and Council reserve the right to reject all offers that may be made.

Plans may be seen, and specification obtained, on application to B. D. FROST, Superintending Engineer, at the Engineers' Office in North Adams, Mass., or to B. H. LATROBE, consulting Engineer, at his office, 49 Lexington Street, Baltimore, Md.

ALVAH CROCKER,
TAPPAN WENTWORTH,
S. W. BOWERMAN,

July 4

Pushing himself hard in March, Latrobe departed his home on Thursday the twelfth and first went to Wilmington, Delaware, where he stopped to look at the drawing of an engine made years earlier for the Hoosac Tunnel work. He does not indicate whether it was an engine for a pump or for a hoist, but this stop

Latrobe's Travels, 1868

- Saturday, 22 February, train New York to Boston

- Thursday, 27 February, train Boston to Shelburne Falls; sledge Shelburne Falls to Tunnel; return to Charlemont

- Friday, 28 February, sledge Charlemont to Shelburne Falls; train on to Fitchburg

- Saturday, 29 February, train Fitchburg to Boston and Boston to Stonington, CT; ferry on to New York City

- Thursday, 12 March, train Baltimore to Wilmington and on to New York City; night train to Troy, NY

- Friday, 13 March, train Troy to North Adams

- Monday, 16 March, train (Western Railroad) North Adams to Boston via Pittsfield

- Thursday, 19 March, Boston to New York City

seems to have been precipitated by continuing discussion about the pumps at the west-shaft, so it can be assumed that he was studying a pump engine. Completing his business there, Latrobe took the train to New York City, where he transferred to the night train for the journey to Troy, New York. At 7 a.m., he was in Troy, where he boarded the 8 a.m. train to North Adams.

Immediately after arriving Friday morning in North Adams, Latrobe met with Crocker. After such an exhausting trip, he notes that he went to bed before his normal time. He was up early the next day, Saturday, 14 March, and departed with the commissioners at 7:30 a.m. for the west shaft. The group went down the shaft and to both the east and west headings. In his diary, he describes "wading in water all the time and at the west heading in a pouring shower bath." The party also stopped at the nitro-glycerin works, but Mowbray was nowhere to be found. Since there was no work on Sunday, Latrobe attended services at the Congregational Church, a block down Main Street from the Wilson House, where he was staying. Latrobe observed in his diary that the Reverend Washington Gladden's sermons were excellent and the choir equally good. Gladden, by his own writings, acknowledged he was a minister who practiced a religion that laid hold upon life (a social gospel), and, based on the comment in his diary, Latrobe must have liked his espousal of the idea to realize the Kingdom of God in this world. On Monday, he took the Western Railroad's train to Boston via Pittsfield, arriving at five o'clock in the afternoon.

Latrobe met with Governor Bullock on Tuesday morning and later with Doane, whose engineering office was across the Charles River in Charlestown. Later in the day, he met with Mowbray. After the meetings, Latrobe spent the day in his room at the Tremont House, writing his report and preparing calculations for the commissioners.

Latrobe's Travels, 1868

- Wednesday, 27 May, carriage Baltimore to Philadelphia
- Thursday, 28 May, train Philadelphia to New York City; New York City to Peekskill
- Friday, 29 May, train Peekskill to Troy and Troy to North Adams
- Saturday, 30 May, over the Mountain to east end
- Sunday, 31 May, east end to Shelburne Falls
- Monday, 1 June, train Shelburne Falls to Fitchburg
- Tuesday, 2 June, train Fitchburg to Boston
- Wednesday, 3 June, Boston to Windsor, VT
- Monday, 15 June, Baltimore to Boston
- Monday, 22 June, Baltimore to New York City
- Tuesday, 23 June, New York City to North Adams via Albany

The pace continued to be hectic. The following day, Tuesday, 18 March, Commissioners Wentworth and Bowerman paid a call before a noon meeting at the State House. In the evening after dinner, Latrobe met with Doane and ex-Commissioner Shute. Before departing for New York City on Thursday, he was in conference with the Governor's Council.

In late May, Latrobe once more made an arduous trip to North Adams. Leaving Baltimore by carriage, he traveled to Philadelphia on Wednesday the twenty-seventh. The next day, he traveled by train to New York City and then transferred to a northbound train to Peekskill, New York. Arriving in Peekskill just after 1 a.m. the following day, he then transferred to a train heading up the Hudson River to Troy. From there, he transferred to the Troy and Boston Railroad's train bound for North Adams, where he finally arrived late Friday afternoon. He had a busy Saturday visiting the west shaft, Mowbray's nitro-glycerin factory, the central shaft, and the work at the east end of the Tunnel. Descendants of Moses Rice, the earliest settler of the Deerfield Valley, had opened an inn near the east portal, so Latrobe, instead of recrossing the Mountain to North Adams, chose this as his resting place for the night. On Sunday, he made a pleasant drive down the valley, arriving at Shelburne Falls at sunset (His diary says drove down to Shelburne Falls, it is not clear if he rented a horse or took a stage).

On Monday, 1 June, it was back to Tunnel business, as Latrobe caught the train to Fitchburg for a quick visit; the next day, he was on Crocker's Fitchburg Railroad headed to Boston. Arriving at the Tremont House, he noted in his diary, "I have got to be well known" here. He immediately had visitors, first of whom was Elias Derby, Crocker's troubadour cohort from twenty years earlier during the Fitchburg Railroad fights. Derby was followed by Commissioner Wentworth. Things were nearing a conclusion on Wednesday, 3 June. Latrobe spent the day at the State House and wrote in his diary that the result was favorable to the Tunnel. The next day, he departed first to Windsor, Vermont, to examine a drilling machine, and then he headed for his home in Maryland. Latrobe's repeated visits to the tunnel were probably to gather the information he needed to develop an estimate of the cost to complete the bore. Governor Bullock and the tunnel men needed a cost number for the legislation they were seeking to enact. They needed a number all parties would accept and trust as reliable.

The Tunnel Bill to which they had all contributed passed on Thursday, 11 June. Latrobe was not present, but he was back in Boston five days later, at the State House with Crocker and Wentworth. Many matters still had to be settled, so, on 23 June, Latrobe and Crocker met the governor and his council in North Adams, where they all visited the west shaft and Mowbray's factory. Latrobe complained of a headache from the nitro-glycerin, but soon he said he was feeling better. The next day, they again visited the west shaft.

Immediately after he met with the Governor, Latrobe began writing to men he viewed as competent to complete the work of boring through the Hoosac Mountain. Back in 1863, when Latrobe was chief engineer for the Pittsburgh and Connellsville Railroad, he and Francis "Frank" Shanly, a Canadian engineer/contractor, had exchanged correspondence regarding work on a section of the road. Frank Shanly did submit a tender to perform part of the work. Now he wrote Shanly and enclosed the advertisement for contractors to take up the Hoosac Tunnel challenge.

Baltimore, June 29, 1868

Francis Shanly Co.

Toronto, Canada W.

I enclose to you an advertisement which speaks for itself. If you have nothing better on hand, I hope you will visit the Tunnel and give the Commonwealth of Massachusetts a tender for it. The money to finish it is all appropriated and there can be no trouble as to funds, no State being in better credit than she is, or able to dispose of her securities at short notice.[153]

It is the sort of work that might suit you well.

Yours, Ben H. Latrobe, Consg. Engr.

Latrobe's Travels, 1868

- Monday, 10 August, Baltimore to West Point
- Tuesday, 11 August, West Point to North Adams
- Friday, 14 August, carriage North Adams to east end; train east end to Deerfield
- Saturday, 15 August, Deerfield to Baltimore
- Saturday, 22 August, Baltimore to Boston
- Wednesday, 26 August, Boston to Baltimore
- Thursday, 27 August, Baltimore to North Adams
- Tuesday, 1 September, carriage over the Hoosac; train east end to Boston.
- Thursday, 3 September, train Boston to Worcester
- Friday, 4 September, train Worcester to Boston.
- Saturday, 5 September, Boston to Baltimore

Written on the side was a note: "The specifications will be ready at North Adams in about 10 days." It was without a doubt exactly the type of challenge Shanly and his older brother, Walter, were seeking. These two experienced engineers, working in Canada and the United States, had probably built as many miles of railroad as any man, even Latrobe with his Baltimore and Ohio experience.

Crocker was also busy encouraging contractors to bid on the Tunnel. He wrote to A. Cohen and Company in London, suggesting that the firm might have an advantage by bringing cheaper labor over from England. They did not submit a bid, but Crocker wrote again after the bids were opened and thanked them for considering the work.[154]

Latrobe was back at the Wilson House in North Adams on Tuesday, 11 August. In his diary, he wrote that he had an interesting conversation with Superintending Engineer Frost, but he does not disclose what was discussed. Still, the two men were of a similar mind concerning contractors, and the discussion might well have been about the amount of freedom an engineer could allow a contractor in executing the work. The next day, while Latrobe was in the office, Crocker arrived, and the diary entry states: "Crocker in office, polite but reserved. Nothing said about the tunnel on either side." There was obviously some difference of opinion and friction between the two men.

On Thursday, Latrobe drove to the west end and the central shaft and paid a visit to Mowbray at the acid works. Then on Friday, 14 August, he crossed the Hoosac Mountain in a carriage and was met on the other side by the president and the superintendent of the Vermont and Massachusetts Railroad, who had come from Greenfield on a special train. At the end of July, B. N. Farren had pushed the tracks of the Troy and Greenfield Railroad to the Hoosac Tunnel Station on the north side of the Deerfield River,[155] so the two gentlemen took

Latrobe back to Greenfield on the special train. Again Latrobe does not reveal conversations in his diary, but the Vermont and Massachusetts had a rental agreement with the Commonwealth to operate its trains on the Troy and Greenfield Railroad tracks that Farren had completed, so the discussion might have centered on the issue of freight charges for the contractor selected to complete the Tunnel. Their railroad would benefit, because it provided the best means of delivering equipment and supplies to the Tunnel work on the east side of the Hoosac Mountain.

It seems that Latrobe departed for home the next day, but the following Saturday he was on an express train bound for Boston, where he again resided at the Tremont House until Tuesday, 25 August. For some reason, he hurried home to Baltimore on Wednesday, only to turn around the following day and make the tiresome journey to North Adams. On 28 August, three days before the bids were to be submitted, Latrobe was in North Adams answering contractor questions. The following day, a Saturday, Latrobe and Frost visited the central shaft to check on the rebuilding of the above ground works. From the top of the Mountain, they proceeded to the east end of the Tunnel. Before returning to North Adams, they had dinner at Rice's Hotel near the Hoosac Tunnel Station.

Now there was nothing more Crocker, Latrobe, or Governor Bullock could do—the interested contractors were busy sharpening their pencils and trying to estimate the cost of completing the Tunnel through the Mountain. Sunday found Latrobe back at the Congregational Church for services, and on Monday he was at the engineer's office in North Adams. On Tuesday, 1 September, the day the contractors' prices were received, Latrobe and Frost drove over the Mountain to Rice's Hotel and Latrobe took the 1:30 p.m. train to Boston. Latrobe met Commissioner Wentworth Thursday morning and handed over two proposals he had carried from North Adams. At 5:30 p.m., he was on the train to Worcester to meet with Governor Bullock at his home. The next day, Friday, 4 September, Latrobe returned to Boston early and went to the State House, where, together with the Governor, his council, and the three Tunnel commissioners, the bids were opened. The next day, Governor Bullock allowed Latrobe to retire, so he headed home to Baltimore.

Crocker's Nightmare

Twelve bids were submitted to complete all of the work. These were reviewed and certified by the three commissioners—Crocker, Wentworth, and Bowerman—together with Engineers Latrobe and Frost. The low bid of $4,027,780 was submitted by Carpenter, Odiorne, and Gardner.[156] Walter Shanly was of the opinion these were a group of Scottish men from Lake Superior.[157] Uran Brother & Company (some reports list them as Emery, Uran & Co.[158]) submitted the second-lowest bid, but they were $410,000 above the Carpenter group. At $4,623,069, Francis and Walter Shanly of Canada came in third. (Francis Shanly was the gentleman to whom Latrobe had written about bidding on the contract.) The fourth-lowest bid came from Jacob Humbird & Son. Humbird, a contractor from Cumberland, Maryland, had completed work for the Chesapeake and Ohio Canal and Latrobe's Baltimore and Ohio Railroad, so he probably was another of those contacted by Latrobe. While Jacob Humbird & Son bid $4,690,183 the fifth-lowest bid by Clark, Lyon, Hayden, Byron & Malone was only $467 above their offer. There were two other very interesting bids: Thomas Doane, together with someone named Stanton, submitted a bid of $4,881,766, and Herman Haupt submitted a bid for $5 million. With five good bids, most were happy, but the game was not over!

The Governor and his council, at the urging of Latrobe, had stipulated that the contractor post a guarantee. This was not part of the legislation, which did, however, include a 20 percent retainage requirement. In other words, every time the contractor earned a payment for completing work, only 80 percent would actually be paid until the entire project was completed. In addition, the offered contract required the contractor to turn over to the Commonwealth $500,000 in securities. This supplemental guarantee was also to be retained until the work was completed. Only when all of the work was completed would the securities be returned and the 20 percent retainage be paid to the contractor. The Commonwealth, however, would pay interest on the amounts withheld.

At the meeting of Governor Bullock and the council on Monday, 7 September, the contract for completing the Hoosac Tunnel was offered to Messrs. Carpenter, Odiorne, and Gardner—on condition that they deposit with the state treasurer the required $500,000 guarantee, in bonds, on or before 12 September.[159] Carpenter, Odiorne, and Gardner could not or would not provide the guarantee, so their bid for completion of the Hoosac Tunnel was rejected.[160] These gentlemen told the Governor this requirement was not part of the legislation and it could not be asked of them. These penalizing contractual requirements and their results were what Crocker had feared. They were probably the basis for Crocker's dispute with Latrobe. As a result of the rejection of the Carpenter group's offer, the Governor and his council ordered the commissioners to suspend all work at the east end and at the east heading at the west shaft.[161] This order also stopped Mowbray's nitro-glycerin trials.

Next the contract was offered to the second-lowest bidder, but these men also declined to furnish the necessary securities. So, on 5 October, the secretary of the Commonwealth sent a Western Union telegram to Francis Shanly in Toronto, Canada. The secretary's message asked whether the Shanlys would be prepared to deposit the half-million-dollar guarantee (in public bonds or stocks)—and, if so, to please travel to Boston immediately. Frank Shanly had no extra money, and his bachelor brother Walter, while having some reserve funds, had nothing approaching such a large sum.[162] They tried to raise the funds from their capitalist friends, but they could not do so on short notice. One friend who seemed seriously interested was Peter Redpath, who was a director of the Bank of Montreal but he was primarily engaged in his family's sugar refinery business. Redpath, however, went off to Cuba, probably on matters connected with the sugar business, before anything could be arranged.[163] Because Commissioners Crocker and Wentworth feared the Tunnel would be abandoned by the Governor if an acceptable contractor could not be found, they worked behind the scenes in late October to keep the Shanlys and the other bidders in the game.[164]

Walter Shanly, the older brother, was the better-known engineer, having been the chief engineer on railroad projects in both the United States and Canada. James Worrall, a contractor from Harrisburg, Pennsylvania, had worked in upstate New York on a railroad project where Walter Shanly was the chief engineer. Worrall had in the past worked on projects under Latrobe. Worrall did not divulge the source of his information, but he wrote to Shanly in early November, expressing an optimistic opinion: "[T]he whole matter seems according to my lights to be still in abeyance; there will probably be time to perfect arrangements."[165] Nevertheless, Shanly did not receive this letter until 18 November, when he returned to Montreal from a visit to Halifax. When he arrived home, and before he could even open his mail, Commissioner Wentworth was at his door, ready to explain the situation with the bids. All proposals over $4,750,000 had been thrown aside, he reported, and he was in Montreal because the Governor's Council and particularly the Governor were desirous that the Shanlys be awarded the contract. He told Walter the status of the other bidders: Jacob Humbird, the bidder just above the Shanlys, would not hear of the

$500,000 deposit. Clark, Lyon, Hayden, Byron & Malone, who were almost tied with Humbird, were trying very hard to get the guarantee, but everyone assumed they would fail. Wentworth wanted Walter to travel to Boston and speak with the Governor and his council. He even mentioned to Walter the fact that it was necessary to conclude the contract before the first week in January, when the legislature would come into session.[166] Crocker and Wentworth were fearful the new legislature might rescind the legislation if a contract was not executed before the members assembled. After the meeting with Wentworth, and finally having time to read the letter from Worrall, Walter wrote to his brother Frank, telling him he had made up his mind to go to Boston.[167] Before departing Montreal the next day, he wrote another letter to Frank in which he instructed his brother to see another Canadian contractor whom they might take in as a partner, particularly considering their need for financial support in gathering funds for the security.[168]

Walter made the journey south and met privately with Governor Bullock on Friday, 20 November. Emerging from the meeting, he was met by Wentworth, who was anxious for the Shanlys to succeed. Crocker was staying in the background, but Wentworth made it clear a great many people believed "a large proportion of the Council, the Governor included, wish to throw over the Tunnel Question altogether, in the expectation of being able to carry a reversal of the act granting the appropriation."[169] He went on to say, "[T]he Springfield and Western Railroad interests generally are working Heaven and Earth to delay the letting. The Governor is a Springfield or Worcester man, hence his originating the $500,000 security stipulation." The comments about the Governor were most certainly nothing more than fear about the situation and the fate of the Tunnel. Governor Bullock was originally from a very small village northwest of Crocker's Fitchburg, and the closest railroad to his roots was the Vermont and Massachusetts Railroad, which now ran to the east end of the Tunnel. He was a fiscal conservative whose aim was not to stop the Tunnel but to stop the financial bleeding it caused. He was well aware of the Commonwealth's past experiences with the Troy and Greenfield Railroad, with Herman Haupt, with the commissioners, and with contractors in the previous year.

At the time these negotiations between Walter Shanly and the Governor were taking place, Crocker was trying to help the low bidder, the firm of Carpenter, Odiorne, and Gardner, obtain the necessary security. Just as in the days when Haupt was having trouble with Governor Andrew, Crocker was, as always, primarily interested in the completion of the Tunnel. He wrote to Sidney

Dillon in New York in late November, encouraging him to provide the security for Carpenter, Odiorne, and Gardner.[170] At that moment, however, Dillon was deeply involved in completing America's first transcontinental railroad. He was an engineer by profession and he had built a section of the Western Railroad in his early years. Throughout the 1860s, he was one of the principal contractors building the Union Pacific Railroad, and in 1874 he would become president of the Union Pacific.

On the day before he wrote Dillon, Crocker had an interview with Governor Bullock, trying—without success—to persuade him to change the security requirement. After writing to Dillon, Crocker wrote to Lieutenant Governor William Claflin, a Tunnel supporter. This letter exhibited all of Crocker's fears about the possibility of Bullock's ending the Tunnel scheme by insisting on the security requirement. He implored Claflin, "What can be done?" and closed with "God save me."[171] On that busy letter writing Tuesday, Crocker also wrote to B. N. Farren, the trusted tube-building contractor. He pleaded with Farren to find the security funds and take the contract.[172] Farren responded the very next day, but he had no wish to make another proposal.[173]

Shanly stayed in Boston over the weekend and returned to Montreal on Monday, 23 November, the day Crocker had his interview with the Governor. Before departing, Walter sent a letter to his brother, describing the situation, and another letter to James Worrall, the Pennsylvania engineer, inquiring whether he could find good men who would come into the partnership and bring part of the security. It was a reenactment of Herman Haupt's trying to find financially sound partners. Shanly did make one point clear: If he and his brother got the contract, he would "look after the work and keep all straight on the ground and underground."[174] He would not be a visiting overseer like Haupt.

When Shanly reached Montreal, he made the rounds of friends to seek financial support, but the results were disappointing. In a letter to his brother Frank, he commented about one of their friends: "[H]e is such an unsatisfactory old beggar, that I got little out of him." But in the same letter, he mentioned an idea he was beginning to formulate to satisfy Governor Bullock. "There would be no trouble in getting $500,000 to carry on the work, but I do not think it possible to find people willing to lock it up."[175] If they could find financing for the work up until they earned $500,000 in payments from the Commonwealth, maybe Bullock would relent on the posting of securities.

Walter Shanly now feared they would lose the contract when the incoming Governor, William Claflin, succeeded Bullock on 7 January 1869.

Latrobe's Travels, 1868

• Wednesday, 9 December, Baltimore to North Adams

• Thursday, 10 December, North Adams to Boston

• Mid-December, Boston to Plymouth Rock and Plymouth to Baltimore

All believed Claflin, a known Tunnel supporter, would not require the security, so the contract would go to the low bidder, Carpenter, Odiorne, and Gardner, whom Crocker had been backing by contacting Dillon for help with the security. Crocker even wrote Bullock on 27 November with the idea that he would get Dillon to come up from New York City and meet with the Governor in Worcester. Crocker wrote letters to Dillon on 8 and 12 December, but nothing came of his efforts.[176] There was tension and fear on all sides. Walter Shanly feared what the incoming Governor would do and Crocker feared that the incoming session of the General Court might overturn the Tunnel Act.

Walter Shanly must have made the offer of substituting the first $500,000 of work for the desired security. Since the prices in the contract included profit, he was confident he and his brother would only need $400,000 to keep the work going until Commonwealth payments were received.[177] Both Latrobe and Walter Shanly arrived in Boston on Friday, 11 December. Latrobe had first gone to North Adams on Wednesday and then traveled to Boston the following day. On Friday, there was a five-hour meeting with the Governor's Council. Crocker was in attendance for this meeting.[178] The next day, Latrobe produced a draft contract—the Governor was going to accept the Shanlys' offer. Still, Latrobe went early to the State House and had a confidential conversation with Governor Bullock before submitting the contract.[179] Latrobe's document was extremely rigid, with "terribly hard clauses about forfeiture in case"[180] of not meeting monthly stipulated rates of progress. Walter protested, and the Governor's Council agreed that the conditions were too stringent. Elias Derby was present, representing the Shanlys. Finally, Derby and the attorney general for the Commonwealth reached an agreement on details. They were to produce a draft document the next week.

It was a very tense meeting, and Latrobe considered the rejection of his draft contract a personal affront, so he handed in his resignation.[181] Maybe to soothe his nerves, he attended a production of Handel's *Messiah* in the evening. Before departing Boston the next week, he also visited Plymouth Rock.

Walter Shanly, in a letter to his brother four days later, related more details of Saturday's bargaining session: "Latrobe is the hardest man I ever had to deal with. There is no equity in his nature. Frost is so small as to be utterly contemptible." Even without the presence of Latrobe, matters dragged on with more meetings and discussions. Shanly became convinced Governor Bullock was trying to delay the contract. On Friday, 18 December, the opposition was given a chance to voice its concerns. The first spokesman to appear before the council was the Tunnel's old archenemy, Frank Bird. His argument was the same as voiced in his many pamphlets: Let's not pour more money down this hole. At this point, Walter Shanly was ready to go home to Montreal. After listening to all the opposing opinions, he wrote to his brother late Friday evening to say he believed "the best course to pursue would be not to go near them again till sent for."[182]

But instead of going home to Canada on Saturday, Shanly headed west to the Tunnel. He wanted to get some facts about changes the Governor wanted written into the contract. He went into Farren's brick tube on the west side of the Mountain and visited Haupt's old tunnel, below and west of the tube. Based on where he spent his time while at the Tunnel, it seems the issue was about control of water in the west shaft and the flow from Farren's brick tube. The water from the bore flowed into Herman Haupt's old tunnel. The old Haupt tunnel started farther down the Mountain and provided the only natural drainage route to avert the need for pumping the water pouring from the bore. Since he could not support a tunnel through the porridge stone, Doane had followed Latrobe's recommendation and made an open cut as far as possible into the west side of the Mountain. This was a deep excavation, a pit, with no natural drainage outlet. Its bottom was at the level of the Tunnel line, and the original commissioners and later Crocker had never purchased the land beyond the Tunnel entrance for the rail line into North Adams. Connecting Haupt's tunnel to Doane's pit provided the only drainage for the west bore unless pumps were employed. Crocker, with his concern for not spending money unless progress could be shown, had not wanted to purchase the land for the route from this hole westward to North Adams. As a result of these decisions, Farren's tube into the west flank of the Mountain started in the bottom of this pit. Until the issue of the railroad route was settled and the flank of the Mountain was removed to the tunnel grade, the only way to remove water without pumping was via Haupt's old tunnel. The proposed contract did not include building the railroad to North Adams, so the Shanly brothers would be at the mercy of future decisions and the work of others when it came to drainage from the Tunnel at this location.

Additionally, the Governor seems to have wanted the Shanlys to lower their prices for the work on the west side of the Mountain, but, after a close examination of Doane's hole and the water situation, Walter would not agree to any reduction in price. Even before Shanly made the trip to North Adams,

Governor Bullock had told him he would execute the contract, so this price question seems to have been more of a request than a contract-defeating matter. Walter had even written his brother on 19 December, saying that the "Governor says he will execute Contract Wednesday [23 December]."[183] But there was one more day of delay. It was a wearing two weeks, but on Christmas Eve Walter Shanly was finally able to telegraph his brother:

December 24, 1868

Montreal Telegraph Company
From Boston to F. Shanly
Contract signed. I leave for Montreal today.

W. Shanly

Arriving back in Montreal on Christmas morning, Walter found no celebration. A letter was awaiting him from Frank in Toronto. It contained the sad news that Frank's baby, who had been ill when Walter departed Canada, had died on 21 December. Walter wrote Frank immediately to say that if he had known more about the child's condition, he would have returned sooner to be with Frank and his wife, Louise.

At this point, Crocker was also exhausted, and in a letter to Tappan Wentworth after Christmas, he bled his spleen: "When I consider the tunnel survived Herman Haupt, the Oily Latrobe, and the Central Shaft [probably meaning the deadly accident] and how I was resisted, the Good Lord hast delivered the tunnel."[184]

12

Walter and Francis Shanly

*The long and well contested competition
for the contract to complete the Hoosac Tunnel, and
its final award to parties outside the United States,
naturally give rise to the question—who are these
favored parties?*

— *The Adams Transcript*, vol. 29, no. 8
(21 January 1869)

Finally, in late 1868, the contract between the Commonwealth of Massachusetts and the Shanly brothers was signed. After months of delay and the airing of too many arguments, the war of words over the issue of completing the Hoosac Tunnel was settled. The cost of completing the Tunnel through the Hoosac Mountain was now set by contract at $4,592,000.[1] During the final negotiations, Walter Shanly had been persuaded to cut $31,000 from his bid price, but he still felt confident. This reduction supposedly represented work accomplished by the commissioners.

It was not the first time a Hoosac contractor had felt self-confident. In 1854, Edward W. Serrell believed he could complete the Tunnel for $3,500,000. And in 1855 Herman Haupt was satisfied with the contract price he negotiated! By now, Alvah Crocker, the man persistently found behind the Hoosac Tunnel scenes, was happy but tired, and his wife, Lucy A. Fay, was suffering. She would be dead in three years. Crocker and Lucy Fay set off for Europe in early 1869 and did not return to Massachusetts until August. The jousting in Boston had been wearisome for Walter Shanly, as he wrote to his younger brother: ". . . my patience was at last so completely exhausted."[2] Arriving in Montreal on Christmas Day of 1868 and discovering that his brother's youngest child had died, he immediately drafted a sympathy letter. Nonetheless, later the same day, he sent Frank a second letter, it was all business: "We must have an early meeting." Urging Frank to be in Montreal on Tuesday of the following week for a meeting, he continued,

Hoosac Tunnel Contract.

W^m & F. Shanly.—

The within document is the original Contract. I sealed it up just as it is in Feby: 1869 when going to Commence work on the Tunnel and gave it to H. Hogan, St Lawrence Hall, to put away in his safe. He mislaid it and it never turned up until last week when searching for other papers he chanced upon this one. I have not broken the seal: Let it stay as it is: W.S. 2/10/96.

"We have a poor, miserable, narrow-minded d---l for Engineer [Frost], but must only manage to get on without his help."[3] The statement proved Walter Shanly's clairvoyance.

Like the Baldwins, the Shanly brothers had begun their engineering careers building canals. Even with the award of the Hoosac Tunnel contract to the Canadian Shanlys, the web of connections among the engineers involved with the Tunnel enterprise remained strong. In 1821, Loammi Baldwin had journeyed south to Pennsylvania to assume the position of chief engineer for the Union Canal Company. Thirty years later, when that company was finally forced by economics to yield to Baldwin's arguments about lock widths, it was Frank Shanly who went south in late 1850 from railroad work in New York to accept an engineer's position on the canal. The Shanlys had one further Baldwin trait: They considered civil engineering a profession. This was especially true in the case of Walter, and it was important for him to maintain his independence. Just as such an attitude had been the cause of Baldwin's troubles on the Union Canal, it would be the source of the Shanlys' later troubles with Benjamin Frost, the engineer overseeing the Hoosac Tunnel contract for the Commonwealth.

A Family from Ireland

Five years after Herman Haupt, age fourteen, embarked on his steamboat journey up the Hudson River to West Point, the Shanly brothers—Walter, age nineteen, and Francis, age sixteen—made a similar journey up the river. Born the same year as Haupt, Walter Shanly immigrated to Canada from Ireland with his family. He and his brothers would soon learn they had no more liking for the drudgery of farm life than did Haupt. Walter and Francis Shanly did not have the advantage of a West Point engineering education, but they turned to engineering for their livelihoods.

The Shanly family could trace its Irish ancestors back to the twelfth century in County Leitrim in northwestern Ireland. There were few literate folk around, and medieval scribes were often not consistent in spellings, but their clan name was MacSheanlaoich or Mac Seanlaoich.[4] By the sixteenth century, the name in the genealogical records had evolved into MacShanly. In 1652, when Oliver Cromwell defeated the Irish Catholic Confederation and Royalist coalition, with which MacShanly was aligned, the family somehow managed to retain their ownership of extensive lands in the county. From Walter Shanly's narrative of the family history, his branch of the clan continued in the Catholic faith but anglicized the family name further by dropping the *Mac*. The loss of the Shanly estates occurred in 1699, when the Catholic King James II of England was defeated by William, the rival Protestant claimant to the throne. Captain William Shanly, who then held title to the family estates, fought on the side of King James, so the family land was seized and given to an Englishman. A friend, however, purchased from the new owner a few parcels and a home for the captain, whose eldest son, James, then came into possession of this acreage. With James's death, it passed to his son, also named William Shanly. Nonetheless, things did not improve, and the last of the family holdings were sold in 1764.

The landless William Shanly had four sons, the eldest named William. The other three sons were James, Tobias, and Michael. The youngest, Michael, followed in his great-grandfather's footsteps and became an officer in the Drogheda Dragoons. He married a wealthy widow and rose to the rank of captain before retiring in 1787. This Shanly, the second to reach the rank of captain in the Dragoons, had three sons—Robert, William, and James. The youngest, James, earned a degree at Trinity College Dublin, spent time in London studying law, and then returned to practice in Dublin. Because he did not seek to advance himself as far as his father thought he should, he was disinherited. His marriage to a merchant's daughter, Frances Elizabeth Mulvany of Dublin, spurred this break. While the couple lived in Dublin, Frances bore James Shanly a daughter and four sons. In 1815, William Shanly, oldest brother of Captain Michael Shanly, died. This brother had never married, but he had acquired land and he had a better regard for all three of Captain Shanly's sons. As a result, he left his property to James Shanly and his two older brothers.

James Shanly, the lawyer, sold his part of the land inheritance to his brother Robert, but he kept his uncle's thriving business of estate management for absentee landlords. Because of the confiscations by Cromwell and King William, about a third of the land in Ireland was owned by absentee landlords in the 1800s.[5] James Shanly believed estate management would provide him a better living, so he gave up his law practice, departed Dublin, and leased a country home in Queen's County (now Laois County), about fifty miles southwest of Dublin.

The change allowed James to apply his knowledge of law in a practical manner, but, more importantly, he could now live the life of a country gentleman. As one chronicler of the times noted, estate management provided a nineteenth-century man the opportunity to live an eighteenth-century life.[6] The new family residence was a leased country home called the Abbey.

After the move, the family continued to grow with the birth of the future Hoosac engineers: Walter in 1817 and Francis in 1820. At the Abbey, the belief that they were gentlemen was bred into Walter and Francis (who was called Frank). In his history of the family, Walter Shanly would write that the Abbey ". . . created impressions on the mind of him who now writes that have had no uncertain influence on his seventy subsequent years and which still make the place of his birth a bright oasis. . . ."[7]

Three days after giving birth to Frank, Frances Mulvany died.[8] As a result of her death, and of James Shanly's desire to give his sons a good education, he

1815/1816 James Shanly moves family to the "Abbey"

11 October 1817 Walter Shanly is born at the "Abbey"

29 October 1820 Francis (Frank) Shanly is born at the "Abbey"

1825 James Shanly moves his family to Norman's Grove

June 1836 The Shanly family reaches New York City

November 1836 First Shanly home in London, Canada

1837 Hamilton Killaly is appointed engineer for the Welland Canal

1838 The Shanlys build Thorndale

Spring 1840 Hamilton Killaly is appointed chairman of the Board of Works

October 1840 Walter Shanly leaves Thorndale to become an engineer

moved the family in 1825 from the Abbey to Norman's Grove, an estate ten miles northwest of Dublin. At the time of the move, James was a widower with seven young boys ranging in age from fourteen to five, but in August of the same year, his ten-year-old son, Cuthbert, died at their new home. Sons Charles Dawson (1811), William (1813), and James (1815) had been born before the move to the Abbey, while Coote Nisbitt (1819) was born at the Abbey between Walter and Francis. This brood must have been too much for James to manage alone, because in 1827 he married his deceased wife's younger sister, Ellen Mulvany.[9]

A book published in 1837 listed for the parish of Dunboyne, in the barony of Dunboyne, county of Meath: "J. Shanley residing at the gentleman's seat of Norman's Grove."[10] During the family's residency at Norman's Grove, the boys had private tutors, and the oldest, Charles Dawson Shanly, was sent to Trinity College Dublin, an institution with 240 years of tradition when he entered. He would graduate in 1834 with a BA, the only son of James Shanly to receive a university education. William Shanly, the next oldest son, was articled (apprenticed) to a civil engineer in Liverpool, but he contracted tuberculosis and died in 1833. At home, Walter and Francis had no fewer than six tutors, who took them through the works of Quintus Horatis (Horace) the Roman lyric poet, Homer the Greek poet, and Euclid the Greek mathematician. They were also enrolled in a drawing academy, took lessons from a French master, and attended chemistry lectures.

After ten years at Norman's Grove, James Shanly decided to move his family to Canada. Though a landless man could make a good living as an estate manager in Ireland, he saw no future for the boys in the country of their birth. On 25 October 1835, he held an auction at Norman's Grove and disposed of everything they could not carry to Canada. The family spent the rest of the winter completing the preparations for their transatlantic crossing. Finally, in the spring of 1836, the Shanlys departed and reached New York City in June. Walter Shanly, in a letter home, called New York City "abominable." To his eye, the finest streets in New York were equivalent to the filthiest streets in Dublin. After a stay in the city of more than two weeks, the family traveled by steamboat up the Hudson River to Albany, where they embarked on an Erie Canal boat for the journey west to Oswego, New York, on Lake Ontario. While his wife and the boys remained behind in Oswego, James Shanly proceeded into Upper Canada to purchase a suitable farm. ("Upper" in this case refers to the upper reaches of the St. Lawrence River.) Compared with the Abbey and Norman's Grove, the farm James purchased near the town of London was primitive.

The next leg of the journey for the family was a steamboat voyage westward across Lake Ontario to Hamilton, Canada, just above Niagara Falls. Finally, in mid-November, with their baggage piled into wagons, the family traveled seventy-five miles farther west to London, on the peninsula between Lake Erie on the south and Lake Huron on the north. One hundred miles farther to the southwest in the United States lay Detroit, then the capital of the Michigan Territory. Michigan would not become a state until 1837. There was daily stage service between Detroit and Chicago, which then had a population under 5,000. In Canada, Toronto was one hundred miles to the northeast of London. It took two trips with fully loaded wagons to move all of the belongings the family had carried from Ireland. Walter and Francis Shanly stayed behind in Hamilton to repack heavy baggage for the second wagon trip. James Shanly then returned to Hamilton and made the final trek with his two boys.

As a former Dublin lawyer, Shanly had chosen a farm located close to the home of a fellow Irishman, Hamilton Hartley Killaly. It proved a fateful choice. Killaly was likewise from Dublin and held both a BA and an MA from Trinity College. His father, John A. Killaly was a prominent engineer who had worked on the extension of the Grand Canal in Ireland. The eighty-two-mile-long Grand Canal connected Dublin with the River Shannon in the west. In 1823, when the senior Killaly was directing engineer for the extension of the Grand Canal to Ballinasloe, in Galway, he secured for his son the position of superintending engineer. Because of that experience gained in Ireland, Hamilton Killaly would quickly rise to prominence as a civil engineer in Canada.

At first, the Shanly boys attacked the farm work in Canada with enthusiasm, but the novelty soon waned. These young gentlemen were not prepared for the drudgery of clearing stumps and the other toils of growing crops. In 1837, Hamilton Killaly was appointed engineer of the Welland Canal Company, which connected Lake Ontario with Lake Erie on the Canadian side of Niagara Falls. At about the same time as Killaly's appointment, James Shanly thought he and his boys needed more land, so he purchased six hundred acres a few miles northeast of their original farm. There they built a country home in 1838. A gentleman's farm needed a name, so they christened the place Thorndale, and Walter Shanly took an active part in building it. His two remaining older brothers, Charles and James, found the life so distasteful they soon departed to pursue their own careers. Charles Shanly joined the militia and his brother James apprenticed himself to a lawyer in London, Canada. Walter, now the oldest son remaining at home, stayed for only two additional years. He remained only because he felt an obligation to his father, but the experience of remaining under such circumstances alienated him from the family.[11] He had always been a reserved and sensitive boy who considered himself lacking in the artistic gift his father esteemed and a coolness had developed between father and son.

The Killaly School

In the spring of 1840, Hamilton Killaly was appointed chairman of the Board of Works for the United Canadas. Walter Shanly, during his boyhood years at Thorndale, had been treated almost like a beloved son by Killaly. Probably because Killaly had observed the way Walter accepted responsibility for managing his father's farm, he knew the young man had potential. Killaly's new role required him to move to Montreal, where he was in a position to dispense professional employment. Walter was hopeful that his surrogate father would provide him the opportunity to escape the farm labors at Thorndale. There were long months of waiting, but finally Killaly returned for Walter in October 1840. With Walter Shanly's departure, only two of the original tribe of boys remained on the farm: Frank and Coote. At twenty, Frank was strong and bold, but he was a fun-loving young man. Coote was intelligent but lacked confidence.

Arriving in Montreal with Killaly, Walter Shanly immediately went to work under Nicol Hugh Baird, the chief engineer for the Chambly Canal. Baird had learned about canal building in Scotland under his father, Hugh Baird. The canal project, just east of the city of the same name on the Richelieu River, had a total length of twelve miles, with nine locks. However, there was a problem: Shanly was only on the temporary payroll, and when the work was stopped after only a month, his employment came to an abrupt end. But it seems Killaly's influence saved him once more. By the middle of January, he was named inspector for Montreal roads, a job for which he had no previous experience. It lasted through the summer of 1841. Even with Killaly's help, his engineering experience over almost two years amounted to only two short periods of employment. Leaving the farm had provided only limited productive experience. But finally, in July of 1842, Walter Shanly was appointed subassistant engineer on the Beauharnois Canal, with a royal salary of £175 annually.

This 14.7-mile-long canal on the south side of the St. Lawrence River would provide a connection between Lake St. Louis and Lake St. Francis, while bypassing three sets of rapids. Its northern or downstream terminus (the St. Lawrence River flows from southwest to northeast) would be about twenty-five miles west of Montreal. Walter's appointment proved an auspicious assignment.

The assistant engineer who supervised Shanly proved incompetent, and though the man was retained on the staff, the new subassistant engineer began reporting directly to J. B. Mills, the engineer-in-charge. Not yet having full authority or pay, Shanly at least was acting as an assistant engineer. By the fall, the canal route was approved and the design of the locks was completed. Contractor bids were quickly solicited, and the work commenced. Shanly was now assigned to inspect the work and keep records of contractor performance for pay purposes. In the spring of 1843, his workload increased as the weather allowed the contractors to be more productive. He proved himself reliable, a trait Killaly had noted earlier, and by autumn Walter Shanly, only three years from the farm at Thorndale, was promoted to the position of assistant engineer.

The engineer-in-charge had a second canal project to oversee, so Shanly assumed more of the engineering responsibilities by 1844. His responsibilities increased even more so beginning in March, because the other assistant engineer resigned in February. Before long, reports on the progress of the work, while being signed by the engineer-in-charge, were all in Shanly's hand.[12] The grounding the Shanly boys had received in the classics had honed their rhetorical skills and made them expert report writers.

In the spring of 1845, before the canal opened, the engineer-in-charge was moved to another canal project, and Shanly was tasked with having the works completed by the first of July. He did not make the deadline, but he was a hard-nosed

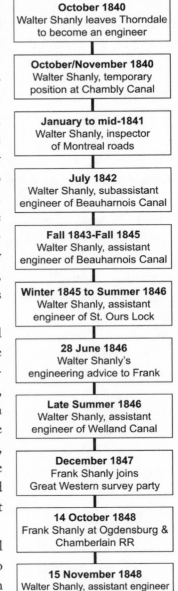

taskmaster, and the work was only a month and a half late.[13] It was a good lesson about the importance of meeting schedules in terms of cost to complete the work and in terms of how project owners evaluated engineers. Three years of handling technical and administrative details made Walter Shanly an engineer.[14] Those

October 1840
Walter Shanly leaves Thorndale to become an engineer

October/November 1840
Walter Shanly, temporary position at Chambly Canal

January to mid-1841
Walter Shanly, inspector of Montreal roads

July 1842
Walter Shanly, subassistant engineer of Beauharnois Canal

Fall 1843-Fall 1845
Walter Shanly, assistant engineer of Beauharnois Canal

Winter 1845 to Summer 1846
Walter Shanly, assistant engineer of St. Ours Lock

28 June 1846
Walter Shanly's engineering advice to Frank

Late Summer 1846
Walter Shanly, assistant engineer of Welland Canal

December 1847
Frank Shanly joins Great Western survey party

14 October 1848
Frank Shanly at Ogdensburg & Chamberlain RR

15 November 1848
Walter Shanly, assistant engineer at Ogdensburg & Chamberlain RR

three years had also given Walter Shanly an appreciation of the laboring man who built the great works. On the Beauharnois Canal, a flood of southern Irish navvies applied for work. (In the British system, manual laborers were known as "navvies.") Shanly saw them crushed by stones, kicked by horses, and drowned under the water in the locks. Perhaps from his own farm experience, but definitely on this project, he came to understand the workingman's burden. A good navvy with pick, shovel, and wheelbarrow could move twenty tons of earth a day, but he needed to be properly fed and treated with respect. Walter Shanly, a standoffish gentleman who could be very cold with peers he did not respect, had acquired a unique ability to relate to the fellows who actually did the work.

In 1840, achieving the status of engineer was attained by performance in the field. After his Beauharnois Canal performance, the board of works valued Walter Shanly as a civil engineer. He was, therefore, immediately assigned to the St. Ours Locks on the Richelieu River. The Chambly Canal, of which the locks were a part, would allow navigation between the St. Lawrence River and Lake Champlain. Completion of this lock and the canal would provide a route to the canals in New York State.

The board obviously had confidence in Walter Shanly's judgment and ability to write succinct reports—over the years, they sent him on various other assignments requiring such skill. He went off to estimate the cost to survey Lake St. Louis and to investigate the work being performed at the Welland Canal, on the Canadian side of the Niagara River and its falls. All of this canal work and his employment depended on Canadian government financing.

The British government passed the Act of Union in 1840 and a parliament was created in Canada. In the summer of 1846, this parliament, seeking more control over the spending of government funds, abolished the Board of Works and created the Department of Public Works, with a nonengineer as chief commissioner. Shanly's benefactor, Hamilton Killaly, was made chief engineer within the new organization, but he lost his ability to dispense patronage. The new chief commissioner moved Shanly to the Welland Canal project, under Samuel Keefer.

Between 1827 and 1833, Keefer had served an engineering apprenticeship under Erie Canal veterans who guided the original Welland Canal work. The original canal was twenty-seven miles long and eight feet deep, with forty wooden locks. Later, Keefer worked on other Canadian canals and was a well-recognized canal engineer by the 1840s.

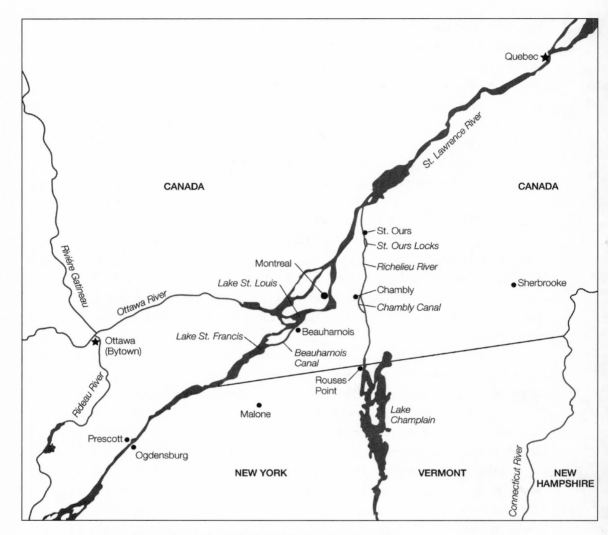

Location of Beauharnois and Chambly Canals, Canada

Actually, the commissioner had given Shanly a choice: the Welland Canal or a position overseeing road improvements. Believing it would better prepare him for future railroad work, he chose the Welland. In a September letter to his brother Frank, Walter made the reason for his decision quite clear: "I made a very great sacrifice of personal comfort at the shrine of engineering knowledge."[15]

At the time he moved to the Welland Canal project, the number of locks was being reduced to twenty-seven, and all of the replacement locks were to be constructed of limestone. This gave Walter Shanly his first exposure to masonry construction, and he learned his lesson well. Already he recognized where the future engineering opportunities would lie. In the same September letter to his brother, he wrote, "I mean myself to leave no means untried to obtain a situation on it [the Great Western Rail-Road Co.]."[16] This railroad was originally incorporated as the London and Gore Railroad Company on 6 May 1834. The name was changed to the Great Western Rail-Road Co. in 1845. In 1853, the company became the Great Western Railway. John M. Forbes, Erastus Corning, and John W. Brooks were all members of a committee to procure American subscriptions for building the Great Western.[17] In fact, Forbes was chair of the committee.

By the summer of 1844, Frank Shanly had decided to leave the farm, but he could not make a go of the few outside jobs he found around London. From the family correspondence, it is clear he had an imprudent streak. Throughout his life, it would surface on many occasions and lead to severe consequences.[18] Too much gaiety was not conducive to responsible work, and he was back at Thorndale by the following spring. Since his older brother seemed to be doing well as an engineer, Frank wrote Walter in the summer of 1846 about possible opportunities as an engineer. Responding to his brother's inquiries, Walter's letter of 28 June 1846 advised: ". . . touch up your knowledge of figures, mathematics, etc. Read Gregory's Practical Mechanics and anything else in the line you can lay hold of."[19] Like his older brother, Frank did not have an easy go of landing his first engineering job, but he was persistent. In December, he secured a junior position on a Great Western Railway survey party, but the winter work caused him to suffer snow blindness.[20] Nevertheless, he proved capable, and he was promoted to compass man in June 1847. Unfortunately, the promotion was short-lived, as the work concluded in early August.

Walter Shanly was providing his younger brother with living funds, so when Frank failed to find employment, his older brother summoned him to the Welland Canal project. Frank now began to help his brother with the office work and to become thoroughly exposed to the duties of an engineer. Through the winter, the brothers lived together in Port Robinson, a town bisected by the canal. During a few months in early 1848, Frank Shanly's name even appeared on the paymaster's records as office assistant.[21]

For all of Frank Shanly's attachment to frivolous living, he was serious about engineering. The notebook he kept during this period includes information on the structural details of locks, the mixture proportions for batching concrete, and materials prices. He was also creating for himself a reference book of mathematical formulas for calculating areas, volumes, and forces. He copied these from other sources, probably from books lent to him by his brother.²² But the Department of Public Works had not adequately controlled its use of funds, so the payroll was cut in July 1848. Frank Shanly once again had to strike out in search of a job. This time, believing there was railroad work in the United States, he traveled south, landing in Massachusetts by September. Friends took him to railroad construction sites, but he had no offers of employment. He even wrote to Engineer A. F. Edwards of Alvah Crocker's Vermont and Massachusetts Railroad. Two years later, Edwards would be chief engineer of the Troy and Greenfield Railroad, and he would draw the first plans describing the size of Crocker's Hoosac Mountain Tunnel. There is no record in Frank Shanly's correspondence that Edwards responded to the young man's letter seeking employment.

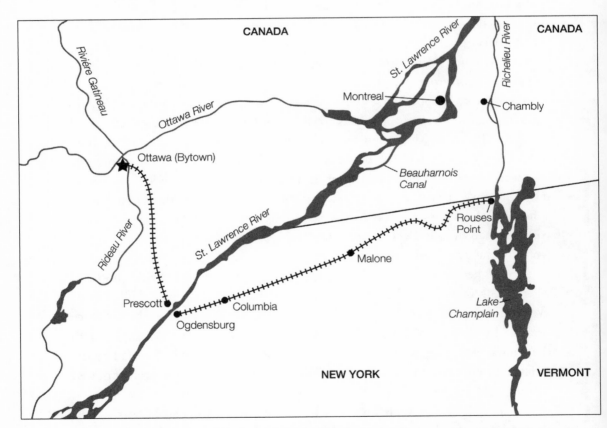

The Northern Railroad of New York, 1848–50 (Ogdensburg to Lake Champlain)

Hearing of a soon-to-be-built railroad across northern New York, Frank next traveled to Ogdensburg, New York. (The name at that time was Ogdensburgh; in 1868, the village removed the *h* from its name.) On Thursday, 12 October, he arrived in this port town on the St. Lawrence River, directly across from Prescott, Canada. Two days later, he was put to work in the engineer's office, drawing a profile of the proposed Northern Railroad of New York. The line was to run from Ogdensburg to Rouses Point on Lake Champlain. The 118-mile route would connect with the Vermont Central Railroad on the Vermont side of Lake Champlain, and the Vermont Central connected with Alvah Crocker's Vermont and Massachusetts Railroad in Massachusetts. The final leg of the linkage to Boston was Crocker's other railroad, the Fitchburg. The contractor who had signed on to build the eastern section of New York's Northern Railroad was Sewell F. Belknap of Vermont, the builder of Crocker's Fitchburg Railroad.

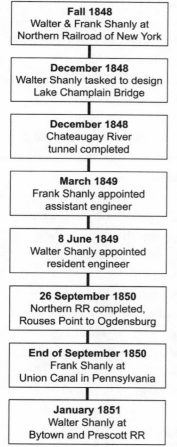

Fall 1848
Walter & Frank Shanly at Northern Railroad of New York

December 1848
Walter Shanly tasked to design Lake Champlain Bridge

December 1848
Chateaugay River tunnel completed

March 1849
Frank Shanly appointed assistant engineer

8 June 1849
Walter Shanly appointed resident engineer

26 September 1850
Northern RR completed, Rouses Point to Ogdensburg

End of September 1850
Frank Shanly at Union Canal in Pennsylvania

January 1851
Walter Shanly at Bytown and Prescott RR

A major portion of the capital to support the construction of this railroad came from Boston capitalists. Alvah Crocker's friend Elias Derby wrote a report that examined the estimated cost and potential of the Northern Railroad. Derby's report was part of a pamphlet published in Boston: *The Northern Railroad in New York with Remarks on The Western Trade.* His report included an evaluation of the railroad's commercial potential and quoted parts of an engineering study prepared by James Hayward.[23] Hayward was the engineer who, together with James Baldwin, had written the report counseling construction of the Western Railroad in Massachusetts. The words of Derby and Hayward must have held sway with the moneymen of Boston, because, by the next year, four Boston men—including Abbott Lawrence—were company directors. Within two years, a Boston man, T. P. Chandler, was president. On 15 November, when Walter Shanly arrived in Ogdensburg to join his brother, the chief engineer straightaway sent him to work as the assistant engineer for the Eastern Division at Malone, sixty miles to the east. Frank Shanly was now located in Ogdensburg while his older brother lodged in a hotel in a Malone hotel. Walter Shanly described the Malone hotel as ". . . the dammedest hole I ever was in."[24] The main street of Malone's business section at this time was lined from end to end with hitching posts and rails. In 1840, the village proper boasted 670 residents. By 1845, a census of the town, which included the surrounding area, listed the population at 3,634, with almost an equal number of cattle: 3,558.[25]

Railroad Engineers

Charles L. Schlatter (generally referred to as Colonel Schlatter), chief engineer for the Northern Railroad of New York, had in 1839 and the early 1840s been principal engineer to the canal commissioners in Pennsylvania. As a state engineer, he had directed the original surveys for a railroad from Harrisburg to Pittsburgh.[26] His work was the preliminary effort for a railroad across Pennsylvania, a railroad Herman Haupt was later instrumental in building. Now, less than ten years since those original surveys, and while Haupt was laboring in Pennsylvania, the Shanly brothers would perform similar railroad-building tasks in New York and receive their railroad-engineering education from Colonel Schlatter.

John Edgar Thomson, chief engineer for the Pennsylvania Railroad, charged Haupt with designing and constructing the most important bridge of the Pennsylvania Railroad, the span across the Susquehanna River. Colonel Schlatter charged Walter Shanly with designing the most important bridge of the Northern Railroad of New York, the span across the outlet of Lake Champlain at Rouses Point, where the lake flows north into the Richelieu River.[27]

The bridge Shanly was tasked to design was ". . . a tremendous concern,—14 spans of 150' each,—besides the swing bridges of 60' each."[28] Walter Shanly had never designed a major bridge! So, less than a week later, he wrote to Frank and requested that he send him Nicholson's *Carpenter's Guide*.[29] He was probably referring to *The Carpenter's New Guide* by Peter Nicholson—the first edition was published in 1792 and the second edition in 1808. The Shanly brothers, like the Baldwins, collected engineering books. Soon after arriving in Ogdensburg, Frank Shanly purchased *A Treatise on Surveying: containing the theory and practice* by John Gummere; *An Elementary Course of Civil Engineering* by D. H. Mahan; and *Scribner's Engineers' and Mechanics' Companion* by J. M. Scribner. During this period Walter Shanly received his introduction to tunnel work.[30]

The Northern Railroad had a number of large rivers to cross. In the case of the Chateaugay River, the original plan was to construct a masonry bridge. Located about ten miles east of Malone village, the Chateaugay flows north, but after crossing into Canada, it turns northeast and runs parallel to the St. Lawrence before joining the St. Lawrence southwest of Montreal. At the proposed site of the Chateaugay River railroad bridge, the rock was unsuitable for supporting the foundation of a heavy masonry bridge, but this was not discovered until 1848. The decision was then made to divert the river through a tunnel cut in solid rock, fill the old ravine of the river, and then place the railroad crossing on an embankment above the tunnel.[31] The proposed embankment at this location was to be 160 feet high.[32]

After Shanly had moved to Malone, he visited the railroad's tunnel work and was undeniably impressed. His letter to Frank in Ogdensburg described the tunnel as ". . . a magnificent work and worth going any distance to see."[33] At the time, most of Frank's work was in the office at Ogdensburg, making drawings. His one visit to the field was not nearly as exciting as his brother's visit to the tunnel. In the cold of January 1849, he was sent out along the route to make a table listing all of the private railroad crossings the company would have to build.[34]

During the winter, Walter made a trip to Rouses Point on Lake Champlain to inspect the site where the bridge he was designing would cross the lake. The design of this bridge was a real challenge for Shanly, and the letters to his brother acknowledge how hard he was working to become a bridge engineer: ". . . in the office every night till 10 o'clock. Send me only my large trunk, box of books, snow shoes and long boots."[35] In another letter to his brother, he revealed that he was then working seven days a week.

At the proposed bridge site, he surveyed the shore of the lake. Another reason for going in the winter—when the lake was a solid sheet of ice—was to take soundings to determine the water depth. He could walk across the frozen lake to the location of each of each proposed bridge pier, cut a hole in the ice, drop a weighted line, and resolve the question of how tall to make the masonry piers on which the bridge superstructure would rest. By the second week of January 1849, he had completed plans for the watertight cofferdams—the temporary structures he planned to use for facilitating dry construction of the bridge piers in the lake. Railroad engineer Walter Shanly was very pleased when the plans were approved by Colonel Schlatter and Frank Shanly's boss, the resident engineer in Ogdensburg.[36] The following month, the colonel asked Walter Shanly to estimate the cost of the bridge. It was an extremely important task, though he might not have fully realized its importance at the time. Colonel Schlatter was preparing his report for the financiers in Boston, and cost was always on their minds.

Shanly would make another excursion to Rouses Point in late March to study the effect of the lake ice as it broke up in the spring. Sometimes he could express himself in a most amusing manner. On this occasion, he wrote, "I have just got orders to strike my tent [and] to pitch it again at Rouse's Point."[37] He needed to know ". . . what kind of pranks it [the ice] plays in moving off."[38] Engineers are always concerned about floating ice damaging a bridge, and Walter Shanly was learning to carefully observe the physical environment of his work.

But there would be no problem with floating ice; by a vote of 106 to 80, the Vermont legislature refused the railroad's request to build the bridge.[39] The Champlain boatmen argued that the bridge would hinder navigation on the lake.

At this moment, the railroad engineering opportunities for Walter and Francis Shanly rested not on hard work but on fate. The moneymen in Boston who were backing the Northern Railroad were not pleased with this development concerning the bridge or the general state of construction affairs. The fate of the Shanlys' continued engineering employment rested with these financiers, who met with Colonel Schlatter in the Tremont House—the same hotel where Walter Shanly and the key decisionmakers for the Hoosac Tunnel contract would gather twenty years later.

News of the discontentment in Boston reached both Shanly brothers in April. Later they learned that control of the railroad had passed to the men in Boston, and a new president had been installed, a Boston man. The two Canadian engineers had no idea what to expect in terms of their future employment.

From his camp on Lake Champlain, Walter Shanly wrote, "[T]he game is up. This infernal Bridge business has played H--- with everything."[40] Finally, on 8 June, he learned his fate. Colonel Schlatter sent him a letter informing him of his appointment as resident engineer for the Western Division of the Northern Railroad! At a salary of $1,200 per annum![41] The Boston men now followed the farsighted construction practice of the Western Railroad in Massachusetts, so Shanly was directed to construct all the Western Division bridges with double tracks.

Even before Walter learned of his promotion, his brother was made assistant engineer of the Western Division, so the younger brother was now working directly for the older. Two days later, they were instructed to drive the work with all deliberate speed, with deep cuts to be excavated and all bridges built that season if possible.[42] Shanly's navvies with their wheelbarrows would be hard put to move the glacial deposits of diluvial soils (accumulations of sand and gravel) found along the route.

Almost immediately after Walter Shanly assumed the resident engineer's position, the letters between the two brothers became more technical. The younger brother was effectively learning his engineering by correspondence course. The older brother's letters covered everything from construction means and methods to machinery. Writing to his brother about a hammer for pile driving that he was to have cast, Walter advised: "[T]he smaller the hammer the greater its liability to split the pile."[43] In the case of bridge building, Walter Shanly wanted the work organized like an assembly line—each man did one particular task and another man followed, completing the next task.[44] Moreover, the older brother provided advice and instructions about paying close attention to the types of soil being excavated. Frank Shanly found himself being questioned repeatedly about the materials being excavated in his section—could they be used somewhere on the project or should they be wasted?

With the onset of fall and freezing weather, construction work typically would have slowed, but the men sitting comfortably in Boston had other ideas. The heavy cuts through the hills to provide a smooth road were on the western end, approaching Ogdensburg. The completion of those excavations controlled when the Northern Railroad would open to through traffic, so Walter Shanly was ordered to carry on vigorously all winter.[45] As winter turned into spring and spring into summer, the pace of the work only increased. In May, President T. P. Chandler, spokesman for the Boston crowd, told Shanly he was depending on him and his brother to complete the Western Division. Walter, the resident engineer, passed the comment on to his brother, adding: "We must do it, though when done, we will get no thanks for it."[46]

By early June, the trains were running from Rouses Point as far west as the village of Chateaugay.[47] Track laying was moving along so fast that Shanly said it was "coming on like lightning."[48] Passenger trains from Rouses Point reached Malone on 19 September 1850. A week later, the Northern Railroad line was continuous from Rouses Point to Ogdensburg. The construction work was finished, the contractors were departing, and Frank Shanly once again was looking for new opportunities.

Before the month of September was out, Frank joined James Worrall in Pennsylvania. Worrall had met the Shanlys while working as one of the contractors for the Northern Railroad. He was more than just a builder, he was also an engineer. Frank Shanly had overseen the work of Worrall's crews for the previous two years, and before he departed, Worrall asked the Shanly brothers to join him on the enlargement of the Union Canal. Worrall and the Shanlys had not always seen eye-to-eye during construction of the railroad, but they had developed respect for one another and a mutual confidence in the abilities each possessed. Worrall also knew the brothers had the ability to manage projects spread across miles of terrain. Frank Shanly accepted Worrall's offer and became his principal assistant engineer for the Union Canal work.

There were rumors of railroad work about to start across the St. Lawrence River in Canada,[49] so Walter Shanly stayed on in Ogdensburg to close out the construction accounts of the Northern Railroad. It was distasteful work: "I am getting heartily sick of the whole concern, and perceive that I am going to have a disagreeable berth."[50] Going down the rails of the line on a handcar a month and a half after the opening celebration, he found the whole line a deserted and cheerless place. He wrote to his brother on 14 November: "Nothing has a more dreary aspect for me than a large work, upon which I have been engaged, just after completion, when the bustle and excitement of urging it forward has subsided."[51]

New Challenges

Union Canal engineer Frank Shanly would make his headquarters in Pine Grove, Pennsylvania, but his first letters to his brother were from Harrisburg, the state capital, about ten miles upriver from Middletown, where the Union Canal joined the Susquehanna River. (Middletown is more famous today because it is only three miles from the infamous Three Mile Island.) Finally, in January 1851, Frank Shanly settled in at Pine Grove, an anthracite-coal transportation hub in the narrow Swatara Creek Valley. A 180-square-mile coalfield runs northeast to southwest across this part of Pennsylvania and during the mid-1800s, it was the largest coal-producing field in the Commonwealth of Pennsylvania. For this reason, the enlargement of the Union Canal was extremely important. From the High Dam on Swatara Creek, which was built the year before Frank arrived, the Pine Grove feeder canal provided the water for the summit crossing of the main canal. This dam was located just to the north of Pine Grove.

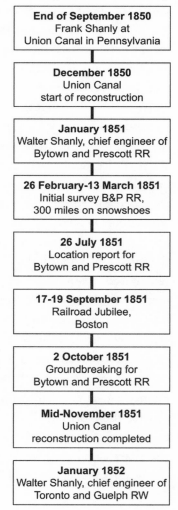

End of September 1850
Frank Shanly at
Union Canal in Pennsylvania

December 1850
Union Canal
start of reconstruction

January 1851
Walter Shanly, chief engineer of
Bytown and Prescott RR

26 February-13 March 1851
Initial survey B&P RR,
300 miles on snowshoes

26 July 1851
Location report for
Bytown and Prescott RR

17-19 September 1851
Railroad Jubilee,
Boston

2 October 1851
Groundbreaking for
Bytown and Prescott RR

Mid-November 1851
Union Canal
reconstruction completed

January 1852
Walter Shanly, chief engineer of
Toronto and Guelph RW

As a principal assistant engineer, Frank Shanly was responsible for approximately twenty miles of canal enlargement and for increasing the size of the locks from eight and a half feet by seventy-five feet in length to seventeen feet by ninety feet in length. He had two assistant engineers to handle the field-work, but contract administration and design were his responsibility. At this point in his career, Frank was very competent handling contractors but weak when it came to design. Soon his brother's ongoing correspondence course began providing needed design information: "Will send you . . . in a day or two, sketch of aqueduct."[52]

On the first of December, Walter Shanly informed his brother that the Bytown and Prescott Railway people, across the St. Lawrence River, had elected him engineer for their line. (Bytown became Ottawa on New Year's Day in 1855.) This decision was made without consulting Shanly. He also mentioned the Great Western Railway in Canada, where matters looked pretty promising for a construction start. Ten days later, but still with no authentic job offers in hand, he wrote to his brother to tell him he had resigned from the Northern Railroad but would be staying on until January to settle up matters, as there always seemed to be another piece of paperwork.[53] As the month of December progressed, he continued to send engineering correspondence lessons south to Pennsylvania. These primarily discussed the design of locks. Walter Shanly described the wooden quoin post they had used on the Welland Canal. (These are the posts that rotate and to which the lock gates are attached.) In his letter, he explained how the quoins were attached at their tops to the stone lock walls with metal straps, how an iron rod at the bottom allowed the gate to pivot, and how important it was for the post to be fitted tightly against the stone side walls of the lock. Always the mentoring brother, he concluded: "Send me a tracing of any plan you may have adopted and I will let you know if there is anything wrong about it."[54]

As his brother's assistant engineer, Frank Shanly seems to have handled much of the bookwork pertaining to paying the contractors on the Northern Railroad. Walter Shanly, situated in Ogdensburg, pored over the books but could not make heads or tails of his brother's notations. Finally, he bundled up every-thing and shipped the package to Pennsylvania. On New Year's Day of 1851, he wrote to Frank, urging him to return the books "as soon as you can get it decently finished. . . ."[55] Working nights, at the same time that he was preparing designs for the Union Canal enlargement, Frank completed the tedious task. Walter must have sent his brother some of the material earlier, because the completed estimate book was returned by express from Pottsville on 16 January 1851. In a letter mailed the same day, Frank let his brother know that the project had taken him nearly three weeks.[56] The younger Shanly was extremely good at this type of work, and he would be called upon many times in the future to review the books of other engineers and report his conclusions as to what had actually taken place during the construction of a project.

The question of the quoins came up again in early January 1851. Frank Shanly wrote Walter to say they intended to use three-piece hollow quoins because it was not possible to get large timbers from the forest in this location.[57] While he completed the designs for his seventeen locks, several aqueducts, and a number of bridges satisfactorily he experienced the same canal leakage problems that had plagued Loammi Baldwin on the Middlesex Canal. Walter Shanly gave Frank advice that the Proprietors on the Middlesex Canal could have used: ". . . put in two feet, good [puddling], it will hold any head of water you have to provide against."[58]

The Union Canal enlargement work did not start until December 1850 because the canal company wanted the revenue from a full season of shipping. But once ice made the canal unnavigable, it was drained and the contractors set to work. With the construction underway, Frank Shanly proved a skilled manager, and the enlargement work was completed in one work season, between December 1850 and mid-November 1851. The achievement of completing the work on time and at nearly the estimated costs, together with the design work, established Frank Shanly's reputation as a competent civil engineer.

The celebration of Walter Shanly's appointment as chief engineer for the Bytown and Prescott Railway was a grand event. On 24 January 1851, he described the proceedings in a long letter to his brother, beginning with the line: "I woke up this morning a 'Chief.'"[59] He had departed Ogdensburg on Monday the twentieth for Bytown, crossed the St. Lawrence River, and traveled the twenty-five miles to Kemptville before nightfall. The next day, when he was about five miles from Bytown, "a number of splendid private Sleighs . . ." met him and took him to the town's principal hotel. The next day, there was a meeting at the Town Hall, where all were invited to acquire stock in the railroad company. Shanly took two shares in his name and one share in Frank's name. Thirteen directors of the company were then elected, after which the meeting was adjourned and everyone went to the hotel for lunch. After lunch, the directors of the Bytown and Prescott Railway held their first meeting; elected a president, John McKinnon; and told

Walter Shanly they desired his services as chief engineer. When they invited him to name a fair figure for his remuneration, he told them not less than £600 per year, and then withdrew. In the evening, at a dinner for about 125 people, McKinnon announced they had engaged the "honored guest as Chief engineer." Shanly then related that the occasion required he say a few words, but "I had to get upon my legs and having a good deal of Champagne on board said something that caused more cheers. . . ."[60]

Walter's letter after these events inquired whether Frank would like to join him again as "a lousy" assistant. In a second letter three days later, he asked the question once again: "Do you want to go on Location?" Walter Shanly was now the boss; he could pick his engineering corps and control the work, so he laid out his plan in the second letter: "I am going to make a cheap road [in terms of cost to the owners] for the Bytown folk and 'put it through' quicker than any road yet heard of."

Following the same reasoning Haupt had applied and for which he had been chastised on the Troy and Greenfield Railroad, Walter wanted first to get the railroad open to revenue-generating traffic and then improve the line. He proposed using temporary wooden structures instead of more costly masonry culverts. But he would build these sufficiently high to leave room for the masonry to be done easily later.

"I will call my first Engine the 'Rideau' and run her from the St. Lawrence [River] to Ottawa in 1852."[61] But his engine dream never came true. In 1851 or 1852, an engine named the "Rideau," a woodburner, was built by the Essex Company of Lawrence, Massachusetts, the mill town Charles Storrow had planned and built. It traveled to Ogdensburg over the rails of New York's Northern Railroad, which Walter Shanly had built. But there the dream ended. At the time, the Bytown and Prescott did not have funds to purchase the locomotive, so the Northern Railroad placed her in service.[62]

While Walter Shanly was struggling to get his new railroad started, his brother once again seems to have taken time off to enjoy the finer things of a gentleman's life. He loved art, literature, and fine music, and he regularly attended church. So, sometime in January of 1851, he slipped down from the mountains and his engineering work and visited Philadelphia for one of Jenny Lind's ninety-three concerts under P. T. Barnum's sponsorship. While in Boston and making Crocker's railroad station tower famous, she stayed at Walter Shanly's favorite hotel, the Revere House.

A month after his appointment as chief engineer, Walter Shanly was still in Ogdensburg. With his limited knowledge of the land between Bytown and

Prescott, he was now thinking he needed to survey four possible routes before making a final decision.[63] The previous month, while in Bytown, he had written to his brother about three of the routes.[64] He also asked his brother for the third time whether he would come to help.

On 26 February, Walter Shanly, accompanied by two axemen, entered the cedar swamp north of Prescott, bound for Bytown, fifty miles away. They were tramping the "miserable country," as he called it, on snowshoes. His surveying instrument for these initial inspections of the ground was a small pocket compass. The first journey through the swamps was over a course he dubbed the "Western Route." The party aimed for Kemptville, where their route crossed the Rideau River and stayed to the west of the river. In letters to his brother, he described his experiences: "I had to put up with hard livings and strange bedfellows." We had to "beg shelter from some log-hut farmer or else get into a disreputable tavern, thinking myself lucky if I could get a lump of fat pork to swallow and a pint of whiskey to gulp before going into a narrow and unclean bed with, as I did on one occasion, an aged Dutchman for my companion."[65]

Sixteen days later, they emerged in Bytown. After a Sunday in Bytown, he turned around and made the trek again over what he called the "Eastern Route." On reaching Prescott, he repeated the adventure on the "Middle or Direct Route," with a return on another Kemptville route but keeping to the east of the Rideau River. He was five weeks out and had walked more than three hundred miles on snowshoes, except for one day when he made seventeen miles on bare ground. "I have had wet feet and hard feeding for thirty-six consecutive days nearly. However, I have done all I wanted to do and know more about the country from Prescott to Bytown than any other live man, don't care who he is."[66] Five days after completing these grueling treks, he submitted a report on the four routes.[67] Following his recommendation, the directors approved the Kemptville route, east of the Rideau.

Frank Shanly did not accept his brother's invitation to return to Canada, so Walter assembled his engineering corps from those who had worked with him on the Northern Railroad. From experience, he well knew how much work was required to design and construct a railroad, but the directors and the president he rated as "D—d't fools in a business point of view." He complained, "I was very busy in my office . . . and was disturbed half a dozen times one day by the President rushing in to try and force me out to play cricket. . . ."[68] But even with the disturbances, Shanly had his report ready on the final location of the railroad by 26 July.

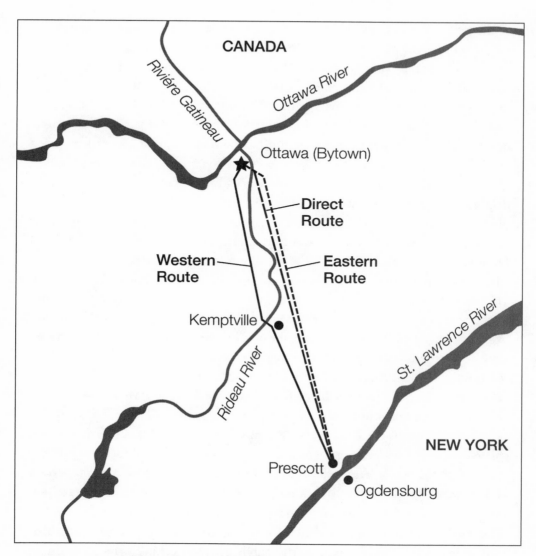

Walter Shanly's Prescott to Bytown Railroad survey routes

A Gala in Boston

Bostonians were very proud of their railroad system, including the links to Canada. They viewed these links as providing an advantage over New York City and the Erie Canal. To call attention to the new rail connections, the city orchestrated a three-day Railroad Jubilee in September of 1851. Walter Shanly sat down to dinner on the Boston Common along with Lord Elgin, governor general of Canada; President Millard Fillmore of the United States; and 4,000 other guests. Two days after the event, he wrote to his brother from New York City, noting, "I have seen Boston, and like the look of the City."[69] After the months of hard work in the wilderness, Shanly arrived at the party intending to enjoy himself, and he had always enjoyed champagne. "I got rather snippy on an excess of champagne one day and continuing in that state until a late hour at night." In fact, it lasted until three the next morning.

Just as the senior Loammi Baldwin had done during his trip to Philadelphia to secure the services of the English engineer William Weston, Walter Shanly used the Boston trip to study engineering works. On his way back to Canada, Walter traveled via the New York and Erie Railroad across New York to Dunkirk on Lake Erie. En route, he was impressed with the Starrucca Viaduct, which the Erie Canal engineers had constructed at Lanesboro, Pennsylvania. This stone arch bridge is 1,040 feet long, with fifty-foot spans, and the clearance to the valley below is one hundred feet. It was impressive and it was beautiful. Walter Shanly could build a railroad cheaply, but he still appreciated engineering works constructed with an eye for beauty. He positioned the line into Bytown so the trains would be silhouetted against the noble Ottawa River.[70] Later he said, referring to the Starrucca Viaduct, "[I]f I had time I would have lain over a day to examine that magnificent work."

Reaching Lake Erie, he took a small steamer to Buffalo. There was a gale blowing, but he ". . . sternly refused to part with [his] breakfast." In Buffalo, he overnighted on the American side of the Niagara River and then pushed on to Lewiston. There he hired a carriage and rode across the New Suspension Bridge,[71] which Edward Serrell, holder of the first Hoosac Tunnel contract, had completed only six months earlier. Shanly was back in Bytown by 1 October 1851, just in time to participate in the public groundbreaking, which the directors had scheduled for the second day of October. Even before the festivities occurred, though, Shanly had a contractor clearing the entire woodland route of the new railroad. He was prepared to follow the clearing immediately with several grading contracts.

At the end of October, friends asked Walter whether he was available to engineer the Toronto and Guelph Railway. Once again, he immediately wrote to his brother, "Can you come in . . . ,"[72] and the same day he had a telegram delivered to Frank: "How soon could you come to Canada?" On Friday, 5 December, Walter Shanly met with the directors of the Toronto and Guelph Railway, who

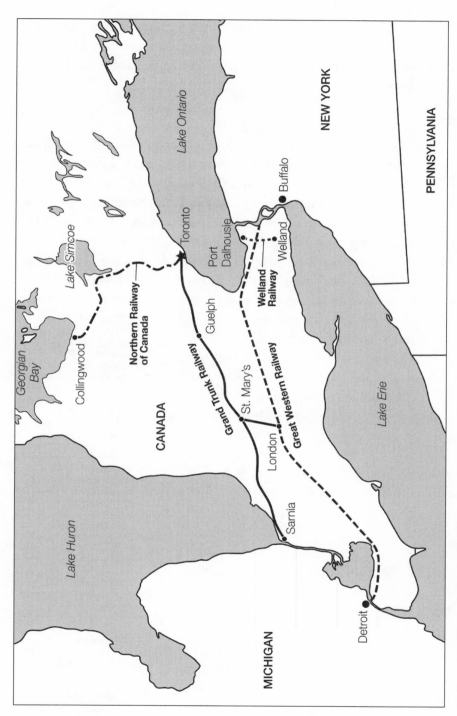

Railroads of Canada in the 1850s

were a little astonished when he laid his demands on them. He required £600 a year and sole control over appointment of his engineering staff. During the evening, they did not capitulate to his demands, but by January of 1852, he was gathering his staff.

Surveys

Walter Shanly now had his dream position—chief engineer for a railroad company with the necessary financial strength to build. On 3 January 1852, the secretary of the railway gave him definite instructions to proceed. His brother Frank agreed to join him on the Toronto and Guelph Railway, so now Walter Shanly could direct the engineering of two railroads with confidence and collect full pay from both companies. Though Frank Shanly had to make two short trips back to Pennsylvania, he had concluded his engagement with the Union Canal. On the first of January 1852, James Worrall, the engineer who had enticed Frank to go south to the canal work, gave him a letter praising his performance in Pennsylvania. Even Robert B. Davidson, president of the Union Canal, provided a gracious letter.[73] But the most important letter Frank received came from Walter on 26 January: "[Y]ou are hereby appointed Principal Assistant Engineer. . . ." For some reason, the senior brother would not yet anoint the younger with the prestigious title of resident engineer.

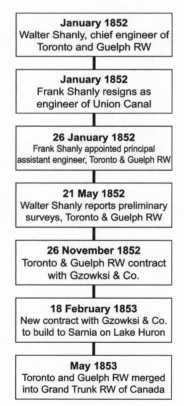

Just as with the snowshoe treks of the previous winter, Walter Shanly was out for the first two weeks of January in 1852, making his own examination of the ground between Toronto and Guelph. By 23 January, he was back in Toronto and made an initial report of his findings to the board.[74] He immediately sent his brother to Georgetown to direct the more extensive surveys needed to design the railroad, while he hurried to Prescott, as the Bytown and Prescott Railway needed his attention. By the middle of March, Walter was back in Toronto and going over the survey data his brother had assembled. Soon even more detailed data were compiled, and Frank began to plot routes and calculate grades. Walter Shanly took this material and

January 1852
Walter Shanly, chief engineer of Toronto and Guelph RW

January 1852
Frank Shanly resigns as engineer of Union Canal

26 January 1852
Frank Shanly appointed principal assistant engineer, Toronto & Guelph RW

21 May 1852
Walter Shanly reports preliminary surveys, Toronto & Guelph RW

26 November 1852
Toronto & Guelph RW contract with Gzowksi & Co.

18 February 1853
New contract with Gzowksi & Co. to build to Sarnia on Lake Huron

May 1853
Toronto and Guelph RW merged into Grand Trunk RW of Canada

worked it into a masterful report to settle the question of the railroad's footprint. As soon as a route decision was made, orders went out to the survey parties to stake the line along the ground. In fact, to mislead and deter other railroads, some surveys had been pushed farther west.

By May, the Engineering Department was encamped in a Toronto office. While the company had funds to pay for all the surveys and the office, there was no money to pay for construction. The total cost of the railroad, construction and equipment, was estimated at £355,000, and the company coffers held only £10,000 in cash. Still, bids were accepted and two companies offered to work on credit. Finally, on 26 November, a contract was signed with C. S. Gzowski & Co. The railroad would supply company bonds of £210,000 and municipalities along the route would supply £145,000 worth of their bonds.[75] The "& Co." of Gzowski & Co. referred to three partners in the firm: Alexander Tilloch Galt, Luther H. Holton, and David Lewis MacPherson, men with political connections and capital. A. T. Galt, a consummate politician, served as the first Canadian minister of finance in 1867. D. L. MacPherson was a businessman and political figure. Years later, he would serve as minister of the interior. L. H. Holton was a prosperous Montreal businessman with activities spanning steamboats, railroads, iron mining, banking, and real estate.

Casimir Stanislaus Gzowski was born in the "Kingdom of Poland," but in 1815 his country was incorporated into Russia. When Casimir was seventeen, his father secured for him a position in the Imperial Corps of Engineers, so he received an education in architecture and surveying in Russia. Nevertheless, he later served with the Polish nationalists who were defeated by the Russians. After confinement in Austria, he arrived in the United States as a refugee in March 1834. He learned English and found a job as a clerk in Pittsfield, Massachusetts, just south of North Adams. Later he returned to engineering and built a section of the Erie Railroad through western New York. In 1842, he moved to Canada. Gzowski was the engineer who managed the firm for the financial men, who remained in the background. Their company had secured the Toronto and Guelph contract, but funds were still lacking. Now Galt, one of the background men, moved to center stage to contribute his expertise. He departed for England to sell the bonds their company had received as payment for the railroad work.[76]

During the fall, as the Shanly brothers prepared for the contractor to begin work, Frank Shanly was promoted to resident engineer. On the first of December, Gzowski informed the engineers that his subcontractors were moving to their respective work sites. There was excitement now, as the brothers prepared to show their true abilities. Then the Shanly engineering world was turned upside down. On 18 February 1853, the railroad company signed a new contract with C. S. Gzowski & Co. This contract extended the line 125 miles farther west, to Sarnia on Lake Huron.[77] But this extension of the route was only the beginning.

On 26 March, when Frank Shanly attempted to start the survey of the route extension, he was blocked by snow. At the same time, Walter Shanly turned down an offer to be the chief engineer for the Allegheny Valley Railway from Pittsburgh to Olean, New York, as he prepared to head west to meet his brother. Before he could depart, however, Gzowski informed him that Galt had convinced the London bankers to make the Toronto and Guelph the western leg of the Grand Trunk Railway of Canada. Gzowski also informed Shanly of the decision in London to appoint him as chief engineer of the Grand Trunk Railway's Western Division.[78] Within four days, Walter was busy changing bridge designs to conform to the wishes of the new owners, because the London bankers wanted a railroad built to English standards. When money had been short, Shanly had planned to build wooden trestles and bridges, but now the designs would be changed to iron-girder bridges or stone-arch culverts.

A Professional Engineer

Walter Shanly was a professional engineer who, like Loammi Baldwin Jr. and Benjamin Latrobe, believed his duty was to serve as a technically knowledgeable agent for owners. Then, on the first of July 1853, the Grand Trunk Railway of Canada introduced a new concept. Going forward, the engineers would be paid by the contractor. This was probably because the contractors had secured the money in England and they saw Shanly's engineering department as a burdensome expense. The new arrangement would effectively place the engineers under the control of C. S. Gzowski & Co. The company also sought to reduce the number of engineers and construction inspectors. Fortunately, Shanly had forewarning of these changes and had been able to alert his staff about pending reductions.

Nevertheless, an explosive clash between Walter Shanly and the contractor was not long in

May 1853
Toronto and Guelph RW merged into Grand Trunk RW of Canada

July 1853
New engineering organization for Grand Trunk RW

25 December 1854
Bytown & Prescott Railway's first train reaches Bytown

1 June 1856
Frank Shanly released from Toronto and Guelph RW

1856-1857
Walter Shanly surveys Ottawa to Georgian Bay Canada

November 1856-June 1859
Frank Shanly engineer-in-charge of Port Dalhousie & Thorold RW

January 1858
Walter Shanly general manager & chief engineer, Grand Trunk RW

coming. An inspector working under Frank Shanly found the foundation work for one of the Humber River Bridge piers to be unsatisfactory. After Gzowski examined the work himself, he wrote to Frank Shanly, saying, "[T]he material will make substantial strong work."[79] The bridge had eight freestanding brick piers. The issue related to the stone foundations under one of the piers. Chief Engineer Walter Shanly wrote to his brother: ". . . the masonry must be done right if we have to fight C. S. G. & Co. every day in the week; and if more moral force is wanting, I will give it by visiting every piece of work every week in the season if necessary."[80]

It was a discouraging time for Walter Shanly. He had turned down the Allegheny Valley Railway job in the United States and the Caughnawaga Canal project in Canada (a proposed canal to connect the St. Lawrence River and Lake Champlain). Now he was questioning those career decisions. The new engineering organization would have stretched the inspecting engineer across sixty to seventy miles of railroad.[81] Shanly continued to fight for his engineers, and finally it was agreed that the engineering corps would be retained but they were transferred to Gzowski & Co. They would now report to and be paid by the contractor. Gzowski was a skilled civil engineer, but his experience was primarily with canals. Because Shanly trusted Gzowski as an engineer, he accepted this new arrangement.[82] But Shanly remained as chief engineer for the Toronto-to-Sarnia section of the Grand Trunk Railway. He would demand quality construction, but he understood it was not his role to direct how the work was accomplished. He stated this very plainly in a letter to his brother in 1854: "The Engineers have no call whatsoever to meddle with contractors' affairs. . . ."[83]

The Humber River Bridge work proceeded, although after the disagreement between Frank and the contractor, Walter Shanly kept a close personal watch on the Humber River Bridge masonry.[84] In February of 1854, he questioned the quality of the bricks being used to construct the bridge piers. This time, Gzowski supported him, and better bricks were used to complete the piers. (A century later, Hurricane Hazel in 1954 would damage many bridges across the Humber, but Shanly's Grand Trunk Railway bridge would remain undisturbed.) The younger Shanly did not espouse the same notions about being a professional engineer as his older brother, so he was comfortable under the new hierarchy. The contractors were paying interest on the borrowed money, so the work was pushed hard through the 1853 work season.

Frank Shanly married Louisa Saunders of Guelph on 28 September 1853. His brother traveled from Toronto to Guelph for the ceremony. The bride was the daughter of an English gentleman, Thomas Saunders, who resided near the town. The bride's mother, Lucy Ann (née Willcocks), was from a Dublin family acquainted with the Shanlys for generations. Following their marriage, the couple rented a well-furnished townhouse in Toronto.[85] During the following month, Frank Shanly decided to bid with others for the construction of a section of railroad in New York. Walter Shanly received the letter announcing the project and counseled his brother to speak first with Stephen Walker, who had been a contractor for the Northern Railroad. He was someone Walter trusted, and, fifteen years later, he would offer the Shanlys financing assistance with the Hoosac Tunnel contract.[86]

Late November and December of 1853 found Walter Shanly again dealing with the financially strapped Bytown and Prescott Railway. Some money had become available, so he succeeded in paying the contractors. About half of the steel rails for the line arrived in the fall of 1853, and the contractors began laying these on 24 April 1854, from Prescott northward. As the laying commenced, Walter would grumble to his brother about the lack of funds. He was frustrated, but he felt an obligation to see the road completed.[87] Finally, the first train reached Bytown on Christmas Day of 1854.

The Shanlys were also being pushed to complete the Grand Trunk work. In June of 1854, Walter Shanly requested from his brother detailed statements of the accomplished work and estimates of what was yet to be done. This was for the purpose of reporting to the Grand Trunk Railway's board. He wanted the information so he could prepare one of his comprehensive reports. Two months later, he again wrote to Frank for a detailed estimate—this time for a board meeting scheduled for August. The company decided to push the work through the winter of 1854–55 so that track laying could start in the spring of 1855.

But as early as the spring of 1854, Walter Shanly's involvement with the railroad had been changing. He was transitioning from engineering to management. As with John Brooks's early trips to Michigan nine years earlier, Walter Shanly was sent to Michigan to seek access for Canadian railroads into the United States. Brooks had been able to purchase the Michigan Central Railroad for John Forbes and the moneymen of Boston. Now Canadians were investigating a similar involvement with the Michigan Northern Railroad.[88] In the process of making the move from engineering to railroad operations, Walter Shanly found himself traveling with S. P. Bidder, general manager of the Grand Trunk Railway. At the same time, the railroad's need for the engineers was obviously drawing to an end, and brother Frank began to worry about his future. In July 1855, Gzowski gave him a letter indicating he would probably be retained for another year, and he was kept on the payroll until 1 June 1856. The formal opening of the line from Toronto to Guelph occurred on 14 June 1856. The festive train had five cars and was stocked with a liberal supply of champagne, Walter Shanly's favorite beverage.

Walter Shanly, 1863, age 46 (courtesy McCord Museum, Montreal)

Careers Diverge

With the Grand Trunk Railway completed, the careers of the two Shanly brothers diverged. They continued to be very close and would on occasion work together, but their personalities, as well as their different professional strengths, led them toward fundamentally dissimilar projects. In November 1856, Frank Shanly went off to be the engineer-in-charge for a twenty-five-mile segment of the Port Dalhousie and Thorold Railway (later named the Welland Railway).[89] His survey work was completed by the end of February 1857, and construction started in April. The railroad itself was completed by January of 1858, but terminal work kept the engineers going until June 1859.

Walter Shanly stayed on with the Grand Trunk in 1856, setting up a permanent engineering staff.[90] In December, he wrote to his brother: "I only remain because they imagine it will look better—in fact for some reason or other they seem scared at the notion of my going."[91] Early in 1857, he confirmed an intention to leave the railway, but they retained him for planning the construction of grain elevators. Besides his railway work, he was taking on consulting work during these years, including in July of 1856 a canal-route survey to join Ottawa with Georgian Bay. Shanly had no interest in surveying the 430 miles of wilderness the route would cover, so he employed trusted colleagues for the fieldwork.

January 1858 Walter Shanly general manager & chief engineer, Grand Trunk RW
January 1860 Frank Shanly to England for Northern Railway contract
30 September 1860 Frank Shanly signs contract with Northern Railway
June 1862 Walter Shanly, Grand Trunk Railway farewell dinner
Early 1863 Frank Shanly excursion to Europe
June 1863 Walter Shanly elected to Parliament

The upper or northern part of the route was under the direction of James Stewart. Walter spent a month with Stewart, even paddling part of the route. Afterward, Stewart wrote to Frank, also a friend: "He [Walter] was convivially abusive of me and spent a fair share of the time drinking brandy and grumbling."[92] This visit to the wilderness seems to have allowed Walter some relief from the paperwork/boardroom imprisonment of the Grand Trunk.

In January 1858, at the age of forty, Walter Shanly became the general manager and chief engineer of the Grand Trunk Railway—at the time, the world's longest railroad. He now faced the challenge of developing a management system to match the complexities of the railway's long-distance operations. It was the same task Herman Haupt and John Edgar Thomson had faced at the Pennsylvania Railroad six years earlier. Walter had an up-and-down first year as general manager. When the English masters sent out a man whom they appointed to the position of general manager, Shanly took this as a personal slight and resigned. But soon the Canadian board and the new manager quarreled, so the Englishman resigned. Walter Shanly was quickly reinstated. At the beginning of 1859, his title was changed to general traffic manager, and he reported directly to the board. Now he managed the operations of a line with thousands of men under his control, held a prestigious position, was paid a grand annual salary of $7,300, and had responsibility for operating a railway stretching from the Atlantic Ocean to Detroit. But it was the wrong job for a man of his temperament. For a start, he did not hold in high esteem many of the men on the board to which he reported. Even worse, particularly for a man who considered himself a gentleman, he bridled under the public criticism he received because of the position. He took personally the accusations of graft, distribution of free passes, political influence, and poor service.[93]

After four-plus years, Walter offered his resignation. The president of the Grand Trunk Railway twice tried to convince him to stay, but Shanly just did not like such a public position. There was a grand farewell dinner in Montreal for the man who had commanded a workforce of 3,000 men. He was known for his short temper, yet all of those men who worked for the railway placed their signatures in a bound book given to Walter Shanly at the June 1862 dinner. His rigid, aloof personality may have kept him apart in some respects, but Shanly was a man who cared about people, and he conveyed his sense of caring to those below him, those who did the work. The surveyor James Stewart captured this in his letter to Frank Shanly: "He [Walter] found the wilderness and earthy company of his fellow engineers a welcome. . ." repose.[94] The man who took Shanly's place as general manager of the Grand Trunk Railway in 1862 was C. J. Brydges, formerly managing director for the Great Western Railway.[95]

Politician, Manufacturer, Banker

After leaving the Grand Trunk Railway, Walter Shanly sought to establish himself in other occupations. All of these were completely different from his previous dogged efforts to become a professional engineer. In the course of the year following his departure from the railway, the respected professional engineer either decided on his own or was persuaded by associates to enter politics. As a result of this decision, by May 1863 he was stumping in the backcountry of the Grenville South Riding, which included the town of Prescott. (The term *riding* is used in Canada to define an electoral district.) He did not live in the district, but he did own land there, and he had business connections from his earlier Bytown and Prescott Railway engineering days.[96]

The book of signatures from the men of the Grand Trunk Railway exposes a very different man from the standoffish professional engineer, and his campaign habits reflected a previously carefully concealed side of his personality. Walter Shanly had an ability to communicate with the common man. During the campaign, he would make a habit of stopping here and there for a chat at an isolated farmhouse. This willingness to communicate with all constituents of the district proved a winning tactic. When the votes were counted, Shanly defeated by a considerable margin the man who had held the seat for the twelve previous years. In August, Quebec welcomed him for the opening of Parliament. He had won the election, but he was not a public speaker, so he seldom rose to address any measure. He was respected, however, because his engineering training made him a clear thinker. The leaders of his party recognized his talent, and he was immediately assigned to the Committee on Canals, Railways, and Telegraph Lines.

Walter Shanly's second nonengineering activity came two years later, when he became involved with a small starch-manufacturing operation in his Grenville South Riding. In 1858, two gentlemen in the riding had established a small factory to produce starch from corn. The firm became successful and made money for its owners because Canada had a thirty percent tariff on imported starch. By the early 1860s, they needed to bring in more capital and expand the plant, which was located on the St. Lawrence River northeast of Prescott. W. T. Benson, one of the original partners, must have approached Shanly about investing in the new company. As a member of Parliament, Shanly was in a position to influence the government's tariff policy, which was crucial to the success of the company. Benson, having earlier bought out his partner, was by this time the sole owner of the company.

A prospectus for the new company was issued in January of 1865, and it listed Walter Shanly as one of five provisional directors.[97] Benson remained the largest single shareholder, but merchants from Montreal purchased large blocks of stock, making them the new company's major shareholders. At the first shareholders' meeting, Walter Shanly, member of Parliament and holder of twenty Edwardsburg Starch Company shares, was elected president. Two of the major Montreal stockholders were John Redpath and his son, Peter, to whom Shanly turned for financial support in securing the Hoosac Tunnel contract.[98] Shanly was not a passive president—he attended the monthly board meeting, played a leading role in the management of the company,[99] and held the presidency for some twenty years.

Shanly's third nonengineering activity engaged him even farther afield. In February 1865, he presented two petitions in Parliament, one of which was for the incorporation of a bank.[100] The petitions read: ". . . of C. J. Brydges and others, of the City of Montreal; . . ."[101] One of the "others" was Walter Shanly. Five years later, he was a director and president of the Mechanics Bank of Montreal. It appears he held four hundred shares in his own name and another four hundred shares in trust.[102]

The year 1866 marked the end of Walter Shanly's term in Parliament, and he decided not to stand for reelection. Parliament was an environment in which his gentlemanly countenance ran counter to the antics of those around him. But his electors encouraged him to reconsider, and his brother believed he would be useful in Parliament—useful in terms of prodding the government to invest in railroads. Frank Shanly wrote, "The very prestige of your being in 'the House' will be a matter of strength to me. . . ."[103]

Canada had reorganized itself politically during Shanly's first term in Parliament. On 1 July 1867, it became the federal Dominion of Canada, or the Canadian Confederation. The Confederation included the provinces of New Brunswick, Nova Scotia, Ontario, and Quebec. Parliament for the Confederation would have a lower house, the House of Commons, and an upper house, the Senate. Walter Shanly reversed his previous decision and became a candidate for the House of Commons in 1867. The result was the same—he easily won the election, and he was again appointed to the Committee on Canals, Railways, and Telegraph Lines. In the spring of 1869, however, he would miss almost the entire second legislative session because of the need to organize the Hoosac Tunnel work. But when he ran a third time in 1872, success did not come to one who was absent in Massachusetts.

Frank Shanly, Contractor

Frank Shanly was not as skillful as his older brother when it came to designing engineering works. He was better at coordinating work tasks and handling the office details of managing work. After their Grand Trunk Railroad experience, both brothers were seeking to increase their financial wealth, so while Walter Shanly turned to politics, manufacturing, and banking, Frank Shanly judged contracting would make him rich.

When the Port Dalhousie and Thorold Railway work finished in 1859, Frank began looking for contracting opportunities. He set his sights on a railroad project where he believed he had a competitive advantage: Walter had been engaged as a consultant to prepare an estimate of the cost to rebuild the track of the Northern Railway of Canada from Toronto to Collingwood, a distance of about ninety-five miles. It was a $1 million project to stabilize embankments, lay new ballast and rails, and remove all of the wooden trestle bridges and replace them with masonry and iron.[104] Frank Shanly knew the work would go to the British contractor Thomas Brassey, who had the resources to finance the project for the railway company. He would be able to accept Northern Railway bonds as payment and not require cash. Men like Frank Shanly needed to work for cash, so they wanted to be Brassey's subcontractors. Brassey's experience building the eastern leg of the Grand Trunk Railway proved to the British contractor his need for a trusted Canadian in charge of construction so far from his home base.

Accordingly, Frank Shanly traveled to England in January 1860 to appeal directly to Brassey for the work. He returned to Canada with a promise that he would be engaged as a subcontractor. Frank was helped in achieving this by his performance in building the Port Dalhousie and Thorold Railway—the influential moneymen in London were well satisfied with his previous work.[105] Shanly must have taken Brassey at his word, because even before he had a signed contract, he set up an office in Toronto and moved Louisa and their three children into a rented house on the outskirts of the city.[106]

Finally, on 20 September 1860, Frank Shanly and Brassey concluded a contract that specified monthly payments to Shanly, the subcontractor. Shanly was now on the other side of a contract, with the engineers inspecting *his* work, but he had no intention of doing the work personally and supervising crews. He found men whom he knew from previous projects, and these subsubcontractors did the actual work. He contracted out all the masonry to a contractor he trusted, but their agreement included a stipulation that the man use stone from a quarry on Shanly's property. The subsubcontractor would be paid for work performed, but he would also pay Shanly for the stone taken from the quarry. Shanly did not have to design any of the Northern Railway work. His job was to manage, so he had no engineering staff, but he did hire one inspector—a man who had worked with him as an assistant engineer on the Port Dalhousie and Thorold Railway.[107]

The work was originally scheduled to be completed in 1861, but there were delays, many of which were not caused by Shanly or his management of the subsubcontractors. Finally, at the end of 1862, the line was handed over to the Northern Railway. Shanly must have made a good profit, because he took a six-week excursion to England, France, and Ireland in early 1863. In addition, his financial records reveal he held clear title to thirty-three £100 Northern Railway bonds.

June 1863
Walter Shanly
elected to Parliament

1864/65
Frank Shanly Maritime
Provinces Railway report

Summer 1865
Frank Shanly, Grand Trunk
Railway to Chicago report

March 1866
Frank Shanly, chief engineer, Chicago
& Michigan Grand Trunk Railway

1 July 1867
Canadian Confederation

September 1867
Walter Shanly elected to
second term in Parliament

June 1868
Hoosac Tunnel letter from
Latrobe to Frank Shanly

After Shanly returned from his pleasure trip and began looking for work, the situation was bleak. When he submitted a bid to build the Montreal and Vermont Junction Railway, it was rejected. Then he submitted a bid to upgrade the Erie and Niagara Railway; it, too, was rejected. In 1864, he proposed building a lightweight railway (a railway not capable of handling heavy freight traffic) north of the Grand Trunk's line. The company was organized in June, but there was no money. The American Civil War had impacted the London money markets, so no new railroads were being built in Canada during the first half of the 1860s. These were very lean years for railroad builders.[108]

During this period, contracting offered nothing but unemployment. Frank Shanly knew how to pursue work, however, and soon he found something matched to his skills. He had done consulting work as far back as 1853, when he had arbitrated a construction dispute between the Ontario, Simcoe, and Huron Railway (predecessor of the Northern Railway of Canada) and one of its contractors. In such matters, he was known for his ability to render impartial judgments and to write exceptionally lucid reports.

In November 1864, the Grand Trunk Railway hired him to report on the commercial viability of railways in the three Maritime Provinces—New Brunswick, Nova Scotia, and Prince Edward Island. This was almost certainly in preparation for the Canadian Confederation then being seriously discussed. New Brunswick and Nova Scotia became members when the original Confederation occurred in 1867, and Prince Edward Island entered in 1873. (The Maritimes and Newfoundland and Labrador are together known as the Atlantic Provinces; Newfoundland and Labrador delayed entry into the Confederation until 1949.)

Frank Shanly, as a consulting engineer, spent almost three months probing the workings of the existing railways in the Maritimes. He assessed their business activity and the quality of their construction and maintenance. The report he produced described the business potential of all the lines and contained recommendations for constructing two branch lines. This successful foray into consulting led to further such assignments. C. J. Brydges, Walter Shanly's partner in the Mechanics Bank, came forward in the summer of 1865 and hired Frank to investigate routes by which the Grand Trunk Railway could reach as far as Chicago. After spending six weeks on the ground in Michigan, he submitted his report. Brydges and local promoters endorsed the proposed route and Frank Shanly became chief engineer in March 1866. He had stated his terms in the same manner as his brother had done in 1851 to the management of the Toronto and Guelph Railway: $10,000 per annum and authority to appoint his own assistants. His terms were accepted, and Frank immediately went to work for the Chicago and Michigan Grand Trunk Railway. His grand position lasted all of six months—the promoters were unable to raise the money necessary to construct the line.[109]

Frank Shanly, the eternal optimist, believed a railroad-building boom was about to occur. The Civil War was over in the United States, Confederation had been achieved in Canada, and business was coming back to life. He wrote: "[T]he 'scramble' is about to take place."[110] The only problem for Shanly at that moment was the need to support his large family. The expected scramble was in the future, but *when* in the future? By July 1867, he and Louisa had seven children, so he was again soliciting consulting jobs. Railroad construction did start in Canada, and he submitted a bid for a line, but the work went to another contractor. In the case of a second railroad contract, his brother advised him not to bother submitting a bid because of the project's entanglement with politics.[111] Then, in June 1868, Benjamin Latrobe's unsolicited letter arrived with the advertisement for completing the Hoosac Tunnel.

Frank and his brother pursued the contract as a partnership, but because Frank's youngest child was ill, Walter Shanly went to Boston alone and negotiated with the Massachusetts governor and his council. Furthermore, it was Walter Shanly's political, banking, and merchant associates who provided the backing so that the partnership could meet the Commonwealth's requirement of performing $500,000 worth of work before the contractor would see the first payment. It was true that Frank Shanly had worked with James Worrall in Pennsylvania on the Union Canal, but still Worrall communicated with the older brother, providing advice during the negotiations and indicating his willingness to come in as a subcontractor. The two brothers had not worked closely together on a project for fifteen years. In the meantime, Walter Shanly, a bachelor, had become more rigid in his ways. He was a successful man, while his younger brother—notwithstanding his wife and seven children—still clung to some of his frivolous habits.[112] Walter Shanly had invested in manufacturing and banking and Frank Shanly had gone off to Europe on vacation. In truth, the Hoosac Tunnel adventure was Walter Shanly's. Although there was no open disharmony between the brothers, Frank Shanly was busy drawing up proposals for other railroad projects even in January 1869, while Walter Shanly was struggling to organize the miners and secure transfer of machinery from the Commonwealth for the massive Hoosac Tunnel project.

13

A Flood and the Great Nitro Explosion

Hemmed in with hills, whose heads aspire
Abrupt and rude, and hung with woods;
Amid these vales I touch the lyre,
Where devious Hoosac rolls his floods.

—William Cullen Bryant, "Descriptio
Gulielmopolis," in Arthur Latham Perry, *Williamstown
and Williams College* (self-published), 340.

THOSE OPPOSED TO THE Tunnel had pressed the central shaft construction mandate on the commissioners in 1863, believing the task would be too difficult and expensive to complete. Not in the way anticipated by the opposition, the central shaft mandate nevertheless almost collapsed the Hoosac Tunnel dream with the tragic 1867 accident. Many believe the accident had accomplished the goals of the opposition. But the perseverance and penny-pinching of Alvah Crocker kept the work going after the accident, and Crocker accepted the suggestion Benjamin Latrobe had been pressing on the commissioners—to contract out the work. After the shaft accident, Latrobe said, "I have never wavered in my opinion that the contract system is the only one by which the work can be done with economy and expedition. . . ."[1] Crocker then used contracting as a cover to convince the Governor and the legislature to continue the Tunnel project. So in January 1869, the Shanlys, contract in hand, assumed the difficult task not only of tunneling through the Hoosac Mountain but also of completing a shaft 1,028 feet straight down into the heart of the Mountain.

24 December 1868 Walter Shanly & Governor Bullock sign Hoosac Tunnel contract
26 March 1869 Transfer of machinery from the Commonwealth
29 March 1869 Shanlys begin mining east bore
5 April 1869 Shanlys begin mining bores from west shaft
20 May 1869 Shanlys begin excavating central shaft
2 July 1869 Shanlys begin mining west bore
6 August 1869 Excursion train to east bore
26 August 1869 *Adams Transcript* editor visits Tunnel Cascade
4 October 1869 The Great Flood
18 November 1869 Thanksgiving Day Charles Browne fuse accident

A Slow Start

Once the news of the Shanlys' Hoosac contract spread everyone in Massachusetts was anxious to learn about these bold men from Canada—men willing to accept the challenge of tunneling the Hoosac when so many had failed. Consequently, a correspondent for the *Boston Traveller* visited North Adams to report on the resumption of the work, but primarily to give readers a sketch of Walter Shanly: "He is well made, gentlemanly appearing, and standing I should say about five feet nine with a light complexion, and open ruddy countenance and a beaming, bright blue eye."[2] The correspondent confirmed what many in Canada had come to appreciate from Shanly's election victories and the 3,000 signatures scratched in the farewell book given him by the men of the Grand Trunk Railway. All of the Tunnel workers spoke of Walter Shanly as the "best man who has yet had any connection with the undertaking."[3] He might have held himself aloof, but he always considered the welfare of the workingman. Somewhere in his psyche was a reminder of his physical labors on his father's farm.

Immediately after Christmas in 1868, the Shanly brothers made their way to North Adams. Like Crocker, they moved into the elegant Wilson House. Work did not resume until 25 January,[4] and even then it was only work on the supporting facilities. The start by the Shanlys mirrored the practice of Thomas Doane and the commissioners years earlier: No miners were set to work immediately to pound steel against rock in the bowels of the Hoosac Mountain. These were men who took time to think, study, and plan their attack.

Frank Shanly turned his attention first to erecting buildings at the east and west portals of the Tunnel and at the central shaft.[5] At the same time, Walter Shanly must have made the rounds in Canada to find financial supporters. Thanks to those efforts, he managed to borrow $600,000 to finance the work until he and his brother could fulfill the contractual obligation of completing $500,000 worth of work before being able to collect anything from the Commonwealth. It was a repeat of Haupt's need to finance $100,000 increments of work before being paid.

Besides the money issue and the need to repair the machinery Crocker had neglected the previous year, the delay in resuming mining of the Hoosac was caused by months of haggling over arrangements for assuming possession of the machines and property belonging to the Commonwealth. The sale of the Commonwealth property to the Shanlys was not completed until 26 March, a Friday. So on Monday 29 March, miners began to attack the heading on the east side of the Mountain.[6] At the west shaft, mining resumed on Monday, 5 April.

According to the news reports, the Shanlys were following Frank Shanly's contracting model with the use of subcontractors to perform the actual work. The two brothers were strictly project managers. Hocking & Holbrook[7] was their subcontractor at the west end, driving the excavation for the brick arch and the two bores from the bottom of the west shaft. (Isaac S. Browne and the *Troy Daily Times* of New York spelled the name as "Hawkins," while the *Adams Transcript*, Massachusetts Senate Reports, and Van Nostrand's *Engineering Magazine* used "Hocking." For consistency, "Hocking" is used throughout this book.) Hocking & Holbrook would take over the brickyard and brick tubing work when B. N. Farren completed his contract with the Commonwealth.

John Hocking had come to the United States in 1852 on the ship *Oregon* from Penzance, Cornwall, England. This area of England had a strong mining history. During the 19th century it was an important mining district for both copper and tin. So it can be assumed he was a miner. After arriving in New York City, he moved west to Johnstown, Pennsylvania, where a miner could expect to find employment. By 1854, however, he had moved to Adams, and he was involved with the Tunnel work from the beginning. Hocking had seen miners' strikes, so when his men went on strike for an eight-hour day in June, he refused to capitulate to their demands. After two weeks, "their point not having been gained," they returned to work.[8] Other subcontractors working on the west side of the Mountain included Dawe & Dobson, Doisgenoit, Gregory, and Callihan & Co.[9]

One newspaper editor had called the Tunnel opponents the "barking dogs" who made the General Court hideous; with the Shanlys' slow start, the pack of hounds began to cry once again. In June, the *Springfield Republican*, mouthpiece for the Western Railroad, printed an article about the lack of Tunnel progress. The first line was a chorus to Frank Bird's earlier barking: "The Hoosac

Tunnel is quite as unsatisfactory under its new management as it ever was, but the Shanlys are so close-mouthed that we don't hear so much about it."[10] The *Report of the Commissioners upon the Troy and Greenfield Railroad and Hoosac Tunnel for the year 1868* contained a note about the depth of the central shaft as of 1 February 1869.[11] The note indicated the Shanlys had increased the depth three feet since taking over the work, but the report was erroneous, for the shaft had again filled with water after Crocker stopped all work the year before. The Shanlys did not begin bailing out the flooded shaft until 5 April, and it took two weeks just to pump out the water. Their efforts to increase the depth of the central shaft did not begin until 20 May.[12] Progress or no progress, the North Adams paper took a positive view of the commissioners' note and announced: ". . . leaving 447 ft to be completed."[13]

Even the *Springfield Republican* had come to admire some of the Hoosac Tunnel work. Months earlier, the paper had praised B. N. Farren's brickwork tube into the west face of the Hoosac Mountain. In early February 1869, with the Shanlys in North Adams and preparing to assume responsibility for tunneling, Farren completed his last contract with the Commonwealth for pressing the brick tube into the Mountain.[14] The *Republican*'s article described a two-foot square stone culvert Farren had constructed below the grade of the Tunnel to drain the water from the terribly demoralized rock on the west side of the mountain. Water held in the rock had been the major culprit causing the difficulties of mining into the western flank of the Mountain. During a Senate hearing in 1874, Engineer Edward Philbrick testified to the occasional need to pump out 1,000 gallons per minute.[15]

The final line of the article in the *Springfield Republican* reported the quantity of water continually flowing out of the Tunnel via this culvert as eight hundred gallons per minute.[16] Now Farren was gone and the water continued to flow, but the Shanlys did not resume work on the west heading until 2 July.[17] If Walter Shanly had read some of the local newspapers when he visited the Tunnel before signing the contract, he might have had a better understanding about the amount of water pouring from the fissures in the rock of the Mountain. In November 1868, *The Hampshire Gazette* had noted, "Water pours out of the west end of the Tunnel sufficient to carry a saw mill."[18] When subcontractor Doisgenoit took over the work from Farrren, he proceeded to drive the central drain into the western flank of the Mountain. Here was another case where the Shanlys took time to improve the construction process by removing the old ventilation and compressed-air pipes and putting new ones in their place.[19]

390 Builders of the Hoosac Tunnel

The Shanlys suffered the same treatment the commissioners and Doane had endured for not going directly to work. Nevertheless, these were methodical builders who devoted time to organizing their projects. Organization and attention to detail were the keys to the way they approached their work. They knew tunneling was dangerous work, and the central shaft fire had proven how quickly many could perish. So, to manage the work at the central shaft, they chose their men very carefully. Cornelius Redding was installed to supervise the mining of the shaft. He was a young married man, thirty-eight years old, from Middleboro, Massachusetts, a small village between Boston and Cape Cod. Redding was an exceptionally experienced hand, having survived the perils of mining in California and Australia, as well as war service.[20]

No one wanted a recurrence of the previous disaster, so the Shanlys first built platforms every twenty-five feet down into the fire-damaged hole. James Laurie, the new consulting engineer for the Commonwealth, complained about the slowness in building the platforms, but he noted that it was caused by a "scarcity of carpenters."[21] Laurie brought unique historical knowledge of the Tunnel work to the Governor and Engineer Frost. He was a link to the Baldwin engineers because of his friendship with James F. Baldwin dating back to 1848, when the two men helped found the Boston Society of Civil Engineers.[22] James Baldwin served as the society's first president. Laurie had also been engaged in 1862 as a consultant to the original commissioners appointed by Governor John Andrew. He was the engineer most critical of Haupt's Green River Bridge, and, considering Haupt's difficulty in boring into the porridge stone on the west side of the Mountain, he fully supported Latrobe's advice concerning the benefits of an open cut.

The new platforms Shanly installed in the central shaft were supported on heavy timbers fitted into notches carved in the rock of the Mountain. Nonetheless, even before the men had been at the work six months, there was a serious accident. Five miners on the lowest platform in the shaft—still sixty feet from the bottom—had entered the derrick bucket to ascend the shaft, but when the operator released the line brake to begin the hoist, the bucket jerked down so violently three men were thrown out. Two of the men were killed instantly as they crashed against the floor of the shaft, and the third was seriously injured.[23] After seeing the shattered bodies, several men quit the shaft work, leaving the work gangs shorthanded and causing a further delay.[24]

An Electric Fuse

Even under the Shanlys' careful management, accidents continued at all of the work locations. At the west shaft, John Dunstan, an Englishman, was gravely injured and two other men were slightly hurt by a misfire during a night shift in early August. After the explosives in one of the boreholes failed to go off, Dunstan went forward to reprime the charge. As he approached, however, it exploded, nearly tearing away his right hand and destroying both of his eyes.[25]

Earlier in the year, an article in the trade magazine the *Manufacturer and Builder* asserted: "Probably nine tenths of the accidents which occur in the use of powder for mining arise from difficulties inseparable from the use of common tape fuse." A tape fuse consisted of a continuous train of fine gunpowder twisted or enfolded in paper, cotton, or hemp. The article continued: "These dangers are in a great measure obviated by the use of the electric fuse."[26] The failure of charges to detonate had repeatedly killed or maimed miners at the Hoosac Tunnel. Charles and Isaac Browne, brothers employed at the Tunnel, were very familiar with the danger. Daily they worked around the explosives and witnessed the results of misfired charges. Even before the August accident, the older brother, Charles Albert Browne, had set to work to perfect an electrical blasting fuse (more commonly referred to today as a blasting cap).

Firing multiple charges electrically required development of two components: (1) a reliable battery or machine to generate an electric spark of sufficient strength to fire the fuse; and (2) a fuse sensitive to electricity. This fuse, moreover, had to ignite with enough force to cause all of the explosive material placed in the borehole to detonate. The original search for an electric fuse at the Hoosac had occurred when Doane began experimenting with explosives other than black powder. He had tried firing multiple boreholes simultaneously on several occasions and had found the technique yielded better breakage of the rock. He knew that if it was possible to fire multiple holes simultaneously, the miners would be able to increase the rate of advancing the Tunnel through the Mountain.

Doane experimented with Colonel Taliaferro Shaffner's "magneto-electrical" system for initiating the explosions, but the Shaffner machine could fire only five shots simultaneously. He also tried Abel fuses made in England and an English frictional battery, but these were expensive and could not be obtained from Europe in the necessary quantities. So the search for a reliable fuse turned to manufacturers in the United States. Inventors in New York City, Boston, and other locations around the country understood the advantage offered by firing multiple holes simultaneously, and they were working to develop an electric fuse.

In fact, as far back as the middle of the previous century, men had experimented with using electricity to fire explosives. In 1750, Benjamin Franklin fashioned an electric blasting fuse by confining crushed black powder in a paper tube with wires leading into both ends.[27] He then used wadding to seal the ends of his tube. The two wires were spaced close together but not touching. When he sent an electrical charge through the wires, a spark resulted at the gap and fired the fuse, which in turn ignited the main charge of black powder.

George Mowbray patented a fuse in July 1869 (U.S. Patent no. 93,113), but it was not satisfactory. He had a particular interest in finding a solution to the fuse problem because the contractors preferred to use his nitro-glycerin only if fuses were available. If there were no fuses, the contractors went back to black powder.[28]

The crux of the fuse problem was the need to find a stable chemical compound with sufficient strength to cause ignition of the bulk explosive material loaded in the borehole. The compound used in the fuse had to be sensitive to the electrical charge, but it also had to be stable so that it did not ignite until the electrical charge was applied. In 1830, the *Journal of the Franklin Institute* ran an article describing how Moses Shaw, in New York, fired several charges of gunpowder simultaneously using an electric spark through a compound of fulminate silver.[29] Fulminates are salts of fulminic acid (molecular formula HCNO or $H_2C_2N_2O_2$). These compounds, however, are very explosive and consequently very dangerous to handle. Mowbray obtained a second patent in November 1869 (no. 96,465) for a compound he claimed "not to be so dangerous to handle as fulminate of mercury,"[30] which others had used to create fuses.

Charles and Isaac Browne

The Browne brothers were natives of the Tunnel environs, Charles having been born in Adams and Isaac in Cheshire, just south of Adams. Charles Browne, born in 1842, held an incredibly diverse series of jobs before arriving at the Tunnel sometime in 1868. His employment immediately prior to moving home to North Adams was with the Bishop Gutta Percha Company in New York City. The Gutta Percha Company manufactured electrical wires coated and insulated with gutta-percha, a natural latex material. Isaac Browne believed that Samuel C. Bishop, owner of the company, was trying to perfect an electric fuse on the pattern of the Abel fuse,[31] which was developed by the chemist Sir Frederick Augustus Abel at the Woolwich Arsenal in England. Browne had joined the Gutta Percha Company specifically to support Bishop's effort to develop an electric fuse. Once he returned to North Adams, the Commonwealth employed him at the west shaft as a statistician.

Bishop had probably enticed Browne to join him because, prior to joining the Gutta Percha Company, he had worked for Colonel Shaffner's United States Blasting Oil Company in Keedysville, Maryland. Keedysville is situated about three miles northeast of the 17 September 1862 Antietam Battle field—the bloodiest one day battle of the civil war.

Because of his association with Shaffner, Browne was familiar with explosives and the need for a reliable electric fuse. Where Browne learned his chemistry is a murky question, as his earlier employment included working in Troy, New York, for P. A. Palmer, a stove dealer, and William E. Marsden, an auctioneer. Palmer held a patent for a "heating elevated oven" (Letter Patent no. 7,672, 24 September 1850). Later Browne worked in Thomas Holbrook's grocery store on Eagle Street in North Adams. Thomas Holbrook was the brother of William Holbrook of the Hocking & Holbrook firm, hired by the Shanlys to mine the Tunnel on the North Adams side of the Mountain. Between all of these diverse employments, Charles Browne even spent time teaching school, but his brother Isaac only refers to the location of that experience as "somewhere in the Union." The use of the term "the Union" likely reflects the sentiments in the North during the period of the Civil War.

When the Shanlys arrived at the Tunnel, the Oriental Powder Company of Boston was supplying the electric fuses then being used. The company manufactured blasting powder at its mills on the Presumpscot River in Maine, and it was the fourth-largest supplier of powder to the federal forces during the Civil War. The firm was located originally in Portland, Maine, but by 1869, when the Shanlys began using its products, it had moved to Boston. In 1868, while working for the company, H. Julius Smith developed and patented (23 June 1868: no. 79,268; 23 November 1869: no. 97,241) an instantaneous electric fuse. His fuse used a mercury fulminate mixture through which ran a high-resistance platinum bridge wire. Smith also developed and manufactured a plunger-type electric blasting machine weighing about sixteen pounds.[32] His original blasting machines were sometimes referred to as "The Smith Battery." These had superseded the imported English frictional machines.

Those tinkering with fulminates were playing a dangerous game with what George Mowbray termed an "over-sensitive" material.[33] Mowbray quoted another gentleman dabbling in the development of fuses, Joseph Dowse of Lockport, Illinois, as urging "that parties unaccustomed to the preparation of fulminates had better leave this preparation alone." Even Julius Smith had experienced accidents; on one occasion, his fuses exploded, "penetrating the fleshy part" of his thigh and burning his "eyelashes, eyebrows, and face severely."[34] On another occasion in 1869, when he was loading fuses into a bag, they exploded, severely burning and injuring him and a gentleman who was standing beside him at the time.

After he returned to North Adams in 1868, Charles Browne dedicated all of his leisure time in an attempt "to construct an electric fuse which would meet the requirements of conditions at the tunnel, where great dampness was proving detrimental; causing in many instances" misfires.[35] Browne had experience with the manufacture of fuses, and he knew there were problems with the Smith fuse when it was used under the damp conditions at the Tunnel. He had serious objections to using fulminate of copper in a fuse: It was liable to lose its effectiveness with age, rendering it unreliable. These were the problems Browne was seeking to overcome. His absorption in this quest led him to abandon his job with the Commonwealth and to dedicate all of his time to overcoming the fuse problems.

During the period when Charles Browne was employed by the Commonwealth, his brother Isaac was working at the east end of the Tunnel, in charge of the blasting with both black powder and Mowbray's nitro-glycerin.[36] He later described the job "as the stupidest thing he'd ever done in his life."[37] But after Charles quit the Commonwealth's employ, Isaac transferred to the west shaft. In early 1869, the brothers shared a room on the second floor of a building next to Rice's Drug Store on Main Street in North Adams. In an adjoining room, Charles Browne conducted his chemical experiments and hand-manufactured fuses. When he succeeded in producing a workable fuse, he convinced the Shanlys to try it in the Tunnel. The Browne fuse proved superior to the Smith fuse then being used, but Charles Browne was not able to supply the fuse in sufficient quantities to meet the blasting needs at the Tunnel. Consulting Engineer James Laurie would complain of this in his September 1869 report to the governor.[38]

After the trial usage of his fuse and the Shanlys' request for a substantial supply, Browne moved his laboratory and manufacturing operation into an old cheese house behind his father's farmhouse at 932 South Church Street, two miles south of town.[39] The house and shop were about one-third of a mile from the Tunnel's west portal and three-quarters of a mile from the west shaft. Here at the cheese house he employed five or six hands who strained to assemble an adequate supply of fuses for the Tunnel work.

Optimism

The Shanlys' subcontractors initially had difficulty finding men willing to work in the damp darkness of the Tunnel. The men of New England and New York had a keen awareness of all the previous accidents, and there were persistent fears of not being paid.[40]

But the Shanlys had one advantage: Their fixed-price contract with the Commonwealth under the 1868 legislation (333d chapter of the Acts of 1868) had taken much of the fight out of Frank Bird and the Western Railroad.[41] As the papers reported, the Shanlys had "not the difficulties of opposition to contend with that ruined General Haupt and delayed the work half a score of years."[42] But this transfer of the entire risk associated with successfully completing the Hoosac Tunnel would later become an issue to the detriment of the Shanlys.

Walter and Frank also had another advantage that had eluded Haupt. Thanks to the persistence of Alvah Crocker and Charles Burleigh, there was now a working pneumatic drill. It still needed modifications, but it was better than anything previously put into the hands of the Hoosac miners. The brothers understood the critical need to use every advantage in mining the Hoosac, so they spent time studying the merits of the Burleigh rock drill and the explosive compounds. Their study of the drill's performance caused Frank Shanly to adopt the Burleigh drill exclusively and to place orders for a large supply of improved drills from the Fitchburg company.[43] The number of drills in the hands of the miners increased as fast as they could be manufactured and sent to the Mountain.[44]

The new Burleigh drills operated with a pressure of fifty pounds per square inch and would strike the rock anywhere from 250 to 300 blows per minute— instead of the sixty hammer strokes of a good miner.[45] Such power allowed the advance of drill holes at a rate ten times faster than Haupt and Doane averaged with manual drills and hammers. A year later, Walter Shanly would state: "The use of the Burleigh drill saved about two thirds of the expense of drilling. The expense of labor would have been, I think, fully three times the cost of machine-drilling. To have done the work by hand-drilling would have taken, I should estimate, not less than twelve years."[46] In addition, the compressed air served a double purpose: driving the drills as well as supplying fresh air to the miners when it was exhausted at the end of a drill stroke.

To supply the necessary power for the lifts and compressors at the west shaft, the Shanlys immediately added two new boilers and began preparations for two additional ones. They did not want to suffer a deficiency for steam to power the pumps and the lift or a deficiency of compressed air, as Crocker had experienced during the penny-pinching days of rigorous political oversight the previous year. When modifications were finished, the compressors at the west shaft had about eight times the installed capacity of those used by the Commonwealth.[47] To prevent work stoppages from low water in the Deerfield River during the summer months and anchor ice in winter, the Shanlys erected buildings at the east portal to accommodate four additional compressors powered by steam.[48, 49]

Doane and Crocker, together with Mowbray, had worked out how to use nitro-glycerin effectively and to fire the charges with electricity. By 1869, Mowbray had his nitro-glycerin factory well established, and the Shanlys were, except for enlargements, soon employing nitro-glycerin for all rock blasting at the west shaft.[50] The *American Railway Times* reported in May that a correspondent had witnessed some 250 cubic yards of rock thrown down in two blasts using Mowbray's nitro-glycerin in four cartridges, each of one pound six ounces. The nitro cartridges were inserted in 1¼-inch-diameter drill holes. The holes for the nitro blasts were at first drilled about six feet into the rock.[51] Soon there would be experiments to determine the optimum depth of boreholes when using Mowbray's nitro-glycerin, and, before the work was completed, miners would use more than half a million pounds of his "soup" to shatter the rock of the Hoosac Mountain.

By August 1869, a reporter from the *Boston Traveller* ventured an opinion about when the Tunnel would be completed. To the delight of Tunnel supporters, his conjecture was reprinted in the *Adams Transcript*. First he speculated that if the Shanlys could maintain their rate of advance, the central shaft would reach its final grade within one year. He next reported that the miners at the east end had passed through the decomposed slate and were now into a softer rock, thus increasing their progress to about eighty-five feet per month. He expected that the miners at the west shaft could better the eighty-five-feet-per-month rate. He based his timeline on completion of the central shaft, which would allow the opening of two more faces for the miners to work. If all those conditions were met, he believed that, barring any unexpected occurrence, a locomotive would "shriek through the tunnel by the 4th of July 1873."[52] It was quite a bold prophecy, especially considering all the past occurrences and failures!

Before the month was out, however, low water in the Deerfield River compelled a reduction in the number of operating drills at the east bore. The steam boilers and compressor ordered by the Shanlys had been delivered, but they were not yet completely assembled and operating. At the west heading from the west shaft, the miners encountered what was described as hard-to-drill quartz rock. (This was a mistaken classification, as the Mountain is mica schist all along the Tunnel. Mica schist contains quartz and mica as its main minerals. At some locations, the rock is crystallized more than at others; this is particularly true from the central shaft to the west shaft.) The miners were still using the old Burleigh drills and awaiting the arrival of the new ones. Those delays were followed by a trial run with the new Burleigh drills at the central shaft. But hopes for improved progress were dashed when the approximately 500-pound drills[53] proved too cumbersome and unwieldy to work efficiently in the confined space of the shaft.[54]

Nine months after the *Boston Traveller*'s prediction, the Commonwealth's superintending engineer, Benjamin Frost, calculated the final completion as March 1874.[55] This was a prediction of when trains would run through the Tunnel, not simply when daylight would be visible through the Mountain. He had the advantage of nine months of additional knowledge about how unanticipated events had affected the progress of boring the Mountain.

In the same edition of the *Adams Transcript* that carried the hopeful *Boston Traveller* scenario for Tunnel completion, there was a paragraph describing a peaceful spot above the entrance into the east bore—the site of a waterfall the editor referred to as the Tunnel Cascade. The *Transcript* article urged Tunnel "visitors who have an eye to the beautiful and grand" not to miss this inspiring spot. The editor ended his short piece with the enticement, "This alone is worth a journey to the East End."[56]

The Tunnel Cascade was located roughly six hundred yards above the entrance into the east bore. The water from the cascade ran past the Tunnel in Cascade Brook just to the north of the entrance into the bore. Doane had dammed this brook in order to pipe water into the Tunnel for washing out the drill holes.

Accidents or not, everyone wanted to visit the Hoosac Tunnel. In early August 1869, a special excursion train ran from Greenfield with twenty-six cars carrying 1,800 passengers to the east end of the Tunnel. To make the excursion, curious individuals traveled to Greenfield from as far as Whately, ten miles to the south, and Montague, five miles to the southeast. It was a festive occasion, and the train conductors even allowed passengers to climb onto the top of the cars. On the return trip, one passenger was knocked off the train as the cars crossed a bridge west of Shelburne Falls. It seems the train did not stop and the report in the North Adams paper simply stated: "[I]f he was not killed he must have been nearly so."[57]

The Flood

No rays of sunlight pierced the skies over the Hoosac Mountain on Sunday morning, 3 October 1869, and the shadowy heavens soon released a torrential rain. Throughout the day, the intensity of the deluge increased, and by evening the rivers on both sides of the Mountain were running high. During the night, an evil black sky continued to discharge torrents of water on the Hoosac Mountain. The rain gauge of Albert Hopkins, professor of natural philosophy and astronomy at Williams College, recorded six inches over the two days: 3 and 4 October.[58] To the east in Fitchburg, Dr. Jabez Fisher's gauge had a reading of 7.53 inches. The rivers running through North Adams "burst their banks and flooded the village in all directions, mill dams were carried away, and bridges swept downstream."[59] The unforeseen had occurred. As Monday afternoon wore on, the rain abated, but torrents of water still raced down the east and west sides of the Hoosac Mountain. Along the north branch of the Hoosic River, families were driven from their homes by the floodwaters that "roared and dashed through doors and windows."[60]

At the west end of the Tunnel, a brook had "formally crossed the line of the Tunnel [about 350 feet west of the entrance to the bore], but it had been diverted by the State into a canal." When this brook broke through the banks of the canal at about 10 a.m. Monday,[61] the water rushed into the earthen backfill immediately behind the extreme western part of the brick arch. This was the section of brick arch constructed in the open trench and later backfilled with earth and rock. Carrying great quantities of earth and stone, the water cut away about twenty-five feet of the backfill material and then poured into the west-end pit between the Tunnel bore and the old Haupt tunnel. The Shanlys had laid rails through the old Haupt tunnel, as it provided the only route for hauling excavated rock from the Tunnel bore without having to hoist the material out of the pit. This pit situation existed because the Commonwealth still had not decided to pursue the work of excavating the side of the Mountain and building the rail line to North Adams. Soon the debris plugged the Haupt tunnel. Once this occurred, the water began to flow over the top of the Haupt tunnel until a segment collapsed, giving vent to a portion of the floodwaters.[62]

Once the Haupt tunnel was plugged, Farren's culvert—which had carried water from the west bore and dumped it through the old tunnel and down to the Hoosic River—began to flow in the opposite direction, rapidly flooding the west bore of the Tunnel. So sudden was the surge that in ninety minutes the water rose fifteen feet above the brick arch at the entrance to the bore.[63] As the water rose in the arched Tunnel, it pushed water through the adit (a small, nearly horizontal bore to provide drainage and ventilation) connecting the eastward Tunnel bore from the west side of the mountain with the westward bore from the west shaft. At the moment when the bank of the canal gave way and the floodwaters began to surge into the Tunnel, seventy-five miners were at work at the header from the west face, and at the east and west headers from the west shaft.

West-end photo taken in 1868 before the Shanlys connected it to the Haupt tunnel. The end of B. N. Farren's brick tube is clearly shown. (courtesy of the North Adams Public Library)

Because of the incoming water, the men mining eastward from the west face of the Mountain could not exit the bore by the way they had entered. Fortunately, Doane, when trying to locate solid rock on the west side of the Mountain, had excavated wells along the line of the Tunnel, and one of these—referred to

as the "brick shaft"—provided the men with an exit. John Hocking, the subcontractor, and his two sons John and James Hocking, were later cited in the papers
for their efforts to save the trapped miners.[64] At the brick shaft, John Hocking Jr.,
riding a timber from the shaft, fought the current of the rushing waters to seize
a twelve-year-old lad who was working in the bore. James Hocking was able to
sling a rope to the struggling miner James Kelly when the Tunnel was nearly full
of water. In the disaster the Hocking's lost only one man, a miner named Richard
Barryman, who had just reported for his first day of work. Unfamiliar with the
Tunnel, he was seen floating on a timber, but the current carried him toward the
east end header, beyond a possible escape up the shaft.

When the canal broke into the excavation, the senior Hocking had
mounted his horse and with great speed rode to the west shaft to shout a warning
there. He seized a light and descended the shaft. Starting westward from the
bottom of the shaft, he guided miners who were fleeing eastward from the rising
water. Before the day was over, the pit between the west end and the Haupt
tunnel was filled with soggy earth and debris, and the entire tunnel to the far
eastward heading from the west shaft was full of water. The debris dam at the
Haupt tunnel was so tight that water still stood a foot above the top of the brick
arch at the west portal on 13 October. On the day after the flood, John Hocking
put a large force of men to work clearing the estimated 5,000 cubic yards of
debris,[65] but the dam resisted their efforts for almost three weeks.[66]

On the east side of the Mountain, the brook from the Tunnel Cascade
had rushed down the ravine in exactly the way Edward Serrell had feared. The
volume of water in the brook coming down the ravine was so great and of such
force that it carried down a mass of boulders and earth. On this side of the
Mountain, there was no excavation, so, as the water slowed, the mass was deposited on the level ground in front of the Tunnel—but it did not block the Tunnel.
Fortunately, there was natural drainage into the Deerfield River, so the waters
backed only half a mile into the Tunnel and all the miners survived the flood.[67]

The tracks from Greenfield to the Tunnel were severely damaged. In
the case of the canal between the Great Dam on the Deerfield River and the
compressor building, several locations along its outer slope were washed away.[68]
The dam proper withstood the raging waters, but the sheathing planks on the
lower apron were stripped off. At the lower end, hydrodynamic cavitation—
created when the water hemmed in by the wing walls of the dam was released—
excavated an eight-to-nine-foot hole in the rock immediately below the dam.[69]
But the damage to the canal was minor when compared with the loss of the Troy

and Greenfield Railroad, which the Shanlys were using to bring heavy supplies to the east bore.

At Shelburne Falls—between seven o'clock on the Monday morning of the flood until one in the afternoon—the Deerfield River rose during some hours at the rate of six feet per hour.[70] The bridge over the Deerfield River at Shelburne Falls was washed out. After the flood, the railroad had to rely on stages with six-horse coaches to haul passengers westward from Greenfield. On reaching the Deerfield River, the railroad's stage could not cross, so the passengers were ferried across and provided another stage for the ride as far as Charlemont, where they were again ferried across the river because of yet another washed-out bridge. There was still a third ferry crossing at Zoar before the passengers could reach North Adams. The railroad tried to put on a good face by announcing that the ferry crossings added "greatly to the novelty of the trip."[71] But the Shanlys were now forced to drag heavy supplies over the Hoosac Mountain. As late as March 1870, the Vermont and Massachusetts Railroad—which operated the Troy and Greenfield for the Commonwealth from Greenfield to the east bore of the Tunnel—was still pleading with the Commonwealth to repair the track and bridges.[72]

At the west bore, it took three weeks to remove the soggy earth and debris and to drain the Tunnel so mining could resume.[73] The brick tube Farren had constructed into the porridge stone withstood the flood and appeared "as sound and strong as when it was laid,"[74] but the work of continuing the brick arching was not resumed until the last week of November 1869.

Thanksgiving Day Accident

President Ulysses S. Grant issued a proclamation in October 1869 recommending Thursday, 18 November, be observed as a day of thanksgiving and of praise and prayer to Almighty God. But Charles Browne decided he had to attend to his fuse work, even if the president had declared a Thanksgiving Day. Continuing the effort to perfect his fuse, he retreated to his father's old cheese house, where he suffered a tragic accident while working a batch of fulminate of copper on a glass plate with a spatula.[75] The mass exploded in his face, leaving him blind.[76] It was the type of accident Mowbray had feared and had been trying to circumvent by his own efforts to devise a safe fuse.

Charles's brother Isaac was standing beside him when the accident occurred, but his head was turned and he escaped injury. He led Charles into their father's house and sent for Dr. N. S. Babbitt, the surgeon who was repeatedly called upon to treat injured Tunnel workmen.[77] Dr. Babbitt held a medical degree from Williams College. Originally he had practiced in South Adams, but he moved to North Adams in 1846, and he had been treating maimed Tunnel workers since the very beginning of the work. After a day or two, Charles Browne seemed improved—he could even tell the time by the clock on the wall. But the improvement did not continue, inflammation followed, and he began to suffer great pain.

Isaac Browne then took his brother to Boston, where he was examined by Dr. Hasket Derby. The Brownes did not indicate who recommended Dr. Derby to them, but it may have been another case of Alvah Crocker's having a hand in Hoosac Tunnel matters. Dr. Derby was the son of Crocker's friend Elias H. Derby.[78] Hasket Derby had been born eight years before the two railroad troubadours had set sail for Europe seeking steel rails for the Fitchburg Railroad, so Crocker must have known him as a lad.

Dr. Derby was a graduate of Amherst College and Harvard Medical School. After serving for a year at the Massachusetts General Hospital, he went abroad to study diseases of the eye and become practiced in surgical procedures for eye problems. Over a period of three years, he studied in Vienna, Berlin, Paris, and London under the most eminent doctors of the era. He practiced at the Massachusetts Charitable Eye and Ear Infirmary for thirty years, but it could not absorb all of his patients, so he established an eye clinic at Carney Hospital in Dorchester, south of Boston.[79] Dr. Derby had previously treated a man who had suffered an accident with fulminate of copper at Julius Smith's shop. The man from Smith's shop at the Oriental Powder Company was treated immediately after the accident, and, even though his sight was not perfect, he could get around without assistance.

At Carney Hospital, Dr. Derby operated on Charles Browne's damaged eyes, but the procedure failed to restore his sight. Fifty-four years after the accident, Isaac Browne wrote, "It was a great mistake that we did not take him to Derby, or some skilled oculist, at once, tho' we had every reason to believe that he was doing well."[80] Even though Charles Browne was in competition with Julius Smith for the development of a blasting fuse, Smith graciously hosted Charles at his home in Boston while he was being treated by Dr. Derby.

After his brother's accident, Isaac Browne quit his job at the Tunnel and became the eyes Charles now lacked. Within the year, the two men, working at the small factory in the old cheese house, were able to meet the demand for fuses at the Tunnel, and their fuse became the one of choice for the Hoosac Tunnel

Browne electrical fuse

blasting.[81] The brothers (both names are on the patents) received Letter Patent no. 108,324 in October 1870, Letter Patent no. 128,945 in July 1872 and their improved electric fuse was granted Letter Patent no. 158,672 in January 1875.[82]

Charles and Isaac Browne's ingenious fuse made use of the heat generated by the resistance of a fine wire through which an electrical current was passed to explode the sensitive explosive material. Like Mowbray and Smith, the Brownes used fulminate of mercury, but they added antimony to lessen the danger from the oversensitive material.

The fuse consisted of a hollow cylinder of wood, about 1¼ inches long and ½ inch in diameter, one end of which was closed. Into the open end they thrust a little wooden plug that had a hollow bottom. In the hollow of this plug was confined the very sensitive fulminate, and the points of two copper wires separated by a small space. These wires were connected with two others that entered the main cylinder on either side.

The fulminate in the plug served to prime the fuse; the main chamber of the cylinder was filled with a less-sensitive and less-costly explosive material. The electric spark, leaping from the one copper wire to the other in the little primer, would ignite the cap and thus explode the fuse.[83] This explosion of the fuse in turn caused the charge in the borehole to explode—be it black powder or Mowbray's nitro-glycerin. Before the Shanlys finished holing through the Mountain, they would use thousands of blasting fuses provided by the Browne brothers.

An Unsatisfactory Year

It had taken the Shanlys from January to April 1869 to complete the arrangements for taking over the machinery belonging to the Commonwealth and to commence work. For the six months prior to April, no one worried about maintaining the mechanical equipment at the Tunnel, so the machinery was in need of major repairs[84] and the central shaft had filled with three hundred feet of water.[85] Still, from the end of March until 23 December 1869, the Shanlys had advanced the bore on the east side of the Mountain 1,199 feet, driven the central shaft down another 205 feet, completed 221 feet of brick tubing into the Mountain on the west side, and repaired the damage done by the October flood.[86] In addition, the Shanlys constructed a railroad bridge over the Deerfield River at the east end and began hauling waste rock over it to build the embankment needed to connect with the terminus of the railroad from Greenfield.[87] The contract with the Commonwealth required them to deposit excavated material "when directed within three thousand feet from either end of the Tunnel."[88] But soon Benjamin Frost was also requiring them to level the dumped material to a particular grade. Walter Shanly's premonitions about the Commonwealth engineer were coming true.

When the new General Court was organized in January 1870, Governor William Claflin, in his opening message, addressed the Shanlys' Hoosac Tunnel contract and noted the time it had taken for the Commonwealth to complete the transfer of machinery, and the delay caused by the flood, but he went on to say that the contractor had not made as much progress as desired by the authorities in charge of the work.

Although the Governor complimented the Shanlys for increased progress during the last two months of 1869, he pointed out that, for the previous six months, they had fallen short according to the rates specified in the contract.[89] This was a reference to the expectations of Benjamin Frost and James Laurie, who had jointly sent a letter to the Shanlys advising them of the need to increase their labor force "up to such a standard as shall enable you to satisfy the full requirement" of the contract.[90] Governor Claflin concluded by stating: "Up to January 1, the Messrs. Shanly had nearly accomplished work to the amount of the guaranty-fund of $500,000." From the Shanlys' perspective, this acknowledged the Commonwealth's acceptance of one year of contractor work gratis; the Commonwealth had expended no funds for all the brothers did accomplish. It also doomed the brothers to completion of the Hoosac Tunnel—or to a fate of forfeiting half a million dollars to the Commonwealth.

The Joint Standing Committee of 1869 on the Troy and Greenfield Railroad and Hoosac Tunnel was of a very different persuasion than Governor Claflin and Engineer Frost. While acknowledging the Shanlys might have fallen short of achieving the specified contract requirements for penetrating the Mountain, the committee—including Moses Kimball, a longtime antagonist of the Tunnel scheme—had only words of praise in its report: "We feel called upon to say generally, that every portion of this stupendous work showed a capacity, thoroughness and energy in its prosecution which speak well for the contractors, and give the best assurance that the work will be completed by them, and within the time prescribed by the contract."[91]

The Governor's speech may have been posturing against the claim Walter Shanly had already drawn up in his typical gentlemanly terms. Shanly argued that "the Brook or Watercourse which caused the damage [to the west bore] is wholly within the limits of and connected with the 'Farren Section.'" Yet it seemed the Commonwealth now sought to require the Shanlys to redesign the Farren brickwork and make it twice as thick.[92] While Farren's tube had withstood the flood, the engineers employed by the Commonwealth believed it should be strengthened. Frank Shanly wrote to the governor and his council on 14 December 1869 stating that "their neighbor the State, had no right to inflict on them in the first instance [the flood from the brook] and secondly, that having so injured them, it has no right to make gain out of its own wrong-doing by calling upon the contractors to pay the greater or any part of the cost not alone of restoring the State property to the condition it was in previous to 4 October, 1869." This was probably a reference to the need to replace the backfill material the flood had washed away from around the Farren tube. It appeared that Mr. Frost—the Shanlys did not refer to him as Engineer Frost—was anticipating Frank Shanly's letter, as his reply bears the same date as the letter of complaint. Walter Shanly responded to Frost on 16 December, complaining about the way the Commonwealth engineer was rating their contract performance: by value and not by measurement in feet, as stated in the contract.

Walter Shanly might have been correct in his appraisal of Engineer Frost the previous year, but here he was mistaken about who was actually making the complaint against him and his brother. The reliance on value (a work item multiplied by a set dollar value instead of the work accomplished, feet of bore advanced) of completed work was the way James Laurie measured progress, and he was basically correct, as Walter Shanly would acknowledge four years later in an appeal to the Commonwealth for additional compensation. The contract had been bid as fixed prices (dollars) for the performance of specific work items. When the Shanlys submitted their bid, it specified $16 per cubic yard of Tunnel enlargement, and similarly there were prices for all the other identified items of work. If the contract had been executed in this manner, Shanly would have been correct about how the work should be measured. But the final agreement was written differently, and that is what led to Walter Shanly's harsh remarks about Frost. Latrobe had submitted to the Governor and his council a lump-sum contract based on Shanly's prices applied to quantities of work. Shanly would later testify before a Senate committee concerning this question about the type of contract: "I at once assented, provided the engineers, Messrs. Latrobe and Frost, then present, would assure me that the quantities had been carefully and accurately ascertained."[93] The question of an accurate accounting of the work quantities was one of the reasons for his quick trip to the Tunnel before finally signing the contract.

To support Walter and Frank Shanly's points about the lack of cooperation by the Commonwealth engineer, Shanly reminded Frost that he still had not responded to their letters of 29 July and 28 August 1869. Like Haupt, who was still trying to secure what he was owed, the Shanlys would soon learn it was very difficult to convince the Commonwealth of Massachusetts to pay its just debts.

The Great Nitro Explosion

Engineers Frost and Laurie were not pleased with the rate of progress, and they definitely wanted to pressure Shanly into exerting greater effort in completing the Tunnel. Frost also took a dim view concerning the quality of their work. The North Adams paper in January 1870 announced the Commonwealth's employment of a "competent man at the west end" of the Hoosac Tunnel to see that the brick arching was "properly done, by having sufficient tiers of brick and the proper proportion of cement and sand" in the mortar.[94] The west bore troubled the Shanlys just as it had Haupt and Doane. Even after Farren completed his brick tube, the Shanlys were still mining through soft veins of rock on the west side of the Mountain, so the need for brick arch would be carried forward for another year.[95] Additionally, after the flood, Frost was directing the Shanlys to strengthen Farren's tube. The dispute over this directive would be long-running.

Accidents continued to plague the work. Though no lives were lost, the first terrifying accident of 1870 occurred at the Tunnel's east end. On the night of 16 March, the nitro magazine on the east side of the Mountain—containing 400 pounds of Mowbray's soup—blew up.[96] People within a twenty-mile radius were startled by the explosion. It seems the flames in a stove caught the magazine building on fire and no one dared fight the conflagration. Memories were still fresh of a similar explosion at an east-end magazine in September 1869, when three men were killed.[97]

Mowbray was producing nitro-glycerin and the Browne brothers were perfecting their fuse, but the Shanlys and their superintendent at the central shaft, Cornelius Redding, continued the search for better and safer explosives. In May, Walter Shanly gave a talk about the Hoosac Tunnel at the Boston

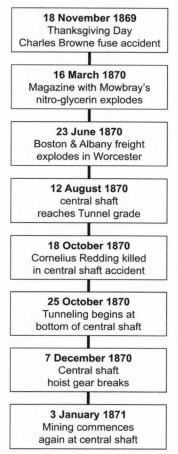

18 November 1869
Thanksgiving Day
Charles Browne fuse accident

16 March 1870
Magazine with Mowbray's
nitro-glycerin explodes

23 June 1870
Boston & Albany freight
explodes in Worcester

12 August 1870
central shaft
reaches Tunnel grade

18 October 1870
Cornelius Redding killed
in central shaft accident

25 October 1870
Tunneling begins at
bottom of central shaft

7 December 1870
Central shaft
hoist gear breaks

3 January 1871
Mining commences
again at central shaft

Board of Trade. He referred to the progress at the west shaft, saying it had not been steady because of trials with a new explosive compound called dualin being pressed on the market by Carl Dittmar (Patent no. 98,854, 18 January 1870). It was a mixture of sawdust treated with nitro-glycerin.[98] Henry Drinker, in his monumental 1878 work on tunneling, gives the composition of Dittmar's dualin as 50 percent nitro-glycerin, 30 percent fine sawdust, and 20 percent nitrate of potassa.[99] The nitro-glycerin part of the dualin Dittmar manufactured was described as a fluid of milky, reddish, or white color with a consistency varying from ordinary syrup to thick broth. The nitro-glycerin Mowbray produced was chemically pure and had the transparency of clear water.[100] During his talk, Shanly went on to say, "At the Central Shaft Mr. Redding is trying dualin with his usual determination to succeed in what he undertakes. . . ."[101]

Carl Dittmar had attended the Prussian Military Academy and the Royal Artillery and Engineers' School before serving as a lieutenant in the Prussian Army. He worked with Alfred Nobel to establish an explosive manufacturing plant at the isolated location of Krümmel, southeast of Hamburg. Nobel's permit from the government for his nitration-producing process at Krümmel required he guarantee an adequate distance between the nitrate work and the manufacture of ignition fuses. In 1866, after Dittmar retired from the army, he became an assistant to Nobel, conducting experiments with solid absorbents of nitro-glycerin. He left Nobel, or was dismissed by him, in the fall of 1867.[102] Accounts differ as to what actually transpired. He emigrated to the United States in 1869 and started his own explosives business with his brother Hugo and Gottlieb (George) F. Burkhardt. It seems they were manufacturing Carl Dittmar's compound at Burkhardt's brewery in Roxbury, Massachusetts. Burkhardt, another German, had opened his brewery in 1850 and had the distinction of brewing the first lager beer in Boston.

In 1867, the Western Railroad merged with the Boston and Worcester

Railroad to become the Boston and Albany Railroad. The Boston and Albany had leased trackage between Pittsfield and North Adams. This connection at Pittsfield was off their main line to Albany, but it allowed the Boston and Albany to deliver goods by rail from Boston to North Adams. The Shanlys were dependent on this line for delivery of supplies after the flood of 1869 destroyed all of the bridges on the rail line from Greenfield to the Tunnel.

During the first half of 1870, the Shanlys, while evaluating the effectiveness of Dittmar's explosive compound, repeatedly ordered dualin from him in Boston. At the same time, they were ordering most of the fuses they needed from Julius Smith in Boston. Subsequently, at noon on 23 June, as a Boston and Albany freight train passed through Worcester, it "suddenly blew up destroying track, cars, property, and buildings."[103] The shock of the explosion was felt and heard twenty-five miles away. One news report claimed that "a gentleman who was on a pond in South Spencer (ten miles away) fishing at the time says that the fishes were seen to jump from the water at the time of the explosion."[104] The car that exploded was carrying a box containing 1,000 fuses manufactured by Smith's Oriental Powder Company in Boston and ten cases—1,000 pounds—of dualin manufactured by Dittmar in Neponset, southwest of Boston.[105] This information came to light during an inquest the following day.

A *New York Times* article about the explosion stated: "The boxes mentioned were directed to Shanly of North Adams, one of the Hoosick Tunnel contractors, and he will be examined before the jury." The Shanlys were building the Tunnel against which, for so long, the Western Railroad had fought, and now the Tunnel builders were causing the railroad's track and trains to disappear in a stupefying flash of sound and light. An action of tort suit by the railroad soon followed in the Supreme Judicial Court against Walter and Francis Shanly. Boston and Albany Railroad officials claimed ignorance of the presence of such dangerous freight. At the trial, no one could prove exactly what happened: Did the fuses catch fire and explode, causing the dualin also to detonate, or did the dualin explode and ignite the fuses? Mowbray believed the nitro-glycerin oozed from the dualin sawdust, flowed through the floor of the freight car and onto the rails, and exploded when hammered by the wheels of the car. But the "how" was not the real question.

The complaint alleged the Shanlys wrongfully requested Dittmar to manufacture a "compound in an unusually dangerous manner, more explosive and powerful" than he had previously made, and to send the compound to them at North Adams on the Boston and Albany Railroad.[106] While the court ruled that from previous law it is the duty of the sender to give notice of a dangerous article, the court continued and ruled in favor of the Shanlys, stating there is no ground for holding the consignee liable for the negligence and improper conduct of others. The decision, however, was not rendered until early 1873.[107]

The accident in Worcester and the lawsuit failed to deter the Shanlys from experiments with dualin. Throughout the year, they conducted six experiments with Dittmar's compound. The effectiveness of the dualin was measured against previous experiments with Mowbray's nitro-glycerin, which was found to work best in holes drilled to a depth of eight feet. In holes of such depth, the Mowbray explosive consistently threw out all the rock. This was the performance standard Dittmar needed to match or exceed. He had repeatedly not been able to do so, and each time he had returned to his factory to formulate a stronger compound. In late November 1870, 1,500 pounds of dualin were delivered to the Tunnel. With great expectation, Dittmar arrived on 28 November to superintend the experiments. Over a period of three days, dualin was substituted for the nitro-glycerin in the eight-foot-deep holes drilled at the east header. "The dualin was utterly unable to move the rock." Dittmar insisted that the problem was the effect of the cold weather on his compound, so the charges were warmed before being loaded into the holes. The results were no better. Only when the depth of a hole was reduced to two feet could the dualin remove the rock, but this was no better than what black powder could achieve. Because the original intent had been to conduct tests at both the east heading and the central shaft, four hundred pounds had been teamed up the Mountain, but the trial at the bottom of the central shaft was abandoned after the failure at the east heading.[108]

Dispute Between the Engineers

Another dispute was smoldering in 1870, but this one involved the two engineers working for the Commonwealth and monitoring the performance of the Shanlys' Tunnel work. Consulting Engineer James Laurie, in one of his earliest monthly reports to the governor, urged that Benjamin Frost begin preparing in tabular form a summary of all work done during the month and all the remaining work, with a time estimate for completion based on the contractors' rate of progress. This manner of presenting progress was never adopted by Frost for monthly reports, and it frustrated Laurie. Frost did, however, adopt a format similar to this for his annual report at year's end.

In February of 1870, Laurie complained to the Governor about not being able to get the report, and he also complained about the quantities of excavation

Frost was using to calculate Shanly's payments, insinuating there had been errors in the certified pay due the contractor. Laurie was even so bold as to accuse Frost of trying to hide his errors. He wrote, "I became convinced that there were serious blunders and discrepancies which he [Frost] was trying to hide and cover up."[109] Consulting Engineer Laurie, who had once worked with those aligned with the Western Railroad, was often accused of being against the Shanlys, but, as Senate hearings in 1874 and 1875 would reveal, his accusations about Frost's hiding true quantities were correct in several instances.[110]

Pushing Frost to complete the monthly estimates in a timely manner, Laurie used the argument of being fair to the contractor. The Shanlys were being paid for their work on a monthly schedule, and the estimate needed to be in Boston by the fifteenth of the month so they could collect their money per the contract with the Commonwealth.

Laurie's efforts were to no avail, so in April 1870 he calculated the March estimate in the tabular form he was advocating. In late April, the council sent Laurie the April estimate for his approval. Again he reiterated his position and reminded the Commonwealth of the contract specification to pay the "contractors on or before the fifteenth day of each month following the performance of the work."[111] While reviewing the April estimate, he called attention to several details he believed were incorrect. Replying to the Governor, Laurie alleged that Frost was paying twice for some work, paid the full amount for incomplete work, and allowed payment for work in advance of its execution. In May, Laurie made similar accusations against Frost. Both Frank and Walter Shanly, when acting in a capacity similar to the one Frost now held, had always been careful about paying their subcontractors. If there were any real problems with the pay estimates, they surely would have complained, and this is one area of their dealings with Frost where the official records never indicate a dispute.

In June Laurie's attacks on Frost changed. The work at the central shaft was rapidly approaching the Tunnel level, and it would then be necessary to establish the alignment of the Tunnel at the bottom of the shaft. At a meeting of the Governor's Council in April, Frost claimed that the lines run by him were "within ¼ or ½ inch of those run by Mr. Doane," but in May Laurie discovered that Frost had not used Doane's mark at the lining tower east of the Deerfield River on Rowe's Neck to run his line. Laurie complimented the quality of Doane's work, stating in his report to the Governor that "his work and station points bear evidence of intelligent purpose and correctness."[112] Then Laurie added another accusation at the very end of a letter to Frost about the alignment: "I hope you notified the contractors that at the east end heading they were above grade."[113]

Laurie voiced additional complaints against Frost in July, but in August he had a more serious grievance. The Shanlys' miners were only days away from driving the central shaft to the Tunnel elevation provided by Frost. Laurie now pointed out the need for reliable levels and noted that the engineer had not yet run these over the Hoosac Mountain. When Frost ran a new line of levels from the west end of the Tunnel, there was a discrepancy of 5¼ inches from the earlier notes.[114] Laurie was well acquainted with surveying and survey instruments, having begun his professional career as an apprentice to an instrument maker before working as a civil engineer in his native Scotland. He repeated this charge about the survey in his September report.[115] On 13 January 1871, he wrote his last report to Governor Claflin, still complaining about the surveys.[116] His fights with Frost had become too much for the Governor, so Laurie was dismissed and replaced by Edward S. Philbrick of Boston as the Commonwealth's Consulting Engineer. Engineer Philbrick's first tasks was to verify "the accuracy of the lines on independent examination."[117] Philbrick found no fault with the surveys. Frost's surveys and/or the surveys conducted by Frost's assistant engineers were excellent, as would be proven when Shanly completed the Tunnel through the Mountain.

The Central Shaft

Two accidents late in 1870 deprived the Shanlys of their most skilled builders. At the central shaft, Superintendent Cornelius Redding, a mining foreman,[118] and a miner were killed on 18 October when, "descending the shaft in the bucket the rope gave way."[119] At the time, fifty feet of water filled the bottom of the shaft, and the three men drowned before aid could reach them.

At the west shaft, the hoisting was done in heavy cages; at the central shaft, large copper buckets with a volume of about one cubic yard[120] were used to carry out the blasted rock and to lower and raise the men. The buckets were attached to a square wooden frame braced with metal crossbars. The wooden hoist frame slid along wooden guide rails that extended the full height of the shaft. The frame prevented the bucket from swinging back and forth. The rate of ascent or descent was very fast—only two minutes for the full 1,000 feet. The miners would stand in the bucket, stand on its rim, or stand on the wooden frame while holding onto whatever they could get their fingers around.[121] One reporter commented: "Their life-long experience in such holes in the ground has made them reckless of danger. When the whistle blows for the shift of hands, every man on the bottom wants to come up in the first bucket and generally

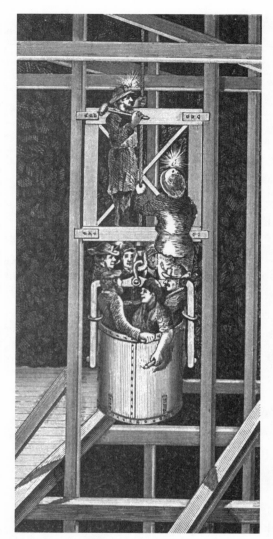

Central-shaft bucket

the whole dozen of them do all come up at once."[122] But the Redding accident was not caused by such foolish behavior. Cornelius Redding lost his life because when an old wire rope was replaced on the hoisting drum, someone did not attach it properly.[123]

The second accident occurred at the west shaft and resulted in the death of John Hocking Jr., the subcontractor's son, one of the heroes the previous year when the west bore flooded. He was killed instantly on 29 November when a huge stone broke loose from the roof of the Tunnel and fell on his head. Although only twenty-two, he had proven his character and resourcefulness during the flood. At the time of the accident, he was overseeing a crew of twenty men working in the bore.[124]

The loss of Cornelius Redding was especially disturbing. Adding thirty-one feet of depth per month for 14½ months, he had driven the shaft to the Tunnel grade. In the year of Crocker's control and up until the fire, the average rate for increasing the depth of the shaft had been only nineteen feet per month. The excavation of the central shaft reached its final depth on 12 August 1870.[125] Between 13 August and 25 October, the miners trimmed the sides of the shaft and strengthened the timbering and elevator guides.[126] This was Walter Shanly's standard approach. Planning for the continuous stress of the future tunneling work, he had the hoisting engine overhauled and he removed the old pipes and pumping equipment inherited from the Commonwealth. Because of the suspension of pumping while they installed new mains and larger-capacity pumps, the bottom of the shaft had again filled with water and into this water-filled hole Redding rode the bucket down the shaft.

The first engineering question after the central shaft excavation supposedly reached the Tunnel grade was to verify the elevation at the bottom of the shaft. Had Shanly's miners, as directed by the engineers, actually cut the shaft to the proper depth? The second question needing to be answered very precisely concerned the directions for mining the two bores from the bottom of the shaft. Both questions were the responsibility of Benjamin Frost. The Commonwealth engineers needed to project the line of the Tunnel down a dripping black hole 1,028 feet deep and set reference points so Shanlys' men mining east and west from the shaft would meet the bores coming from the east and west sides of the Mountain.

Frost found an exceptionally talented engineer, Carl O. Wederkinch, to accomplish this critical survey. He was a young Dane who, after graduating from the University of Copenhagen,[127] had emigrated to the United States. When Wederkinch departed Denmark, he was completely ignorant of the English language. Landing in New York City the handicap forced him to take a job as a common laborer while he strove to master the language. As his language skills improved, he found work as a machinist and then drifted to Boston, where he was engaged as an instrument maker,[128] the same trade about which Loammi Baldwin had inquired for his son Loammi Jr. Both of these trades, machinist and instrument maker, would serve Wederkinch well at the central shaft. He would later craft many of his own instruments.

At the central shaft, Wederkinch was "clad in the uncouth miner's dress of the region." He was the life and spirit of the work at the shaft and was described as "possessing a face so frank, so fresh, so full of vigor and earnestness that it at once attracted and held attention."[129] The responsibility for projecting the Tunnel line from the top of the shaft to the bottom of the 1,028-foot hole now fell to this man. Along the line of the Tunnel, the shaft had an open distance of slightly less than twenty-three feet—an extremely short distance for projecting a line accurately to guide the work of the miners. Frost almost lost this exceptional surveyor in another central shaft accident. Riding down one day, Wederkinch was showered by pieces of iron when a machine above broke into fragments, fortunately the engineer was unharmed.[130]

Before Wederkinch surveyed his accurate line, Tunnel header excavation based on initial measurements commenced in both east and west directions. This was done because the surveyors needed to set points to mark the line in the roof of the Tunnel beyond the central shaft. So on 25 October, the miners began hammering on blast holes at the bottom of the shaft for starting the Tunnel. If there was a need to correct the excavation based on the initial line, it could be accomplished when the full Tunnel was excavated. The space at the bottom of the shaft was still very limited, so this work had to be accomplished by hand drilling and black powder. The mining continued until the night of 7 December, when the gear teeth on the hoisting machinery failed. With no way to lift the buckets of broken rock from the bottom of the shaft, mining had to cease. Walter Shanly had been at the shaft the entire time.[131] Under his eye, the men penetrated sixty feet eastward and eighty-seven feet westward[132] before the gear splintered. Repairing the gear took until midnight on Christmas Day. But while the machinery was out of service, water again accumulated in the shaft, so mining did not commence again until 3 January 1871.[133] Then Wederkinch began to set an accurate Tunnel line for the miners. The engineers had what was described as a "colossal transit instrument"[134] specially manufactured for this survey work.

One of the first steps in projecting such a line to the bottom of a shaft was to drop plumb bobs from the Tunnel line where it crossed the top of the shaft. The two plumb bobs dropped at the extreme edges of the oval would serve to mark the line at the bottom of the 1,028-foot shaft. But Wederkinch had to initially overcome several small yet unique problems because of the extreme depth of the shaft. During the cold nights atop the Mountain, the air at the bottom of the shaft would be warmer than the air at ground level above, so it would rush up the shaft. These currents of moving air would disturb the necessary perfect vertical drop of the plumb bobs. Spiders would also cause problems. The accuracy of the alignment could be seriously impaired by spiders attaching their webs to the plumb-bob line and introducing alignment errors by drawing the line to the walls of the shaft.[135]

Wederkinch's solution for transferring an accurate Tunnel alignment to the bottom of the shaft was to establish an accurate line at the top of the shaft. He machined two vertical plate verniers, each having a vertical slit or opening in the middle. The vertical slit was arranged to move horizontally along a scale. The scale permitted the engineer to take a precise reading of the location of the vertical slit. These verniers were fixed to the upper works of the shaft.

To set his verniers, Wederkinch made repeated sightings through his transit of the Tunnel alignment across the top of the shaft under different atmospheric conditions. He then used the average of these measurements to position the verniers atop the stone walls of the shaft. Finally, he carefully stretched two fine steel wires from vernier to vernier across the shaft.[136] These two wires rested against the opposite sides of the vernier slits. This accurately established the Tunnel line at the top of the shaft. Once he had the Tunnel line established at the surface, Wederkinch positioned two copper wires holding fifteen-pound brass plumb bobs through the two parallel wires resting against the slits of the verniers. One brass plumb bob was at each side of the shaft opening. His two plumb-bob wires extended to the bottom of the shaft, with the bobs hanging in buckets of water on the Tunnel floor. The man was like a watchmaker operating on a grand scale. To protect against the effects of air currents, dripping water, and spiders, he enclosed the copper wires in wooden tubes. Still he found the plumbs had an oscillating motion of some extent in an elliptical orbit.[137]

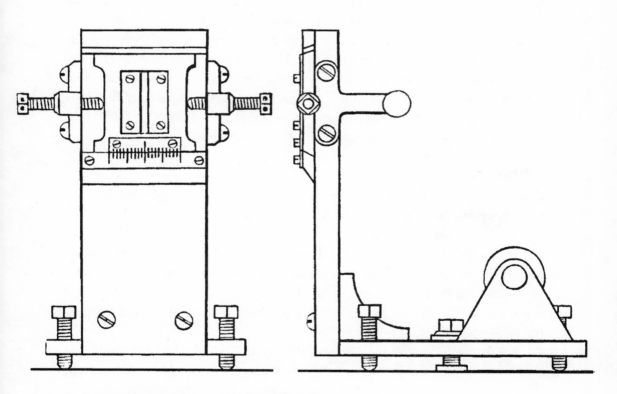

Carl O. Wederkinch's Hoosac Tunnel verniers

At the bottom of the shaft, Walter Shanly had his men erect an elevated floor. It was positioned a few feet below the roof of the Tunnel and served as a work platform for Wederkinch and his surveyors. Working from the elevated floor, Wederkinch placed a second set of horizontal verniers directly in front of the oscillating vertical plumb wires. Francis D. Fisher, an engineer with Wederkinch, described how they drilled holes in the roof of the short section of Tunnel that Shanly's miners had excavated and drove wooden plugs into these holes. The verniers at the bottom of the shaft were different from those used at the top. Wederkinch was especially clever in developing solutions to the very difficult surveying problem of establishing the Tunnel direction at the bottom of the shaft. Each of the verniers he made for use at the bottom consisted only of a simple piece of metal divided into decimals of a foot instead of using the normal and unwieldy twelve inches. These he secured to the wooden plugs driven into the roof of the Tunnel. Once again, he made repeated trials of plumb-wire observations against the divided metal strips, and he used the average of these readings to fix the Tunnel alignment.[138] The remaining Tunnel documents do not record the number of readings Wederkinch and his fellow surveyors made at either the top of the shaft or in the Tunnel, but, considering the accuracy of the line he established, it was probably several hundred or more at each location.

Progress

During 1870, the Commonwealth finally completed the repairs to the railroad line between Greenfield and the east end of the Hoosac Tunnel. The line opened for reduced-speed rail traffic on the Fourth of July, and the final work was completed in late autumn. The Joint Standing Committee on the Hoosac Tunnel[139] blamed the necessary repairs partly on "imperfections and deficiencies in original construction" [Farren's work] but acknowledged that the "exceptional trials to which the works were subjected" during the October 1869 flood were the major culprit.

At the end of the year, Benjamin Frost did concede that "the heading at the east and west ends" had made nearly continuous advances. He went on to say, "[T]he progress may be deemed a fair exhibit of what could be accomplished with the means at command, in view of the nature of the material encountered."[140] The forces organized by the Shanlys had pushed the east bore 1,515 feet and the west bore 1,203 feet, for a total increase in Tunnel length of more than half a mile. In his report of 28 January 1871 Frost ventured that the Tunnel would be complete by 15 March 1874. The final item in his report was a strong reminder about the need to complete the railroad between the west portal of the Tunnel and North Adams. He specifically warned the committee about the danger from the canal above the west bore and the fact that until the open cut was made for the railroad extension to North Adams, the only escape for water flowing from the Tunnel was the old Haupt tunnel. He closed with a warning about the possibility of a disaster similar to the flood of 1869.

Frank Shanly

As the first two years of the Tunnel work progressed, Frank Shanly was at the Hoosac site less and less. He had gone to North Adams with Walter in January 1869, but even as he executed the building program to support the work, it became apparent his heart was not in the Tunnel project. His older brother was the leader, the negotiator of the contract, and the successful man everyone recognized. It was Walter who promised the investors in Canada he would manage the affair. There are no records of disharmony between the brothers, but Frank Shanly soon began to submit proposals on his own for other railroad projects.[141]

Very early during his sojourn in North Adams, Frank joined forces with a contractor from Canada to submit a price for constructing a section of the Rondout and Oswego Railroad in New York.[142] The line was to run from Rondout (now Kingston) westward for sixty miles to Oneonta. It was an important connection because Rondout—on the Hudson River fifty miles south of Albany—was at the eastern terminus of the Delaware and Hudson Canal. Frank and his partner, Richard Jones from Port Hope, Canada, agreed on prices for the work and the railroad company accepted their proposal—but then the railroad failed to execute the contract. It was an interesting combination of talent. Thirty years earlier, Richard Jones had been the Methodist minister in Port Hope, but he seemed to have held many jobs, including moving mail for the government.

After the disappointment of losing the contract, the partners persisted in their search for a project. Five months later, in May 1869, they bid on another railroad project. This time they were successful. Again the venture had an interesting feature: Benjamin Latrobe was the chief engineer. On the strength of their promise to bring workers from Canada, the Pittsburgh and Connellsville Railroad granted them a contract to build twenty-three miles of line. After the contract was signed, Frank wrote to Latrobe: "I will not be able to give much time to the work, but my partners will surely give satisfaction."[143] The only problem for Frank Shanly and his partners was that each believed the other would supervise the work, it was a repeat of Haupt's initial assumption about the Hoosac Tunnel work. They subcontracted their project to local Pennsylvania firms and then seemed to have gone their merry ways. During the 1869 work season, construction moved forward satisfactorily but by March 1870, the subcontractors began to abandon the job for better-paying work elsewhere.

By late 1870, Frank Shanly was dividing his time between the Hoosac Tunnel with his brother and other jobs he had taken in Canada.[144] He tried to withdraw from the partnership to build the Pittsburgh and Connellsville Railroad, but the railroad refused to release him from his obligations. Latrobe's temper flared, and he threatened to seize all of the assets on the project. Perhaps remembering the 1868 Hoosac Tunnel negotiations and believing Walter was a silent member of the partnership, Latrobe even threatened to go against Walter Shanly, who actually held no interest in the partnership. When the railroad company began withholding payments for the monthly estimates, Frank and his partners had to dig into their pockets and use their own money to finish the project. They finally completed the work in March of 1871.

From late 1869 onward, the Pennsylvania debacle was only a small sideshow to Frank's other construction contracts. Over the next five years, his company in Canada would build more than two hundred miles of railroad in Ontario. On some of the early contracts in Canada, his brothers Walter and James were guarantors.[145] In early 1871, Frank established an office on York Street in Toronto, and by April he had employed more than a dozen men to manage all of his contracts. His efforts to become a rich man kept him on a continuous travel schedule, shuttling to and from North Adams, Boston, Pittsburgh, and Toronto. He spread himself much too thin so in late 1869, Frank and Walter Shanly ended their Hoosac Tunnel partnership. Walter paid Frank $50,000 over and above what he had already been paid, and Frank allowed Walter to continue to use his name in the partnership.[146]

Transporting Nitro-Glycerin

Walter Shanly took the Burleigh drill, George Mowbray's tri-nitro-glycerin, Charles Browne's electric fuse, and Thomas Doane's idea for a drill carriage and, by late 1870, had united them into a smooth-running tunneling operation. Some of the important lessons for using these four important innovations came about accidentally or as the result of accidents. The Worcester train explosion had been tragic, but it highlighted the importance of keeping the explosive material and the fuses separated.

With the close of 1870, Washington Gladden published an article in *Scribner's Monthly* describing his tour of the Hoosac mining operations.[147] "Clothed in a tarpaulin and rubber boots for protection against the water," which dripped continuously and abundantly from the Tunnel roof, Gladden journeyed into the bore penetrating the east side of the Hoosac Mountain. He was first on a small platform car pulled by the locomotive the Shanlys had procured. Looking around at his fellow passengers, he noticed a man with a basket "containing a dozen, more or less, of tin"[148] tubes. These were 1½ inches in diameter, between 1½ and 2 feet long, and were closed at the end with a large cork. He was riding beside cartridges of Mowbray's nitro-glycerin.

When they arrived at the rock face of the Tunnel bore, the corks were removed from the tubes and each cork was perforated with a small hole. Browne fuses were now readied. With the fuse on the cartridge side of the cork, its wires were pushed through the perforation. The fuse was then pushed into the cartridge by the cork as it again sealed the tin tube, but now the short ends of the insulated copper wires from the fuse projected from the cork. After these arrangements were completed, the cartridges were carefully placed in the holes where Burleigh's wonderful drills had pounded drill steel into the rock. Doane's drill-carriage idea for mounting the heavy Burleigh drills was now an iron framework resting on rollers. After the drill carriage was moved back from the face the miners were preparing to blast, two strong plank doors were positioned between the carriage and the rock face, to provide protection from flying rock.

After all of the cartridges were placed in the drill holes, the fuse wires were connected to long wires that were in turn connected to the electrical machine located a safe distance back behind the plank doors. When the miners withdrew to a safe location, the crank on the electrical machine was rotated a few turns, resulting in a "stunning reverberation."[149]

Mowbray gave a lecture on explosives at Martin's Hall in North Adams on Tuesday evening, 24 January 1871. The week prior to the lecture, he wrote a letter to the *Adams Transcript*, reputing the dangers of using nitro-glycerin. Asserting that his nitro-glycerin was safe for blasting, the chemist went on to list all of the nitro-glycerin accidents over the three years of its use at the Tunnel. His letter in the *Transcript* claimed only one man was killed, and that accident occurred because of a fuse problem. Apparently the miners had been using an old tape fuse, and when the explosion did not occur as expected, a miner had gone forward to investigate. As had happened many times with black powder, the charge exploded just as the miner "imprudently approached it."[150]

Mowbray did admit to other accidents, but these were not specifically mining accidents. One accident occurred when blasters placed a can of nitro-glycerin on a stove to thaw it. The resulting explosion claimed three lives. On another occasion at Mowbray's magazine, "a man had gone to bathe" and there was an explosion. Everyone assumed the victim urinated on the glycerin, but Mowbray listed the accident as "cause unknown."

Greater awareness of the effects of heat and cold on tri-nitro-glycerin came about as the result of an important accident recorded by Mowbray in his book *Tri-Nitro-Glycerin*. During the winter of 1867 and 1868, W. P. Granger, the Tunnel engineer, wanted to use nitro-glycerin to remove an ice obstruction at the Great Dam on the Deerfield River. The scientific literature stated, and Mowbray's own beliefs at the time were, "that when congealed, the slightest touch or jar was sufficient to explode nitro-glycerin."[151] Granger asked Mowbray to pack ten cartridges so that he could carry them from the nitro-glycerin factory in North Adams to the other side of the Mountain safely in the cold weather. Mowbray warmed the cartridges to ninety degrees and packed them in a box with sawdust that he had also heated to ninety degrees. He and Granger placed the box on the back of the sleigh and covered the box with a buffalo robe for the nine-mile trip over the Hoosac Mountain. Starting down the east side of the Mountain, Granger lost control of the sleigh. It overturned, throwing the engineer and the box of cartridges into the snow. Granger believed himself a dead man, as horse, sleigh, and he went flying, but there was no explosion. When he retrieved the cartridges from the snow, they were frozen solid. He righted his sleigh, found the horse, and, with the cartridges at his feet, proceeded to the dam, "thinking a heap but saying nothing."[152]

Arriving at the ice obstruction, Granger attached a fuse to the cartridges and inserted them into the ice. He was using a common tape fuse to fire the cartridges, so, after lighting the tape, he drew back a safe distance. There was a sharp crack but no explosion. The fuse had exploded in the congealed nitro-glycerin, but Mowbray's product had not exploded. Granger then tried a second time, with the same result. Only after he had thawed the nitro-glycerin could he get it to explode. Granger's episode thus provided a true understanding of the effects of temperature on nitro-glycerin and the safest way to transport the explosive.

Accidents

The year 1870 concluded with another tragic accident at the east end. Early on 26 December, the large boardinghouse caught fire, and a boarder named Brown perished in the flames on the second floor. Another boarder, named McGowan, was so badly burned that he died the next day. A third man jumped from a window and was seriously injured.[153]

In the first two weeks of 1870, three men were injured at the west shaft in a nitro-glycerin accident. Patsy Carns, John Wolf, and a third man listed only as Flynn were unlucky enough to set up their drilling machine over some spilled nitro-glycerin. As soon as they engaged their drill, the nitro exploded, scattering broken debris around the drill and causing painful wounds to the men.[154] This occurred the week before Mowbray's lecture on the safety of his soup.

All the eminent geologists, including President Edward Hitchcock of Amherst College, had always expressed a "dry tunnel" opinion when questioned about the Hoosac Mountain. Hitchcock had even testified to this at legislative hearings in 1853 and 1854.[155] Nonetheless, the real villain in 1871 would again be water—water that no one expected.

14

"Fail in the Tunnel"

Our estimate [of cost] will be based upon
President Hitchcock's opinion, the highest authority,
that the quantity of water to be met with, except in
the secondary formation at the west end,
will not be as large as to be seriously troublesome.

—*Senate No. 93, Report of the Commissioners*
upon the Troy and Greenfield Railroad and Hoosac Tunnel
(Boston: Wright & Potter, 1863), 54.

EDWARD HITCHCOCK WAS CALLED to appear before the committees of the General Court in 1851 and 1854 regarding the Hoosac Tunnel. On both occasions, the gentlemen questioned him about the presence of water in the rock of the Hoosac Mountain. Hitchcock, a native of Deerfield, was educated at Deerfield Academy before spending two years studying theology at Yale College. In 1818, Yale awarded him an honorary master's (AM) degree.[1] This distinction was probably given because of the technical articles he published in the *American Journal of Science and Arts*, edited by Yale Professor Benjamin Silliman. In 1825, Hitchcock returned to Yale for three months to study chemistry before his appointment as professor of chemistry and natural history at Amherst College. He had a passion for investigating the natural world, and in 1830 the Commonwealth of Massachusetts appointed him its first geologist. His January 1854 testimony about the rock of the Hoosac Mountain included the statement:

> *Water will undoubtedly be found near the surface, and elsewhere to some extent, but I have an impression, or rather an opinion, that this Tunnel will be found to go below where the water percolates, unless the layers are found to be more broken than I suppose they are. . . . I have an impression that this Tunnel will be found dry, after penetrating a considerable distance from the surface.*[2]

3 January 1871
Mining begins
again at the central shaft

27 March 1871
Flood at the west heading
from the central shaft

7 August 1871
New pumps started
at the central shaft

8 August 1871
Pump foundation fails
at the central shaft

2 October 1871
New pump again set to work
at the central shaft

6 October 1871
Bearing plate under
the new pump fractures

31 October 1871
New pump begins lifting
water from the central shaft

November 1871
Mining again commences
eastward from the central shaft

December 1871
Mining again commences
westward from the central shaft

January 1872
McClallan & Walker begin
railroad to North Adams

Rocks Full of Water

From the bottom of the central shaft, Walter Shanly in early 1871 had his miners tearing at the very heart of the Hoosac Mountain in search of miners boring toward them from headers started years earlier by Edward Serrell, Herman Haupt, and Thomas Doane. One gang of miners was driving a header eastward to meet the bore from the Deerfield River side of the Mountain, while a second gang was working westward to meet the miners working toward them from the Hoosic River side. At the time, there was not enough Tunnel length at the bottom of the shaft for drawing the pneumatic drills back from the flying rock of a blast. Therefore, the miners, just as in the days of Haupt, were drilling blast holes purely by muscle power. This would be the practice until the Tunnel could be extended a sufficient length to protect the drills during a blast. As a result of this hand drilling situation, the rate of advance for the two headers was slow.[3]

At the bottom of the shaft, Shanly also had miners blasting out a sump to catch the water seeping from the heart of the Mountain.[4] The intake for the pump used to remove water from the shaft was placed in this sump. Finally on Monday, 27 March, the two headers were separated by sufficient distance so the pneumatic drills could be introduced to speed the work. But no drills were lowered down the shaft that day—ill fortune again struck the Tunnel enterprise. The Hoosac saga had its political drama, but it was also a saga of the Mountain's Great Spirit against the engineers and miners. On this day, as Shanly's miners drove their bore westward from the central shaft, a water-bearing vein, encountered a few days earlier, released a flood into the short section of Tunnel at the bottom of the shaft. At more than 1,028 feet from the surface of the Hoosac Mountain, the miners had struck what Hitchcock had deemed improbable. Attempts to stop the flow proved fruitless, and the flood soon began to gain on the pump.[5] Even Engineer Frost had to admit that the "water came into the central section, exceeding the capacity of the pump."[6] Shanly, Frost, and the miners all remained hopeful the water came from a pocket and would soon run dry.[7]

To supplement the hard-pressed pumps, Shanly withdrew the miners from the Tunnel and began bailing the water with the buckets normally used for lifting rock from the bottom of the shaft.[8] But two weeks later, it was clear this was no pocket. The flow of water did not diminish, and there was no indication it would eventually run dry. A story in the North Adams paper related how the pumps at the central shaft were unable to keep the Tunnel dry. Even with the combined effort of pumps and buckets, the water from the westward header had, in two weeks, flooded the central shaft to a depth of sixteen feet. The article in the paper described how Shanly was excavating the header westward as a top cut, so, trying to put a positive spin on the crisis, the paper announced that the water was only four feet above the floor of the header![9]

The paper's statement, however, was not completely correct. Shanly planned and directed the mining from the central shaft based on the fact that the grade directly under the shaft was the high point of the Tunnel—the Tunnel grade descended from the short level section at the central shaft toward each portal. Because of this design feature, when the Tunnel was completed, water would naturally drain from the high point at the central shaft out the east and west ends. But if the miners now excavated down to the final floor grade from the central shaft, water would have accumulated at the two headers until the Tunnel was completed as both headers would collect water like sumps. Therefore, to keep his miners working in dry conditions, Shanly had the header work from below the central shaft start at the bottom elevation of the Tunnel's high point and angle upward in both directions toward the top of the Tunnel. Consequently, all of the water seeping from the rock veins of the Mountain, flowed back to the central shaft, where it was collected in the sump and pumped to the surface. At the surface, an outlet pipe discharged the water into an underground culvert and the culvert conveyed the flow into a ravine running down the side of the Mountain.[10] Even though Shanly was an engineer who planned his work carefully, the engineers for the Commonwealth would continually attack his planning and execution of the Hoosac mining.

Consulting Engineer Edward Philbrick blamed Shanly for the delay resulting from this unexpected flood in the heart of the Mountain. At the Senate hearing three years later, he expressed his feelings to Attorney General Charles

Train: "I think these delays would certainly have been foreseen and avoided if Mr. Shanly had thought it his business to have provided for the water before finding it."[11] While Philbrick did not take over as consulting engineer until 7 February 1871[12] it is hard to believe he was unaware of the refurnishing work Shanly had done at the central shaft in the fall of 1870 after the shaft reached the Tunnel depth. Shanly had at that time replaced the Commonwealth's old pumping equipment and installed new mains and larger-capacity pumps.

The Joint Standing Committee took a different view of Shanly's foresight in planning the work. In the report for 1871, these gentlemen of the General Court commended Shanly for placing steam compressors in service on the east side of the Mountain. This was because many had predicted earlier the effect of occasions when ice or low water in the Deerfield River would deprive the contractor of the turbine compressors dependent on the river's water supply. Lack of water in turn meant a lack of compressed air to keep the drills working. The contractor from Canada was prepared for such situations.[13] By early January of 1871, Shanly had his steam compressors in operation.[14] The Committee also made it clear that the Shanlys were spending their own money anticipating the needs of the work: "The Messrs. Shanly derive no direct compensation from the Commonwealth for all their provisions of costly machinery for pumping and hoisting, or for their labor of many months in completing and setting them in place. . . ."[15] From the beginning, it was Walter Shanly who had borrowed the money to keep the work going, and it was he who was liable to the creditor—not his brother Frank, who was now engaged in his own projects in Canada. Therefore, it was not "Messrs. Shanly" but Walter Shanly who was spending the money.

East and West Bores

Besides the unexpected flood, there was an additional costly incident at the Hoosac Tunnel project in April 1871. On 1 April, about forty feet of the old Haupt tunnel on the west side of the Mountain collapsed. Because the Commonwealth had still not decided on the railroad line between the Tunnel and North Adams, the Haupt tunnel provided the most efficient route for removing the rock debris from the bore. Without the Haupt tunnel, all excavated rock had to be lifted out of the Doane pit by derrick. This situation was the result of the decision by the first commissioners and Thomas Doane to excavate as far into the Mountain as possible with an open cut. Doane, and Alvah Crocker after him, had effectively dug a pit from which they began to bore into the Mountain while using the old Haupt tunnel to remove the debris. Consequently, until Hocking &

Holbrook could clear the blockage in the Haupt tunnel, mining of the eastward bore would be delayed.

Even, Consulting Engineer Philbrick had advised Governor Claflin and the Governor's Council about the importance of constructing the two miles of railroad between the west portal of the Tunnel and the North Adams station, but no action was taken on the matter.[16] Philbrick may have blamed Shanly for the flooding at the central shaft, but he clearly believed the contractor would complete the Tunnel in three years. Therefore, he counseled the Governor about the large amount of work required to complete the needed two miles of railroad.

Philbrick's warning, combined with Shanly's progress in boring the Mountain, finally convinced the Governor and his council that the Tunnel was no longer a dream. As a result, they directed Benjamin Frost to move forward with building the railroad to North Adams and thus eliminate the pit situation at the west end. During the summer, after Frost established the location of the tracks, agents for the Governor and his council finally purchased the necessary land.[17] In November of 1871, when Frost invited bids for the two miles of excavation and culvert work, he received eighteen proposals. The Governor and council selected C. McClallan & Son of Chicopee, in partnership with T. M. Walker of Springfield, for the job. The $149,300 contract stipulated completion of the work before the first day of November in 1873.

Charles McClallan originally from Lancaster, Massachusetts, about eleven miles southeast of Fitchburg, had gone to Springfield in 1820 as a seventeen-year-old. There he apprenticed himself to the master mason Charles Stearns. By 1832, he had established his own company, and over the years he proceeded to build most of the mid-nineteenth-century brick buildings in Chicopee and Holyoke. His company also built a stone dam on the Chicopee River. The firm of T. M. Walker & Co. advertised itself as house painter and decorator. It was an interesting partnership for building a railroad.

Maybe the only positive news for Shanly during the first half of the year was the repair of the broken hoisting machinery at the west shaft. On 5 March, the iron shaft for transmitting power from the steam engine to the elevator drums at the west shaft had twisted in half, shattering one of the iron drums. With no operating elevator, the miners could not easily reach the work, and it was impossible to remove the excavated rock, so mining operations were halted for a month. By April, mining at the west shaft could be resumed, as there was once again an operating elevator to carry the men and to raise the broken rock from the Tunnel.[18] But Shanly seems to have had difficulty securing good-quality iron shafts for his hoisting equipment. This new shaft broke in late August, after only five months of use. But Shanly was ready with a plan to keep the miners boring into the Mountain.[19] He had his miners enter the bore by way of the small adit between the Tunnel at the bottom of the shaft and the brick arched bore from the west side of the Mountain. The miners continued to drill and blast, but the excavated rock was left to be hoisted when the hoisting engine was repaired.

At the east header, the miners made good progress throughout 1871. Shanly now had use of a small locomotive he had christened the "Gov. Claflin." Because he purchased the locomotive after the flood he had to muscle it over the Hoosac Mountain. It carried the miners into the Mountain and brought out the shattered rock. At this point in time, the tracks penetrated about four-fifths of a mile into the Mountain. But at the header beyond the track, the faithful mules still had to drag the dump cars to the locomotive.[20] While a bottom header was now being used on the east side of the mountain, the top header approach was continued on the west side of the Mountain.

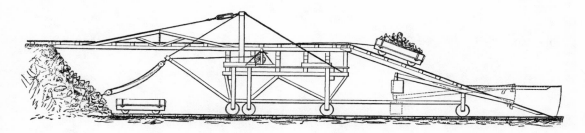

Carriage arrangement at the west end to move blasted rock from the top bench[21]

A rough tramway ran out to the high bank above the Deerfield River, and the dump cars unloaded the broken rock on the brink of the river. This pile of rock was slowly pushing itself farther out into the waters of the Deerfield.[22] Shanly was also using the Deerfield River railroad bridge he had completed in 1869 and dumping broken rock on the far side of the river to build the railroad embankment needed there.[23]

Half a mile downriver, on the north bank at the end of the railroad from Greenfield, stood the Hoosac Tunnel Station. Three small hotels[24] had sprung up around the station for travelers and Tunnel visitors. Travelers who wanted to go farther west would board a stage for the trip over the Mountain to North Adams.

The stage crossed over the Deerfield River on a wagon bridge and proceeded along the old road in the direction of the Tunnel. At the bend in the Deerfield River, stage riders had a good view of the little octagonal superintendent's building. If they looked west toward the Hoosac Mountain, they could glimpse a small stone survey station (or alignment tower) built by Doane. This survey station was centered directly on the line of the Tunnel. The woods above the Tunnel still retained the slashed line Doane's surveyors had cut through the Hoosac Mountain forest years earlier. A traveler who turned and looked to the east would have seen another survey tower high above the Deerfield River on Rowe's Neck, the mountain immediate to the east. Because this tower was perched on the edge of an almost vertical cliff, it was of a different configuration but still of sturdy construction, as it was vital to the surveyors' work of maintaining the Tunnel alignment.

Alignment tower, east bore.

Superintendent's office, east bore

If a visitor desired to see the central shaft, the *Boston Daily Globe* recommended following the surveyor's path up the Mountain: "There is no difficulty in finding or in keeping it." The writer, who used the nom de plume "Flaneur" (French for "stroller"), did warn the adventurous hiker that "the hill is steep in some places, nearly perpendicular in others, level in none."[25]

The superintendent's building was probably occupied at this time by Augustus Woodbury Locke, who was Frost's assistant engineer in charge of the

eastern division of the Tunnel until the heading from the east side met the bore
from the central shaft. Locke was from Rye, New Hampshire, a small town on
the Boston Post Road, which connected Boston to Maine. After being educated
in academies in his home state, he spent a year and a half in the U.S. Navy as a
seaman before attending Massachusetts Institute of Technology. Prior to joining
Frost, he served in the United States Coastal Survey. Consequently, Locke was a
very qualified surveyor. He would later stay on in North Adams and become the
manager of the Troy and Greenfield Railroad and Hoosac Tunnel.[26]

The *Boston Daily Globe* announced there was no difficulty in obtaining
permission from the superintendent, near the Tunnel mouth, to go in on the
debris train.[27] The paper failed to mention that sitting on the broken rocks during
the exit journey was not very comfortable. Still, many travelers took the time to
don a slicker and rubber boots for an adventure into the yawning black hole. In
the heat of summer, the cool atmosphere of the Tunnel, fifty-four degrees, was
welcoming, but many timid souls quickly returned to the sunlight, having been
terrified by the unearthly clangor, the ghoulish voices, and the black gloom.[28]

Those ghoulish voices came from the miners driving their Burleigh drills
into the very heart of the Mountain. These brawny English, French Canadian,
and Irish miners were clustered on and about two huge iron drill-carriers. Now
Shanly was attaching six drills like hydra heads to each carrier. A miner with
his drill clamped securely to the carrier frame aimed his heavy machine in the
appointed direction. The drill holes were driven in a pattern designed to produce
the best breakage of the rock. After the rock from the previous blast was cleared
away, the carriers were pushed up against the rock face of the Mountain and
positioned in the proper location. Before the Burleigh drills began their rattle,
screw grippers running through the carrier were rotated so the gripper on the
end of the screw pressed tightly against the surrounding rock. With the screw
grippers set firmly against the roof and floor of the Mountain, the carrier would
not move when its drills beat on the rock of the mountain and created the needed
blast holes. The cylinder of the Burleigh machines drove the drill steel against
the rock so hard that Shanly had to purchase three tons of drill steel each month
to replace what these machines consumed.[29] Blacksmiths stationed at the east
end, the central shaft, and the west shaft were kept constantly busy sharpening
blunted drill steel until the steel was too short for use in the drills. Once all
the blast holes were completed, the carrier grippers were released and the drill-
carriers were pushed back a safe distance.

With the rock face cleared, brave men with their cans of nitro-glycerin went forward to load the holes. Counting all the locations of mining work, Shanly was using three tons of Mowbray's soup each month to carve his way through the Mountain.[30] When everything was ready, the charges of nitro-glycerin were fired and the bowels of the Mountain trembled. After the terrifying noise, there was a cloud of smoke and dust, but soon the eight-inch-diameter ventilation pipe supplied sufficient air to drive out the smoke and let the miners resume their work.[31]

Monster Machines

The four-inch pump installed by the Commonwealth, and the equipment Shanly installed later, quickly proved inadequate when the westward-boring miners struck the rock vein literally bursting with water. So once the flood overwhelmed the pump, Shanly was compelled to increase the pumping capacity at the shaft. But there were no large pumps readily available in North Adams, so securing such pumps, delivering them to the Tunnel, and completing the installation of these monster machines took time—four long months.

Finally, on 7 August, two Cornish pumps with eleven-inch plungers and three feet of stroke were firmly set on the pump foundations built by the Commonwealth years earlier. The pump rod for these pumps reached the full 1,028 feet to the bottom of the shaft and weighed twenty-six tons. The weight was so great the rod had to be partly balanced at the top by a counterweight of stacked iron weighing thirteen tons.

One of the two pumps was slightly larger than the other. It had a ten-inch-diameter pipe to raise the water. The smaller pump had a seven-inch pipe.[32] Each pump was really several pumps on one rod, raising the water to the surface in four lifts of 250 feet each from tanks sited on the rebuilt platforms in the shaft. These pumps did ten strokes a minute. When the fifteen-foot-di-ameter drive wheel for the pumps was set in motion, the monsters began the process of lifting water from the bottom of the shaft. But after just one day, the old pump foundations constructed by the Commonwealth started to crumble.[33] Before the pumps could vibrate themselves into a mass of useless pieces, Shanly had to suspend the removal of water.

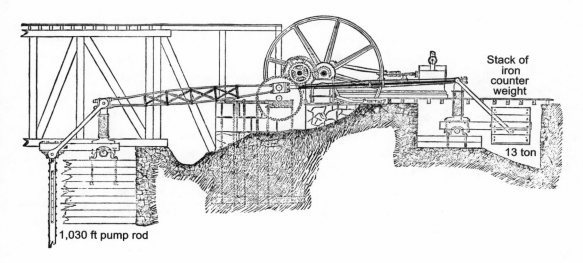

Stack of
iron
counter
weight

13 ton

1,030 ft pump rod

Pumping machinery at the central shaft with 15-foot-diameter wheel[34]

A month later, the *Adams Transcript* carried a short paragraph describing the new and much larger pump foundation being built by Shanly's crews. The newspaper, probably in reference to the larger pump, described the machinery as "the great pump." The massive foundation was to be fourteen feet long, eight feet wide, and fourteen feet thick. Shanly was depending on mass to dampen the pump vibrations. The total weight of this new foundation was given as two hundred tons of masonry, with the top two and a half feet being made of granite from a quarry at Monson, Massachusetts. Monson is about sixty miles south of Deerfield, so if the granite came by train to either North Adams or the eastern end of the Tunnel, it was still necessary to haul it up the Hoosac Mountain to the central shaft.[35] The stage running from the Hoosac Tunnel depot on the east side of the Mountain to North Adams could cross the Mountain in an hour and a quarter,[36] but oxen pulling a load of granite up the slope was another matter.

On Monday, 2 October, six months after the miners struck the water-logged vein of rock west of the central shaft, Shanly again set his monster pumps to work. But once more fate intervened. After only four days, the cast-iron bearing plate under the pumps fractured, causing yet another delay. The bearing plate was replaced, but securing the iron and completing the work took almost a full month. Finally, on 31 October, the pumps were set to work lifting water from the shaft. Because of the flood and the repeated pump problems, mining at the bottom of the central shaft had been set back almost seven months.

Early on during the flooding, the old pump did at times control the accumulation of water to a limited extent, and some mining took place in the eastward direction, beginning the last week of July. Work continued through August and part of September, but the mining was suspended completely in September during construction of the new pump foundations. Shanly was constantly juggling his workforce—adding men when it was possible to mine more faces in the Tunnel, letting men go, and reassigning men to more urgent tasks. After 1 November 1871, the new pumps worked satisfactorily.[37] As the pump gained on the floodwaters, Shanly added men to the crew, and the eastward mining was resumed once more in late November. Finally, in December, he added still more miners and resumed the attack on the rock veins west of the central shaft. During 1871, the men working at the bottom of the shaft had managed to excavate a total of 277 feet eastward and 153 feet into the water-filled vein to the west.[38]

Argument

Engineer Benjamin Frost failed to comprehend the water situation, remarking in his report to the Joint Standing Committee on the Troy and Greenfield Railroad and Hoosac Tunnel for the year 1871:

> *The delays of the past year show the urgent importance of forthwith undertaking a provision of additional pumping machinery with capacity sufficient to remove the increased flow of water now anticipated in the further progress of the excavation.*

During the year of water problems in the central shaft, a very strained relationship developed between Frost and Shanly, because Frost continued to push Shanly about the requirements in the contract for him to mine both eastward and westward from the central shaft at prescribed monthly rates. Frost wanted the miners to persist in the effort to bore into the Mountain's water-filled rock veins west of the central shaft, and Shanly refused to take the risk of being flooded out and losing the opportunity to at least mine to the east. Shanly's evaluation of Frost three years earlier during the contract negotiations had not been favorable, but now the clear-eyed Canadian had to restrain himself. Even though Shanly had spent large sums of money lifting water instead of rock up the 1,028-foot central shaft, Frost still wanted him to persist in efforts to bore into the water-filled rock west of the shaft. Shanly later asserted that the pumping had cost him "$10,000 a month" for twenty months.[39]

Walter and Frank Shanly had accepted the risk of a lump-sum contract, based on the accuracy of the measurements and calculations Frost had made of the quantities of work to be performed. During the contract negotiations in December 1868, when Shanly was asked whether he "would accept the engineers' measurements" and take the contract for a single fixed amount, he at once assented—"provided the engineers, Messrs. Latrobe and Frost, then present would assure [him] that the quantities had been carefully and accurately ascertained."[40] As an engineer, Shanly understood the difficulty of fixing the exact quantities of rock to be excavated. Measurements could not be taken at every foot of Tunnel length, but by common practice they are taken at some fixed distance, such as 25-, 50-, or 100-foot intervals—so there are always errors in the computations introduced by differences at locations between the points measured. Shanly was well aware that some of these errors would be in his favor while others would favor the Commonwealth.[41] If the measurements by the engineer happened to fall where the Tunnel had not been cut to the full dimension, the calculations would indicate more rock removal for the contractor. But perhaps at an intermediate point where no measurements were taken, the true condition was overexcavation of the Tunnel dimensions, so the contractor would not have to drill and blast the quantity of rock calculated by the engineer. These are the random errors common to engineering practice.

Shanly expected, however, that the measurements were carefully determined, and he had asked at the meeting whether that was true. One of his first encounters with the sloppiness of Frost's measurements came when it was discovered that Shanly would have to construct the central drain from the east portal. Frost had certified that the drain was properly constructed for a certain distance and no work would be required. But the drain was not built as stated, and Shanly, to meet the requirements of his contract, had to deepen and correct previous work executed by the Commonwealth.[42] Apparently the drain had been covered with broken rock and other debris, so Frost had not made a close inspection of it to verify whether it was constructed per the Tunnel plan.

Later, members of a Senate Committee on Claims would write: "It further appears to our satisfaction that during the prosecution of this work the course of the engineers of the Commonwealth towards the contractors was not such as the latter were entitled to expect."[43] Under questioning by the senators, Walter Shanly, ever the gentleman, clearly stated how Frost had approached the tunneling of the Hoosac:

> *I would prefer not to have had the question asked me, but as it has been asked, I will answer it. I always felt—I always was made to feel—this: "You have got to follow that specification. Fail in the tunnel, if you*

*will; but if you do, you must not fail in carrying out the specification."
That was what was always dinned into me. "You must follow that
specification, even if it should be destructive of the ultimate progress of
the tunnel."*[44]

Now Frost, with Edward Philbrick standing firmly behind him but in
the background, threatened Shanly with the withholding of contract payments
if the contractor did not proceed with mining into the water-filled vein of rock
west of the central shaft.

The central shaft was an oval twenty-seven feet long, with a width of
only fifteen feet. Within its curved perimeter, there was only 318 square feet of
open space. The surveyor Carl Wederkinch, to maintain the line of the Tunnel
for the miners, regularly made his descent to the bottom of the shaft in the
bucket and fully understood the physical space limitations. But Frost, judging
from his comments and reports, seems to have lacked an appreciation for the
space required to support all of the operations necessary to drive the Tunnel
bores into the Mountain. If miners were to descend the shaft and work, it was
necessary to supply them with air and to control the water seeping into the shaft.
There were pipes for compressed air to drive the drills, and provide ventilation
air, and more pipes for pumping water. There were the pump rods and the tanks
on the platforms. And still Frost wanted more! Had he forgotten about the space
necessary for the rock-removal buckets?

The first use of this limited space was for the buckets used to remove the
blasted rock and lower the miners 1,028 feet into the forbidding pit. These dual
but not exclusive requirements controlled Shanly's approach to the work. The
huge wooden building surmounting the shaft contained steam engines for the
two pumps, five air compressors, and the hoist. The buckets required space in the
oval, as did the pump pipes and the pipes delivering air from the compressors.
There was little room to cram more pipes into the 318-square-foot space through
the rock.

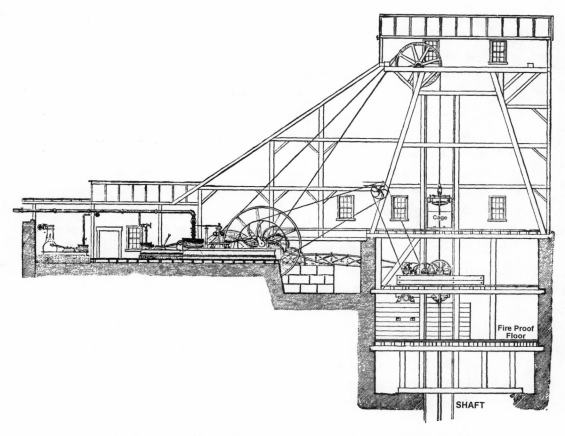

Cutaway view across the 15-foot dimension of the central-shaft machinery house, showing the gearing for the pump and the elevator[45]

In his resolute manner, Shanly would continue trying to explain that mining operations were controlled by the limited area available within the confines of the shaft, but Engineer Frost was blinded by the contract specifications, which dictated rates of progress for boring into the Mountain in both an east and a west direction from the bottom of the central shaft. He remained adamant that the contractor had to meet those specifications.

In February of 1874, after it was all over, Shanly testified before the Committee of the General Court on the Hoosac Tunnel concerning the issue of trying to bore westward: "We made an effort to proceed, working in that rock, but finally abandoned it in May [1871]. We concluded to put in very large pumps, to enable us to work eastward, but found the central shaft would not be sufficient for the pumps that would be necessary to remove the water, were we to continue working westward."[46]

It seemed many could only see problems, and there were always problems for those who attempted to bore the Hoosac Mountain. Nevertheless, 1871 was a year of significant progress. Even with all the delays in mining from the bottom of the central shaft, the total linear feet of heading for the year was 3,553 feet—almost twice the distance covered in 1869. Over on the more troublesome west side of the Mountain, where B. N. Farren had previously completed 931 feet of brick-arched tunnel for the Commonwealth, Shanly completed an additional 1,043½ feet during the year. By the quantities expressed in the bid documents, Shanly had to do only 227½ feet more of brick arching before the "porridge stone" problem would finally be put to rest. At the end of 1871, even the pessimistic Frost was predicting daylight through the Mountain by April of 1874.

In October 1871, with optimism about the Tunnel's eventual completion running high, friendlier folks from Boston visited Saratoga, New York, to advocate for a railroad line westward from the Hoosac Tunnel. Alvah Crocker's ally Elias H. Derby attended the meeting, proclaiming to all how Boston capitalists were confident a railroad via Oswego and the Shore Line could compete with any other line. He noted the probability of completion of the Hoosac Tunnel in 1873 and the great advantage of Boston as a harbor for commerce with Europe.[47]

While some made predictions and others made proposals, the miners toiled on, braving the dangers of boring through the Mountain. The stalwart men still seemed to be maimed or killed with regularity. In mid-October, a miner named Terry Columbus met instant death while attempting to "pick out" a charge that had failed to explode. His coworker Reuben Bottrell, standing a few paces back, was seriously injured by the explosion.[48]

The year closed with Alvah Crocker, who was in Europe on holiday, being elected to the U.S. Congress on the Republican ticket.[49] Crocker would finish the unexpired term of William B. Washburn, who had resigned his seat to become Governor of Massachusetts. Congressman Crocker was slated to take his seat in the Forty-Second Congress on 2 January 1872.

Perseverance

On 1 January 1872, there remained 2,721 feet of Hoosac Mountain rock between Shanly's miners boring the east header westward from the Deerfield River and those toiling to meet them from the central shaft.[50] The Deerfield would maintain an unusually constant flow during that year, keeping the turbine wheels

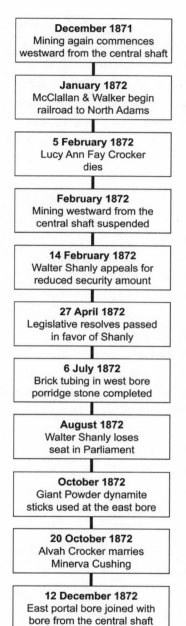

December 1871
Mining again commences
westward from the central shaft

January 1872
McClallan & Walker begin
railroad to North Adams

5 February 1872
Lucy Ann Fay Crocker
dies

February 1872
Mining westward from the
central shaft suspended

14 February 1872
Walter Shanly appeals for
reduced security amount

27 April 1872
Legislative resolves passed
in favor of Shanly

6 July 1872
Brick tubing in west bore
porridge stone completed

August 1872
Walter Shanly loses
seat in Parliament

October 1872
Giant Powder dynamite
sticks used at the east bore

20 October 1872
Alvah Crocker marries
Minerva Cushing

12 December 1872
East portal bore joined with
bore from the central shaft

driving and the air compressors turning, and thus providing the air necessary for all the drills at the east bore.[51] This reduced Shanly's cost for driving the east header, as wood to fire the steam engines did not have to be purchased, but still money would be a problem for the contractor. At the central shaft, the boilers driving the pumps and the hoist were consuming six hundred cords of wood per month.[52]

Confidence in Shanly's ability to complete the Tunnel caused the *Report of the Joint Standing Committee on the Troy and Greenfield Railroad and the Hoosac Tunnel for 1872* to include a statement about additional work needed to complete a through-line railroad from the Hoosac Tunnel Station on the east side of the mountain to North Adams. The question of controlling the flow of the Cascade Brook—and the need to permanently divert the brook from the Tunnel and the railroad embankment connecting the Tunnel portal with the railroad bridge across the Deerfield River—was another critical item the committee report addressed. After the flood of 1869, Shanly had built barriers to confine the brook. However, his temporary rails for dumping waste rock from the Tunnel did not follow the line of the permanent railroad, and his barriers would have to be removed to allow for grading the permanent roadbed.

Alvah Crocker, the driving force behind the Hoosac Tunnel, should have been celebrating the contractor's success in driving the Tunnel, but his wife of twenty-one years was desperately ill. Lucy Ann Fay Crocker had been sick for some time, and by January 1872 her life was "despaired of," so Crocker, instead of traveling to Washington to take his seat in the U.S. Congress, remained in Fitchburg to comfort her. Her health had been the main reason for their trip to Europe. She expired on Monday, 5 February. So, for the second time, Crocker was a widower.

Thomas Doane, the former chief engineer, returned to North Adams in March 1872 to visit friends in the village. Since leaving the Tunnel, Doane had gone west to build railroads in Iowa and Nebraska for the ex-Tunnel commissioner John Brooks. Following completion of the Burlington and Missouri River Railroad through Crete, Nebraska, Doane had taken up residence in the new town. Like Shanly, he was a favorite in North Adams, and the town gave him a cordial welcome.[53]

An Appeal

On Wednesday, 14 February, Walter Shanly appeared before the Joint Standing Committee on the Troy and Greenfield Railroad and the Hoosac Tunnel to request a reduction in the amount of funds the Commonwealth held as security for the completion of the Tunnel. He was represented before the committee by Charles Allen, the former attorney general of Massachusetts. Allen, an 1847 graduate of Harvard, was from Greenfield, where he practiced law until 1862. As a result, he was well acquainted with the financial and political struggles of all who attempted to bore a Tunnel through the Hoosac Mountain.

Under the terms of the Shanlys' Hoosac Tunnel contract, the first $500,000 of earnings were retained by the Commonwealth as security for the completion of the Tunnel. Additionally, the Commonwealth retained 20 percent of all pay estimates after the brothers had earned $2,500,000 of the contract amount. By the first day of 1872, the contract earnings were $2,059,971.[54] Therefore, Shanly could expect at some point in 1872 to have total earnings greater than $2,500,000, and the Commonwealth would begin to withhold 20 percent of his future earnings in addition to the half a million dollars it was already holding as security. In fact, based on what he did eventually earn in 1872, the Commonwealth withheld $77,206[55] in addition to the $500,000. Like Herman Haupt before him, Walter Shanly struggled monthly to find the funds needed to pay the bills and keep the work going. The cost of pumping water at the central shaft, in particular, was a severe drain on his financial resources, an expense he had not anticipated.

Allen pleaded with the committee to reduce the security held by the Commonwealth to $350,000. He stressed three events, which he called "unforeseen obstacles," as having caused Shanly to spend much more money than anticipated and to leave him "crippled for means."[56] These unforeseen obstacles were: the flood of 1869, forcing the expenditure of extra funds for the removal of the debris from the west bore; the lack of water in the Deerfield River in 1871, forcing the use of steam power to keep the compressors running (the boilers consumed many a cord of expensive wood); and the floods from the rock vein at the central shaft, with the tremendous cost of pumping water out of a 1,028-foot-deep shaft. The combination of these circumstances had embarrassed Shanly financially and left him with little ready cash to maintain the work.

Consulting Engineer Philbrick appeared before the Committee and criticized Shanly's command of the tunneling operations. He took issue with the work of trimming the Tunnel to the required finish dimensions and the tardiness of Shanly's performance in excavating at all the points required by the contract. In February, after mining about eighty-five feet westward from the central shaft into another water-filled vein, Shanly, fearful of completely flooding the work at the bottom of the central shaft, suspended all attempts to continue mining to the west.[57] Philbrick's comments were, therefore, a continuation of the argument about not mining west from the central shaft. Allen, in response, pointed out that at other points the excavation was proceeding at rates greater than those in the contract. For the previous year, 1871, the work accomplished from the east face of the Hoosac was 25 percent in excess of the contract rate. Philbrick concluded his assault against the request by stating that "he did not think that they [Walter and Francis] could possibly complete the contract by October 1874—the time specified."[58] In response, Shanly stated positively that he could put additional men on as he pleased and do the work in a hurry. His words carried their usual resolute tone, and he made an excellent impression on the committee, but the legislators decided to visit the Tunnel before deciding on the matter.[59] Spring was approaching, and maybe the gentlemen simply wanted to take a train ride through what the *Boston Daily Globe* correspondent considered the most picturesque river valleys in New England, those of the Miller and Deerfield rivers.[60] The *Globe*, while describing the Deerfield Valley, called the attention of its readers to the fact that railroad engineers would, in the very near future, again try their skill at building a railroad between the river and the valley's steep rock walls.

The legislators' ride to the Tunnel would be on the Troy and Greenfield Railroad—a line that Haupt had originally built as cheaply as possible, B. N. Farren had rebuilt, and the Commonwealth had repaired after the flood of 1869. It was now generating a little revenue. The bridges were rebuilt and the route was back in service, but much still needed to be done, because the steel rails of the line wandered along precipitous ridges cut by the river without the slightest regard to the railroad's need for level ground. As Shanly neared completion of the bore, the issue of the railroad would soon gain the committee's attention—and later the attention of every politician in Massachusetts. This would become the new battleground for those who did not want to see a competing railroad from Boston to Albany.

In early April, the *Adams Transcript* pleaded Shanly's cause, giving a detailed listing of security beyond the $500,000 cash the Commonwealth was holding back pending completion of the work. The list included $200,000 worth of machinery on the ground at the east and west bores and at the central shaft; stored supplies valued at $30,000; and $20,000 of wood cut and stored for use in fueling the boilers.[61] Summing up the value of all the items listed, the *Transcript* concluded that the Commonwealth was already holding security of $750,000 in material goods and should, therefore, reduce the cash amount to $350,000.

The article claimed the Commonwealth was not paying the contractor interest on the retainage funds it held, yet the contractor had to pay interest on borrowed funds. The *Transcript*'s arguments followed those made by Haupt years earlier. Time was being wasted chasing money—time the contractor and the Commonwealth could more profitably apply to the work of boring a Tunnel through the Hoosac Mountain. The *Transcript* editor, in the last paragraph of his appeal, focused on the underlying issue. There were still factions who did not want to see the Hoosac Tunnel completed, and those with a vested interest in another railroad were making innuendos about Shanly's request.[62]

Shanly did not get all of what he wanted, but the legislature did provide some relief! It granted the Governor and his council authority to advance Shanly $100,000 from the reserve fund, "upon execution by the contractor of a mortgage to the Commonwealth" on the machinery "now owned and employed by them in the said work to secure the repayment of the same."[63]

Tunnel enemies must have had a hand in writing that resolve. While the Commonwealth was actually lending Shanly use of his own money, he was obliged to pay 5 percent interest on this "gracious" loan. It seems Edward Philbrick was also able to jab Shanly about not excavating all of the bores to the specifications of the contract. The resolve stipulated that the Governor and his council could, at their discretion, remit the reservation of the 20 percent retainage when "the contractors shall have so advanced the work as to comply with the conditions of the contract as to the rate and amount of progress and mode of construction required." Benjamin Frost acknowledged in a later report that Shanly did take the loan and execute the mortgage on his machinery. As further relief, the Commonwealth, under the resolve, issued Shanly $200,000 in interest-free certificates,[64] but he seems to have not made use of these in 1872.[65]

As with the financial problems, some things never seemed to change at the Tunnel. The accidents continued, even as hundreds of miners struggled against the Mountain. In mid-1871, Shanly had 699 men working underground and another 116 on the surface in support of the miners.[66] On 29 February 1872 (a leap year), there was another accident at the central shaft. Eighteen-year-old John McCann was killed by the accidental discharge of some nitro-glycerin. He was the shaker holding the steel drill against a rock as two other miners, Joseph Donavan and Patrick Fitzgerald, pounded away with their hammers. This rock, thrown out by an earlier blast, was so massive the men had to drill a blast hole into it so a charge could be loaded and the monster broken into smaller fragments. Unbeknownst to the miners, however, the rock held an earlier borehole loaded with nitro. When their drill steel struck the cap buried in the rock, the nitro exploded, ripping off McCann's arm and shooting rock fragments into Fitzgerald's eyes. Donavan was only slightly injured.

Progress

The citizens of North Adams, who had watched the Tunnel project since Edward Serrell's first efforts in 1855, began to have a sense the work was nearing completion. Beginning in 1872, the *Adams Transcript* began to post progress reports on the first of each month. The first such report in early May 1872 offered the following statistics: east end, 131 feet; central shaft, eastward 98 feet and westward no progress; west end, 140 feet.[67]

The work of building the railroad embankment on the east side of the Deerfield River was completed in April. This embankment was wide enough for laying four railroad tracks. Shanly interpreted the contract as only requiring him to provide the material for the embankment, but Frost made him grade it. Even after this work was completed, a short length of excavation was necessary before the roadbed would reach the Hoosac Tunnel Station. Bids for performing the needed excavation were invited in September, and a contractor began work in November to complete the roadbed to the station.[68]

In May, Shanly—prodded by Frost—again attempted to mine westward from the central shaft. According to the *Transcript*, the miners achieved all of fourteen feet before giving up the effort in the face of more veins full of water.[69]

On Saturday, 6 July, a milestone was reached in tunneling the Hoosac Mountain. Hocking & Holbrook, Shanly's subcontractor, who had taken over the brick tubing work through the porridge stone (what the Irishmen called the "live ells" on the Hoosac's west flank), finished the construction of the brick tube (or arch) for the distance required by the contract specifications. Several members of the legislature attended the ceremonial event, but the placement of the last brick was reserved for Engineer Frost. At the celebration, Frost announced, "This arch is laid."[70] Soon after the ceremony, he directed Shanly to return the brickyard to the Commonwealth, which Shanly did.[71] The next month, Holbrook sold the locomotive he had used to haul brick to J. M. Dwyer. Dwyer was a subcontractor working for C. McClallan & Son and T. M. Walker. His subcontract included excavating the approach to the Tunnel from North Adams.[72] During the next year, Dwyer would discover solid rock blocking the route to the Tunnel. Haupt and Doane had battled "ells," but now Dwyer had to purchase a drill and blast his way to the Tunnel with Mowbray's nitro-glycerin. Unlike Shanly's miners working underground, Dwyer was able to use a steam shovel to load the cars hauling away the waste material.[73]

Driving the Tunnel work, dealing with Engineer Frost, and struggling continually to finance the work were tasks consuming all of Walter Shanly's attention, so it did not come as a surprise in August 1872 when he lost his seat in the Canadian Parliament.[74] His friends had pushed him into seeking the seat the first time, and while he took pleasure in participating on committees addressing engineering matters he disliked political fights. The loss did not seem to affect him, but maybe this was because he was completely absorbed in driving the Tunnel.

Shanly cared about his miners and took steps to improve safety practices, but another deadly blasting accident at the heading from the west shaft occurred in September. David E. Witto, an experienced blaster, had just loaded four holds for a blast with nitro-glycerin, but he had not yet finished connecting the charges to the battery when two of the holes exploded. The blast killed Witto and his partner, Michael Harrington. John Scolley, a lad of about fourteen, who carried steel drills for hand drilling, was close by, and flying rock shattered his left arm.[75] The thirty-eight-year-old Witto, a native of Cornwall, England, left a wife and six children. What pieces of his body the men could find were buried under an apple tree on a farm in Clarksburg, a village on the Hoosic River just northeast of North Adams. About two gallons of nitro-glycerin from the two unexploded holes drained into the fractured rock at the bottom of the Tunnel. As a warning to other miners, the location of the spilled nitro-glycerin was marked with drill holes on each side.[76]

When the *Adams Transcript* posted the Tunnel progress report for August, it announced that the miners boring westward from the east side of the Mountain could distinctly hear the drills of the miners working toward them from the central shaft. Shanly and his faithful miners, who were burning four tons of candles a month to illuminate their dreary way,[77] had now reduced the distance separating the two crews to less than seven hundred feet. In October, another sign of Tunnel success came with the renomination of Alvah Crocker to Congress. The *Adams Transcript* made a recommendation to the people of Western Massachusetts on Crocker's behalf. The paper called Alvah Crocker, the consistent advocate of the Hoosac Tunnel, "a sound, practical, business man."[78] Crocker was elected with 14,919 votes to 4,589 cast for his Democratic competitor.[79] On 20 October, Crocker married Minerva Cushing.

There was another deadly accident in October, this time at the heading for the bore on the east side of the Mountain. When one charge from a previous blast had failed to explode, the men decided it was less dangerous to drill past it instead of attempting to pick it out. But the driller, Michael Cunningham, set the drill steel too close to the unexploded charge, and it detonated. Cunningham left a wife and two children. Three other miners were severely injured by the blast.[80]

After these nitro-glycerin accidents, Shanly engaged special supervisors for the blasting work. This was yet another of his attempts to protect his miners, who continually scoffed at the dangers of their work.[81] These tragedies spurred Shanly to experiment again with other explosives. This time, he tried what miners referred to as "Giant Powder," though it was not a powder. It was more powerful than black powder but less sensitive than liquid nitro-glycerin.[82] Giant Powder was a nitro-glycerin paste in a cartridge: dynamite.[83] Julius Bandmann established his Giant Powder Works in 1867 and began producing cartridges of dynamite in 1868 at an establishment in Rock House Gulch in San Francisco's Mission District. When the plant blew up a year later, he moved to a site in the sand dunes south of what is now Golden Gate Park.

These dynamite cartridges seemed to be more sensitive to electric firing, giving them an advantage. Because of the favorable results, Shanly continued to use Giant Powder cartridges during November and December, with increased rates of progress in boring the Mountain. But Giant Powder had one disadvantage: it took about twenty minutes to clear the Tunnel of the fumes, and the clearing was only achieved by running all the air compressors at full discharge.[84]

Misfires and accidental explosions of nitro-glycerin were not the only threats to life around the Tunnel work sites in the late fall of 1872. Scarlet fever was raging through the cluster of miners' homes surrounding the central shaft, with forty cases reported in November.[85] Even Benjamin Frost was susceptible to accidents. In early December, while driving over the Mountain, his sleigh got away from him and was demolished in the resulting crash. The engineer, however, escaped without serious injury.[86]

Amazing Accomplishment

The junction between the bore from the east side of the Hoosac Mountain at the Deerfield River and the eastward bore from the central shaft was finally achieved on 12 December 1872.[87] For several days before the linkage was accomplished, the miners could clearly hear one another on each side of the separating rock wall. To protect themselves in case a blast on the opposite side should shatter the wall, they arranged a set of code signals for indicating when a blast would be fired. On 10 December, to further eliminate the danger, Walter Shanly established an operational plan for executing the junction. The men working the east heading, which was being driven at the bottom and about seven feet high for the full width, were to continue drilling and blasting. The miners on the central shaft side were to stop blasting. On Wednesday, 11 December, it was thought the rock wall was about fourteen feet thick, so Shanly ordered the drilling of a hole eighteen feet deep. The hole did not let air through, and an attempt with a slightly longer drill was similarly unsuccessful. Shanly was personally supervising the operation. He first went to the east header and could distinctly hear every blow from the other side. He then left the header and went to the central shaft. With a reporter from the *Chicago Daily Tribune* tagging along, he descended to the Tunnel. Afterward, the reporter wrote about the ride to the bottom of the shaft: "You go down as if you were a stone dropped from the hand."[88]

On Thursday, 12 December, the work continued. A blast was fired at about 11:30 in the morning, but the rock wall remained. The next blast created cracks, allowing the miners to pass a stick through from one heading to the other. While the miners prepared the next blast, Shanly and the reporter ascended to the pure air of the mountaintop to have their mid-day meal. Afterward, they descended to the bottom of the shaft just as the final blast was fired. This blast created a hole through which the faces of the gnomes on the other side appeared. A few blows of a hammer enlarged the opening, and a lad named John Harrigan dropped through to receive shouts and cheers from the men. Timothy Buckley followed almost immediately and was cheered as heartily as Harrigan had been. This lively celebration occurred at four o'clock in the afternoon. Immediately afterward, the reporter and Shanly returned to North Adams.[89] Once the opening was made, the central shaft acted like an immense chimney, producing a strong draft through the length of the eastern section of the Tunnel.[90]

Everyone was thrilled about the achievement, but the *Adams Transcript* did not report any special celebration. Four days later, the *Boston Daily Globe* announced: "[C]ontractors quarreled and false prophets insisted in the newspapers that the project never could be and never would be carried out." The editor of the paper probably was grinning as he wrote that the news "was received with a feeling of intense gratification, not only in the immediate locality, but throughout the Commonwealth. The completion of that portion of the task, though the labor of months yet remains to be accomplished, is the virtual crowning of the work."[91]

Heretofore, water was lifted more than 1,028 feet up the central shaft, but now, with the joining of the two headers, it would only have to be raised about twelve feet[92] over the high point of the tunnel below the shaft. Once over the high point, gravity would carry it through the east portal and into the Deerfield River.[93] This was just a joining of headers, and the miners still had considerable work to bring the Tunnel to its completed shape and grade, but Shanly's persistence in the face of criticism by Frost had relieved him of a great cost and the risk of the Tunnel's being flooded beyond his pumps' capacity. Shanly, as he had promised, immediately set a crew of miners to work excavating westward from the central shaft, and they progressed twenty feet into the wet rock before the end of 1872.

Edward Philbrick sent a letter to the editor of the *Boston Daily Advertiser*, praising the excellence of the survey work in guiding the miners to a successful meeting of the two bores. He commended no individual by name, but he attributed the successful joining to "the persistent industry of the engineering corps." While failing to mention Carl Wederkinch by name, he vividly described the conditions under which the engineer had repeatedly conducted his surveys with endless patience amid falling rocks and suffocating smoke, surrounded by the most depressing circumstances of danger, darkness, filth, and monotony. Philbrick may well have been describing his own personal distaste for venturing into the Tunnel. He closed by saying that the engineers working in the dark of the bores had "none of the exhilaration which attends ordinary field work in the open air."[94]

Joined by Frost and other Tunnel engineers, Philbrick had spent a day connecting the Tunnel survey lines, planning to make whatever modifications might be required. He therefore claimed to be the first person to measure the discrepancy between the survey lines from the central shaft and the east portal. The lateral difference between the two lines was just five-sixteenths of an inch, an amazing accomplishment! Having less than twenty-three feet of distance to fix a direction, and twenty-plus feet at the bottom of a smoky pit just over a thousand feet in depth, Wederkinch had managed to determine an almost perfect line from the central shaft.

A check of the vertical lines for the grade of the Tunnel against the levels run by Frost over the Hoosac Mountain in 1870 yielded a similar degree of accuracy. The vertical error was one-tenth of a foot, or 1.2 inches.

Philbrick gloried in this engineering wonder and could attribute it to the engineers as a group, but he lacked the capacity to praise the individual. Wederkinch, whom Shanly often praised for persistence and for being present when needed in the Tunnel, received not a mention in Philbrick's letter to the *Boston Daily Advertiser.* Similarly, Thomas Doane, the engineer who had established the survey line over the Hoosac Mountain and built the essential alignment towers for permanently referencing the line, received no credit for the accomplishment. With great care, Doane had established permanent line markers at each portal. The one at the east portal was in a very solid thirteen-foot-square building with lime masonry walls on a dry masonry foundation.[95] Pictures show the one at the west portal as being protected by a wooden building, which may have been the result of the original alignment tower's being destroyed when the commissioners decided to do an open cut into the Mountain and start the Tunnel farther to the east. The easternmost lining tower was on Rowe's Neck, the ridge across the Deerfield River and to the east of the Hoosac Mountain. The exact type and configuration of this control point was not reported. Moving westward from the Deerfield River, the next three mountaintop towers were all of the same design and construction as the one at the east portal. These were located on Whitcomb Hill, the east summit of the Hoosac Mountain; Spruce Hill, the west summit of the Hoosac Mountain; and Notch Mountain, across the valley to the west of the Hoosac Mountain. At the central shaft, there was a stone table on the centerline of the Tunnel. The transit used by engineers, dressed in suits and ties, for establishing the centerline across the central shaft was mounted on this sturdy table. Because the building over the shaft was missing a board or two, it was possible to sight through the structure to one of the two towers on the Hoosac summits and take a backsight on the other.

Stone transit table at the central shaft (courtesy of The State Library of Massachusetts)

Railroad to North Adams

McClallan & Son and Walker were making good progress grading the railroad to North Adams. Nevertheless, they, like everyone else who attempted to work on the grand project, met the unexpected. In their case, the problem was the approach cut to the west portal, where the material they encountered delayed their work, and even Engineer Frost described it as being unfavorable.[96] At the end of the year, Frost remarked that he expected McClallan & Son and Walker to complete the excavation into Shanly's pit at the west end long before the need for it would arise. But Frost was thinking in terms of building the railroad to North Adams and not about the fact that Shanly's subcontractor Holbrook had to remove material via the old Haupt tunnel. Since 1869, when Shanly began work, the old Haupt tunnel had twice been blocked, and each blockage delayed Shanly's mining of the west bore.

By June of 1872, McClallan & Son and Walker had nearly completed two of the required masonry arched culverts between the Tunnel and North Adams. In addition, they had the steam shovel owned by J. M. Dwyer[97] working its way into Ives Hill. The gangs supporting the shovel were carting the excavated material to a lower meadow to construct the embankment toward North Adams.[98]

All of this work was only for grading the roadbed for a single-track railroad. At the end of the year, a committee of the General Court would advise the Senate of the need for a further appropriation to grade the line for a second track, to construct the bridge superstructures, and to provide and lay the rails. The Committee followed this modest counsel with one of even greater importance. The members alerted the legislature and the Governor about the need to establish a method for the "ultimate control and management" of the nearly forty-four miles of railroad the Commonwealth would own in the very near future. The completion of the Hoosac Tunnel would give Massachusetts unrestricted ownership of a railroad extending from Greenfield to the New York border with Vermont, because title to the Southern Vermont Railroad was vested in the Commonwealth.

3,125 feet to Daylight

When Governor William Claflin left office in January 1872, William B. Washburn succeeded him. Washburn was from Winchendon, Massachusetts, a small community just to the northwest of Fitchburg. In 1858, he moved to Greenfield, where he became president of the Greenfield National Bank. Consequently, he was very familiar with the history of the Hoosac Tunnel project and the Troy and Greenfield Railroad. He had personally witnessed the legislative fights concerning the Tunnel, since he served in the Senate in the early 1850s and in the House from 1853 to 1855. His cousin Emory Washburn, as Governor of Massachusetts in 1854, signed the first Tunnel loan bill, granting the Troy and Greenfield Railroad $2 million in Commonwealth bonds.

The Governor's message to the Massachusetts legislature in early January 1873 contained only praise for "the contractors" who had opened "the Hoosac Tunnel from the eastern portal to the Central Shaft."[99] So that no uncertainty

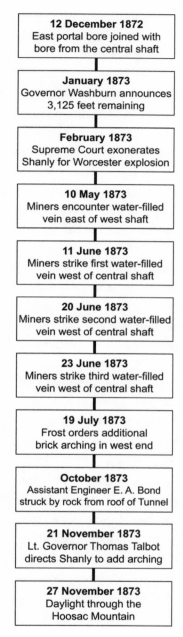

12 December 1872
East portal bore joined with bore from the central shaft

January 1873
Governor Washburn announces 3,125 feet remaining

February 1873
Supreme Court exonerates Shanly for Worcester explosion

10 May 1873
Miners encounter water-filled vein east of west shaft

11 June 1873
Miners strike first water-filled vein west of central shaft

20 June 1873
Miners strike second water-filled vein west of central shaft

23 June 1873
Miners strike third water-filled vein west of central shaft

19 July 1873
Frost orders additional brick arching in west end

October 1873
Assistant Engineer E. A. Bond struck by rock from roof of Tunnel

21 November 1873
Lt. Governor Thomas Talbot directs Shanly to add arching

27 November 1873
Daylight through the Hoosac Mountain

could remain as to what was about to happen, Washburn told the legislature and the gallery of onlookers that Shanly would penetrate the remaining 3,125 feet of rock before the end of the year. The Governor followed this good news with a warning about the need to bring the railroad from Greenfield up to standard so the Commonwealth could "obtain the business naturally coming to the seaboard by way of the Tunnel."[100] The Commonwealth would soon have to decide how it would operate its Tunnel. Washburn noted that the funds for building the Tunnel were drawn from the public treasury, and, therefore, every railroad should be allowed to intersect through it on a fair and equitable basis. Before Shanly even achieved daylight through the Mountain, a new Hoosac Tunnel political fight emerged about who would control passage through the Tunnel.

While the Mountain kept the temperature in the Tunnel in the mid-fifties, many a Tunnel workman had frozen to death in the bitter winter cold above ground, but on 6 January, the cold caused a different kind of accident. The engine and the tender of the morning train from the Hoosac Tunnel Station to Shelburne Falls were thrown from the track by ice that coated the steel rails. The engineer and the fireman went down a twenty-foot bank with the steel horse, but fortunately the passenger cars remained on the track and no one suffered serious injury.[101]

By early 1873, the news stories in the *Adams Transcript* were all excitement about completion of the Tunnel. As in the previous year, the paper published progress reports in the first edition of each month. On 6 February, the paper announced that 2,832 feet remained to be completed, "being 192 feet more than half-a-mile."[102]

The same edition of the *Transcript* carried a story about the replacement of the wire ropes at the central shaft. Consulting Engineer Philbrick continually attacked Walter Shanly for not organizing the work and for not being prepared for "the expected," especially in the case of the water-filled rock veins. Yet the facts published in the *Adams Transcript* repeatedly contradict Philbrick's testimony before legislative committees. Shanly had replaced the old Commonwealth pumps at the central shaft and he had attempted to improve blasting safety by employing special supervisors. Now, not only did he replace the wire rope, but he imported high-quality wire rope from England. During the last week of January, the workmen placed two steel wire ropes of more than 1,000 feet on the hoisting drums at the central shaft. While the ropes were being replaced, however, the miners were obliged to make the 1,028-foot ascent and descent on the ladders between the platforms in the shaft.[103]

More good news came in early February, when the Supreme Court of Massachusetts rendered its decision in the suit by the Boston and Albany Railroad against Walter Shanly and others for damages caused by the dualin explosion at Worcester in 1870. Shanly was exonerated. Dittmar and Burkhardt, manufacturers of the dualin, and the Oriental Powder Company, manufacturers of the electric fuses, were found jointly liable.[104]

Although the final outcome of the suit exonerated Shanly, accidents with explosive materials continued at the Tunnel. On Monday, 17 February, some nitro-glycerin that had spilled the previous September in the west bore detonated when the miners set off a blast twenty feet from the spot. The nitro-glycerin, lying hidden in the broken rock, was left from the accident that had killed David E. Witto. No one was hurt by the sudden explosion, but it did tear up about thirty feet of the track used by the muck-removal cars.

Like the nitro blasts shattering the rock of the Hoosac Mountain, Governor Washburn's address to the legislature in January had shattered political thinking across the Commonwealth. The troubling question centered on control of the Tunnel route: Should several railroads in the Commonwealth be consolidated to assume control of the Tunnel? Everyone understood this to mean the consolidation of Crocker's two railroads—the Fitchburg and the Vermont and Massachusetts—with the Troy and Greenfield. Such a consolidation would provide a through line from Boston to New York by way of the Tunnel. The *Worcester Spy*, published on the home turf of the Boston and Albany Railroad, made a rather bold and untrue statement: "The state never expended a dollar on the Western Railroad." The *Spy* continued, arguing that the Commonwealth "assumed the whole work on the tunnel and has spent millions. It is state work, done for the benefit of the whole State, and the State should not part with its control."[105]

As Shanly stood on the verge of completing the Tunnel through the Hoosac Mountain, politicians and commercial interests in Massachusetts were slowly awaking to a looming change in railroad access to the West. As this fact became evident, it is not known whether Oliver Wendell Holmes ordered his ascension robe. He had published another volume of his Breakfast Table series, *The Poet of the Breakfast Table*, the previous year. It contained some of his usual clever remarks, such as: "The sound of a kiss is not so loud as that of a cannon, but its echo lasts a great deal longer."

No longer did anyone claim a Tunnel could not be driven through the Hoosac Mountain. Even as the new political fight over the Tunnel brewed, Shanly remained steady in his management of the work. With the joining of the two east-section headers, the number of miners at the east end was reduced from 300 to 190. While there was still enlargement work to be completed in the east section, major mining in the Tunnel was now limited to the two headers seeking to find each other somewhere in the west section. One header had miners working westward from the central shaft and the other was being mined eastward from the west shaft. As February wore on, Shanly moved part of the machinery from the machine shop at the east end to the central shaft and discharged five machinists.[106]

But even enlargement work was dangerous. On the same day as the nitro-glycerin accident in the west bore, a stone fell from the ceiling of the east bore, striking Jeremiah Leary and breaking his skull and a leg. He was carried to his boarding place, where he died the next day.

Another Argument

As the cold winds and freezing temperatures of winter departed the Mountain, Shanly's miners continued to make good progress. The Burleigh drills were unrelenting in their pounding of the rock in front of both the central shaft and the west shaft headers. But on Saturday, 10 May, the miners driving the heading from the west shaft opened an immense pocket of water. The trapped water emerged from the rock with such force that it surged forty-three feet in a stream almost twelve inches in diameter.[107] The miners were driven from the work, but in the west bore there was no need to pump water up a shaft. Slowly the flow diminished as the water found its way out of the Tunnel via the central drain and then poured through Haupt's old tunnel to the Hoosic River.

A week later, the miners were able to return to their drills and resume work. The delay caused by the flood slowed the progress for the month of May, but when the *Adams Transcript* gave its report in early June, the distance between the two headers was only 1,664 feet.[108] In the five months since Governor Washburn's speech, Shanly's miners had closed the gap by 1,461 feet.

Many distinguished engineers had been associated with the Tunnel over the years, but now, with success so near, the Hoosac Tunnel became a work of special interest to engineering professionals. Periodicals such as the *Journal of the Franklin Institute*, the *Manufacturer and Builder*, and railroad-specific journals were publishing monthly reports on the progress of Shanly's Hoosac miners. As a result of this interest from the professionals, engineering students at Rensselaer Polytechnic Institute in Troy, New York, visited the Tunnel in May.

When the Tunnel's two bores on the eastern side of the Mountain were joined, about 1,000 feet of bench rock remained to be removed east of the central shaft. This bench was a result of the way Shanly had directed the miners to excavate the header eastward from the shaft at a slight upward angle so that water would flow to the sump below the central shaft. Removal of this bench was completed on 12 June, and water then flowed naturally from the high point of the Tunnel at the bottom of the central shaft eastward to the Deerfield River.[109] This milestone finally eliminated the need to pump water from the Tunnel. Nonetheless, the lifting engine and the compressors at the top of the central shaft were consuming about six hundred cords of wood monthly.

It was fortunate the bench no longer existed, because, on the day before the clearance was achieved, the miners driving the header westward from the central shaft struck another rock vein full of water, driving the miners from their drills until the flow dissipated. Work then resumed, but nine days later, on Friday, 20 June, another water-filled vein was struck. After that flow weakened, the miners returned to work, but a third vein was penetrated on the following Monday. This third vein released water at a rate equal to the combined flow of the previous two sources.[110] The encounters with these three water-filled rock veins proved the wisdom of Shanly's refusal the previous year to continue mining westward from the central shaft.

Possibly because of his experience with the devastating train explosion in Worcester, Shanly had issued orders forbidding the carrying of powder or nitro, the primers into which the fuses were fixed, and fuses close together. The three components necessary to fire a blast were always supposed to be transferred into the Tunnel separately and not brought into close contact until the drill holes were being prepared for a blast. The order applied to all types of explosives:

nitro-glycerin, the new Giant Powder, and the old black powder that was still used for some minor blasting. Also, because of the danger from the locomotive's sparks, which constantly fell upon the cars, the blaster (the miner responsible for loading the explosives) was supposed to place the powder on the rear car of the train. It was also the duty of the blaster to ride with the powder and watch for fires. Nevertheless, when the shift of miners entered the east end of the Tunnel at midnight on 29 June, the blaster rode on the rear car and placed forty pounds of Giant Powder no. 2 together with a dozen primers on the first car behind the locomotive.[111]

Francis Kingsley, the engineer, pulled his levers and the train loaded with explosives and miners moved forward into the black hole. But before the train reached the work area, there was a terrible explosion. Miner Stephen Brown was killed instantly; the head of Henry Ferns, a tool boy, was blown off; the body of Michael Campbell, another miner, exhibited no serious external wounds, but he was dead. Two others—Dennis McFayden, a miner, and Timothy Lynch, a boy—lived a short time but also died. The body of Francis Kingsley was thrown forward on the lever of the engine, but he somehow managed to stop the train. When they removed his mangled body, they had to tear him from the lever. Everyone expected he would soon be dead, but miraculously—minus one ear blown off by the explosion—he recovered.

Giant Powder no. 2 can burn and not explode, so the explosion was attributed to the primers placed next to the Giant Powder, as these will explode when exposed to flame. The man guilty of the carelessness was uninjured by the explosion, but he was "threatened with personal violence" by the other miners.[112] Reportedly he left the region as soon as possible.

In the spring, the builders working on the 9.3-mile-long St. Gotthard railroad tunnel in Switzerland placed an order for the Browne electric fuses now made famous at the Hoosac Tunnel. So Charles Browne, the blind fuse maker, together with his brother, Isaac, sailed for Europe in June. Supposedly it was a business trip to introduce their electric fuses to tunnel builders, but the brothers still hoped something could be done to improve Charles's sight, so they intended to visit "oculists" (ophthalmologists) in Europe.[113]

At the beginning of July, the *Adams Transcript* reported that only 1,407 feet of Mountain remained to be bored. Mining operations now seemed to be moving smoothly, and all were expecting daylight through the Mountain before the end of the year. But ever since the February death of Jeremiah Leary from a stone falling from the Tunnel ceiling, there had been increased concern about an issue Frost and Philbrick had been discussing—the need for additional arching. The first definite transmittal to Shanly of a decision for additional lengths of brick arch came in mid-July.[114]

ENGINEER'S OFFICE, HOOSAC TUNNEL,

NORTH ADAMS, MASS., July 19, 1873

Messrs. F. Shanly & Co.—I make the following approximate estimate of quantity of brick which will be required to complete the arching of the Tunnel, under your contract: —

West end section, 344 lineal feet, ... 855 M brick

East end section,   40 lineal feet, ... 106 M brick

Add allowance for waste in providing quantities at brick-yard. Mr. Holbrook, contractor of brick, informs me that he is now ready to receive your orders, and to proceed with the manufacture of brick for your use.

Yours, respectfully, Benj. D. Frost

The specifications Shanly had received in 1868 for "the work required to be done at the Hoosac Tunnel upon the Troy and Greenfield Railroad" called for the contractor to submit a bid for arching part of the Tunnel and being paid per thousand bricks laid. This requirement was included in the section addressing work at the west end. The specification had a further sentence giving the "estimated amount of bricks, four million."[115] The specifications for the eastern section were different and used the following language: "As the rock is sufficiently hard to prevent apprehensions from falls and slides, estimates will be made only of quantities within the exterior line prescribed for the Tunnel."

Later, during the contract negotiations with Governor Claflin, the distance to be arched at the west end under the Shanly contract was set at 1,270 feet, and the four million bricks were thought to be the quantity needed to complete such a length, based on a fixed thickness of arch. During the discussions with the Governor, someone questioned whether the ground might be so bad as to require an extra thickness of arch. Therefore, as a contingency, the brick quantity in the contract was increased by half a million. The contract between Shanly and the Commonwealth specified the amount of bricks as not to exceed

4,500,000. During the discussions with the Governor and his council, the added bricks were explicitly included if there was a need for a *thicker* arch. The quantity change was not envisioned based on an increased *length* of arch. Increased length of arch involved an increase in the excavation quantity, as it would be necessary to mine space for the arch. Shanly would be paid for 4,500,000 bricks, so the change was intended to reduce the risk of needing additional bricks.

The order from Engineer Frost accurately absorbed the unused portion of bricks left after the prescribed distance of arch was completed in August of 1872, when Frost had laid the last brick with his own hand. Shanly did not contest the 344 feet of additional arch at the western end of the Tunnel, and he promptly sought to procure the needed bricks. In gross terms, about 260 feet of the additional arch length directed by Frost was an extension of the arch finished in 1872. Another eighty feet of the arching was for one or two places within the limits of the west bore.[116] The making of the bricks for the west end took the rest of 1873, so the actual arching work would not be performed until 1874.

The forty feet of arching at the east end was another matter. It would require going back and enlarging the excavated Tunnel circumference by five feet. Believing that the contract did not bind him to arch outside of the west end section, Shanly would, early the next year, appeal to the General Court for relief from the order to arch the forty feet at the east end. Though it was not really relevant to his argument, he would ask why, after taking back the brickyard, the Commonwealth waited almost a year before demanding additional arching.

Consulting Engineer Philbrick, who seemed to enjoy criticizing Shanly's operations before politicians, always had rock-solid excuses and explanations for his own actions. In this case, he spoke to the committee of the General Court reviewing the arching argument early in March 1874: "There was 40 feet in the east which I always knew would require arching, a little soft section which was timbered at once when it was opened. But the Tunnel had not pierced the mountain when it was first found, and I considered there was no need of carting bricks over the mountain to arch 40 or 50 feet when, by waiting till afterwards, we could easily cart them through; it was only a month's work."[117] By his statement before the committee, it appears the man who had stated that he "had no official communications with the contractors" appeared to believe he could nonetheless plan Shanly's operations and work sequences. Philbrick issued these statements when called before the committee Shanly appealed to in February 1874 for relief from performing work beyond what he believed was required by the contract. Shanly was forced to seek relief in this manner because, on 31 October, the order to arch as directed was repeated. On 21 November, Lieutenant-Governor Thomas Talbot, in his capacity as chairman of the Hoosac Tunnel Committee of the Governor's Council, wrote to Shanly, directing him to "proceed at once with the arching that Mr. Frost had ordered in the east and west divisions" of the Tunnel.[118]

Talbot had a most interesting relationship with the Tunnel and the Tunnel engineers. In 1825, he had worked in a weaving firm in Williamsburg, Massachusetts, a small mill community below the Deerfield River and south-west of Greenfield. This coincided with the period when Loammi Baldwin was tromping through the woods of northern Massachusetts surveying a canal route from Boston to the Hudson River. The relationship became much closer in the 1850s, when Thomas Talbot and his brother Charles acquired the water rights of the defunct Middlesex Canal. In 1857, the brothers would establish their textile mill in North Billerica. The mill drew its water from a dam constructed by the elder Loammi Baldwin to provide water for his Middlesex Canal. A dispute played out in the legislature concerning this dam and the water rights drew Talbot into politics. Having served on the Governor's Council from 1864 to 1869, he should have been very familiar with the terms of the Hoosac Tunnel contract.

Whiskey, Nitro, and Falling Rocks

At the beginning of August 1873, the *Adams Transcript* reported that 1,119 feet of Tunnel remained to be opened;[119] in September, the figure was down to 868 feet.[120]

Some accidents at the Tunnel work sites had a comical air. A local paper reported that the wife of one miner sent him to buy a jug of molasses. The miner, who believed there was a better use for the money, returned home with a jug of whiskey. His wife took one whiff of the jug and then squared herself, with eyes flashing, before exclaiming, "Where's them molasses?" The miner smiled, winked pleasantly, and, waving his left hand propitiatingly, replied, "Them's they." The article concluded by saying the miner would recover, but the jug was hopelessly demoralized.[121]

An accident had proven it was safe to handle Mowbray's nitro-glycerin when it was in the frozen state, but it had to be thawed before it could be used for blasting rock. On a Thursday night in September, David Bourdon, an assistant blaster, went to the magazine at the central shaft to retrieve some nitro for a blast. At the time, the magazine contained about 630 pounds of the temperamental explosive. On that evening, the quantity he needed had already been thawed and was ready for use. What exactly happened is not known, but it was assumed that the magazine building caught fire from the lamp Bourdon carried. Evidently he realized his danger and attempted to escape. He was able to put about fifty feet of distance between himself and the magazine when the nitro exploded. The shock waves from the explosion on the Hoosac Mountain were so great that the residents of Pittsfield, more than twenty miles to the southwest, assumed an earthquake had shaken their village.[122]

Where the magazine had once stood, morning light revealed only a deep hole in the ground. The shock waves from the explosion flung Bourdon to the ground with such force his broken body never moved again. The following morning, the man's body was taken to Canada, his homeland.

On Tuesday of the following week, twenty-year-old William Hicky was killed when a blast was set off at the east end. The young miner had retreated from where the blast was to be fired, and because there were no wooden doors at the location, as at the header with the drill carriages, he placed himself behind a box on the same side of the bore as the shot. When the blast was fired, a stone was thrown against the opposite wall of the Tunnel and it bounced back across the bore, hitting Hicky in the head. He was killed instantly.[123]

Even the engineers experienced accidents. In early October, while Frost's assistant engineer, E. A. Bond, was working at the central shaft, a rock fell from the roof of the Tunnel, striking his head. The rock knocked him senseless, but Bond was more fortunate than many. He was wearing a miner's hat with a tin shield from which hung his miner's lamp. The "rock struck the lamp, jamming it all out of shape and cut through the tin shield, inflicting a wound from which the blood flowed profusely,"[124] but the funny hat-lamp arrangement afforded just enough protection to prevent a skull fracture and saved his life. Within a short time, the engineer was quite himself again.

The accidents of September and the opening days of October did not slow header progress; in fact, the westward progress from the central shaft in September was the greatest single month's advance ever, 184 feet.[125] At this time, Shanly had the miners driving the header the full width of the Tunnel, twenty-four feet, with an eight-foot depth. They now had seven Burleigh drills attached to the carriage with compressed air piped down the central shaft. At the end of September, the *Adams Transcript* reported that the separation between the two headers was down to 552 feet.[126] By the second of October, the miners working the two headers could hear the sound of the others' drills through 550 feet of rock. The anticipation of daylight through the Mountain was building, and Governor Washburn and the Tunnel Committee of his council visited North Adams in late October.[127]

The question of additional arching arose again in October, when the miners working from the central shaft encountered a fifty-foot-thick vein of soft decomposed mica-slate. To work through this weak material, it was necessary to timber the bore, and everyone seemed to agree it would have to be arched with brick.[128]

Through the Mountain!

As a guest of Chief Engineer Frost, Benjamin H. Latrobe visited North Adams and the Tunnel works in September. Latrobe expressed gratification to see Shanly nearing completion of the Tunnel. He took pride in the success following the Commonwealth's decision to use the contract method to complete the Tunnel,[129] since he had always advocated contracting the work to a private builder. In September, Shanly started paying bonuses to the miners if the advance of a heading was greater than 125 feet per month. For every foot beyond the 125 feet, each man received an extra two dollars.

In October, a contract for constructing fifty feet of stone arching at the western entrance to the Tunnel was let to John Hawkins.[130] Shanly also awarded a contract to McClallan & Son and Walker for the façade at the very western end of the Tunnel. These experienced masons were the ones who already had a contract with the Commonwealth for building culverts and grading the road to North Adams. The inscription on the façade at the western entrance would be engraved: "Hoosac Tunnel, 1874."[131]

Forty-eight years after the younger Loammi Baldwin first suggested a tunnel through the Hoosac Mountain, the headline in the *Adams Transcript* edition of 6 November 1873 read: "The Meeting of the Hoosac Tunnel Headings Expected Thanksgiving Week."[132] The story urged the city leaders to organize a celebration of the miners' triumph under the Hoosac Mountain and to smile at all the former naysayers. After the wearying details of the legislative acts connected with the struggle, the slanders, the jealousies of rival railroads, the inventive genius, and the energy lavished on the project, ought not the communities of the area do something in the way of observing the meeting of the headings? A week later, the report from the Tunnel was that 186 feet remained to be cleared.[133]

The first drill to pierce through the last thirteen feet of rock separating the two headers did so on Tuesday night, 25 November. The next day, the miners on each side proceeded to drill twelve six-foot-deep holes around this center point. Through the center-piercing hole, wires were passed from the nitro-loaded central shaft side holes so that when the perimeter holes on the other side were loaded with nitro-glycerin, the holes on both sides would be fired simultaneously. Once all of the drilling was completed, it was officially announced that the final blast would be fired at around two o'clock on Thursday afternoon, Thanksgiving Day.

The *Adams Transcript* reported that hundreds of people left the village to attend the "grand opening, Thanksgiving dinners being forgotten or swallowed (?) up in the great event of the day and of the season."[134] It was a day of low temperatures, "with flickering flakes adding to the whiteness of the already snow-clad earth."[135] In fact, many traveled up the Mountain on sleds. The buckets at the central shaft lowered about six hundred reporters, miners, engineers, and visitors to the Tunnel level. From the bottom of the shaft, they traded the snow for free shower baths as they went stumbling over rocks and waded through water to within 2,000 feet of the header. They covered 750 feet of full Tunnel that the miners had completed from the central shaft. The last 2,000 feet yet to be hiked was through full-width header but with a low, eight-foot ceiling.

Walter Shanly went to the east side of the Mountain to meet about a dozen guests from Boston, including Senator Robert Johnson, chairman of the Joint Standing Committee on the Troy and Greenfield Railroad and Hoosac Tunnel in 1872 and 1873. He met these distinguished guests at the Hoosac Tunnel Station, and the group dined at Rice's Hotel. After lunch, Shanly clad them in rubber and put them on a special train that carried them some two miles into the dark Tunnel.[136] From there, the distinguished guests, like all the other curious folks, splashed through the water to join those who had come down the shaft.

While the crowd at the central shaft waited for Shanly, a group of students from Williams College entertained everyone with vocal music. It was almost three o'clock when Shanly arrived with the distinguished guests. When he was ready, the blasters—Hancock on the east side and Richards on the west side—went forward to make the final preparations. According to Frost, Shanly fired the electric machine at 3:05 p.m. (At the time, the machine was called a "battery.") There was a shout—FIRE!—followed by a thundering explosion and a terrible rumble that reverberated off the Tunnel walls and through the crowd. The blast instantly extinguished every light. Nonetheless, from the crowd in the pitch-dark cavern came loud cheers and shouts. The force of the explosion was stronger in the westward direction, throwing one huge boulder against the wooden doors protecting the drills. It pushed the doors open and smashed a drill as if it had been made of clay.

Shanly advanced toward the broken heading but stopped short to allow one of the blasters to determine whether it was safe to proceed. The crowd wanted to surge forward, but the dense smoke held them in check. Shanly understood the excitement of it all, but he wanted no calamity to occur on this day of success. As a precaution, to warn off reckless adventurers until the blaster returned, he had stationed a staunch six-footer as a guard, with shovel in hand. Finally, at twenty minutes after three, word came back from the blaster. Shanly, with the line of gawkers behind him, advanced to a hole five feet by five and a half feet pierced through the last thirteen feet of Hoosac rock. It was the work of 170 pounds[137] of nitro-glycerin fired by blasters huddled about three hundred feet from the header. The *Hoosac Valley News* gave the quantity of nitro-glycerin used as 150 pounds, but whatever the exact amount, the result—at last—was a continuous Tunnel through the Hoosac Mountain.

When Shanly reached the opening in the rock, he stood aside and allowed Senator Robert Johnson to pass through first. The Honorable Brownell Granger, a House member of the Joint Standing Committee, followed Johnson. Granger was a native of Greenfield, and after three years of civil engineering studies at Norwich University in Vermont, he had worked as an engineer. Finally, Walter Shanly passed through the hole to meet a crowd of some two hundred persons who had gathered on the west side. Engineer Benjamin Frost was there to escort the distinguished guests through the Tunnel to the west end, and when the visitors exited the Tunnel, Wheelers Brass Band and Drum Corps was at the west shaft, playing good music to greet everyone.

There was no formal celebration in the Tunnel, although congratulations were heard all around and many a hand was grasped in a hearty shake. The following week's issue of the *Adams Transcript* heaped praise on Walter Shanly. In concluding its report, however, the paper reminded all not to forget the valuable service Thomas Doane had rendered—Doane was obviously a favorite of the town. Lieutenant-Governor Talbot did not arrive to view the achievement until the following Monday.[138] Before Talbot arrived, Mrs. J. Roscoe had "the honor of being the first woman to pass through the Tunnel."[139] Several weeks later, Walter Shanly would walk through his Tunnel from end to end.[140]

An official statement issued by Engineer Benjamin Frost read, "[M]y lines varied by nine-sixteenths of an inch, and levels by one and one half inches."[141] Consulting Engineer Edward Philbrick congratulated the engineering corps at the Tunnel. He was quoted as saying, "Mr. Frost takes pleasure in acknowledging how largely he has been aided in the attainment of these gratifying results by the vigilance, fidelity and unremitting labor and devotion of his Assistant Engineers, Messrs. F. D. Fisher and C. O. Wederkinch and their assistants Messrs. E. A. Bond, L. E. Blanchard, E. A. Patton, and E. Mowry."[142] Later, Philbrick noted that, when compared on a per-foot-of-tunnel-length basis, the Hoosac surveying had an accuracy fifteen times better than what was accomplished at the Mont Cenis Tunnel in Europe. The Mont Cenis alignment error had been approximately half a yard.[143]

Two weeks after the historic linkage, however, there was another fatal accident from a falling rock in the west section of the Tunnel. A block of rock with an estimated weight of a quarter of a ton fell from the roof of the Tunnel onto a crew of trackmen. Miles O'Grady was killed instantly and Michael Flaherty's leg was crushed. Dr. Babbitt, the surgeon who had treated Charles Browne and who was called to operate on so many Tunnel workers, amputated the leg successfully. Two others, James Barrett and Patrick Mulcahy, were bruised, though not seriously.[144] After the Tunnel opened, Barrett was employed by the railroad and would be fatally injured seven years later when attempting to mount a moving train.[145] While the falling-rock incident did occur after a blast near where the men were working, and could be attributed to the force of the explosion, it was again a warning regarding the need for further arching in the Tunnel. A similar accident would take place in the western part of the Tunnel in the first weeks of 1874, crushing trackman Michael Casey.[146] The need for additional arching in certain sections of the Tunnel was obvious to all the engineers and miners. But the point of contention still centered on the obligations Shanly had assumed when he agreed to the Tunnel contract with the Commonwealth of Massachusetts. Had Shanly, by the words of the contract, obliged himself to build arching outside of the western section?

Trains and Falling Rocks

Here and there a spring of water gushes from the
sides. We splash through some wet places, however,
and have a mind that we do not run against some
stray rock left where it happened to drop.
　　　　—Lucius Holmes, "Hoosac Tunnel—No. 2,"
The Phrenological Journal and Science of Health 58, no. 2
(February 1874): 91.

ONCE WALTER SHANLY PIERCED the Hoosac Mountain and proved the derisive Oliver Wendell Holmes wrong, everyone expected to see trains steaming through the Tunnel by the summer of 1874. The report from the Committee of the General Court overseeing the work in 1873 stated: ". . . it now remains only a question of months, more or less, of further operations, to reach the time when the people of the Commonwealth shall commence to enjoy the practical benefits of the continuous route."[1] Yet, as 1874 drew to a close, Walter Shanly was still in North Adams, and the Commonwealth had not even completed the two and a half miles of track needed to connect the west end of the Tunnel with the village. This connecting track and the even more extensive track improvements needed on the east side of the Mountain were slowly being built, but only after the usual lengthy debates in the chambers of the General Court on Beacon Hill.

　　Shanly visited Chicago in early November 1874 and granted an interview about the Tunnel work to a reporter from the *Chicago Tribune*, at that time a leading voice of Midwest Republicanism.[2] In the interview, Shanly stated the case very plainly: "Until there is such a first class road, the Tunnel will not be of any real advantage to those who expected to be benefitted by its construction."[3]

　　Engineer Benjamin Frost, in conversation with Walter Shanly at the contractor's office on 6 January 1874, asked whether it was Shanly's "opinion that there was a great deal of arching to be done in the central division" of the Tunnel.

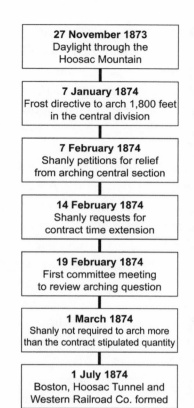

27 November 1873
Daylight through the
Hoosac Mountain

7 January 1874
Frost directive to arch 1,800 feet
in the central division

7 February 1874
Shanly petitions for relief
from arching central section

14 February 1874
Shanly requests for
contract time extension

19 February 1874
First committee meeting
to review arching question

1 March 1874
Shanly not required to arch more
than the contract stipulated quantity

1 July 1874
Boston, Hoosac Tunnel and
Western Railroad Co. formed

Shanly answered by stating he had "always been of that opinion since the day" his miners "struck the wet granite." According to Shanly, there ensued considerable conversation about the matter, and he told Frost the central division arching was not in his contract.[4] The next day, Shanly received a letter from Engineer Frost, directing him to proceed with the excavation necessary for brick arch work from a certain point toward the central shaft. By this directive, the distance that needed to be arched would be 1,800 feet.

In this case, Frost seemed to be acting under a sincere sense of duty as the engineer representing the interest of the Commonwealth. In his report submitted on 20 March 1874 to the Joint Standing Committee on the Troy and Greenfield Railroad and Hoosac Tunnel, he stated: "[T]he necessity of building brick arching in the portions of the Tunnel where no such requirement was included in the original estimate" . . . increases "to a proportional extent, the total cost to the contractor of completing his work."[5]

Falling Rocks

On 20 January, Michael Casey, a trackman working in the Tunnel near the west shaft, was killed instantly when a large rock fell from the roof of the Tunnel.[6] His death, and similar previous accidents, made clear in a terrible way the need for additional arching. Dangerous locations along the length of the Tunnel were marked to warn workmen, and timber bracing was erected at some of the worst places. Shanly acknowledged the need for brick arching, and in his petition of 7 February 1874, to the General Court, he wrote, "[I]t has been apparent for two years and over that more or less of such arching would be required in order to secure perfect safety in the continued use of the Tunnel." The contention between Shanly and the Commonwealth was about who would suffer the expense of building the needed arching. Was Frost correct in his interpretation of the contract requirements and his belief that the work should be accomplished by Shanly? Or was Shanly correct in his understanding of the contract?[7]

In his petition to the legislature seeking relief from the engineer's directive for the contractor to construct additional arching, Shanly reiterated what he considered the important contract terms addressing the arching question. The contract "does not require them [the Shanlys] to arch any portion of the Tunnel except in the west end section." The contractor has "promised to arch a part of the west end section of the Tunnel with bricks, it being specified that the amount of bricks to be laid there should not exceed 4,500,000."[8]

Frost, representing the Commonwealth, took a very different view of the contract, and he was supported by the attorney general, who claimed the Act of 1868 specifically authorized the Governor to contract for the "whole work" of constructing the Hoosac Tunnel. He noted that the fourth page of the contract even referenced the Act of 1868. Concerning the schedule of prices annexed to the contract, the attorney general argued that these were strictly for the purpose of calculating progress payments to the contractor.[9]

While the arching argument was proceeding before the legislative committee, Shanly and his legal counsel appeared on Saturday, 14 February, before the Governor and his council, seeking a six-month extension of the Tunnel contract. This would move the specified completion date from 1 March to 1 September 1874. The contract included a clause stipulating that such an extension could be granted if unforeseen difficulties were encountered. No determination was made by the Governor, and further consideration of the matter was postponed until later in the month.[10]

The first hearing before the committee considering the arching question and Shanly's petition for contractual relief was held on Thursday, 19 February. A week earlier, the *Transcript* of North Adams informed its readers that the committee was inclined to favor the Shanlys. But, as with all other Tunnel matters, nothing was ever certain! During this period of maneuvering, Shanly received a request from President Ulysses Grant, seeking his participation in the expedition the United States was sending to Nicaragua[11] to survey possible routes for an interocean canal.[12] Needless to say, Shanly was too busy with Hoosac Tunnel matters to accept the invitation. Such a request did, however, indicate the high regard in which Walter Shanly was held by his fellow engineers and the U.S. Government.

Shanly and his attorney, Charles Allen, spent the first committee hearing presenting their case. They focused much of their attention on the specifications of the work, contained in the advertisements the Commonwealth issued in the summer of 1868. Shanly's argument was again based on two particular clauses.

The first, which described the work to be performed in the eastern section, stated: "As the rock is sufficiently hard to prevent apprehensions from falls and slides, estimates will be made only of quantities within the exterior line prescribed for the Tunnel."

The second clause upon which Shanly and his lawyer relied stated: ". . . a bid for arching part of the Tunnel, per thousand of bricks laid." The contract specifically set the number of bricks for arching at 4,500,000. So Shanly believed this second clause set a limit on the work the contractor was to perform.[13]

Shanly had to appeal to the General Court because the Governor and his council believed they had the duty to execute the contract but not the power to amend it. The Governor and the council stood by their interpretation and left it to the General Court to clarify the meaning of the words in the document. After Shanly and Allen presented their arguments, the hearing adjourned and the committee members gathered to consult privately about the course they should pursue.

The following day, the hearing reconvened, with the Committee indicating it would hear whatever either side had to offer. On this second day, Shanly explained the tender process and the items of work it required the bidders to price, together with the quantities stated in the tender documents. The original request was for pricing items of work—an "item-bid" request. In the case of a contract made under this type of tender, the builder would be paid according to measured units of work actually performed. Therefore, the cost to the Commonwealth would not be fixed. However, during that discussion with Governor vAlexander Bullock in 1868, someone had suggested it would be more convenient if the contractor took the contract for a lump sum and the contractor would be paid a fixed amount for the project, no matter the actual quantities of work performed.[14] Following Shanly's presentation, the Committee members had many questions about the rock west of the central shaft and Shanly's difficulty in driving the Tunnel through the water-filled material. Attorney General Charles Train then cross-examined Shanly, seeking to stress to the Committee that Shanly had been represented by legal counsel when he agreed to the contract, so he had not been pressured to sign a contract he did not understand.

After Shanly's presentation and cross-examination, Train presented the Commonwealth's legal construct of the contract and the work the contractor was required to perform. He spoke about the 1868 legislation, saying it authorized "one" contract for completion of the Troy and Greenfield Railroad and the Hoosac Tunnel, entirely and thoroughly. "This contract was a contract for the completion of the entire work," he said, and the risks of changes were the responsibility of the contractor.[15] Then Train and Allen engaged in a give-and-take argument about the finer points of the contract's wording. Finally, the committee chairman adjourned the hearing until the following week.

The hearing reconvened on 25 February, with Train again arguing the Commonwealth's objective and purpose of the contract. On this day, Train and Allen argued specifically about the meaning of the words: "the work necessary to complete the Hoosac Tunnel, in accordance with the schedule hereunto appended."[16] Allen declared to the Committee that these words would not have been included if the intent of "the contract was to construct and complete the Hoosac Tunnel." Train once again claimed the words were solely in reference to the calculation of contractor pay.[17] Once again, the hearing adjourned without a decision.

The following week, Consulting Engineer Philbrick testified before the Committee, speaking primarily to the issue of the need for arching. He did not offer an interpretation of the contract. Nevertheless, he did use the occasion to criticize Shanly for refusing to mine westward from the central shaft, supposedly because of the water in the rock. When the Committee chair urged the Governor and Shanly to settle the controversy between themselves, Train seemed to accept the suggestion. But the attorney general wanted Engineer Frost to have his say because of the negative remarks leveled against him during the hearings. Frost did appear, but his comments did not touch on the subject of arching. The thrust of his statement concerned his relationship with the consulting engineer, James Laurie, and accusations about the Tunnel surveys. The hearing adjourned with the chairman instructing the parties to resolve the question quickly.

Three days after the adjournment, there was another deadly explosion at the Tunnel. On Friday, 6 March, the village of North Adams felt the tremor and heard the deep rumble of an accident at the west shaft. A blaster named Patrick Donnelly was using the timekeeper's office at the shaft to prepare cartridges of Giant Powder when an exploder went off, spontaneously setting fire to the cartridges. At the time, about 200 pounds of Giant Powder were in the building. As Donnelly tried to extinguish the fire, he shouted to warn those near the building. When the inevitable explosion occurred, Donnelly was thrown through one of the office windows. He was badly burned and splinters were driven into his body, but he survived. Seeking to help others who might be in the building, James K. Mulaney, a foreman at the blacksmith shop, ran toward the office before the explosion occurred. He had not yet reached the building when the blast shook the earth. The unlucky man was killed instantly when a flying splinter pierced his neck, cutting his jugular vein.[18] The forty-four-year-old Mulaney, who had been born in Ireland, left a wife, five sons, and two daughters. The youngest, a son, was only four years old at the time of his father's death. Mulaney was buried in the Hillside Cemetery of North Adams, where his grave and marker on the hill can be easily found today.

Two weeks after the accident, the *Hoosac Valley News* announced Shanly had prevailed in his argument and would not be required to arch the additional lengths of Tunnel without being paid. The legislative committee even had gracious words for the contractor from Canada: Mr. Shanly is "one of God's noblemen."[19] Still, loose rocks in the Tunnel remained a problem, and it seemed each loose rock took aim at those who were not vigilant.

John Chean was badly injured by a falling rock at the west end of the Tunnel on 18 June.[20] The same day, also at the west end of the Tunnel, Michael Tullman was injured by a falling rock.[21] James Gallaher, a foreman, was killed by a rock falling from the roof at the west end of the Tunnel on 17 July.[22]

On 19 August, a workman named Doherty had his leg broken in three places by a falling rock.[23] James Mack was severely injured by a rock falling from the roof east of the west shaft on 31 August.[24]

On 4 September, James Gladding lingered about three hours before dying after a rock fell on him at the central shaft.[25]

About fifty tons of rock fell from the roof of the Tunnel east of the central shaft on 13 September. It being a Sunday, no laborers were at work in the Tunnel.[26]

In late August, the local papers mentioned that the engineer's office was finally preparing to issue specifications for a separate arching contract. "A notice and specifications will soon be issued from the engineer's office for proposals for the arching contract. The minimum size of the additional excavation required for the brick arch will be about two feet."[27]

Remaining Work

By the first of April in 1874, the workforce at the east end of the Tunnel was down to only twenty men who were engaged in clearing loose rock and laboring on the central drain.[28] Fifty carloads of the flagstones for covering the drain had arrived at the end of March, and part of the crew began working to complete this detail of Shanly's contract. Interestingly, the stone was delivered by the Tunnel's old enemy, the Boston and Albany Railroad, formerly the Western Railroad.[29]

On the other side of the Mountain railcars loaded with granite arrived from Norwich, Connecticut, for erecting the west portal.[30]

Over the years, some men had built solid reputations while toiling to bore the Hoosac Mountain, and now there were opportunities to apply their skills elsewhere. Before the month of April concluded, Engineer Carl Wederkinch accepted an appointment as the chief engineer for the 3.9-mile-long Sutro Tunnel in Nevada.[31] The Sutro Tunnel was designed to provide drainage for the Comstock Lode silver mine without the need for pumping. Within a month, a large number of Hoosac miners departed with Wederkinch for the tunnel work in Nevada.[32] Wederkinch would eventually be employed at a silver mine in Honduras and die there in 1881.[33]

Just as the papers had provided regular reports the previous year on the progress of the two headers pressing together to allow daylight through the Mountain, the local editors now began to report the footage of bottom bench that the crews needed to remove between the west end and the central shaft. Once the full Tunnel length was completely excavated, everyone expected Shanly to begin laying track. On the first of May, the *Adams Transcript* informed its readers 962 feet of bottom bench remained to be removed. To save money, Shanly retired the steam-driven air compressors at the central and west shafts. All compressed air for the drills was now supplied by the water-driven compressors on the Deerfield River at the east end of the Tunnel.[34]

In late May, John Edgar Thomson, president of the Pennsylvania Railroad and Herman Haupt's great mentor, died. Thomson designated most of his considerable estate for the education and care of the female orphans of railroad employees killed while engaged in the discharge of their duties.[35]

At the Hoosac Mountain, the mules hauling the rock out of the west portal were still kept in a barn located in the Tunnel close to the west shaft, but, like many of the miners, they would soon be put out to pasture.[36] The bench removal went quickly, and in early June the papers reported that only 361 feet remained.[37] To speed the work, the miners had proceeded from both east and west ends of the bench, but on Wednesday, 10 June, Shanly halted the miners on the west end. Only about 223 feet remained, and it was too dangerous to have both crews firing Mowbray's soup. The contractor J. M. Dwyer, working for the Commonwealth, was expected to drive his steam shovel through to the west portal that same week.[38] In fact, Dwyer completed the cut on Saturday, 13 June.[39] Finally, the work necessary to join the Tunnel to the railroads on both ends of the Tunnel was nearing completion. Only a few Burleigh drills—tools contributing to Shanly's success in boring the Mountain—were needed now to complete the work. But the drill's reputation had spread far because of its performance at the Hoosac Tunnel. While Burleigh shipped only a few of his masterpieces to the Tunnel in this last year of mining, many were being expressed to Western mines and even beyond: Crocker's Fitchburg friend shipped drills and three of his large air compressors to Peru later in the year. Because the machines would have to be carried to the silver mines high in the Andes by pack animals, they were built in sections, with no individual part weighing more than three hundred pounds.[40]

As the year wore on, even though numerous Tunnel details were still claiming Walter Shanly's attention, it was clear his association with the Tunnel was rapidly drawing to a close. All of those who had come to know Shanly during his five-year struggle with the Mountain were now coming forward to offer him hearty thanks. In June, George Mowbray published the third edition of his little book *Tri-Nitro-Glycerin as Applied in the Hoosac Tunnel*. He dedicated this edition to Walter Shanly. In appreciation, Mowbray wrote:

> *Permit me to dedicate the following pages in token of my appreciation of the indomitable energy, admirable organization, integrity of purpose, and engineering talent which have rescued the Hoosac Tunnel from the mire of politics and rendered it an engineering success.*[41]

By the middle of July, the bench existed no longer, so Shanly discharged another fifty workmen. At the east end of the Tunnel, a 2,500-foot central drain-pipe was installed in the trench and covered. Crews of miners had completed the forty feet of enlargement excavation necessary for the arching ordered by Frost in the east section, and bricklaying was expected to commence before the end of the month.[42] But as summer moved into fall, Shanly was having trouble with McClallan & Son and Walker, his subcontractor building the west façade. These gentlemen had been laggardly in the performance of their contract with the Commonwealth to construct the road to North Adams, and now they were delaying Shanly by not completing all the tasks of their façade contract.

The general feeling of approaching success caused the papers of North Adams to reminisce. The *Hoosac Valley News* carried a story about two men who had come up from Hardwick, Massachusetts, with their carts twenty-three years earlier at the beginning of the tunneling at the east end, and they were still hard at work on the great undertaking.[43] Their names were John Burke and Cornelius Collins. Hardwick is a small community thirty miles southeast of Greenfield. After his tunneling days, Burke worked for the railroad and died eight years later after his foot was severed in a train accident.

But even as the pace of the Tunnel work slackened, fatal accidents continued. James Handlon (or Hanlon),[44] who had labored in the Tunnel for three years, was killed just beyond the west shaft when part of a drill carriage overturned and crushed his head between it and the Tunnel wall.[45] John Hocking (Hawkins), Shanly's faithful subcontractor on the west end, and the miner who directed the arching work after B. N. Farren completed his section for the Commonwealth, died in November. Hocking and his sons were the men who rescued the trapped west-bore miners during the flood of 1869. He reportedly made good money on the arching work, but he had other losses, and after being weighed down by setbacks, he was committed to the State Hospital at Northampton. He had also suffered the loss of his son John in November 1870. After being released from the asylum, he was home when his mental burden became too great to bear.[46]

Even beyond the Berkshire Hills, tragedy followed others involved in the Tunnel drama. Francis W. Bird Jr., the twenty-one-year-old son of Tunnel nemesis Frank Bird, died of heart disease on 10 July at his father's home in East Walpole.[47]

Political Musical Chairs

In 1874, the General Court established the Boston, Hoosac Tunnel and Western Railroad Company. Specifically, chapter 403 of that year's legislation[48] set up a temporary management structure for the Commonwealth's Hoosac Tunnel. In addition, the law replaced and joined the former Troy and Greenfield Railroad and the Southern Vermont Railroad into a consolidated company. Under the authority of chapter 403, the Governor appointed five corporators and on the first of July in 1874, they assumed control of all property owned by the two railroads. Shanly's contract and other pending Hoosac Tunnel contracts remained under the control and authority of the Governor and his council, with Benjamin Frost acting as the agent for the Commonwealth.

The installation of the new corporators was an interesting orchestration of political musical chairs. Charles Sumner, the U.S. senator from Massachusetts who was nearly caned to death on the Senate floor in 1856 after his "Crime Against Kansas" antislavery speech, had died on 11 March 1874. William B. Washburn, who was still Governor and who in January 1873 had first broached the subject of how the Commonwealth should exercise control of the completed Hoosac Tunnel, was elected by the Senate of the Commonwealth to Sumner's

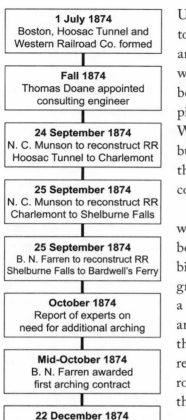

1 July 1874
Boston, Hoosac Tunnel and
Western Railroad Co. formed

Fall 1874
Thomas Doane appointed
consulting engineer

24 September 1874
N. C. Munson to reconstruct RR
Hoosac Tunnel to Charlemont

25 September 1874
N. C. Munson to reconstruct RR
Charlemont to Shelburne Falls

25 September 1874
B. N. Farren to reconstruct RR
Shelburne Falls to Bardwell's Ferry

October 1874
Report of experts on
need for additional arching

Mid-October 1874
B. N. Farren awarded
first arching contract

22 December 1874
Shanly's Hoosac Tunnel
contract certified complete

U.S. Senate seat on 30 April.[49] With his election to the U.S. Senate, Washburn resigned from office, and Lieutenant Governor Thomas Talbot, who had written the harsh letter to Shanly about arching, became the acting Governor. All of this transpired only three years after Alvah Crocker assumed Washburn's seat in the U.S. House when Washburn resigned after being elected Governor. Now, the ex-Governor, Senator Washburn, was named a corporator.

The other men appointed as corporators were Charles Francis Adams Jr., Paul A. Chadbourne, Stephen M. Crosby, and Solomon B. Stebbins. Adams, a graduate of Harvard (1856) was the great-grandson of President John Adams. He was a lawyer by profession and noted for his studies and articles on railroad matters. After service in the Union Army during the War of Rebellion, he received an appointment to the Massachusetts Railroad Commission; from 1869 to 1879, he chaired the commission.

Chadbourne was at the time of his appointment president of Williams College, a position he had assumed in July 1872.[50] At the ceremony when he was installed, James A. Garfield, the future U.S. president, gave the address on behalf of the alumni. Prior to Chadbourne's return to Williams, his alma mater, he taught chemistry and natural history at Bowdoin College in Maine and then served as president at the University of Wisconsin from 1867 to 1870.

Crosby, from Williamsburg, Massachusetts, was a member of the Commonwealth's Senate in 1871 and a man much engaged in railroad matters. A few years earlier, he had been a member of the House, where he had served on a committee—along with the old Tunnel foe Francis Bird—to consider the filling-in of part of Boston's South Bay.

Stebbins, the fifth corporator, was appointed after the other four had conducted their first meeting on 29 July. He was originally from Ludlow, Massachusetts, a village just west of Springfield, but at the age of twenty he moved to

Boston, where he engaged in the grain and flour business.[51] In 1861, he served in the House of Representatives of the General Court and in 1866, the Senate. In 1873, he became a member of the board of aldermen for the City of Boston, a position he would hold until 1877.[52]

At the first meeting of the corporation, Washburn was chosen as president and Crosby assumed the role of secretary. The four gentlemen divided their work, with Washburn and Chadbourne handling contracts and construction and Adams and Crosby attending to questions of law and railroad connections. When Stebbins joined the corporators, he provided assistance to both groups. During the first week of August, the corporators made a thorough examination of the railroad property.[53]

They found the Troy and Greenfield Railroad to be in an exceedingly unsatisfactory condition. These were men of action, so Engineer W. P. Granger—Doane's west shaft engineer in 1866 and the man who discovered it was better to keep Mowbray's nitro-glycerin frozen—was immediately hired as chief engineer of the new company and tasked to make surveys for improving the railroad between the Tunnel and Greenfield. At the same time, Edwin Stratton was hired as assistant engineer. He had previously been chief engineer for the Boston, Barre and Gardner Railroad. Following the example set by the Western Railroad during its original construction, the corporators directed the engineers to plan the construction of bridges and all masonry work with provisions for a double-track railroad, even though only a single track would be laid at first. Believing they were also in need of an engineer with wide experience, they decided to hire Thomas Doane as consulting engineer.[54] Since leaving the Hoosac Tunnel work in January 1867, Doane had been chief engineer of the Burlington and Missouri River Railroad in Nebraska. In approximately four years, he completed 241 miles of railroad and established a steam ferryboat service for crossing the Missouri River.[55]

Although Frost was preparing to let an arching contract for the Governor and his council, the corporators were directed by section 5 of the legislation to appoint five or more experts to examine the Tunnel separately and ascertain how much needed to be arched in order to ensure safe passage of trains. Accordingly, geologists Thomas S. Hunt and James Hall, together with civil engineers Josiah Brown, Daniel L. Harris, and Thomas Doane, were engaged to examine and report on the need for further arch work.[56]

At the time of his appointment, Thomas Hunt was professor of geology at Massachusetts Institute of Technology. Prior to joining MIT, he had held positions with the Geological Survey of Vermont and the Canadian Geological Survey.[57] Some authorities credit Hunt as being the first to propose the theory linking climate change with concentrations of carbon dioxide in the atmosphere. James Hall was originally from Hingham, Massachusetts, but had left Massachusetts to study at Rensselaer Polytechnic Institute in Troy, New York. He remained at RPI for a number of years as a professor of chemistry and natural science before being appointed state geologist for New York.[58]

Josiah Brown, from Fall River, Massachusetts, was professionally more noted for directing the construction of mill complexes. During the days when Crocker was acting as the Tunnel superintendent, Brown had examined the pumping operation at the west shaft and advised Crocker about using steam-driven pumps.[59] Daniel Harris, the railroad engineer from Springfield, was engaged in bridge building and closely associated with the Western Railroad. As president of the Connecticut River Railroad, he had in the past often served the Western as a voice opposing the Hoosac Tunnel.[60]

Expert Opinions

Shanly was not selected to perform the extra arching under the contract Frost let for the Governor and the Executive Council in 1874. This work was to be performed using a special $300,000 appropriation voted the previous year and dedicated especially for additional arching.[61] It was estimated that this amount of money would be sufficient to complete the 1,800 feet of additional arching agreed upon by Engineers Frost and Philbrick. Their cost estimate was based on the need for laying the usual five courses of bricks, but experience had shown the need to sometimes make the arch eighteen bricks thick. The increased thickness would mean 9,000 bricks instead of 2,000 per lineal foot. Moreover, the thicker walls required more hydraulic cement, two and a half barrels for the thinner section as opposed to nine barrels for a thick arch.[62]

B. N. Farren, the arching master from years earlier, was awarded the work in mid-October 1874. Farren was now making Greenfield his home, and it was estimated it would take him about a year to complete the work.[63] At this time, he was also closely associated with Alvah Crocker in the Montague Paper Company of Turners Falls. When the paper company was incorporated in 1871, Crocker became president and Farren was a director. The builder from Pennsylvania had done very well in northern Massachusetts.

As Farren prepared to undertake this new arching contract, the five experts descended on the Tunnel to issue their opinions as to what additional arching might be necessary following Farren's work. Even before the first expert on the need for additional arching made an appearance, Farren secured another contract associated with the Tunnel. He would build the wing wall at the eastern portal to protect the Tunnel from another Cascade Brook flood.

Geologist Hunt visited the Tunnel in late September and spent five days examining the broken rock through which the bore penetrated; his report was purely about the rock mass. Hunt's scientific training led him to describe the differences in rock mass as "from very soft and flaky mica-schist to a gneiss of great hardness and strength," as always is the case in the Appalachians. He hesitated to express an opinion as to the amount of arching, because it was a matter in which civil engineers are more competent, but he still provided a thorough analysis, including a cautionary note to the corporators to consider the effects of winter frost upon the Tunnel.[64]

The following week, James Hall, the other geologist, arrived in North Adams to inspect the bore through the Mountain. He submitted a much more detailed report to Chadbourne, identifying by location some 7,900 feet as definitely needing arching and another 2,000 feet as of doubtful stability and probably needing arching. His report explained how the removal of millions of cubic feet of rock had disturbed the equilibrium of pressure and tension established through geological ages. He believed the Mountain was now seeking to "restore equilibrium of pressure and tension." Furthermore, he counseled the corporators to consider the continuing effects of water, air, and frost on the stability of the rock. He specifically advised that they consider ways to divert water dripping through the sides of the arch.[65]

After an examination of the Tunnel rock exposed by the bore, Josiah Brown gave his opinion as to the need for arching. He believed that 3,112 feet needed to be arched in the east section and 5,379 feet in the west section. But he went on to inform the corporators that the true need could not be ascertained until "after the sides and roof have been trimmed and all loose pieces removed."[66] The report submitted to Chadbourne by Daniel Harris consisted of only two pages and was basically just a summary. It recommended 11,081 feet of arching, with about half in the west section and the remainder in the east section closer to the central shaft.[67]

When Doane arrived to make his inspection, Walter Shanly provided him with three men to assist in his examination of the dark bore. These men carried lamps on long poles to light the roof as Doane walked the length of the Tunnel. They also carried an iron ram attached to another pole. This instrument was used by Doane to test the rock of the Tunnel roof. Engineer Locke accompanied Doane when he walked the eastern section on 30 September. The next day, Doane covered half of the western section with Engineer Cole. Finally, on the third day, Engineer Fisher joined Doane while he covered the remaining distance to the west shaft.[68] Doane believed 5,670 feet definitely needed to be arched, and, like Hall, he provided a very detailed list of needs by location. And he added a stipulation similar to the warning issued by Brown. Until the trimming and removal of loose rock was completed, "no human wisdom can determine exactly what must be done nor how much." Doane made a summary tabulation of the individual reports. Doane and Harris were in almost complete agreement as to locations needing brick arch work, with Harris reporting a greater total length. The difference resulted because Harris either accepted a section as safe or recommended arching. He never considered the effect of further trimming to provide a better understanding of the need, while Doane in many cases recommended trimming before a final judgment was made. Neither Hunt nor Brown considered further trimming, and again this largely explained the difference between their recommendations and those of Doane. Hall did consider trimming, but his much higher recommendation concerning the distance in need of arching seemed to stem from a more critical attitude.

In his report of 13 October, Doane offered four specific suggestions to the corporators for further consideration. First, he warned about the effect of freezing weather on exposed brick masonry. In effect, he said the masonry will always be saturated and would not tolerate freezing without loss of stability. In response to this problem, he advised that they consider the need for doors at the Tunnel portals. Hall had voiced a similar concern in his report:

> *I am not advised as to the intention regarding protection against freezing; but I am informed by the superintendent of the eastern division that the frost penetrated from the portal for more than half a mile; and that the amount of dripping water from the roof was sufficient to form icicles from roof to floor, and thence gradually up, filling the interstices.*[69]

Doane's second suggestion addressed the shape of the Tunnel roof in the section driven with a top header. He took pains to explain clearly to the nonengineer corporators how, in excavating this section, some 9,702 feet, enormous amounts of nitro-glycerin were used in single, simultaneous blasts. Such blasting had shattered the rock forming the roof of the Tunnel to a greater depth, causing some of it to fall away but "leaving other portions of it insecure."[70] This, he noted, was an important factor for consideration in assessing the safety of the Tunnel.

Doane's third suggestion explained the relationship between roof shape and rock stability. Driving the Tunnel with a top heading eliminated the need for drilling vertical holes upward and eased the work in other ways, but it did not create a stable roof shape. The resulting roof in these sections was very flat and did not have the arch shape needed to promote stability. Fourth, Doane believed the flow of air through the Tunnel would not have any effect on disintegration of the rock, as the locations of the soft seams where this might happen would all be supported by arching.

Engineer Philbrick was not one of those selected to review the need for arching but, acting in his capacity as consultant for the Tunnel, he submitted a report to Governor Talbot on 31 July. His report was included in those assembled by the corporators. Doane, however, did not include Philbrick's analysis in the summary table he prepared for the corporators. After inspecting the length of the Tunnel with Engineer Frost, Philbrick opined that a further length of 1,600 feet needed to be arched to ensure the safe passage of trains. He had conducted his inspection in a manner similar to that of Doane—by using lanterns hung on poles and with long-handled hammers to sound the rock. As a final thought, Philbrick suggested in his report that it might be cheaper to bring brick from Greenfield by rail.[71]

Home to Canada

The corporators had at their disposal an appropriation of $1.5 million for improving the Commonwealth's Troy and Greenfield Railroad. Therefore, following the advice of engineers Granger and Doane, these gentlemen quickly reached decisions concerning necessary changes and improvements. By early September, bids were solicited for track work between the eastern portal of the Hoosac Tunnel and Charlemont; five bids were received. On 24 September, William Washburn signed a contract for this work with a completion date of 1 December 1874.[72]

Norman Carmine Munson, a railroad contractor with a history reaching back to the opening days of Crocker's Fitchburg Railroad, was the low bidder to straighten and repair this section of the road. He would remove the old iron rails and lay new steel rails purchased by the Commonwealth.[73] Leaving his hometown of Hinesburgh (Hinesburg), Vermont,[74] at an early age, Munson began his railroad career as a laborer on the Boston and Worcester Railroad. Based on when the Boston and Worcester was constructed, he was probably thirteen or fourteen when he first went to work. A few years later, he was a subcontractor building some fifteen miles of Crocker's Fitchburg Railroad from South Acton to Marlboro. This was part of the S. F. Belknap contract, so he must have performed the work for Belknap. There may have been a connection between the two men, as Belknap was also from Vermont. In 1848, Munson returned to the Fitchburg Railroad and built the line's second track from Concord to Fitchburg. During both of Munson's engagements with the Fitchburg, Samuel Felton was Crocker's engineer.

After Felton left to become president of the Philadelphia, Wilmington, and Baltimore Railroad, Munson followed him and was employed between 1854 and 1857 as the contractor to straighten the track alignment near Havre de Grace, Maryland.[75] But Munson's greatest claim to fame was the filling-in of Boston's Back Bay. To accomplish this feat, he purchased gravel-pit land in Needham and ran gravel trains carrying the needed material into Boston. In 1862, he delivered more than 100,000 cars of gravel fill to Boston's Back Bay. He was similarly engaged in hauling material to fill the mudflats adjacent to Loammi Baldwin's old Mill Dam.[76]

Before the end of September, Washburn signed two other contracts to complete similar work for the improvement of the alignment and quality of the railroad structures from Charlemont to Bardwell's Ferry. A contract for the eight-mile section from Charlemont to Shelburne Falls went to Munson, and the contract for the five miles from Shelburne Falls to Bardwell's Ferry was awarded to B. N. Farren.[77] Both sections were to be completed by 1 July 1875. The week before these last two contracts were awarded, Governor Talbot and the Executive Council visited the Hoosac Tunnel.

The corporators ordered sixty-pound-per-yard steel rails from the Pennsylvania Steel Company for the contractors to use in replacing the old iron rails of the Troy and Greenfield. Doane, his beard turned gray, was back to complete the Tunnel, and now Samuel Felton, Doane's engineering mentor, was to supply the steel rails from his Bessemer-process mill. After recovering from his shock of paralysis, Felton had become the first president of the Pennsylvania Steel Company in 1865.[78]

A considerable portion of the old iron rails on the Troy and Greenfield Railroad were in extremely poor condition—so poor they were declared unsafe for use. The contractors replaced these immediately. There were other sections of the road between the Tunnel and Greenfield, however, where a substantial amount of work was yet to be done by the contractors, so it was decided not to lay the new steel rails immediately in those locations. The decision was to take the best of the old iron rails and have these rerolled for use in such locations. So the old rails from thirty miles of road extending east from the Mountain to Greenfield were sent to the Washburn Iron Company of Worcester to be rerolled. As payment, the Washburn firm took a portion of the old rails. A similar program was instituted on the west side of the Mountain, but those rails were sent to the Albany and Rensselaer Iron and Steel Company in Troy, New York.[79] This firm was the result of a merger by the Rensselaer Iron Works (owned by John A. Griswold, who in 1858 had helped Haupt purchase the seven miles of rails he needed to qualify for the first loan payment from the Commonwealth) and the Albany Iron Works (of which Erastus Corning Jr. was part owner). It was Corning's father who, years earlier, in combination with John Murray Forbes, had sent John Brooks out to build a railroad to Chicago before Brooks became a Hoosac Tunnel commissioner.

Shanly's Tunnel contract specified fifty-six-pound-per-yard "iron" rails for the track through the Mountain. The Commonwealth now decided to substitute sixty-eight-pound-per-yard "steel" rails for use in the Tunnel.[80] Those rails were to be delivered before the first of October, and Shanly had the necessary ties ready to lay the track. These rails through the Hoosac Tunnel would complete the connection of the Troy and Greenfield Railroad with North Adams.

Governor-elect William Gaston visited the Tunnel, accompanied by the corporators, early in November; a week later, the labor of removing the timber platforms from the central shaft commenced. It was hazardous work, and, not being part of Shanly's contract, it was directly under the control of the Commonwealth. Once the shaft was cleared, the machinery and buildings above would be removed and a curb of masonry would be constructed to prevent anything from falling into the Tunnel.[81] With all of this activity, and Shanly's work nearing completion, everyone was hopeful they would see the Tunnel opened to train traffic before the end of the year. Then, in early December, the *Adams Transcript* announced: "[T]he prospects are fair for a speedy settlement of accounts between the Commonwealth and the Messrs. Shanly, tunnel contractors."[82] The announcement was premised on the visit by Governor Talbot and the council to the Tunnel during the second week of December for the purpose of investigating and settling the contract.[83]

As a result of the visit, Walter Shanly found himself in Boston with the Governor and his council, and, just as during Christmas week six years earlier, the negotiations were tedious. Finally, on 22 December, the Tunnel contract was certified as complete and the Commonwealth of Massachusetts accepted the Hoosac Tunnel and other contractor property. The final contract amount was $4,594,268. There was a deduction of $32,031.60 for the iron rails Shanly would not have to lay through the Tunnel and $4,515.94 for central drain work he had not completed.

Shanly collected for the contract work a warrant for $456,014.80, most of it representing the amount the Commonwealth had withheld from the monthly payments as security. He also collected $27,155.47 for extras the Governor allowed, including the work Frost had ordered for grading the dumped material at the east end.[84] Walter Shanly signed a receipt for these sums but reserved the right to present certain claims later to the General Court. These claims represented matters the Governor believed he had no authority to adjudicate and others the Governor simply disallowed, including Shanly's complaint about the condition of the central drain being misrepresented during the original contract negotiations.[85]

The Mountain Fights Back

Once the Governor issused the certification stating the Tunnel Contract was completed, all work on the Tunnel immediately became the responsibility of the Commonwealth under the direction of its engineers. Frost had not recommended the purchase by the Commonwealth of the tracks Shanly had laid in the Tunnel for his work trains, so, on the morning of the settlement, workmen began removing the worn rails. For the time being, Frost retained responsibility for the work in the Tunnel. In mid-1875, he and Granger, who was hired by the corporators, would have their responsibilities split, with Frost looking after the Tunnel work but also having responsibility for the road from the West side of the Mountain to the Vermont state line.

Granger would have responsibility for the rebuilding of the road from the Tunnel to Greenfield, and Doane would continue as consulting engineer.[86] The office for the Commonwealth's Troy and Greenfield Railroad and Hoosac Tunnel was established in Greenfield. On 1 July 1875, the Commonwealth's railroad reverted to being the Troy and Greenfield Railroad from the previous Boston, Hoosac Tunnel and Western Railroad Company—the name used during the one year the corporators were in charge. No decision had been made in 1874 concerning the relocation of the road's alignment from Bardwell's Ferry into Greenfield. The old line entered Greenfield half a mile south of the depot, and all trains were obliged to back up from the depot to that point when going westward. It was hoped a new route would eliminate this situation. On the west side of the Mountain in North Adams, the so-called Little Hoosac Tunnel was being enlarged. To level the grade of the tracks, the bottom of this tunnel was to be lowered eight feet. Farren secured this work in February 1875, with the tunnel slated to be ready for service by the Fourth of July.[87]

The experts gave their opinions as to the amount of arching necessary after Farren finished his contract, and the General Court appropriated funds for the additional arching. While Shanly was urged by the Commonwealth's manager of the Troy and Greenfield Railroad to bid on the new arching work, he declined to do so. At fifty-eight, Shanly was ready to return home to Canada. Coote Shanly, his dearest sibling, had died in April 1874, and at some point earlier he learned the true state of Frank Shanly's finances, including many loans for which Walter was liable as a cosigner.

Four days after Walter Shanly settled his contract with the Commonwealth, Alvah Crocker—the eternal spark driving the epic Hoosac Tunnel struggle—died at his home in Fitchburg.

22 December 1874 Shanly's Hoosac Tunnel contract certified complete
26 December 1874 Death of Alvah Crocker
9 February 1875 Engine "N. C. Munson" makes first passage through Tunnel
1 April 1875 Central shaft cleared by E. A. Bond
5 April 1875 First freight train through Tunnel
17 April 1875 Mrs. H. M. Streeter walks through Tunnel
13 October 1875 First passenger train car through Tunnel
April 1876 Regular passenger train service through Hoosac Tunnel

After bidding adieu to his colleagues in Washington, Crocker had started north to New England for the congressional Christmas break. The journey carried him into the deep cold of the New England winter, and he contracted a cold during the trip. The cold soon turned into pneumonia, which took his life a day later. Fitchburg, the community he had nurtured and helped to build over so many years, was shocked by the loss. In fact, all of northern Massachusetts mourned the passing of their patron. The man who was brought up by the rugged hand of poverty was seventy-three years old when he passed over the Mountain. He knew Shanly had pierced the Mountain, but his eyes never beheld a locomotive dragging a train through the work that epitomized his life.

There was still no track through the Hoosac Tunnel, but the laying of the steel rails to North Adams from the west portal was nearly complete. The

Hoosac Valley News stated the Tunnel situation well: "The rock which was so hard to get through crumbles, slakes off, and falls on exposure to the air, and a steel track would not only be often obstructed, but would be greatly damaged by the rock falling upon it."[88] The paper, commenting on the Shanlys' success in boring the Tunnel through the Hoosac Mountain, spoke one other truth: For all of their "international reputation for grim determination and skill in managing great undertakings," they realized nothing financial for the effort.

Moving into 1875, the only work being pushed at the Tunnel was the clearing of the central shaft. Frost placed E. A. Bond in control of this dangerous task. He contrived a plan to use a movable platform, which he constructed and lowered to the bottom of the shaft in sections. The platform was reassembled at the bottom of the shaft and then raised from above, until it was suspended below each of the levels before being raised to the next one. Bond's crew removed each floor in turn, working up the shaft from the bottom. On this platform he had forty-five experienced miners removing the timber floors and clearing loose rock. The timbers of the disassembled floors were hoisted to the surface in the old mining buckets. The task had started from the bottom of the shaft in November and was more than 500 feet up from the bottom by late January.[89]

Doane and Granger found the double-track bridge over the Deerfield River at the east portal of the Tunnel strained by overloading and from lack of care. It had carried the many cars of broken rock excavated to create the Tunnel. Doane also noted in his report that the bridge "was rather light" in its original construction. Consequently, a third truss was being added in the middle of the bridge, and it was undergoing a thorough repair.[90]

The laying of a single track through the Tunnel commenced the last week of January 1875.[91] For the most part, the track was to be used by Farren in the performance of his arching contract.[92] But during January and February he was busy concentrating on completing the track work east of Shelburne Falls and had not yet begun the Tunnel arching. It was expected his arching contract would take six to eight months. Provision was made in the arching contract "for the daily running of two trains each way through the Tunnel while the work . . ." was ongoing. This was provisional on the Commonwealth's determination of its being desirable even to run trains.

First Passage

The first train to pass through the Hoosac Tunnel did so on Tuesday, 9 February 1875, a bitter-cold winter day.[93] With George H. Cheney at the controls of the coal-burning eight-wheeler "N. C. Munson," three gravel cars and a single boxcar were slowly pulled safely through—from daylight on the east side of the Hoosac Mountain to daylight on the west side. (The locomotive was named for the contractor rebuilding the tracks from the Tunnel to Charlemont.) The time required to cover a distance of less than five miles was, by different estimates printed in the papers, thirty-four, thirty-five, and, according to one writer, thirty-nine minutes. The speed was limited, owing to the condition of the track. It had still not been ballasted, so ties supporting the rails lay directly on the irregular rock floor of the Tunnel. The boxcar was filled with more than 100 passengers, according to one newspaper, but another editor estimated 125 passengers. Consulting Engineer Thomas Doane and his son John, together with Chief Engineer W. P. Granger, Austin Bond, N. C. Munson, James Edwards, and N. G. Healey, managed to crowd into the cab of the locomotive with Cheney.[94] Austin Bond was the newly appointed treasurer of the Troy and Greenfield Railroad. Edwards worked for Munson and was responsible for the work at the east end of the Tunnel; Healey was the master track-layer. Cheney the engineer also had his two sons in the cab with him on this historic run.

The other riders, passengers, and stowaways squeezed into the boxcar. Commonwealth Engineer Benjamin Frost and seventy-six-year-old Dr. E. S. Hawkes of North Adams, a pioneer of the Hoosac Tunnel enterprise, were among those in the boxcar.[95] While there was no public demonstration after the event, the news carried far—two days later, even the *Los Angeles Herald* took notice of the event.[96] Thirty-six years later, seventy-eight-year-old George Cheney would still be living in Williamstown.

With this first passage of a four-car train through the Tunnel, another of those uncanny connections among those associated with the Tunnel existed. While Herman Haupt did not ride the "N. C. Munson" through the Tunnel, this locomotive was of the four driving wheel design (4-4-0) perfected and patented by Henry R. Campbell in Philadelphia. It was over a drawing of this type engine that Haupt labored in Campbell's office during his first year after leaving West Point. Norman Munson purchased this particular locomotive from the Hinkley Locomotive Works in Boston in 1864 for use in transporting sand and gravel to fill Boston's Back Bay, whose tidal flow Loammi Baldwin's Boston Mill Dam, built between 1819 and 1821, had captured.

Riders described the experience of traveling through the Tunnel and looking forward from the cab of the locomotive with the headlight of the engine playing on the walls as providing a sensation like being at the large end of a funnel and looking through the smaller tube. A black spot seems just ahead, but it may be a mile or more away. There is the strange sensation of trying in vain to plunge from the glare of the light into the darkness beyond. The smoke from the engine hangs lazily around the rough-edged rock, the water trickles down the sides or at times falls in deluging streams from above, while there are traces of the drill holes, and discarded implements are scattered on the wayside. As the engine rattles over the uneven track, a slight rope ladder is passed at the central shaft, and the cold air of winter is felt.[97]

The editor of the *Adams Transcript* later provided advice to those adventuresome types who might want to take a train ride through the Tunnel and run the risk ". . . of having your equilibrium disturbed or your personal appearance damaged by any little tunnel irregularities in the way of falling rock or collisions. Get on the right side of some doctor who has a good practice at the East End, take out an accident policy, clean up your conscience a little, leave your wife a lock of your hair, kiss the babies, laugh at your creditors, and improve the first opportunity you have of riding through the tunnel."[98] Frost set crews to work ballasting the track through the Tunnel, and, by the end of the month, the work was completed halfway through the black hole.[99]

During the week of this first passage, George Mowbray had a serious accident while working in his laboratory. He was in the process of preparing a mixture when he broke a bottle, releasing sulfurous fumes that nearly suffocated him before, with irritated eyes, he escaped the confines of his laboratory. It took Mowbray several days to recover from the effects of breathing the fumes.[100]

With the passing of a train through the Tunnel, the political infighting intensified over how the Commonwealth's railroad would be managed and used. Before the end of February, a bill was submitted in the General Court to establish a board of five directors to control the railroad and the Tunnel. The bill also established the right of all railroad companies to use the Tunnel and the Commonwealth's trackage.[101] Like the dreary years it took to bore the Mountain, many more years of political wrangling were ahead before the Commonwealth would finally liberate itself from the Hoosac Tunnel railroad business.

On Monday, 22 February, B. N. Farren set his crews to work at the Little Hoosac Tunnel.[102] To break the rock, the miners were loading their drill holes with Mowbray's soup. On Saturday morning, 13 March, the miners fired a charge with a little extra nitro-glycerin. The blast sent broken rock flying across the river and into the two-story machine shop of James Hunter & Company, breaking 151 panes of glass. A large piece of the Hoosac Mountain had been dragged to this shop for testing mechanical drills in 1864. A year later, Doane had commissioned Hunter to built air compressors for the mechanical drill he hoped would soon be perfected. To keep good men working at the Little Hoosac Tunnel, Farren raised the wages of his miners from $1.37 to $1.50 per day.[103]

In the Tunnel through the Hoosac Mountain, Farren now had sixty men employed under the supervision of R. B. Campbell. They were working day and night, laying the bricks for the much-needed arching.[104] To light all of the work locations, Farren used fifty large kerosene oil torches.[105] Campbell, who was from Turners Falls, had previously worked with Farren on the west end during the early arching years, so he and Farren now had thirteen years of experience working together. The men in the Tunnel were scattered along its length at the various points where brick arching was needed—locations marked by the engineers working for Frost. As the loose rock was removed from the roof and walls, it was piled along the track and later carried out on railroad cars. The bricks were laid with waterproof cement.[106] By the first of April, E. A. Bond completed clearing the central shaft.[107] At the bottom of the stonework Doane had built from the ground surface to the top of the rock, Bond built a heavy floor to seal the shaft. Farren was, with his usual energy, proceeding with the arching in the Tunnel, and with the central shaft now sealed, all were hopeful freight service would soon be passing through the Mountain.

Finally, at ten o'clock in the evening of Monday, 5 April 1875, the Hoosac Tunnel went into operation for freight trains. A train from Troy, New York, bound for Boston, left the depot in North Adams and headed for the Tunnel. George H. Cheney was again at the controls, but this time the twenty-two cars of corn were drawn by the engine "Deerfield." The engine "Robinson," driven by Robert Clark, was at the rear, pushing. The pusher would be employed only as far as the central shaft. R. B. Campbell, Farren's supervisor, hopped a ride on the freight through the Tunnel, together with a few others. It took the long train something like forty-five minutes to cover the five miles through the Mountain.[108] On the same day, a railroad car with 12,000 pounds of furniture left Leominster for the Tunnel.[109] Both trains were detained at Bardwell's Ferry, between Shelburne Falls and Greenfield, because a flood the previous week had swept away two spans of the bridge over the Deerfield River. Even before the flood arrangements had been made with the Keystone Bridge Company of Philadelphia to replace the old wooden structure with a new iron-truss bridge.[110] George T. Wiswell, the road-master of the Commonwealth's Troy and Greenfield Railroad,[111] was to have charge of the work, using a gang of railroad workers. But all expected a temporary fix to be executed by Thursday, and then the freights could be sent on to their destinations.

In announcing the opening of the Tunnel for freight trains, the *American Railroad Journal* reported a contract had been signed to bring five hundred cars of coal directly from mines in Pennsylvania to Fitchburg. The *Journal* also noted that fifty freight cars were being built by Ranlet Manufacturing Company in Laconia, New Hampshire, for Crocker's old Fitchburg Railroad. These were to be painted coffee brown and lettered in white: "Hoosac Tunnel Line—Fitchburg Railroad." The first ten cars were ready by the middle of March. There was great expectation for the Hoosac Tunnel line, as the *Journal* closed its article by predicting that offices for the line would be opened by the first of June in all the leading shipping points.[112]

Farren's arching contract obliged him to carry on the work in such a way as to allow the passage of eight to ten trains during the day.[113] Accordingly, the Fitchburg Railroad contracted with him to haul the trains with his locomotives "—and to have sole responsibility and charge of same through the Tunnel"[114] from the east portal to the station in North Adams, a distance of seven miles.

A Passenger Train?

A few weeks after the first freight completed its passage, Mrs. H. M. Streeter walked completely through the Tunnel from the Hoosac Tunnel Station on the east end to North Adams. She had arrived at the station in the afternoon and, being anxious to reach her home that evening, she undertook the tiresome walk.[115] Mrs. Streeter's husband held the lease on and operated the Wilson House, the hotel where Alvah Crocker had encamped during the years he directed the Hoosac Tunnel work. When the lease expired later in 1875, Mr. Streeter and his Tunnel-hiking wife moved to California.[116]

Even though Walter Shanly was released from the Hoosac Tunnel contract in 1874, he would visit Massachusetts many times over the next ten years while trying to recoup the extra expenses incurred in completing the work. He would repeatedly present petitions and memorials to the General Court for dealing with the unexpected flow of water encountered west of the central shaft, for having to conform to the requirement beyond what was specified by the contract but imposed by the Commonwealth's engineers, and for the necessity of removing a large quantity of rock beyond the Tunnel lines that were stipulated in the contract.[117] These efforts were very frustrating to a man of his character, but in late 1874 and in 1875, family matters were his greatest burden and probably the reason for his unwillingness to pursue further Hoosac Tunnel work.

The death of his brother Coote[118] and the knowledge of Frank's shaky financial situation weighed heavily on him. Frank built well, but he seldom made money, and now Walter found himself liable for his brother's debts. Walter and Frank must have been in North Adams settling matters on the Saturday Mrs. Streeter walked through the Tunnel. The brothers, however, had to change their plans and depart for Jacksonville, Florida, at this time to attend the funeral of their brother Charles Dawson Shanly. Dawson's death cast yet another cloud on Walter's outlook. He had spent most of the preceding months in Boston arguing his case. The majority of the Committee on Claims presented a resolve (a bill) directing the Commonwealth to pay $112,000 out of the treasury to Walter and Francis Shanly as full settlement of their claims. The minority submitted a resolve to pay $226,495, and a dissenting report by Isaac Pratt Jr. submitted a resolve specifying $37,837.61.[119] But none of these resolves met with a sustaining vote in the General Court, so Shanly like Haupt so many times before, left Massachusetts empty-handed.

By mid-May, B. N. Farren had completed construction of the rails between the west portal and the depot of the Troy and Boston Railroad in North Adams. The railroad's road-master was building a new depot at Zoar and would also replace the old Hoosac Tunnel Station.[120] In North Adams, he had crews building the foundations for an iron turntable. But before regular passenger service could safely commence, more of Farren's arching work in the Tunnel needed to be completed. Realizing the Hoosac Tunnel work was rapidly coming to an end, E. A. Bond, in late April, resigned his position with Benjamin Frost and the engineering corps. He immediately found employment with Farren, supervising the arching and excavation of the Little Hoosac Tunnel.[121]

In May 1875, when the Commonwealth reorganized the management of the Hoosac Tunnel from an engineering operation into a railroad management structure, Jeremiah Prescott, previously with the Eastern Railroad of Massachusetts as superintendent from 1855 to the spring of 1875, was confirmed as manager of the Troy and Greenfield Railroad.[122] The Eastern Railroad connected Boston with Portland, Maine. Prescott, originally from Hampton Falls, New Hampshire, had begun his railroad career as a conductor for the Eastern in 1844. He resigned from the Eastern in March to take the new position. It was a most remarkable appointment, as Prescott, in his position as superintendent of the Eastern, was at least partially responsible for two serious train accidents in Massachusetts. The operating rules for the Eastern Railroad forbade conductor acceptance of verbal instructions, but Prescott would often give such instructions personally, and this practice led to trouble many times.[123]

First there was the September 1862 collision at Hamilton, near Salem, Massachusetts, a tragedy resulting in the deaths of five persons and injuries to about thirty-five others. A coroner's jury laid the blame on Prescott, who resigned but soon resumed his old position. Nine years later, in August 1871, a disaster in Revere, Massachusetts resulted in thirty killed and fifty-seven injured.[124] Again the accident was the result of Prescott's verbal orders not being understood by a locomotive engineer. In this case, the Bangor Express train out of the Boston Station plowed into the rear car of a stopped train headed to Beverly, Massachusetts. The express engine surged two-thirds of the way into the rear passenger car, packed with some seventy-five travelers. Those not crushed were roasted or scalded to death by the fire ignited by broken oil lamps and steam escaping from the locomotive's boiler, which rested inside the car. At the time, Charles Francis Adams was head of the Massachusetts Railroad Commission, but he took no action against Prescott and instead blamed the conductor of the stopped train, who failed to send the brakeman to the rear to flag down the Bangor Express.[125] The president of the company resigned, but "Superintendent Prescott, who seemed to be disaster proof, was retained as superintendent of the Eastern Railroad."[126]

Prescott's departure from the Eastern Railroad may have been prompted by the 1873 publication of a pamphlet titled *The Eastern Railroad of Massachusetts: Its Blunders, Mismanagement and Corruption*. The pamphlet was written by Charles W. Felt of Salem, who had spent years as assistant superintendent under Prescott, and it clearly described Prescott's actions in both accidents.

During May, about twenty-five loaded freight cars were hauled through the Tunnel each day, but there was still no passenger service. Farren had begun excavation for the arching in the western section, and by this time he had completed almost three hundred feet of arching in the eastern section.[127] As 1875 moved into June, the buildings at the central shaft were removed and the machinery was dismantled, preparatory to their sale.[128] But even with daylight through the Mountain and freight trains cautiously making the passage, the "Great Spirit" of the Hoosac Mountain battled the engineers and workers. On Friday morning, 11 June, forty tons of Hoosac Mountain rock fell from the Tunnel roof and blocked passage. This was in a section two thousand feet east of the west shaft where Farren's miners had completed their excavations prior to placement of the brick arching. The eleven o'clock work train going through the Tunnel struck the rock pile, badly wrecking two cars. The engine was pushing the cars, so the engineer did not see the rock pile until it was too late.[129] Ten days later, the Mountain belched another large quantity of rock from the roof of the Tunnel.[130] Farren, besides dealing with all the falling rock, was still having trouble with the blasting at the Little Hoosac Tunnel. In June, a blast again threw rock a little farther than planned and destroyed a town bridge over the tracks of the Troy and Boston Railroad.

In June, Farren hauled 531 freight cars through the Tunnel. With the Troy and Greenfield Railroad coming into operation on Wednesday, 7 July, Farren began attaching a passenger car to the freight train he hauled through the Tunnel from North Adams each morning at six o'clock. For those wanting to return, the car was attached to the westbound 6:30 evening freight train.[131] Farren was collecting the passage toll for the railroad: seventy-five cents per passenger and $1.50 per freight car.[132] As service improved, freight traffic was slowly increasing. During July, as Farren still struggled with the arching work, 811 freight cars passed through. Most of the loaded traffic was from the west, headed east: 511 cars, with 436 being loaded. Only 188—or less than half of the cars going west—were loaded.[133]

October 1875

On Wednesday, 13 October, an engine and one passenger car from Boston bound for Troy, New York, reached North Adams via the Tunnel. Aboard were Governor William Gaston, the former Mayor of Boston, and a party of Commonwealth officials, including ladies. The train was pulled by a new engine, named after the Governor, and was decorated profusely with flags and bunting in honor of the occasion.[134]

A week later, Herman Haupt and Henry Cartwright descended on North Adams to see the Tunnel.[135] For the month of October, 895 loaded freight cars moved east through the Tunnel, with most of it being cotton from the southwest, destined for mills in Massachusetts. But the cotton cars were sent back empty, so the number of loaded cars moving west was only 255 in October. As 1875 drew to a close, B. N. Farren's crews were still struggling to restrain the rock of the Hoosac Mountain. During November of 1875, he had five hundred hands working day and night in the Tunnel, laying about 50,000 bricks per day![136] To support the bricklaying, he arranged in September for 1,400 carloads of brick from Rondout, New York. These were to be delivered at the rate of ten carloads daily.[137] The falling rock now seemed a greater problem than the Irishman's "ells" of the Haupt and early Doane years. But the work was slowly—to some, ever so slowly—being accomplished.

In January 1876, the Commonwealth began to dispense with the engineers employed to oversee the work of its contractors. The Governor's Council was supposed to travel through the Tunnel by special train in mid-January 1876, but the Mountain managed to delay their travel on the appointed day by once again dropping a pile of rocks on the tracks.[138] Less than a month later, on 8 February, the Mountain repeated the performance and dumped a ten-foot-high pile of rocks in the same general area as the Mountain's January display of displeasure. The pile was so great this time that the evening train through the Tunnel had to be canceled because Farren's crews could not clear the mass in a single day.[139] The following week, the *Adams Transcript* reported the engineers were considering arching another 1,000 to 1,500 feet of Tunnel.[140]

With the opening of the General Court in 1876, Walter Shanly was back in Boston carrying a petition for $150,000 of extra compensation for losses he sustained during the Hoosac Tunnel work. His claim this time concerned the large amount of rock excavation beyond the designated "tunnel lines," for which he was "paid nothing—nor did their contract entitle them to pay therefor; but as matters turned out"[141] benefited the Commonwealth where arching was proved necessary. Even Chief Engineer Frost admitted that where the arching was required, Shanly's argument was true. He calculated the amount of excavation for the benefit of the Commonwealth at 22,628 cubic yards, and at the lowest rate paid for such work—namely, $10 per yard—the value would be $226,280.

Walter Shanly was well respected, but no funds were forthcoming from the Commonwealth. Nevertheless, the people of North Adams and the Deerfield Valley were especially appreciative of what Shanly had accomplished. They were well aware of his battles with the Mountain and his perseverance in the face of so many seemingly overwhelming challenges. As a memento of their esteem, the citizens got together and purchased a gold-headed ebony cane for him. On Friday evening, 17 March, there was a truly touching presentation ceremony at the Arnold House hotel in North Adams. On the cane were images of the west end of the Tunnel, a profile of the Mountain, and a view of the east end. The top of the cane bore an inscription: "Presented to Walter Shanly, contractor of the Hoosac Tunnel, from the citizens of North Adams, Mass."

Shanly, never one for speeches, on this occasion delivered a heartfelt acceptance to those in attendance, but his words were really addressed to the community at large. After mentioning difficulties encountered both inside and outside the Mountain, he proceeded:

> *I still always felt that the good will of the people was with me, and many a time, in my solitary rides over the Hoosac mountain, in what I will call the "dark days," when I sometimes doubted if I could live through and overcome the obstacles encountered, the friendly, warm greeting of the mountain farmers, as they stopped to ask if all were well with me, have cheered me up, and given me new strength and fresh courage, causing me to feel that, let the worst come to the worst, I had the people at my back anyhow.*[142]

It was an occasion reminiscent of the farewell dinner held when he left the Grand Trunk Railway. In Canada, the book presented to him in 1862 contained the signatures of working men. The cane presented to him in North Adams was a very expensive one procured in New York City, and its cost was borne by many who had no personal intimacy with Shanly. This fact greatly added to his gratification.

At the end of April, the Troy and Greenfield Railroad, together with the Fitchburg Railroad, began running daily passenger trains between North Adams and Boston. The eastbound train departed North Adams at 6 a.m. and arrived in Boston at 2:22 p.m., while the westbound departed Boston at 11:10 a.m. and reached North Adams at 6:45 p.m.[143]

Toward the end of May, with the arching work neared completion, Farren began discharging his Tunnel workers. E. A. Bond, who had gone from Tunnel engineer under Benjamin Frost to employment with contractor Farren, was now appointed freight agent for the railroad in North Adams. Engineer Frost seems to have grown attached to North Adams, so, before the year was out, he left his position with the Commonwealth, opened an office in the village, and established permanent residence. The Tunnel arching work was completed on 30 June 1876 and in early 1877, Farren would travel to Philadelphia and wed Caroline F. Atkinson.

The Troy and Greenfield Railroad had only one track, but the masonry and seven of the sixteen bridges were constructed for two tracks. The iron bridge at Bardwell's Ferry over the Deerfield River was 585 feet long, and the one over the Green River in Greenfield was 569 feet long. The old bridges were gone, and the new iron ones were now in service. In total, 7,573 lineal feet of Tunnel were supported by arch work, including the fifty feet of stone arch at the west portal. To control the train traffic, a telegraph station was established at each end of the Tunnel, with a connecting wire run through the Tunnel. Consequently, on 17 July 1876, the Tunnel was finally opened without restriction, and through trains began clouding it with their smoke.

After so many years of hope, failures, work, and trials, passenger trains immediately began express service between Boston and Troy. A passenger standing on the rear platform of one of the trains wrote of the experience: "Emerging from the western portal, it requires a moment for our eyes to become accustomed to the change, for we are now spinning along in the sunshine, past the green fields and the woods. We look back from the rear car up at that mighty barrier, the tallest peaks of which seem to pierce the sky, and far down we see a hole surmounted by an arch of stone, which, as we leave it, dwindles to a tiny spot."[144]

Epilogue

ALVAH CROCKER'S DREAM WAS finally realized on 1 February 1887, when the Commonwealth of Massachusetts sold its Troy and Greenfield Railroad and Hoosac Tunnel to the Fitchburg Railroad. For this prize, Crocker's Fitchburg Railroad gave the Commonwealth $5 million in its own bonds and $5 million in its common stock.

Of those who had taken up the crusade to achieve daylight through the Hoosac Mountain, many did not live long enough to rejoice when the first trains made their way regularly between Boston and Troy. There were a few toilers, however, who continued in the professional practice of engineering, and their lives, in almost mystical ways, would be intertwined as they pursued the business of building railroads across the country. For the Shanly brothers and Herman Haupt, however, the "Great Spirit" of the Mountain seemed to have won the battle.

Francis Shanly

Although Frank and Walter Shanly had taken the Hoosac Tunnel contract in partnership, it was the older brother, Walter, who handled the negotiations with the Commonwealth and courted the investors needed to finance their battle with the Hoosac Mountain. By 1870, Frank was dividing his time between the Tunnel work and his own projects in Canada. The official separation came on 20 October 1871, when Frank signed a formal statement authorizing his brother to act jointly for them.[1]

Though the details for all the various contracts are not available, the records indicate Frank Shanly and Company built more than 200 miles of railroad in Canada between 1870 and 1874, while Walter was struggling with the trials of piercing the Mountain in Massachusetts. This Canadian railroad work represented contracts valued at almost $2 million. In many instances, however,

Frank Shanly either was unable to meet the contract time requirements or experienced labor problems. In other cases, his assumptions about the work proved faulty and he incurred greater expenses in fulfilling the contract requirements. Worst of all, some railroad companies simply ran out of money, and Frank's firm was not paid for the work performed.

Still banking on a big profit from the Hoosac Tunnel contract, and believing his next project would be a grand success, Frank and his contracting company went merrily along and assumed all was well. Finally, Walter, who was liable as a cosigner for many of Frank's various loans, realized his brother's dire situation. He found himself jointly responsible with Frank for $95,000 in bank debt and another $37,000 in floating debt, while Frank's firm had only $34,500 in paper assets. The climax occurred in 1874, when the railroad boom in Canada ground to a screeching halt. Frank Shanly was in ruins. His household furnishings were sold at a sheriff's sale in January 1874.[2] The ambitious and high-living engineer/contractor was fifty-four years old, with nine children still living under his roof. Walter, in his role as cosigner on many of the loans, had to reach into his own savings to pay his brother's mountain of debt. After a two-year absence and burdened with a feeling of obligation, Frank returned to the Hoosac Tunnel work in early 1874, but there is no indication the partnership was reestablished.

In the second half of 1875, Frank Shanly returned to engineering work—first for the Canadian government and then for the City of Toronto. He also had consulting assignments on the side and even began to bid again on railroad construction work. Although he desperately needed the income, he disliked working for the City of Toronto as he was forced to maintain regular office hours, thus restricting his freedom. Relief came in June 1880 with his appointment as the chief engineer of the Intercolonial Railway. He then resigned from the Toronto position.[3]

By this time, Walter Shanly, using what little he had made on the Hoosac Tunnel contract, had paid off $109,636 of Frank's outstanding loans. Even though Walter might not have expected his younger brother ever to repay this large debt, this graciousness still did not solve Frank's financial problems, and it left a pall on the older brother's outlook on life. Despite Walter's help, Frank remained burdened with a large number of small debts that were beyond his means to pay. Frank had always lived well beyond his means, but age and life now began to dampen his spirits.

Between his 1880 appointment to the Intercolonial Railway position and August 1882, Frank lost three of his children to the angel of death. The third to succumb was his son Cuthbert, for whom he had held great hopes. He had even had the youth appointed as his secretary at the Intercolonial Railway. After Cuthbert died, Walter wrote to a friend that his brother never again held up his head.[4]

Less than two months later, Frank Shanly, railroad engineer, died while riding on a night train to Ottawa. The date was 12 September 1882. The notice to Walter was a cold telegram stating, "Body taken off here and is waiting to be removed by relative." So once again the noble elder brother took up the task of untangling and settling the younger brother's debts.

Walter Shanly

The work of driving a Tunnel through the Hoosac Mountain had come to an end, but Walter Shanly still faced the daunting task of collecting the money he believed the Commonwealth owed him for completing the bore. He and his brother had accepted the Hoosac Tunnel challenge with the expectation that they would make money. At the age of fifty-eight, he returned to Montreal burdened by the mountain of his brother's debt. He was duty-bound and legally required to repay the loans, but the obligation affected his spirit. He penned a note on his Hoosac Tunnel accounts, giving vent to his frustration: "[T]he very large liabilities I had unwittingly assumed for my reckless and utterly uncalculating brother Frank"[5] swallowed the small surplus left from the Hoosac contract. In need of income, he became an engineering consultant. Until late 1879, he served the Quebec provincial government in resolving disputes dealing with the construction of railroads.

Furthermore, there was still the need to repay the $600,000 of working capital he had borrowed to carry the Tunnel work forward until the earnings passed the $500,000 retainage the Commonwealth had demanded. He had paid back a small portion of this loan in the early years of the work, but he still owed the interest and a large amount of principal when he settled with Massachusetts. The Shanly records do not give an exact accounting of the interest, but if one assumes he had reduced the principal to $500,000 by partial payments during the first and second years of the work, and if the interest rate for the loan was six percent, the accumulated interest alone at the end of 1874 (when Shanly collected his final payment from the Commonwealth) would have amounted to more than $200,000.

In the case of the huge Hoosac Tunnel loan, fortune cast a smile on Walter Shanly. Shanly's correspondence leads to the conclusion that Alexander

Tilloch Galt was the source of the loan.[6] The matter was apparently a very private arrangement between Shanly and Galt.

Shanly's relationship with Galt dated back to 1851, when Shanly was chief engineer for the Toronto and Guelph Railway. Additionally, the British-born Galt was a man with political connections and capital—he had managed to convince the London bankers to make the Toronto and Guelph the western leg of Canada's Grand Trunk Railway. Nonetheless, he seems to have suffered his own financial reverses after making the loan to Shanly, but his creditors failed to discover the Hoosac loan. So when Shanly came forward to repay the debt, Galt was happy to accept the return of the principal amount and to forgo the interest if Shanly would continue to remain silent about the matter. As a result Shanly did not have to come up with the large amount of accrued interest and the identity of the lender remained undisclosed. In his Hoosac accounts, Shanly wrote, "Not even my bookkeeper knew from where the working capital came. . . ."[7]

Over the next twelve years, Shanly would make multiple trips to Boston, attempting to dislodge money from the Commonwealth based on the Hoosac Tunnel work he was forced to perform beyond his contractual responsibilities. The Mechanics Bank in Montreal also experienced difficulties in mid-1875. Years earlier, Shanly had been a director and then president of this bank. He had stepped in as a vice president[8] when the bank was in trouble. Still, the bank was forced to write down the shareholders' capital, and Shanly suffered a $20,000 loss.[9]

His letters to his brother Frank indicate he spent most of February 1877 at the Revere House in Boston, while making his case before a Committee of the General Court.[10] Even though the Committee recommended a payment of $125,000 to settle the matter, no resolution was passed, so Shanly returned to Canada no richer for all the effort. In 1881, 1882, and 1884, he continued with his appeals to the Commonwealth.[11] Finally, in 1887, he received $79,495.62 of additional compensation and the matter was closed.[12]

After Frank Shanly's death in 1882, Walter took on responsibility for his brother's widow, Louisa, and the six surviving children. One life insurance policy, not encumbered by a lien, allowed Mrs. Shanly to purchase a house in Toronto, but Walter Shanly continued to pay the family's household expenses for many years.

In 1878, Walter Shanly became chief engineer for the Canada Atlantic Railway, which was being built from Ottawa to join the Vermont Central

Railroad across the St. Lawrence River. This was again one of those déjà-vu convergences in the engineering experiences of those who came together at the Hoosac Mountain. The Vermont Central was the railroad Crocker had supported in his quest to bring steel rails to northern Massachusetts, and it was Crocker who had sent Samuel Felton early in 1844 to survey a route for the line of the Vermont Central.[13]

In 1885, when Walter Shanly was seventy years old, he was once again elected to the House of Commons, representing Grenville South. He would spend six more years in Parliament before retiring in 1891. Just as during his earlier terms, he shied away from the general business of the House and spoke only on engineering matters. Even into his seventies, he continued his involvement with the Edwardsburg Starch Company. On the professional side, he had a role in founding the Canadian Society for Civil Engineering. In the 1890s, however, he distanced himself from all these pursuits and focused on history as his avocation.

Walter Shanly, civil engineer, died in Montreal on 17 December 1899. He was interred in the family plot at Arva, near London, Ontario.

Thomas Doane

After perfecting his engineering skills in Loammi Baldwin's Charlestown office, Thomas Doane began his association with the Hoosac Mountain challenge when he was appointed chief engineer of the Hoosac Tunnel in 1863 under Commonwealth commissioners John W. Brooks, Samuel M. Felton, and Alexander Holmes. Doane was born on 20 September 1821 in Orleans, Massachusetts, and died on 22 October 1897 in West Townsend, Vermont.

He resigned his position as chief engineer of the Hoosac Tunnel work in 1867, when Alvah Crocker assumed direction of the effort, but he returned in 1874 as consulting engineer for the Commonwealth and was present to see the first trains complete their passage through the Tunnel. When he left the Tunnel in 1867, he again partnered with John Brooks, building railroads for the Boston moneymen led by John Murray Forbes. He went westward in 1869 as chief engineer and superintendent of the Burlington and Missouri River Railroad in Nebraska (B&MR-N). He built a subbranch from the road's original route across Iowa. His diligent efforts had rails going to Lincoln, Nebraska, by the summer of 1870, and by September 1872, the rails of the B&MR-N joined the Union Pacific Railroad at Kearney, Nebraska. In 1872, the B&MR-N became part of the Chicago, Burlington, and Quincy Railroad (CB&Q). These corporate matters reflected consolidations of ownerships controlled by Boston money. Doane named the towns along this land-grant railroad in alphabetical order, using New England names—Dorchester, Exeter, Harvard, and Lowell are examples. The Commonwealth retained Doane as a consultant on the Troy and Greenfield Railroad and Hoosac Tunnel until 1877.

As acting chief engineer for the Northern Pacific Railroad, Doane headed west again in 1879. During his one-year tenure, he organized the engineering corps of the railroad and led location work in the Dakotas and Washington Territory. During the winter, he stretched track across the thick ice of the Missouri River, which facilitated the rapid delivery of materials for the next construction season.

A year later, he was in West Virginia, locating a railroad in a manner reminiscent of Loammi Baldwin's canal-location days, with overnights in wayside taverns. During a twelve-day stint, he prepared a route profile covering more than 150 miles while traveling on horseback with a single guide. For this survey, he determined elevations using an aneroid barometer.

Massachusetts was Doane's home and his office was in Charlestown, so he had no lack of engineering employment with the many railroads centering on Boston. While in Nebraska between his Hoosac engagements, he was instrumental in the founding of Doane College, a liberal-arts institution in Crete, twenty miles west of Lincoln, on the Big Blue River.

During the last twenty years of his life, Doane was an active member of the Boston Society of Civil Engineers and served as its president for nine years. In 1882, he became a member of the American Society of Civil Engineers. With a sincere sense of civic duty, Doane served as a director of the Associated Charities of Boston and as vice president of the Hunt Asylum for Destitute Children. In the tradition of Loammi Baldwin, he was a man of convictions and integrity: "Work done by him must be good work or none."[14] His grave is in the old family burial ground in Orleans, Massachusetts.

Samuel M. Felton

In 1851 when Samuel Felton became president of the Philadelphia, Wilmington, and Baltimore Railroad (PWBRR), he handed over Loammi Baldwin's Charlestown engineering practice to Thomas Doane. Felton then established his residence in Philadelphia and turned the PWBRR into a profitable road. In 1857, while president of the PWBRR, Felton put the locomotive *Daniel Webster* into regular service. It was probably the first really successful coal burning passenger engine in regular service upon any railroad in the United States.

As a Hoosac Tunnel commissioner between 1862 and 1865, Felton again worked with Doane. The strain of operating the strategically important PWBRR during the Civil War caused him to resign all of his positions in early 1865. But he seems to have quickly regained his health following his attack of paralysis and became president of the Pennsylvania Steel Company later in the year. The company was the first firm in the United States to manufacture steel railroad rails using the Bessemer process.

During the years after the Civil War, Felton served as a director for numerous railroads, including his old Philadelphia, Wilmington, and Baltimore; the Northern Pacific Railroad (1870 to 1873, some six years before Thomas Doane served as its chief engineer); the Ogdensburg and Lake Champlain Railroad, the road Walter and Frank Shanly built; and the Pennsylvania Railroad (1873 to 1883). In 1869, President Ulysses Grant appointed Felton a commissioner to inspect the Union Pacific and the Central Pacific Railroads.

Felton was born on 17 July 1809 in West Newbury, Massachusetts, and died at his home in Philadelphia on 24 January 1889.

John W. Brooks

The physical collapse Brooks suffered in 1866, during the legislative fight with Herman Haupt, almost cost him his life. It caused him, like Felton, to resign his position as president of the Michigan Central Railroad and to step away from all of the other duties he was handling at the time for John Murray Forbes. In 1865, James F. Joy, the lawyer and Brooks's partner from the Michigan Central, became president of the Chicago, Burlington, and Quincy Railroad. With rest, Brooks recovered and regained his strength by 1867. He then went out to Iowa to become the head of the Burlington and Missouri River Railroad. This explains the call for Doane to build the Nebraska line, because in 1869 Brooks became president of the B&MRR-N, the land-grant extension of the road in Nebraska.

Tragedy befell Brooks when he joined the attorney Joy in a scheme to pay themselves as contractors with funds advanced to the CB&Q for building roads in Iowa.[15] In 1875, when Forbes discovered their siphoning of funds, he purged both men from his railroads. In a very short time, thirty years of friendship and professional confidence dissolved. Brooks was unrepentant, and the association was completely destroyed. Perhaps it was the stress of this break, but again Brooks was stricken with serious health issues, so he retired to his home in Boston. It was not a happy retirement, and this time his health did not return.

Despite his poor health, Brooks decided to sail for Europe in May 1881. He settled in Heidelberg, Germany, hoping the climate would help, but he died five months later, on 16 September.

Herman Haupt

His engagement in the service of the Union Army probably saved Herman Haupt from further embarrassment in attempting to bore the Hoosac Mountain without the aid of a workable pneumatic drill and nitro-glycerin. Later historians have acclaimed Haupt's magnificent railroad and bridge building work during the Civil War as monuments to his true greatness as an engineer. After the war, he found employment in 1870 as chief engineer of the Shenandoah Valley Railroad, then as general manager of the Richmond and Danville Railroad, and later as general manager of the Piedmont Air-Line Railway between Richmond, Virginia, and Atlanta, Georgia. His service to the railroads ended in 1876, when he undertook to build an oil pipeline for the Pennsylvania Transportation Company. Critics of the idea pointed to his failure at the Hoosac Mountain in order to discredit his cost estimates. By the fall of 1878, Haupt had procured the necessary right-of-way for a pipeline from the Allegheny River to Baltimore and was preparing to let contracts for the laying of pipe, but he left the project later in the year.

In 1881, Haupt became general manager of transportation for the Northern Pacific Railroad—two years after Thomas Doane's stint as chief engineer for the Northern. He held the manager's position until 1885, when he became general superintendent. He left the Northern Pacific the following year.

Haupt and his wife purchased the Mountain Lake Hotel (now the Mountain Lake Lodge), a resort west of Blacksburg in the Shenandoah Mountains of Virginia. As with many of his other speculative adventures, it was never a success. After 1892, he started and served as president of the General Compressed Air and Power Company. In 1899, he became president of another adventure, the National Nutrient Company—a scheme to produce powdered and condensed milk. Like Frank Shanly, Herman Haupt died in a Pullman compartment on a speeding train while journeying from New York City to Philadelphia on 14 December 1905. He was buried in the family plot at West Laurel Hill Cemetery, Bala Cynwyd, Pennsylvania, just outside of Philadelphia.

His death marked the end for all the Hoosac Tunnel engineers. The last as with the rest had passed into the earth they all once strived so mightily to bore.

Things Never Change

One of the last claims against the Commonwealth of Massachusetts for work performed on Boston's $14-billion Central Artery project, the "Big Dig," was settled in November 2014, fifteen years after the work was completed. The Commonwealth finally agreed to a $88.7-million final settlement. The claim involved engineering changes on tunneling the contractor team performed and for the extra cost caused by differing soil conditions.[16]

Endnotes

Introduction

1   "Hoosac Tunnel Matters," *Hoosac Valley News*, vol. 24, no. 20 (14 January 1864).

2   "A Great Bore," *Adams News & Transcript*, vol. 25, no. 34 (20 July 1865).

3   "Central Shaft," *Senate No. 102, Report of the Joint Standing Committee of 1867 on the Hoosac Tunnel and Troy and Greenfield Railroad* (March 1868), p. 5.

4   "Progress on the Hoosac Tunnel," *American Railway Times* 19, no. 45 (9 November 1867).

5   Ibid.

6   "The Hoosac Tunnel," *New York Times* (18 November 1867).

7   Henry S. Drinker, *Tunneling, Explosive Compounds, and Rock Drills* (New York: John Wiley, 1878), 693.

Chapter 1

1   Michael D. Coe, *The Line of Forts* (Lebanon, NH: University Press of New England, 2006), 7.

2   Edward Manning Ruttenberg, *History of the Indian Tribes of Hudson's River* (Albany, NY: J. Munsell, 1872), 376.

3   William B. Browne, *The Mohawk Trail: Its History and Course* (Pittsfield, MA: Sun Printing Co., 1920), 35.

4   Nancy Woloch, *Women and the American Experience* (New York: McGraw-Hill, 2006), 26.

5   T. J. Brasser, "Mahican," in *Handbook of North American Indians*, vol. 15 (Washington, DC: Smithsonian Institution Press, 1978), 199.

6   Timothy Dwight, *Travels in New England and New York*, vol. 3 (New Haven, CT: S. Converse, Printer, 1822), 166.

7   H. G. Rowe and C. T. Fairfield, *North Adams and Vicinity Illustrated* (North Adams, MA: The Transcript Publishing Co., 1898), 13.

8   Henry D. Thoreau, "Monday," in *A Week on the Concord and Merrimack Rivers* (Princeton, NJ, 1904), 146.

9   Dwight, *Travels in New England and New York*, vol. 1, 26.

10   John Greenleaf Whittier, "The Grave by the Lake," *The Atlantic Monthly* (May 1865).

11   Brasser, "Mahican," 199.

12   Jean Jarvie, "The Mohawk Indians," in *Stories from Our Hills* (Adams, MA: Lamb Printing Co., 1926), 28.

13   Shirley W. Dunn, *The Mohicans and Their Land 1609–1730* (Fleischmanns, NY: Purple Mountain Press, 1994), 46.

14   Grace Greylock Niles, *The Hoosac Valley: Its Legends and Its History* (New York: G. P. Putnam's Sons, 1912), 15.

15   David Hackett Fischer, *Champlain's Dream* (New York: Simon & Schuster, 2008), 253.

16   Dunn, *The Mohicans and Their Land 1609–1730*, 8; Dwight, *Travels in New England and New York*, vol. 4, 129: they "were called by the early Dutch colonists Mohikanders."

17   Ruttenberg, *History of the Indian Tribes of Hudson's River*, 100.

18   *Voyages of Samuel de Champlain*, ed. Edmund F. Slafter (Boston: Prince Society, 1878), 210–11.

19   Fischer, *Champlain's Dream*, vol. 2, 261.

20   Francis Parkman, *Pioneers of France in the New World* (Boston: Little, Brown, 1897).

21   Bruce G. Trigger, "Early Iroquoian Contacts with Europeans," in *Handbook of North American Indians*, vol. 15, 348.

22   Franklin Leonard Pope, "The Western Boundary of Massachusetts," in *Four Papers of the Berkshire Historical and Scientific Society* (Pittsfield, MA: Berkshire Historical and Scientific Society, 1886), 37.

23   George Bancroft, *History of the United States, from the Discovery of the American Continent*, vol. 3 (Boston: Little, Brown, 1843), 141.

24   Ruttenberg, *History of the Indian Tribes of Hudson's River*, 159.

25   Bancroft, *History of the United States,* vol. 3, 146.

26   John Adams Aiken, "The Mohawk Trail," in *History and Proceedings of the Pocumtuck Valley Memorial Association 1905–1911*, vol. 5 (Deerfield, MA: Pocumtuck Valley Memorial Association, 1912), 338.

27 Ruttenberg, *History of the Indian Tribes of Hudson's River*, 172.

28 Bancroft, *History of the United States*, vol. 3, 179.

29 Emma Lewis Coleman, *New England Captives Carried to Canada between 1677 and 1760 During the French and Indian Wars*, vol. 1 (Portland, ME: Southworth Press, 1925), 198.

30 Bancroft, *History of the United States*, vol. 3, 184.

31 *A new map of New England, New York, New Jersey, Pennsylvania, Maryland and Virginia* (1676). Publisher: Robert Morden (1650–1703); William Berry, *A new map of New England, New York, New Jersey, Pennsylvania, Maryland and Virginia* (1685). Sold by John Thornton, Robert Morden, and Phillip Lea.

32 Bancroft, *History of the United States*, vol. 3, 212.

33 Coleman, *New England Captives Carried to Canada between 1677 and 1760*, vol. 2, 42.

34 John Williams, *The Redeemed Captive, Returning to Zion* (Boston, 1707).

35 Coleman, *New England Captives Carried to Canada between 1677 and 1760*, vol. 2, 42.

36 Browne, *The Mohawk Trail*, 116.

37 James Russell Trumbull, *History of Northampton Massachusetts from its Settlement in 1654*. vol. 1 (Northampton, MA: Press of Gazette Printing Co., 1898), 498.

38 Bancroft, *History of the United States*, vol. 3, 215.

39 Ibid., 223.

40 Josiah Gilbert Holland, *History of Western Massachusetts: The Counties of Hampden, Hampshire, Franklin, and Berkshire*, vol. 2, part 3 (Springfield, MA: Samuel Bowles and Company, 1855), 330.

41 Aiken, "The Mohawk Trail," 343.

42 Holland, *History of Western Massachusetts*, vol. 2, part 3, 328.

43 Niles, *The Hoosac Valley*, 67.

44 Jarvie, "Beginnings in North Adams," in *Stories from Our Hills*, 103.

45 Christopher Clark, *Iron Kingdom—The Rise and Downfall of Prussia, 1600–1947* (Cambridge, MA: Harvard University Press, 2006), 183–95.

46 Ruttenberg, *History of the Indian Tribes of Hudson's River*, 204.

47 Percy Whiting Brown, *History of Rowe Massachusetts* (Boston: Old Colony Press, 1921, privately printed), 11–16.

48 Niles, *The Hoosac Valley*, 128.

49 Jarvie, "Fort Massachusetts," in *Stories from Our Hills*, 45.

50   Browne, *The Mohawk Trail*, 17.

51   A. L. Perry, "Fort Shirley," *Bay State Monthly* 3, no. 5 (October 1885): 345.

52   Jarvie, "Fort Massachusetts," in *Stories from Our Hills*, 53.

53   Ruttenberg, *History of the Indian Tribes of Hudson's River*, 206.

54   Jarvie, "The Battle of Bennington," in *Stories from Our Hills*, 81.

55   W. F. Spear, *History of North Adams, Mass. 1749–1885* (North Adams, MA: Hoosac Valley News Printing House, 1885), 1.

56   Ibid.

57   Ibid., 13.

58   Aiken, "The Mohawk Trail," 344.

59   Donald M. Murray, "Thoreau's Uncivil Man Rice," *The New England Quarterly* 56, no. 1 (March 1983): 103–9.

60   Henry David Thoreau, *A Week on the Concord and Merrimack Rivers* (Princeton, NJ: Princeton University Press, 1980).

61   Browne, *The Mohawk Trail*, 19.

62   Ibid., 21.

63   Aiken, "The Mohawk Trail," 346, 347.

64   Jarvie, "Beginnings of North Adams," in *Stories from Our Hills*, 105.

65   Browne, *The Mohawk Trail*, 24.

66   Ibid.

67   Ralph Waldo Emerson, "The Concord Hymn" (1837).

68   Bancroft, *History of the United States*, vol. 7, 339.

69   *History of the Connecticut Valley in Massachusetts*, vol. 2 (Philadelphia: Louis H. Everts, 1879).

70   Ibid.

71   Ibid.

72   Bancroft, *History of the United States*, 385.

73   Spear, *History of North Adams, Mass.*, 1.

74   Frederic J. Wood, *The Turnpikes of New England* (Boston: Marshall Jones Company, 1919), 66.

75   Washington Gladden, *From Hub to the Hudson with Sketches of Nature, History and Industry in North-Western Massachusetts* (Boston: The New England News Company, 1869), 99.

Chapter 2

1   *Report of the Commissioners of the State of Massachusetts, on the Routes of Canals from Boston Harbour to Connecticut and Hudson Rivers* (Boston: True and Green, State Printers, 1826), 10.

2   *Innovate Boston! Shaping the Future from Our Past: Four Amazing Centuries of Innovation* (Boston: Boston History & Innovation Collaborative, 2006), 32.

3   William H. Pease and Jane H. Pease, *The Web of Progress: Private Values and Public Styles in Boston and Charleston, 1828–1843* (Athens: University of Georgia Press, 1991), 23.

4   Noble E. Whitford, "Chapter XXIV. The Canals as a School of Engineering," in *Supplement to the Annual Report of the State Engineer and Surveyor of the State of New York* (Albany, NY: Brandow Printing Company, 1906), 788.

5   Ibid., 786 (D. S. Gregory writing in 1866).

6   Richard G. Weingardt, "Ellen Henrietta Swallow Richards and Benjamin Wright," *Leadership and Management in Engineering*, ASCE 4, no. 4 (October 2004): 156–60.

7   Rev. L. Thompson, "Loammi Baldwin," in *History of Middlesex County, Massachusetts, with Biographical Sketches of Many of Its Pioneers and Prominent Men*, vol. 1, comp. D. Hamilton Hurd (Philadelphia, 1890), 446.

8   John R. Galvin, *The Minute Men, The First Fight: Myths and Realities of The American Revolution* (New York: Pergamon–Brassey's International Defense Publishers, 1989), 14.

9   Samuel Sewall, *The History of Woburn, Middlesex County, Mass., from the Grant of Its Territory to Charlestown, in 1640, to the Year 1860* (Boston: Wiggin and Lunt Publishers, 1868), 385.

10 This date is from Edward F. Johnson's *Woburn Records of Births, Deaths, and Marriages from 1640 to 1873* (p. 15), published in 1890, and is based on the records of the town clerk. It asserts that the record reads: "Loammi, s. of James and Ruth, Jan. 10, 1744." It might also be noted that the town clerk who made the record was James Fowle, Esq., the father of Loammi Baldwin's first wife, Mary Fowle. William R. Cutter and Edward F. Johnson, in their *Transcript of Epitaphs in Woburn First and Second Burial-Grounds* (1890), detail on p. 56. Inscribed on the marble tablet of Loammi

Baldwin's obelisk is: "Born Jan. 10, 1744–45, son of James and Ruth (Richardson) Baldwin." C. C. Baldwin, without stating his source, on page 627 of his 1881 book, *The Baldwin Genealogy from 1500 to 1881,* uses January 10, 1744/5 for Loammi Baldwin's date of birth.

11   Frank Warren Coburn, *The Battle of April 19, 1775,* 2nd ed. (Lexington, MA: Lexington Historical Society, 1922), 33.

12   Sewall, *The History of Woburn, Middlesex County, Mass.,* 362.

13   Thompson, "Loammi Baldwin," in *History of Middlesex County, Massachusetts,* vol. 1, 447.

14   Coburn, *The Battle of April 19, 1775,* 2nd ed., 34.

15   Mark M. Boatner III, *Encyclopedia of the American Revolution* (New York: David McKay Co., 1966).

16   Thompson, "Loammi Baldwin," in *History of Middlesex County, Massachusetts,* vol. 1, 448 (from diary of Loammi Baldwin).

17   Galvin, *The Minute Men, The First Fight,* 171.

18   Richard Frothingham Jr., *History of the Siege of Boston, and of the Battles of Lexington, Concord, and Bunker Hill,* 2d ed. (Boston: C. C. Little and J. Brown, 1851), 74.

19   Galvin, *The Minute Men, The First Fight,* 201.

20   Thompson, "Loammi Baldwin," in *History of Middlesex County, Massachusetts,* vol. 1, 447.

21   Abram English Brown, *Beneath Old Roof Trees* (Boston: Lee and Shepard, 1896), 321.

22   Thompson, "Loammi Baldwin," in *History of Middlesex County, Massachusetts,* vol. 1, 449.

23   Charles C. Chase, "Lowell," in *History of Middlesex County, Massachusetts,* vol. 2, 5.

24   Timothy Flint, ed., "Canals," *The Western Monthly Review* 1 (June 1827): 73.

25   Sewall, *The History of Woburn, Middlesex County, Mass.,* 391.

26   Christopher Roberts, *The Middlesex Canal 1793-1860* (Cambridge, MA: Harvard University Press, 1938), 39.

27   Dirk J. Struik, *Yankee Science in the Making* (Boston: Little, Brown, 1948), 26.

28   Peter Force, *American Archives,* fourth series, vol. 2 (Washington, DC, 1839), 902.

29   Daniel Hovey Calhoun, *The American Civil Engineer: Origins and Conflict* (Cambridge, MA: Technology Press, MIT, 1960), 12.

30   Caleb Eddy, *Historical Sketch of the Middlesex Canal* (Boston: Samuel N. Dickinson Printer, 1843), 3 (charter signed 22 June 1793 by John Hancock, Governor of the Commonwealth).

31   Ibid.

32   Ibid., 4.

33   Mary Stetson Clarke, *The Old Middlesex Canal* (Easton, PA: Center for Canal History and Technology, 1974), 23.

34   Joseph Stancliffe Davis, *Essays in the Earlier History of American Corporations*, no. 4 (Cambridge, MA: Harvard University Press, 1917), 175.

35   Peter J. Guthorn, *British Maps of the American Revolution* (Monmouth Beach, NJ: Philip Freneau Press, 1972), 24–27.

36   Georgius Agricola, *De Re Metallica*, Book V (1556), 104.

37   Père Jean-Francois, *La Science des Eaux* (Rennes, 1653), 165.

38   9 November 1793, Knox MMS, XXXIV, 138.

39   Richard Shelton Kirby, "William Weston and His Contribution to Early American Engineering," *Transactions of the Newcomen Society for the Study of the History of Engineering and Technology* 16 (1935–36): 112.

40   Irving Stone, *Those Who Love* (New York: Doubleday, 1965), 524.

41   Rennie to William Vaughan, London, 6 March 1798 (copy: Corporate Records).

42   Frederick K. Abbott, *The Role of the Civil Engineer in Internal Improvements: The Contributions of the Two Loammi Baldwins, Father and Son, 1776–1838* (PhD dissertation, Columbia University, 1952), 22.

43   Nathaniel B. Shurtleff, *A Topographical and Historical Description of Boston* (Boston: Printed by Request of the City Council, 1871), 417.

44   Clarke, *The Old Middlesex Canal*, 26.

45   Roberts, *The Middlesex Canal 1793-1860*, 5.

46   Charles Shaw, *Topographical and Historical Description of Boston* (Boston: Oliver Spear, 1817), 120.

47   Shurtleff, *A Topographical and Historical Description of Boston*, 418.

48   Kirby, "William Weston and His Contribution to Early American Engineering," 118.

49   George Adams, *Geometrical and Graphical Essays Containing a General Description of the Mathematical Instruments used in Geometry, Civil and Military Surveying* (London, 1791), plate XVII, fig. 3.

50   Copy of memo for Captain Scott, 1794, Baldwin Manuscripts, Loammi Baldwin, 1744–1807, Baker Library, Harvard University.

51   A. W. Skempton and Joyce Brown, "John and Edward Troughton, Mathematical Instrument Makers," *Notes and Records of the Royal Society of London* 27, no. 2 (February 1973): 233–49.

52   Kirby, "William Weston and His Contribution to Early American Engineering," 127.

53   George L. Vose, *A Sketch of the Life and Works of Loammi Baldwin, Civil Engineer* (Boston: Press of Geo. H. Ellis, 1885), 1.

54   Report of William Weston to the Directors of the Middlesex Canal, 2 August 1794, Manuscripts Division, Baldwin Papers, Baker Library, vol. 4.

55   Struik, *Yankee Science in the Making*, 116.

56   Report of November 1794, Baldwin Manuscripts, Loammi Baldwin, 1744–1807, Baker Library, Harvard University.

57   George Edward Ellis, *Memoir of Sir Benjamin Thompson, Count Rumford, with notices of his daughter* (Boston: Estes and Lauriat, 1871), 370–76.

58   Kerby A. Miller, Arnold Schrier, Bruce D. Boling, and David N. Doyle, *Irish Immigrants in the Land of Canaan* (New York: Oxford University Press, 2003), 283 (the original James Patton letter written March 1839 from Asheville, NC, in *Letters of James Patton, One of the First Residents of Asheville, North Carolina, to his Children*, 1845).

59   Clause concerning "puddle gutters" inserted in banking job contracts: Baldwin Manuscripts, Loammi Baldwin, 1744–1807, Baker Library, Harvard University.

60   Lorin L. Dame, "The Middlesex Canal," *Bay State Monthly* 2, no. 2 (November 1884): 98.

61   Memo. of Supt. to Committee, 27 May 1802: copy in Baldwin Manuscripts, Baker Library, Harvard University.

62   Marcus Vitruvius Pollio [ca. 90–20 BC], *De Architectura*, book II, chapter VI, section 1.

63   John Smeaton, *A Narrative of the Building and a Description of the Construction of the Edystone [sic] Lighthouse* (London: Printed for the Author, 1791), 108, 109.

64 "Note on 'Terra Puzzolana'": Proprietors of the Middlesex Canal, Corporate Records, 3 November 1795.

65 William Vaughan to Charles Vaughan, London, 9 March 1798: Proprietors of the Middlesex Canal, Corporate Records. Vaughan states he sent a copy of Smeaton's Works by Mr. Apthorp.

66 "Annual Report of the President and Directors of the Board of Public Works, Richmond," in *North American Review and Miscellaneous Journal* 8, no. 22 (1818/19): 16.

67 Report, 23 July 1798: copy in Baldwin Manuscripts, Baker Library, Harvard University.

68 Charles Riborg Mann, *A Study of Engineering Education*, bulletin no. 11 (1918), Carnegie Foundation for the Advancement of Teaching: 3.

69 Roberts, *The Middlesex Canal 1793–1860*, 93.

70 Ibid., 122.

71 "Baldwin, Loammi," in *The National Cyclopaedia of American Biography*, vol. 10 (1900), 302.

72 Julius A. Stratton and Loretta H. Mannix, *Mind and Hand: The Birth of MIT* (Cambridge, MA: MIT Press, 2005), 666.

Chapter 3

1 William Richard Cutter and William Frederick Adams, *Genealogical and Personal Memoirs Relating to the Families of the State of Massachusetts* (New York: Lewis Historical Publishing Company, 1910), 579.

2 Frederick K. Abbott, *The Role of the Civil Engineer in Internal Improvements: The Contributions of the Two Loammi Baldwins, Father and Son, 1776–1838* (PhD dissertation, Columbia University, 1952), 61.

3 J. Elfreth Watkins, "The Beginnings of Engineering," *Transactions of the American Society of Civil Engineers* 24, no. 5 (May 1891): 330 (read at the annual convention on 28 June 1890).

4 James Gregory McGivern, *First Hundred Years of Engineering Education in the United States, 1807–1907* (Spokane, WA: Gonzaga University Press, 1960), 8.

5 George L. Vose, *A Sketch of the Life and Works of Loammi Baldwin, Civil Engineer* (Boston: Press of Geo. H. Ellis, 1885), 10.

6   Benson J. Lossing, "The War on the New England Coast in 1814," in *The Pictorial Field-Book of the War of 1812* (New York: Harper and Brothers, 1896), 892.

7   Edward C. Carter II, "The Engineer as Agent of Technological Transfer: The American Career of Benjamin Henry Latrobe, 1796–1820," in *Benjamin Henry Latrobe & Moncure Robinson: The Engineer as Agent of Technological Transfer* (Wilmington, DE: Eleutherian Mills–Hagley Foundation, 1975), 14–15.

8   *Report of the Secretary of the Treasury on the Subject of Public Roads and Canals made in pursuance of a resolution of Senate of March 2, 1807* (Washington, DC: R. C. Weightman, 1808), 79.

9   Ibid., 104.

10   Sarah Knight, *The Private Journal of a Journey from Boston to New York in the Year 1704* (Albany, NY: Frank H. Little, 1865), 25.

11   *Annual Report of the President and Directors of the Board of Public Works to the Legislature of Virginia* (19 December 1816).

12   Baldwin, June 25, 1816: Baldwin Manuscripts, Loammi Baldwin, 1780–1838, Baker Library, Harvard University.

13   Simon Winchester, *Krakatoa: The Day the World Exploded* (New York: Harper, 2005), 292.

14   Haraldur Sigurdsson, Professor of Oceanography and Volcanology at the University of Rhode Island (www.uri.edu/news/releases/?id=3467; viewed 10 June 2014).

15   Thomas R. Ryan, *Orestes A. Brownson* (Huntington, IN: Our Sunday Visitor, 1976), 23.

16   The date was 20 November, according to Abbott, *The Role of the Civil Engineer in Internal Improvements*, 96.

17   E. W. Howe, *Proceedings of the Boston Society of Civil Engineers*: 87 (read at regular meeting 15 December 1880).

18   Wilbur W. Davis, "The History of Boston Disclosed in the Digging of the Commonwealth Avenue Underpass and Other Traffic Tunnels," *Proceedings of the Bostonian Society Annual Meeting* (January 1938): 29–31.

19   Nathaniel B. Shurtleff, *A Topographical and Historical Description of Boston* (Boston: Printed by Request of the City Council, 1871), 424.

20   Abbott, *The Role of the Civil Engineer in Internal Improvements*, 107.

21 Loammi Baldwin letters, 1 October and 22 November 1821, Baldwin Manuscripts, Loammi Baldwin, 1780–1838, Baker Library, Harvard University.

22 Ibid.

23 Loammi Baldwin letters, 10 February, 6, 10, and 17 March 1822, Baldwin Manuscripts, Baker Library, Harvard University.

24 Abbott, *The Role of the Civil Engineer in Internal Improvements*, 114.

25 Loammi Baldwin letter, 1 December 1822, Baldwin Manuscripts, Baker Library, Harvard University.

26 Loammi Baldwin letter, 5 January 1823, Baldwin Manuscripts, Baker Library, Harvard University.

27 "Annual Report of the President and Managers of the Union Canal Company," *The National Gazette* (Philadelphia), vol. IV, no. 1263 (Tuesday, 30 November 1824).

28 L. Baldwin, *Letters of the Union Canal of Pennsylvania*, first published in the *Boston Daily Advertiser* (44 pages, n.d.).

29 Edward Chase Kirkland, *Men, Cities, and Transportation: A Study in New England History, 1820–1900* (Cambridge, MA: Harvard University Press, 1948), 102, 103.

30 F. E. Turneaure, "The Engineering School and the Engineer," *Journal of the Western Society of Engineers* 22, no. 1 (January 1917): 7.

31 H. G. Good, "New Data on Early Engineering Education," *Journal of Educational Research* 29, no. 1 (September 1935): 39.

32 Julius Rubin, "Canal or Railroad? Imitation and Innovation in the Response to the Erie Canal in Philadelphia, Baltimore, and Boston," *Transactions of the American Philosophical Society* 51, no. 7 (1961): 15.

33 Abbott, *The Role of the Civil Engineer in Internal Improvements*, 129.

34 Vose, *A Sketch of the Life and Works of Loammi Baldwin*, 13.

35 Rubin, "Canal or Railroad?" 80.

36 *Report of the Commissioners of the State of Massachusetts, on the Routes of Canals from Boston Harbour to Connecticut and Hudson Rivers* (Boston: True and Green, State Printers, 1826), 67.

37 Correspondence with Steven Turner, Smithsonian Institution, October 2008.

38 *Report of the Commissioners of the State of Massachusetts*, 14.

39   John Hills, *A plan and section of the country, from Connecticut River to the tide water at Milton, in the State of Massachusetts* (1791): map located in the Special Collections of the State Library of Massachusetts, Boston.

40   *Report of the Commissioners of the State of Massachusetts*, 44.

41   Eleanor Gilmartin, "John Fitch—A Man for Our Times," Fitchburg Historical Society (fall 2008).

42   Loammi Baldwin, *Plan and profile of surveys made under the directions of Nathan Willis, Elihu Hoyt & H.A.S. Dearborn to ascertain the practicability of making a canal from Boston Harbor to Connecticut River* (1825): map located in the Special Collections of the State Library of Massachusetts, Boston.

43   *Report of the Commissioners of the State of Massachusetts*, 53.

44   Ibid., 132.

45   Ibid., 145.

46   Ibid., 152.

47   Ibid., 184.

48   Abbott, *The Role of the Civil Engineer in Internal Improvements*, 145.

49   Charles B. Stuart, *Lives and Works of Civil and Military Engineers of America* (New York: D. Van Nostrand, 1871), 121.

50   "Bunker Hill Monument," *Christian Register* 4, no. 19 (14 May 1825): 75.

51   D. Hamilton Hurd, *History of Norfolk County, Massachusetts, with Biographical Sketches of Many of Its Pioneers and Prominent Men*, (Philadelphia: J. W. Lewis & Co., 1884), 357.

52   Jane Molloy Porter, *Friendly Edifices* (Portsmouth, NH: Peter E. Randall Publisher, 2006), 167, 178, 186.

53   Edward Chase Kirkland, *Men, Cities, and Transportation: A Study in New England History, 1820–1900*, vol. 1 (New York: Russell & Russell, 1948), pp. 102, 103.

54   Alvin F. Harlow, *Steelways of New England* (New York: Creative Age Press, 1946), 32.

55   Abbott, *The Role of the Civil Engineer in Internal Improvements*, 146.

56   Gridley Bryant to James F. Baldwin, 21 January 1828: Baldwin Manuscripts (XXXVI), Baker Library, Harvard University.

57   *Report of the Board of Directors of the State of Massachusetts on the Practicability and Expediency of a Rail-Road from Boston to the Hudson River, and from Boston to Providence* (Boston: Press of the *Boston Daily Advertiser*, 16 January 1829): 13.

58   Ibid., 70.

59   Rubin, "Canal or Railroad?" 89.

60   *Report of the Board of Directors of the State of Massachusetts on the Practicability and Expediency of a Rail-Road*, 54.

61   Ibid., 55.

62   Peter Mensen & Co., New York, Manuscript #609, Canvass White Collection, Rare and Manuscript Collections, Cornell University Library, Ithaca, NY. Frank Edgar Grizzard Jr, *The Documentary History of the Construction of the Buildings at the University of Virginia*, 1817–1828, in note 780 for chapter 11, "The Final Years: 1826–1828," PhD dissertation, University of Virginia, states: "The cisterns were lined with White's Patent Hydraulic Cement, purchased from the New York firm of Peter Remsen & Co." So there is some confusion regarding the spelling of the company's name.

63   *Directions for Using White's Patent Hydraulic Cement*, Peter Mensen & Co., New York, (Manuscript #609, Canvass White Collection, *Rare and Manuscript Collections*, Cornell University Library, Ithaca, N.Y.)

64   Richard Shelton Kirby and Philip Gustave Laurson, *The Early Years of Modern Civil Engineering* (New Haven, CT: Yale University Press, 1932), 265.

65   Robert W. Lesley, *History of the Portland Cement Industry in the United States* (Philadelphia: American Cement Company, 1924), 15.

66   Grizzard, *The Documentary History of the Construction of the Buildings at the University of Virginia*, appendix T: "Selected Documents Related to the Water Works and Fire Apparatus."

67   Peter A. Ford, "Charles S. Storrow, Civil Engineer: A Case Study of European Training and Technological Transfer in the Antebellum Period," *Technology and Culture* 34, no. 2 (April 1993): 279–81.

68   Ibid., 280.

69   John R. Freeman, "Mr. Chas. S. Storrow and the Lawrence Scientific School," *Engineering News* 28, no. 36 (September 1, 1892): 207.

70   Abbott, *The Role of the Civil Engineer in Internal Improvements*, 170.

71   Vose, *A Sketch of the Life and Works of Loammi Baldwin*, 17.

72   *Boston Daily Advertiser and Patriot* (25 June 1833). (Nathan Hale's paper was the *Boston Daily Advertiser* from 1813 to 1831 and the *Boston Daily Advertiser and Patriot* from 1832 to 1835.)

73   Abbott, *The Role of the Civil Engineer in Internal Improvements*, 184.

74 John A. Roebling's "Delaware Aqueduct" on the Delaware & Hudson Canal in Pennsylvania, the "Roebling Bridge" over the Ohio River at Cincinnati, and the "Brooklyn Bridge" are all recognized as National Historic Civil Engineering Landmarks. Although the Brooklyn Bridge was designed by John A. Roebling, it was built under the supervision of his son, Washington Augustus Roebling. Benjamin Henry Latrobe's "Philadelphia Municipal Water Supply" is a National Historic Civil Engineering Landmark, and his son is recognized as a collaborator on the "Baltimore & Ohio Roundhouse" at Martinsburg, West Virginia, which is also a National Historic Civil Engineering Landmark.

75 Abbott, *The Role of the Civil Engineer in Internal Improvements*, 195.

76 Loammi Baldwin to James, 6 June 1834: Baldwin Manuscripts, Loammi Baldwin, 1780–1838, Baker Library, Harvard University.

77 Charles S. Storrow, *Treatise on Water-Works for Conveying and Distributing Supplies of Water* (Boston: Hilliard, Gray, and Co., 1835).

78 James F. Baldwin to Loammi Baldwin II, 27 May 1835: Baldwin Manuscripts (XXXVII), Baker Library, Harvard University.

79 Cutter and Adams, *Genealogical and Personal Memoirs Relating to the Families of the State of Massachusetts*, 582.

Chapter 4

1 Doris Kirkpatrick, *The City and the River* (Fitchburg, MA: Fitchburg Historical Society, 1971), 176.

2 Herman Haupt Papers (MS#269), Manuscripts and Archives, Yale University Library.

3 Rufus C. Torrey, *History of the Town of Fitchburg, Massachusetts* (Fitchburg, MA: J. Garfield Printer, 1836), 18.

4 William Bond Wheelwright and Sumner Kean, *The Lengthened Shadow of One Man* (Fitchburg, MA: Crocker, Burbank and Company, 1957) 3.

5 Torrey, *History of the Town of Fitchburg, Massachusetts*, 5.

6 Frederick A. Currier, "Stage Coach Days and Stage Coach Ways," *Proceedings of the Fitchburg Historical Society* 1 (1897): 78 (read 18 February 1895).

7 William H. Pease and Jane H. Pease, *The Web of Progress: Private Values and Public Styles in Boston and Charleston, 1828–1843* (Athens: University of Georgia Press, 1991), 4.

8   William A. Emerson, *Fitchburg, Massachusetts, Past and Present* (Fitchburg, MA: Blanchard & Brown, 1887), 183.

9   Crane, *Historic Homes and Institutions and Genealogical and Personal Memoirs*, vol. 4, 239.

10 Ellery Bicknell Crane, *Historic Homes and Institutions and Genealogical and Personal Memoirs of Worcester County, Massachusetts, with a History of Worcester Society of Antiquity* (New York/Chicago: Lewis Publishing, 1907), 239.

11 Richard H. McKey Jr., "Elias Hasket Derby and the American Revolution," *Essex Institute Historical Collections* 97 (July 1961): 166.

12 C. T. Crocker, *A Biography of Alvah Crocker I—by his son* (not published, no date; copy in the Fitchburg Historical Society collection), 1.

13 Ibid.

14 Elias Nason, *A Gazetteer of the State of Massachusetts, with Numerous Illustrations on Wood and Steel* (Boston: B. B. Russell, 1874), 292.

15 David Wilder, *The History of Leominster, or the Northern Half of the Lancaster New or Additional Grant* (Fitchburg, MA: Reveille Office, 1853), 125.

16 Crocker, *A Biography of Alvah Crocker I—by his son*, 1.

17 "Crocker, Alvah," in *Dictionary of American Biography*, vol. 4 (1930), 551–52.

18 William Bond Wheelwright, *Life and Times of Alvah Crocker* (Boston: privately printed, 1923), 3.

19 Address of Mr. Benjamin F. Butler of Massachusetts, Memorial Addresses on the Life and Character of Alvah Crocker (a Representative from Massachusetts), delivered in the Senate and House of Representatives, Forty-Third Congress, Second Session, 20 February 1875.

20 *The Tariff: Remarks of Hon. Alvah Crocker of Massachusetts*, House of Representatives, 16 May 1872, 2.

21 Judith A. McGaw, *Most Wonderful Machine: Mechanization and Social Change in Berkshire Papermaking, 1801–1885* (Princeton, NJ: Princeton University Press, 1987), 45.

22 *History of Leominster, MA: Jonas Kendall* [4-2005], from Leominster Historical Society, author unknown, Transcribed by C. J. Bagley.

23 Crocker, *A Biography of Alvah Crocker I—by his son*, 2.

24 Wilder, *The History of Leominster*, 85.

25 Wheelwright, *Life and Times of Alvah Crocker*, 5.

26   Byron Weston, "History of Paper Making in Berkshire County, Massachusetts, U.S.A.," *Collections of the Berkshire Historical and Scientific Society* (Pittsfield, MA, 1895), 19.

27   Crocker, *A Biography of Alvah Crocker I—by his son*, 2.

28   Ibid.

29   Ibid.

30   McGaw, *Most Wonderful Machine*, 29.

31   Crocker, *A Biography of Alvah Crocker I—by his son*, 3.

32   Dard Hunter, *Papermaking: The History and Technique of an Ancient Craft*, 2nd ed. (New York: Alfred A. Knopf, 1947), 355.

33   Ibid.

34   Ibid., 355–56.

35   Ibid., 358.

36   Kirkpatrick, *The City and the River*, 171.

37   Wheelwright, *Life and Times of Alvah Crocker*, 10.

38   Kirkpatrick, *The City and the River*, 171.

39   Wheelwright, *Life and Times of Alvah Crocker*, 11.

40   Crocker, *A Biography of Alvah Crocker I—by his son*, 3.

41   Torrey, *History of the Town of Fitchburg, Massachusetts*, 11.

42   Josiah Gilbert Holland, *History of Western Massachusetts: The Counties of Hampden, Hampshire, Franklin, and Berkshire* (Springfield, MA: Samuel Bowles and Company, 1855), 417.

43   *Biographical Encyclopedia of Massachusetts of the Nineteenth Century*, vol. 2 (Boston: Metropolitan Publishing and Engraving Co., 1883), 138.

44   Alvah Crocker, "The Bill for the More Speedy Completion of the Troy and Greenfield Railroad": speech in the Senate, 18 April 1862, 4.

45   "Railroad to Vermont," *Columbian Centinel* 4720 (4 July 1829), 1.

46   William W. Wheildon, *Memoir of Solomon Willard: Architect and Superintendent of the Bunker Hill Monument* (Boston: Bunker Hill Monument Association, 1865), 229.

47   Ibid.

48   Charles B. Stuart, *Lives and Works of Civil and Military Engineers of America* (New York: D. Van Nostrand, 1871), 122.

49   Pease and Pease, *The Web of Progress*, 208.

50   Crocker, *A Biography of Alvah Crocker I—by his son*, 5.

51   Ibid., 6.

52   Ralph Waldo Emerson, *Journals of Ralph Waldo Emerson with Annotations*, vol. 10 (Boston: Houghton Mifflin, 1914), 313–14.

53   *Fitchburg Sentinel*, vol. 3, no. 45 (11 November 1841).

54   "A Railroad to Fitchburg," *Fitchburg Sentinel*, vol. 3, no. 46 (18 November 1841).

55   John A. Garraty and Mark C. Carnes, gen. eds., *American National Biography*, vol. 5 (New York: Oxford University Press, 1999), 745.

56   Currier, "Stage Coach Days and Stage Coach Ways," 176.

57   Caroline E. MacGill and Balthasar Henry Meyer, *History of Transportation in the United States before 1860* (Washington, DC: Carnegie Institution, 1917), 317.

58   "Railroad Meeting," *Fitchburg Sentinel*, vol. 3, no. 51 (23 December 1841).

59   "Rail Road Circular," *Fitchburg Sentinel* (23 December 1841).

60   Henry A. Willis, "The Early Days of Railroads in Fitchburg," *Proceedings of the Fitchburg Historical Society, 1892–1894*, vol. 1 (1895): 32.

61   *Annual Reports of the Railroad Corporations in the State of Massachusetts for 1845* (1846). Massachusetts General Court, Committee on Railways and Canals, 22.

62   Thomas Doane and Charles Harris, "Samuel Morse Felton," *Journal of the Association of Engineering Societies* 11, no. 4 (April 1892): 203.

63   Alvin F. Harlow, *Steelways of New England* (New York: Creative Age Press, 1946), 237.

64   Willis, "The Early Days of Railroads in Fitchburg," vol. 1, 33.

65   Doane and Harris, "Samuel Morse Felton," 203.

66   Stephen Salsbury, *The State, the Investor, and the Railroad: The Boston & Albany, 1825–1867* (Cambridge, MA: Harvard University Press, 1967), 141.

67   Crocker, "The Bill for the More Speedy Completion of the Troy and Greenfield Railroad," 7.

68   "An Act to Establish the Fitchburg Rail-road Company," *Acts and Resolves passed by the Legislature of Massachusetts in the Year 1842 (Winter Session)* [approved by the governor, 3 March 1842], chap. 84, p. 535.

69   Willis, "The Early Days of Railroads in Fitchburg," 35.

70   Thomas Morris Longstreth, *Hide-out* (New York: Macmillan, 1947).

71   "Regular monthly meeting, Fitchburg Historical Society, December 17, 1894," *Proceedings of the Fitchburg Historical Society*, vol. 2 (1897): 9.

72 "Fitchburg Railroad," *American Railroad Journal and Mechanics' Magazine* 16, no. 427 (August 1843): 253.

73 Willis, "The Early Days of Railroads in Fitchburg," vol. 1, 34.

74 Ibid., 35.

75 Charles J. Kennedy, "The Early Business History of Four Massachusetts Railroads," *Bulletin of the Business Historical* Society 25, no. 1 (March 1951): 63.

76 William B. Dana, "Railroad and Steamboat Statistics," *Merchants' Magazine and Commercial Review* 10 (January–June 1844): 382.

77 Kennedy, "The Early Business History of Four Massachusetts Railroads," 63.

78 William Appleton and W. H. Swift, *Massachusetts Railroads 1842 to 1855* (Boston: J. H. Eastburn's Press, 1856), 11.

79 Ralph L. Rusk, *The Letters of Ralph Waldo Emerson*, vol. 3 (New York: Columbia University Press, 1939), 339.

80 Samuel Morse Felton (Sr.) Collection, Baker Library, Harvard University.

81 Willis, "The Early Days of Railroads in Fitchburg," vol. 1, 36.

82 Alvah Crocker, "Rejoinder to the Reply of a Committee Appointed by the Iron Trade in Philadelphia," Washington, DC (1844), 9.

83 Sohier and Welch Collection, Baker Library, Harvard University.

84 Arthur M. Johnson and Barry E. Supple, *Boston Capitalists and Western Railroads: A Study in the Nineteenth-Century Investment Process*, Harvard Studies in Business History 23 (Cambridge, MA: Harvard University Press, 1967), 19.

85 Ibid., 55.

86 Ibid.

87 George W. Cullum, *Biographical Sketch of Captain William H. Swift of the Topographical Engineers, United States Army, 1832–1849* (New York: A. G. Sherwood & Co., 1880).

88 Doane and Harris, "Samuel Morse Felton," 203.

89 Charles J. Kennedy, "The Eastern Rail-Road Company to 1855," *The Business History Review* 31, no. 1 (Spring 1957): 100–101.

90 Harlow, *Steelways of New England*, 237.

91 "Fitchburg Railroad," *American Railroad Journal and Mechanics' Magazine*, 253.

92 Willis, "The Early Days of Railroads in Fitchburg," vol. 1, 43.

93   Francis B. C. Bradlee, *Eastern Railroad*, 2nd ed. (Salem, MA: Essex Institute, 1922), 11.

94   George Kraus, *High Road to Promontory—Building the Central Pacific (now Southern Pacific) across the High Sierra* (Palo Alto, CA: American West Publishing Company, 1969).

95   Kirkpatrick, *The City and the River*, 178.

96   *Specifications for Grading & C.*, Samuel Morse Felton (Sr.) Collection, Baker Library, Harvard University.

97   A. Crocker, *Diary*, cover embossed with "A. Crocker, Fitchburg": copy held by Fitchburg Historical Society.

98   E. H. Derby, *Two Months Abroad* (Boston: Redding & Co., 1844), 16.

99   Ibid.

100   Ibid., 58.

101   Carter Goodrich, "Government Promotion of American Canals and Railroads 1800—1890," *The Mississippi Valley Historical Review*, 47, no. 2 (September 1960): 128.

102   Holland, *History of Western Massachusetts: The Counties of Hampden, Hampshire, Franklin, and Berkshire*, 417.

103   Justin Winsor, *The Memorial History of Boston, including Suffolk County, Massachusetts, 1630–1880*, vol. 4 (Boston: Ticknor and Company, 1881), 132.

104   Mason Arnold Green, *Springfield 1636–1886: History of Town and City* (Springfield, MA: C. A. Nichols & Co., 1888), 417.

105   Holland, *History of Western Massachusetts: The Counties of Hampden, Hampshire, Franklin, and Berkshire*, 418.

106   Ibid.

107   Ibid.

108   Ralph W. Hidy, *The House of Baring in American Trade and Finance: English Merchant Bankers at Work, 1763–1861* (Cambridge, MA: Harvard University Press, 1949), 261.

109   Ibid.

110   Salsbury, *The State, the Investor, and the Railroad*, 147.

111   Hidy, *The House of Baring in American Trade and Finance*, 261, 273.

112   Herbert Collins Parsons, *A Puritan Outpost: A History of the Town and People of Northfield, Massachusetts* (New York: Macmillan, 1937). (Samuel Clesson Allen Jr. (1793–1860) was in the legislature from 1837 to 1843.)

113   Hidy, *The House of Baring in American Trade and Finance*, 283.

114 Salsbury, *The State, the Investor, and the Railroad*, 150.

115 George L. Vose, "Sketch of the Life of George W. Whistler," *Contributions of the Old Residents' Historical Association* (Lowell, Massachusetts) 3, no. 4 (July 1887): 347.

116 Forest G. Hill, *Roads, Rails, and Waterways: The Army Engineers and Early Transportation* (Norman: University of Oklahoma Press, 1957), 145.

117 Salsbury, *The State, the Investor, and the Railroad*, 161.

118 Kennedy, "The Early Business History of Four Massachusetts Railroads," 70.

119 Salsbury, *The State, the Investor, and the Railroad*, 155.

120 Edward Chase Kirkland, *Men, Cities, and Transportation: A Study in New England History, 1820–1900*, vol. 1 (New York: Russell & Russell), 159.

121 Kirkland, *Men, Cities, and Transportation*, 390.

122 Kirkland, *Men, Cities, and Transportation*, 275.

123 Alvah Crocker Diaries, Fitchburg Historical Society.

124 Wheelwright, *Life and Times of Alvah Crocker*, 30.

125 Doane and Harris, "Samuel Morse Felton," 203.

126 Willis, "The Early Days of Railroads in Fitchburg," 454.

127 Crocker, "Rejoinder to the Reply of a Committee Appointed by the Iron Trade in Philadelphia," Washington, DC.

128 Lewis Henry Haney, *A Congressional History of Railways in the United States to 1850*, Bulletin of the University of Wisconsin, no. 211, Economics and Political Science Series, vol. 3, no. 2 (1906): 310.

129 Wheelwright, *Life and Times of Alvah Crocker*, 32.

130 Crocker, "Rejoinder to the Reply of a Committee Appointed by the Iron Trade in Philadelphia," Washington, DC.

131 Haney, *A Congressional History of Railways in the United States to 1850*, 308.

132 Wheelwright, *Life and Times of Alvah Crocker*, 32.

133 Crocker, "Rejoinder to the Reply of a Committee Appointed by the Iron Trade in Philadelphia," Washington, DC, 18–19.

134 Wheelwright, *Life and Times of Alvah Crocker*, 34.

135 MacGill and Meyer, *History of Transportation in the United States before 1860*, 335.

136 Henry David Thoreau, "Sounds," in *Walden or Life in the Woods* (New York: Vantage Books, 1991), 127.

137 Ralph Waldo Emerson, "Thoreau Memorial Address," published originally in *Atlantic Monthly* 10, no. 58 (August 1862): 239–49. Emerson gave the address at the funeral service in May 1862.

138 Thoreau, "Economy," in *Walden or Life in the Woods*, 36.

139 Clayton Hoagland, "The Diary of Thoreau's 'Gentle Boy,'" *The New England Quarterly* 28, no. 4 (December 1955): 489.

140 *Bunker Hill Aurora & Boston Mirror*, Charlestown, MA (8 March 1845).

141 Ibid.

142 Alvah Crocker, letter to S. M. Felton dated 8 January 1844, Samuel Morse Felton (Sr.) Collection, Baker Library, Harvard University.

143 Terrence E. Coyne, *The Hoosac Tunnel* (PhD dissertation, Clark University, Worcester, MA, April 1992), 43.

144 Wheelwright, *Life and Times of Alvah Crocker*, 27.

145 "Massachusetts Railroads . . . 1849," *American Railway Times*, 2, no. 18 (9 May 1850).

146 Salsbury, *The State, the Investor, and the Railroad*, 280.

147 "Whittemore, Thomas," in *New American Supplement to the New Werner Twentieth Century Edition of the Encyclopaedia Britannica* (1907), 545.

148 "Vt. and Mass. Railroad," *The Weekly Transcript*, vol. 7, no. 1 (6 September 1849), 2.

Chapter 5

1 "New Route from Boston to Troy," North Adams (MA) *Weekly Transcript*, vol. 4, no. 30 (25 March 1847).

2 "Rail Road Meeting," *Weekly Transcript*, vol. 5, no. 9 (28 October 1847).

3 "Railroad Meeting," *Weekly Transcript*, vol. 5, no. 10 (4 November 1847).

4 "Section 2," in *Troy and Greenfield Railroad Act of Incorporation*, 9 February 1848.

5 Edward C. Kirkland, "The Hoosac Tunnel Route: The Great Bore," *New England Quarterly* 20, no. 1 (March 1947): 93.

6 "Troy and Greenfield Railroad," *Weekly Transcript*, vol. 7, no. 36 (9 May 1850), 2.

7 "Troy & Greenfield Railroad," *Gazette & Courier* (Greenfield, MA) (22 February 1875).

8 *Gazette & Courier* (1 December 1873).

9 "Letter from Judge Grennell," *Gazette & Courier* (1 March 1875).

10　*Act 2 of 1848*, 13 November 1848, Vermont State Archives.

11　"Troy and Boston," *American Railroad Journal* 6, no. 24 (15 June 1850): 374.

12　"Letter from Judge Grennell," *Gazette & Courier* (1 March 1875).

13　"Troy and Greenfield Railroad," *American Railway Times* 3, no. 15 (10 April 1851).

14　Gary S. Brierley, "Construction of the Hoosac Tunnel 1855 to 1876," *Journal of the Boston Society of Civil Engineers Section, American Society of Civil Engineers* 6, no. 3 (October 1976): 178.

15　"Rail Road News," *Scientific American* 5, no. 49 (24 August 1850).

16　"Gardner's Rock Drill," *American Railway Times* 5, no. 45 (10 November 1853).

17　"Drill," in *New International Encyclopaedia*, vol. 6 (1903), 305.

18　David W. Brunton and John A. Davis, *Modern Tunneling*, 2nd ed. (New York: John Wiley, 1922), 19.

19　Brierley, "Construction of the Hoosac Tunnel 1855 to 1876," 178.

20　*The Hoosac Tunnel: A Brief Report of the Hearing of the Troy and Greenfield Railroad Company Petitioners for a Loan of Two Millions, before A Joint Special Committee of the Legislature of Massachusetts* (Boston: Thurston, Torry & Emerson, Printers, Boston, 1853), 28.

21　Brierley, "Construction of the Hoosac Tunnel 1855 to 1876," 177.

22　Peter M. Molloy, "Nineteenth-Century Hydropower: Design and Construction of Lawrence Dam, 1845–1848," *Winterthur Portfolio* 15, no. 4 (Winter 1980): 320.

23　Ibid., 322.

24　"The Hoosac Tunnel," *Scribner's Monthly* (December 1870), 145.

25　"Letter from Rev. Dr. Crawford," *Gazette & Courier* (22 December 1873).

26　"Troy & Greenfield Railroad," *Gazette & Courier* (22 February 1875).

27　"The Troy and Greenfield Railroad," *American Railway Times* 3, no. 3 (16 January 1851).

28　"Fitchburg Railroad Company," *American Railway Times* 3, no. 6 (6 February 1851).

29　"The Troy and Greenfield Railroad Company," *American Railway Times* 3, no. 7 (13 February 1851).

30　*Pittsfield Sun*, vol. 52, no. 2663 (2 Oct 1851), 2.

31　"Troy and Greenfield Railroad—Loan of State Credit," *American Railway Times* 3, no. 13 (27 March 1851).

32 "Troy and Greenfield Railroad," *American Railway Times* 3, no. 15 (10 April 1851).

33 Ibid.

34 "Loan of the State Credit to the Troy and Greenfield Railroad Company," *American Railway Times* 3, no. 14 (3 April 1851).

35 Ibid.

36 "Troy and Greenfield Railroad," *Weekly Transcript*, vol. 8, no. 32 (10 April 1851).

37 "The Hoosac Tunnel," *Pittsfield Sun*, vol. 51, no. 2639 (17 April 1851), 2.

38 "Troy and Greenfield Railroad," *American Railway Times* 3, no. 16 (17 April 1851).

39 "The Tunnel," *Weekly Transcript*, vol. 8, no. 33 (17 April 1851).

40 *The Memorial of the Western Railroad Corporation relating to the Application of the Troy and Greenfield Railroad for a State Loan of Two Millions of Dollars* (16 April 1851), 3–4.

41 "Postscript," *Weekly Transcript*, vol. 8, no. 37 (15 May 1851), 3.

42 "Troy and Greenfield Railway," *American Railway Times* 3, no. 29 (17 July 1851).

43 "Troy and Greenfield Railroad," *American Railway Times* 3, no. 40 (2 October 1851).

44 Ibid.

45 "The Hoosac Tunnel," *American Railway Times* 4, no. 6 (5 February 1852).

46 Copy of the handwritten contract is in the Troy and Greenfield Railroad file, Baker Library, Harvard University.

47 Arthur W. Brayley, *History of the Granite Industry of New England* (Boston: The National Association of Granite Industries of the United States, 1913), 74.

48 Paul Wood, "Tools and Machinery of the Granite Industry, Part III," *The Chronicle of the Early American Industries Association* 59, no. 4 (December 2006): 139.

49 Brayley, *History of the Granite Industry of New England*, 88.

50 "Mechanics and Useful Arts," in *The Annual of Scientific Discovery: or Yearbook of Facts in Science and Art* (Boston: Gould, Kendall, and Lincoln, 1850), 49.

51 *Journal of the Franklin Institute*, Philadelphia (1852): 164.

52 "Report of the Board of Managers—The Twenty fifth Annual Fair 1852," in *Eleventh Annual Report of the American Institute of the City of New York* (Albany: Charles van Benthuysen, printer, 1853), 73.

53 Ibid.

54 "The Rock Tunnelling Machine," *American Railway Times* 4, no. 10 (4 March 1852).

55 "To Capitalists," *New York Times* (2 July 1852).

56 "The Hoosac Tunnel," *American Railway Times* (5 February 1852).

57 *American Railway Times* 4, no. 19 (6 May 1852): Souther's Works at South Boston. *American Railway Times* 4, no. 43 (21 October 1852): machine shop in South Boston. *American Railway Times* 5, no. 5 (3 February 1853: machine was commenced at South Boston in the month of December 1851. *Weekly Transcript* 10, no. 2 (1852), 2: "Globe Works, South Boston." Souther's business, located on Foundry Street, was known as the Globe Works and Globe Locomotive Works.

58 *The Hoosac Tunnel: A Brief Report of the Hearing of the Troy and Greenfield Railroad Company*, 18.

59 "The Rock Tunnelling Machine," *American Railway Times* (4 March 1852).

60 "The Hoosac Tunnel," *American Railway Times* (6 May 1852).

61 "The Mountain Borer," *American Railway Times* 4, no. 27 (1 July 1852).

62 *The Hoosac Tunnel: A Brief Report of the Hearing of the Troy and Greenfield Railroad Company*, 29.

63 "The Hoosac Tunnel," *American Railway Times* (6 May 1852).

64 "Tunnelling the Hoosac," *Scientific American* 7, no. 41 (26 June 1852), 326.

65 "Hoosac Mountain—The Great Tunnel," *American Railway Times* 4, no. 43 (21 October 1852).

66 "A Visit to the Tunnel Machine," *American Railway Times* 4, no. 36 (2 September 1852).

67 "Tunnels—Hoosac and others," *Appletons' Mechanics' Magazine and Engineers' Journal* 3, no. 5 (1 May 1853): 106.

68 "A Visit to the Tunnel Machine," *American Railway Times* (2 September 1852).

69 "Hoosac Tunnel Borer," *Barre Gazette* (Barre, MA), vol. 19, no. 6 (13 August 1852), 2.

70 "The Hoosac Tunnel Borer," *American Railway Times* 4, no. 34 (19 August 1852).

71 "The Hoosac Tunnelling Machine," *American Railway Times* 5, no. 5 (3 February 1853).

72 "The Tunnel Borer," *Weekly Transcript*, vol. 10, no. 2 (9 September 1852), 2.

73 "Hoosac Mountain—The Great Tunnel," *American Railway Times* (21 October 1852).

74 "The Hoosac Tunnel, United States," *Civil Engineer and Architect's Journal* 18, no. 253 (April 1855): 133.

75 *Journal of the Proceedings of the General Railroad Conventions held at Springfield, August 24th and 25th, 1852* (New Haven, CT: T. J. Stafford, 1852): 5, 7.

76 Ibid., 12.

77 "The Hoosac Tunnelling Machine," *American Railway Times* (3 February 1853).

78 *The Hoosac Tunnel: A Brief Report of the Hearing of the Troy and Greenfield Railroad Company*, 4.

79 "The Hoosac Tunnel," *Pittsfield Sun* (24 March 1853).

80 *The Hoosac Tunnel: A Brief Report of the Hearing of the Troy and Greenfield Railroad Company*, 8.

81 "The Hoosac Tunnel," *Pittsfield Sun* (24 March 1853).

82 *The Hoosac Tunnel: A Brief Report of the Hearing of the Troy and Greenfield Railroad Company*, 8.

83 Ibid., 9.

84 Two notes, dated 10 July 1853, to Batchelder and Butler for $100 each, the first payable immediately and the second in ten days: Troy and Greenfield Papers, Baker Library, Harvard University.

85 "To Capitalists," *New York Times* (2 July 1852).

86 "American Patents," *Journal of the Franklin Institute of the State of Pennsylvania, for the Promotion of the Mechanic Arts* (third series, vol. 23, whole no. vol. 53, 1852): 164

87 George Glover Crocker, *From the Stage Coach to the Railroad Train and the Street Car* (Boston: W. B. Clarke, 1900), 10.

88 *The Hoosac Tunnel: A Brief Report of the Hearing of the Troy and Greenfield Railroad Company*, 26.

89 Ibid.

90 Ibid., 58.

91 *Hoosac Tunnel, Speech of Ansel Phelps, Jr., Counsel for the Remonstrants* (Boston: Eastburn's Press, 6 April 1853), 31.

92 Ibid., 19.

93 "The Hoosac Tunnel Bill Defeated," *Weekly Transcript*, vol. 10, no. 39 (26 May 1853), 3.

94 Ibid.

95 "Troy and Greenfield Railroad Meeting," *Weekly Transcript*, vol. 10, no. 44 (30 June 1853).

96 Francis M. Thompson, *History of Greenfield Shire Town of Franklin County Massachusetts*, vol. 2 (Greenfield, MA: T. Morey & Son, 1904), 822.

97 George Adams, *The Massachusetts Register for the Year 1853* (Boston: Damrell and Moore, 1853), 100.

98 Troy and Greenfield Railroad Meeting," *Weekly Transcript* (30 June 1853).

99 "Troy and Greenfield Railroad Company," *American Railway Times* 5, no. 24 (30 June 1853).

100 "Massachusetts Constitutional Convention," *New York Daily Times* (18 May 1853).

101 *Journal of the Constitutional Convention of the Commonwealth of Massachusetts, begun and held in Boston, on the Fourth Day of May, 1853* (Boston: White & Potter, 1853), 33.

102 Ibid., 44.

103 *Official Report of the Debates and Proceedings in the State Convention assembled May 4th, 1853, to Revise and Amend the Constitution of the Commonwealth of Massachusetts*, vol. 2 (1853), 641.

104 *Journal of the Constitutional Convention of the Commonwealth of Massachusetts*, 213.

105 "Hoosac Tunnel Convention," *American Railway Times* 5, no. 40 (6 October 1853).

106 "Hoosac Tunnel Convention," *American Railway Times* 5, no. 41 (13 October 1853).

107 "Tunnel Borer," *Barre Patriot*, vol. 10, no. 5 (12 August 1853).

108 "Miscellanies," *Mining Magazine: Devoted to Mines, Mining Operations, Metallurgy, etc., etc.* 1, no. 5, (November 1853), 552.

109 John Timbs, *The Year-Book of Facts in Science and Art: Exhibiting the Most Important Discoveries & Improvements of the Past Year* (London: Lockwood & Co., 1854), 27.

110 *Report of Cases Argued and Determined in the Superior Court of the City of New York*, vol. 4 (1861), 407.

111 "The New Tunneling Machine," *Weekly Transcript*, vol. 11, no. 18 (29 December 1853), 3.

112 Henry S. Drinker, *A Treatise on Explosive Compounds, Machine Rock Drills and Blasting* (New York: John Wiley, 1883), 193.

113 Terrence E. Coyne, *The Hoosac Tunnel* (PhD dissertation, Clark University, Worcester, MA, April 1992), 76.

114 "The Hoosac Tunnel State Loan," *American Railway Times* 6, no. 8 (23 February 1854).

115 Coyne, *The Hoosac Tunnel*, 77.

116 "The Hoosac Tunnel State Loan," *American Railway Times* (23 February 1854).

117 Coyne, *The Hoosac Tunnel*, 77.

118 Edward Chase Kirkland, *Men, Cities, and Transportation: A Study in New England History, 1820–1900*, vol. 1 (New York: Russell & Russell, New York, 1948), 398.

119 Ibid., 397.

120 "The Hoosac Tunnel State Loan," *American Railway Times* (23 February 1854).

121 Kirkland, *Men, Cities, and Transportation*, 400.

122 "To Contractors, Hoosac Tunnel," *American Railway Times* 6, no. 16 (20 April 1854).

123 *King's Hand Book of Boston*, 7th ed. (Cambridge, MA: Moses King, 1885), 357.

124 Kirkland, "The Hoosac Tunnel Route: The Great Bore," 100.

125 "The Tunnel Route to the West," *American Railway Times* 6, no. 24 (15 June 1854).

126 "Serrell, Edward Wellman," in *The Twentieth Century Biographical Dictionary of Notable Americans*, vol. 9 (Boston: The Biographical Society, 1904).

127 "Serrell, Edward Wellman," in *Dictionary of American Biography*, vol. 8 (New York: Charles Scribner's Sons, 1963), 592.

128 "Serrell, Edward Wellman," in *Appleton's Cyclopaedia of American Biography*, vol. 5 (New York: D. Appleton and Company, 1888), 464.

129 "Serrell, Edward Wellman," in *The Twentieth Century Biographical Dictionary of Notable Americans*.

130 Ibid.

131 Edward W. Serrell, "Description of an Instrument for Rapid Surveying," *Journal of the Franklin Institute of the State of Pennsylvania for the Promotion of the Mechanic Arts* (third series, vol. 28, no. 5, 1854): 304–6.

132 "Gen. Serrell Married," *New York Times* (8 September 1900).

133 "Lewiston and Queenston Suspension Bridge," *Scientific American* 5, no. 31 (30 April 1850): 242.

134 William Pool, *Landmarks of Niagara County, New York* (Syracuse, NY: D. Mason & Company, 1897), 296.

135 Edward W. Serrell, "Considerations Respecting the Hoosac Tunnel," *Journal of the Franklin Institute of the State of Pennsylvania for the Promotion of the Mechanic Arts* (third series, vol. 29, no. 1, 1855): 11–12.

136 "The Hoosac Tunnel," *American Railway Times* 7, no. 5 (1 February 1855).

137 "Troy and Greenfield Railroad Co.—Hoosac Tunnel," *American Railroad Journal* 11, no. 5, whole no. 981, vol. 28 (3 February 1855): 76.

138 "Troy and Greenfield Railroad," *Weekly Transcript*, vol. 12, no. 25 (15 February 1855).

139 "The Tunnel Railroad," *Weekly Transcript*, vol. 12, no. 34 (19 April 1855).

140 "Troy & Greenfield Railroad," *Weekly Transcript*, vol. 12, no. 38 (17 May 1855).

141 "The Troy and Greenfield Railroad and Hoosac Tunnel," *American Railway Times* 7, no. 34 (23 August 1855).

142 "Troy & Greenfield Railroad," *Weekly Transcript*, vol. 12, no. 49 (2 August 1855).

143 *Massachusetts Senate Document 163* (Boston: Wright & Potter, State Printers, 1855).

144 "Troy & Greenfield Railroad," *Weekly Transcript*, vol. 12, no. 43 (21 June 1855).

145 Ibid.

146 "The Fight," *The Pittsfield Sun*, vol. 56, no. 2882 (13 December 1855), 2.

147 Herman Haupt Chapman, "Origin of the Hoosac Tunnel [n.d.]," *Haupt*, Haupt Papers, Manuscripts and Archives, Yale University Library, Box 13, Folder 223, p. 5.

148 "Letter from Mr. Dawes," *Weekly Transcript*, vol. 13, no. 17 (20 December 1855).

149 "The Tunnel Affray," *Weekly Transcript*, vol. 13, no. 16 (13 December 1855).

150 "A Meeting of the Directors of the Troy and Greenfield Railroad," *Weekly Transcript*, vol. 13, no. 17 (20 December 1855).

151 "Troy & Greenfield Railroad," *Weekly Transcript*, vol. 12, no. 38 (17 May 1855).

152 *The Boston Traveller* (8 March 1855).

153 James A. Ward, *That Man Haupt*: A Biography of Herman Haupt (Baton Rouge: Louisiana State University Press, 1973), 60.

Chapter 6

1 Robert Fulton, "On the Formation of Canals, and the Mode of extending them into every District," in *A Treatise on the Improvement of Canal Navigation* (London: I. and J. Taylor at the Architectural Library, 1796), 22

2 James Arthur Ward III, *That Man Haupt: A Biography of Herman Haupt* (PhD dissertation, Louisiana State University, 1969), 111.

3 H. Haupt, *Suspension of Work on Hoosac Tunnel: Communication from H. Haupt, Chief Engineer* (1861), 3.

4 Haupt, *Haupt Family in America*, pp. 5, 14, 16; Haupt Papers, Yale University Library, Box 13, Folder 221.

5 William Henry Haupt, *Haupt Family in America* (Chariton, IA: self-published, 1924), and Israel D. Rupp, *A Collection of Upwards of Thirty Thousand Names of German, Swiss, Dutch, French and Other Immigrants in Pennsylvania from 1727 to 1776* (Philadelphia: IG. Kohler, 1876).

6 At age fourteen, Herman Haupt, the great-grandson, would choose to use the original spelling of the family name.

7 Haupt Papers, Yale University Library, Box 17, Folder 221.

8 Haupt Papers, Yale University Library, Box 17, Folder 294.

9 Herman Haupt, *Memoirs of Herman Haupt Up to the Age of 21 when He Married, 1889* [n.d.], p. 3. The Historical Society of Pennsylvania, Haupt Family Documents and Letters, Doc. Box 17.

10 "The Haupt Family in Bucks and Philadelphia Counties," Haupt Papers, Yale University Library, Box 17, Folder 292.

11 Ibid., Box 13, Folder 221.

12 Ibid.

13 Ibid.

14 Ward, *That Man Haupt*, 10.

15   Haupt, *Memoirs of Herman Haupt Up to the Age of 21 when He Married, 1889*, 1.
16   Ward, *That Man Haupt*, 10.
17   Haupt, *Memoirs of Herman Haupt*, 3.
18   Ibid., p. 5.
19   Letter, M. Boyd to John Haupt, 24 October 1828, Haupt Papers, Yale University Library, Box 1, Folder 3.
20   Haupt, *Memoirs of Herman Haupt*, 9.
21   United States Military Academy, Cadet Application Papers, 1831, National Archives, frames 296–301.
22   Haupt, *Memoirs of Herman Haupt*, 12.
23   Ibid., p. 16.
24   Herman Haupt, photography from Herman Haupt Papers (MS 269), Manuscripts and Archives, Yale University Library, Box 20, Folder 331.
25   Anna Margaretta Haupt, photography from Herman Haupt Papers (MS 269), Manuscripts and Archives, Yale University Library, Box 20, Folder 332.
26   Photostat of official order, Haupt Papers, Yale University Library, Box 1, Folder 3.
27   Stephen E. Ambrose, *Duty, Honor, Country: A History of West Point* (Baltimore: John Hopkins University Press, 1966), 122.
28   Forest G. Hill, *Roads, Rails, & Waterways: The Army Engineers and Early Transportation* (Norman: University of Oklahoma Press, 1957), 59.
29   Terry S. Reynolds, *The Engineer in America: A Historical Anthology from Technology and Culture* (Chicago: University of Chicago Press, 1991), 17.
30   Order no. 72, Adjutant General Office, Washington, DC, 1 October 1835, Photostat of official order, Haupt Papers, Yale University Library, Box 1, Folder 3.
31   Haupt, *Memoirs of Herman Haupt*, 20.
32   Ibid.
33   Caroline E. MacGill and Balthasar Henry Meyer, *History of Transportation in the United States before 1860* (Washington, DC: Carnegie Institution, 1948), 311.
34   Anthony J. Bianculli, *Trains and Technology: The American Railroad in the Nineteenth Century, vol. 1: Locomotives* (Newark: University of Delaware Press, 2001), 74.

35 Alfred W. Bruce, *The Steam Locomotive in America: Its Development in the Twentieth Century* (New York: W. W. Norton, 1952), 25.

36 Herbert T. Walker, "The Evolution of the American Locomotive," *Scientific American Supplement* 43, no. 1113 (1 May 1897): 17792.

37 Edwin P. Alexander, *Iron Horses: American Locomotives, 1829–1900* (New York: W. W. Norton, 1941), 32.

38 Haupt, *Memoirs of Herman Haupt*, 21.

39 Charles Aeneas Shaw, *Tales of a Pioneer Surveyor* (Longman Canada, 1970), 12.

40 Haupt, *Memoirs of Herman Haupt*, 30.

41 Shaw, *Tales of a Pioneer Surveyor*, 13–38.

42 Haupt, *Memoirs of Herman Haupt*, 31.

43 Ibid.

44 Herman Haupt's letters address her as Anna, but the name engraved on her tombstone in the West Laurel Hill Cemetery in Bala Cynwyd, PA, is "Anne."

45 Anna Cecelia Keller, photography from Herman Haupt Papers (MS 269), Manuscripts and Archives, Yale University Library, Box 13, Folder 222.

46 Herman Haupt, *Reminiscences of General Herman Haupt* (Milwaukee: Wright & Joys Co., 1901), 311.

47 Samuel Gring Hefelbower, *The History of Gettysburg College, 1832–1932* (Gettysburg, PA: Gettysburg College, 1932), 144.

48 "List of American Patents issued in December, 1839," *Journal of the Franklin Institute*, third series, vol. 1 (1841): 107.

49 Oakridge, photography from Herman Haupt Papers (MS 269), Manuscripts and Archives, Yale University Library, Box 20, Folder 335.

50 Silvio Bedini, "History Corner: Samuel Wright Mifflin," *Professional Surveyor* 16, no. 8 (November/December 1996).

51 Haupt, *Reminiscences of General Herman Haupt*, xiv.

52 *American National Biography* (1999). Oxford University Press under the auspices of the American Council of Learned Societies, Vol. 13, p. 246.

53 John E. Semmes, *John H. B. Latrobe and His Times, 1803–1891* (Baltimore: Norman, Remington & Co., 1917), 84.

54 Ibid., 285.

55 John Thomas Scharf, *History of Baltimore City and County, from the Earliest Period to the Present Day* (Philadelphia: Louis H. Everts, 1881), 348.

56   "Biographical Sketch of Benjamin H. Latrobe," *Van Nostrand's Eclectic Engineering Magazine* 5, no. 31 (July 1871): 2.

57   *Hints on Bridge Construction, by an engineer.* The copy in the Library of Congress (TG153.H37), is dated 1842. Haupt, in *Reminiscences of General Herman Haupt* (p. xi), says it was published in 1841.

58   Herman Haupt, *General Theory of Bridge Construction* (Philadelphia: D. Appleton & Company, 1851).

59   Haupt, *Reminiscences of General Herman Haupt,* xv.

60   Herman Haupt, "Description of an Iron Arched Bridge of 133 Feet Span, Across the Canal on Section 5 of the Pennsylvania Central Railroad," *Journal of the Franklin Institute,* third series, vol. 18 (September 1849): 181–84.

61   Haupt, *General Theory of Bridge Construction.*

62   Ward, *That Man Haupt,* 49.

63   Ibid., 51.

64   Julius Rubin, "Canal or Railroad? Limitations and Innovation in the Response to the Erie Canal in Philadelphia, Baltimore, and Boston," *Transactions of the American Philosophical Society* 51, no. 7 (1961): 49–50.

65   Eliza Cope Harrison, ed., *Philadelphia Merchant: The Diary of Thomas P. Cope, 1800–1851* (South Bend, IN: Gateway Editions, 1978), 495.

66   James A. Ward, "Power and Accountability on the Pennsylvania Railroad," *The Business History Review* 49, no. 1 (Spring 1975): 41.

67   Daniel R. Goodwin, "Obituary Notice of Samuel Vaughan Merrick, Esq.," *Proceedings of the American Philosophical Society* 11, no. 81 (January 1869): 585.

68   Henry Butler Allen, "The Franklin Institute of the State of Pennsylvania," *Transactions of the American Philosophical Society,* new series, vol. 43, no. 1 (1953): 275.

69   Haupt, *Reminiscences of General Herman Haupt,* xvi.

70   Harrison, *Philadelphia Merchant,* 531.

71   Ibid.

72   *First Annual Report of the Directors of the Pennsylvania Railroad Co. to the Stockholders* (Philadelphia: Crissy & Markley, Printers, 1847), p. 5.

73   Harrison, *Philadelphia Merchant,* 531.

74   James A. Ward, *J. Edgar Thomson: Master of the Pennsylvania* (Westport, CT: Greenwood Press, 1980), 26.

75   Ward, *That Man Haupt,* 66.

76 Mary G. Cumming, *Georgia Railroad & Banking Company* (Augusta, GA: Walton Printing Co., 1945), 67.

77 Henry Pettit, "Obituary Notices of Members Deceased. Joseph Miller Wilson, A.M., C.E.," *Proceedings of the American Philosophical Society* 42, no. 174 (May–December 1903): ii.

78 Solomon W. Roberts, "Obituary Notice of Edward Miller, Civil Engineer," *Proceedings of the American Philosophical Society* 12, no. 86 (1871): 581–86.

79 Solomon W. Roberts, "Reminiscences of the First Railroad over the Allegheny Mountain" (read before the Historical Society of Pennsylvania, 8 April 1878), *The Pennsylvania Magazine of History and Biography* 2, no. 4 (1878): 378.

80 Daniel Hovey Calhoun, *The American Civil Engineer: Origins and Conflict* (Cambridge, MA: Harvard University Press, 1960), 82.

81 *First Annual Report of the Directors of the Pennsylvania Railroad Co.*, p. 6.

82 Hubertis M. Cummings, "James D. Harris and William B. Foster, Jr., Canal Engineers," *Pennsylvania History* 24, no. 3 (July 1957): 191–206.

83 George H. Burgess and Miles C. Kennedy, *Centennial History of the Pennsylvania Railroad Company* (Pennsylvania Railroad Co., 1949), 46.

84 Christopher T. Baer, *A General Chronology of the Pennsylvania Railroad Company, Its Predecessors and Successors and Its Historical Context*, "PRR Chronology 30 June 1847" (April 2005 ed.).

85 Harrison, *Philadelphia Merchant*, 547.

86 Ward, *That Man Haupt*, 25.

87 Haupt, *Reminiscences of General Herman Haupt*, xvii.

88 J. Edgar Thomson, "Second Annual Report of the Chief Engineer, 15 November 1849," *Third Annual Report of the Directors of the Pennsylvania Railroad Co. to the Stockholders* (Philadelphia: Crissy & Markley, Printers, 1849), p. 55.

89 James A. Ward, "Herman Haupt and the Development of the Pennsylvania Railroad," *The Pennsylvania Magazine of History and Biography* 95, no. 1 (January 1971): 77.

90 Herman Haupt to John Edgar Thomson (p. 29 of his letterbook), 9 December 1861, Haupt Papers, Yale University Library, Box 2, Folder 34.

91 Ward, *That Man Haupt*, 27.

92 H. Haupt, "Report of the Superintendent of Transportation, 31 December 1850," *Fourth Annual Report of the Directors of the Pennsylvania Railroad Co. to the Stockholders* (Philadelphia: Crissy & Markley, Printers, 1851), p. 41.

93 Harrison, *Philadelphia Merchant*, 558.

94 Herman Haupt, *Reminiscences of Early History of the Pennsylvania Railroad Company* [n.d.], typed manuscript, National Museum of American History, Smithsonian Institution, Haupt file, p. 7.

95 James A. Ward, "Power and Accountability on the Pennsylvania Railroad," *The Business History Review* 49, no. 1 (Spring 1975): 45.

96 MacGill and Meyer, *History of Transportation in the United States before 1860*, 392.

97 Haupt, *Reminiscences of Early History of the Pennsylvania Railroad Company*, p. 8.

98 Ibid., p. 9.

99 Ibid., p. 17.

100 Letter, T. A. Marshall to J. Edgar Thomson, 26 August 1852, Haupt Papers, Yale University Library, Box 1, Folder 6.

101 James A. Ward, "A New Look at Antebellum Southern Railroad Development," *The Journal of Southern History* 39, no. 3 (August 1973): 417.

102 Letter, J. Edgar Thomson to T. A. Marshall, 2 September 1852, Haupt Papers, Yale University Library, Box 1, Folder 6.

103 Ward, *That Man Haupt*, 48.

104 Ward, "Herman Haupt and the Development of the Pennsylvania Railroad," 93.

105 H. Haupt, *Report of the Final Location of the Southern Railroad from Brandon, Mississippi, to the Alabama Line, in the Direction of Charleston and Savannah* (Philadelphia: T. K. and P. G. Collins, Printers, 1853).

106 Haupt, *Reminiscences of Early History of the Pennsylvania Railroad Company*, p. 19.

107 *Sixth Annual Report of the Directors of the Pennsylvania Railroad Co. to the Stockholders* (Philadelphia: Crissy & Markley, Printers, 1853), p. 34.

108 J. Edgar Thomson, "Third Annual Report of the Chief Engineer, 31 December 1850," *Fourth Annual Report of the Directors of the Pennsylvania Railroad Co. to the Stockholders* (Philadelphia: Crissy & Markley, Printers, 1 January 1851), p. 19.

109 Ibid.

110 *Sixth Annual Report of the Directors of the Pennsylvania Railroad Co. to the Stockholders*, p. 34.

111 J. Edgar Thomson, "Fourth Annual Report of the Chief Engineer, 15 January 1852," *Fifth Annual Report of the Directors of the Pennsylvania Railroad Co. to the Stockholders* (Philadelphia: Crissy & Markley, Printers, 1852), p. 15.

112 H. Haupt, "Seventh Annual Report of the Chief Engineer, 25 January 1854," *Seventh Annual Report of the Directors of the Pennsylvania Railroad Co. to the Stockholders* (Philadelphia: Crissy & Markley, Printers, 1854), p. 28.

113 Ibid., p. 42.

114 *Eighth Annual Report of the Directors of the Pennsylvania Railroad Company, to the Stockholders* (Philadelphia: Crissy & Markley, Printers, 1855), p. 4.

115 Ibid., p. 22.

116 *Ninth Annual Report of the Directors of the Pennsylvania Railroad Company, to the Stockholders* (Philadelphia: Crissy & Markley, Printers, 1856), p. 30.

117 Baer, *A General Chronology of the Pennsylvania Railroad Company, Its Predecessors and Successors and Its Historical Context.*

118 Burgess and Kennedy, *Centennial History of the Pennsylvania Railroad Company*, 786.

119 Haupt to Christian Spangler, 7 March 1864, Haupt Papers, Yale University Library, Box 4.

120 Ward, "Power and Accountability on the Pennsylvania Railroad," 50.

121 Benjamin Homans, *The United States Railroad Directory for 1856* (New York: B. Homans, 1856), 59. *Troy and Greenfield Rail Road and Hoosac Tunnel—History and Present Condition of the Enterprise* (n.d.; written after 1857), Historical Collections, Baker Library, Harvard Business School, p. 2, refers to Lane as "President of the Northwestern R. R. Co. of Pennsylvania." Ward, *That Man Haupt*, p. 56, refers to Lane as "President of the North Western Railroad Company in Pennsylvania."

122 Herman Haupt Chapman, *Haupt*, "Origin of the Hoosac Tunnel (n.d.)," Haupt Papers, Yale University Library, Box 13, Folder 223, p. 6. Herman Haupt Chapman was the grandson of Herman Haupt. In the early 1950s, using his grandfather's papers, which had been given to his father, Fred Chapman, he wrote a long biography of Herman Haupt. After Herman Haupt Chapman's death, the papers were given to Yale University.

123 Chapman, *Haupt*, "Origin of the Hoosac Tunnel," p. 6.

124 *History of Butler County, Pennsylvania* (Chicago: Waterman, Watkins & Co., 1883), chapter 8.

125 Ibid., chapter 4.

126 Ibid., chapter 21.

127 "A Meeting of the Directors of the Troy and Greenfield Railroad," North Adams (MA) *Weekly Transcript*, vol. 13, no. 17 (20 December 1855).

128 Chapman, *Haupt*, "Origin of the Hoosac Tunnel," p. 8.

129 Ward, *That Man Haupt*, 60; Haupt, *A Short History of the Hoosac Tunnel*, 3.

130 "Report of James Laurie, on the Troy & Greenfield Railroad and Hoosac Tunnel," *Report of the Commissioners Upon the Troy and Greenfield Railroad and Hoosac Tunnel to His Excellency the Governor, and the Honorable the Executive Council of the State of Massachusetts* (23 February 1863), p. 146.

Chapter 7

1 Herman Haupt Chapman, "Dealing with Serrell, Galbraith, and Subcontractor [n.d.]," *Haupt*, Haupt Papers, Manuscripts and Archives, Yale University Library, Box 13, Folder 224, p. 1.

2 Henry Varnum Poor, *History of the Railroads and Canals of the United States of America*, vol. 1 (New York: J. H. Schultz & Company, 1860), 466.

3 Chapman, "Origin of the Hoosac Tunnel [n.d.]," *Haupt*, Haupt Papers, Yale University Library, Box 13, Folder 223, p. 9.

4 *House No. 174, Commonwealth of Massachusetts, Petition of the Troy & Greenfield Railroad Corporation* (12 April 1856), 18.

5 Benjamin Homans, *The United States Railroad Directory for 1856* (New York: B. Homans, 1856), 59.

6 James A. Ward, *That Man Haupt: A Biography of Herman Haupt* (Baton Rouge: Louisiana State University Press, 1973), 63.

7 Chapman, "Dealing with Serrell, Galbraith, and Subcontractor," 2.

8 James A. Ward, *J. Edgar Thomson: Master of the Pennsylvania* (Westport, CT: Greenwood Press, 1980), 178.

9 Chapman, "Origin of the Hoosac Tunnel," 9.

10 Ward, *That Man Haupt*, 64.

11 Letter, Edward W. Serrell to Board of Directors, Troy and Greenfield Railroad, Troy and Greenfield Railroad Papers, Historical Collections, Baker Library, Harvard University.

12 Chapman, "Dealing with Serrell, Galbraith, and Subcontractor," 4.

13 Ward, *That Man Haupt*, 65.

14 Contract between H. Haupt and Company and the Troy and Greenfield Railroad Company, 30 July 1856, Troy and Greenfield Railroad Papers, Historical Collections, Baker Library, Harvard University; "Report of James Laurie, on the Troy & Greenfield Railroad and Hoosac Tunnel," *Report of the Commissioners Upon the Troy and Greenfield Railroad and Hoosac Tunnel to His Excellency the Governor, and the Honorable the Executive Council of the State of Massachusetts,* 23 February 1863, 147.

15 Chapman, "Haupt's Contracts and Dealings with the Troy and Greenfield Railroad Company [n.d.]," *Haupt*, Haupt Papers, Yale University Library, Box 13, Folder 223, p. 2.

16 Carl R. Byron, *A Pinprick of Light: The Troy and Greenfield Railroad and Its Hoosac Tunnel* (Shelburne, VT: New England Press, 1995), 15.

17 "Report of James Laurie, on the Troy & Greenfield Railroad and Hoosac Tunnel," 147.

18 Robert A. Hodge, "Gaslight! The Story of the Fredericksburg Gas Company," *Fredericksburg* [VA] *Times Magazine* (August 1977).

19 Henry Cartwright later referred to himself as "Engineer and Contractor": Haupt Papers, Yale University Library, Box 11, letter dated 26 May 1875.

20 *The Weekly Transcript* (17 October 1856).

21 "Troy and Greenfield Railroad," *Weekly Transcript*, vol. 13, no. 39 (22 May 1856).

22 Ibid.

23 Ibid.

24 Herman Haupt, *Reminiscences of General Herman Haupt* (Milwaukee: Wright & Joys Co., 1901), xxi.

25 "The Hoosac Tunnel—An Inside View," *Adams Transcript*, vol. 13, no. 49 (10 September 1859).

26 "Trip to the Hoosac Tunnel," *Adams Transcript*, vol. 17, no. 42 (19 July 1860).

27 Ibid.

28 Ibid.

29 *Eighth Annual Report of the Directors to the Stockholders of the Connecticut River Railroad, for Eleven Months ending Nov. 30, 1852,* C. W. Chapin, President, Springfield (28 December 1852), 5.

30 Chas. E. Fisher, "Daniel L. Harris," Bulletin no. 32, *The Railway & Locomotive Historical Society* (October 1933): 10.

31 Edward Chase Kirkland, *Men, Cities, and Transportation: A Study in New England History 1820–1900*, vol. 1 (New York: Russell & Russell, 1948), 405.

32 "Report of the Hoosac Tunnel Committee," *Weekly Transcript*, vol. 14, no. 36 (7 May 1857).

33 Henry S. Drinker, *Tunneling, Explosive Compounds, and Rock Drills* (New York: John Wiley, 1878), 323

34 "Report of the Hoosac Tunnel Committee," *Weekly Transcript* (7 May 1857).

35 Terrence E. Coyne, *The Hoosac Tunnel* (PhD dissertation, Clark University, Worcester, MA, April 1992), 106.

36 "Gov. Gardner has Vetoed the Tunnel Bill," *Weekly Transcript*, vol. 14, no. 36 (28 May 1857).

37 Ibid.

38 "Tunnels," *American Engineer* (18 July 1857), 11.

39 Byron, *A Pinprick of Light*, 17.

40 Chapman, "The Wilson Boring Machine [n.d.]," *Haupt*, Haupt Papers, Yale University Library, Box 13, Folder 224, p. 1, puts the total cost to Haupt at $22,272.40.

41 Chs. Wilson, of Springfield, Massachusetts, Machine for Tunneling Rocks, &c., Specification of Letters Patent No. 14,483, dated 18 March 1856.

42 "Hoosac Tunnel," *Hoosac Valley News*, vol. 1, no. 3 (2 September 1857).

43 *Hoosac Valley News*, vol. 1, no. 5 (16 September 1857).

44 Chapman, "The Southern Vermont Railroad [n.d.]," *Haupt*, Haupt Papers, Yale University Library, Box 13, Folder 230, p. 1.

45 Byron, *A Pinprick of Light*, 11.

46 Ward, *That Man Haupt*, 70.

47 "Troy and Greenfield Railroad," *Weekly Transcript*, vol. 14, no. 41 (11 June 1857).

48 Ward, *That Man Haupt*, 71.

49 Galbraith to the board of directors, Troy and Greenfield Railroad, July 13, 1857, Troy and Greenfield Railroad Papers, Historical Collections, Baker Library, Harvard University.

50 Ward, *That Man Haupt*, 74 (quoting letter of 17 August 1857).

51 Ibid., 75.

52 Ibid., 78.

53 Ibid., 79. Contract between H. Haupt and Troy and Greenfield Railroad Company, 18 February 1858, Troy and Greenfield Papers, Historical Collections, Baker Library, Harvard University.

54 Edward Chase Kirkland, "The Hoosac Tunnel Route: The Great Bore," *The New England Quarterly* 20, no. 1 (March 1947): 99.

55 Ward, *That Man Haupt*, 80.

56 "Hoosac Tunnel," *Hoosac Valley News*, vol. 1, no. 24 (27 January 1858).

57 "Local Intelligence," *Adams Transcript*, vol. 15, no. 19 (13 February 1858).

58 *Hoosac Valley News*, vol. 1, no. 31 (26 March 1858).

59 "Good News for the Hoosac Tunnel," *Hoosac Valley News*, vol. 1, no. 35 (14 April 1858).

60 "Troy and Greenfield Railroad," *Adams Transcript*, vol. 15, no. 28 (17 April 1858).

61 "Rapid Progress of the Railroad to Troy," *Adams Transcript*, vol. 15, no. 35 (5 June 1858).

Chapter 8

1 "Railroad Items," *Adams Transcript*, vol. 15, no. 45 (14 August 1858).

2 "Visit to Hoosac Mountain," *Adams Transcript* (14 August 1858).

3 Ibid.

4 Edward Chase Kirkland, *Men, Cities, and Transportation: A Study in New England History, 1820–1900*, vol. 1 (New York: Russell & Russell), 404.

5 James A. Ward, *That Man Haupt* (Baton Rouge: Louisiana State University Press, 1973), 81.

6 F. W. Bird, *The Road to Ruin: or the Decline and Fall of the Hoosac Tunnel* (Boston: Wright & Potter, 1862).

7 *The Troy & Greenfield Railroad: Argument of E. Hasket Derby, Esq., Delivered Feb. 29th, 1856 Before a Joint Special Committee of the Legislature of Massachusetts, in Behalf of the Troy and Greenfield Railroad Company, Petitioners for a State Subscription to Their Stock* (Boston: Bazin & Chandler, 1856).

8 Ward, (1973). *That Man Haupt*, 82: attachment of Elias H. Derby against the Troy and Greenfield Railroad, 2 October 1858.

9   *The Argument of E. H. Derby, Esq. in Favor of a State Loan to the Vermont and Massachusetts Railroad Co. before the Joint Committee on Railroads and Canals of the Legislature of Massachusetts, March 1855* (Boston: Dutton and Wentworth, 1855).

10   Ward, *That Man Haupt*, 82; Herman Haupt Chapman, "The State Loan Fund [n.d.]," *Haupt*, Haupt Papers, Yale University Library, MS#269, Box 13, Folder 224, p. 3.

11   "Report of James Laurie, on the Troy & Greenfield Railroad and Hoosac Tunnel," *Report of the Commissioners Upon the Troy and Greenfield Railroad and Hoosac Tunnel to His Excellency the Governor, and the Honorable the Executive Council of the State of Massachusetts*, 23 February 1863, 151.

12   Chapman, "The Southern Vermont Railroad [n.d.]," *Haupt*, Haupt Papers, Yale University Library, MS#269, Box 13, Folder 230, p. 2.

13   Chapman, "Herman Haupt's Family Life [n.d.]," *Haupt*, Haupt Papers, Yale University Library, MS#269, Box 13, Folder 233, p. 1, Letter from Herman to his daughter Mary, 1 December 1858.

14   Ward, *That Man Haupt*, 83.

15   "Report of James Laurie, on the Troy & Greenfield Railroad and Hoosac Tunnel," 151.

16   H. Haupt letter to General John E. Wool, 25 September 1858, published in the *Adams Transcript*, vol. 16, no. 9 (4 December 1858).

17   Henry S. Drinker, *Tunneling, Explosive Compounds, and Rock Drills* (New York: John Wiley, 1878), 154.

18   J. W. Fowle, caveat filed 9 May 1849 to J. J. Couch's patent no. 6237.

19   *Adams Transcript*, vol. 16, no. 18 (5 February 1859).

20   *Hoosac Valley News*, vol. 2, no. 25 (3 February 1859).

21   "Good News!" *Adams Transcript*, vol. 16, no. 24 (19 March 1859).

22   "The Hoosac Tunnel," *Scientific American* 22, no. 7 (1870); Bird, *The Road to Ruin:* diagram opposite p. 6.

23   Fred Harvey Harrington, *Fighting Politician Major General N. P. Banks* (Philadelphia: University of Pennsylvania Press, 1948), 41.

24   Ibid., 3.

25   Ibid., 47.

26   Bird, *The Road to Ruin*, 3.

27   Ward, *That Man Haupt*, 86; based on letters from Haupt to Cartwright, 24 March and 2 April 1859.

28   *Adams Transcript*, vol. 16, no. 37 (18 June 1859).

29   Letter, Haupt to Cartwright, 2 August 1859, Haupt Papers, Yale University Library, MS#269, Box 2, Folder 22.

30   *Hoosac Valley News*, vol. 2, no. 44 (16 June 1859).

31   "Hoosac Tunnel," *Adams Transcript*, vol. 16, no. 36 (11 June 1859).

32   Haupt Papers, Yale University Library, MS#269, Box 18, Folder 312, p. 18.

33   "Visit to the Hoosac Tunnel," *Adams Transcript*, vol. 16, no. 51 (24 September 1859).

34   H. G. Rowe and C. T. Fairfield, *North Adams and Vicinity Illustrated* (North Adams, MA: The Transcript Publishing Co., 1898), 26.

35   "Railroad Items," *Adams Transcript*, vol. 16, no. 37 (18 June 1859).

36   *Hoosac Valley News*, vol. 2, no. 48 (14 July 1859).

37   Ibid.

38   "The Hoosac Tunnel—An Inside View," *Adams Transcript*, vol. 16, no. 49 (10 September 1859).

39   Letter, Haupt to Cartwright, 30 November 1859, Haupt Papers, Yale University Library, MS#269, Box 2, Folder 23.

40   Ward, *That Man Haupt*, 89; Drinker, *Tunneling, Explosive Compounds, and Rock Drills*, 3d ed., 201.

41   Herman Haupt, *Tunneling by Machinery* (Philadelphia: H. G. Leisenring's Steam Printing House, 1867), 4.

42   Chapman, "Herman Haupt's Contribution to the Invention of the Pneumatic Rock Drill [n.d.]," *Haupt*, Haupt Papers, Yale University Library, Box 13, Folder 228, p. 5.

43   Haupt, *Tunneling by Machinery*, 5.

44   Payments by state treasurer to Troy and Greenfield Railroad Co. (12 July 1861): Haupt Papers, Yale University Library, MS#269, Box 11, Folder 201.

45   "The Hoosac Tunnel—An Inside View," *Adams Transcript* (10 Sept 1859).

46   Letter, Haupt to Cartwright (2 April 1860), Haupt Papers, Yale University Library, MS#269, Box 2, Folder 21.

47   H. Haupt, "Reply of the General Superintendent of the Pennsylvania Railroad, To a Letter from a Large Number of Stockholders of the Company, Requesting Information in Reference to the Management of the Road" (20 January 1852), John W. Barriger III National Railroad Library, University of Missouri, St. Louis, p. 32.

48   Letter, Haupt to Cartwright (2 April 1860).

49   Ward, *That Man Haupt*, 244.

50   Ibid., 249.

51   *Hoosac Valley News*, vol. 3, no. 28 (23 February 1860).

52   *House Document No. 185, Commonwealth of Massachusetts, 1860*, partially reprinted in the *Hoosac Valley News*, vol. 3, no. 34 (5 April 1860).

53   "Statement of Col. Ezra Lincoln," *House No. 235, Commonwealth of Massachusetts*, 4 April 1862, p. 53.

54   *Acts and Resolutions passed by the General Court of Massachusetts, in the year 1860*, pp. 157–62.

55   Letter, Steever to Haupt (11 April 1860), Haupt Papers, Yale University Library, MS#269, Box 2, Folder 26.

56   Charles Dungan to Haupt (13 April 1860), cited in "1860—Responsibility Shifts to the State," p. 21, Haupt Papers, Yale University Library, MS#269, Box 18, Folder 311.

57   "1860—Responsibility Shifts to the State."

58   Ward, *That Man Haupt*, 94.

59   Ibid., 95.

60   Ibid; Fred Chapman, "Chap. XVI [n.d.]," *Haupt*, Haupt Papers, Yale University Library. It is difficult to determine exactly how much Haupt "appropriated," but he did pay the note to Spangler (Spangler, Howell, and Burroughs) for $60,000 with interest and Derbyshire's $33,000, according to the summary of the Haupt ledger, p. 23.

61   *Hoosac Valley News*, vol. 3, no. 44 (14 June 1860).

62   *Hoosac Valley News*, vol. 3, no. 52 (9 August 1860).

63   Ibid.

64   Ron Powers, *Mark Twain: A Life* (New York: Simon and Schuster, 2005), 183.

65   *Hoosac Valley News*, vol. 3, no. 3 (15 September 1859).

66   *Hoosac Valley News*, vol. 4, no. 6 (20 September 1860).

67   *Hoosac Valley News* (15 September 1859).

68   *Hoosac Valley News*, vol. 3, no. 19 (22 December 1859).

69   *Hoosac Valley News*, vol. 3, no. 20 (29 December 1859).

70   *Hoosac Valley News*, vol. 3, no. 48 (12 July 1860).

71   *Adams Transcript*, vol. 17, no. 37 (14 June 1860).

72   *Adams Transcript*, vol. 17, no. 34 (24 May 1860).

73   Letter, Haupt to Cartwright, 2 May 1860, Haupt Papers, Yale University Library, MS#269, Box 2, Folder 26.

74   Letter, Stuart Gwynn to Anna Cecilia Haupt, 25 June 1860, Haupt Papers, Yale University Library, MS#269, Box 2, Folder 27.

75   *Hoosac Valley News*, vol. 4, no. 9 (11 October 1860).

76   Ibid.

77   *Hoosac Valley News*, vol. 4, no. 3 (30 August 1860).

78   Thomas Doane and Charles Harris, "Samuel Morse Felton—A Memoir," *Journal of the Association of Engineering Societies* 11, no. 4 (April 1892): 210–13.

79   *House No. 235, Commonwealth of Massachusetts*: "Statement of Col. Ezra Lincoln," 4 April 1862, p. 51.

80   Ibid., p. 52.

81   Letter, Haupt to Cartwright, 13 December 1860, Haupt Papers, Yale University Library, MS#269, Box 2, Folder 30.

82   *Report of the Commissioners upon the Troy and Greenfield Railroad and Hoosac Tunnel to His Excellency the Governor, and the Honorable the Executive Council of the State of Massachusetts*, 28 February 1863, p. 22, *Senate No. 93, Commonwealth of Massachusetts* (Senate, 25 February, House 26 February).

83   Chapman, "Governor John A. Andrew [n.d.]," *Haupt*, Haupt Papers, Yale University Library, p. 9; Andrew to Haupt, 22 January 1861, Haupt Papers, Yale University Library, Box 13, Folder 230.

84   Ward, *That Man Haupt*, 99; Herman Haupt, *Reminiscences of General Herman Haupt* (Milwaukee: Wright & Joys Co.), xxiii.

85   Ward, *That Man Haupt*, 99.

86   Ibid.

87   Letter, Haupt to Cartwright, 14 February 1861, Haupt Papers, Yale University Library, MS#269, Box 2, Folder 32.

88   *Hoosac Valley News and Transcript*, vol. 21, no. 36 (25 April 1861); *Gazette and Courier* (Greenfield, MA), vol. 24, no. 8 (29 April 1861).

89   "Statement of C. L. Stevenson," *House No. 235, Commonwealth of Massachusetts*, 4 April 1862, p. 75.

90   Ibid.

91   Ibid.

92   Ward, *That Man Haupt*, 100; Daniel Harris to Moses Kimball, 1 May 1861, Troy and Greenfield Papers.

93   Ward, *That Man Haupt*, 101; Letter, Haupt to Cartwright, 29 April 1861, Haupt Papers, Yale University Library, MS#269, Box 2, Folder 32, and

cited in Chapman, "Chap. XI [n.d.]," *Haupt*, pp. 10–11, Haupt Papers, Yale University Library, MS#269.

94 Letter, Haupt to Andrew, 18 January 1861, copy in Haupt Papers, Yale University Library, MS#269 Box 2, Folder 31, original in J. A. Andrew Papers, Massachusetts Historical Society, Boston.

95 Letter, H. W. Green to Haupt, 1 June 1861, Haupt Papers, Yale University Library, MS#269, Box 2, Folder 33.

96 Chapman, "William W. Whitwell [n.d.]," *Haupt*, p. 3, Haupt Papers, Yale University Library, Box 13, Folder 230.

97 Letter, Haupt to Cartwright, 26 June 1861, Haupt Papers, Yale University Library, MS#269, Box 2, Folder 33.

98 Letter, Haupt to Cartwright, 27 June 1861, Haupt Papers, Yale University Library, MS#269, Box 2, Folder 33.

99 Summons from Secretary Stanton, 22 April, 1862, Haupt Papers, Yale University Library, Box 18, Folder 312.

100 "Hoosac Tunnel Bill," *American Railroad Journal*, second quarto series, vol. 18, no. 18, whole no. 1,359, vol. 35 (3 May 1862): 330.

Chapter 9

1 Oliver Wendell Holmes, "Latter-Day Warnings," *The Complete Poetical Works of Oliver Wendell Holmes*, 1908 ed., p. 154. Alfred E. Cumming was the first non-Mormon territorial governor of Utah, 1857, protected from Brigham Young's Mormon militia by federal troops under Colonel Albert Sidney Johnson. William Miller (1782–1849) and his followers preached that everyone should sell their goods because the end of the world was imminent.

2 Duncan Yaggy, *John Forbes: Entrepreneur* (PhD dissertation, Brandeis University, Waltham, MA, June 1974), 547.

3 Thomas C. Cochran, *Railroad Leaders, 1845–1890: The Business Mind in Action* (New York: Russell & Russell, 1965), 34.

4 "Hoosac Tunnel Bill," *American Railroad Journal*, second quarto series, vol. 18, no. 18, whole no. 1,359, vol. 35 (3 May 1862): 330.

5 F. W. Bird, *The Hoosac Tunnel: Our Financial Maelstrom* (Boston: Wright & Potter Printers, 1866), 9.

6 Ibid.

7   Abner Forbes and J. W. Greene, *The Rich Men of Massachusetts* (Boston: Fetridge and Company, 1851), 182.

8   F. W. Bird, letter to "My Dear Governor [John A. Andrew]," 15 May 1862, Massachusetts Historical Society, microfilm P-344, Box 9, File 6.

9   Eras M. Curare, letter to "Gov. Andrew," 17 May 1862, Massachusetts Historical Society, microfilm P-344, Box 9, File 6.

10   Bird, *The Hoosac Tunnel*, 11.

11   Terrence E. Coyne, *The Hoosac Tunnel* (PhD dissertation, Clark University, Worcester, MA, April 1992), 182.

12   Alvah Crocker, Troy and Greenfield Railroad speech of Hon. Alvah Crocker on *The Bill for the More Speedy Completion of the Troy and Greenfield Railroad*, in the Senate of Massachusetts, 15 April 1862 (published as a 39-page pamphlet).

13   *Hoosac Valley News and Transcript*, vol. 23, no. 4 (11 September 1862).

14   Yaggy, *John Forbes: Entrepreneur*, 209.

15   Oliver Wendell Holmes, "The Professor's Story," *Atlantic Monthly* 5, no. 27 (January 1860): 91–93.

16   John Lauritz Larson, "John Woods Brooks," in *Encyclopedia of American Business History and Biography: Railroads in the Nineteenth Century*, ed. Robert L. Frey (New York: 1988).

17   Frank Walker Stevens, *The Beginnings of the New York Central Railroad: A History* (New York: G. P. Putnam, 1926).

18   Irene D. Neu, *Erastus Corning: Merchant and Financier, 1794–1872* (Ithaca, NY: Cornell University Press, 1960), p. 75.

19   Arthur M. Johnson and Barry E. Supple, *Boston Capitalists and Western Railroads: A Study in the Nineteenth-Century Investment Process*, Harvard Studies in Business History 23 (Cambridge, MA: Harvard University Press, 1967), 101.

20   Neu, *Erastus Corning: Merchant and Financier*, 30.

21   Alfred D. Chandler Jr., "Patterns of American Railroad Finance, 1830–50," *The Business History Review* 28, no. 3 (September 1954): 257.

22   Cochran, *Railroad Leaders, 1845–1890*, 36.

23   Chandler, "Patterns of American Railroad Finance, 1830–50," 257.

24   Alvin F. Harlow, *The Road of the Century: The Story of the New York Central* (New York: Creative Age Press, 1947), 218.

25   Henry Greenleaf Pearson, *An American Railroad Builder: John Murray Forbes* (Boston/New York: Houghton Mifflin, 1911), 31.

26 "The Genesis of the Rail," *The Frisco-Man* 10, no. 5 (May 1916): 10 (published by the St. Louis–San Francisco Railway Company, Frisco Building, St. Louis, MO).

27 J. M. Forbes, *Reminiscences of John Murray Forbes*, vol. 1 (Boston: George H. Ellis, 1902), 275–78.

28 Neu (1960). *Erastus Corning: Merchant and Financier*, 74.

29 John W. Brooks, *Report upon the Merits of the Michigan Central Rail-Road as an Investment for Eastern Capitalists* (New York: Van Norden & Ameran, Printers, 1846).

30 Neu, *Erastus Corning: Merchant and Financier*, 75.

31 John Lauritz Larson, *Bonds of Enterprise: John Murray Forbes and Western Development in America's Railway Age* (Boston: Harvard Business School, 1984), 36.

32 *Journal of the Senate of Michigan* (1846), 274–75.

33 Johnson and Supple, *Boston Capitalists and Western Railroads*, 91.

34 Larson, *Bonds of Enterprise*, 111.

35 Charles J. Kennedy, "The Early Business History of Four Massachusetts Railroads," *Bulletin of the Business Historical Society* 25, no. 1 (March 1951): 59.

36 Kennedy, "The Early Business History of Four Massachusetts Railroads—III," *Bulletin of the Business Historical Society* 25, no. 3 (September 1951): 196.

37 Larson (1984). *Bonds of Enterprise*, 46.

38 Richard C. Overton, *Burlington Route: A History of the Burlington Lines* (New York: Alfred A. Knopf, 1965), xxvi.

39 Johnson and Supple, *Boston Capitalists and Western Railroads*, 162.

40 Ibid., 170.

41 Ibid., 174.

42 Justin Winsor, *The Memorial History of Boston, including Suffolk County, Massachusetts, 1630–1880*, vol. 4 (Boston: Ticknor and Company, 1881), 24.

43 Yaggy, *John Forbes: Entrepreneur*, 544.

44 Thomas C. Cochran, *Railroad Leaders, 1845–1890*, 37.

45 Commonwealth of Massachusetts Commission Document, Felton Papers, 1839–1920, Box 2, Folder 1, Historical Society of Pennsylvania, Philadelphia.

46 Andrew to Felton, letter of 22 May 1862, Felton Papers, 1839–1920, Box 2, Folder 1, Historical Society of Pennsylvania, Philadelphia.

47 Thomas Doane and Charles Harris, "Samuel Morse Felton—A Memoir," *Journal of the Association of Engineering Societies* 11, no. 4 (April 1892): 199–215.

48 William Bond Wheelwright, *Life and Times of Alvah Crocker* (Boston: privately printed, 1923), 39.

49 A. Crocker to Felton, letter of 25 May 1862, Felton Papers, 1839–1920, Box 2, Folder 1, Historical Society of Pennsylvania, Philadelphia.

50 E. Appleton to Felton, letter of 26 May 1862, Felton Papers, 1839–1920, Box 2, Folder 1, Historical Society of Pennsylvania, Philadelphia.

51 J. Brooks to Felton, letter of 9 June 1862, Felton Papers, 1839–1920, Box 2, Folder 1, Historical Society of Pennsylvania, Philadelphia.

52 "Charles Storer Storrow," *Engineering News* 29, no. 7 (16 February 1893): 147.

53 J. Brooks to Felton, letter of 14 June 1862, Felton Papers, 1839–1920, Box 2, Folder 1, Historical Society of Pennsylvania, Philadelphia.

54 Charles S. Storrow, "Report on European Tunnels," *Report of the Commissioners Upon the Troy and Greenfield Railroad and Hoosac Tunnel, Senate Document 93*, Commonwealth of Massachusetts, 28 February 1863, p. 5.

55 "Charles Storer Storrow," *Engineering News* (16 February 1893): 147.

56 Charles S. Storrow, *Of the Celestial Motions* (mathematical thesis no. 354, 28 April 1829), Harvard University Archives.

57 "Charles Storer Storrow," *Engineering News* (16 February 1893): 147.

58 Peter A. Ford, "Charles S. Storrow, Civil Engineer: A Case Study of European Training and Technological Transfer in the Antebellum Period," Technology and Culture 34, no. 2 (April 1993): 284–87.

59 Ibid., 288–89.

60 *The Merrimack River* (n.d.), Lowell National Historical Park, National Park Service.

61 Peter A. Ford, "'Father of the Whole Enterprise': Charles S. Storrow and the Making of Lawrence, Massachusetts, 1845–1860," *Massachusetts Historical Review*, vol. 2 (2000): 76–117.

62 Peter M. Molloy, "Nineteenth-Century Hydropower: Design and Construction of Lawrence Dam, 1845–1848," *Winterthur Portfolio* 15, no. 4 (Winter 1980): 320.

63 H. Haupt to Felton, letter of 16 June 1862, Felton Papers, 1839–1920, Box 2, Folder 1, Historical Society of Pennsylvania, Philadelphia.

64 "Hoosac Tunnel," *Hoosac Valley News and Transcript*, vol. 22, no. 50 (31 July 1862).

65 "The Troy and Greenfield Commission," *American Railway Times* 14, no. 32 (9 August 1862).

66 *Senate Document 93, Report of the Commissioners Upon the Troy and Greenfield Railroad and Hoosac Tunnel*, Commonwealth of Massachusetts, March 1863.

67 Charles B. Stuart, "Benjamin H. Latrobe," *Lives and Works of Civil and Military Engineers of America* (New York: D. Van Nostrand, 1871), 246.

68 James MacFarlane, *An American Geological Railway Guide* (New York: D. Appleton and Company, 1890), 341.

69 James Morton Callahan, *Semi-Centennial History of West Virginia* (Charleston, WV: Semi-Centennial Commission of West Virginia, 1913), 117.

70 George L. Vose, *Manual for Railroad Engineers and Engineering Students* (Boston: Lee and Shepard, 1878), 101.

71 Ibid., 102.

72 Anthony J. Bianculli, *Trains and Technology: The American Railroad in the Nineteenth Century, vol. 4: Bridges and Tunnels, Signals* (Newark: University of Delaware Press, 2003), 97.

73 James D. Dilts, *The Great Road: The Building of the Baltimore & Ohio, The Nation's First Railroad, 1828–1853* (Stanford, CA: Stanford University Press, 1993), 369.

74 Ibid., 257.

75 Elmer F. Farnham, *The Quickest Route: The History of the Norwich & Worcester Railroad* (Chester, CT: Pequot Press, 1973), 13–17.

76 "Troy and Greenfield Railroad," *Hoosac Valley News*, vol. 23, no. 6 (25 September 1862).

77 "Appendix," *Senate Document 93, Report of the Commissioners Upon the Troy and Greenfield Railroad and Hoosac Tunnel*, Commonwealth of Massachusetts (March 1863), p. 125.

78 Copy of letter from Andrew to Brooks, 13 December 1862, Felton Papers, 1839–1920, Box 2, Folder 1, Historical Society of Pennsylvania, Philadelphia.

79 Copy of letter from Andrew to Brooks, 16 December 1862, Felton Papers, 1839–1920, Box 2, Folder 1, Historical Society of Pennsylvania, Philadelphia.

80 Louisa May Alcott, *Hospital Sketches* (Boston: J. Redpath, Boston, 1863), 9.

81 Ibid., 33.

82 Copy of letter from Brooks to Felton, 27 December 1862, Felton Papers, 1839–1920, Box 2, Folder 1, Historical Society of Pennsylvania, Philadelphia.

83 Copy of letter from Latrobe to Felton, 31 December 1862, Felton Papers, 1839–1920, Box 2, Folder 1, Historical Society of Pennsylvania, Philadelphia.

84 J. W. Brooks, "Superintendent and Engineers Report," *Second Annual Report of the Directors of the Michigan Central Rail-Road Company to the Stockholders* (Boston: Eastburn's Press, 1848), 23.

85 J. M. Forbes, *Second Annual Report of the Directors of the Michigan Central Rail-Road Company to the Stockholders* (Boston: Eastburn's Press, 1848), 3.

86 Abraham Lincoln, *Proclamation* [Emancipation], 22 September 1862.

87 "Troy and Greenfield Rail Road," *Hoosac Valley News & Transcript*, vol. 23, no. 22 (15 January 1863).

88 *Senate No. 93, Report of the Commissioners upon the Troy and Greenfield Railroad and Hoosac Tunnel* (March 1863), p. 5.

89 "Mr. Latrobe's View of the Hoosac Tunnel," *American Railway Times* 15, no. 20 (16 May 1863).

90 Benj. H. Latrobe, "Report on the Hoosac Tunnel," *Senate No. 93, Report of the Commissioners upon the Troy and Greenfield Railroad and Hoosac Tunnel* (March 1863), p. 129.

91 Ibid., p. 130.

92 "Mr. Latrobe's View of the Hoosac Tunnel," *American Railway Times* 15, no. 21 (23 May 1863).

93 Benj. H. Latrobe, "Report on the Hoosac Tunnel," *Senate No. 93, Report of the Commissioners upon the Troy and Greenfield Railroad and Hoosac Tunnel* (March 1863), p. 132.

94 Ibid., p. 135.

95 Charles S. Storrow, "Report on European Tunnels," *Senate No. 93, Report of the Commissioners upon the Troy and Greenfield Railroad and Hoosac Tunnel* (March 1863), p. 34.

96   Ibid., p. 51.

97   Ibid., p. 117.

98   Ibid., p. 111.

99   Ibid., p. 87.

100   Ibid., p. 109.

101   Henry M. Burt, *Memorial Tributes to Daniel L. Harris* (Springfield, MA: privately printed, 1880), 160, 176.

102   James Laurie, "Report on the Troy and Greenfield Railroad," *Senate No. 93, Report of the Commissioners upon the Troy and Greenfield Railroad and Hoosac Tunnel* (March 1863), p. 156.

103   Ibid., p. 160.

104   Ibid., p. 163.

105   Benj. H. Latrobe, "Report on the Hoosac Tunnel," *Senate No. 93, Report of the Commissioners upon the Troy and Greenfield Railroad and Hoosac Tunnel* (March 1863), p. 126.

106   Charles S. Storrow, "Report on European Tunnels," *Senate No. 93, Report of the Commissioners upon the Troy and Greenfield Railroad and Hoosac Tunnel* (March 1863), p. 117.

107   James Laurie, "Report on the Troy and Greenfield Railroad," *Senate No. 93, Report of the Commissioners upon the Troy and Greenfield Railroad and Hoosac Tunnel* (March 1863), pp. 184–85.

108   Ibid., p. 184.

109   "Report on the Troy and Greenfield Railroad," *Senate No. 93, Report of the Commissioners upon the Troy and Greenfield Railroad and Hoosac Tunnel* (March 1863), p. 62.

110   "The Hoosac Tunnel," *Hoosac Valley News and Transcript*, vol. 23, no. 31 (19 March 1863).

111   "The Hoosac Tunnel," *Hoosac Valley News and Transcript*, vol. 23, no. 36 (23 April 1863).

112   "Hoosac Tunnel," *Hoosac Valley News*, vol. 23, no. 34 (9 April 1863).

113   N. H. Egleston, "The Story of the Hoosac Tunnel," *The Atlantic Monthly* 49, no. 293 (March 1882): 294.

114   William Z. Ripley, *Railroads: Finance and Organization* (New York: Longmans, Green, 1920), pp. 14–15.

115   *Senate No. 59, Report on the Hoosac Tunnel and Troy and Greenfield Railroad by the Joint Standing Committee of 1866* (Boston: Wright & Potter, 1867), 55.

116 Brooks to Andrew, letter of 23 July 1863, Felton Papers, 1839–1920, Box 3, Historical Society of Pennsylvania, Philadelphia.

117 Draft of Executive Department order by Andrew, 2 June 1863, Felton Papers, 1839–1920, Box 3, Historical Society of Pennsylvania, Philadelphia.

118 Herman Haupt Chapman. *Biography of Herman Haupt* [n.d.], "1863: The State Studies Its Problem," p. 4 (typewritten manuscript paged anew each chapter, written in the early 1950s), Haupt Papers, Sterling Library, Yale University, Box 18, Folder 312.

119 "Hoosac Tunnel," *American Railroad Journal* 19, no. 27, whole no. 1,420, vol. 36 (4 July 1863): 625.

120 *Hoosac Valley News and Transcript*, vol. 23, no. 41 (28 May 1863).

121 Brooks to Felton, letter of 25 July 1863, Felton Papers, 1839–1920, Box 3, Historical Society of Pennsylvania, Philadelphia.

122 Alfred Alder Doane, *The Doane Family: I. Deacon John Doane, of Plymouth, II. Doctor John Done, of Maryland, and Their Descendants*, 4th ed. (Long Island City, NY: Apollo Books, 1984), 444.

123 Timothy T. Sawyer, *Old Charlestown* (Boston: J. H. West Co., 1902), 114.

124 Doane, *The Doane Family*, 444.

125 Chapman, *Biography of Herman Haupt*, "Operations Under the Tunnel Commission (22)—1863: The State Studies Its Problem," p. 8, Haupt Papers, Sterling Library, Yale University, Box 13, Folder 234.

126 *Report on the Investigating Committee of the Vermont Central Railroad Co.* (Boston: George C. Rand, July 1853), 16.

127 William Richard Cutter, *Genealogical and Personal Memoirs*, vol. 1 (New York: Lewis Historical Publishing Company, 1910), 407.

128 *Fourth Annual Report of the Directors of the Vermont Central Railroad Company* (Montpelier, VT: E. P. Walton & Sons, 1849), 15.

129 Sawyer, *Old Charlestown*, 114.

130 Argument of E. H. Derby, Esq., on behalf of the Old Colony Rail-Road Company, 7 April 1848, Massachusetts Historical Society, Box 1848.

131 Dorchester and Milton Branch Railroad Company bond [1858], issue date 5 February 1867, Massachusetts Historical Society, Ms. N-49.17.

132 Cutter, *Genealogical and Personal Memoirs*, 407.

133 Henry V. Poor, *History of the Railroads and Canals of the United States of America*, vol. 1 (New York: J. H. Schultz & Company, 1860), 112.

134 W. Williams, *Appleton's Railroad and Steamboat Companion* (New York: Geo. S. Appleton, 1848), 85, and map between 84 and 85.

135 "Married," *New Hampshire Sentinel* (Keene, NH), vol. 52, no. 46 (14 November 1850).

136 Doane, *The Doane Family*, 445.

137 "Brig. Gen. Haupt," *Hoosac Valley News and Transcript*, vol. 23, no. 48 (12 July 1863).

138 "Hoosac Tunnel," *Hoosac Valley News and Transcript*, vol. 23, no. 52 (13 August 1863).

139 Copy of Commissioners' Report to Gov. Andrew, dated 30 December 1863, p. 4, Felton Papers, 1839–1920, Box 3, Historical Society of Pennsylvania, Philadelphia.

140 *Hoosac Valley News*, vol. 24, no. 2 (27 August 1863).

141 Chapman, *Biography of Herman Haupt*, "Operations Under the Tunnel Commission (22)—1863: The State Studies Its Problem," p. 8, Haupt Papers, Sterling Library, Yale University, Box 13, Folder 234.

142 "Hoosac Tunnel," *Hoosac Valley News*, vol. 24, no. 4 (10 September 1863).

143 *Hoosac Valley News*, vol. 24, no. 5 (17 September 1863).

144 Copy of Commissioners' Report to Gov. Andrew, dated 30 December 1863, p. 6, Felton Papers, 1839–1920, Box 3, Historical Society of Pennsylvania, Philadelphia.

145 Henry S. Drinker, "Surveying-Work of the Hoosac Tunnel," in *Tunneling, Explosive Compounds, and Rock Drills* (New York: John Wiley, 1878), 906 (the description was prepared by Edward S. Philbrick with contributions by Thomas Doane).

146 Copy of Commissioners' Report to Gov. Andrew. dated 30 December 1863, p. 7, Felton Papers, 1839–1920, Box 3, Historical Society of Pennsylvania, Philadelphia.

147 Drinker, "Surveying-Work of the Hoosac Tunnel," in *Tunneling, Explosive Compounds, and Rock Drills*, 906.

148 "John H. Temple," *Proceedings of the American Academy of Arts and Sciences*, whole series, vol. 13 (1878): 449–51.

149 "General Haupt," *Hoosac Valley News*, vol. 24, no. 8 (3 October 1863).

150 "The Hoosac Tunnel," *American Railway Times* 15, no. 42 (17 October 1863).

151 Copy of Commissioners' Report to Gov. Andrew, dated 30 December 1863, p. 7, Felton Papers, 1839–1920, Box 3, Historical Society of Pennsylvania, Philadelphia.

152 Ibid., p. 8.

153 Ibid., p. 5.

154 Ibid., p. 3.

155 Ibid., p. 11

156 Ibid.

157 Ibid., pp. 13–14.

158 *Annual Reports, Michigan Central Railroad* (1855, 1856, 1857), Corporate Records Division, Baker Library, Harvard University.

159 Duncan Yaggy, *John Forbes: Entrepreneur* (PhD dissertation, Brandeis University, Waltham, MA, June 1974), 327–28.

160 Drinker, *Tunneling, Explosive Compounds, and Rock Drills*, 690.

161 Ibid., 691.

Chapter 10

1 Theseus [pseudonym of Edward Hamilton], *Death of Our Minotaur* (Boston, 1868), 4.

2 Ibid., 3.

3 "Killed and Wounded," *Hoosac Valley News and Transcript*, vol. 24, no. 39 (19 May 1864).

4 *Hoosac Valley News*, vol. 24, no. 27 (25 February 1864).

5 "Fatal Accident at the Hoosac Tunnel," *Hoosac Valley News and Transcript*, vol. 24, no. 30 (17 March 1864).

6 Frank Preston Stearns, "Frank W. Bird, and the Bird Club," in *Cambridge Sketches* (Philadelphia: J. B. Lippincott Company, 1905), 162–79.

7 Ibid.

8 Theseus, *Death of Our Minotaur*, 12.

9 Thomas Doane, "Report of Chief Engineer, 12 September 1864," *House No. 3* (January 1865), p. 23.

10 "Hoosac Tunnel Matters," *Hoosac Valley News and Transcript*, vol. 24, no. 20 (14 January 1864).

11 "The Hoosac Tunnel," *Scientific American*, new series, vol. 13, no. 17 (21 October 1865): 260–61.

12 *Hoosac Valley News*, vol. 24, no. 49 (28 July 1864).

13 Henry S. Drinker, *Tunneling, Explosive Compounds, and Rock Drills* (New York: John Wiley, 1878), 159

14 *Hoosac Valley News*, vol. 24, no. 51 (11 August 1864).

15 "Hoosac Tunnel," *Hoosac Valley News and Transcript*, vol. 24, no. 52 (18 August 1864.

16 *Hoosac Valley News and Transcript*, vol. 25, no. 1 (25 August 1864).

17 *Hoosac Valley News and Transcript*, vol. 25, no. 10 (27 October 1864).

18 "Official Visit to the Tunnel," *Hoosac Valley News and Transcript*, vol. 25, no. 10 (27 October 1864).

19 Ibid.

20 Drinker, *Tunneling, Explosive Compounds, and Rock Drills*, 237.

21 Thomas Doane, "Safety cages for west shaft of Hoosac Tunnel, 1864," *Hoosac Tunnel Photographs*, The State Library of Massachusetts, files: ocn496810869.jpg.

22 David McNeely Stauffer, *Modern Tunnel Practice* (New York: Engineering News Publishing Co., 1906), 53.

23 Drinker, *Tunneling, Explosive Compounds, and Rock Drills*, 287.

24 "Hoosac Tunnel," *Hoosac Valley News and Transcript*, vol. 24, no. 52 (18 Aug 1864).

25 "Hoosac Tunnel," *Hoosac Valley News and Transcript*, vol. 24, no. 52 (18 August 1864).

26 Ibid.

27 Drinker, *Tunneling, Explosive Compounds, and Rock Drills*, 235.

28 Doane, "Report of Chief Engineer, 19 September 1864," *House No. 3* (January 1865), p. 16.

29 Ibid., p. 19.

30 Doane, "Elevation and some sections of the dam built in the Deerfield River to secure a water power for compressing air for the Hoosac Tunnel work, 1864," *Hoosac Tunnel Photographs*, The State Library of Massachusetts, files: ocn496814076.jpg.

31 Ibid., p. 18.

32 F. W. Bird, *The Hoosac Tunnel: Its Condition and Prospects* (Boston: Wright & Potter, Printers, 1865), 11.

33 Doane, "Report of Chief Engineer, 19 September 1864," *House No. 3* (January 1865), p. 18.

34 *Report of the Commissioners*, 20 December 1864, *House No. 3* (January 1865), p. 2.

35 "The Hoosac Tunnel," *Hoosac Valley News and Transcript*, vol. 25, no. 21 (12 January 1865).

36 "Troy and Greenfield Railway," *American Railway Times* 17, no. 11 (18 March 1865).

37 *Hoosac Valley News*, vol. 25, no. 7 (6 October 1864).

38 *Hoosac Valley News*, vol. 25, no. 11 (3 November 1864).

39 "The Hoosac Tunnel," *Hoosac Valley News and Transcript*, vol. 25, no. 23 (26 January 1865).

40 Doane, "Report of Chief Engineer, 19 September 1864," *House No. 3* (January 1865), p. 13.

41 "Chap. 210," *Acts and Resolves passed by the General Court of Massachusetts in the Year 1865* (Boston: Wright & Potter, approved 9 May 1865), pp. 610–11.

42 "Another Andersonville Prisoner Returned Home," *Hoosac Valley News*, vol. 25, no. 17 (15 December 1864).

43 "Pneumatic and Steam Drill," *Hoosac Valley News and Transcript*, vol. 25, no. 20 (5 January, 1865).

44 "Greenpoint Industries," *The Newtown Register* (Long Island, NY) (14 February 1878).

45 Theseus, *Death of Our Minotaur*, 3.

46 *American Railway Times* 17, no. 31 (5 August 1865).

47 Bird, *The Hoosac Tunnel*.

48 Ibid., 4.

49 Terrence E. Coyne, *The Hoosac Tunnel* (PhD dissertation, Clark University, Worcester, MA, 1992), 208.

50 H. Haupt, *Hoosac Tunnel Insufficiency of Air* (Boston: Wright & Potter, 25 April 1866), 3.

51 "A Sorry Bird," *Hoosac Valley News and Transcript*, vol. 25, no. 22 (19 January 1865).

52 Theseus, *Death of Our Minotaur*, 14.

53 Ibid., 15.

54 *Senate No. 220, Report on the Troy and Greenfield Railroad and the Hoosac Tunnel by the Joint Special Committee of 1865* (April 1866), p. 5.

55 Doane, "Report of Chief Engineer, 19 September 1864," *House No. 3* (January 1865), p. 20.

56 "Hoosac Tunnel," *Hoosac Valley News and Transcript*, vol. 25, no. 23 (26 January 1865).

57 "Hoosac Tunnel," *Adams News & Transcript*, vol. 25, no. 41 (7 September 1865).

58 *Adams News & Transcript*, vol. 25, no. 44 (28 September 1865).

59 "Accident at the West Shaft," *Adams News & Transcript*, vol. 25, no. 44 (28 September 1865).

60 Drinker, *Tunneling, Explosive Compounds, and Rock Drills*, 237.

61 "Hoosac Tunnel," *Adams News & Transcript*, vol. 25, no. 40 (31 August 1865).

62 *Senate No. 59, Report on the Hoosac Tunnel and Troy and Greenfield Railroad by the Joint Special Committee of 1866* (February 1867), p. 16.

63 "Hoosac Tunnel," *Adams News & Transcript*, vol. 25, no. 41 (7 September 1865).

64 Ibid.

65 Ibid.

66 Drinker, *Tunneling, Explosive Compounds, and Rock Drills*, 237.

67 "Hoosac Tunnel," *Adams News & Transcript*, vol. 25, no. 41 (7 September 1865).

68 Ibid.

69 "Hoosac Tunnel," *Hoosac Valley News and Transcript*, vol. 25, no. 23 (26 January 1865).

70 "Hoosac Tunnel," *Adams News & Transcript*, vol. 25, no. 41 (7 September 1865).

71 "West End," *Adams News & Transcript*, vol. 25, no. 29 (15 June 1865).

72 "Local Paragraphs," *Adams News & Transcript*, vol. 25, no. 45 (5 October 1865).

73 "Hoosac Tunnel," *Adams News & Transcript* (7 September 1865).

74 Ibid.

75 *Adams News & Transcript*, vol. 25, no. 43 (21 September 1865).

76 Drinker, *Tunneling, Explosive Compounds, and Rock Drills*, 287.

77 "Hoosac Tunnel," *Adams News & Transcript* (7 September 1865).

78 "Gen. Butler Visits the Hoosac Tunnel," *Adams News & Transcript*, vol. 25, no. 47 (19 October 1865).

79 Shelby Foote, *The Civil War: A Narrative. Vol. 3: Red River to Appomattox* (New York: Random House, 1974), pp. 739–40.

80 "Gen. Butler Visits the Hoosac Tunnel," *Adams News & Transcript*, (19 October 1865).

81 *Adams News & Transcript*, vol. 25, no. 48 (26 October 1865).

82 "Bird after the Tunnel," *Adams News & Transcript*, vol. 25, no. 46 (12 October 1865).

83 "Election Notes," *Adams News & Transcript*, vol. 25, no. 50 (9 November 1865).

84 "The Hoosac Tunnel Question," *American Railway Times* 11, no. 45 (17 November 1865).

85 "The Hoosac Tunnel, Shall it be Abandoned!" *American Railway Times* 17, no. 47 (25 November 1865).

86 Ibid.

87 "How Shall we Pass the Hoosac Mountain?" *American Railway Times* 17, no. 48 (2 December 1865).

88 "Hoosac Tunnel," *Adams News & Transcript*, (7 September 1865).

89 Ibid.

90 *House No. 4, Commissioners' Report, for 1865* (January 1866), p. 8; Drinker, *Tunneling, Explosive Compounds, and Rock Drills*, 159.

91 Thomas Doane and Charles Harris, "Samuel Morse Felton—A Memoir," *Journal of the Association of Engineering Societies* 11, no. 4 (April 1892): 214–15.

92 *Senate No. 220, Report on the Troy and Greenfield Railroad and the Hoosac Tunnel by the Joint Special Committee of 1865* (April 1866), p. 11.

93 *Senate No. 59, Report on the Hoosac Tunnel and Troy and Greenfield Railroad by the Joint Special Committee of 1866* (February 1867), p. 24.

94 Ibid., 23.

95 Ibid., 25–27.

96 Herman Haupt Chapman, "1866 Hope Revives [n.d.]," Haupt Papers, Yale University Library, MS#260, Box 18, Folder 314, p. 17.

97 T. Doane, "Diagram No. 2 and Diagram No. 3," *House No. 30, Annual Report of the Commissioners on the Troy and Greenfield R.R. and Hoosac Tunnel* (Boston: Wright & Potter, 1867).

98 *Senate No. 59, Report on the Troy and Greenfield Railroad and Hoosac Tunnel by the Joint Special Committee of 1866* (February 1867), p. 15.

99 D. Hamilton Hurd, *History of Worcester County, Massachusetts, with Biographical Sketches of many of its Pioneers and Prominent Men*, vol. 1 (Philadelphia: J. W. Lewis & Co., 1889), 315.

100 Ibid., 315–16.

101 Ibid., 276.

102 Ibid., 277.

103 Ibid.

104 *Bay State Monthly: A Massachusetts Magazine* 2, no. 6 (March 1885).

105 "Miscellaneous Summary," *Scientific American* 9, no. 20 (14 November 1863): 307.

106 "Miscellaneous Summary," *Scientific American* 12, no. 16 (15 April 1865): 307.

107 *House No. 375, Report of the Evidence on the Claim of Charles Burleigh together with the Argument of Counsel, before the Committee on the Hoosac Tunnel and Troy and Greenfield Railroad* (Boston: Wright & Potter, 1874), p. 3.

108 Hurd, *History of Worcester County, Massachusetts,* vol. 1, 281.

109 William A. Emerson, *Fitchburg, Massachusetts: Past and Present* (Fitchburg, MA: Blanchard & Brown, 1887), 219.

110 Joseph G. Edgerly, "Fitchburg, Mass.," *New England Magazine,* new series, vol. 12, no. 3 (May 1895), 335.

111 Doris Kirkpatrick, *The City and the River,* vol. 1 (Fitchburg, MA: Fitchburg Historical Society, 1971), pp. 308–9.

112 Hurd, *History of Worcester County, Massachusetts,* vol. 1, 318.

113 *House No. 3, Commissioners' Report for 1864* (January 1865), p. 9.

114 "Appendix I: Report of Chas. S. Storrow, on European Tunnels, 28 November 1862," *Senate No. 93* (Boston: Wright & Potter, 1863), p. 87.

115 *House No. 4, Massachusetts Legislative Reports* (1866), p. 14.

116 Henry S. Drinker, *A Treatise on Explosive Compounds, Machine Rock Drills and Blasting* (New York: John Wiley, 1883), 260.

117 "Stephen F. Gates," *Annals of the Massachusetts Charitable Mechanic Association, 1795-1892* (Boston: Press of Rockwell and Churchill, 1892), p. 461.

118 *House No. 375, Report of the Evidence on the Claim of Charles Burleigh,* p. 3.

119 Chapman, "1866 Hope Revives [n.d.]," manuscript, Haupt Papers, Yale University Library, MS#260, Box 18, Folder 314, p. 10.

120 "The Hoosac Drill," *Adams News & Transcript,* vol. 26, no. 18 (5 April 1866).

121 Chapman, "1866 Hope Revives," p. 19.

122 Haupt, *1866 Hoosac Tunnel: Facts about Machinery, &c.,* directed to President and Directors of Troy and Greenfield Railroad Company, and to Commissioners of Hoosac Tunnel (27 March 1866), p. 12.

123 Haupt, *Tunneling by Machinery: Description of Perforators and Plans of Operations in Mining and Tunneling* (Philadelphia: H. G. Leisenring's Steam Printing House, 1867).

124 "The Hoosac Drill," *Adams News & Transcript*, vol. 26, no. 18 (5 April 1866).

125 *House No. 375, Report of the Evidence on the Claim of Charles Burleigh*, p. 3.

126 Letter, Haupt to Cartwright, 11 May 1866, Haupt Papers, Yale University Library, MS#260, Box 4, Folder 67.

127 Letter, Haupt to his wife, 15 May 1866, Haupt Papers, Yale University Library, MS#260, Box 4, Folder 66.

128 James M. Shute, *Rejected Papers in Relation to the Hoosac Tunnel* (Boston: Wright & Potter, 1868), 5.

129 *House No. 30, Annual Report of the Commissioners on the Troy and Greenfield Railroad and Hoosac Tunnel* (Boston: Wright & Potter, 1867), p. 5.

130 *Senate No. 59, Report on the Hoosac Tunnel and Troy and Greenfield Railroad, by the Joint Standing Committee of 1866* (Boston: Wright & Potter, 1867), p. 34.

131 "Rock Drilling Machine," *American Railway Times* 18, no. 13 (31 March 1866): 103.

132 *House No. 30, Annual Report of the Commissioners on the Troy and Greenfield Railroad and Hoosac Tunnel*, (Boston: Wright & Potter, 1867), diagram 1 opposite p. 33.

133 *Senate No. 59, Report on the Hoosac Tunnel and Troy and Greenfield Railroad, by the Joint Standing Committee of 1866* (Boston: Wright & Potter, 1867), p. 34.

134 *House No. 375, Report of the Evidence on the Claim of Charles Burleigh*, p. 3.

135 Ibid., p. 4.

136 Ibid., pp. 10–11.

137 Shute, *Rejected Papers in Relation to the Hoosac Tunnel*, 6.

138 Wilbur F. Brigham, *Brigham's Early Hudson History*, comp. and ed. Katherine Johnson and Lewis Halprin (Hudson, MA: Hudson Historical Society and Museum, 2010).

139 "Troy and Greenfield Railroad," *Adams News & Transcript*, vol. 26, no. 44 (4 October 1866).

140 *Senate No. 59, Report on the Hoosac Tunnel and Troy and Greenfield Railroad, by the Joint Standing Committee of 1866* (Boston: Wright & Potter, 1867), p. 41.

141 Ibid., p. 42.

142 Doane, "Report of Chief Engineer, 19 December 1866," *House No. 30.
     Annual Report of the Commissioners on the Troy and Greenfield R.R. and
     Hoosac Tunnel* (Boston: Wright & Potter, 1867), p. 21.

143 *House No. 30, Annual Report of the Commissioners on the Troy and Greenfield
     Railroad and Hoosac Tunnel* (Boston: Wright & Potter, 1867), p. 40.

144 "Scientific Blasting—Nitro-Glycerin," *Scientific American* 15, no. 22, new
     series (24 November 1866): 353.

145 Drinker, *A Treatise on Explosive Compounds, Machine Rock Drills, and
     Blasting*, 65.

146 "Annual Report of the Commissioner of Patents for the Year 1866, vol.
     II," *House of Representatives Ex. Doc. No. 109*, No. 60,572 (Washington,
     DC, 1866), pp. 1561–62.

147 *Adams News & Transcript*, vol. 26, no. 46 (18 October 1866).

148 *Senate No. 59, Report on the Hoosac Tunnel and Troy and Greenfield Railroad,
     by the Joint Standing Committee of 1866* (Boston: Wright & Potter, 1867), p.
     38.

149 *Adams News & Transcript*, vol. 27, no. 5 (3 January 1867).

150 *Adams News & Transcript*, vol. 27, no. 746 (10 January 1867).

Chapter 11

1 Richard Herndon, *Boston of To-Day* (Boston: Post Publishing Company,
   1892), 15–16.

2 Washington Gladden, *From the Hub to the Hudson* (Boston: The New
   England News Company, 1869), 109.

3 *Adams Transcript*, vol. 27, no. 10 (10 February 1867).

4 James M. Shute, *Rejected Papers in Relation to the Hoosac Tunnel* (Boston:
   Wright & Potter, 1868), 7.

5 Gladden, *From the Hub to the Hudson*, between pp. 112 and 113.

6 *The Berkshire Hills*, American Guide Series, Federal Writers Project of the
   Works Progress Administration for Massachusetts (New York: Funk &
   Wagnalls, 1939), 2.

7 *Senate No. 102, Report on the Troy and Greenfield Railroad and the Hoosac
   Tunnel by the Joint Special Committee of 1867* (Boston: Wright & Potter,
   March 1868), p. 2.

8   James D. Dilts, *The Great Road* (Stanford, CA: Stanford University Press, 1993), 378–79.

9   *House No. 359, Letter of Hon. Charles Hudson* (Boston: Wright & Potter, May 1868), p. 11.

10 *Senate No. 59, Report on the Hoosac Tunnel and Troy and Greenfield Railroad by the Joint Special Committee of 1866* (February 1867), p. 11.

11 "The Hoosac Tunnel," *Journal of the Franklin Institute* 56, no. 1 (July 1868): 5–6.

12 Robert Scott Burn, *The Steam-Engine: Its History and Mechanism* (London: H. Ingram and Co., 1854), 47.

13 Edward Whymper, *Scrambles Amongst the Alps in the Years 1860–69*, 2nd ed. (London: John Murray, 1871), 72.

14 *The Berkshire Hills*, 3.

15 "Drill, ye Tarriers, Drill" is an American folk song of 1888, attributed to Thomas F. Casey. *Tarrier* is a vernacular British term for a manual laborer. Often it refers to those involved with blasting and explosives.

16 "Accidents—Casualties," *Senate No. 20, Report of the Hon. Alvah Crocker, Commissioner, acting as Superintendent, of work upon the Troy and Greenfield Railroad and the Hoosac Tunnel by the Joint Special Committee of 1867* (Boston: Wright & Potter, January 1868), p. 74.

17 "A Terrible Accident at the Tunnel," *Adams Transcript*, vol. 27, no. 19 (11 April 1867).

18 *Adams Transcript*, vol. 27, no. 23 (9 May 1867).

19 "Eureka Company v. Bass, Adm'r." Reports of Cases Argued and Determined in the Supreme Court of Alabama during the December Term 1886, (Montgomery: Joel White, 1887), p. 206.

20 *Adams Transcript*, vol. 27, no. 26 (30 May 1867).

21 *Senate No. 289, Letters of John W. Brooks Esq., Chairman of Commissioners of Troy & Greenfield Railroad, and Hoosac Tunnel to Hon. Tappan Wentworth, Chairman of Legislative Committee* (12 May 1866), p. 18.

22 *House No. 3, Commissioners' Report upon the Troy and Greenfield Railroad and Hoosac Tunnel* (12 January 1865), p. 8.

23 *Senate No. 59, Report on the Hoosac Tunnel and Troy and Greenfield Railroad by the Joint Special Committee of 1866* (February 1867), p. 32.

24 Larry C. Hoffman, "The Rock Drill and Civilization," *Invention & Technology* 15, no. 1 (Summer 1999).

25   *House No. 375, Report of the Claim of Charles Burleigh together with the Argument of Counsel before the Committee on the Hoosac Tunnel and Troy and Greenfield Railroad* (Boston: Wright & Potter, May 1874), p. 4.

26   Henry S. Drinker, *Tunneling, Explosive Compounds, and Rock Drills* (New York: John Wiley, 1878), 158–65.

27   "Report of Chief Engineer," *House No. 30, Annual Report of the Commissioners on the Troy and Greenfield R.R. and Hoosac Tunnel* (Boston: Wright & Potter, Boston, January 1867), p. 20.

28   "The Hoosac Tunnel Drills," *Scientific American* 18, no. 1 (4 January 1867): 2–3.

29   *Improvement in Rock-Drilling Machines,* Letters Patent No. 59,960, United States Patent Office, 27 November 1866.

30   *House No. 375, Report of the Claim of Charles Burleigh,* p. 85.

31   "An Act to promote the progress of useful arts, and to repeal all acts and parts of acts heretofore made for that purpose," Chapter 357, *Patent Act of 1836,* Ch. 357, 5 Stat. 117 (4 July 1836).

32   *Improved Steam Drilling Machine,* Reissue No. 2,275, United States Patent Office (5 June 1866).

33   *House No. 375, Report of the Claim of Charles Burleigh,* p. 8. Copies of two letters from H. A. Willis, Treasurer, Burleigh Rock Drill Co., to Messrs. Crosby and Gould (19 and 20 February 1872), Archives of the Fitchburg Historical Society, Fitchburg, Massachusetts.

34   *House No. 375, Report of the Claim of Charles Burleigh,* p. 59.

35   Ibid., p. 56.

36   Ibid., p. 4.

37   Ibid., p. 66.

38   "Joseph W. Fowle's Patent," *The Congressional Globe containing The Debates and Proceedings of the Second Session Forty-Second Congress,* Office of the Congressional Globe, City of Washington (19 March 1872), pp. 1819–43.

39   De Volson Wood, letter to the Committee of Patents in the House of Representatives (3 April 1872), Archives of the Fitchburg Historical Society, Fitchburg, Massachusetts.

40   *Congressional Directory,* 1st ed. Compiled for the use of the Congress by Ben: Perley Poore, Clerk of Printing Records (Washington, DC: Government Printing Office, 15 January 1872), 25.

41   "Report of Chief Engineer," *House No. 30, Annual Report of the Commissioners on the Troy and Greenfield R.R. and the Hoosac Tunnel,* p. 20.

42 Ibid., p. 33.

43 "Rock Drilling Machine," *American Railway Times* 18, no. 13 (31 March 1866).

44 "Report of Chief Engineer," *House No. 30, Annual Report of the Commissioners on the Troy and Greenfield R.R. and the Hoosac Tunnel,* drawing no. 1, between pp. 32 and 33.

45 *Improvement in Rock-Drilling Machines,* Letters Patent No. 59, 960.

46 "Report of Consulting Engineer," *Senate No. 20, Report of the Hon. Alvah Crocker, Commissioner, acting as Superintendent,* (Boston: Wright & Potter, January 1868), p. 52.

47 *House No. 375, Report of the Claim of Charles Burleigh,* p. 27.

48 Hoffman, "The Rock Drill and Civilization."

49 "Consulting Engineer's Report," *House No. 30, Annual Report of the Commissioners on the Troy and Greenfield R.R. and Hoosac Tunnel* (Boston: Wright & Potter, January 1867), p. 77.

50 "Hoosac Tunnel," *American Railroad Journal,* second quarto series, vol. 24, no. 9, whole no. 1,663, vol. 41 (29 February 1868): 201.

51 *Adams Transcript,* vol. 27, no. 10 (7 February 1867).

52 Shute, *Rejected Papers in Relation to the Hoosac Tunnel,* 9.

53 "The Tunnel Under Contract," *Adams Transcript,* vol. 27, no. 27 (6 June 1867).

54 *House No. 395, Letter of Hon. Charles Hudson* (Boston: Wright & Potter, May 1868), p. 9.

55 "The Tunnel Under Contract," *Adams Transcript* (6 June 1867).

56 Shute, *Rejected Papers in Relation to the Hoosac Tunnel,* 9.

57 "Hoosac Tunnel," *Adams Transcript,* vol. 27, no. 36 (8 August 1867).

58 "The Hoosac Tunnel," *American Railway Times* 19, no. 32 (10 August 1867).

59 "Dull, Gowan and White the Loser," *Adams Transcript,* vol. 27, no. 47 (24 October 1867).

60 Benj. H. Latrobe, "Report of Consulting Engineer," *Senate No. 20, Report of the Hon. Alvah Crocker, Commissioner,* (Boston: Wright & Potter, January 1868), p. 33.

61 "Hoosac Tunnel," *Frank Leslie's Illustrated Newspaper* (20 December 1873), 245.

62 Ibid.

63   "Central Shaft," *Senate No. 102, Report of the Joint Standing Committee of 1867 on the Hoosac Tunnel and the Troy and Greenfield Railroad* (March 1868), p. 5.

64   "The Origin of the Fire," *Adams Transcript* (24 October 1867).

65   "The Hoosac Tunnel Disaster," *New York Times* (24 October 1867), 2.

66   "Fatal Accident at the Central Shaft," *Adams Transcript*, vol. 27, no. 37 (15 August 1867).

67   *The Berkshire Hills*, 3.

68   "Troy and Greenfield Railroad," *Adams Transcript*, vol. 27, no. 44 (3 October 1867).

69   Nathaniel Hawthorne, *Passages from the American Note-Books* (Boston: James R. Osgood and Company, 1873), 142.

70   *The Berkshire Hills*, 3.

71   Jonah 2:1.

72   "Terrible Accident at the Central Shaft!" *Adams Transcript* (24 October 1867).

73   "The Origin of the Fire," *Adams Transcript* (24 October 1867).

74   "The Hoosac Tunnel Disaster," *New York Times* (24 October 1867), 2.

75   "Accidents—Casualties," *Senate No. 20, Report of the Hon. Alvah Crocker, Commissioner*, p. 74.

76   "The Hoosac Tunnel Disaster," *New York Times* (24 October 1867), 2.

77   "Accidents—Casualties," *Senate No. 20, Report of the Hon. Alvah Crocker, Commissioner*, p. 74.

78   "Terrible Accident at the Central Shaft!" *Adams Transcript* (24 October 1867).

79   "The Hoosac Tunnel," *Scribner's Monthly* (December 1870), 158.

80   "The Hoosac Tunnel Disaster," *Springfield Republican*, vol. 24, no. 251, whole no. 7220 (22 October 1867), 2.

81   "Terrible Accident at the Central Shaft!" *Adams Transcript* (24 October 1867).

82   Ibid.

83   *Senate No. 102, Report of the Joint Standing Committee of 1867 on the Hoosac Tunnel and the Troy and Greenfield Railroad*, p. 5.

84   "The Hoosac Tunnel Disaster," *New York Times* (24 October 1867), 2.

85   *Senate No. 102, Report of the Joint Standing Committee of 1867 on the Hoosac Tunnel and the Troy and Greenfield Railroad*, p. 5.

86 "Terrible Accident at the Central Shaft!" *Adams Transcript* (24 October 1867).

87 *Senate No. 102, Report of the Joint Standing Committee of 1867 on the Hoosac Tunnel and the Troy and Greenfield Railroad*, p. 5.

88 "Terrible Accident at the Central Shaft!" *Adams Transcript* (24 October 1867).

89 *Senate No. 102, Report of the Joint Standing Committee of 1867 on the Hoosac Tunnel and the Troy and Greenfield Railroad*, p. 5.

90 Ibid.

91 Terrible Accident at the Central Shaft!" *Adams Transcript* (24 October 1867).

92 *Senate No. 102, Report of the Joint Standing Committee of 1867 on the Hoosac Tunnel and the Troy and Greenfield Railroad*, p. 5.

93 "The Hoosac Tunnel Disaster," *New York Times* (24 October 1867), 2.

94 *Senate No. 102, Report of the Joint Standing Committee of 1867 on the Hoosac Tunnel and the Troy and Greenfield Railroad*, p. 5.

95 Ibid.

96 Terrible Accident at the Central Shaft!" *Adams Transcript* (24 October 1867).

97 "The Hoosac Tunnel Disaster," *New York Times* (24 October 1867), 2.

98 "Terrible Accident at the Central Shaft!" *Adams Transcript* (24 October 1867).

99 *Senate No. 102, Report of the Joint Standing Committee of 1867 on the Hoosac Tunnel and the Troy and Greenfield Railroad*, p. 5.

100 Ibid.

101 "Terrible Accident at the Central Shaft!" *Adams Transcript* (24 October 1867).

102 *Senate No. 102, Report of the Joint Standing Committee of 1867 on the Hoosac Tunnel and the Troy and Greenfield Railroad*, p. 5.

103 Ibid.

104 Ibid., p. 6.

105 Ibid.

106 Shute, *Rejected Papers in Relation to the Hoosac Tunnel*, 13.

107 "The Hoosac Tunnel," *New York Times* (18 November 1867).

108 "Railroad Meeting at Northampton," *Adams Transcript*, vol. 27, no. 51 (21 November 1867).

109 "Explosion in Greenwich-Street; Fortunate Escape of a Hotel and its
     Inmates—Twenty-four Persons Wounded—No one Mortally," *The New
     York Times* (6 November 1865).

110 *The Berkshire Hills*, 4.

111 "Nitro-Glycerin," *Scientific American* 1015, no. 24 (8 December 1866): 397.

112 Geo. M. Mowbray, "Report of the Operative Chemist," *Senate No. 20,
     Report of the Hon. Alvah Crocker, Commissioner*, p. 71.

113 Samuel P. Bates, *Our County and Its People: A Historical and Memorial
     Record of Crawford County, Pennsylvania* (Alfred, NY: W. A. Fergusson &
     Company, 1899), 401.

114 Ibid., 421.

115 *The Berkshire Hills*, 4.

116 Titusville, PA, *Morning Herald*, 28 October 1868.

117 Geo. M. Mowbray, *Tri-Nitro-Glycerin as applied in the Hoosac Tunnel,
     Submarine Blasting, Etc., Etc., Etc.* (North Adams, MA: James T.
     Robinson & Son, 1872), 44.

118 Geo. M. Mowbray, "Report of the Operative Chemist," *Senate No. 20,
     Report of the Hon. Alvah Crocker, Commissioner*, p. 71.

119 "Commissioners' Report," *House No. 192, Report of the Commissioners upon
     the Troy and Greenfield Railroad and Hoosac Tunnel* (Boston: Wright &
     Potter, March 1869), p. 36.

120 "Report of Consulting Engineer, 20 December 1867," *Senate No. 20,
     Report of the Hon. Alvah Crocker, Commissioner*, p. 45.

121 "Opening of the Railroad to Shelburne Falls," *Adams Transcript*, vol. 28,
     no. 5 (2 January 1868).

122 "Tunnel Commissioners," *Adams Transcript*, vol. 28, no. 10 (6 February
     1868).

123 J. E. A. Smith, *The History of Pittsfield (Berkshire County), Massachusetts,
     from the Year 1800 to the Year 1876* (Springfield, MA: C. W. Bryan & Co.,
     1876), 623.

124 "Fire at the West Shaft," *Adams Transcript*, vol. 28, no. 13 (27 February
     1868).

125 "Superintending Engineer's Report, 24 December 1868," *House No. 192,
     Report of the Commissioners upon the Troy and Greenfield Railroad and Hoosac
     Tunnel*, p. 60.

126 "Commissioners' Report," *House No. 192, Report of the Commissioners upon
     the Troy and Greenfield Railroad and Hoosac Tunnel*, p. 24.

127 "The Hoosac Tunnel Commissioners," *American Railway Times* 20, no. 7 (15 February 1868).

128 *Catalogue of the Officers and Alumni of Rutgers College* (Trenton, NJ: State Gazette Publishing Co., 1916), 103.

129 "Superintending Engineer's Report, 24 December 1868," *House No. 192, Report of the Commissioners upon the Troy and Greenfield Railroad and Hoosac Tunnel*, p. 67.

130 Ibid., p. 66.

131 Ibid., p. 63.

132 *Adams Transcript*, vol. 28, no. 11 (13 February 1868).

133 *Adams Transcript*, vol. 28, no. 10 (6 February 1868).

134 "The Ballou Claim," *Adams Transcript*, vol. 28, no. 17 (26 March 1868).

135 *Adams Transcript*, vol. 28, no. 23 (7 May 1868).

136 *Adams Transcript*, vol. 28, no. 18 (2 April 1868).

137 "The Tunnel Bill Passed," *Adams Transcript*, vol. 28, no. 28 (11 June 1868).

138 Benj. H. Latrobe, *Senate No. 6, Report of Benj. H. Latrobe Consulting Engineer, on the Troy and Greenfield Railroad and Hoosac Tunnel* (Boston: Wright & Potter, January 1869), p. 6.

139 F. W. Bird, *The Last Agony of the Great Bore* (Boston: E. P. Dutton, 1868), 36.

140 "Tunnel Bill Passed," *Adams Transcript*, vol. 28, no. 27 (4 June 1868).

141 Bird, *The Last Agony of the Great Bore*, 4.

142 "The Hoosac Tunnel," *American Railway Times* 20, no. 40 (3 October 1868).

143 Bird, *The Last Agony of the Great Bore*.

144 Ibid., 37.

145 Ibid., 49.

146 Theseus [pseudonym of Edward Hamilton], *Death of Our Minotaur* (Boston, 1868), 14.

147 "To Tunnel Contractors," *American Railway Times* 20, no. 27 (4 July 1868).

148 "The Hoosac Tunnel," *Adams Transcript*, vol. 28, no. 33 (16 July 1868).

149 *Adams Transcript*, vol. 28, no. 35 (30 July 1868).

150 Ibid.

151 *Adams Transcript*, vol. 28, no. 37 (13 August 1868).

152 Benj. H. [Benjamin Henry] Latrobe, 1807–1878, *Pocket Diary 1868, Jan. 1–Dec. 31* (barcode 48188-10), Archival Collections, PPA Library, The Athenaeum of Philadelphia..

153 Latrobe, letter to Francis Shanly, 29 June 1868, Francis Shanly fonds [record group], Archives of Ontario, Toronto, Fonds F647, Hoosac Tunnel Series A-21.

154 Crocker to A. Cohen, letter dated 7 September 1868, Crocker Letterbook 1868, Fitchburg Historical Society, Fitchburg, Massachusetts, p. 62.

155 Alfred R. Field, 22 December 1868, "Report of the Chief Engineer," *House No. 192, Report of the Commissioners upon the Troy and Greenfield Railroad and Hoosac Tunnel*, p. 70.

156 "Statement of Commissioners on Troy and Greenfield Railroad and Hoosac Tunnel," *Senate No. 6, Report of Benj. H. Latrobe consulting engineer on the Troy and Greenfield Railroad and Hoosac Tunnel* (Boston: Wright & Potter, January 1869), p. 13.

157 Walter Shanly, letter to Frank Shanly (first letter), 18 November 1868, Francis Shanly fonds, Archives of Ontario, Toronto.

158 "The Hoosac Tunnel," *American Railroad Journal*, second quarto series, vol. 24, no. 43, whole no. 1,697, vol. 41 (24 October 1868): 1031.

159 *American Railroad Journal*, second quarto series, vol. 24, no. 37, whole no. 1,691, vol. 41 (12 September 1868): 889.

160 "The Hoosac Tunnel," *American Railroad Journal*, second quarto series, vol. 24, no. 40, whole no. 1,694, vol. 41 (3 October 1868): 968.

161 Ibid.

162 Richard Wallace White, *The Civil Engineering Careers of Frank and Walter Shanly, c.1840–c.1890* (PhD thesis, University of Toronto, 1995), 312–14.

163 Ibid., 313.

164 Crocker to Wentworth, letter dated 23 October 1868, Crocker Letterbook 1868, Fitchburg Historical Society, pp. 111–12.

165 James Worrall, letter to Walter Shanly, 5 November 1868, Francis Shanly fonds, Archives of Ontario, Toronto.

166 Walter Shanly, letter to Frank Shanly (first letter), 18 November 1868, Francis Shanly fonds, Archives of Ontario, Toronto.

167 Walter Shanly, letter to Frank Shanly (second letter, same date), 18 November 1868, Francis Shanly fonds, Archives of Ontario, Toronto.

168 Walter Shanly, letter to Frank Shanly, 19 November 1868, Francis Shanly fonds, Archives of Ontario, Toronto.

169 Walter Shanly, letter to Frank Shanly, 21 November 1868, Francis Shanly fonds, Archives of Ontario, Toronto.

170 Crocker to Dillon, letter dated 24 November 1868, Crocker Letterbook 1868, Fitchburg Historical Society, p. 138.

171 Crocker to Claflin, letter dated 24 November 1868, Crocker Letterbook 1868, p. 139.

172 Crocker to Farren, letter dated 24 November 1868, Crocker Letterbook 1868, p. 137.

173 Copy of Farren letter to Crocker, Crocker Letterbook 1868, p. 145.

174 Walter Shanly, letter to Worrall, 21 November 1868, Francis Shanly fonds, Archives of Ontario, Toronto.

175 Walter Shanly, letter to Frank Shanly, 26 November 1868, Francis Shanly fonds, Archives of Ontario, Toronto.

176 Crocker to Dillon, letters dated 8 and 12 December 1868, Crocker Letterbook 1868, Fitchburg Historical Society, pp. 166, 179.

177 Walter Shanly, letter to Frank Shanly, 21 December 1868, Francis Shanly fonds, Archives of Ontario, Toronto.

178 Benj. H. Latrobe, *Pocket Diary 1868, Jan. 1–Dec. 31*, Archival Collections, PPA Library, The Athenaeum of Philadelphia.

179 Ibid.

180 Walter Shanly, letter to Frank Shanly, 12 December 1868, Francis Shanly fonds, Archives of Ontario, Toronto.

181 Ibid.

182 Walter Shanly, letter to Frank Shanly, 18 December 1868, Francis Shanly fonds, Archives of Ontario, Toronto.

183 Walter Shanly, letter to Frank Shanly, 19 December 1868, Francis Shanly fonds, Archives of Ontario, Toronto.

184 Crocker to Wentworth, letter dated 28 December 1868, Crocker Letterbook 1868, Fitchburg Historical Society, p. 194.

Chapter 12

1 "The Hoosac Tunnel to Be Completed," *New York Times* (29 December 1868), 5.

2 Walter Shanly, letter to Frank Shanly, Christmas morning 1868, Francis Shanly fonds [record group], Archives of Ontario, Toronto, Ontario, Canada, Fonds F647, Hoosac Tunnel Series A-21.

3 Walter Shanly, second letter to Frank, Christmas Day 1868, Francis Shanly fonds, Archives of Ontario, Toronto.

4   Walter Shanly, *The Canadian Shanlys: Whence they came and how they got to Thorndale*, 1896, PA057, Canadian Railroad Historical Association Archives and Document Center, Saint Constant, Quebec, Canada.

5   P. J. Duffy, "Irish Landholding structures and population in the mid-nineteenth century," *Maynooth Review* 3, no. 2 (December 1977): 18.

6   G. E. Mingay, *Rural Life in Victorian England* (London: William Heinemann, 1977), 126–29.

7   Shanly, *The Canadian Shanlys*, 15.

8   "Shanly, Francis (Frank)," in *Dictionary of Canadian Biography Online, 1881–1890*, vol. 11, gen. ed. John English (Toronto/Quebec: University of Toronto/Université Laval, 2000).

9   Walter Shanly, "The Family Tree of James Shanly (1778–1857)," in *The Canadian Shanlys*.

10   Samuel Lewis, *A Topographical Dictionary of Ireland, Comprising the Several Counties, Cities, Boroughs, Corporate, Market, and Post Towns, Parishes, and Villages, with Historical and Statistical Descriptions*, vol. 1 (London: S. Lewis & Co., 1837), 568.

11   Richard Wallace White, *The Civil Engineering Careers of Frank and Walter Shanly, c.1840–c.1890* (PhD dissertation, University of Toronto, 1995), 31.

12   *Beauharnois Canal, Report on the state of work from 1844*, National Archives of Canada, RG 11, vol. 94 (1844).

13   White, *The Civil Engineering Careers of Frank and Walter Shanly*, 79.

14   Archives Nationales du Québec à Montréal (ANQM), P464, Fonds Walter Shanly.

15   Walter Shanly to Frank Shanly, 3 September 1846, Archives of Ontario, Toronto, Shanly Papers, MU2731, Walter Shanly correspondence.

16   Ibid.

17   *Report upon the Merits of the Great Western Railroad, Canada West: by a Committee of its American Friends* (Boston: Eastburn's Press, 1851), 3–4.

18   White, *The Civil Engineering Careers of Frank and Walter Shanly*, 48.

19   Walter Shanly to Frank Shanly, 28 June 1846, Archives of Ontario, Shanly Papers.

20   Ibid., 3 March 1847.

21   Frank Shanly notebook, Archives of Ontario, Shanly Papers, MU2714, pay records March and April 1848.

22   Ibid.

23 J. G. Hopkins, *The Northern Railroad in New York with Remarks on The Western Trade* (Boston: S. N. Dickinson & Co., 1847), 30–31.

24 Walter Shanly to Frank Shanly, 6 December 1848, Archives of Ontario, Shanly Papers, MU2714.

25 Frederick J. Seaver, *Historical Sketches of Franklin County and several Towns, with many Short Biographies* (Albany, NY: J. B. Lyon Company, 1918), 436.

26 Charles L. Schlatter, *Second Report of Charles L. Schlatter, Principal Engineer in the Service of the State of Pennsylvania, to the Canal Commissioners, relative to the Continuous Railroad from Harrisburg to Pittsburg* (Harrisburg: James S. Wallace, 1841).

27 "Northern (New York) Railroad Report," *American Railroad Journal*, second quarto series, vol. 4, no. 46, whole no. 657, vol. 21 (11 November 1848): 724.

28 Walter Shanly to Frank Shanly, 6 December 1848, Archives of Ontario, Shanly Papers, MU2714.

29 Ibid., 12 December 1848.

30 White, *The Civil Engineering Careers of Frank and Walter Shanly*, 117.

31 *Report of the Directors of the Northern Rail Road Company* (Ogdensburgh, New York: Hitchcock & Smith, 1848), p. 4.

32 *The Railroad Jubilee: An Account of the Celebration Commemorative of the Opening of Railroad Communication between Boston and Canada* (Boston: J. H. Eastburn, 1852).

33 Walter Shanly to Frank Shanly, 12 December 1848, Archives of Ontario, Shanly Papers.

34 White, *The Civil Engineering Careers of Frank and Walter Shanly*, 93.

35 Walter Shanly to Frank Shanly, 26 December 1848, Archives of Ontario, Shanly Papers, MU2714.

36 Ibid., 8 January 1849.

37 Ibid., 21 March 1849.

38 Ibid., 29 March 1849.

39 *Report of the Directors of the Northern Rail Road Company* (Boston: T. R. Marvin, 1849), p. 7.

40 Walter Shanly to Frank Shanly, 17 April 1849, Archives of Ontario, Shanly Papers, MU2731.

41 Ibid., 9 June 1849.

42 Ibid., 10 June 1849.

43 Ibid., 7 March 1850.

44   Ibid., 21 March 1850.

45   Ibid., 9 September 1849.

46   Ibid., 9 May 1850.

47   Frank Walker, *Daylight Through the Mountain* (Montreal: The Engineering Institute of Canada, 1957), 157.

48   Walter Shanly to Frank Shanly, 9 August 1850, Archives of Ontario, Shanly Papers, MU2731.

49   Ibid., 1 December 1850.

50   Ibid., 11 November 1850.

51   Ibid., 14 November 1850.

52   Ibid., 16 November 1850.

53   Ibid., 10 December 1850.

54   Ibid., 23 December 1850.

55   Ibid., 1 January 1851.

56   Frank Shanly to Walter Shanly, 16 January 1851, Archives of Ontario, Shanly Papers, MU2720.

57   Ibid., 2 January 1851.

58   Walter Shanly to Frank Shanly, 24 February 1851, Archives of Ontario, Shanly Papers, MU2731.

59   Ibid., 24 January 1851.

60   Ibid.

61   Walter Shanly to Frank Shanly, 27 January 1851.

62   Walker, *Daylight Through the Mountain*, 198–199.

63   Walter Shanly to Frank Shanly, 24 February 1851.

64   Ibid., 24 January 1851.

65   Ibid., 16 March 1851.

66   Ibid., 2 April 1851.

67   W. Shanly, *Report No. 1, To the President and Directors of the Bytown and Prescott Railway Company* (Prescott, Ontario: Bytown and Prescott Railway Office, 7 April 1851).

68   Walter Shanly to Frank Shanly, 13 July 1851.

69   Ibid., 21 September 1851.

70   W. Shanly, *Report No. 2, To the President and Directors of the Bytown and Prescott Railway Company* (Prescott, Ontario: Bytown and Prescott Railway Office, 26 July 1851).

71   Walter Shanly to Frank Shanly, 3 October 1851.

72   Ibid., 23 October 1851.

73   Walker, *Daylight Through the Mountain*, 246–247.

74   Walter Shanly, *Report on the Preliminary Surveys of the Toronto & Guelph Railway* (Toronto: Brewer, McPhail and Co., 1851), p. 6.

75   *Second Annual Report, Toronto and Guelph Railway Company* (Toronto: Henry Rowsell, 6 June 1853), pp. 10–11.

76   White, *The Civil Engineering Careers of Frank and Walter Shanly*, 150–151.

77   Walter Shanly to Frank Shanly, 14 March 1853, Archives of Ontario, Shanly Papers.

78   Ibid., 31 March 1853.

79   White, *The Civil Engineering Careers of Frank and Walter Shanly*, 162.

80   Walter Shanly to Frank Shanly, 10 August 1853, Archives of Ontario, Shanly Papers.

81   Ibid., 4 August 1853.

82   White, *The Civil Engineering Careers of Frank and Walter Shanly*, 159, 160.

83   Walter Shanly to Frank Shanly, 2 November 1853.

84   Frank Shanly to Walter Shanly, 21 August 1853, Archives of Ontario, Shanly Papers, MU2691.

85   Shanly, *The Canadian Shanlys*, 34–35.

86   Walker, *Daylight Through the Mountain*, 283.

87   Walter Shanly to Frank Shanly, 17 May 1854, Archives of Ontario, Shanly Papers, MU2731.

88   Walter Shanly, *Report on the Port Huron & Lake Michigan ("Michigan Northern") Railway* (Toronto: Brewer, McPhail and Co., 1854).

89   White, *The Civil Engineering Careers of Frank and Walter Shanly*, 206–207.

90   Ibid., 270.

91   Walter Shanly to Frank Shanly, 1, 7, and 12 December 1856, Archives of Ontario, Shanly Papers, MU2731.

92   Stewart to Frank Shanly, 16 November 1856, Archives of Ontario, Shanly Papers, MU2720.

93   White, *The Civil Engineering Careers of Frank and Walter Shanly*, 279.

94   Stewart to Frank Shanley, 16 November 1856.

95   "Brydges, Charles John," in *Dictionary of Canadian Biography Online, 1881–1890*, vol. 11.

96   White, *The Civil Engineering Careers of Frank and Walter Shanly*, 283.

97   Ibid., 304.

98   Ibid., 304–305.

99 George F. Benson, *Historical Record of the Edwardsburg and Canada Starch Companies* (Montreal: Canada Starch Co., 1958), 25–29.

100 White, *The Civil Engineering Careers of Frank and Walter Shanly*, 307.

101 *Journals of the Legislative Council of the Province of Canada*, Third session, Eighth Provincial Parliament, vol. 24 (1865), pp. 57, 78, 86.

102 Walker, *Daylight Through the Mountain*, 407.

103 White, *The Civil Engineering Careers of Frank and Walter Shanly*, 294.

104 Archibald Currie, *The Grand Trunk Railway of Canada* (Toronto: University of Toronto Press, 1957), 265.

105 White, *The Civil Engineering Careers of Frank and Walter Shanly*, 212.

106 Ibid., 214.

107 Ibid., 215.

108 Ibid., 220.

109 Ibid., pp. 223–224.

110 Ibid., 225.

111 Ibid.

112 Ibid., 228.

Chapter 13

1 *Senate No. 20, Report of the Hon. Alvah Crocker, Commissioner, acting as Superintendent, of the work upon the Troy and Greenfield Railroad and Hoosac Tunnel together with the Reports of the Chief and Consulting Engineers* (Boston: Wright & Potter, 1868), p. 50.

2 *Adams Transcript*, vol. 29, no. 31 (1 July 1869).

3 Ibid.

4 Ibid.

5 Frank Walker, *Daylight Through the Mountain* (Montreal: The Engineering Institute of Canada, 1957), 378.

6 *Senate No. 58, Report of the Joint Standing Committee of 1869 on the Troy and Greenfield Railroad and Hoosac Tunnel* (Boston: Wright & Potter, 1870), p. 4.

7 Isaac S. Browne, letter to Bert Browne (progeny of Charles A. Browne) from New London, CT, 25 May 1923, copy in North Adams Public Library, North Adams Vault, Call #385 Browne, Status Storage.

8 "The Tunnel Strike," *Adams Transcript*, vol. 29, no. 29 (17 June 1869).

9   "Reports of James Laurie, late Consulting Engineer on the Hoosac Tunnel," *Senate No. 283* (Boston: Wright & Potter, May 1871), pp. 2–3.

10   *Adams Transcript* (reprint from the *Springfield Republican*), vol. 29, no. 29 (17 June 1869).

11   *House No. 192, Report of the Commissioners upon the Troy and Greenfield Railroad and Hoosac Tunnel, for the year 1868* (Boston: Wright & Potter, 1869), profile drawing between pp. 26 and 27.

12   *Senate No. 58, Report of the Joint Standing Committee of 1869 on the Troy and Greenfield Railroad and Hoosac Tunnel*, p. 4.

13   "Hoosac Tunnel," *Adams Transcript*, vol. 29, no. 18 (1 April 1869).

14   *Senate No. 58, Report of the Joint Standing Committee of 1869 on the Troy and Greenfield Railroad and Hoosac Tunnel*, p. 4.

15   *Senate No. 300, Evidence and Arguments on the Petition of Walter and Francis Shanly before the Committee on the Hoosac Tunnel and Troy & Greenfield Railroad* (Boston: Wright & Potter, 1874), p. 93.

16   "The West End Tunnel," *Adams Transcript*, vol. 29, no. 12 (18 February 1869).

17   *Senate No. 58, Report of the Joint Standing Committee of 1869 on the Troy and Greenfield Railroad and Hoosac Tunnel*, p. 4.

18   "Hoosac Tunnel," *Hampshire Gazette* (Northampton, MA), 16 November 1868.

19   "Reports of James Laurie, late Consulting Engineer on the Hoosac Tunnel," *Senate No. 283*, p. 4.

20   M. T. Runnels, *History of Sanbornton, New Hampshire. Vol. 2: Genealogies* (Boston: Alfred Mudge & Son, 1881), 222.

21   "Reports of James Laurie, late Consulting Engineer on the Hoosac Tunnel," *Senate No. 283*, p. 3.

22   Henry Petroski, "The Civil Engineer," *American Scientist* 90 (March–April 2002): 121.

23   "Accident at the Tunnel," *Adams Transcript*, vol. 29, no. 31 (1 July 1869).

24   "Reports of James Laurie, late Consulting Engineer on the Hoosac Tunnel," *Senate No. 283*, p. 8.

25   "Accident at the West Shaft," *Adams Transcript*, vol. 29, no. 36 (5 August 1869).

26   "Improved Electric Fuse," *Manufacturer and Builder* 1, no. 4 (April 1869): 116.

27   N. S. Greensfelder, "Shot Firing by Electricity," *The Coal Industry* 5, no. 9 (September 1922): 391.

28   "Reports of James Laurie, late Consulting Engineer on the Hoosac Tunnel," *Senate No. 283*, p. 10.

29   *Journal of the Franklin Institute* 6 (October 1830): 218.

30   Henry S. Drinker, *Tunneling, Explosive Compounds, and Rock Drills* (New York: John Wiley 1878), 96.

31   Browne, letter to Bert Browne, 25 May 1925.

32   Heinrich Schellen, *Magneto-Electric and Dynamo-Electric Machines* (New York: D. Van Nostrand, 1884), 154.

33   Geo. M. Mowbray, *Tri-Nitro-Glycerin as applied in the Hoosac Tunnel, Submarine Blasting, Etc., Etc., Etc.* (North Adams, MA: James T. Robinson & Son, 1872), 93.

34   Mowbray, *Tri-Nitro-Glycerin*, 94.

35   Browne, letter to Bert Browne, 25 May 1925.

36   Ibid.

37   Mark E. Rondeau, "Cemetery Walk: Whistling Past the Graveyard," story told by North Adams historian Paul Marino, iBerkshires.com, North Adams, MA, 11 July 2003: http://www.iberkshires.com/story/11446/Cemetery-walk-Whistling-past-the-graveyard.html?ss_id=1794, viewed 6 July 2013.

38   "Reports of James Laurie, late Consulting Engineer on the Hoosac Tunnel," *Senate No. 283*, p. 10.

39   *Historic Resources of the City of North Adams, Massachusetts* (partial inventory), NPS Form 10-900, National Park Service, U.S. Department of the Interior (received 12 September 1985, entered 25 October 1985), p. 6.

40   "Reports of James Laurie, late Consulting Engineer on the Hoosac Tunnel," *Senate No. 283*, p. 8.

41   *Senate No. 300, Evidence and Arguments on the Petition of Walter and Francis Shanly before the Committee on the Hoosac Tunnel and Troy & Greenfield Railroad*, p. 60.

42   "When Will the Tunnel Be Completed," *Adams Transcript*, vol. 29, no. 39 (26 August 1869).

43   "Burleigh's Rock Drill," *American Railway Times* 21, no. 21 (22 May 1869).

44   Walker, *Daylight Through the Mountain*, 45.

45   N. H. Egleston, "The Story of the Hoosac Tunnel," *Atlantic Monthly* 49, No. 293 (March 1882): 295.

46   Drinker, *Tunneling, Explosive Compounds, and Rock Drills*, 328.

47   "The Hoosac Tunnel," *American Railway Times* 21, no. 18 (1 May 1869).

48   "Work at the Tunnel," *Adams Transcript*, vol. 29, no. 35 (29 July 1869).

49   "Reports of James Laurie, late Consulting Engineer on the Hoosac Tunnel," *Senate No. 283*, p. 6.

50   Ibid., p. 7.

51   "The Hoosac Tunnel," *American Railway Times* (1 May 1869).

52   "When Will the Tunnel Be Completed," *Adams Transcript* (26 August 1869).

53   "The Hoosac Tunnel," in *The Science Record for 1872*, ed. Alfred E. Beach (New York: Munn & Company, 1872), 186.

54   "Reports of James Laurie, Late Consulting Engineer on the Hoosac Tunnel," *Senate No. 283*, p. 9.

55   *Senate No. 58, Report of the Joint Standing Committee of 1869 on the Troy and Greenfield Railroad and Hoosac Tunnel*, p. 8.

56   "Tunnel Cascade," *Adams Transcript* (26 August 1869).

57   *Adams Transcript*, vol. 29, no. 37 (12 August 1869).

58   *Senate No. 58, Report of the Joint Standing Committee of 1869 on the Troy and Greenfield Railroad and Hoosac Tunnel*, pp. 18–19.

59   "The Great Flood," *Adams Transcript*, vol. 29, no. 45 (7 October 1869).

60   Ibid.

61   *Senate No. 58, Report of the Joint Standing Committee of 1869 on the Troy and Greenfield Railroad and Hoosac Tunnel*, p. 9.

62   "Reports of James Laurie, late Consulting Engineer on the Hoosac Tunnel," *Senate No. 283*, (May 1871). p. 11.

63   "The Great Flood," *Adams Transcript* (7 October 1869).

64   Ibid.

65   "Reports of James Laurie, late Consulting Engineer on the Hoosac Tunnel," p. 12 (estimate made by Engineer Frost).

66   *Senate No. 58, Report of the Joint Standing Committee of 1869 on the Troy and Greenfield Railroad and Hoosac Tunnel*, p. 10.

67   "The Hoosac Tunnel," *Adams Transcript*, vol. 29, no. 47 (21 October 1869).

68   "Reports of James Laurie, late Consulting Engineer on the Hoosac Tunnel," *Senate No. 283*, p. 12.

69   Ibid., p. 14.

70 *Gazette and Courier* (Greenfield, MA) (11 October 1869), 2.

71 "The Hoosac Tunnel," *Adams Transcript* (21 October 1869).

72 "Vermont and Massachusetts Railroad," *American Railroad Journal*, second quarto series, vol. 26, no. 10, whole no. 1,768, vol. 43 (5 March 1870): 259.

73 "The West Shaft of the Tunnel," *Adams Transcript*, vol. 29, no. 48 (28 October 1869).

74 "The Tunnel—the Brick Arching Stands," *Adams Transcript*, vol. 30, no. 1 (2 December 1869).

75 Browne, letter to Bert Browne.

76 William Lowell Putman, *Great Railroad Tunnels of North America* (Jefferson, NC: McFarland & Company, 2011), 70.

77 John C. Rand, *One Thousand Representative Men Residents in the Commonwealth of Massachusetts A.D. 1888–'89* (Boston: First National Publishing Company, 1890), 26.

78 Benjamin W. Dwight, *The History of the Descendants of Elder John Strong, of Northampton, Mass.*, vol. 1 (Albany, NY: Joel Munsell, 1871), 634.

79 Myles Standish, "Dr. Hasket Derby," in *Transactions of the American Ophthalmological Society*, vol. 14, part 1 (Philadelphia: American Ophthalmological Society, 1915), 1.b2–4.

80 Browne, letter to Bert Browne.

81 Rondeau, "Cemetery Walk: Whistling Past the Graveyard."

82 *Improvement in Electric Fuses*, Charles A. Browne and Isaac S. Browne of North Adams, MA, United States Patent Office, Letters patent No. 158,672, 12 January 1875.

83 Washington Gladden, "The Hoosac Tunnel," *Scribner's Monthly* 1, no. 2 (December 1870): 150.

84 "The Hoosac Tunnel," *Adams Transcript*, vol. 30, no. 7 (13 January 1870).

85 Walker, *Daylight Through the Mountain*, 43.

86 "The Hoosac Tunnel," *American Railway Times* 22, no. 1 (1 January 1870).

87 "Reports of James Laurie, late Consulting Engineer on the Hoosac Tunnel," *Senate No. 283*, p. 25.

88 *Senate No. 150, Committee on claims, to whom was referred the memorial of Walter and Francis Shanly concerning the Hoosac Tunnel, Report* (Boston: Wright & Potter, April 1875), p. 10.

89 "The Organization of the Legislature—Message of Gov. Claflin," *Adams Transcript*, vol. 30, no. 7 (13 January 1870).

90 "Reports of James Laurie, late Consulting Engineer on the Hoosac Tunnel," *Senate No. 283*, p. 15.

91 *Senate No. 58, Report of the Joint Standing Committee of 1869 on the Troy and Greenfield Railroad and Hoosac Tunnel*, p. 3.

92 Walker, *Daylight Through the Mountain*, 379.

93 *Senate No. 300, Evidence and Arguments on the Petition of Walter and Francis Shanly before the Committee on the Hoosac Tunnel and Troy & Greenfield Railroad*, p. 38.

94 *Adams Transcript*, vol. 30, no. 9 (27 January 1870).

95 *Senate No. 55, Report of the Joint Standing Committee on the Troy and Greenfield Railroad and Hoosac Tunnel for the year 1870*, p. 5.

96 *Adams Transcript*, vol. 30, no. 17 (24 March 1870).

97 "Reports of James Laurie, late Consulting Engineer on the Hoosac Tunnel," *Senate No. 283*, p. 12.

98 *Senate No. 300, Evidence and Arguments on the Petition of Walter and Francis Shanly before the Committee on the Hoosac Tunnel and Troy & Greenfield Railroad*, p. 90.

99 Drinker, *Tunneling, Explosive Compounds, and Rock Drills*, 85.

100 Mowbray, *Tri-Nitro-Glycerin*, 69.

101 "Hoosac Tunnel," *Adams Transcript*, vol. 30, no. 30 (23 June 1870).

102 Henrik Schück and Ragnar Sohlman, *The Life of Alfred Nobel*, trans. Brian and Beatrix Lunn (London: Heinemann, 1929), 101.

103 "The Worcester Explosion," *Public Document No. 35, Second Annual Report of the Board of Railroad Commissioners* (Boston: Wright & Potter, 1871), pp. 27–28.

104 "The Worcester Explosion—One Thousand Exploders in One Car," *New York Times*, 25 June 1870.

105 Ibid.

106 "Boston and Albany Railroad Company vs. Walter Shanly & others. Thomas Carney vs. Same," in *Cases Argued and Determined in the Supreme Judicial Court for the County of Worcester, October Term 1871, at Worcester, Massachusetts, Reports 107* (Boston: H. O. Houghton and Company, 1873), 568–81.

107 "The Shanly's [sic] Win Their Suit," *Adams Transcript*, vol. 33, no. 12 (13 February 1873).

108 "Hoosac Tunnel," *Adams Transcript*, vol. 31, no. 2 (8 December 1870).

109 "Reports of James Laurie, late Consulting Engineer on the Hoosac Tunnel," *Senate No. 283*, p. 30.

110 *Senate No. 150, Committee on claims, to whom was referred the memorial of Walter and Francis Shanly concerning the Hoosac Tunnel* (27 April 1875).

111 "Reports of James Laurie, late Consulting Engineer on the Hoosac Tunnel," *Senate No. 283*, p. 364.

112 Ibid., p. 42.

113 Ibid., p. 43 (letter to Benjamin D. Frost from Laurie, 26 May 1870, New York).

114 Ibid., p. 46.

115 Ibid., p. 48.

116 "Reports of James Laurie, late Consulting Engineer on the Hoosac Tunnel," *Senate No. 330, Supplement to Senate No. 283* (Boston: Wright & Potter, May 1871), p. 10.

117 *Senate No. 300, Evidence and Arguments on the Petition of Walter and Francis Shanly before the Committee on the Hoosac Tunnel and Troy & Greenfield Railroad*, p. 85.

118 "Reports of James Laurie, late Consulting Engineer on the Hoosac Tunnel," *Senate No. 330, Supplement to Senate No. 283*, p. 3.

119 "Accident at the Central Shaft," *Adams Transcript*, vol. 30, no. 47 (20 October 1870).

120 "Reports of James Laurie, late Consulting Engineer on the Hoosac Tunnel," *Senate No. 283*, p. 52.

121 Gladden, "The Hoosac Tunnel," *Scribner's Monthly* (December 1870): 156.

122 Ibid.

123 "Reports of James Laurie, late Consulting Engineer on the Hoosac Tunnel," *Senate No. 330, Supplement to Senate No. 283*, p. 3.

124 "Fatal Accident at the West Shaft," *Adams Transcript*, vol. 31, no. 1 (1 December 1870).

125 *Senate No. 55, Report of the Joint Standing Committee on the Troy and Greenfield Railroad and Hoosac Tunnel for the year 1870*, p. 8.

126 Drinker, *Tunneling, Explosive Compounds, and Rock Drills*, 244.

127 J. L. Harrison, "How the Tunnel-Headings Were Made to Meet," in *The Great Bore* (North Adams, MA: Advance Job Print Works, 1891), 27.

128 *Engineering News* 8 (23 July 1881): 292.

129 Harrison, "How the Tunnel-Headings Were Made to Meet," 26.

130 Egleston, "The Story of the Hoosac Tunnel," 299.

131 "Hoosac Tunnel," *Adams Transcript*, vol. 31, no. 2 (8 December 1870).

132 *Senate No. 55, Report of the Joint Standing Committee on the Troy and Greenfield Railroad and Hoosac Tunnel for the year 1870*, p. 98.

133 Ibid., p. 8.

134 "The Hoosac Tunnel," *Adams Transcript*, vol. 30, no. 50 (10 November 1870).

135 "Miscellaneous Spiders and Engineers," *RSA Journal* (published by the Royal Society for the Encouragement of Arts, Manufactures and Commerce, London), vol. 39 (17 July 1891).

136 George L. Vose, *Manual for Railroad Engineers and Engineering Students* (Boston: Lee and Shepard, 1883), 70.

137 Egleston, "The Story of the Hoosac Tunnel," 302.

138 Francis D. Fisher, "Discussion," "Tunnel Surveying of Division No. 6, New Croton Aqueduct," in *Transactions of the American Society of Civil Engineers* 23 (July–December 1890): 33.

139 *Senate No. 55, Report of the Joint Standing Committee on the Troy and Greenfield Railroad and Hoosac Tunnel for the year 1870*, pp. 2–3.

140 Ibid., p. 8.

141 Richard Wallace White, *The Civil Engineering Careers of Frank and Walter Shanly, c.1840–c.1890* (PhD dissertation, University of Toronto, 1995), 228.

142 Jones to Frank Shanly, 21 January 1869, "Rondout and Oswego," Archives of Ontario, Shanly Papers, MU2690.

143 Frank Shanly and partners to Latrobe, 1 June and 18 June 1869, "Pittsburgh and Connellsville Railroad," Archives of Ontario, Shanly Papers, MU2688.

144 White, *The Civil Engineering Careers of Frank and Walter Shanly*, 230.

145 "Contract between Frank Shanly and the Toronto, Grey, & Bruce Railway, 18 November 1869," Tenders & Contracts, Archives of Ontario, Shanly Papers, MU2710.

146 "Hoosac Tunnel Correspondence," 18 November 1869, Archives of Ontario, Shanly Papers, MU2678.

147 Gladden, "The Hoosac Tunnel," *Scribner's Monthly* (December 1870): 143–59.

148 Ibid., 150.

149 Ibid., 151.

150	Mowbray, "Nitro-Glycerine at the Hoosac Tunnel," *Adams Transcript*, vol. 31, no. 9 (26 January 1871).

151	Mowbray, *Tri-Nitro-Glycerin*, 3d ed. (New York: D. Van Nostrand, 1872), 45.

152	Ibid.

153	"Fire at the East End of the Tunnel," *Adams Transcript*, vol. 31, no. 5 (29 December 1870).

154	*Adams Transcript*, vol. 31, no. 8 (19 January 1871).

155	*Senate No. 300, Evidence and Arguments on the Petition of Walter and Francis Shanly before the Committee on the Hoosac Tunnel and Troy & Greenfield Railroad*, pp. 7–9.

Chapter 14

1	Edward Wilton Carpenter and Charles Frederick Morehouse, *The History of the Town of Amherst, Massachusetts* (Amherst, MA: Carpenter & Morehouse, 1896), 175.

2	*Senate No. 300, Evidence and Arguments on the Petition of Walter and Francis Shanly before the Committee on the Hoosac Tunnel and Troy & Greenfield Railroad* (Boston: Wright & Potter, May 1874), p. 8.

3	*Senate No. 250, Report of the Joint Standing Committee on the Troy and Greenfield Railroad and the Hoosac Tunnel, for the year 1871.* (Boston: Wright & Potter, March 1872), p. 10.

4	Ibid.

5	"Central Shaft," *Adams Transcript*, vol. 31, no. 18 (30 March 1871).

6	*Senate No. 250, Report of the Joint Standing Committee on the Troy and Greenfield Railroad and the Hoosac Tunnel, for the year 1871*, p. 10.

7	"Central Shaft," *Adams Transcript* (30 March 1871).

8	*Senate No. 250, Report of the Joint Standing Committee on the Troy and Greenfield Railroad and the Hoosac Tunnel, for the year 1871*, p. 10.

9	"Hoosac Tunnel," *Adams Transcript*, vol. 31, no. 19 (6 April 1871).

10	*Senate No. 201, Report on the Troy and Greenfield Railroad and Hoosac Tunnel by the Joint Standing Committee for 1873* (Boston: Wright & Potter, April 1874), p. 13.

11	*Senate No. 300, Evidence and Arguments on the Petition of Walter and Francis Shanly before the Committee on the Hoosac Tunnel and Troy & Greenfield Railroad*, p. 94.

12 Henry S. Drinker, *Tunneling, Explosive Compounds, and Rock Drills* (New York: John Wiley, 1878), 247.

13 *Senate No. 250, Report of the Joint Standing Committee on the Troy and Greenfield Railroad and the Hoosac Tunnel, for the year 1871*, p. 5.

14 Ibid., p. 9.

15 Ibid., p. 6.

16 *Senate No. 169* (Boston: Wright & Potter, April 1871), p. 2.

17 *Senate No. 250, Report of the Joint Standing Committee on the Troy and Greenfield Railroad and the Hoosac Tunnel, for the year 1871*, p. 13.

18 *Senate No. 300, Evidence and Arguments on the Petition of Walter and Francis Shanly before the Committee on the Hoosac Tunnel and Troy & Greenfield Railroad*, p. 94.

19 "West Shaft," *Adams Transcript*, vol. 31, no. 39 (24 August 1871).

20 "Hoosac Tunnel," *Adams Transcript* (2 January 1873; reprinted from the *Boston Traveller*).

21 Drinker, "Fig. 129," in *Tunneling, Explosive Compounds, and Rock Drills*, 246.

22 "The Hoosac Tunnel," in *The Science Record for 1872*, ed. Alfred E. Beach (New York: Munn & Company, 1872), p. 176.

23 *Senate No. 201, Report of the Joint Standing Committee on the Troy and Greenfield Railroad and the Hoosac Tunnel, for the year 1872*, p. 3.

24 Flaneur ("Stroller"), "Hoosac Village," *Boston Daily Globe* (1 November 1872), 2.

25 Ibid.

26 *Proceedings of the American Society of Civil Engineers* (New York: American Society of Civil Engineers 19 (October 1893), 172–73.

27 Rambler, "Hoosac Tunnel," *Boston Daily Globe* (28 August 1872), 2.

28 "The Hoosac Tunnel," in *The Science Record for 1872*, 182.

29 "Hoosac Tunnel," *Adams Transcript* (2 January 1873; reprinted from the *Boston Traveller*).

30 Ibid.

31 "The Hoosac Tunnel," in *The Science Record for 1872*, 189.

32 "Hoosac Tunnel," *Adams Transcript* (2 January 1873; reprinted from the *Boston Traveller*).

33 *Senate No. 250, Report of the Joint Standing Committee on the Troy and Greenfield Railroad and the Hoosac Tunnel, for the year 1871*, p. 10.

34 Drinker, "Fig. 615," in *Tunneling, Explosive Compounds, and Rock Drills*, 641.

35 *Adams Transcript*, vol. 31, no. 43 (21 September 1871).

36 Ibid.

37 *Senate No. 250, Report of the Joint Standing Committee on the Troy and Greenfield Railroad and the Hoosac Tunnel, for the year 1871*, p. 11.

38 Ibid., p. 9.

39 "Hoosac Tunnel," *Adams Transcript* (2 January 1873; reprinted from the *Boston Traveller*).

40 *Senate No. 300, Evidence and Arguments on the Petition of Walter and Francis Shanly before the Committee on the Hoosac Tunnel and Troy & Greenfield Railroad*, p. 38.

41 *Senate No. 150, Massachusetts General Court, Senate Committee on Claims, to whom was referred the memorial of Walter and Francis Shanly concerning the Hoosac Tunnel* (April 1875), p. 12.

42 Ibid., p. 10.

43 Ibid., p. 7.

44 Ibid.

45 Drinker, "Fig. 614," in *Tunneling, Explosive Compounds, and Rock Drills*, 640.

46 *Senate No. 300, Evidence and Arguments on the Petition of Walter and Francis Shanly before the Committee on the Hoosac Tunnel and Troy & Greenfield Railroad*, p. 42.

47 "Hoosac Tunnel," *Adams Transcript*, vol. 31, no. 45 (5 October 1871).

48 *Adams Transcript*, vol. 31, no. 47 (19 October 1871).

49 *Adams Transcript*, vol. 32, no. 5 (28 December 1871).

50 *Senate No. 250, Report of the Joint Standing Committee on the Troy and Greenfield Railroad and the Hoosac Tunnel, for the year 1871*, p. 12.

51 *Senate No. 201, Report of the Joint Standing Committee on the Troy and Greenfield Railroad and the Hoosac Tunnel, for the year 1872*, p. 22.

52 "Hoosac Tunnel," *Adams Transcript*, vol. 32, no. 51 (14 November 1872).

53 *Adams Transcript*, vol. 32, no. 17 (21 March 1872).

54 *Senate No. 250, Report of the Joint Standing Committee on the Troy and Greenfield Railroad and the Hoosac Tunnel, for the year 1871*, p. 18.

55 *Senate No. 201, Report of the Joint Standing Committee on the Troy and Greenfield Railroad and the Hoosac Tunnel, for the year 1872*, p. 22.

56 "Hoosac Tunnel," *Adams Transcript*, vol. 32, no. 12 (15 February 1872).

57   *Senate No. 201, Report of the Joint Standing Committee on the Troy and Greenfield Railroad and the Hoosac Tunnel, for the year 1872*, p. 21.

58   "Hoosac Tunnel," *Adams Transcript* (15 February 1872).

59   Ibid.

60   Rambler, "Hoosac Tunnel," *Boston Daily Globe* (28 August 1872). 2.

61   "Hoosac Tunnel Contract," *Adams Transcript*, vol. 32, no. 19 (4 April 1872).

62   Ibid.

63   "Chap. 47. Resolves in Favor of the Contractors for the Construction of the Hoosac Tunnel," *Acts and Resolves passed by the General Court of Massachusetts in the year 1872* (Boston: Wright & Potter, 1872), pp. 352–53.

64   *Senate No. 201, Report of the Joint Standing Committee on the Troy and Greenfield Railroad and the Hoosac Tunnel, for the year 1872*, p. 20.

65   "The Hoosac Tunnel and its Connections," *Adams Transcript*, vol. 33, no. 7 (7 January 1873).

66   *Adams Transcript*, vol. 31, no. 23 (4 May 1871).

67   "Progress of Hoosac Tunnel for April 1872," *Adams Transcript*, vol. 32, no. 24 (9 May 1872).

68   *Senate No. 201, Report of the Joint Standing Committee on the Troy and Greenfield Railroad and the Hoosac Tunnel, for the year 1872*, p. 10.

69   "Progress of Hoosac Tunnel for May 1872," *Adams Transcript*, vol. 32, no. 29 (13 June 1872).

70   *Adams Transcript*, vol. 32, no. 33 (11 July 1872).

71   *Senate No. 300, Evidence and Arguments on the Petition of Walter and Francis Shanly before the Committee on the Hoosac Tunnel and Troy & Greenfield Railroad*, p. 25.

72   *Adams Transcript*, vol. 32, no. 38 (15 August 1872).

73   *Hoosac Valley News*, vol. 6, no. 31 (13 August 1873).

74   *Adams Transcript* (15 August 1872).

75   "Accident at the West Shaft," *Adams Transcript*, vol. 32, no. 42 (12 September 1872).

76   "Explosion at the West Shaft," *Adams Transcript*, vol. 33, no. 13 (20 February 1872).

77   *Adams Transcript*, vol. 32, no. 51 (14 November 1872).

78   "Hon. Alvah Crocker of Fitchburg," *Adams Transcript*, vol. 32, no. 47 (17 October 1872).

79   *Biographical Encyclopaedia of Massachusetts of the Nineteenth Century*, vol. 2 (Boston: Metropolitan Publishing and Engraving Company, 1883), p. 141.

80   "Another Accident," *Adams Transcript*, vol. 32, no. 46 (10 October 1872).

81   "West End, Hoosac Tunnel," *Adams Transcript* (10 October 1872)

82   Ibid.

83   "East End, Hoosac Tunnel," *Adams Transcript*, vol. 32, no. 52 (21 November 1872).

84   Ibid.

85   *Adams Transcript* (14 November 1872).

86   "Runaway," *Adams Transcript*, vol. 33, no. 2 (5 December 1872).

87   *Senate No. 201, Report of the Joint Standing Committee on the Troy and Greenfield Railroad and the Hoosac Tunnel, for the year 1872*, p. 22.

88   "The Hoosac Tunnel," *Chicago Daily Tribune* (17 December 1872), 7.

89   Ibid., 7.

90   "Progress of the Hoosac Tunnel," *Scientific American* 27, no. 26 (28 December 1872): 401.

91   "The Hoosac Tunnel," *Boston Daily Globe* (16 December 1872), 4.

92   *Senate No. 201, Report of the Joint Standing Committee on the Troy and Greenfield Railroad and the Hoosac Tunnel, for the year 1872*, p. 21.

93   "Opening between Central Shaft and East End Hoosac Tunnel, Effected," *Adams Transcript*, vol. 33, no. 3 (12 December 1872).

94   "Engineering Skill and the Tunnel," *Adams Transcript*, vol. 33, no. 5 (26 December 1872).

95   Thomas Doane, "Details of the Instrument Houses used in Surface Alignment of the Hoosac Tunnel (drawing, 1863)," Massachusetts State Library, Photos 385.8 H78, nos. 15 and 16.

96   *Senate No. 201, Report of the Joint Standing Committee on the Troy and Greenfield Railroad and the Hoosac Tunnel, for the year 1872*, p. 24.

97   *Adams Transcript* (15 August 1872).

98   *Adams Transcript* (13 June 1872).

99   "The Hoosac Tunnel and its Connections," *Adams Transcript*, vol. 33, no. 7 (7 January 1873).

100 Ibid.

101 *Adams Transcript* (7 January 1873).

102 "Progress of Hoosac Tunnel to February 1st 1873," (1873). *Adams Transcript*, vol. 33, no. 11 (6 February 1873).

103 "Central Shaft," *Adams Transcript* (6 February 1873).

104 "The Shanly's [*sic*] Win their Suit," *Adams Transcript*, vol. 33, no. 12 (13 February 1873).

105 "Hoosac Tunnel—the New Bedford Mercury," *Adams Transcript*, vol. 33, no. 13 (20 February 1873).

106 "Hoosac Tunnel," *Adams Transcript* (20 February 1873).

107 "Hoosac Tunnel," *Adams Transcript*, vol. 33, no. 25 (15 May 1873).

108 "Hoosac Tunnel," *Adams Transcript*, vol. 33, no. 29 (12 June 1873).

109 "Hoosac Tunnel," *Adams Transcript*, vol. 33, no. 31 (26 June 1873).

110 Ibid.

111 "Hoosac Tunnel, Terrible Accident at the East End," *Adams Transcript*, vol. 33, no. 32 (3 July 1873).

112 Ibid.

113 Ibid.

114 *Senate No. 300, Evidence and Arguments on the Petition of Walter and Francis Shanly before the Committee on the Hoosac Tunnel and Troy & Greenfield Railroad*, p. 25.

115 Ibid., pp. 12–13.

116 Ibid., p. 43.

117 Ibid., p. 89.

118 Ibid., p. 44.

119 "Progress of the Hoosac Tunnel," *Adams Transcript*, vol. 33, no. 37 (7 August 1873).

120 "Progress of Hoosac Tunnel During August, 1873," *Adams Transcript*, vol. 33, no. 42 (11 September 1873).

121 *Hoosac Valley News*, vol. 6, no. 16 (30 April 1873).

122 "A Terrific and Fatal Explosion," *Adams Transcript*, vol. 33, no. 43 (18 September 1873).

123 "A Man Killed at the East End of Hoosac Tunnel," *Adams Transcript* (18 September 1873).

124 "A Narrow Escape," *Adams Transcript*, vol. 33, no. 46 (9 October 1873).

125 "The Advancement of the Heading," *Adams Transcript*, (9 October 1873).

126 "Progress of Hoosac Tunnel," *Adams Transcript* (9 October 1873).

127 "The Turning of the Hoosac River," *Adams Transcript*, vol. 33, no. 49 (30 October 1873).

128 "Hoosac Tunnel," *Adams Transcript* (30 October 1873).

129 *Hoosac Valley News*, vol. 6, no. 34 (3 September 1873).

130 *Hoosac Valley News*, vol. 6, no. 38 (1 October 1873).

131 *Hoosac Valley News,* vol. 6, no. 41 (22 October 1873).

132 "The Meeting of the Hoosac Tunnel Headings Expected Thanksgiving Week," *Adams Transcript,* vol. 33, no. 50 (6 November 1873).

133 *Adams Transcript,* vol. 33, no. 51 (13 November 1873).

134 "The Hole Through the Mountain," *Adams Transcript,* vol. 34, no. 2 (4 December 1873).

135 "Hoosac Tunnel Open," *Hoosac Valley News,* vol. 6, no. 47 (3 December 1873).

136 Ibid.

137 "The Hole Through the Mountain," *Adams Transcript* (4 December 1873).

138 Ibid.

139 Ibid.

140 *Hoosac Valley News,* vol. 6, no. 49 (17 December 1873).

141 "Hoosac Tunnel Open," *Hoosac Valley News* (3 December 1873).

142 Ibid.

143 *Adams Transcript,* vol. 34, no. 3 (11 December 1873).

144 *Adams Transcript,* vol. 34, no. 4 (18 December 1873).

145 *Eleventh Annual Report of the Board of Railroad Commissioners* (Boston: Rand, Abery & Co., 1880), p. 95.

146 "Fatal Accident at the Tunnel," *Adams Transcript,* vol. 34, no. 9 (22 January 1874).

Chapter 15

1 *Senate No. 201, Report on the Troy & Greenfield Railroad and Hoosac Tunnel by the Joint Standing Committee for 1873* (Boston: Wright & Potter, 1874), p. 4.

2 Harris L. Dante, "The Chicago Tribune's 'Lost' Years, 1865–1874," *Journal of the Illinois State Historical Society* 58, no. 2 (Summer 1965): 164.

3 "The Hoosac Tunnel," *Hoosac Valley News,* vol. 7, no. 45 (19 November 1874).

4 *Senate No. 300, Evidence and Arguments on the Petition of Walter and Francis Shanly before the Committee on the Hoosac Tunnel and Troy & Greenfield Railroad* (Boston: Wright & Potter, May 1874), pp. 44–45.

5 *Senate No. 201, Report on the Troy & Greenfield Railroad and Hoosac Tunnel by the Joint Standing Committee for 1873,* p. 21.

6 "Fatal Accident at the Tunnel," *Adams Transcript*, vol. 34, no. 9 (22 January 1874).

7 *Adams Transcript*, vol. 34, no. 10 (29 January 1874).

8 *Senate No. 300, Evidence and Arguments on the Petition of Walter and Francis Shanly before the Committee on the Hoosac Tunnel and Troy & Greenfield Railroad*, pp. 44–45.

9 Ibid., pp. 60–65.

10 "The Hoosac Tunnel," *Adams Transcript*, vol. 34, no. 13 (19 February 1874).

11 "The Piercing of the American Isthmus," *Manufacturer and Builder* 11, no. 6 (June 1879): 188.

12 *Adams Transcript*, vol. 34, no. 12 (12 February 1874).

13 *Senate No. 300, Evidence and Arguments on the Petition of Walter and Francis Shanly before the Committee on the Hoosac Tunnel and Troy & Greenfield Railroad*, pp. 12–13.

14 Ibid., p. 38.

15 Ibid.

16 Ibid., p. 67.

17 Ibid., p. 79.

18 "Terrible Explosion at the West Shaft—The Sad Death of James Mulaney," *Adams Transcript*, vol. 34, no. 16 (12 March 1874).

19 "Settled," *Hoosac Valley News*, vol. 7, no. 10 (19 March 1874).

20 *Hoosac Valley News*, vol. 7, no. 24 (25 June 1874).

21 Ibid.

22 "Hoosac Tunnel," *Adams Transcript*, vol. 34, no. 35 (23 July 1874).

23 *Hoosac Valley News*, vol. 7, no. 33 (27 August 1874).

24 *Hoosac Valley News*, vol. 7, no. 34 (3 September 1874).

25 *Hoosac Valley News*, vol. 7, no. 35 (10 September 1874).

26 *Hoosac Valley News*, vol. 7, no. 36 (17 September 1874).

27 "Hoosac Tunnel," *Adams Transcript*, vol. 34, no. 38 (13 August 1874).

28 *Hoosac Valley News*, vol. 7, no. 13 (9 April 1874).

29 *Hoosac Valley News*, vol. 7, no. 11 (26 March 1874).

30 *Hoosac Valley News*, vol. 7, no. 18 (14 May 1874).

31 *Hoosac Valley News*, vol. 7, no. 14 (16 April 1874)

32 *Hoosac Valley News* (14 May 1874).

33 "Personal," *Engineering News*, vol. VIII, (23 July 1881), 292.

34 "Hoosac Tunnel," *Adams Transcript*, vol. 34, no. 24 (7 May 1874).

35   *Adams Transcript*, vol. 34, no. 30 (18 June 1874).

36   Lucius Holmes, "Hoosac Tunnel—No. 2," *The Phrenological Journal and Science of Health* 58, no. 2 (February 1874): 91.

37   *Hoosac Valley News*, vol. 7, no. 22 (11 June 1874).

38   "Hoosac Tunnel," *Adams Transcript*, vol. 34, no. 29 (11 June 1874).

39   *Hoosac Valley News*, vol. 7, no. 23 (18 June 1874).

40   *Hoosac Valley News*, vol. 7, no. 47 (3 December 1874).

41   Geo. M. Mowbray, *Tri-Nitro-Glycerin as Applied in the Hoosac Tunnel*, 3d ed. (North Adams, MA: James T. Robinson & Son, 1874).

42   *Hoosac Valley News*, vol. 7, no. 27 (16 July 1874).

43   *Hoosac Valley News*, vol. 7, no. 36 (17 September 1874).

44   "Killed at the Hoosac Tunnel," *Adams Transcript*, vol. 34, no. 37 (6 August 1874).

45   *Hoosac Valley News*, vol. 7, no. 30 (6 August 1874).

46   *Hoosac Valley News*, vol. 7, no. 46 (26 November 1874).

47   "Death of Francis W. Bird, Jr.," *Adams Transcript*, vol. 34, no. 35 (23 July 1874).

48   "Chapter 403," *Acts and Resolves passed by the General Court of Massachusetts in the year 1874* (Boston: Wright & Potter, 1874), pp. 460–62.

49   George Lowell Austin, *The History of Massachusetts from the Landing of the Pilgrims to the Present Time* (Boston: Estes & Lauriat, 1876), 554.

50   *Williams College Inauguration of Pres. P. A. Chadbourne* (Williamstown, MA: 1872).

51   "The Hoosac Tunnel Commission," *New York Times* (7 September 1874), 2.

52   Alfred Noon, *The History of Ludlow Massachusetts*, 2nd ed. (Springfield, MA: Springfield Printing and Binding Company, 1912), 314.

53   *House No. 9, Boston, Hoosac Tunnel and Western Railroad Company, Report of the Corporators* (Boston: Wright & Potter, 1875), p. 3.

54   Ibid., pp. 3–4.

55   F. W. D. Holbrook, "Memoirs of Deceased Members, Thomas Doane," in *Proceedings of the American Society of Civil Engineers* 24, no. 4 (April 1898): 304.

56   "Chapter 403, Section 5," *Acts and Resolves passed by the General Court of Massachusetts in the year 1874*, p. 462.

57   Frank Dawson Adams, *Biographical Memoir of Thomas Sterry Hunt, 1826–1892*, vol. 15 (Washington, DC: National Academy of Sciences, 1932).

58   "Dr. James Hall Is Dead," *New York Times* (9 August 1894).

59 "Letter from Josiah Brown, 23 December 1867," *Senate No. 20, Report of the Hon. Alvah Crocker, commissioner, acting as Superintendent, of work upon the Troy & Greenfield Railroad and Hoosac Tunnel* (Boston: Wright & Potter, 1868), p. 70.

60 Henry M. Burt, ed., *Memorial Tributes to Daniel L. Harris with Biography and Extracts from his Journal and Letters* (Springfield, MA: Henry M. Burt, Printer, 1880), 194.

61 "The Hoosac Tunnel Nearly Done With," *Hoosac Valley News* (17 September 1874).

62 Ibid.

63 *Adams Transcript*, vol. 34, no. 48 (22 October 1874).

64 "Appendix A: Report of Experts, Report of T. Sterry Hunt, 12 October 1874," *House No. 9, Boston, Hoosac Tunnel and Western Railroad Company, Report of the Corporators* (Boston: Wright & Potter, 1875), pp. xxv–xxxvi.

65 "Appendix A: Report of Experts, Report of James Hall, 10 October 1874," *House No. 9, Boston, Hoosac Tunnel and Western Railroad Company, Report of the Corporators*, pp. iii–xxi.

66 "Appendix A: Report of Experts, Report of Josiah Brown, 13 October 1874," *House No. 9, Boston, Hoosac Tunnel and Western Railroad Company, Report of the Corporators*, pp. xxxv–xxxvi.

67 "Appendix A: Report of Experts, Report of D. L. Harris, 16 October 1874," *House No. 9, Boston, Hoosac Tunnel and Western Railroad Company, Report of the Corporators*, pp. xxxvii–xxxviii.

68 "Appendix A: Report of Experts, Report of Thomas Doane, 13 October 1874," *House No. 9, Boston, Hoosac Tunnel and Western Railroad Company, Report of the Corporators*, pp. xxxix–lviii.

69 "Appendix A: Report of Experts, Report of James Hall," p. ix.

70 "Appendix A: Report of Experts, Report of Thomas Doane," p. xxxiv.

71 "Appendix A: Report of Experts, Report of Edward S. Philbrick, 31 July 1874," *House No. 9, Boston, Hoosac Tunnel and Western Railroad Company Report of the Corporators*, pp. lix–lxiv.

72 *Senate No. 50, First Annual Report of the Manager of the Troy & Greenfield Railroad and Hoosac Tunnel* (Boston: Wright & Potter, 1876), p. 6.

73 *Hoosac Valley News*, vol. 7, no. 37 (24 September 1875).

74 Myron A. Munson, *The Munson Record: A Genealogical and Biographical Account of Captain Thomas Munson and His Descendants*, vol. 2 (New Haven, CT: Munson Association, 1895), 916.

75 Ibid., 932.

76 William A. Newman and Wilfred E. Holton, *Boston's Back Bay: The Story of America's Greatest Nineteenth-Century Landfill Project* (Boston: Northeastern University Press, 2006), 131.

77 *Adams Transcript*, vol. 34, no. 45 (1 October 1874).

78 Thomas Doane and Charles Harris, "Samuel Morse Felton: A Memoir," *Journal of the Association of Engineering Societies* 11, no. 4 (April 1892): 214, 215.

79 *Senate No. 50, First Annual Report of the Manager of the Troy & Greenfield Railroad and Hoosac Tunnel*, p. 6.

80 Ibid., p. 5.

81 "Hoosac Tunnel," *Adams Transcript*, vol. 34, no. 52 (19 November 1874).

82 *Adams Transcript*, vol. 35, no. 3 (10 December 1874).

83 *Hoosac Valley News*, vol. 7, no. 48 (10 December 1874).

84 "The Hoosac Tunnel," *New York Times* (26 December 1874), 3.

85 "The Hoosac Tunnel Contractors," *Hoosac Valley News*, vol. 7, no. 51 (31 December 1874).

86 *Senate No. 50, First Annual Report of the Manager of the Troy & Greenfield Railroad and Hoosac Tunnel*, p. 8.

87 *Adams Transcript*, vol. 35, no. 13 (18 February 1875).

88 "The Tunnel Not to Be Opened for Trains until Next Summer," *Hoosac Valley News*, vol. 7, no. 49 (17 December 1874).

89 "Hoosac Tunnel," *Adams Transcript*, vol. 35, no. 10 (28 January 1875).

90 "Appendix C: Report of Thomas Doane, 23 December 1874," *House No. 9, Boston, Hoosac Tunnel and Western Railroad Company, Report of the Corporators*, p. cx.

91 "Hoosac Tunnel," *Adams Transcript* (28 January 1875).

92 *House No. 9, Boston, Hoosac Tunnel and Western Railroad Company, Report of the Corporators*, p. 8.

93 J. L. Harrison, *The Great Bore: A Souvenir of the Hoosac Tunnel* (North Adams, MA: Advance Job Print Works, 1891), 19.

94 "First Train through Hoosac Tunnel," *Fitchburg Sentinel* (10 February 1875).

95 "First Train through the Hoosac Tunnel," *New York Observer and Chronicle* (18 February 1875), 54.

96 "The Hoosac Tunnel," *Los Angeles Herald*, vol. 3, no. 115 (11 February 1875), 2.

97   "The Tunnel by the Head-Light of an Engine," *Adams Transcript*, vol. 35, no. 18 (25 March 1875).

98   Ibid.

99   *Adams Transcript*, vol. 35, no. 15 (4 March 1875).

100   *Adams Transcript*, vol. 35, no. 13 (18 February 1875).

101   "Hoosac Tunnel," *Adams Transcript*, vol. 35, no. 14 (25 February 1875).

102   *Adams Transcript* (25 February 1875).

103   *Adams Transcript*, vol. 35, no. 20 (8 April 1875).

104   *Adams Transcript*, vol. 35, no. 17 (18 March 1875).

105   *Senate No. 50, First Annual Report of the Manager of the Troy & Greenfield Railroad and Hoosac Tunnel*, p. 22.

106   "The Hoosac Tunnel," *Scientific American* 35, no. 7, new series (1876): 102.

107   *Adams Transcript*, vol. 35, no. 19 (1 April 1875).

108   "The First Freight Train Through the Hoosac Tunnel," *Adams Transcript*, vol. 35, no. 20 (8 April 1875).

109   "The Hoosac Tunnel Route Open," *American Railroad Journal* 21, no. 16, second quarto series (17 April 1875): 508.

110   *Senate No. 50, First Annual Report of the Manager of the Troy & Greenfield Railroad and Hoosac Tunnel*, p. 7.

111   Ibid., p. 10.

112   "The Hoosac Tunnel Route Open," *American Railroad Journal* (17 April 1875): 508.

113   *Senate No. 50, First Annual Report of the Manager of the Troy & Greenfield Railroad and Hoosac Tunnel*, p. 17.

114   Ibid., p. 21.

115   "Personals," *Adams Transcript*, vol. 35, no. 22 (22 April 1875).

116   W. F. Spear, "Chapter 8, Public Houses," in *History of North Adams, Mass., 1749–1885* (North Adams, MA: Hoosac Valley News Printing House, 1885), 60–61.

117   *Senate No. 282, Shanly Petition* (Boston: Wright & Potter, April 1884).

118   Walter Shanly, *The Canadian Shanlys: Whence they came and how they got to Thorndale*, 1896, PA057, Canadian Railroad Historical Association Archives and Document Center, Saint Constant, Quebec, Canada.

119   *Senate No. 150, The Shanly Petition* (Boston: Wright & Potter, April 1875).

120   *Senate No. 50, First Annual Report of the Manager of the Troy & Greenfield Railroad and Hoosac Tunnel*, p. 11.

121   *Adams Transcript*, vol. 35, no. 23 (29 April 1875).

122 *American Railroad Journal* 31, no. 22, second quarto series (29 May 1875): 699.

123 Francis B. C. Bradlee, "The Eastern Railroad," *Historical Collections of the Essex Institute* 53, no. 1 (January 1917): 6.

124 Charles W. Felt, *The Eastern Railroad of Massachusetts: Its Blunders, Mismanagement & Corruption* (Liverpool, UK: Miss J. Green, 1873), 6–7.

125 Bradlee, "The Eastern Railroad," *Historical Collections of the Essex Institute*, 21.

126 Ibid., 22.

127 *American Railroad Journal* (29 May 1875): 701.

128 *Adams Transcript*, vol. 35, no. 28 (3 June 1875).

129 *Adams Transcript*, vol. 35, no. 30 (17 June 1875).

130 *Adams Transcript*, vol. 35, no. 31 (24 June 1875).

131 *Adams Transcript*, vol. 35, no. 33 (8 July 1875).

132 *Adams Transcript*, vol. 35, no. 36 (29 July 1875).

133 *American Railroad Journal* 31, no. 37, second quarto series (11 September 1875): 1157.

134 *Adams Transcript* 35, no. 48 (21 October 1875).

135 "Personals," *Adams Transcript*, vol. 35, no. 49 (28 October 1875).

136 "Hoosac Tunnel Line," *American Railroad Journal* 31, no. 47, second quarto series (20 November 1875): 1476.

137 *Adams Transcript*, vol. 35, no. 44 (23 September 1875).

138 "The Governor's Council and the Hoosac Tunnel," *Adams Transcript*, vol. 36, no. 9 (20 January 1876).

139 *Adams Transcript*, vol. 36, no. 12 (10 February 1876).

140 *Adams Transcript*, vol. 36, no. 13 (17 February 1876).

141 *Adams Transcript*, vol. 36, no. 10 (27 January 1876).

142 "A Present to Walter Shanly," *Adams Transcript*, vol. 36, no. 18 (23 March 1876).

143 "Troy and Greenfield," *Adams Transcript*, vol. 36, no. 23 (27 April 1876).

144 *Cambridge Tribune*, vol. 17, no. 26 (1 September 1894), 7.

Epilogue

1 Frank Walker, *Daylight Through the Mountain* (Montreal: The Engineering Institute of Canada, 1957), 403.

2   Richard Wallace White, *The Civil Engineering Careers of Frank and Walter Shanly, c.1840–c.1890* (PhD dissertation, University of Toronto, 1995), 243–44.

3   Ibid., 260.

4   Walter to Bellen, 22 October 1882, Walter Shanly Correspondence, Shanly Papers, Archives of Ontario, Toronto, MU2725.

5   *Account of Walter Shanly and Frank Shanly on the Hoosac Tunnel contract*, June 1875, Hoosac Tunnel Miscellaneous, Shanly Papers, Archives of Ontario, MU2678.

6   Walter Shanly to Francis Shanly, 23 and 25 December 1868, Hoosac Tunnel Correspondence [Galt's offer to the Shanlys], Shanly Papers, Archives of Ontario, MU2678.

7   Ibid.

8   White, *The Civil Engineering Careers of Frank and Walter Shanly*, 417.

9   Ibid., 324.

10 Walker, *Daylight Through the Mountain*, 408–409.

11 *Senate No. 282, Shanly Petition, by the Committee on Claims* (Boston: Wright & Potter, April 1884), p. 7.

12 "Resolve in favor of Walter Shanly," *Chapter 105, Acts and Resolves passed by the General Court of Massachusetts in the year 1887* (Boston: Wright & Potter, 1887), p. 1173.

13 Thomas Doane and Charles Harris, "Samuel Morse Felton," *Journal of the Association of Engineering Societies* 11, no. 4 (April 1892): 203.

14 Desmond FitzGerald, C. Frank Allen, and Chas. A. Pearson, "Thomas Doane—A Memoir," *Journal of the Association of Engineering Societies* 24, no. 1 (January 1900): 73–80.

15 John Lauritz Larson, "Chicago, Burlington & Quincy Railroad," in *Encyclopedia of American Business History and Biography: Railroads in the Nineteenth Century*, ed. Robert L. Frey (New York: Facts on File, 1988), 48.

16 "'Big Dig' Change-Order Battle Set to end after 15 Years," *ENR engineering News-Record*, (16/22 December 2014), p. 14.

Bibliography

Books

Adams, Frank Dawson. *Biographical Memoir of Thomas Sterry Hunt, 1826–1892*, vol. 15 (Washington, DC: National Academy of Sciences, 1932).

Adams, George. *Geometrical and Graphical Essays Containing a General Description of the Mathematical Instruments used in Geometry, Civil and Military Surveying* (London, 1791).

Adams, George. *The Massachusetts Register for the Year 1853* (Boston: Damrell and Moore, 1853).

Agricola, Georgius. *De Re Metallica*, Book V (1556).

Aiken, John Adams. *History and Proceedings of the Pocumtuck Valley Memorial Association 1905–1911*, vol. 5 (Deerfield, MA: Pocumtuck Valley Memorial Association, 1912).

Alcott, Louisa May. *Hospital Sketches* (Boston: J. Redpath, Boston, 1863).

Alexander, Edwin P. *Iron Horses: American Locomotives, 1829–1900* (New York: W. W. Norton, 1941).

Ambrose, Stephen E. *Duty, Honor, Country: A History of West Point* (Baltimore: John Hopkins University Press, 1966).

American National Biography, vol. 5 & 13 (New York: Oxford University Press, under the auspices of the American Council of Learned Societies, 1999).

Appleton, William and W. H. Swift. *Massachusetts Railroads 1842 to 1855* (Boston: J. H. Eastburn's Press, 1856).

Appleton's Cyclopaedia of American Biography, vol. 5 (New York: D. Appleton and Company, 1888).

Austin, George Lowell. *The History of Massachusetts from the Landing of the Pilgrims to the Present Time* (Boston: Estes & Lauriat, 1876).

Baldwin, L. *Letters of the Union Canal of Pennsylvania*, first published in the *Boston Daily Advertiser* (44 pages, n.d.).

Bancroft, George. *History of the United States, from the Discovery of the American Continent*, vol. 3 (Boston: Little, Brown, 1843).

Bates, Samuel P. *Our County and Its People: A Historical and Memorial Record of Crawford County, Pennsylvania* (Alfred, NY: W. A. Fergusson & Company, 1899).

Benson, Barbara E. *Benjamin Henry Latrobe & Moncure Robinson: The Engineer as Agent of Technological Transfer* (Wilmington, DE: Eleutherian Mills–Hagley Foundation, 1975).

Benson, George F. *Historical Record of the Edwardsburg and Canada Starch Companies* (Montreal: Canada Starch Co., 1958).

The Berkshire Hills, American Guide Series, Federal Writers Project of the Works Progress Administration for Massachusetts (New York: Funk & Wagnalls, 1939).

Bianculli, Anthony J. *Trains and Technology: The American Railroad in the Nineteenth Century, vol. 1: Locomotives* (Newark: University of Delaware Press, 2001).

Bianculli, Anthony J. *Trains and Technology: The American Railroad in the Nineteenth Century, vol. 4: Bridges and Tunnels, Signals* (Newark: University of Delaware Press, 2003).

Biographical Encyclopaedia of Massachusetts of the Nineteenth Century, vol. 2 (Boston: Metropolitan Publishing and Engraving Company, 1883).

Boatner, Mark M. III. *Encyclopedia of the American Revolution* (New York: David McKay Co., 1966).

Bradlee, Francis B. C. "The Eastern Railroad," *Historical Collections of the Essex Institute* 53, no. 1 (January 1917).

Bradlee, Francis B. C. *Eastern Railroad*, 2nd ed. (Salem, MA: Essex Institute, 1922).

Brigham, Wilbur F. *Brigham's Early Hudson History*, comp. and ed. Katherine Johnson and Lewis Halprin (Hudson, MA: Hudson Historical Society and Museum, 2010).

Brown, Abram English. *Beneath Old Roof Trees* (Boston: Lee and Shepard, 1896).

Brown, Percy Whiting. *History of Rowe Massachusetts* (Boston: Old Colony Press, 1921, privately printed).

Browne, William B. *The Mohawk Trail: Its History and Course* (Pittsfield, MA: Sun Printing Co., 1920).

Brayley, Arthur W. *History of the Granite Industry of New England* (Boston: The National Association of Granite Industries of the United States, 1913).

Bruce, Alfred W. *The Steam Locomotive in America: Its Development in the Twentieth Century* (New York: W. W. Norton, 1952).

Brunton, David W. and John A. Davis. *Modern Tunneling*, 2nd ed. (New York: John Wiley, 1922).

Burgess, George H. and Miles C. Kennedy. *Centennial History of the Pennsylvania Railroad Company* (Pennsylvania Railroad Co., 1949).

Burn, Robert Scott. *The Steam-Engine: Its History and Mechanism* (London: H. Ingram and Co., 1854).

Burt, Henry M. *Memorial Tributes to Daniel L. Harris with Biography and Extracts from his Journal and Letters* (Springfield, MA: privately printed, Henry M. Burt, Printer, 1880).

Byron, Carl R. *A Pinprick of Light: The Troy and Greenfield Railroad and Its Hoosac Tunnel* (Shelburne, VT: New England Press, 1995).

Calhoun, Daniel Hovey. *The American Civil Engineer: Origins and Conflict* (Cambridge, MA: Technology Press, MIT, 1960).

Callahan, James Morton. *Semi-Centennial History of West Virginia* (Charleston, WV: Semi-Centennial Commission of West Virginia, 1913).

Carpenter, Edward Wilton and Charles Frederick Morehouse. *The History of the Town of Amherst, Massachusetts* (Amherst, MA: Carpenter & Morehouse, 1896).

Catalogue of the Officers and Alumni of Rutgers College (Trenton, NJ: State Gazette Publishing Co., 1916).

Chase, Charles C. *History of Middlesex County, Massachusetts*, vol. 2. (Boston: Estes and Lauriat, 1880).

Clark, Christopher. *Iron Kingdom—The Rise and Downfall of Prussia, 1600–1947* (Cambridge, MA: Harvard University Press, 2006).

Clarke, Mary Stetson. *The Old Middlesex Canal* (Easton, PA: Center for Canal History and Technology, 1974).

Coburn, Frank Warren. *The Battle of April 19, 1775*, 2nd ed. (Lexington, MA: Lexington Historical Society, 1922).

Cochran, Thomas C. *Railroad Leaders, 1845–1890: The Business Mind in Action* (New York: Russell & Russell, 1965).

Coe, Michael D. *The Line of Forts* (Lebanon, NH: University Press of New England, 2006).

Coleman, Emma Lewis. *New England Captives Carried to Canada between 1677 and 1760 During the French and Indian Wars*, vol. 1 and 2 (Portland, ME: Southworth Press, 1925).

Crane, Ellery Bicknell. *Historic Homes and Institutions and Genealogical and Personal Memoirs of Worcester County, Massachusetts, with a History of Worcester Society of Antiquity* (New York/Chicago: Lewis Publishing, 1907).

Crocker, A. *Diary*, cover embossed with "A. Crocker, Fitchburg": copy held by Fitchburg Historical Society.

Crocker, C. T. *A Biography of Alvah Crocker I—by his son* (not published, no date; copy in the Fitchburg Historical Society).

Crocker, George Glover. *From the Stage Coach to the Railroad Train and the Street Car* (Boston: W. B. Clarke, 1900).

Cullum, George W. *Biographical Sketch of Captain William H. Swift of the Topographical Engineers, United States Army, 1832–1849* (New York: A. G. Sherwood & Co., 1880).

Cumming, Mary G. *Georgia Railroad & Banking Company* (Augusta, GA: Walton Printing Co., 1945).

Currie, Archibald. *The Grand Trunk Railway of Canada* (Toronto: University of Toronto Press, 1957).

Cutter, William Richard. *Genealogical and Personal Memoirs*, vol. 1 (New York: Lewis Historical Publishing Company, 1910).

Cutter, William R. and Edward F. Johnson. *Transcript of Epitaphs in Woburn First and Second Burial-Grounds* (Woburn, MA: Andrews, Cutler & Co., 1890).

Cutter, William Richard and William Frederick Adams. *Genealogical and Personal Memoirs Relating to the Families of the State of Massachusetts* (New York: Lewis Historical Publishing Company, 1910).

Davis, Joseph Stancliffe. *Essays in the Earlier History of American Corporations*, no. 4 (Cambridge, MA: Harvard University Press, 1917).

Derby, E. H. *Two Months Abroad* (Boston: Redding & Co., 1844).

Dictionary of American Biography (New York: Charles Scribner's Sons, under the auspices of the American Council of Learned Societies, 1930).

Dilts, James D. *The Great Road: The Building of the Baltimore & Ohio, The Nation's First Railroad, 1828–1853* (Stanford, CA: Stanford University Press, 1993).

Doane, Alfred Alder. *The Doane Family: I. Deacon John Doane, of Plymouth, II. Doctor John Done, of Maryland, and Their Descendants*, 4th ed. (Long Island City, NY: Apollo Books, 1984).

Drinker, Henry S. *Tunneling, Explosive Compounds, and Rock Drills* (New York: John Wiley, 1878).

Drinker, Henry S. *A Treatise on Explosive Compounds, Machine Rock Drills and Blasting* (New York: John Wiley, 1883).

Dwight, Benjamin W. *The History of the Descendants of Elder John Strong, of Northampton, Mass.*, vol. 1 (Albany, NY: Joel Munsell, 1871).

Dwight, Timothy. *Travels in New England and New York*, vol. 1, 3, and 4 (New Haven, CT: S. Converse, Printer, 1822).

Dunn, Shirley W. *The Mohicans and Their Land 1609–1730* (Fleischmanns, NY: Purple Mountain Press, 1994).

Eddy, Caleb. *Historical Sketch of the Middlesex Canal* (Boston: Samuel N. Dickinson Printer, 1843).

Ellis, George. Edward *Memoir of Sir Benjamin Thompson, Count Rumford, with notices of his daughter* (Boston: Estes and Lauriat, 1871).

Emerson, Ralph Waldo. *Journals of Ralph Waldo Emerson with Annotations*, vol. 10 (Boston: Houghton Mifflin, 1914).

Emerson, William A. *Fitchburg, Massachusetts, Past and Present* (Fitchburg, MA: Blanchard & Brown, 1887).

Farnham, Elmer F. *The Quickest Route: The History of the Norwich & Worcester Railroad* (Chester, CT: Pequot Press, 1973).

Felt, Charles W. *The Eastern Railroad of Massachusetts: Its Blunders, Mismanagement & Corruption* (Liverpool, UK: Miss J. Green, 1873).

Fischer, David Hackett. *Champlain's Dream* (New York: Simon & Schuster, 2008).

Foote, Shelby. *The Civil War: A Narrative. Vol. 3: Red River to Appomattox* (New York: Random House, 1974).

Forbes, Abner and J. W. Greene. *The Rich Men of Massachusetts* (Boston: Fetridge and Company, 1851).

Forbes, J. M. *Reminiscences of John Murray Forbes*, vol. 1 (Boston: George H. Ellis, 1902).

Force, Peter. *American Archives*, fourth series, vol. 2 (Washington, DC, 1839).

Frothingham, Richard Jr. *History of the Siege of Boston, and of the Battles of Lexington, Concord, and Bunker Hill*, 2d ed. (Boston: C. C. Little and J. Brown, 1851).

Fulton, Robert. *A Treatise on the Improvement of Canal Navigation* (London: I. and J. Taylor at the Architectural Library, 1796).

Galvin, John R. *The Minute Men, The First Fight: Myths and Realities of The American Revolution* (New York: Pergamon–Brassey's International Defense Publishers, 1989).

Gladden, Washington. *From Hub to the Hudson with Sketches of Nature, History and Industry in North-Western Massachusetts* (Boston: The New England News Company, 1869).

Green, Mason Arnold. *Springfield 1636–1886: History of Town and City* (Springfield, MA: C. A. Nichols & Co., 1888).

Guthorn, Peter J. *British Maps of the American Revolution* (Monmouth Beach, NJ: Philip Freneau Press, 1972).

Haney, Lewis Henry. *A Congressional History of Railways in the United States to 1850*, Bulletin of the University of Wisconsin, no. 211, Economics and Political Science Series, vol. 3, no. 2 (1906).

Harlow, Alvin F. *Steelways of New England* (New York: Creative Age Press, 1946).

Harlow, Alvin F. *The Road of the Century: The Story of the New York Central* (New York: Creative Age Press, 1947).

Harrington, Fred Harvey. *Fighting Politician Major General N. P. Banks* (Philadelphia: University of Pennsylvania Press, 1948).

Harrison ed., Eliza Cope. *Philadelphia Merchant: The Diary of Thomas P. Cope, 1800–1851* (South Bend, IN: Gateway Editions, 1978).

Harrison, J. L. *The Great Bore: A Souvenir of the Hoosac Tunnel* (North Adams, MA: Advance Job Print Works, 1891).

Haupt, Herman. *General Theory of Bridge Construction* (Philadelphia: D. Appleton & Company, 1851).

Haupt, H. *Hoosac Tunnel Insufficiency of Air* (Boston: Wright & Potter, 25 April 1866).

Haupt, Herman. *Tunneling by Machinery: Description of Perforators and Plans of Operations in Mining and Tunneling* (Philadelphia: H. G. Leisenring's Steam Printing House, 1867).

Haupt, Herman. *Reminiscences of General Herman Haupt* (Milwaukee: Wright & Joys Co., 1901).

Haupt, Herman. *Reminiscences of Early History of the Pennsylvania Railroad Company* [n.d.], typed manuscript, National Museum of American History, Smithsonian Institution, Haupt file.

Haupt, William Henry. *Haupt Family in America* (Chariton, IA: self-published, 1924).

Hawthorne, Nathaniel. *Passages from the American Note-Books* (Boston: James R. Osgood and Company, 1873).

Hefelbower, Samuel Gring. *The History of Gettysburg College, 1832–1932* (Gettysburg, PA: Gettysburg College, 1932).

Herndon, Richard. *Boston of To-Day* (Boston: Post Publishing Company, 1892).

Hidy, Ralph W. *The House of Baring in American Trade and Finance: English Merchant Bankers at Work, 1763–1861* (Cambridge, MA: Harvard University Press, 1949).

Hill, Forest G. *Roads, Rails, and Waterways: The Army Engineers and Early Transportation* (Norman: University of Oklahoma Press, 1957).

History of Butler County, Pennsylvania (Chicago: Waterman, Watkins & Co., 1883).

History of the Connecticut Valley in Massachusetts, vol. 2 (Philadelphia: Louis H. Everts, 1879).

History of Leominster, MA: Jonas Kendall [4-2005], from Leominster Historical Society, author unknown, Transcribed by C. J. Bagley.

Holland, Josiah Gilbert. *History of Western Massachusetts: The Counties of Hampden, Hampshire, Franklin, and Berkshire*, (Springfield, MA: Samuel Bowles and Company, 1855).

Holmes, Oliver Wendell. *The Complete Poetical Works of Oliver Wendell Holmes* (Boston: Houghton Mifflin Company, 1908).

Homans, Benjamin. *The United States Railroad Directory for 1856* (New York: B. Homans, 1856).

Hopkins, J. G. *The Northern Railroad in New York with Remarks on The Western Trade* (Boston: S. N. Dickinson & Co., 1847).

Hunter, Dard. *Papermaking: The History and Technique of an Ancient Craft*, 2nd ed. (New York: Alfred A. Knopf, 1947).

Hurd, D. Hamilton. *History of Worcester County, Massachusetts, with Biographical Sketches of many of its Pioneers and Prominent Men*, vol. 1 (Philadelphia: J. W. Lewis & Co., 1889).

Innovate Boston! Shaping the Future from Our Past: Four Amazing Centuries of Innovation (Boston: Boston History & Innovation Collaborative, 2006).

Jarvie, Jean. *Stories from Our Hills* (Adams, MA: Lamb Printing Co., 1926).

Jean-Francois, Père. *La Science des Eaux* (Rennes, 1653).

Johnson, Arthur M. and Barry E. Supple. *Boston Capitalists and Western Railroads: A Study in the Nineteenth-Century Investment Process*, Harvard Studies in Business History 23 (Cambridge, MA: Harvard University Press, 1967).

Johnson, Edward F. *Woburn Records of Births, Deaths, and Marriages from 1640 to 1873* (Woburn, MA: 1890).

King's Hand Book of Boston, 7th ed. (Cambridge, MA: Moses King, 1885).

Kirby, Richard Shelton and Philip Gustave Laurson. *The Early Years of Modern Civil Engineering* (New Haven, CT: Yale University Press, 1932).

Kirkland, Edward Chase. *Men, Cities, and Transportation: A Study in New England History, 1820–1900* (Cambridge, MA: Harvard University Press, 1948).

Kirkpatrick, Doris. *The City and the River* (Fitchburg, MA: Fitchburg Historical Society, 1971).

Knight, Sarah. *The Private Journal of a Journey from Boston to New York in the Year 1704* (Albany, NY: Frank H. Little, 1865).

Kraus, George. *High Road to Promontory—Building the Central Pacific (now Southern Pacific) across the High Sierra* (Palo Alto, CA: American West Publishing Company, 1969).

Larson, John Lauritz. *Bonds of Enterprise: John Murray Forbes and Western Development in America's Railway Age* (Boston: Harvard Business School, 1984).

Lesley, Robert W. *History of the Portland Cement Industry in the United States* (Philadelphia: American Cement Company, 1924).

Lewis, Samuel. *A Topographical Dictionary of Ireland, Comprising the Several Counties, Cities, Boroughs, Corporate, Market, and Post Towns, Parishes, and Villages, with Historical and Statistical Descriptions*, vol. 1 (London: S. Lewis & Co., 1837).

Longstreth, Thomas Morris. *Hide-out* (New York: Macmillan, 1947).

MacFarlane, James. *An American Geological Railway Guide* (New York: D. Appleton and Company, 1890).

MacGill, Caroline E. and Balthasar Henry Meyer. *History of Transportation in the United States before 1860* (New York: Reprinted by Peter Smith 1948).

MacGill, Caroline E. and Balthasar Henry Meyer. *History of Transportation in the United States before 1860* (Washington, DC: Carnegie Institution, 1948).

Mann, Charles Riborg. *A Study of Engineering Education*, bulletin no. 11, Carnegie Foundation for the Advancement of Teaching (Boston: The Merrymount Press, 1918).

McGaw, Judith A. *Most Wonderful Machine: Mechanization and Social Change in Berkshire Papermaking, 1801–1885* (Princeton, NJ: Princeton University Press, 1987).

McGivern, James Gregory. *First Hundred Years of Engineering Education in the United States, 1807–1907* (Spokane, WA: Gonzaga University Press, 1960).

The Merrimack River (n.d.), Lowell National Historical Park, National Park Service.

Miller, Kerby A., Arnold Schrier, Bruce D. Boling, and David N. Doyle. *Irish Immigrants in the Land of Canaan* (New York: Oxford University Press, 2003).

Mingay, G. E. *Rural Life in Victorian England* (London: William Heinemann, 1977).

Mowbray, Geo. M. *Tri-Nitro-Glycerin as applied in the Hoosac Tunnel, Submarine Blasting, Etc., Etc., Etc.* (North Adams, MA: James T. Robinson & Son, 1872).

Munson, Myron A. *The Munson Record: A Genealogical and Biographical Account of Captain Thomas Munson and His Descendants*, vol. 2 (New Haven, CT: Munson Association, 1895).

Nason, Elias. *A Gazetteer of the State of Massachusetts, with Numerous Illustrations on Wood and Steel* (Boston: B. B. Russell, 1874).

National Cyclopaedia of American Biography, (New York: James T. White & Co.) vol. 10 (1900).

Neu, Irene D. *Erastus Corning: Merchant and Financier, 1794–1872* (Ithaca, NY: Cornell University Press, 1960).

Newman, William A. and Wilfred E. Holton. *Boston's Back Bay: The Story of America's Greatest Nineteenth-Century Landfill Project* (Boston: Northeastern University Press, 2006).

Niles, Grace Greylock. *The Hoosac Valley: Its Legends and Its History* (New York: G. P. Putnam's Sons, 1912).

Noon, Alfred. *The History of Ludlow Massachusetts*, 2nd ed. (Springfield, MA: Springfield Printing and Binding Company, 1912).

Overton, Richard C. *Burlington Route: A History of the Burlington Lines* (New York: Alfred A. Knopf, 1965).

Parkman, Francis. *Pioneers of France in the New World* (Boston: Little, Brown, 1897).

Parsons, Herbert Collins. *A Puritan Outpost: A History of the Town and People of Northfield, Massachusetts* (New York: Macmillan, 1937).

Pearson, Henry Greenleaf. *An American Railroad Builder: John Murray Forbes* (Boston/New York: Houghton Mifflin, 1911).

Pease, William H. and Jane H. Pease. *The Web of Progress: Private Values and Public Styles in Boston and Charleston, 1828–1843* (Athens: University of Georgia Press, 1991).

Pictorial Field-Book of the War of 1812 (New York: Harper and Brothers, 1896).

Pollio, Marcus Vitruvius [ca. 90–20 BC], *De Architectura*.

Pool, William. *Landmarks of Niagara County, New York* (Syracuse, NY: D. Mason & Company, 1897).

Poor, Henry Varnum. *History of the Railroads and Canals of the United States of America*, vol. 1 (New York: J. H. Schultz & Company, 1860).

Porter, Jane Molloy. *Friendly Edifices* (Portsmouth, NH: Peter E. Randall Publisher, 2006).

Powers, Ron. *Mark Twain: A Life* (New York: Simon and Schuster, 2005).

Proceedings of the American Society of Civil Engineers (New York: American Society of Civil Engineers (October 1893).

Putman, William Lowell. *Great Railroad Tunnels of North America* (Jefferson, NC: McFarland & Company, 2011).

The Railroad Jubilee: An Account of the Celebration Commemorative of the Opening of Railroad Communication between Boston and Canada (Boston: J. H. Eastburn, 1852).

Rand, John C. *One Thousand Representative Men Residents in the Commonwealth of Massachusetts A.D. 1888–89* (Boston: First National Publishing Company, 1890).

Reynolds, Terry S. *The Engineer in America: A Historical Anthology from Technology and Culture* (Chicago: University of Chicago Press, 1991).

Ripley, William Z. *Railroads: Finance and Organization* (New York: Longmans, Green, 1920).

Roberts, Christopher. *The Middlesex Canal 1793-1860* (Cambridge, MA: Harvard University Press, 1938).

Rowe, H. G. and C. T. Fairfield. *North Adams and Vicinity Illustrated* (North Adams, MA: The Transcript Publishing Co., 1898).

Runnels, M. T. *History of Sanbornton, New Hampshire. Vol. 2: Genealogies* (Boston: Alfred Mudge & Son, 1881).

Rupp, Israel D. *A Collection of Upwards of Thirty Thousand Names of German, Swiss, Dutch, French and Other Immigrants in Pennsylvania from 1727 to 1776* (Philadelphia: IG. Kohler, 1876).

Rusk, Ralph L. *The Letters of Ralph Waldo Emerson*, vol. 3 (New York: Columbia University Press, 1939).

Ruttenberg, Edward Manning. *History of the Indian Tribes of Hudson's River* (Albany, NY: J. Munsell, 1872).

Salsbury, Stephen. *The State, the Investor, and the Railroad: The Boston & Albany, 1825–1867* (Cambridge, MA: Harvard University Press, 1967).

Sawyer, Timothy T. *Old Charlestown* (Boston: J. H. West Co., 1902).

Scharf, John. Thomas *History of Baltimore City and County, from the Earliest Period to the Present Day* (Philadelphia: Louis H. Everts, 1881).

Schellen, Heinrich. *Magneto-Electric and Dynamo-Electric Machines* (New York: D. Van Nostrand, 1884).

Schück, Henrik and Ragnar Sohlman. *The Life of Alfred Nobel*, trans. Brian and Beatrix Lunn (London: Heinemann, 1929).

Seaver, Frederick J. *Historical Sketches of Franklin County and several Towns, with many Short Biographies* (Albany, NY: J. B. Lyon Company, 1918).

Semmes, John E. *John H. B. Latrobe and His Times, 1803–1891* (Baltimore: Norman, Remington & Co., 1917).

Sewall, Samuel. *The History of Woburn, Middlesex County, Mass., from the Grant of Its Territory to Charlestown, in 1640, to the Year 1860* (Boston: Wiggin and Lunt Publishers, 1868).

Shanly, Walter. *Report on the Port Huron & Lake Michigan ("Michigan Northern") Railway* (Toronto: Brewer, McPhail and Co., 1854).

Shaw, Charles. *Topographical and Historical Description of Boston* (Boston: Oliver Spear, 1817).

Shaw, Charles Aeneas. *Tales of a Pioneer Surveyor* (Longman Canada, 1970).

Shurtleff, Nathaniel B. *A Topographical and Historical Description of Boston* (Boston: Printed by Request of the City Council, 1871).

Shute, James M. *Rejected Papers in Relation to the Hoosac Tunnel* (Boston: Wright & Potter, 1868).

Smeaton, John. *A Narrative of the Building and a Description of the Construction of the Edystone [sic] Lighthouse* (London: Printed for the Author, 1791).

Smith, J. E. A. *The History of Pittsfield (Berkshire County), Massachusetts, from the Year 1800 to the Year 1876* (Springfield, MA: C. W. Bryan & Co., 1876).

Spear, W. F. *History of North Adams, Mass. 1749–1885* (North Adams, MA: Hoosac Valley News Printing House, 1885).

Stauffer, David McNeely. *Modern Tunnel Practice* (New York: Engineering News Publishing Co., 1906).

Stevens, Frank Walker. *The Beginnings of the New York Central Railroad: A History* (New York: G. P. Putnam, 1926).

Stone, Irving. *Those Who Love* (New York: Doubleday, 1965).

Storrow, Charles S. *Treatise on Water-Works for Conveying and Distributing Supplies of Water* (Boston: Hilliard, Gray, and Co., 1835).

Stratton, Julius A. and Loretta H. Mannix. *Mind and Hand: The Birth of MIT* (Cambridge, MA: MIT Press, 2005).

Struik, Dirk J. *Yankee Science in the Making* (Boston: Little, Brown, 1948).

Stuart, Charles B. *Lives and Works of Civil and Military Engineers of America* (New York: D. Van Nostrand, 1871).

Thompson, Francis M. *History of Greenfield Shire Town of Franklin County Massachusetts*, vol. 2 (Greenfield, MA: T. Morey & Son, 1904).

Thompson, L. *History of Middlesex County, Massachusetts, with Biographical Sketches of Many of Its Pioneers and Prominent Men*, vol. 1, comp. D. Hamilton Hurd (Philadelphia: J. W. Lewis &Co., 1890).

Thoreau, Henry D. *A Week on the Concord and Merrimack Rivers* (Princeton, NJ, 1904).

Thoreau, Henry David. *Walden or Life in the Woods* (New York: Vantage Books, 1991).

Timbs, John. *The Year-Book of Facts in Science and Art: Exhibiting the Most Important Discoveries & Improvements of the Past Year* (London: Lockwood & Co., 1854).

Torrey, Rufus C. *History of the Town of Fitchburg, Massachusetts* (Fitchburg, MA: J. Garfield Printer, 1836).

Trigger, Bruce G. *Handbook of North American Indians*, vol. 15 (Washington, DC: Smithsonian Institution Press, 1978).

Trumbull, James Russell. *History of Northampton Massachusetts from its Settlement in 1654*. vol. 1 (Northampton, MA: Press of Gazette Printing Co., 1898).

Twentieth Century Biographical Dictionary of Notable Americans, vol. 9 (Boston: The Biographical Society, 1904).

Vose, George L. *Manual for Railroad Engineers and Engineering Students, 1ˢᵗ ed.* (Boston: Lee and Shepard, 1878).

Vose, George L. *Manual for Railroad Engineers and Engineering Students, 2nd ed.* (Boston: Lee and Shepard, 1883).

Vose, George L. *A Sketch of the Life and Works of Loammi Baldwin, Civil Engineer* (Boston: Press of Geo. H. Ellis, 1885).

Voyages of Samuel de Champlain, ed. Edmund F. Slafter (Boston: Prince Society, 1878).

Walker, Frank. *Daylight Through the Mountain* (Montreal: The Engineering Institute of Canada, 1957).

Ward, James A. *That Man Haupt: A Biography of Herman Haupt* (Baton Rouge: Louisiana State University Press, 1973).

Ward, James. A. *J. Edgar Thomson: Master of the Pennsylvania* (Westport, CT: Greenwood Press, 1980).

Wheelwright, William Bond. *Life and Times of Alvah Crocker* (Boston: privately printed, 1923).

Wheelwright, William Bond and Sumner Kean. *The Lengthened Shadow of One Man* (Fitchburg, MA: Crocker, Burbank and Company, 1957).

Wheildon, William W. *Memoir of Solomon Willard: Architect and Superintendent of the Bunker Hill Monument* (Boston: Bunker Hill Monument Association, 1865).

Whitford, Noble E. *Supplement to the Annual Report of the State Engineer and Surveyor of the State of New York* (Albany, NY: Brandow Printing Company, 1906).

Whymper, Edward. *Scrambles Amongst the Alps in the Years 1860–69*, 2nd ed. (London: John Murray, 1871).

Wilder, David. *The History of Leominster, or the Northern Half of the Lancaster New or Additional Grant* (Fitchburg, MA: Reveille Office, 1853).

Williams College Inauguration of Pres. P. A. Chadbourne (Williamstown, MA: 1872).

Williams, John. *The Redeemed Captive, Returning to Zion* (Boston, 1707).

Williams, W. *Appleton's Railroad and Steamboat Companion* (New York: Geo. S. Appleton, 1848).

Winchester, Simon. *Krakatoa: The Day the World Exploded* (New York: Harper, 2005).

Winsor, Justin. *The Memorial History of Boston, including Suffolk County, Massachusetts, 1630–1880*, vol. 4 (Boston: Ticknor and Company, 1881).

Woloch, Nancy. *Women and the American Experience* (New York: McGraw-Hill, 2006).

Wood, Frederic J. *The Turnpikes of New England* (Boston: Marshall Jones Company, 1919).

Dissertations

Abbott, Frederick K. "The Role of the Civil Engineer in Internal Improvements: The Contributions of the Two Loammi Baldwins, Father and Son, 1776–1838" PhD dissertation, Columbia University, 1952.

Coyne, Terrence E. "The Hoosac Tunnel" PhD dissertation, Clark University, Worcester, MA, April 1992.

Ward, James Arthur III. "That Man Haupt: A Biography of Herman Haupt" PhD dissertation, Louisiana State University, 1969.

White, Richard Wallace. "The Civil Engineering Careers of Frank and Walter Shanly, c.1840–c.1890" PhD thesis, University of Toronto, 1995.

Yaggy, Duncan. "John Forbes: Entrepreneur" PhD dissertation, Brandeis University, Waltham, MA, June 1974.

Articles

Allen, Henry Butler. "The Franklin Institute of the State of Pennsylvania," *Transactions of the American Philosophical Society*, new series, vol. 43, no. 1 (1953).

"Annual Report of the President and Managers of the Union Canal Company," *National Gazette* (Philadelphia), vol. IV, no. 1263 (Tuesday, 30 November 1824).

Bedini, Silvio. "History Corner: Samuel Wright Mifflin," *Professional Surveyor* 16, no. 8 (November/December 1996).

"'Big Dig' Change-Order Battle Set to end after 15 Years," *ENR engineering News-Record*, (16/22 December 2014).

"Biographical Sketch of Benjamin H. Latrobe," *Van Nostrand's Eclectic Engineering Magazine* 5, no. 31 (July 1871).

Brierley, Gary S. "Construction of the Hoosac Tunnel 1855 to 1876," *Journal of the Boston Society of Civil Engineers Section, American Society of Civil Engineers* 6, no. 3 (October 1976).

"Bunker Hill Monument," *Christian Register* 4, no. 19 (14 May 1825).

Chandler, Alfred D. Jr. "Patterns of American Railroad Finance, 1830–50," *Business History Review* 28, no. 3 (September 1954).

Cummings, Hubertis M. "James D. Harris and William B. Foster, Jr., Canal Engineers," *Pennsylvania History* 24, no. 3 (July 1957).

Currier, Frederick A. "Stage Coach Days and Stage Coach Ways," *Proceedings of the Fitchburg Historical Society* 1 (1897).

Dame, Lorin L. "The Middlesex Canal," *Bay State Monthly* 2, no. 2 (November 1884).

Dana, William B. "Railroad and Steamboat Statistics," *Merchants' Magazine and Commercial Review* 10 (January–June 1844).

Dante, Harris L. "The Chicago Tribune's 'Lost' Years, 1865–1874," *Journal of the Illinois State Historical Society* 58, no. 2 (Summer 1965).

Davis, Wilbur W. "The History of Boston Disclosed in the Digging of the Commonwealth Avenue Underpass and Other Traffic Tunnels," *Proceedings of the Bostonian Society Annual Meeting* (January 1938).

Doane, Thomas and Charles Harris. "Samuel Morse Felton—A Memoir," *Journal of the Association of Engineering Societies* 11, no. 4 (April 1892).

"Drill," in *The New International Encyclopaedia*, vol. 6 (New York: Dodd Mead & Co., 1903).

Duffy, P. J. "Irish Landholding Structures and Population in the Mid-Nineteenth Century," *The Maynooth Review* 3, no. 2 (December 1977).

Egleston, N. H. "The Story of the Hoosac Tunnel," *Atlantic Monthly* 49, no. 293 (March 1882).

Emerson, Ralph Waldo. "Thoreau Memorial Address," *Atlantic Monthly* 10, no. 58 (August 1862).

Fisher, Chas. E. "Daniel L. Harris," Bulletin no. 32, *Railway & Locomotive Historical Society* (October 1933).

Fisher, Francis D. "Discussion," "Tunnel Surveying of Division No. 6, New Croton Aqueduct," *Transactions of the American Society of Civil Engineers* 23 (July–December 1890).

"Fitchburg Railroad," *American Railroad Journal and Mechanics' Magazine* 16, no. 427 (August 1843)

FitzGerald, Desmond, C. Frank Allen, and Chas. A. Pearson. "Thomas Doane—A Memoir," *Journal of the Association of Engineering Societies* 24, no. 1 (January 1900).

Flint, Timothy ed. "Canals," *Western Monthly Review* 1 (June 1827).

Ford, Peter A. "Charles S. Storrow, Civil Engineer: A Case Study of European Training and Technological Transfer in the Antebellum Period," *Technology and Culture* 34, no. 2 (April 1993).

Ford, Peter A. "'Father of the Whole Enterprise': Charles S. Storrow and the Making of Lawrence, Massachusetts, 1845–1860," *The Massachusetts Historical Review*, vol. 2 (2000).

Freeman, John R. "Mr. Chas. S. Storrow and the Lawrence Scientific School," *Engineering News* 28, no. 36 (September 1, 1892).

Gilmartin, Eleanor. "John Fitch—A Man for Our Times," Fitchburg Historical Society (fall 2008).

Gladden, Washington. "The Hoosac Tunnel," *Scribner's Monthly* 1, no. 2 (December 1870).

Good, H. G. "New Data on Early Engineering Education," *Journal of Educational Research* 29, no. 1 (September 1935).

Goodwin, Daniel R. "Obituary Notice of Samuel Vaughan Merrick, Esq.," *Proceedings of the American Philosophical Society* 11, no. 81 (January 1869).

Goodrich, Carter. "Government Promotion of American Canals and Railroads 1800–1890," *The Mississippi Valley Historical Review* 47, no. 2 (September 1960).

Greensfelder, N. S. "Shot Firing by Electricity," *The Coal Industry* 5, no. 9 (September 1922).

Harrison, J. L. "How the Tunnel-Headings Were Made to Meet," in *The Great Bore* (North Adams, MA: Advance Job Print Works, 1891).

Hoagland, Clayton. "The Diary of Thoreau's 'Gentle Boy,'" *New England Quarterly* 28, no. 4 (December 1955).

Hodge, Robert A. "Gaslight! The Story of the Fredericksburg Gas Company," *Fredericksburg* [VA] *Times* Magazine (August 1977).

Hoffman, Larry C. "The Rock Drill and Civilization," *Invention & Technology* 15, no. 1 (Summer 1999).

Holbrook, F. W. D. "Memoirs of Deceased Members, Thomas Doane," *Proceedings of the American Society of Civil Engineers* 24, no. 4 (April 1898).

Holmes, Lucius. "Hoosac Tunnel—No. 2," *Phrenological Journal and Science of Health* 58, no. 2 (February 1874).

Holmes, Oliver Wendell. "The Professor's Story," *Atlantic Monthly* 5, no. 27 (January 1860).

"The Hoosac Tunnel," in *The Science Record for 1872*, ed. Alfred E. Beach (New York: Munn & Company, 1872).

Howe, E. W. "Mill Dam," *Proceedings of the Boston Society of Civil Engineers* (1881).

"Improved Electric Fuse," *Manufacturer and Builder* 1, no. 4 (April 1869).

Kennedy, Charles J. "The Early Business History of Four Massachusetts Railroads," *Bulletin of the Business Historical Society* 25, no. 1 (March 1951).

Kennedy, Charles J. "The Early Business History of Four Massachusetts Railroads–III," *Bulletin of the Business Historical Society* 25, no. 3 (September 1951).

Kennedy, Charles J. "The Eastern Rail-Road Company to 1855," *Business History Review* 31, no. 1 (Spring 1957).

Kirby, Richard Shelton. "William Weston and His Contribution to Early American Engineering," *Transactions of the Newcomen Society for the Study of the History of Engineering and Technology* 16 (1935–36).

Kirkland, Edward C. "The Hoosac Tunnel Route: The Great Bore," *New England Quarterly* 20, no. 1 (March 1947).

Larson, John Lauritz. "Chicago, Burlington & Quincy Railroad," *Encyclopedia of American Business History and Biography: Railroads in the Nineteenth Century*, ed. Robert L. Frey (New York: Facts on File, 1988).

Larson, John Lauritz. "John Woods Brooks," *Encyclopedia of American Business History and Biography: Railroads in the Nineteenth Century*, ed. Robert L. Frey (New York: Facts on File, 1988).

McKey, Richard H. Jr. "Elias Hasket Derby and the American Revolution," *Essex Institute Historical Collections* 97 (July 1961).

"Mechanics and Useful Arts," in *The Annual of Scientific Discovery: or Year-book of Facts in Science and Art* (Boston: Gould, Kendall, and Lincoln, 1850).

"Miscellanies," *Mining Magazine: Devoted to Mines, Mining Operations, Metallurgy, etc., etc.* 1, no. 5, (November 1853).

"Miscellaneous Spiders and Engineers," *RSA Journal* (published by the Royal Society for the Encouragement of Arts, Manufactures and Commerce, London), vol. 39 (17 July 1891).

Molloy, Peter M. "Nineteenth-Century Hydropower: Design and Construction of Lawrence Dam, 1845–1848," *Winterthur Portfolio* 15, no. 4 (Winter 1980).

Murray, Donald M. "Thoreau's Uncivil Man Rice," *New England Quarterly* 56, no. 1 (March 1983).

Petroski, Henry. "The Civil Engineer," *American Scientist* 90 (March–April 2002).

Perry, A. L. "Fort Shirley," *Bay State Monthly* 3, no. 5 (October 1885).

Pettit, Henry. "Obituary Notices of Members Deceased. Joseph Miller Wilson, A.M., C.E.," *Proceedings of the American Philosophical Society* 42, no. 174 (May–December 1903).

"The Piercing of the American Isthmus," *Manufacturer and Builder* 11, no. 6 (June 1879).

Pope, Franklin Leonard. "The Western Boundary of Massachusetts," in *Four Papers of the Berkshire Historical and Scientific Society* (Pittsfield, MA: Berkshire Historical and Scientific Society, 1886).

"Regular monthly meeting, Fitchburg Historical Society, December 17, 1894," *Proceedings of the Fitchburg Historical Society*, vol. 2 (1897).

"Northern (New York) Railroad Report," *American Railroad Journal*, second quarto series, vol. 4, no. 46, whole no. 657, vol. 21 (11 November 1848).

Roberts, Solomon W. "Obituary Notice of Edward Miller, Civil Engineer," *Proceedings of the American Philosophical Society* 12, no. 86 (1871).

Roberts, Solomon W. "Reminiscences of the First Railroad over the Allegheny Mountain" (read before the Historical Society of Pennsylvania, 8 April 1878), *Pennsylvania Magazine of History and Biography* 2, no. 4 (1878).

Rubin, Julius. "Canal or Railroad? Imitation and Innovation in the Response to the Erie Canal in Philadelphia, Baltimore, and Boston," *Transactions of the American Philosophical Society* 51, no. 7 (1961).

"Shanly, Francis (Frank)," *Dictionary of Canadian Biography Online, 1881–1890*, vol. 11, gen. ed. John English (Toronto/Quebec: University of Toronto/ Université Laval, 2000).

Skempton, A. W. and Joyce Brown. "John and Edward Troughton, Mathematical Instrument Makers," *Notes and Records of the Royal Society of London* 27, no. 2 (February 1973).

Standish, Myles. "Dr. Hasket Derby," *Transactions of the American Ophthalmological Socie*ty, vol. 14, part 1 (Philadelphia: American Ophthalmological Society, 1915).

Stearns, Frank Preston. "Frank W. Bird, and the Bird Club," *Cambridge Sketches* (Philadelphia: J. B. Lippincott Company, 1905).

"Stephen F. Gates," *Annals of the Massachusetts Charitable Mechanic Association, 1795–1892* (Boston: Press of Rockwell and Churchill, 1892).

"The Genesis of the Rail," *Frisco-Man* 10, no. 5 (May 1916): 10 (published by the St. Louis –San Francisco Railway Company, Frisco Building, St. Louis, MO).

"John H. Temple," *Proceedings of the American Academy of Arts and Sciences*, whole series, vol. 13 (1878).

Turneaure, F. E. "The Engineering School and the Engineer," *Journal of the Western Society of Engineers* 22, no. 1 (January 1917).

Vose, George L. "Sketch of the Life of George W. Whistler," *Contributions of the Old Residents' Historical Association* (Lowell, Massachusetts) 3, no. 4 (July 1887).

Ward, James A. "Herman Haupt and the Development of the Pennsylvania Railroad," *Pennsylvania Magazine of History and Biography* 95, no. 1 (January 1971).

Ward, James A. "A New Look at Antebellum Southern Railroad Development," *Journal of Southern History* 39, no. 3 (August 1973).

Ward, James A. "Power and Accountability on the Pennsylvania Railroad," *Business History Review* 49, no. 1 (Spring 1975).

Watkins, J. Elfreth. "The Beginnings of Engineering," *Transactions of the American Society of Civil Engineers* 24, no. 5 (May 1891).

Weingardt, Richard G. "Ellen Henrietta Swallow Richards and Benjamin Wright," *Leadership and Management in Engineering*, ASCE 4, no. 4 (October 2004).

Weston, Byron. "History of Paper Making in Berkshire County, Massachusetts, U.S.A.," *Collections of the Berkshire Historical and Scientific Society* (Pittsfield, MA, 1895).

Whittier, John Greenleaf. "The Grave by the Lake," *Atlantic Monthly* (May 1865).

Willis, Henry A. "The Early Days of Railroads in Fitchburg," *Proceedings of the Fitchburg Historical Society, 1892–1894*, vol. 1 (1895).

Newspapers

Adams News & Transcript (North Adams, MA)
Adams Transcript (North Adams, MA)
American Railroad Journal (New York City, NY)
American Railway Times (Boston, MA)
Barre Gazette (Barre, MA)
Barre Patriot (Barre, MA)
Boston Daily Globe (Boston, MA)
Boston Traveller (Boston, MA).
Bunker Hill Aurora & Boston Mirror (Charlestown, MA)
Cambridge Tribune (Cambridge, MA)
Chicago Daily Tribune (Chicago, IL)
Columbian Centinel (Boston, MA)
Fitchburg Sentinel (Fitchburg, MA)
Frank Leslie's Illustrated Newspaper (New York City, NY)
Gazette & Courier (Greenfield, MA)
Hoosac Valley News (North Adams, MA)
Hoosac Valley News & Transcript (North Adams, MA)
Los Angeles Herald (Los Angeles, CA)
New Hampshire Sentinel (Keene, NH)
New York Observer and Chronicle (New York City, NY)
New York Times (New York City, NY)
Newtown Register (Long Island, NY)
Pittsfield Sun (Pittsfield, MA)
Springfield Republican (Springfield, MA)
Weekly Transcript (North Adams, MA)

Periodicals

American Railroad Journal and Mechanics' Magazine (New York City, NY)
Appletons' Mechanics' Magazine and Engineers' Journal (New York City, NY)
Bay State Monthly: A Massachusetts Magazine (Boston, MA)
Civil Engineer and Architect's Journal (London, England)
Engineering News and American Railway Journal (New York City, NY)
Hampshire Gazette (Northampton, MA)
*Journal of the Franklin Institute of the State of Pennsylvania for the Promotion of the
      Mechanic Arts* (Philadelphia, PA)
Merchants' Magazine and Commercial Review (New York City, NY)
New England Magazine (Boston, MA)
Scientific American (New York City, NY)
Scribner's Monthly (New York City, NY)
Titusville Morning Herald (Titusville, PA)

Pamphlets

Bird, F. W. *The Road to Ruin: or the Decline and Fall of the Hoosac Tunnel*
      (Boston: Wright & Potter, 1862).
Bird, F. W. *The Hoosac Tunnel: Its Condition and Prospects* (Boston: Wright &
      Potter, Printers, 1865).
Bird, F. W. *The Hoosac Tunnel: Our Financial Maelstrom* (Boston: Wright &
      Potter Printers, 1866).
Bird, F. W. *The Last Agony of the Great Bore* (Boston: E. P. Dutton, 1868).
Crocker, Alvah. "Rejoinder to the Reply of a Committee Appointed by the Iron
      Trade in Philadelphia," (Washington, DC: 1844).
Crocker, Alvah. Troy and Greenfield Railroad speech of Hon. Alvah Crocker
      on *The Bill for the More Speedy Completion of the Troy and Greenfield
      Railroad*, in the Senate of Massachusetts, 15 April 1862 (Boston: Wright
      & Potter, 1862).
Haupt, Herman. *1866 Hoosac Tunnel: Facts about Machinery, &c.*, directed to
      President and Directors of Troy and Greenfield Railroad Company, and to
      Commissioners of Hoosac Tunnel (27 March 1866).
*The Memorial of the Western Railroad Corporation relating to the Application of
      the Troy and Greenfield Railroad for a State Loan of Two Millions of Dollars*
      (Boston: Eastburn's Press, 16 April 1851).
Theseus [pseudonym of Edward Hamilton], *Death of Our Minotaur* (Boston,
      1868).

Speeches

Butler, Benjamin F. Address of Mr. Benjamin F. Butler of Massachusetts, Memorial Addresses on the Life and Character of Alvah Crocker (a Representative from Massachusetts), delivered in the Senate and House of Representatives, Forty-Third Congress, Second Session, 20 February 1875.

Crocker, Alvah. "The Bill for the More Speedy Completion of the Troy and Greenfield Railroad": speech in the Massachusetts Senate, 15 April 1862 (Boston: 1862).

Crocker, Alvah. *The Tariff: Remarks of Hon. Alvah Crocker of Massachusetts*, House of Representatives, 16 May 1872.

Derby, E. H. *The Argument of E. H. Derby, Esq. in Favor of a State Loan to the Vermont and Massachusetts Railroad Co. before the Joint Committee on Railroads and Canals of the Legislature of Massachusetts, March 1855* (Boston: Dutton and Wentworth, 1855).

Derby, Hasket. *The Troy & Greenfield Railroad: Argument of E. Hasket Derby, Esq., Delivered Feb. 29th, 1856 Before a Joint Special Committee of the Legislature of Massachusetts, in Behalf of the Troy and Greenfield Railroad Company, Petitioners for a State Subscription to Their Stock* (Boston: Bazin & Chandler, 1856).

Lincoln, Abraham. *Proclamation* [Emancipation], 22 September 1862.

Phelps, Ansel Jr. *Hoosac Tunnel, Speech of Ansel Phelps, Jr., Counsel for the Remonstrants* (Boston: Eastburn's Press, 6 April 1853).

Acts

"An Act to Establish the Fitchburg Rail-road Company," *Acts and Resolves passed by the Legislature of Massachusetts in the Year 1842 (Winter Session)* [approved by the governor, 3 March 1842], chap. 84.

"Section 2," in *Troy and Greenfield Railroad Act of Incorporation*, 9 February 1848.

Act 2 of 1848, 13 November 1848, Vermont State Archives. (charter for the Southern Vermont Railway Company)

Acts and Resolutions passed by the General Court of Massachusetts, in the year 1860.

"Chap. 210," *Acts and Resolves passed by the General Court of Massachusetts in the Year 1865* (Boston: Wright & Potter, approved 9 May 1865).

"Chap. 47. Resolves in Favor of the Contractors for the Construction of the Hoosac Tunnel," *Acts and Resolves passed by the General Court of Massachusetts in the year 1872* (Boston: Wright & Potter, 1872).

"Chapter 403," *Acts and Resolves passed by the General Court of Massachusetts in the year 1874* (Boston: Wright & Potter, 1874).

"Resolve in favor of Walter Shanly," *Chapter 105, Acts and Resolves passed by the General Court of Massachusetts in the year 1887* (Boston: Wright & Potter, 1887).

Public Documents

Baer, Christopher T. *A General Chronology of the Pennsylvania Railroad Company, Its Predecessors and Successors and Its Historical Context*, "PRR Chronology 30 June 1847" (April 2005 ed.).

Baldwin. Baldwin Manuscripts, Loammi Baldwin, 1744–1807, Baker Library, Harvard University.

Browne, Isaac S. letter to Bert Browne (progeny of Charles A. Browne) from New London, CT, 25 May 1923, copy in North Adams Public Library, North Adams Vault, Call #385 Browne, Status Storage.

Congressional Directory, 1st ed. Compiled for the use of the Congress by Ben: Perley Poore, Clerk of Printing Records (Washington, DC: Government Printing Office, 15 January 1872).

Crocker. Letterbook 1868, Fitchburg Historical Society, Fitchburg, MA.

Derby, Argument of E. H. Derby, Esq., on behalf of the Old Colony Rail-Road Company, 7 April 1848, Box 1848. Massachusetts Historical Society.

Dorchester and Milton Branch Railroad Company bond [1858], issue date 5 February 1867, Massachusetts Historical Society, Ms. N-49.17.

Doane, Thomas. "Safety cages for west shaft of Hoosac Tunnel, 1864," *Hoosac Tunnel Photographs*, State Library of Massachusetts, files: ocn496810869. jpg.

———, "Elevation and some sections of the dam built in the Deerfield River to secure a water power for compressing air for the Hoosac Tunnel work, 1864," *Hoosac Tunnel Photographs*, The State Library of Massachusetts, files: ocn496814076.jpg.

Felton. Samuel Morse Felton (Sr.) Collection, Baker Library, Harvard University.

Felton Papers, 1839–1920, Historical Society of Pennsylvania, Philadelphia.

Haupt, H. John W. Barriger III National Railroad Library, University of Missouri, St. Louis.

Haupt. Haupt Family Documents and Letters, Historical Society of Pennsylvania.

Haupt. Herman Haupt Papers, Manuscripts and Archives, Yale University Library.

Haupt. United States Military Academy, Cadet Application Papers, 1831, National Archives, frames 296–301.

Gov. Andrew. Microfilm P-344, Box 9, File 6. Massachusetts Historical Society.

Journal of the Senate of Michigan (1846).

Journals of the Legislative Council of the Province of Canada, Third session, Eighth Provincial Parliament, vol. 24 (1865).

Latrobe, Benj. H. *Pocket Diary 1868, Jan. 1–Dec. 31*, (barcode 48188-10), Archival Collections, PPA Library, Athenaeum of Philadelphia.

Middlesex Canal. Proprietors of the Middlesex Canal, Corporate Records, (Center for Lowell History, University of Massachusetts-Lowell).

Rondeau, Mark E. "Cemetery Walk: Whistling Past the Graveyard," story told by North Adams historian Paul Marino, iBerkshires.com, North Adams, MA, 11 July 2003: http://www.iberkshires.com/story/11446/Cemetery-walk-Whistling-past-the-graveyard.html?ss_id=1794, viewed 6 July 2013.

Shanly, Walter. *The Canadian Shanlys: Whence they came and how they got to Thorndale*, 1896, PA057, Canadian Railroad Historical Association Archives and Document Center, Saint Constant, Quebec, Canada.

Shanly, Walter. Archives Nationales du Québec à Montréal (ANQM), P464, Fonds Walter Shanly.

Shanly, Francis fonds [record group], Archives of Ontario, Toronto, Archives of Ontario.

Shanly Papers: MU2678, MU2688, MU2690, MU2691, MU2710, MU2714, MU2720, MU2725, MU2731, Archives of Ontario, Toronto, Archives of Ontario.

Sohier and Welch Collection. Baker Library, Harvard University.

Storrow, Charles S. *Of the Celestial Motions* (mathematical thesis no. 354, 28 April 1829), Harvard University Archives.

Troy and Greenfield Papers. Baker Library, Harvard University.

White. Canvass White Collection, Rare and Manuscript Collections, Cornell University Library, Ithaca, NY.

Worcester Explosion

"The Worcester Explosion," *Public Document No. 35, Second Annual Report of the Board of Railroad Commissioners* (Boston: Wright & Potter, 1871).

"Boston and Albany Railroad Company vs. Walter Shanly & others. Thomas Carney vs. Same," in *Cases Argued and Determined in the Supreme Judicial Court for the County of Worcester, October Term 1871, at Worcester, Massachusetts, Reports 107* (Boston: H. O. Houghton and Company, 1873).

Collections of the State Library of Massachusetts, Boston

Hills, John. *A plan and section of the country, from Connecticut River to the tide water at Milton, in the State of Massachusetts* (1791): map.

Baldwin, Loammi. *Plan and profile of surveys made under the directions of Nathan Willis, Elihu Hoyt & H.A.S. Dearborn to ascertain the practicability of making a canal from Boston Harbor to Connecticut River* (1825): map.

Journal of the Proceedings of the General Railroad Conventions held at Springfield, August 24th and 25th, 1852 (New Haven, CT: T. J. Stafford, 1852).

Journal of the Constitutional Convention of the Commonwealth of Massachusetts, begun and held in Boston, on the Fourth Day of May, 1853 (Boston: White & Potter, 1853).

Doane, Thomas. "Details of the Instrument Houses used in Surface Alignment of the Hoosac Tunnel (drawing, 1863)," Photos 385.8 H78, nos. 15 and 16.

Commonwealth of Massachusetts

The Hoosac Tunnel: A Brief Report of the Hearing of the Troy and Greenfield Railroad Company Petitioners for a Loan of Two Millions, before A Joint Special Committee of the Legislature of Massachusetts (Boston: Thurston, Torry & Emerson, Printers, Boston, 1853).

Senate No. 163 (Boston: Wright & Potter, State Printers, 1855).

House No. 174, Petition of the Troy & Greenfield Railroad Corporation (Boston: Wright & Potter, State Printers, 12 April 1856).

House No. 235, Troy & Greenfield Railroad (Boston: Wright & Potter, State Printers, 4 April 1862).

Senate No. 93, Troy and Greenfield Railroad and Hoosac Tunnel (Boston: Wright & Potter, State Printers, 12 March 1863).

House No. 3, Troy and Greenfield Railroad and Hoosac Tunnel (Boston: Wright & Potter, State Printers, 12 January 1865).

Senate No. 220, Report on the Troy and Greenfield Railroad and the Hoosac Tunnel by the Joint Special Committee of 1865 (April 1866).

Senate No. 289, Letters of John W. Brooks Esq., Chairman of Commissioners of Troy & Greenfield Railroad, and Hoosac Tunnel to Hon. Tappan Wentworth, Chairman of Legislative Committee (12 May 1866).

House No. 30, Annual Report of the Commissioners on the Troy and Greenfield R.R. and Hoosac Tunnel (Boston: Wright & Potter, January 1867).

Senate No. 59, Report on the Hoosac Tunnel and Troy and Greenfield Railroad by the Joint Standing Committee of 1866 (Boston: Wright & Potter, February 1867).

Senate No. 102, Report on the Troy and Greenfield Railroad and the Hoosac Tunnel by the Joint Special Committee of 1867 (Boston: Wright & Potter, March 1868).

Senate No. 20, Report of the Hon. Alvah Crocker, Commissioner, acting as Superintendent, of work upon the Troy and Greenfield Railroad and the Hoosac Tunnel together with the Reports of the Chief and Consulting Engineers (Boston: Wright & Potter, January 1868).

House No. 359, Letter of Hon. Charles Hudson (Boston: Wright & Potter, May 1868).

Senate No. 6, Report of Benj. H. Latrobe Consulting Engineer, on the Troy and Greenfield Railroad and Hoosac Tunnel (Boston: Wright & Potter, January 1869).

House No. 192, Report of the Commissioners upon the Troy and Greenfield Railroad and Hoosac Tunnel (Boston: Wright & Potter, March 1869).

Senate No. 58, Report of the Joint Standing Committee of 1869 on the Troy and Greenfield Railroad and Hoosac Tunnel (Boston: Wright & Potter, February 1870).

Senate No. 55, Report of the Joint Standing Committee on the Troy and Greenfield Railroad and Hoosac Tunnel for the year 1870 (Boston: Wright & Potter, February 1871).

Senate No. 169 Communication from Edward S. Philbrick, Consulting Engineer, upon building of a railroad at North Adams, (Boston: Wright & Potter, April 1871).

Senate No. 283, Reports of James Laurie, late Consulting Engineer on the Hoosac Tunnel, (Boston: Wright & Potter, May 1871).

Senate No. 330, Supplement to Senate No. 283, Reports of James Laurie, late Consulting Engineer on the Hoosac Tunnel, (Boston: Wright & Potter, May 1871).

Senate No. 250, Report of the Joint Standing Committee on the Troy and Greenfield Railroad and the Hoosac Tunnel, for the year 1871. (Boston: Wright & Potter, March 1872).

Senate No. 201, Report on the Troy and Greenfield Railroad and Hoosac Tunnel by the Joint Standing Committee for 1873 (Boston: Wright & Potter, April 1874).

Senate No. 300, Evidence and Arguments on the Petition of Walter and Francis Shanly before the Committee on the Hoosac Tunnel and Troy and Greenfield Railroad (Boston: Wright & Potter, May 1874).

House No. 375, Report of the Evidence on the Claim of Charles Burleigh together with the Argument of Counsel, before the Committee on the Hoosac Tunnel and Troy and Greenfield Railroad (Boston: Wright & Potter, May 1874).

House No. 9, Boston, Hoosac Tunnel and Western Railroad Company, Report of the Corporators (Boston: Wright & Potter, January 1875).

Senate No. 150, Committee on claims, to whom was referred the memorial of Walter and Francis Shanly concerning the Hoosac Tunnel (27 April 1875).

Senate No. 50, First Annual Report of the Manager of the Troy & Greenfield Railroad and Hoosac Tunnel (Boston: Wright & Potter, February 1876).

Senate No. 282, Committee on claims, to whom was referred the Petition of Walter Shanly (Boston: Wright & Potter, April 1884).

Patents

"An Act to promote the progress of useful arts, and to repeal all acts and parts of acts heretofore made for that purpose," Chapter 357, *Patent Act of 1836*, Ch. 357, 5 Stat. 117 (4 July 1836).

"Annual Report of the Commissioner of Patents for the Year 1866, vol. II," *House of Representatives Ex. Doc. No. 109*, No. 60,572 (Washington, DC, 1866).

Improved Steam Drilling Machine, Reissue No. 2,275, United States Patent Office (5 June 1866).

Improvement in Electric Fuses, Charles A. Browne and Isaac S. Browne of North Adams, MA, United States Patent Office, Letters patent No. 158,672, 12 January 1875.

Improvement in Rock-Drilling Machines, Letters Patent No. 59,960, United States Patent Office, 27 November 1866.

"Joseph W. Fowle's Patent," *The Congressional Globe containing The Debates and Proceedings of the Second Session Forty-Second Congress*, Office of the Congressional Globe, City of Washington (19 March 1872).

De Volson Wood, letter to the Committee of Patents in the House of Representatives (3 April 1872), Archives of the Fitchburg Historical Society, Fitchburg, Massachusetts.

Wilson, Chs. Machine for Tunneling Rocks, &c., Specification of Letters Patent No. 14,483, dated 18 March 1856.

Public Reports

Annual Report of the President and Directors of the Board of Public Works to the Legislature of Virginia (19 December 1816).

"Annual Report of the President and Directors of the Board of Public Works, Richmond," in *North American Review and Miscellaneous Journal* 8, no. 22 (Boston: Cummings and Hilliard, 1818/19).

Annual Reports of the Railroad Corporations in the State of Massachusetts for 1845 (1846). Massachusetts General Court, Committee on Railways and Canals.

Beauharnois Canal, Report on the state of work from 1844, National Archives of Canada, RG 11, vol. 94 (1844).

Eighth Annual Report of the Directors to the Stockholders of the Connecticut River Railroad, for Eleven Months ending Nov. 30, 1852, C. W. Chapin, President, Springfield (28 December 1852).

Eleventh Annual Report of the Board of Railroad Commissioners (Boston: Rand, Abery & Co., 1880).

"Eureka Company v. Bass, Adm'r." Reports of Cases Argued and Determined in the Supreme Court of Alabama during the December Term 1886, (Montgomery: Joel White, 1887).

Haupt, H. *Report of the Final Location of the Southern Railroad from Brandon, Mississippi, to the Alabama Line, in the Direction of Charleston and Savannah* (Philadelphia: T. K. and P. G. Collins, Printers, 1853).

Historic Resources of the City of North Adams, Massachusetts (partial inventory), NPS Form 10-900, National Park Service, U. S. Department of the Interior (received 12 September 1985, entered 25 October 1985).

Official Report of the Debates and Proceedings in the State Convention assembled May 4th, 1853, to Revise and Amend the Constitution of the Commonwealth of Massachusetts, vol. 2 (Boston: White & Potter, printers, 1853.)

Report of Cases Argued and Determined in the Superior Court of the City of New York, vol. 4 (1861).

Report of the Secretary of the Treasury on the Subject of Public Roads and Canals made in pursuance of a resolution of Senate of March 2, 1807 (Washington, DC: R. C. Weightman, 1808).

Report of the Commissioners of the State of Massachusetts, on the Routes of Canals from Boston Harbour to Connecticut and Hudson Rivers (Boston: True and Green, State Printers, 1826).

Report of the Board of Directors of the State of Massachusetts on the Practicability and Expediency of a Rail-Road from Boston to the Hudson River, and from Boston to Providence (Boston: Press of the *Boston Daily Advertiser*, 16 January 1829).

"Report of the Board of Managers—The Twenty fifth Annual Fair 1852," in *Eleventh Annual Report of the American Institute of the City of New York* (Albany: Charles van Benthuysen, printer, 1853).

Report upon the Merits of the Great Western Railroad, Canada West: by a Committee of its American Friends (Boston: Eastburn's Press, 1851).

Schlatter, Charles L. *Second Report of Charles L. Schlatter, Principal Engineer in the Service of the State of Pennsylvania, to the Canal Commissioners, relative to the Continuous Railroad from Harrisburg to Pittsburg* (Harrisburg: James S. Wallace, 1841).

Bytown and Prescott Railway

Shanly, W. *Report No. 1, To the President and Directors of the Bytown and Prescott Railway Company* (Prescott, Ontario: Bytown and Prescott Railway Office, 7 April 1851).

———. *Report No. 2, To the President and Directors of the Bytown and Prescott Railway Company* (Prescott, Ontario: Bytown and Prescott Railway Office, 26 July 1851).

Michigan Central Rail-Road

Annual Reports, Michigan Central Railroad (Boston: Eastburn's Press, 1855, 1856, 1857), Corporate Records Division, Baker Library, Harvard University.

Brooks, John W. *Report upon the Merits of the Michigan Central Rail-Road as an Investment for Eastern Capitalists* (New York: Van Norden & Ameran, Printers, 1846).

Forbes, J. M. *Second Annual Report of the Directors of the Michigan Central Rail-Road Company to the Stockholders* (Boston: Eastburn's Press, 1848).

Northern Rail Road Company

Report of the Directors of the Northern Rail Road Company (Ogdensburgh, New York: Hitchcock & Smith, 1848).

Report of the Directors of the Northern Rail Road Company (Boston: T. R. Marvin, 1849).

Pennsylvania Railroad

First Annual Report of the Directors of the Pennsylvania Railroad Co. to the Stockholders (Philadelphia: Crissy & Markley, Printers, 1847).

Sixth Annual Report of the Directors of the Pennsylvania Railroad Co. to the Stockholders (Philadelphia: Crissy & Markley, Printers, 1853).

Eighth Annual Report of the Directors of the Pennsylvania Railroad Company, to the Stockholders (Philadelphia: Crissy & Markley, Printers, 1855).

Ninth Annual Report of the Directors of the Pennsylvania Railroad Company, to the Stockholders (Philadelphia: Crissy & Markley, Printers, 1856).

Thomson, J. Edgar. "Second Annual Report of the Chief Engineer, 15 November 1849," *Third Annual Report of the Directors of the Pennsylvania*

Railroad Co. to the Stockholders (Philadelphia: Crissy & Markley, Printers, 1849).

———. "Third Annual Report of the Chief Engineer, 31 December 1850," *Fourth Annual Report of the Directors of the Pennsylvania Railroad Co. to the Stockholders* (Philadelphia: Crissy & Markley, Printers, 1 January 1851).

———. "Fourth Annual Report of the Chief Engineer, 15 January 1852," *Fifth Annual Report of the Directors of the Pennsylvania Railroad Co. to the Stockholders* (Philadelphia: Crissy & Markley, Printers, 1852).

Haupt, H. "Seventh Annual Report of the Chief Engineer, 25 January 1854," *Seventh Annual Report of the Directors of the Pennsylvania Railroad Co. to the Stockholders* (Philadelphia: Crissy & Markley, Printers, 1854).

———. "Report of the Superintendent of Transportation, 31 December 1850," *Fourth Annual Report of the Directors of the Pennsylvania Railroad Co. to the Stockholders* (Philadelphia: Crissy & Markley, Printers, 1851).

Toronto & Guelph Railway

Second Annual Report, Toronto and Guelph Railway Company (Toronto: Henry Rowsell, 6 June 1853).

Shanly, Walter. *Report on the Preliminary Surveys of the Toronto & Guelph Railway* (Toronto: Brewer, McPhail and Co., 1851), p. 6.

Vermont Central Railroad

Fourth Annual Report of the Directors of the Vermont Central Railroad Company (Montpelier, VT: E. P. Walton & Sons, 1849).

Report on the Investigating Committee of the Vermont Central Railroad Co. (Boston: George C. Rand, July 1853).

Index

About the Author

CLIFFORD J. SCHEXNAYDER IS an Arizona State University Eminent Scholar, Emeritus. He received his PhD in Civil Engineering from Purdue University, bachelor's and master's degrees in Civil Engineering from Georgia Tech, and has taught at Louisiana Tech, United States Air Force Academy, and Virginia Tech. Since the early 1980s, he has written about construction at the technical level. Several of his technical papers are historical in content. As a result, he received a Dibner Library Resident Scholar fellowship from the Smithsonian Institution Libraries to research this book.

Since 1995, he has written college-level textbooks for McGraw-Hill, including four editions of *Construction Planning, Equipment, and Methods* and two editions of *Construction Management Fundamentals*. During his early career, he served in the Army Corps of Engineers and later worked as an engineer on major construction projects across the United States. It was during one of his military assignments that he began his two-decade-long fascination with the Hoosac Tunnel. He and his wife, Judy, now live in Branford, Connecticut.

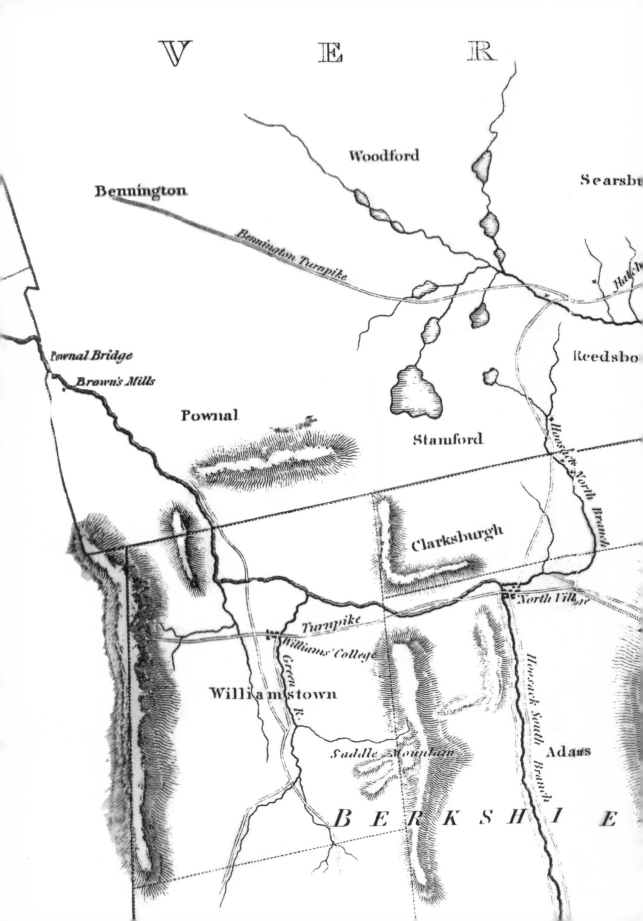